THE SINGING TRADITION OF
CHILD'S POPULAR BALLADS

"What will a Child learn sooner than a Song?"

Alexander Pope, *To Augustus*, 205

"I think that there must be a place in the soul all made of tunes of long ago . . . I know not what are the words But they sing in my soul of the things our Fathers loved."

Charles Ives, Song XLIII (1917)

THE
SINGING TRADITION
OF CHILD'S
POPULAR BALLADS

EDITED BY

BERTRAND HARRIS BRONSON

PRINCETON, NEW JERSEY
PRINCETON UNIVERSITY PRESS
1976

CONTENTS

[v]

[vii]

PREFACE

THOSE WHO make use of this volume will no doubt already have made acquaintance with *English and Scottish Popular Ballads*, edited by George Lyman Kittredge and Helen Child Sargent, and probably, too, will have dipped into the large work of which that is an abridgment: Francis James Child's collection bearing the same title. It is therefore unnecessary to describe the content and scope of those works.

Latterly, an attempt was made by the present editor to supply, in so far as the available records permitted, the musical half of Child's work with a comparable fullness of evidence, not omitting the body of fresh verbal texts collected from the singers along with their tunes. This work was published in four volumes by Princeton University Press, 1959-72, under the title, *The Traditional Tunes of the Child Ballads*.

The present book is intended to perform a service like Kittredge's to Child, by abridging the bigger work with as little distortion as possible, neither departing from the scheme and procedures of the original, nor disturbing the contents by revision of the critical commentary where not required by Addenda in the last volume, nor by introduction of new examples not present in the complete work. This, then, is not to be taken as a revised and updated edition of the other work. The headnotes have not been altered in substance; but they have often been shortened to accord with the change of scale, which in turn entailed the omission of references to variants excluded from the abridgment, and of bibliographical allusions not essential to the text. The only major addition is that of a general introduction, principally designed to further the intelligent use and appreciation of the music of British-American balladry.

In order not to falsify the primary purpose of exhibiting the kinds and scope of change, or continuity, in traditional transmission, it was essential to include representative examples of variation within the groups of tunes belonging to a single ballad. A principle of admission, therefore, was requisite here which differs from that of an editor concerned only to shape an anthology of "the fairest flowers of balladry." Many beauties will surely be discovered in these pages, but the ends of sober study must over-ride the culling of posies for their own sole sake.

The critical reader may naturally ask why some ballads to be found in the larger work have been omitted altogether from the present one. The question is more easily answered in reverse. It is obvious that, where there is an abundance of melodic variants on record, the ballad with such proofs of traditional vitality has the best claims to admission. The bulk of this kind of evidence, we know, has been gathered within the last century from living links in the traditional chain, or, to use the more appropriate figure, from shoots of the living tree. These claims are confirmed, of course, by the existence of earlier texts without tunes; but we do not need them, and for the present purpose they are superfluous. The uncertainties begin when the tune-record is sparse or even solitary. We must then be guided by our confidence in the authenticity of the record, which depends on our reliance on the dependability of the transcriber, his immediate proximity to his source, the accuracy of particulars about singer and circumstance, and the nature of the transcription. Even an inexpert record of a tune, where other factors are satisfactory, may give us more confidence than inclusion in a song-collection edited for publication without attributions to source. But the older the record, the more lenient we become, because of its relative scarcity and consequent interest. The tunes preserved by Ravenscroft and D'Urfey are cases in point with regard to editing; and Robert Scott's attempts to take down the tunes of his aunt, Mrs. Brown, are examples of honest inaccuracy. In such instances opinions may differ, and we may have to fall back on our knowledge or judgment of the tune's apparent validity and idiom. Over all, the aim of the present collection has been to stay as close as possible to credibility in traditional transmission.

Berkeley, Calif., 30 April, 1974

ACKNOWLEDGMENTS

GRATEFUL acknowledgments are due to the many collectors, editors, organizations, and societies, with whose consent the contents of this work have been printed, or reprinted, from collections first issued by them, or else in their keeping. More extensive obligations have been avowed in the four volumes of which the present one is an abridgment. But it is appropriate to renew acknowledgments for the contents of this abridgment. The bare list that follows cannot convey the editor's personal sense of indebtedness for the friendly accord with the work's intention of so many generous contributors.

A primary obligation is acknowledged to the proprietors of manuscripts and sound recordings, to which wherever possible the editor has first turned for basic authority. Where print has been a necessary intermediary, it will be obvious that all instrumental accompaniments supplied have been omitted from the present copy. Transcriptions from sound recordings, when unattributed, are to be charged to the present editor, who has in a very few cases ventured to simplify more meticulous copy by other transcribers.* Foremost among his creditors over all are Dr. Maud Karpeles, who long since gave him free use of the incomparable store amassed by Cecil Sharp on both sides of the Atlantic, together with her own Newfoundland gatherings; and Dr. W. Douglas Simpson, former Librarian of Aberdeen University, who gave equal access to the Gavin Greig manuscripts at King's College, along with the J. B. Duncan tunes of the Child ballads, transcribed by William Walker. Other essential favors of this kind will be specified below. It must be clearly understood that in no case has there been a transfer of copyright from claimant to either editor or publisher of the present work.

In the lists below, Child Ballad numbers are printed in bold face, with variant numbers following.

Aberdeen University, King's College Library, Gavin Greig and J. B. Duncan MSS: **2**, 1; **7**, 25; **12**, 43; **20**, 15; **25**, 2 (Duncan); **40**, 1; **41**, 2; **43**, 13; **46**, 7; **52**, 3; **53**, 74; **58**, 3; **62**, 1 (Duncan); **63**, 2; **83**, 5; **84**, 44; **100**, 4; **106**, 2 (Duncan); **110**, 14; **114**, 9 (Duncan); **163**, 11; **173**, 6, 11.1 (Duncan); **178**, 5; **191**, 4 (Duncan); **196**, 2; **201**, 5 (Duncan); **209**, 4; **212**, 4, 9 (Duncan); **213**, 20; **214**, 28 (Broadwood); **215**, 3 (Broadwood); **216**, 2; **217**, 17; **218**, 2, 3 (Duncan), 5 (Duncan); **219**, 3; **221**, 10 (Duncan); **226**, 7 (Duncan); **228**, 3, 12; **231**, 4 (Duncan); **233**, 11 (Duncan); **235**, 7 (Duncan); **236**, 5 (Duncan), 23; **237**, 4, 6 (Duncan), 7 (Duncan), 9; **240**, 3; **241**, 2 (Duncan); **245**, 2 (Duncan); **252**, 2; **267**, 3; **269**, 3 (Duncan), 4; **274**, 3 (Duncan), 20; **275**, 12 (Duncan); **277**, 5 (Duncan); **279A**, 24 (Duncan); **280**, 7 (Duncan); **281**, 33; **282**, 2, 5, 6 (Duncan); **283**, 1, 25; **287**, 8; **288**, 2; **289**, 2 (Duncan).

(English) Folk Song Society, *Journal:* **2**, 31 (Broadwood), 53 (Vaughan Williams); **4**, 30 (Kidson), 40 (Sharp); **10**, 49 (Kidson), 83 (Kidson); **12**, 97 (Nicholson), 99 (Broadwood); **20**, 4 (Hammond); **24**, 2 (Sharp), 17 (Sharp); **43**, 4 (Sharp), 20 (Amherst), 23 (Vaughan Williams); **46A**, 3 (Hammond); **53**, 12 (Kidson), 34 (Grainger); **54**, 3 (Sharp); **73**, 8 (Broadwood); **78**, 27 (Broadwood), 35 (Sharp); **84**, 2 (Sharp), 28 (Broadwood); **85**, 24 (Gardiner, Guyer), 34 (ditto); **92A**,

* In the case of certain of Mrs. Ailie Munro's transcriptions, he has failed to meet the exacting requirements of the copy kindly put at his disposal. For this, as for other shortcomings, unintended and still unrecognized, he offers apologies and hopes for forgiveness.

1 (Ford), 16 (Hammond); **95,** 4 (Hammond); **100,** 10 (Hammond); **110,** 4 (Sharp), 11 (Sharp); **132,** 6 (Sharp), 11 (Broadwood); **140,** 3 (Gardiner, Vaughn Williams); **144,** 3 (Hammond), 2.1 (Gardiner, Gamblin); **155,** 4 (Sharp), 5 (Newell); **170,** 3 (Sharp); **208,** 3 (Gamblin, Vaughan Williams); **214,** 28 (Broadwood); **215,** 3 Broadwood); **243,** 82 (Hammond); **250,** 12 (Vaughan Williams); **277,** 15 (Gilchrist); **278,** 2 (Hammond); **283,** 12 (Kidson), 38 (Vaughan Williams); **286,** 27 (Merrick); **287,** 3 (Vaughan Williams)

JEFDSS: **12,** 24 (Shuldham-Shaw); **18,** 4 (Kidson; **19,** 1 (Shuldham-Shaw); **213,** 18 (Karpeles).

Folk Music Journal: **106,** 4.1 (Guyer); **125,** 3 (Gardiner, Gamblin); **126,** 5 (Gardiner); **140,** 5.1 (Gardiner); **250,** 12 (Vaughan Williams); **276,** 2 (Hammond); **283,** 38 (Vaughan Williams), 40 (Vaughan Williams); **287,** 3 (Vaughan Williams).

Oxford University Press. C. J. Sharp and Maud Karpeles, *English Folk Songs from the Southern Appalachians,* 1932: **3,** 5; **4,** 106, 135; **7,** 11; **10,** 50, 55; **12,** 14, 53; **13,** 8, 11; **46A,** 7; **49,** 1, 11, 19, 25; **51,** 2; **54,** 16; **65,** 12; **68,** 2, 13, 27, 37; **73,** 103; **74,** 47; **79,** 5, 20, 43; **81,** 27; **84,** 78, 137; **93,** 12; **95,** 33; **99,** 12; **155,** 21; **170,** 5; **200,** 21; **209,** 50; **243,** 9; **272,** 1a, 2; **286,** 43, 94; **295,** 41; **299,** 12.

Maud Karpeles, *Folk Songs from Newfoundland,* 1934: **14,** 3; **17,** 2; **43,** 27; **53,** 101; **73,** 71, 91; **74,** 68; **77,** 3; **248,** 5.

Jean Ritchie Pickow, *Singing Family of the Cumberlands,* 1955: **81,** 15; **84,** 142; **278,** 52.

Harvard University, Houghton Library, MSS: **4,** 95 (Child); **5,** 1 (Ritson); **10,** 79 (Ritson); **12,** 33 (Macmath); **32,** 1 (Ritson); **34,** 1 (Ritson); **42,** 1 (Ritson); **46,** 16 (Barry, Bayard); **47,** 1 (Harris); **53,** 94 (Harris), 112 (Ritson); **54,** 1 (Gilbert); **58,** 5 (Harris); **61,** 1 (Harris); **63,** 1 (Harris); **65,** 1 (Ritson); **68,** 34 (Harris); **75,** 23 (Barry); **77,** 1 (Harris); **81,** 55 (Barry cylinder); **84,** 79 (Harris); **99,** 10 (Ritson), 11 (Macmath); **100,** 22 (Macmath); **106,** 1 (Harris); **114,** 4 (Harris); **157,** 2 (Macmath); **161,** 1 (Sharpe, Macmath); **164,** 1 (Sharpe, Macmath); **169,** 7 (Harris); **173,** 5 (Harris); **182,** 1 (Harris); **222,** 1 (Sharpe, Macmath); **228,** 13 (Macmath); **299,** 3 (Macmath).

Library of Congress, Archive of American Folk Song, Recorded Sound: **3,** 7 (Emrich); **4,** 124 (Halpert); **10,** 67 (Halpert); **18,** 2 (Halpert); **45,** 4 (Cowell); **73,** 21 (Halpert); **93,** 5a (Halpert); **125,** 2 (Kirkland); **132,** 8 (Cowell); **155,** 10b (Karpeles, Cowell); **167,** 8 (Cowell); **200,** 4 (Emrich, Korson), 8 (Lomax), 83 (Foss), 101 (Parler); **209,** 40 (Carlisle); **243,** 78 (Lomax), 98 (Carlisle), 111 (Foss), 129 (Karpeles, Cowell); **274,** 14 (Grimes), 35 (Emrich); **277,** 29 (Warner); **278,** 33 (Halpert), 67 (Lomax); **283,** 18 (Cowell); **285,** 10 (Lomax); **286,** 102 (Halpert); **289,** 30 (Cowell), 40 (Cowell, Powell); **295,** 20 (Eskin).

Edinburgh University, School of Scottish Studies, Recorded Sound: **12,** 35.1 (MacInnes, Munro), 35.2 (Henderson, Lomax, Collinson), 43.2 (Henderson, Porter); **13,** 3.2 (Henderson, Collinson); **19,** 2 (Collinson); **20,** 19.1 (Henderson, Munro); **39,** 2.1 (MacIntyre, Fullarton, Munro); **49,** 13.1 (Henderson, Porter); **53,** 30.2 (Henderson, Collinson); **75,** 32.1 (Henderson, Collinson); **76,** 4.1 (Henderson, Collinson); **77,** 12 (Henderson, Collinson); **106,** 3.2 (Henderson, Collinson); **110,** 17.1 (Henderson, Etherington); **125,** 1 (Henderson, Collinson); **203,** 2 (Collinson), 2.3 (Buchan, Munro), 3.1 (Henderson, Kennedy, Munro); **238,** 10 (Henderson, Collinson); **251,** 8 (Henderson, Collinson); **278,** 68 (Henderson, Collinson); **279,** 6 (Kennedy, Lomax, Johnstone), 17 (Henderson, BHB); **281,** 14 (Henderson, Porter); **293,** 16 (Goldstein, BHB); **299,** 17 (Henderson, Porter).

Edinburgh University Library: MS Dc 1.69; **46A,** 1; **162,** 3.

National Library of Scotland, MSS 840, 843, 1578: **9,** 5 (Lady John Scott/Sharpe); **10,** 81 (ditto); **37,** 2 (Blaikie); **64,** 1 (Lady John Scott/Sharpe); **93,** 27 (Blaikie); **100,** 1 (Blaikie); **163,** 1 (Lady Scott); **173,** 3 (Lady Scott/Sharpe); **187,** 1 (Lady Scott, ?Campbell); **191,** 2 (Blaikie); **203,** 3 (Lady Scott); **206,** 3 (Blaikie); **215,** 1 (Blaikie); **229,** 1 (Blaikie); **231,** 6 (Blaikie); **277,** 1 (Lady Scott/Sharpe); **288,** 1 (Blaikie).

Boosey and Hawkes, Ltd.: L. E. Broadwood, *English Traditional Songs and Carols,* 1908: **78,** 27; **132,** 11. Herbert Hughes, *Irish Country Songs,* 1915: **92A,** 10; **248,** 8. Josephine McGill, *Folk-Songs of the Kentucky Mountains,* 1917: **49,** 29. C. V. Stanford, *The Complete Petrie Collection of Irish Music,* 1902-05: **12,** 61; **273,** 1.

Harvard University Press: W. R. Mackenzie,

Ballads and Sea Songs from Nova Scotia, 1928: **4**, 61; **46**, 13; **88**, 4. Reed Smith, *South Carolina Ballads*, 1928: **95**, 23. E. P. Greenleaf and G. Y. Mansfield, *Ballads and Sea Songs of Newfoundland*, 1933: **17**, 21; **78**, 36. A. K. Davis, Jr., *Traditional Ballads of Virginia*, 1929: **1**, 5; **13**, 22; **18**, 10; **62**, 3; **79**, 48; **85**, 2, 29; **120**, 1; **141**, 1.

Helen Creighton, *Songs and Ballads from Nova Scotia*, 1932: **132**, 12; **139**, 1. *Traditional Songs from Nova Scotia* (with D. H. Senior), 1950: **12**, 48; **12A**, 20; **17**, 22; **20**, 20, 45; **26**, 11; **46A**, 2a; **53**, 6; **73**, 136; **84**, 38; **105**, 18; **106**, 3; **272**, 6.

Society of Antiquaries, Newcastle-upon-Tyne, Telfer MS: **39**, 3.1; **187**, 3; **191**, 5; **193**, 1; **279**, 15; **281**, 4, 35; **289**, 35. J. C. Bruce and J. Stokoe, *Northumbrian Minstrelsy*, 1882: **2**, 22; **7**, 1b; **10**, 7; **112**, 6; **162**, 6; **211**, 1.

Novello and Co., Ltd.: W. A. Barrett, *English Folk-Songs*, 1891: **46A**, 16. C. J. Sharp, *English Folk Songs*, Selected Edition, 1920: **4**, 28a; **12**, 90; **20**, 31; **53**, 92; **126**, 2; **155**, 4; **170**, 3; **200**, 73. C. J. Sharp, gen. ed., *Folk Songs of England*, Bk. II, ed. R. Vaughan Williams, 1908: **209**, 11; **287**, 3. *Folk Songs for Use in Schools*, set 202, 1908: **2**, 36. Set 245, 1913: **55**, 2. Set 274, 1925: **12A**, 15.

Yale University Press: Phillips Barry, F. H. Eckstorm, M. W. Smyth, *British Ballads from Maine*, 1929: **2**, 3; **4**, 81, 101; **12**, 72; **17**, 4; **20**, 6; **46**, 14; **81**, 66; **188**, 7; **199**, 11; **243**, 53; **287**, 10; **289**, 25; **295**, 1.

American Folklore Society, *Journal of American Folklore*: **2**, 23 (Kittredge et al.); **10**, 42 (Smelser); **75**, 53 (Barry, Hudson MS); **81**, 6 (Kittredge); **95**, 1 (Barry, Hudson MS); **155**, 28 (Rinker); **162**, 10 (Barry); **181**, 4 (Parsons, Roberts); **243**, 88 (Treat); **250**, 8 (Hubbard); **295**, 26 (Barry).

Helen Hartness Flanders (with George Brown), *Vermont Folk Songs and Ballads*, 1931: **2**, 6; **4**, 130; **73**, 47. *Country Songs of Vermont*, 1937: **167**, 2; **286**, 71. *Ballads Migrant in New England* (with Margaret Olney), 1953: **13**, 2; **53**, 1; **106**, 4; **132**, 3; **250**, 31.

Folk-Song Society of the North-East, *Bulletin* of the: **51**, 4 (Flanders).

University of Virginia, the Rector, Visitors, and Curator of MSS of the Alderman Library, Winston

Wilkinson MSS: **7**, 23; **10**, 28, 35, 53; **49**, 4, 37; **84**, 60, 63; **277**, 49; **293**, 12.

Charles Taphouse & Son: Frank Kidson, *Traditional Tunes*, 1891: **26**, 3; **53**, 100; **73**, 115; **84**, 33, 94; **110**, 8; **162**, 7; **214**, 36.

J. J. Augustin: Mary O. Eddy, *Ballads and Songs from Ohio*, 1939: **12**, 94; **75**, 46; **93**, 8.

Boston Public Library; Hudson MS: **75**, 53; **95**, 1; **114**, 3a.

B.B.C., Archive of Sound Recording, Marie Slocombe, librarian: **221**, 11; **248**, 9.

L. W. Chappell, *Folk-Songs of the Roanoke and the Albemarle*, 1939: **12**, 8; **85**, 18.

F. M. Collinson & F. Dillon, *Songs from the Countryside*, 1946: **188**, 3; **200**, 42.

Columbia University Press; Dorothy Scarborough, *A Song Catcher in Southern Mountains*, 1937: **75**, 8; **274**, 54.

J. M. Diack, *The New Scottish Orpheus*, 1924: **181**, 5.

Society of Antiquaries, Dublin: P. W. Joyce, *Old Irish Folk Music and Songs*, 1909: **12**, 60; **53**, 9; **248**, 12. *Ancient Irish Music*, 1873: **279**, 13.

University of Florida Press: A. C. Morris, *Folksongs of Florida*, 1950: **20**, 47; **85**, 26.

Theodore G. Garrison, *Forty-five Folk Songs Collected from Searcy County, Arkansas*, 1944: **53**, 105.

New York Public Library: Percy Grainger MSS (by permission of Mrs. Grainger); **45**, 7; **53**, 34.

Dr. Maud Karpeles, MSS: **77**, 9; **105**, 11; **295**, 47. (Subsequently printed in *Folk Songs from Newfoundland*, 1971.)

George Korson, *Pennsylvania Songs and Legends*, 1949: **20**, 22.

Ewan MacColl and Peggy Seeger, private recording: **10**, 3.2.

Ewan MacColl (Goldstein-Riverside recording): **223**, 1; **240**, 5.

Tom Munnelly, private recording: **21**, 2.

University of North Carolina Press: A. K. Davis, Jr., *More Traditional Ballads from Virginia*, 1960: **162**, 5; **278**, 33.

Colm O'Lochlainn, *Irish Street Ballads,* 1939: **278,** 7.

Paisley Central Library, A. Crawfurd MS (by favor of Dr. Emily Lyle): **281,** 1.

Sandy Paton, private recording: **95,** 39.1. (Folk-Legacy recording): **52,** 1.1. (Folkways recording): **286,** 74. L. B. Haggerty & H. Felt (Folk-Legacy): **17,** 4.1.

Plymouth City Libraries, Baring-Gould MSS (Librarian & G. Hitchcock, Esq.) **2,** 15; **299,** 13.

Vance Randolph, *Ozark Folksongs,* Vol. I, 1946: **76,** 16; **95,** 61.

Jean Ritchie, Riverside recording: **74,** 11. Private recording (also Folkways): **76,** 5. Gordon-Pickow Collector Limited Editions recording: **84,** 30, 156.

Peter Shepheard, MSS, private recording: **14,** 7.1; **278,** 69.

Southern Folklore Quarterly: E. C. Kirkland, 1938. **49,** 22.

Ellen Stekert, private recording: **278,** 26.

Evelyn K. Wells, private recording: **210,** 4. *Notes from Pine Mountain Settlement School,* 1935: **7,** 37.

Berkeley, Calif.
May 18, 1975

INTRODUCTION

1

SEVENTY YEARS AGO, George Lyman Kittredge published his invaluable (but tuneless) abridgment of the massive, learned collection of *English and Scottish Popular Ballads* serially issued by his revered master, Francis James Child, between the years 1882 and 1898. Child's work first appeared in ten parts, constituting five big quarto volumes, in an edition of 1,000 copies. The tenth part contains, as a portion of the critical apparatus, an Index of Published Airs, "undertaken for me," writes Child in a preliminary note, and compiled "by my constant friend Mr William Walker, of Aberdeen." It is thus manifest that the Index of Airs was not an afterthought: it was integral to Child's own design. In itself, the List is without discriminations: it contains no evaluative signals of preference, no indication of repeated printings of the same air by successive editors; nor is it quite exhaustive even for its chosen books of reference. The bulk of its contents is extracted from a round half dozen collectors or editors, mainly these: James Johnson, R. A. Smith, G. R. Kinloch, W. Motherwell, W. Christie, and the library men, William Chappell and E. F. Rimbault. Whatever its insufficiencies, its choice of authorities was judicious, and the list of airs is a sizable one. It contains, by careful count, 447 references, sorted by Child's numbers and titles. This total is raised to an even 500 by the addition of fifty-three tunes printed from manuscript. Eleven of these are to ballads not listed in Walker's Index, which contains none but references to tunes previously published. Five of the new tunes were contributed by Walker himself.

Walker's interest in the subject did not flag with the death of Child. While his list contains no citations from Gavin Greig or the Rev. J. B. Duncan, he was later to copy from their enormous Aberdonian collections all the tunes belonging to the Child ballads. His efforts on Child's behalf have received too little acknowledgment. Neither Greig nor Duncan limited their concern with Scottish folk-song to the ballads, and it must have been Walker's insistent preoccupation with that segment of their work which led directly to the selection of their Child material for separate publication. Most of it eventually appeared as *Last Leaves of Traditional Ballads and Ballad Airs*, edited by Alexander Keith, and privately published for the Buchan Club of Aberdeen in 1925. Both Greig and Duncan died in the years of the First World War. But they no doubt concurred in thus limiting the volume, for Walker worked with them on its earlier stages; and he continued to further it after their deaths. He was in fact the custodian of their total collection until it was subsequently donated to the Library of King's College, Aberdeen University. Keith, the nominal and efficient editor of *Last Leaves*, makes personal acknowledgment of Walker's invaluable assistance and encouragement.

Of most of this coming attention to the musical side of research in balladry, Child could have had little premonition. But the American Folklore Society was founded in 1888, and Child, who had just reached the midpoint of his *magnum opus*, was elected its first president. Its English counterpart had been established ten years earlier, and Child was inevitably in touch with all related activities abroad, both in Britain and on the Continent. Among his foreign correspondents were Sabine Baring-Gould and Frank Kidson, each deeply interested in the field-collecting of English folk-song. Their publications, as well as those of Christie, Bruce and Stokoe, W. W. Newell, and Lucy Broadwood, at once found a place in Child's bibliography of sources for his texts. They were all primarily song collections, "made from the mouths of the People." Although Child did not see the music as an essential part of his editorial responsibility, and perhaps could hardly conceive of scholarly ways of incorporating the musical component of his subject with those aspects of it with which he was supremely conversant, it is mere justice to recognize that he did take the requisite first step by instigating the gathering of all existing evidence of tune-records. That objective was more closely bound than he suspected to his effort to collect, by means of circulated appeals to rural school-teachers, whatever scraps of traditional balladry might be recovered from oral sources. But contact at first hand with the bearers of tradition *as song* was what to him was missing, and the lack of it led to disappointingly meagre and even misleading results.

Very soon after Child's death, the essential contact with living tradition began to be supplied. The concentrated efforts of collecting were now turned primarily toward the recovery of the music, which could only be got from the lips of the singers themselves. The singers sang what they liked, and it turned out that, among much else, they were very fond of the traditional ballads which Child had sought, but had found in written records alone. Here, surprisingly, was uncovered a vast treasury of fresh oral versions, which in effect transformed the subject from an antiquarian study to a socio-musicological inquiry grounded in contemporary evidence. There seemed every reason to believe that such evidence could be augmented almost any day by energetic, adventurous, qualified seekers. The (English) Folk Song Society was founded by a relatively small body of enthusiasts in 1898. Their initial antiquarian bias was soon swallowed up and superseded by whole-hearted response to the appeal of the living music discovered by the collectors. This in turn drew in a number of highly gifted musicians who joined the quest, energizing the Society. Cecil Sharp, Ralph Vaughan Williams, and Percy Grainger were among those who contributed their finds to the Society's *Journal*, which soon became the general repository, a kind of national archive, of truly native melody. Until the outbreak of the First World War, this fever of collecting galvanized the activities of the Society.

Unquestionably, Kittredge at Harvard developed a lively interest in all this field-collecting, and gave his influence and encouragement to its furtherance by the award of fellowships and the publication of regional gatherings of folk-song in books and journals. In the summer number of the *Journal of American Folk-Lore*, vol. XXX, 1917, he himself edited an important collection of ballads and songs, gathered and sent him by various collectors on this side of the Atlantic from oral sources: a sort of American supplement to Child, with a score and more of ballad texts and tunes, and multiple bibliographical references and notes; and with an equal number of other folk-songs similarly annotated—enough for a small volume, the spin-off of a busy scholarly life. Kittredge calls it a "report," but a less Olympian figure would have elaborated it into a book.

2

Kittredge commences his famous Introduction to the abridged *Child* with a definition of the Ballad. It will be well to take a close look at this, for it is highly indicative of his point of view, symptomatic of not only his approach to the subject, but that of almost all his scholarly predecessors and contemporaries. "A ballad," he writes, "is a song that tells a story, or—to take the other point of view—a story told in song. More formally, it may be defined as a short narrative poem, adapted for singing, simple in plot and metrical structure, divided into stanzas, and characterized by complete impersonality so far as the author or singer is concerned." It is noteworthy that he immediately swings from song as the primary constituent to a more congenial position, in which the story is primary. But the term *song* is still a little embarrassing, having awkward connotations or overtones that deflect one's train of thought. Consequently, he abandons it in the next sentence, and substitutes *poem*: "a short narrative poem, adapted for singing." If it is *adapted* for singing, we may infer that, when so treated, that is not its natural state. It would have been a straight narrative poem before being adapted for singing. What seems to be implied here is that the poem was independently made, and that the musical accompaniment is added at a subsequent stage in the process of ballad-making; as a composer might *set* his chosen verses to music.

In his hypothetical example of how a ballad might come into being, Kittredge cites "The Hangman's Tree" (Child no. 95). He writes conjecturally of its first performance by the improvising author: "The audience are silent for the first two stanzas and until the first line of the third has been finished. After that, they join in the song" (p. xxvi). Is it not pertinent to ask how the tune got there? Did the audience know it already? Did the "improvising author" invent it as he sang? Did the audience catch it from him before he had completed it? It happens that the tune of this particular version of that ballad was preserved and printed by Child in the musical appendix. It would have been better had Kittredge looked at it again. For the musical statement requires *three* stanzas to reach its conclusion. Moreover, the second half of the second stanza is not a repetition of the first stanza's second half. And if the audience had joined in the song after the first line of the third stanza, there might have been a muddle; for the third stanza opens differently from the other two, and leaves a choice, whether to continue on another course, or to revert either to stanza one or to stanza two. It chooses the last alternative. But, supposing the singers to have achieved some kind of osmotic combination, we may still ask whether it is more reasonable to think that the author improvised the stanza-pattern as he went, or to suppose that he already had it in his head. And if the latter, what was it that he had? A stanza-pattern, or a tune already devised, either his own or one he remembered? We have seen that the tune outruns the stanzaic boundaries. The tune makes musical sense. It is not formless. Its phrases run parallel, or contrast pleasingly. Their cadences balance in a melodic logic. The whole simple structure is aesthetically satisfying, not a random concatenation of notes in meaningless sequence.

How did this come about? As a spontaneous invention, to conform to the evolving structure of the verbal stanza? But we have seen that he already had a three-tiered pattern in mind. This rudimentary ballad is conceived from the start as a total structure built in blocks of three units apiece, each unit matching its counterpart at the next stage, and each block bound into one by the over-riding tune, the last third of which is marked off by a perceptible metrical distinction in its first phrase. The so-called improviser had to know beforehand, both as to text and tune, what the structure was on which he was engaged. His improvisations would have had to be limited to the arbitrary substitution of persons: the rest was premeditated and fixed. So was the climactic conclusion of redemption. If this be spontaneous composition, the creative act is sufficiently complex.

The fact must not be minimized that a simple tune is a powerful organism, with far-reaching effects. Kittredge allows a ballad to be called a song, but this, for him, appears an insignificant concession. It would seem that a ballad read or recited in speech is indistinguishable from a ballad sung. But whoever listens to the same ballad, first read aloud and then sung, must recognize a palpable difference. If, moreover, the ballad is sung, as may often happen, by or in a group gathered for communal, participative enjoyment, and ready to dance to it or to join in chorus or refrain, the contrast is extreme. Furthermore, it is demonstrable that without the impelling music some of the most familiar of our ballads could never have come into recognizable being. Consider, for example, a "play-party" version of "The Two Sisters" (Child no. 10). A single stanza will suffice as evidence:

> Oh sister, sister, please lend me your hand,
>   Bow-wee down,
> Oh sister, sister, please lend me your hand,
>   Bow and balance to me.
> Oh sister, sister, please lend me your hand,
> That you may pull me to dry land.
>   I'll be true to my love,
>   If my love will be true to me.

The tune itself dictates the stanzaic pattern, as mere narrative could never have done; suggests the line repetitions, instigates the choral or refrain elements, and binds the whole into a unity to which all the other stanzas must equally conform. Whatever the alterations of person, action, or consequent mood, this dominant melodic control is never relinquished. Simultaneously, it slows the pace of narrative, evens the impact of diverse action, and lowers the emotional temperature, with the shimmer of atmospheric heat at a distance.

3

Perhaps the lyrical bias of the ballad-*genre*, conceived as song, and marked habitually by overt lyrical stigmata—refrain internal or external, chorus or burden, repeated lines—stands in inherent opposition to the narrative impulse. Narrative, at any rate, does not by its own nature consent to be cut into blocks all of equal size, regardless of the content of each block, whether of action, speech, or description; nor to be further divided into halves and quarter-lengths by line and set rhyme; nor to be submissive to constant interruption and repetition at fixed points throughout its length, at the behest of an arbitrary and relatively uncompromising vehicle imposed to contain it by a power owning another lordship. It may be safely declared that a narrative subjected to such unremitting and inescapable domination, if successful, is a *tour de force*.

In this paradoxical situation, it appears to have been discovered early that there were two satisfactory ways of meeting the challenge and effecting a satisfactory compromise. One, and perhaps the later, avenue of escape from the strait-jacket, was to give the narrative its head, and to reduce the importance of the tune to its essential minimum, cutting down or eliminating the refrain elements and repetitions. An end refrain, when it required only a repeating of the last line of the stanza, could be omitted at will, without destroying the symmetry of the tune. The better, and longer, Robin Hood ballads, the longer battle pieces, and (questionably) the border ballads, seem to have followed this track. To be sure, "Dick o' the Cow" (Child no. 185) and "Jock o' the Side" (Child no. 187) have interlaced refrains, which the tunes require. But the evidence here is sparse on traditional continuity: it rests in the first case on a single example; in the second, it is clear that the tune was drastically modified and simplified as it was handed on—if not, instead, elaborated by the first editor. Scott's "Kinmont Willie" (Child no. 186), which he may himself have composed, is unencumbered with any refrain.

It is worth remembering, however, that the tune is a potent *aide-mémoire*. There are numberless instances of ballads in fragmentary state, where the narrative is so confused, disordered even in its central incidents, or all but forgotten, that everything would have been lost, were it not for the tune. This is often true even of the most popular ballads. Narrative interest, then, is not essential for survival, and still less suspense or climax. But a tune *is* essential. Obviously, the tune has the best chance of being remembered, because it is repeated, as a near-constant, throughout the ballad; and if composed of recurrent phrases, has an even better chance of enduring in the memory. And some words will in all likelihood cling to the notes.

The other way of meeting the dilemma is by accepting and exploiting the lyrical component to the full, surrendering narrative to the indulgence of rhythm in time, repetition, refrain, choral interplay, burden. This is what we acknowledge as typifying the ballad. It is the habit of the accepted favorites, turning a handicap as story into a benefit as song.

<blockquote>

It fell aboot a Martimas time,
  An' a gay time it was then, O,
When oor guidwife had puddins to mak
  An' she boil'd them in the pan, O.
Chorus. The barrin' o' oor door weel, weel, weel
  O, the barrin' o' oor door weel. (no. 275)

</blockquote>

<blockquote>

There wis a wee cooper wha lived in Fife
  Nickity nackity noo' noo' noo'
An' he has gotten a gentle wife
  Hey Wullie Wallacky how John Dougall
  Alane quo Rushety roue' roue' roue' (no. 277)

</blockquote>

There was an old farmer in Yorkshire did dwell
    (*Whistle*)
He had an old wife and he wished her in Hell.
Sing fa la la la, fa la la la,
Sing fa la la liddle la day.   (no. 278)

There was a jolly beggar, an' a beggin he was boun',
    Wi' his fal an' his dal an' his dandie, O,
An' he's taen up his quarters at yon neeper toon,
    Wi' his teerin owrin eerin owrin andie, O.   (no. 279)

Once there was a ship in the Northern Counteree,
The title she went under was the Golden Vanity,
Supposed to have been taken by a Turkish canoe,
    And sunken in the Lowlands low.
    Lowlands, Lowlands low,
    And sunken in the Lowlands low.   (no. 286)

A trooper lad came here last nicht,
    O' ridin he was weary,
A trooper lad came here last nicht,
    When the moon was shinin' clearly.
Chorus.   Bonnie lassie, I'll lie near ye yet,
Bonnie lassie, I'll lie near ye.
An I'll gar all your ribbons reel,
When the mornin's there I'll leave ye.   (no. 299)

4

Of the primary ingredients of a tale—action, character, description—it is noteworthy that folk ballads have relatively little concern for description, limiting it mainly to adjective and epithet—often cliché. Action, moreover, is likely to be hurried over, "leaping and lingering," as Gummere aptly phrased the procedure. The lingering is what holds and fixes attention. On examination, it will oftenest be found to center on a confrontation between two persons; and because ballads are more often than not concerned with some aspect of heterosexual love, a love-relation is likely to be the focus of the episode. But the emotion of love is treated as a fact, not to be described or analyzed as in a love-lyric: rather, accepted as the motivation of speech and consequent action. So that characteristically the typical ballad tends above all to condense into dialogue. Herein is likely to lie the essence of the form, which, one may say, reaches instinctively for dramatic interchange between people, and aspires to the condition of pure drama in some of the most memorable examples of the *genre*. We think at once of "Edward" (Child no. 13) and "Lord Randall" (no. 12), which are dialogue throughout, without the addition of a single third-personal word either of introduction, conclusion, or identification of speakers. The same is true of "The Maid Freed from the Gallows" (no. 95). Cases quite so bare of narrative elements are not common; but they essentialize the form. The high proportion of speech in dialogue, throughout the collection, is a basic feature of balladry; and this holds also of those ballads, mentioned earlier, in which are to be found the greatest degree of narrative. Direct discourse of the persons involved in the action is the native mode of ballad story-telling, and is doubtless the most telling cause of the vivid immediacy of the best of the kind.

> "Is there ony dogs into this toun,
>   Maiden, tell me true."
> "And what wad ye do wi' them,
>   My hinny and my dow?"
>
> "They'll rive a' my mealpocks,
>   And do me meikle wrang."
> "O dool for the doing o't,
>   Are ye the puir man?"   (Child no. 279)

Gerould observes[1] that 80 or 90 of Child's "specimens" "carry out the action almost wholly through dialogue." He specifies the following: Child nos. 176, 178, 180, 193, 195, 200, 203, 205, 208, 232, 233, 241.

<h1 style="text-align:center">5</h1>

The tune is what keeps the ballad syntax simple and straightforward. It controls phrasal structure according to what the ear takes in as a musical unit. Since the thought is conveyed in a series of musical phrases, it must be understood as they are sung, not wait for clarifying essentials; so the meaning of a line is not in suspense, nor often split between two melodic units. The stanza's length and pattern seldom escape the fixed control of the tune, the cadence-points of which determine rhetorical pauses. These are the natural turning-points, and give the tune its balance and proportion, its rationale. In a four-phrase tune, the mid- and final cadences are moments of greater emphasis, marking an equivalent division; and they commonly assert a mutual reference, whether of contrast or reiteration. They are a sort of musical rhyme, and in accord with them the normal ballad-rhyme comes at the end of lines 2 and 4. A familiar example of this chiming is notable in the double-rhyme and melodic balance throughout "Barbara Allen" (Child no. 84). When the fourth line of the quatrain is repeated to make a refrain, the symmetry of the tune is not upset, and the midpoint remains where it was. But alternatively, because of the greater emphasis of phrases 2 and 4, internal refrain is suggested, and these

---

[1] G. H. Gerould, *The Ballad of Tradition*, 1932, p. 85.

lines are often given over to lyric or choral comment of non-narrative sort: as

Binnorie, O Binnorie (2) and
By the bonny mill-dams of Binnorie (4)

Or the pattern may be expanded over-all to the length of a double-strain tune, like that of "The Two Sisters" quoted earlier.

Apart from this kind of lyrical interruption of the narrative, the tune is unfriendly to parenthetical complexities. Conditional clauses tend to precede, not follow, declaratory statement, because this order requires no corrective reconsideration. Consequently, the normal connectives of ballad syntax are progressive ones: *and, when, then, or, for, where, which, that, to* (in order to), *until*, etc.

Because complex verbal statement is not readily conveyed in a regularly repeated succession of chosen notes, it has come about by the natural working of mutual accommodation that ballad characters, restricted to this mode of expression, should be simple, direct, uncomplicated in thought, speech, and act. Typically, each of them takes either the whole tune, or half of it, to carry his unhurried, conventional idea to completion.

He took the second one by the hand
     All a lee and a lonely O
And whipped her around till he made her stand
     On the bonny bonny banks of Vergeo.

O will you be a robber's wife?
     All a lee and a lonely O
Or will you die by my penknife?
     On the bonny bonny banks of Vergeo.

I will not be a robber's wife,
     All a lee and a lonely O
I would rather die by your penknife.
     On the bonny bonny banks of Vergeo.

He took the penknife in his hand,
     All a lee and a lonely O
And it's there he took her own sweet life.
     On the bonny bonny banks of Vergeo.   (Child no. 14)

Speeches of only a single melodic phrase are uncommon, and a phrase divided between two speakers (except for mere identifications of character—as "Lord Thomas said"—) would be very hard to find. It would clutter the sense. Ballad stychomythia proceeds at stanza-pace, as in the example just quoted.

Moreover, the tune does not easily tolerate statements that contradict its established rhythm.

When they occur, the sense is blurred or obliterated. For example:

> Then Willie's ta'en his pistol oot,
> And set it to the minister's breist:
> "O, marry me [i.e., us], marry me, minister,
> Or else I'll be your priest, your priest,
> Or else I'll be your priest."

Here the sense demands an emphatic stress on the possessive "your." But the word falls each time on an unstressed note, and the music over-rides the irony of the threat, so that we hear, not "Or else I'll be yóur priest," but "Or elśe I'll bé your priést."

This raises the question of ironic statement, and we may usually hold it in suspicion when it appears. Thus, in Sir Walter Scott's version of "Thomas the Rhymer" (Child no. 37), we find:

> she pu'd an apple frae a tree—
> "Take this for thy wages, True Thomas,
> It will give thee the tongue that can never lie."

> "My tongue is mine ain," True Thomas said;
> "A gudely gift ye wad gie to me!
> I neither dought to buy nor sell,
> At fair or tryst where I may be.

> "I dought neither speak to prince or peer,
> Nor ask of grace from fair ladye."

In the level rendition of the tune, the irony of his retort is sure to be missed, because it does not *sing*, so as to be distinguished tonally from other stanzas. And if the singer chooses to circumvent the difficulty by extraneous signals, alterations of voice, or other hints of facial expression or gesture, he is flouting the impassive, objective habit of delivery that makes folk-singing often impressive, for the sake of an audience-conditioned dramatic rendition, a self-conscious appeal radically inimical to the *genre* of traditional balladry—a different and individualized art, whatever the adventitious merits of the solo performance.

6

It is seldom possible to follow a particular ballad-variant, text and tune, more than two or three generations back. A living singer will tell us that he "had" the song from a parent or even a grandparent, but his testimony can seldom outreach his own memory. "Since time immemorial" sounds impressive when family tradition is in question, but the proof is usually to seek. Few editors are able to match the assurance with which Dean Christie, in 1876, can assert that his air for some ballad was noted in Buchan by his father, in 1816, from the singing of an aged relative; or that he can follow another distinctly by the same agency to 1756. But, to our regret, both his father and himself "arranged" their melodies after taking them down; and neither was interested in recording the exact texts to which the airs had been sung, contenting themselves with "epitomized" copies taken mainly from Buchan's and Jamieson's published works. We cannot, therefore, even in these well-documented cases, be sure that what the editor published was, in musically significant particulars, what was actually sung a century or a century and a half earlier. The currency of the ballad in the previous century, in a given region and in a familiar form, is, however, established; and its melodic resemblance to later, and occasionally earlier, records might confirm the song's continued life in tradition during that whole period.

For, in spite of incessant slight alteration, tunes have survived in recognizable shape in sufficient quantity to convince any qualified student that a folk melody may in its outlines have existed in tradition for a very long time. It may meanwhile have been borrowed for other uses, been wedded to various texts, secular or sacred, across the intervening years. But it is a durable entity, and has a life of its own, the persistence of which is not to be gainsaid. The vast bulk of our records is comparatively recent, but such evidence as we have controverts the often expressed opinion that tunes change in tradition into a new and quite different shape. They neither change so drastically nor so rapidly as to become unrecognizable in their basic identity over long periods, even, in some cases it may be, over centuries. Therefore, when we can perceive no resemblance between one tune and another, there probably *is* no connection. We ought not lightly to hypothesize that the first has by the action of tradition been gradually transmuted into the second. Departures from continuity, in tunes associated with the "same" ballad (i.e., analogous texts embodying a kindred theme, or story), are undoubtedly common; but it is not likely that unbroken transmission is responsible for the phenomena of divergence. Some alien influence, an *anti*-traditional force, has most probably intervened.

There are indications of longevity among the ballad-tunes other than the all-too-infrequent happy chance of some clerical hand's having set them in musical script at an early date. Although we can never trace a straight linear path for a ballad-tune from generation to generation, since no such connected chain of evidence has ever existed except accidentally for two or three members of the same kin, the tenacity with which folk-tunes cling to some quintessential core of identity, despite all superficial change of their individual notes, metre, sequence of phrase, is one of the most remarkable facts about them. There is, for example, a melodic "family" to which a dozen Child ballad-tunes, as well as a hundred others, belong, which can be traced from the present day, back through the centuries and across national boundaries and every sort of textual subject-matter. It has no inclusive name, but well-known examples can be cited: "How should I your true-love know," "Thomas the Rhymer," "I would I were in my own country," "Hind Horn" ("The Lone Prairie" in the U.S.), "The Cruel Mother." It is at the heart of British folk tradition; it exists in *The Fitzwilliam Virginal Book* (Elizabethan); in a Swedish Latin carol-book, *Piae Cantiones*, 1582; and in an antiphonary of the twelfth century, from Apt, near Avignon, under the name "En Gaudeat."[2] The last-named

[2] See an article, "Some Observations about Melodic Variation in British-American Folk Tunes," in the *Journal of the American Musicological Society*, Vol. III, 1950, pp. 120-134, where 33 examples are quoted.

seems to be related to a liturgical chant, "Corona Aurea," which is the recognized precursor of the widely known French folk song, "La Pernette." The shape of some of our tunes, moreover, more than suggests their kinship with Gregorian melodies. Examples are D'Urfey's tune for Child no. 1, "Riddles Widely Expounded," which resembles, almost note for note, the *Sanctus* in the Mass, "Orbis Factor," of the eleventh century; and the typical tune-pattern of Child no. 4, to be compared with the *Sanctus* of the Easter Mass, *Lux et Origo*.

Such cases as these do not indicate *lineage* in the ordinary sense of parental or filial connections, descent through generations by oral transmission, traceable or not. But they display something equally interesting, and a good deal farther reaching: a melodic pattern, or habit, peculiarly congenial to the mind of western Europe for the last millennium and longer. It re-forms in successive tunes, never quite the same, but with noteworthy resemblance, so that we say they are "related." The basic elements will be a sequence of notes belonging to an established scale, occurring in separable musical phrases, equivalent in duration, usually measured off in units of four pulse-beats each, of which the second and fourth phrases end in cadences normally balancing. Four such phrases typically constitute a tune mutually integrated. Such a structure is the ordinary vehicle of the ballad stanza. This is its simplest form, and it is so omnipresent that it can be found from beginning to end of our melodic culture—from the Ambrosian hymns of the fourth century down, say, to "Casey Jones" of the twentieth:

Laetus dies hic transeat,
Pudor sit ut diluculum,
Fides velut meridies,
Crepusculum mens nesciat

May this day pass in gladness,
May our purity be like the dawn,
Our faith like the noonday,
And may our souls know no twilight.

St. Ambrose, "Splendor paternae gloriae."
(Translated by F. Brittain)

All the great Latin hymns subsequently have used the form.

7

A folk-tune is brief enough to be readily grasped and remembered as a whole: it has an inner unity that makes it *shapely* to the ear and mind. Hence, it is individual, recognizable, and welcome on repetition. As a temporal event, or succession of notes, it consists of a little tour through a sonic landscape; so that as we follow the course we recognize its topography: the setting forth, the approach to a turning-point, a moment of heightened interest, a pause of retrospection or anticipation, a homecoming. It falls naturally into related and relatively equal, self-defining stages of its whole extent, revealing balance, contrast, and decision. The balance normally relies on approximately the same number of stresses in corresponding phrases; the contrast (also an aspect of balance) usually on tonal sequence and management; the decision appears in cadential statement and held, or repeating, notes, like signposts at an intersection. Because the tune is seized as a whole, and because its several parts have these mutual references, we gain already the suggestion of stanzas of a certain pattern and identical length. Since the phrasal cadences get their weight and meaning from their relative emphasis and relation to the tonic (usually the final note), they inherently prompt corresponding verbal emphases, of rhyme or pause. By their perceptible division or separation, they exert, moreover, a pressure on the verbal partner, so that the total syntactical and rhetorical structure is palpably affected, and restricted, by their influence.[3]

So much for the over-all topography. But in order to compare one tune with another, we must consent to a closer analysis. Our first business will be to study melodic contour. By a figure of speech, really strange, but so universally accepted as to seem instinctive, we say the notes of a scale go up or down. (The ancient Greeks did not see it that way.) Now, granting that the voice as a musical instrument can produce theoretically, in unbroken, continuous sequence all possible differences of tonal distinction or pitch, between one note and its octave: for present purposes it will be best to ignore microtones—plus or minus levels, sharp or flat—more precise than the inexact semitones of the diatonic scale, accepting the tuning to which most of us today are accustomed by the equal-tempered piano. If we acknowledge that in fact by this tuning every interval but the octave itself is acoustically incorrect, though the ear accepts it: it should be easy to accommodate the rather flexible intonation of a folk-singer who tends to sharpen certain notes in an ascending phrase, and flatten some when descending. Actuality is more liberal than we recognize or usually admit in our own case, in this field of sound; and, unless for scientific uses, it is unnecessary to record tonal shading beyond the refinement of equal temperament. It is enough to be aware that the notation is no better than approximate.

Equal temperament divides the octave into twelve equal semitones. The whole series forms an octave segment of chromatic notes that remains undifferentiated in kind, whatever the note on which it commences. The chromatic scale therefore has no anchorage on a center tone or tonic, and can be properly considered "unnatural" and artificial. By contrast, the natural, or diatonic, system generates a series of scales markedly differing from one another according to which note is taken as tonic or starting-point. This difference arises from the fact that when the chromatic, or "unnatural," notes are not admitted, a series composed of five whole tones and two semitones is left. If there were nothing but whole tones in the series, the scale would be—and is—equally "unnatural" with the semitonal, chromatic series.

But the position of the semitones in relation to the tonic center determines the character and feeling-quality of the familiar scale, and consequently of the melodies that employ it. We all recognize the difference between a tune in the major and one in the minor. The differences, we find, arise from the fact that, in the major, the semitonal intervals are between the third and fourth, and between the seventh and eighth (or octave) notes of the rising scale, counting from the tonic; and that in the natural melodic minor, the semitones lie between the second and third degrees, and between the fifth and sixth, above the tonic. Confining ourselves to the "white" notes of the piano, a tune anchored on C, without any accidental sharps or flats, would of course exemplify the first, or major, scale; and a tune based on A, again on "white" notes only, would illustrate the second, or minor, scale. Why the shift in the relative position of the semitones with reference to the tonic center should entail psychological consequences, is a mystery which I do not know that anyone has ever satisfactorily explained. But

[3] The foregoing paragraph is borrowed from the editor's essay, "Of Ballads, Songs, and Snatches," printed in his collected papers, *The Ballad as Song*, University of California Press, 1969, p. 308.

an emotional difference has always been felt; and it is still popularly agreed that the first generates cheerfulness in its tunes, and the second, sadness or melancholy. So sure of the fact were the medieval churchmen that, assuming the naughty tunes would normally be built on the cheerful scale, they proscribed its use in sacred music. It was called the *modus lascivus*, and the significance of that requires little Latin to grasp.

By misunderstanding and misinterpretation of the ancient Greek theorists, the medieval theorists came to adopt some of the Greek terminology in mistaken uses. But the latter were perfectly clear as to what scales they meant to designate by the wrong names; so that, in the course of time, the names were generally accepted in their new meaning, and acquired a dignity not to be easily dislodged or replaced by other terms. So long as they are understood in their adopted sense, it is more convenient to continue with them than to invent a fresh set of terms.

To each note of the diatonic series a Greek name was attached to designate that scale of which it served as the center. The scale with C as tonic, the *modus lascivus*, was called the Ionian mode. As our major, it is still the most favorite mode of British-American folk-tunes. The scale with D as tonic, with semitones between second and third, and sixth and seventh, was called the Dorian. The scale with E as tonic, wherein the interval of the semitone lies between the tonic and second degree, and the fifth and sixth, is the Phrygian mode. The scale on F, with semitones between four and five, and seven and eight, is the Lydian. The scale on G, with semitones between three and four, and six and seven, is the Mixolydian. That on A, with semitones between two and three, and five and six—our natural minor—is the Æolian mode. That on B, with semitones between tonic and second, and fourth and fifth, was called the Locrian. Neither the Lydian nor the Locrian is often found in the British-American folk-tradition, though they are accepted elsewhere in Europe.

As at present generally allowed with regard to the major and minor, it was formerly held that all the rest of the modes likewise had emotional overtones, or semantic significance. There was some dispute, or at least difference of opinion, as to the mood expressed by this or that mode; but all agreed that the implications were potentially important, because music had transcendent meaning for many centuries. The music of the spheres, it was felt, might have generated the scales, and, in whatever shape of belief, still kept potent poetic reverberations. Lorenzo merely amplified common faith, when he told Jessica in Belmont:

> There's not the smallest orb which thou beholdst
> But in his motion like an angel sings,
> Still quiring to the young-eyed cherubins;
> Such harmony is in *immortal* souls [including ours],
> But whilst this muddy vesture of decay
> Doth grossly close us in, we cannot hear it.

In the Elizabethan lutenist composer Dowland's translation of an earlier treatise on music, there is an amusing reflection of belief in modal influences. Dowland's book was published in 1609; his original had appeared at Leipzig in 1517. From this work we learn:

The Dorian Moode is the bestower of wisedome, and causer of chastity. The Phrygian causeth wars, and enflameth fury. The Eolian doth appease the tempests of the minde, and when it hath appeased them, luls them asleepe. The Lydian doth sharpen the wit of the dull, and doth make them that are burdened with earthly desires, to desire heavenly things, an excellent worker of good things . . . . every habit of the mind is governed by songs, (as Macrobius writeth) for songs make men sleepy, and wakefull, carefull, and merrie, angry, and merciful, songs do heale diseases, and produce divers wonderful effects (as saith Petrarch), moving some to vain mirth, some to a devout and holy joy, yea oft-times to godly teares (*Micrologus*, 1609, Bk. I. ch. 13, p. 36).

Such attributions may be taken as no more than hearsay, and indeed Dowland himself prefers to stop short of certainty in particulars. But Sir Thomas Browne's more philosophical words, half a century later, throw a sober light on the serious belief in music as a bridge between physics and metaphysics:

. . . even that vulgar and Taverne Musicke, which makes one man merry, and another mad, strikes in mee a deepe fit of devotion, and a profound contemplation of the first Composer. There is something in it of Divinity more than the eare discovers. It is an Hieroglyphicall and shadowed lesson [i.e., piece of music] of the whole world, and Creatures of God; such a melody to the eare, as the whole world, well understood, would afford the understanding. In briefe, it is a sensible fit [extract] of that Harmony, which intellectually sounds in the eares of God (*Religio Medici*, 1643, § 9, pp. 164-5).

Browne perceived in the notes of a simple tune evidences of order, proportion, relationship, which reflected the supernal harmony that he apprehended in the universe, in the planetary and stellar motions, and movements of the human spirit in divine affinity, which enabled him to accept conceptually the music of the spheres. A tune was thus for him an allegorical symbol.

8

For us, however, the matter is of more immediate concern, and we must take a further look at modal habits, not as a question of mere antiquarian curiosity, but for present, practical reasons. The series already named above and differentiated by the position of semitones was not thought up by idle monks to lay down prescriptive rules for those who wished to compose tunes. Quite the contrary. The tunes came into existence without benefit of monastic midwifery—had come, and would continue to come. They came at the behest of musical instincts widely shared among Western peoples. The clerics gave the names to phenomena they found already embodied in uncounted lyrical creations which the singers could not have written down, had they tried. The system of modes was only a useful way of ordering what was already there. The pedantry—if such it was—did not command the product into utterance, but only described and classified it. The tunes arose in a preharmonic stage of melodic invention, which was gradually discarded with the increasing complexity of sophisticated harmonic evolution. But the simpler impulses did not altogether disappear, for they were indeed at the root of all music-making. They persisted, and are found today where they have not been overlaid or obliterated by later musical fashions. As a consequence, the vast bulk of British-American traditional folk-tunes still conforms to those ancient patterns, and it is therefore a matter of present, not antiquarian, concern to familiarize ourselves with this inheritance so as to recognize and distinguish its several characteristics. Since we have no trouble in discriminating between the major and minor modes today, it should not be burdensome to add the recognition of several others to our range of learning. To do so is to enrich our musical experience and pleasure.

Should someone protest that the differences are insignificant, since they are only the shift of a semitone here or there, we easily find by experiment that, whatever the ultimate significance, the effect of these differences is palpable. Let any one take a familiar tune and "translate" it into a different mode, observing his own responses.[4] Suppose, for example, we try the experiment on "Annie Laurie," a tune in the Ionian, or major, mode. For the purpose, we need go no farther than the first two lines, or phrases of the song. They are as follows:

Now, the only difference between the Ionian and Mixolydian scales is that the first has a semitone between its seventh degree and its octave, whereas the latter has the semitone between sixth and seventh. Make this slight alteration, turning the tune into Mixolydian:

Now, again, we find by laying one scale on top of the other, that the Mixolydian differs from the Dorian at only one point, the former having a semitone between third and fourth degrees, the latter between second and third. Make this change, lowering the major third by a semitone:

Once more, the Dorian and Æolian scales are alike except that a semitone of the former lies between the sixth and seventh, and of the latter, between and the fifth and sixth. Make this change by lowering the sixth of the Dorian:

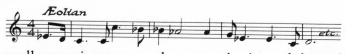

We have now, by small successive steps, made a natural minor of the major tune with which we started. The different effects on the hearer must be left to experience. Of course, the whole tune should be sung through each time, keeping the altered note wherever it occurs in every case, so as to perceive the full effect of each modal shift.

In the present instance, the successive alterations from mode to mode have been made arbitrarily, for purposes of mere illustration. But the fact is that in the course of traditional transmission, similar changes quite often occur. The consequence is that we find the "same" tune—that is, a recognizable variant of the melodic *idea*—appearing in another mode. It may be that another singer learned the tune a different way; or it can happen that a particular singer

[4] It must be understood that change of pitch does not affect the modal scales in traditional singing. What is significant is always the position of the semitones with relation to the tonic.

may instinctively favor one mode or another, so that a bigger proportion of his repertory will show this preference. Because of that possibility, we cannot safely assert that the appearance of a tune in a less "modern," i.e., less familiar, mode—say the Mixolydian or Dorian—is evidence of greater antiquity. But the fact that these practices are congenial to the singer is proof that his ear has been conditioned by tradition to a style of melody that *is* old, being rooted in habits that arose before the major/minor syndrome came in to dominate the scene, and when melody usually made its way without adventitious harmonic assistance, through chordal, or instrumental, accompaniment.

Some pathways from mode to mode are easier, and therefore more likely to be followed, than others. We have seen that only the difference of a note separates the Ionian scale from the Mixolydian, or again, the Mixolydian from the Dorian, or the Dorian from the Æolian. We perceive a closer affinity between the adjacent pairs so listed than if we skipped to a different modal sequence.

But there are many tunes that do not contain all the notes of the full diatonic octave. Ordinarily, where a note is missing, the want is found to occur where a semitone would fill the gap. So that there is a quantity of tunes, otherwise major, lacking the higher or lower seventh which differentiates the Ionian from the Mixolydian scale. And similarly, we find a quantity of tunes lacking the third which distinguishes the Mixolydian from the Dorian. And once again, a number lacking the sixth which divides the Dorian from the Æolian. These hexatonic tunes, therefore, have lost their modal identification as between the pairs. And any hexatonic tune could fill the gap in either direction, by supplying a semitone lower or higher at that point. Thus these gapped tunes are neutral between each pair of modes, and therefore natural bridges.

But we noted at the beginning that every diatonic octave has *two* semitones. And there is another body of tunes, particularly frequent in the Appalachian region, which omits *both* semitones. In so doing, it is clear that these pentatonic tunes have deprived us of the right to say which of *three*, not two, of the modes they would exemplify if their gaps were filled up with notes higher or lower at those places in the scale. So that we can say that each pentatonic is a natural bridge, or channel, whereby each of three modes could pass without effort into either of the other two. For each of the five pentatonic scales, depending on where the gaps lie, is indistinguishable from its three related heptatonic scales. Thus, the first pentatonic coincides, in the notes it possesses, with the Lydian, the Ionian, and the Mixolydian modes. The second pentatonic coincides similarly with the Ionian, the Mixolydian, and the Dorian. The third pentatonic is equally aligned with the Mixolydian, Dorian, and Æolian; the fourth pentatonic, with the Dorian, Æolian, and Phrygian; and the fifth, seldom occurring, with the Æolian, Phrygian, and Locrian.

9

Some tunes, in the range of notes they contain, rise from their tonal center, or tonic, to the octave above. If they extend beyond the octave, it is seldom more than two or three notes higher, or a note or two lower. We say these tunes lie in the *authentic* range, or we call them authentic tunes. Others, however, swing both above and below their tonic center, seldom more than to the upper fifth, or to the fourth note below, counting downward. They have therefore a range equivalent to the authentic class, but their proper octave lies from the lower fifth to the upper fifth, or the lower "dominant" to upper "dominant." (The dominant counting upward is a fifth higher than the tonic, but counting down, is a fourth lower.) Such tunes, with their tonic in the approximate center of their range, are called *plagal* tunes. The important fact is that the tonal center is not altered by the shift of range. But the distinction is valid because the melodic shape of the tune is quite different. For example, "Annie Laurie" is an authentic tune (though extended to two tones above the octave); "Afton Water" ("Flow gently, Sweet Afton," Burns's familiar song) is a plagal tune. When the tune, still keeping its tonal center as before, descends to the lower dominant but rises also to the full octave above the tonic, we call it *mixed*. These rough distinctions are observed throughout the present collection, and are indicated by the symbols a (authentic), m (mixed), and p (plagal). They apply equally to all the modes exemplified.

Now, it is further to be observed, in comparing one mode with another, that from another point of view than that described above, the pairs of adjacent modes have significant affinities too important to be overlooked. These are revealed by the plagal tunes. For the *plagal* segment of the Ionian scale is seen to be identical in its octave extent, from lower to upper fifth, with the *authentic* octave of its adjacent mode, the Mixolydian. It follows that, by establishing a new tonic on the Ionian dominant, the tune thereby becomes an authentic Mixolydian tune. It often happens, especially among the Appalachian tunes, that a 5-phrased, plagal major will in its fourth phrase cadence on the lower fifth, and then in the last phrase, instead of ending on the proper tonic, fall to close on that same lower fifth. If then we choose to regard the last note, or "final," as tonic, our major tune has been translated into the adjacent Mixolydian. Since the fifth of the scale is the most satisfying resting-point after the tonic, such an interchange is neither unnatural nor uncommon.

The point may be illustrated in the following two variants of the ballad, "Lord Thomas and Fair Eleanor" (Child no. 73). The first was collected in Somerset by Cecil Sharp. The second was taken down by Sharp in Kentucky. It happens that the latter is pentatonic and the other hexatonic, but the point at issue is not affected. The gaps will be ignored, except on analysis.

106. "Lord Thomas and Elinda"

Sharp MSS., 624/. Also in Baring-Gould and Sharp, [1906], p. 28. Sung by Mrs. Anne Lacey, Drayton, Somerset, August 31, 1905.

p I/M

3. "Lord Thomas and Fair Ellender"

Sharp MSS., 3849/. Also in Sharp and Karpeles, 1932, I,
p. 125(P). Sung by Mrs. Cis Jones, Goose Creek, Ky.,
August 14, 1917.

a π²

We can see that the same affinities obtain between each pair of adjacent modes. Thus, the plagal Mixolydian, regarded simply as a diatonic scale, is identical with the Dorian authentic; the plagal Dorian with the authentic Æolian; and so on round the circle of modes. This, then, is another route whereby tunes pass from mode to mode.

It will probably be helpful at this point to illustrate what has been so far said about modal interconnections and affiliations with a few examples from extant tunes. Not to make too long a search, we can find all we need for the present purpose among the variants of a single rich but musically consistent traditional ballad, "Lord Bateman" (Child's no. 53, "Young Beichan"). Let us take a scattering of tunes that display the way in which melodic stuff can adopt various nearly allied modal patterns without violence to the "idea" of the tune exemplified. In a series of variants, more or less homogeneous, it will usually be found that there is a modal center, around which the majority of variants will cluster most thickly. It is not suggested that any of the variants here shown in succession is derived immediately from its predecessor. It is quite unlikely that any of the singers knew any other variants than his own, and the sequence exhibited here is not intended to demonstrate a logical or rational progression. But it will serve to illustrate the "moving waters" in popular circulation, without other controls than musical instinct acting in accord with inherited community taste—the common sense of tradition.

The first handful of variants shows how the gapped scales can facilitate the transmission of a melodic idea from one modal conformation to another without willful or arbitrary disturbance.

111. [Lord Bateman]

Smith, 1928, pp. 104-6. Sung by Ada Taylor Graham, Columbia, S.C., 1924; learned from her mother and grandmother.

a I

7. "Lord Batesman"

Randolph, I, 1946, pp. 86(E)-88. Sung by Wiley Hembree, Farmington, Ark., December 12, 1941; learned from his parents, near Farmington, c. 1899.

a π[1]

8. "Lord Bateman"

Barry, Eckstorm, and Smyth, 1929, pp. 106(A)-108. Sung by Mrs. Susie Carr Young, Brewer, Maine; learned from family tradition. Melody recorded by George Herzog.

a I/M

24. [Lord Bateman]

Sharp MSS., 735/. Sung by Mrs. James Southwood, Bridgwater, January 1, 1906.

a M

43. [Lord Bateman]

Sharp MSS., 3971/. Sung by Mrs. Bagley, Beattyville, Ky., September 5, 1917.

a π[2]

A gentleman of the courts of England
A gentleman of high degree
He lived uneasy and discontented
Until he took a voyage to sea.

41. [Young Beichan]

Sharp MSS., 3999/2882-83. Also in Sharp and Karpeles, 1932, I, p. 87(J). Sung by Mrs. Frances Carter, Beattyville, Lee County, Ky., September 8, 1917.

a M/D

29. [Lord Bateman]

Sharp MSS., 1071/. Sung by William Stokes, Chew Stoke, August 27, 1906.

a D (inflected III)

Another group of tunes will show how the authentic-plagal relationship can effect similar modal change. Again, it is not insisted here that tunes are under compulsion to alter by rule, falling (or on the contrary rising) from mode to mode. But the group in question exemplifies natural movement in a natural sequence.

4. [Lord Bacon]

Barry MSS., Bk. I, No. 53D. Miss Bessie Osgood's transcript of Perkins MS. 1790, owned by Mrs. Holden, Boston, Mass.

a I

There is a bass in the MS. copy, but no words are given. The Perkins MS. has 2/4, which Barry reduces to 3/4 and also to 4/4.

60. [Lord Bateman]

Sharp MSS., 545/. Sung by Mrs. Fido (70), Langport, August 11, 1905.

p I

22. "Lord Bakeman"

Mackenzie, 1928, p. 392; text, pp. 16-19. Sung by Alexander Harrison, Maccan, Cumberland County, Nova Scotia.

a M

70. "Lord Brechin"

Greig MSS., IV, p. 14; text, Bk. 764, LIV, pp. 50ff. Also in Greig and Keith, 1925, p. 43(B). Sung by Mrs. Cruickshank, New Deer, Aberdeenshire.

p M

109. [Lord Bateman]

Sharp MSS., 3020/. Sung by Miss Aimers, Rothgar, Ireland, at Stratford-on-Avon, August 15, 1914; learned from her mother, who learned it in turn from her mother.

a D

92. [Lord Bateman]

Sharp MSS., 695/772-76. Also in Sharp, 3rd series, 1906, pp. 28-31, with accompaniment; and Sharp, 1907, pp. 22-23. Sung by Henry Larcom(be), Haselbury Plucknett, December 26, 1905.

p D/Æ [Add E♭ to make p D]

This extraordinarily fine copy, it will be observed, is the only variant with minor tonality in this group.

44. "Lord Bateman"

Randolph, I, 1946, p. 85(C). Sung by Miss Jewell Perriman, Jenkins, Mo., February 28, 1941.

a π^3 | Add F♮ and B♭ to make a Æ |

10

The congeries of modal relationships may be most economically displayed in a simple figure, representing the interconnections of the whole diatonic system in its pure state. By "pure" is meant, uncluttered—or unadulterated—by alien influences such as accidental sharps and flats, and unaffected by abnormal scale-gaps not accounted for by the pentatonic and hexatonic scales. It will not be found that such irregular or exceptional aberrations occur with sufficient frequency in the great mass of traditional British-American records to challenge the basic modality of our folk-song. Where these eccentricities appear, they may of course be easily noted by the careful student in each particular case. In an analysis of 4120 tunes of the Child ballads, only 228 were found to have *a*-systematic gaps. More than two-thirds of these were the abnormal absence of the sixth degree of their scale—which suggests that the sixth, modally considered, is felt to be the least essential note of the scale. But why this should be is a mystery, since it does no less than any of the other scale degrees in differentiation.

So far as our extant records show, the seventh is most likely to be "inflected" in the same tune: that is, to be used in both a higher and lower intonation, natural or sharp, as the case may be: no doubt because of the modern harmonic drift toward the "leading-note." But well below 175 of these occur in the total record. Inflected fourths number less than 50; inflected thirds only 35. What is true of the whole body of Child ballad-tunes is not likely to be contradicted by the sum total of our other folk-tunes. So that we may be confident of the solid modal foundation of the whole melodic tradition.

In the figure now presented, it is to be understood that each point or angle of the star-outline represents a distinct modal scale. The outer points are the heptatonic modes, signified by their initial letters. The hexatonic scales appear with a double initial and a figure indicating which degree is missing in each case. The pentatonic scales are numbered at the inner angles, from one to five. The three points with bracketed signatures, joined by dotted lines, are hypothetical, because they lack their proper tonics, and a scale without its tonic is an anomaly. Theoretically, they would complete the intersecting scheme, but are to be ignored.

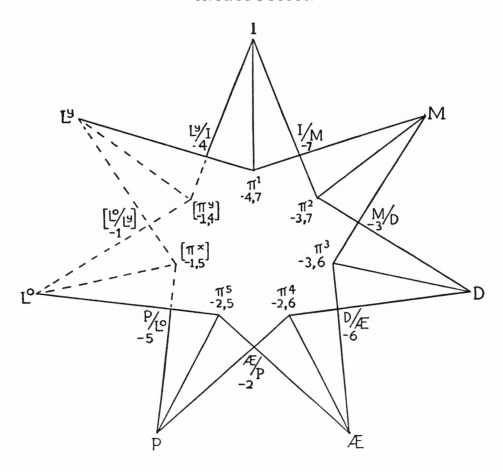

It is pertinent to quote here Gerould's remark, that it is "only by understanding [the processes by which both words and melodies keep continually changing, that] we can find out why ballads and other folk-songs have qualities of their own that are the result neither of blind chance working upon degenerate strays from an ordinary garden of song, nor of a mysterious power somehow resident in the ignorant folk when emotionally stimulated."[5] He quotes Pidal's insistence that "variants are not accidents,"[6] but rather essentials to the process of communal poetizing.

11

Generalizing from the whole mass of tunes in the British-American tradition to which our ballad-texts have adhered, we can discern some deeply grooved melodic pathways through the network of possible variables, which the folk-mind has tended habitually to prefer. They can be briefly summarized: a greater liking for the authentic range; a preference for four-phrase structures, and within these limits, for phrases that do not exactly repeat one another

[5] Gerould, *op. cit.*, p. 165.
[6] M. Pidal, *El Romancero*, 1927, p. 37. Gerould, pp. 169-170.

—ABCD as compared to recurrent patterns of whatever design;[7] a preference for the major galaxy, I/Ly, π^1, I, I/M, M; a strong compulsion to end on, not off, the tonic. When we remember that these are not willful, but communally instinctive, choices, signifying countless unconscious rejections of opposing appeals and possibilities, we acknowledge the power of living tradition.

It is very important to realize that the folk-memory is an active force, not an inert duplicator, so that the choices in question are perpetually being made afresh. There is no fixed original, like an author's signed autograph, to be memorized note for note, and word for word. Just as in the telling of a prose yarn by a practised raconteur, the true folk-singer carries in his or her memory the mental image of a song, malleable in verbal and melodic detail, to be given new realization in every fresh rendition.[8] The differences may be almost unnoticeable, but it is next to impossible for a singer to give an identical repetition of the same song. The notes of the successive stanzas will be affected by the words; the unmemorized words will not be repeated verbatim; the unmemorized notes will be slightly varied as they re-create the tune. The changes will be minute, in accordance with the limited range of traditional idiom. Tradition is a fluid medium, never quite the same, ever renewed. That is what keeps it inexhaustibly interesting and alive.

The Child canon is ordered numerically, according to the narrative themes it contains, each number displaying potentially wide verbal variation. Since it is not musically ordered, it imposes certain restrictions on the order of its tunes. These cannot pass the numerical boundaries arbitrarily fixed by the narrative principle on which it operates. But within the fixed numbered limits, the tunes can be ordered roughly in homogeneous groups, to show their kinship so far as the record permits, and their variety in unity; or, as the case may be, their diversity from time to time.

We can, however, perceive that the tunes themselves refuse to be limited by their textual mates: they have an independent existence, and not infrequently take up with other companions. We shall therefore find favored melodic patterns, or *Gestalten*, reappearing occasionally throughout the range of the whole collection. In broadest outline, the resemblances will appear in the recurrence of the same notes at the same places during the course of the tunes. These will be especially the notes that are accented or stressed so as to give them importance in the shaping of the tune. Thus, the mid-cadence has special weight, in most tunes of the authentic range, and after it the first-cadence note. Then will come the first accented note, and so on. These accents will coincide in a great number of tunes, to mark the contour outlines of the form; so that one can say, for example, that the skeletal outline of a whole mass of tunes will

---

[7] By actual count of nearly 3500 tunes, roughly half are of this pattern. The closest competitor, ABCDE, has fewer than a fifteenth of the total; the next, ABAC, fewer than an eighteenth; the next, ABCDD, a thirtieth. The first two patterns, ABCD and ABCDE together, comprise four and a half times the others combined, even with a further, and obvious pattern, ABAB, added to them. This count, it ought to be said, depends on differentiating phrases by differing cadences.

[8] This is not to deny the continual reappearance of what Samuel Bayard has called "melodic formulae" or "congenial idiomatic expressions." (Cf. his "Prolegomena to a Study of the Principal Melodic Families of British-American Folk Song," in *JAF*, vol. 63, Jan.-Mar. 1950, pp. 1-44.)

conform in the pattern of the first two phrases on the accented sequence of the following degrees of the scale: I V V I, V 8 V V. (The last two accents will most frequently be a held note.) But an almost endless variability gives fleshly substance to this bony structure, and informs it with the breath of individual life.

The Child collection, as said above, was compiled on textual evidence alone, based on the hypothesis that at some point in the past, if not in their present state, all its members had been in oral circulation. The criteria were broad enough to admit specimens of professional minstrelsy like "The Boy and the Mantle" (no. 29), "The Gest of Robin Hood" (no. 117), a long composite made of earlier ballads artfully strung together; and many broadside ballads whose only claim to acceptance was that they were surrogates for genuine pieces of oral literature no longer extant. Among the last sort, is even included one piece worked up by a known author out of semi-traditional matter: Martin Parker's "A True Tale of Robin Hood" (no. 154, printed 1632). And there is, finally, the highly controversial Border Ballad, "Kinmont Willie," made, or remade, by that prince of minstrels, Walter Scott (no. 186). Most of these either lack any traditional music, or are arbitrarily mated for the nonce to a tune.

12

It is a question, therefore, of much more than passing interest to inquire how many, and which, of the Child canon have come down to our day with some sort of melodic record attested by traditional transmission. As we might expect, since the existence of tonal survival was no part of Child's test of popularity, the evidence to be discovered is very unevenly distributed, and by no means commensurate with the whole body of textual records. Over all, better than two-thirds of the numbered themes of Child's "canon" of 305 can be provided with some associated melodic item. It is idle to be more exact, because some attributions are unsubstantiated as traditional, and contrariwise we may still hope for fresh recoveries. As matters stand at present, there are unquestionably above 5000 independent records in existence of traditional variants, excluding unaltered copies transmitted in print or writing. The work of which the present volume is an abridgment contains some 4000 tunes. The distribution, ballad by ballad, ranges from a single tune to as many as 250 variants or versions. Where these are sufficiently alike, or sufficiently distinct, and sufficiently abundant, they can be arbitrarily ordered in groups, according to their sameness or difference. For comparative study, this has been attempted in the collection herein assembled, but without any claim to scientific exactitude.

Far the greater proportion of our extant records are of the present century, and, moreover (probably because of the activity of regional societies along with the devotion of a handful of individual field-collectors), the greater proportion of even this century's harvest is of tunes collected in America. Unfortunately, therefore, we can form no dependable estimate of relative popularity in the singing tradition of previous centuries. Cecil Sharp in Somerset and Gavin Greig in Aberdeenshire showed what could have been accomplished more widely in Britain before the First Great War; and Sharp, by his Appalachian work, was himself the greatest stimulus to subsequent efforts on the western side of the Atlantic. It is an unhappy fact that only three of Child's ballads were set down with their tunes so early as the first decade of the seventeenth century (by Thomas Ravenscroft). It took another century and a half to add another half dozen. The next half-century increased the tally by 150, virtually all Scottish. By the time of Child's death, or to the opening of the present century, we can see from William Walker's bibliographical appendix to Child what had by that time come to light—still bearing in mind that his list is full of duplicate copies, and by no means a guarantee of genuine tradition. G. H. Gerould quotes Carl Engle, whose book on National Music is still consulted. In it he declared, so recently as 1879, that, contrary to the general belief that the English had no native folk-song, the opinion "would probably be found to be only partially correct if search were made in the proper places."[9] Think of it! The Scots, of course, had long taken pride in their musical heritage, and likewise the Welsh and the Irish. But the truth about traditional song in England was largely an undisclosed secret until the day before yesterday.

Since we have no secure basis upon which we can estimate the relative popularity of individual ballads in former generations of singers, we must resort to the strength of late tradition as revealed in widespread and frequent appearance, for the most trustworthy evidence to be had. It is certainly remarkable that Child's first two volumes, in which he placed, on grounds of conjectural age and international diffusion, the ballads with the best claims of venerability, are also with some few exceptions the ones that yield the fullest British-American melodic record of current circulation as living song.

On this basis, it is interesting to make a brief list of general, if not universal favorites. Apart from the first of the lot, which is very far in the lead, it may be said that all are so close that a little diligent field work in likely districts might alter the place of any one of them in a comparative numerical rating. For what it is worth, a tally by tune-count yields the following results in the order given. None of them has left fewer than 125 independent copies in hand at present:

"Barbara Allen" (Child no. 84); "The Outlandish Knight; or Lady Isabel and the Elf-Knight" (no. 4); "Lord Thomas and Fair Eleanor" (no. 73); "The House Carpenter; or The Daemon Lover" (no. 243); "The Gypsy Laddie" (no. 200); "Lord Bateman; or Young Beichan" (no. 53); "The Sweet Trinity; or The Golden Vanity" (no. 286); "Lord Randal" (no. 12).

To decide what has given these particular narrative songs their lead in traditional popularity will not be easy, and had better be left to the interested student for prolonged meditation. It may, however, be said in passing that, although love of some kind is the generative force of all but one, it is not love for its own sake whereon the focus is fixed, but the consequences which ensue. These are most often fatal and inescapable, like an illness from which the victim never recovers. It can also be said without much fear of contradiction that the narrative interest of the first and last, and the concomitant elements of suspense and surprise, are almost negligible. Barbara's antipathy to her lover is seldom motivated, and the deadly spite of Randal's sweet-heart is never explained. The nuncupative testament of Lord Randal, far from seeming a

---

[9] Gerould, *The Ballad of Tradition*, 1932, p. 69.

"climax of relatives," appears more like a device to lengthen the ballad, its items, except the last, occurring in any sequence; and the simple tale of Barbara frequently dissolves into fragments in the folk memory. The same is frequently the case also with "Lady Isabel," of which the action is sometimes so disconnected as to make no narrative sense. There are dozens of exciting stories among the Child ballads, but many of them have not survived in tradition, and a large proportion of those reviewed in Gerould's chapter on Ballad Narratives has lost all trace of the music which would have kept them in circulation. But where the tune has taken strong hold in tradition, it has usually sustained some portion of the story. There are, for example, many who could not summarize the fable, but can sing one stanza of "Mary Hamilton" (no. 173):

> Last nicht there was four Maries,
>   The nicht there'll be but three;
> There was Marie Seton, and Marie Beaton,
>   And Marie Carmichael, and me.

It has now, one hopes, become reasonably clear that the ballad-tunes are essential to an understanding of the ballad as a special *genre*, with its own properties and procedures, its own *modus vivendi* and natural laws. It lives in the air, not on paper.

The present work is intended to represent the parent work of which it is an abridgment, and it was therefore felt to be unjustifiable to depart from the scheme of the original, to introduce new versions of the ballads or proceed on another plan. To make an attractive anthology of an editor's favorite versions would not have been impossible, but it would have falsified and misrepresented the serious purpose: to display the habits of this class of narrative song as they are activated by, and during, the course of oral transmission. One does not learn from solitary specimens anything about the processes of traditional activity, and it was necessary to include as many examples as space permitted in order to show what happens in the traditional interplay of tune and text, as Child showed in his verbal variants what happens to a narrative theme in its passage through many minds and memories. With this object, it was felt wisest to lay emphasis where the evidence was full and revealing, and to omit where it was inadequate or undependable. Kittredge, in his abridgment, aimed to exhibit examples of all members of the Child canon (with four omissions *pudoris causa*). But this was a privilege which the absence of tunes for many interesting and valuable ballad texts— roughly a third of the canon—had already denied to his follower. Those who are most interested in the texts alone will still find Kittredge indispensable—or, rather, Child's own volumes. The present work is by no means put forward as a substitute or up-dated surrogate for either Kittredge or Child. But it does aspire to exhibit an essential aspect of the subject in a manner convenient for serious study.

BERTRAND H. BRONSON

Berkeley 1974

THE SINGING TRADITION OF
CHILD'S POPULAR BALLADS

Riddles Wisely Expounded

CHILD NO. 1

RESTORATION broadsides of this ballad are directed to be sung to the tune of "Lay the bent to the bonny broom," but no contemporary version of the tune has survived. We may, however, presume that the form of it appearing in D'Urfey's *Pills* is true in the main to its predecessors. But the words of the refrain, which give the tune its name, seem more appropriate to a pastoral subject, and may have come over, along with their tune, from a different, if not earlier, song. "Fa la" was a current Elizabethan name for a "ballet," such as Thomas Morley's "Now is the month of Maying."

The tune as D'Urfey has it, with its narrow compass, its avoidance of intervals wider than a step of the scale, and its suggestion of the Dorian mode, hints of an antiquity far higher than the verbal text as printed. Parallels can be found in Gregorian chant.

Probably also the presence in the broadside version (i.e., D'Urfey's text) of rival daughters belongs to a form of the ballad in which they played a more integral part. In Child's fifteenth-century text they are absent, and in late tradition they disappear. The knight was not originally of the marrying kind,

and sounder tradition makes him a fiend, or the devil himself, to be checkmated, rather than confirmed in his choice, by the maid's ability to guess his riddles. It is worth notice that even the earliest text (Child's A*) is already confused, in that the fiend first offers the maid all the wisdom of the world if she will be his "leman," and then abruptly poses his riddles with the threat that *unless* she can answer them she shall be his. The contradiction implies a still earlier life for the ballad, and doubtless arises from homiletic rehandling, out of memories of Christ's temptation. Yet, though inappropriately, the element of amorous appeal enters thus early: it was later to refashion the plot as in the broadsides. This earliest text lacks a refrain, but is in rhyming couplets, which normally admit an interlaced refrain, thereby according with a four-phrased tune.

A slender connection may be made out between the Engiish tunes from D'Urfey to the end of the nineteenth century, and perhaps even doubtfully carried across to the Appalachian examples. It is not strong enough to bind the refrain lines into verbal community, though the interlaced pattern persists.

TUNES WITH TEXTS

GROUP A

1. [A Riddle Wittily Expounded]

D'Urfey, 1719-20, IV, pp. 129-32 (emended).

a D if e♮ (but – VII)

D'Urfey prints the tune in ¢ time throughout; Chappell, in his revision of it (II [1859], p. 531), regularizes in ¾, giving two beats to the last note of the first and third phrases, and changing the signature to G minor. Bruce and Stokoe (1882, pp. 76-78) profess to print from D'Urfey, but again in two flats, regularizing the timing in ¾, and with four alterations in notes: D for initial A, e raised to f in the third bar, the third d in the same bar lowered to c, and the first A in the penultimate bar raised to c.

1. There was a Lady in the North-Country,
   Lay the Bent to the Bonny Broom,
   And she had lovely Daughters three,
   Fa, la la la, fa, la la ra re.

2. There was a Knight of Noble worth,
   Lay the Bent, &c.
   Which also lived in the North,
   Fa, la, &c.

3. The Knight of Courage stout and brave,
   Lay the Bent, &c.
   A Wife he did desire to have,
   Fa la, &c.

4. He knocked at the Lady's Gate,
   Lay the Bent, &c.
   One Evening when it was late,
   Fa la, &c.

5. The youngest Sister let him in,
   Lay the Bent, &c.
   And pinn'd the Door with a Silver Pin,
   Fa la, &c.

6. The second Sister she made his Bed,
   Lay the Bent, &c.
   And laid soft Pillows under his Head,
   Fa la, &c.

7. The Youngest [Sister] that same Night,
   Lay the Bent, &c.
   She went to Bed to this young Knight,
   Fa la, &c.

8. And in the Morning when it was Day,
   Lay the Bent, &c.
   These words unto him she did say,
   Fa la, &c.

9. Now you have had your will (quoth she)
   Lay the Bent, &c.
   I pray Sir Knight you Marry me,
   Fa la, &c.

10. The young brave Knight to her reply'd,
    Lay the Bent, &c.
    Thy Suit, Fair Maid shall not be deny'd,
    Fa la, &c.

[3]

11. If thou can'st answer me Questions three,
    Lay the Bent, &c.
    This very Day I will Marry thee,
    Fa la, &c.

12. Kind Sir, in Love, O then quoth she,
    Lay the Bent, &c.
    Tell me what your three Questions be,
    Fa la, &c.

13. O what is longer than the Way?
    Lay the Bent, &c.
    Or what is deeper than the Sea?
    Fa la, &c.

14. Or what is louder than a Horn?
    Lay the Bent, &c.
    Or what is sharper than a Thorn?
    Fa la, &c.

15. Or what is greener than the Grass?
    Lay the Bent, &c.
    Or what is worse than a Woman was?
    Fa la, &c.

The Damsel's Answer to the Three Questions

16. O Love is longer than the way,
    Lay the Bent, &c.
    And Hell is deeper than the Sea,
    Fa la, &c.

17. And Thunder's louder than the Horn,
    Lay the Bent, &c.
    And Hunger's sharper than a Thorn,
    Fa la, &c.

18. And Poyson's greener than the Grass,
    Lay the Bent, &c.
    And the Devil's worse than the Woman was,
    Fa la, &c.

19. When she these Questions answered had,
    Lay the Bent, &c.
    The Knight became exceeding glad,
    Fa la, &c.

20. And having truly try'd her Wit,
    Lay the Bent, &c.
    He much commended her for it,
    Fa la, &c.

21. And after as 'tis verifi'd,
    Lay the Bent, &c.
    He made of her his lovely Bride,
    Fa la, &c.

22. So now fair Maidens all adieu,
    Lay the Bent, &c.
    This Song I dedicate to you,
    Fa la, &c.

23. I wish that you may Constant prove,
    Lay the Bent to the bonny Broom,

Unto the Man that you do love,
    Fa, la la la, fa, la la ra re.

3. "There was a Lady in the West"

Mason, 1878, p. 31. Also in Broadwood and Maitland, 1893, pp. 6-7. Sung in Northumberland.

p I (but inflected IV)

Reprinted again in the 1908 ed. of Mason, where Miss Mason adds that the song was traditional in her mother's family, the Mitfords, of Mitford, Northumberland. As said above, the D'Urfey tune can be discerned behind the first half of this one.

1. There was a lady in the West,
       Lay the bank with the bonny broom,
   She had three daughters of the best,
       Fa lang the dillo,
           Fa lang the dillo, dillo, dee.

2. There came a stranger to the gate,
       Lay the bank with the bonny broom,
   And he three days and nights did wait,
       Fa lang the dillo,
           Fa lang the dillo, dillo, dee.

3. The eldest daughter did ope the door,
       Lay the bank, &c.
   The second set him on the floor.
       Fa lang, &c.

4. The third daughter she brought a chair,
       Lay the bank, &c.
   And placed it that he might sit there,
       Fa lang, &c.

(To first daughter)

5. "Now answer me these questions three,"
       Lay the bank, &c.
   "Or you shall surely go with me."
       Fa lang, &c.

(To second daughter)

6. "Now answer me these questions six,"
       Lay the bank, &c.,
   "Or you shall surely be Old Nick's."
       Fa lang, &c.

(To all three)

7. "Now answer me these questions nine,"
       Lay the bank, &c.,
   "Or you shall surely all be mine."
       Fa lang, &c.

8. "What is greener than the grass?"
   Lay the bank, &c.
   "What is smoother than crystal glass?"
   Fa lăng, &c.

9. "What is louder than a horn?"
   Lay the bank, &c.
   "What is sharper than a thorn?"
   Fa lang, &c.

10. "What is brighter than the light?"
    Lay the bank, &c.
    "What is darker than the night?"
    Fa lang, &c.

11. "What is keener than an axe?"
    Lay the bank, &c.
    "What is softer than melting wax?"
    Fa lang, &c.

12. "What is rounder than a ring?"
    Lay the bank, &c.
    "To you we thus our answers bring."
    Fa lang, &c.

13. "Envy is greener than the grass,"
    Lay the bank, &c.,
    "Flattery, smoother than crystal glass."
    Fa lang, &c.

14. "Rumour is louder than a horn,"
    Lay the bank, &c.
    "Hunger is sharper than a thorn."
    Fa lang, &c.

15. "Truth is brighter than the light,"
    Lay the bank, &c.
    "Falsehood is darker than the night."
    Fa lang, &c.

16. "Revenge is keener than an axe,"
    Lay the bank, &c.
    "Love is softer than melting wax."
    Fa lang, &c.

17. "The world is rounder than a ring,"
    Lay the bank, &c.
    "To you we thus our answers bring."
    Fa lang, &c.

18. "Thus you have our answers nine,"
    Lay the bank, &c.
    "And we never shall be thine."
    Fa lang, &c.

By permission of Messrs. J. B. Cramer & Co., Ltd., London.

4. [The Three Sisters]

Gilbert, 1823, pp. 65-67. From editor's recollection; Cornish tradition.

Also in Child, 1882-98, I, p. 4(B).

p I

The tune and first stanza are reproduced in facsimile in Sir Richard Terry, *Gilbert and Sandy's Christmas Carols*, 1931, p. xix. It may be observed that the first refrain-line appears under the notes as "Juniper Gentle and Rosemary," not as given in the text below.

1. There were three Sisters fair and bright,
   Jennifer gentle and Rosemaree,
   And they three loved one valiant Knight,
   As the dew flies over the Mulberry tree.

2. The eldest Sister let him in,
   Jennifer gentle and Rosemaree,
   And barred the door with a silver pin,
   As the dew flies over the Mulberry tree.

3. The second Sister made his bed,
   Jennifer gentle and Rosemaree,
   And placed soft pillows under his head,
   As the dew flies over the Mulberry tree.

4. The youngest Sister fair and bright,
   Jennifer gentle and Rosemaree,
   Was resolved for to wed with this valiant Knight,
   As the dew flies over the Mulberry tree.

5. And if you can answer questions three,
   Jennifer gentle and Rosemaree,
   Oh! then, fair Maid, I will marry with thee,
   As the dew flies over the Mulberry tree.

6. What is louder than an horn?
   Jennifer gentle and Rosemaree,
   And what is sharper than a thorn?
   As the dew flies over the Mulberry tree.

7. Thunder is louder than an horn,
   Jennifer gentle and Rosemaree,
   And hunger is sharper than a thorn,
   As the dew flies over the Mulberry tree.

8. What is broader than the way?
   Jennifer gentle and Rosemaree,
   And what is deeper than the sea?
   As the dew flies over the Mulberry tree.

9. Love is broader than the way,
   Jennifer gentle and Rosemaree,
   And hell is deeper than the sea,
   As the dew flies over the Mulberry tree.

10. . . . .
    Jennifer gentle and Rosemaree,
    And now, fair Maid, I will marry with thee,
    As the dew flies over the Mulberry tree.

GROUP B

5. "The Devil's Nine Questions"

Davis, 1929, p. 549; text, pp. 59-60. Sung by Mrs. Rill Martin, Giles County, Va., September 11, 1922; noted by Evelyn Rex. Collected by Alfreda M. Peel.

p π¹

1. "If you don't answer me questions nine,
        Sing ninety-nine and ninety,
    I'll take you off to hell alive,
        And you are the weaver's bonny.

2. "What is whiter than milk?
        Sing ninety-nine and ninety;
    What is softer than silk?
        Say you're the weaver's bonny."

3. "Snow is whiter than milk,
        Sing ninety-nine and ninety;
    Down is softer than silk,
        And I'm the weaver's bonny."

4. "What is louder than a horn?
        Sing ninety-nine and ninety;
    What is sharper than a thorn?
        Sing I am the weaver's bonny."

5. "Thunder's louder than a horn,
        Sing ninety-nine and ninety;
    Death is sharper than a thorn,
        Sing I'm the weaver's bonny."

6. "What is higher than a tree?
        Sing ninety-nine and ninety;
    What is deeper than the sea?
        Sing I'm the weaver's bonny."

7. "Heaven's higher than a tree,
        Sing ninety-nine and ninety;
    And hell is deeper than the sea,
        Sing I'm the weaver's bonny."

8. "What is innocenter than a lamb?
        Sing ninety-nine and ninety;
    What is worse than woman kind?
        Say I'm the weaver's bonny."

9. "A babe is innocenter than a lamb,
        Sing ninety-nine and ninety;
    The devil's worse than woman kind,
        Sing I'm the weaver's bonny."

10. "You have answered me questions nine,
        Sing ninety-nine and ninety;
    You are God's, you're not my own,
        And you're the weaver's bonny."

The Elfin Knight

CHILD NO. 2

THE musical records of this ballad fall into three main groups, each with its own style of verbal refrain. The oldest, one surmises, of the groups is wedded to a broadside graft upon earlier tradition. The text of Child's A does not indicate a tune; but its relation to B is close, and B is directed to be sung "to its own proper tune." B's title—and hence the title of its "proper tune"—is "The Wind hath blawn my Plaid awa"— a form of its last refrain-line. This version has a four-line burden, which begins:

> My Plaid awa, my plaid awa,
> And owre the hills and far awa . . .

The copy is altered from a black-letter broadside, perhaps A, which is nearly identical in these respects, and tentatively dated c. 1670. Tunes, therefore, called either "My plaid awa," or "Oure the hills and far awa," or "The Wind hath blawn my Plaid awa" would, we may suppose, be related to the tune sought; and in fact variants of one and the same tune are found under all three names, in MS. or print, about the turn of the seventeenth century to the early eighteenth. There is, however, no occurrence anywhere of this tune mated with the words of this ballad. The tune is familiar today as the setting of Gay's song in *The Beggar's Opera*, "Were I laid on Greenland's Coast (Air 16)." It is called by Stenhouse (*Illustrations of the Lyric Poetry and Music of Scotland*, 1853, p. 62) an old pipe tune, and it has surely very little of the character of a traditional ballad air. Possibly it was attached arbitrarily to the broadside version: its second strain accommodates the burden, which is lacking in all forms of the ballad picked up in later tradition. Yet the maker of the broadside was obviously close to tradition in this case, and may have had the traditional tune in mind.

Although the relationship of this tune with primary forms of the ballad is very dubious, we cannot dismiss the traditional connection of the interlaced refrain, irrelevant though its content now appears. At a comparatively early period, in Scotland, the ballad was being sung in a form in which the second and fourth phrases were some variation of "Ba, ba, lilly ba," and "The wind has blawn my plaid awa"; and this tradition has persisted into the present century, the tune appearing always in duple rhythm, not as elsewhere in triple. But in this duple-rhythm group, the refrain in America has tended to be sup-

planted by some kind of nonsense syllables—no sharp decline, after all, in meaningful statement.

At about the end of the eighteenth century a different form of the ballad becomes dominant, in which the interlaced refrain-lines are "Parsley, sage, rosemary, and thyme" (or a similar jingle) and "Once she (he) was a true lover of mine." All variants of this group are in a triple rhythm (including 6/8). This is, so far as the record shows, the central and leading tradition for the ballad, and is still in comparatively vigorous life.

Before the middle of the last century, however, a third pattern makes its appearance, with a refrain on the order of "Ivy, sing Ivy," and "Holly, go whistle and Ivy" [*query* if "go whistle" came in when *mistletoe* departed?]. The text of this branch starts with the bequest of an acre of land, the riddle-exchange is altered into a straight catalogue of impossible things performed: the dramatic element descends into simple narrative. A common differentiating feature of the tunes, which in the main are not sharply distinguished from the central group, is that the shorter second verbal phrase forces a compensating lengthening of the accented notes, generally coinciding with the initial vowel of "Ivy."

Of our first group, variants have been recovered from Scotland, New England, and Texas. The Scottish form is darker, and a favorite type in Northern tradition, being found with a number of other texts, e.g., Child Nos. 10, 20, 209, 212, 235, 240. The other members of the group are all in a major tonality, all authentic, and all American. There is no consistency at the mid-pause, but the first phrase usually ends on V.

As can be seen, the sturdiest branch of tradition lies with Group B, which may be called the "True Lover of Mine" group. All refrains of this class *end* with these words, although varying elsewhere. The group as a whole, mainly in a major tonality, displays fascinating variety within its unity. Most of the tunes are in genuinely triple time (but often 6/8), and most of them are four-phrased.

The C group is wholly English. So far as concerns the words, they have generally suited themselves to the nursery. The riddles have lost their dramatic function: the story-line is a straightforward recounting, as narrative, of delightful impossibilities, unchallenged by an opponent.

TUNES WITH TEXTS

GROUP A

1. "The Laird o' Elfin"

Greig MSS., III, p. 139; text, Bk. 739, XXIX, pp. 6off. Also in Greig and Keith, 1925, p. 2(1). Sung by Alexander Robb, New Deer, Aberdeenshire, 1908.

p Æ/D

The tune as printed in the *Rymour Club Miscellanea*, I (1910), p. 201, gives the initial upbeat as D (i.e., C transposed).

1. The Laird o' Elfin stands on yon hill
   Ba-ba-ba leelie ba
And he blows his trumpet loud & shrill
   And the wind blaws aye my plaid awa.

2. O gin I'd that horn in my kist
   Ba &c.
   And then get wedded wi' him next
   And the wind &c.

3. But afore that I do that to thee
   Ba &c.
   A weel-sewed sark ye maun sew to me
   And the wind &c.

4. And ye maun sew it needle-thread free
   Ba &c.
   And a weel-sewed sark ye maun sew to me
   And the wind &c.

5. But afore that I do this to thee
   Ba &c.
   I'll gie ye some wark to do to me
   And the wind &c.

6. I have a little wee acre o' lan'
   Ba &c.
   That's atween the salt seas & the san'
   And the wind &c.

7. And ye maun ploo't wi your bugle horn
   Ba &c.
   And ye maun saw't wi' Indian Corn
   And the wind &c.

8. And ye maun cut it wi' your pen knife
   [Ba &c.]
   And bind it up just as your life
   And the wind &c.

9. And ye maun thrasht in your shee-sole
   Ba &c.
   And ye maun riddle't in yonder moose hole
   And the wind &c.

10. And ye maun winny't in your nieves
    Ba, &c
    And ye maun seek it in your gloves
    And the wind &c.

11. And ye maun stook it on the sea
    Ba &c.
    And a dry sheaf ye maun bring to me
    And the wind &c.

12. Robin Redbreast and the wran
    Ba &c.
    They'll bring me my corn hame
    And the wind &c.

13. And when ye have done a' this wark
    Ba &c.

Come ye to me & ye'll get your sark
   And the wind &c.

3. "Redio-Tedio"

Barry, Eckstorm, and Smyth, 1929, pp. 3-4. Sung by **Mrs.** Susie Carr Young, Brewer, Maine; learned from **Sybil** Emery in 1882. Melody recorded by George Herzog.

a I/M (– VI)

N.B. that Herzog noted this air in 4/4, but in notes of only half the values given above.

1. (*He*) "I want you to make me a cambric shirt,
   Fum-a-lum-a-link, sup-a-loo-my-nee,
   With neither seam or needle-work,
   Redio-tedio, toddle-bod-bedio,
   Fum-a-lum-a-link, sup-a-loo-my-nee."

2. (*She*) "I want you to buy me an acre of land,
   Fum-a-lum-a-link, sup-a-loo-my-nee,
   Between salt water and the sea-sand,
   Redio-tedio, toddle-bod-bedio,
   Fum-a-lum-a-link, sup-a-loo-my-nee.

3. "Plow it o'er with an old buck's horn,
   Fum-a-lum-a-link, sup-a-loo-my-nee,
   Plant it o'er with one peppercorn,
   Redio-tedio, toddle-bod-bedio,
   Fum-a-lum-a-link, sup-a-loo-my-nee.

4. "Reap it down with a peacock's feather,
   Fum-a-lum-a-link, sup-a-loo-my-nee,
   Bind it up with the sting of an adder,
   Redio-tedio, toddle-bod-bedio,
   Fum-a-lum-a-link, sup-a-loo-my-nee.

5. "Thrash it out with a mouse's tail,
   Fum-a-lum-a-link, sup-a-loo-my-nee,
   Cart it in on the back of a snail,
   Redio-tedio, toddle-bod-bedio,
   Fum-a-lum-a-link, sup-a-loo-my-nee.

6. "When you have completed your work,
   Fum-a-lum-a-link, sup-a-loo-my-nee,
   Come to me, you shall have your shirt,
   Redio-tedio, toddle-bod-bedio,
   Fum-a-lum-a-link, sup-a-loo-my-nee."

6. "Scarborough Fair"

Flanders and Brown, 1931, pp. 194-96. Sung by Ola Leonard (Mrs. Ivan W.) Gray, East Calais, Vt., from family tradition. Collected by Sylvia Bliss, Plainfield, Vt. From *Vermont Folk-Songs and Ballads*, edited by Helen Hartness Flanders and George Brown; copyright 1931 by Arthur Wallace Peach.

a I (– VI)

1. "Oh, where are you going?" "I'm going to Lynn,"
    Fellow ma la cus lomely.
  "Give my respects to the lady therein,
    Ma-ke-ta-lo, ke-ta-lo, tam-pa-lo, tam-pa-lo,
    Fellow ma la cus lomely.

2. "Tell her to buy me a yard of cloth,
    Fellow ma la cus lomely.
  And make me a cambric shirt thereof,
    Ma-ke-ta-lo, ke-ta-lo, tam-pa-lo, tam-pa-lo,
    Fellow ma la cus lomely.

3. "Tell her to make it with a gold ring,
    Fellow ma la cus lomely.
  Stitch it and sew it without a seam,
    Ma-ke-ta-lo, ke-ta-lo, tam-pa-lo, tam-pa-lo,
    Fellow ma la cus lomely.

4. "Tell her to wash it in yonder well,
    Fellow ma la cus lomely.
  Where never a drop of water yet fell,
    Ma-ke-ta-lo, ke-ta-lo, tam-pa-lo, tam-pa-lo,
    Fellow ma la cus lomely.

5. "Tell her to dry it on yonder thorn,
    Fellow ma la cus lomely.
  That never was rooted since Adam was born,
    Ma-ke-ta-lo, ke-ta-lo, tam-pa-lo, tam-pa-lo,
    Fellow ma la cus lomely."

6. "Oh, where are you going?" "I'm going to Japan,"
    Fellow ma la cus lomely.
  "Give my respects to this same young man,
    Ma-ke-ta-lo, ke-ta-lo, tam-pa-lo, tam-pa-lo,
    Fellow ma la cus lomely.

7. "Tell him to buy me an acre of land,
    Fellow ma la cus lomely.
  Between the salt sea and the sea sand,
    Ma-ke-ta-lo, ke-ta-lo, tam-pa-lo, tam-pa-lo,
    Fellow ma la cus lomely.

8. "Tell him to plow it with a deer's horn,
    Fellow ma la cus lomely.
  Sow it all over with one pepper corn,
    Ma-ke-ta-lo, ke-ta-lo, tam-pa-lo, tam-pa-lo,
    Fellow ma la cus lomely.

9. "Tell him to reap it with a sea fowl's quill,
    Fellow ma la cus lomely.
  Tan it all up into an eggshell,
    Ma-ke-ta-lo, ke-ta-lo, tam-pa-lo, tam-pa-lo,
    Fellow ma la cus lomely.

10. "And when he has completed his work,
    Fellow ma la cus lomely.
  Come unto me and he shall have his shirt,
    Ma-ke-ta-lo, ke-ta-lo, tam-pa-lo, tam-pa-lo,
    Fellow ma la cus lomely."

GROUP B

15. [The Tasks]

Baring-Gould MSS., CXXVIII(3). Sung by S. Lobb, Mawgan-in-Pyder, Cornwall, April 1893. Noted by F. W. Bussell.

p I

In the MS., the 10th and 8th notes from the end (D and d) are inadvertently written as quarters instead of eighths.
This version commences like "Jog on" (*Dancing Master*, 1650, p. 53, and later), which is the Elizabethan "Hanskin" (Fitzwilliam Book, 1899, II, pp. 494ff.). Also cf. D'Urfey, *Pills*, 1719, IV, p. 32 ("The Catholick Ballad") and IV, p. 37 ("Sir Francis Drake; or, Eighty Eight"); and Chappell, I, pp. 211-13.

22. [Whittingham Fair]

Bruce and Stokoe, 1882, pp. 79-80.

a Æ

1. Are you going to Whittingham fair,
    Parsley, sage, rosemary, and thyme;
  Remember me to one who lives there,
    For once she was a true love of mine.

2. Tell her to make me a cambric shirt,
    Parsley, sage, rosemary, and thyme;
  Without any seam or needlework,
    For once she was a true love of mine.

3. Tell her to wash it in yonder well,
    Parsley, sage, rosemary, and thyme;
  Where never spring water nor rain ever fell,
    For once she was a true love of mine.

4. Tell her to dry it on yonder thorn,
   Parsley, sage, rosemary, and thyme;
   Which never bore blossom since Adam was born,
   For once she was a true love of mine.

5. Now he has asked me questions three,
   Parsley, sage, rosemary, and thyme;
   I hope he will answer as many for me,
   For once he was a true love of mine.

6. Tell him to find me an acre of land,
   Parsley, sage, rosemary, and thyme;
   Betwixt the salt water and the sea sand,
   For once he was a true love of mine.

7. Tell him to plough it with a ram's horn,
   Parsley, sage, rosemary, and thyme;
   And sow it all over with one pepper corn,
   For once he was a true love of mine.

8. Tell him to reap it with a sickle of leather,
   Parsley, sage, rosemary, and thyme;
   And bind it up with a peacock's feather,
   For once he was a true love of mine.

9. When he has done and finished his work,
   Parsley, sage, rosemary, and thyme;
   O tell him to come and he'll have his shirt,
   For once he was a true love of mine.

23. "Strawberry Lane"

Kittredge, JAF, XXX (1917), pp. 284-85. Also in Barry, Eckstorm, and Smyth, 1929, p. 10. Sung by Mr. E. R. Davis, 1914, as remembered from his grandfather, William Henry Banks (born 1834) of Maine.

a Æ/D

1. As I was a-walking up Strawberry Lane,—
   Every rose grows merry and fine,—
   I chanced for to meet a pretty, fair maid,
   Who said she would be* a true-lover of mine.

2. "You'll have for to make me a cambric shirt,—
   Every rose grows merry and fine,—
   And every stitch must be finicle work,
   Before you can be a true-lover of mine.

3. "You'll have for to wash it in a deep well,—
   Every rose grows merry and fine,—
   Where water never was nor rain ever fell,
   Before you can be a true-lover of mine."

(The man goes on to make several more conditions. Finally the girl turns on him thus:)

4. "Now, since you have been so hard with me,—
   Every rose grows merry and fine,—

Perhaps I can be as hard with thee,
   Before you can be a true-lover of mine.

5. "You'll have for to buy me an acre of ground,—
   Every rose grows merry and fine,—
   .   .   .   .
   Before you can be a true-lover of mine.

6. "You'll have for to plough it with a deer's horn,—
   Every rose grows merry and fine,—
   And plant it all over with one grain of corn,
   Before you can be a true-lover of mine.

7 "You'll have for to thrash it in an eggshell,—
   Every rose grows merry and fine,—
   And bring it to market in a thimble,†
   Before you can be a true-lover of mine."

* Or, "wanted to be."
† Or, "And take it to market where man never dwelled."

31. "The Sea Side; or, The Elfin Knight"

Broadwood, JFSS, III (1907), p. 12. Sung by Bridget Geary at Camphire Cappoquin, County Waterford, Ireland, August 1906.

a I/M

1. As I roved out by the sea side,
   (*Ev'ry rose grows merry in time*),
   I met a little girl,
   And I gave her my hand,
   And I says, "Will you be a true lover of mine?

2. If you are to be a true lover of mine
   (*Every rose grows merry in time*),
   You must make me a shirt without needle or seam,
   And it's then you will be a true lover of mine.

3. You must wash it in a spring well,
   (*Every rose grows merry in time*),
   Where the water never ran or the rain never fell,
   And it's then you will be a true lover of mine.

4. You must dry it in a hawthorn tree,
   (*Every rose grows merry in time*),
   That never was blossomed since Adam was born,
   And then you will be a true lover of mine."

5. "Now, Sir, you have questioned me three times three,
   (*Every rose grows merry in time*),

But I might question as many as thee,
And it's then you will be a true lover of mine.

6. You must get me a farm of the best land
(*Every rose grows merry in time*),
Between the salt water and the sea strand,
And it's then you will be a true lover of mine.

7. You must plough it with a goat's horn,
(*Every rose grows merry in time*),
And sow it all over with one grain of corn,
And it's then you will be a true lover of mine.

8. You must thrash it in a sparrow's nest,
(*Every rose grows merry in time*),
And shake it all out with a cobbler's awl,
And it's then you will be a true lover of mine.

9. And when you are done, and finished your work
(*Every rose grows merry in time*),
You can come back to me, and I'll give you your shirt,
And it's then you will be a true lover of mine!"

36. [The Lover's Tasks]

Sharp MSS., 763/826. Also in Sharp and Marson, 3rd series, 1906, pp. 26-27. Sung by William Huxtable, Rowbarton, Taunton, January 15, 1906.

a I

The variants are from the singing of Bessie Huxtable, at Minehead, January 12, 1906. She sang the first refrain line as "O yes, she said, Sweet William and time."
This form of the tune is sung by Clive Carey, on a phonograph record (English Columbia, rec. WA 10685 [DB 335]).

1. Say can you make me a cambric shirt
Sing Ivy Leaf, Sweet William and Thyme,
Without any needle or needle work?
And you shall be a true lover of mine.

2. Yes, if you wash it in yonder well
Sing Ivy Leaf, Sweet William and Thyme,
Where neither springs water, nor rain ever fell,
And you shall be a true lover of mine.

3. Say can you plough me an acre of land
Sing Ivy Leaf, Sweet William and Thyme,
Between the sea and the salt sea strand?
And you shall be a true lover of mine.

4. Yes, if you plough it with one ram's horn
Sing Ivy Leaf, Sweet William and Thyme,
And sow it all over with one pepper corn,
And you shall be a true lover of mine.

5. Say can you reap with a sickle of leather
Sing Ivy Leaf, Sweet William and Thyme,
And tie it all up with a Tom-tit's feather?
And you shall be a true lover of mine.

6. Yes if you gather it all in a sack,
Sing Ivy Leaf, Sweet William and Thyme,
And carry it home on a butterfly's back,
And you shall be a true lover of mine.

Sung by Robert Pope, at Rowbarton, Taunton, January 15, 1906:

1. Say can you make me a cambric shirt
O yes she said Sweet William and time
Without any needle or needle work
And then you shall be a true lover of mine.

2. Wash it all up in yonder wink
Water will never foddle na never know spring.

3. Hang it all out on yonder thorn
Which never bear leaves since Adam was born.

4. Can you plough me an acre of land
Between the sea and the sea sand.

5. Plough it all over with a ram's horn
And sow it all over with one peppercorn.

6. Cut it all down with one strap of leather
And tie it all up in a tom tit's feather.

7. Put it all in to the bottom of sacks
And carry it all home on a butterfly's back.

8. Put it all in to a little mouse's hole
Thrash it all out with a cobbler's awl.

Pope's text appears to be assigned in Sharp's MS. to Bessie Huxtable's and William Huxtable's tune, above. But Pope's name may inadvertently have been written for W. Huxtable's, since Pope belonged to Alcombe, Dunster. Sharp usually tidied up the texts he printed.

GROUP C

53. "An Acre of Land"

Vaughan Williams, *JFSS*, II (1906), p. 212. Sung by Frank Bailey, Coombe Bisset, Wiltshire, August 31, 1904.

p I

1. My father left me an acre of land,
   There goes this ivery (?)
   My father left me an acre of land,
   And a bunch of green holly and ivery.

2. I ploughed it with my ram's horn
   There goes this ivery (?)
   I sowed it with my thimble,
   And a bunch of green holly and ivery.

3. I harrowed it with my bramble-bush,
   There goes etc.
   I reaped it with my penknife,
   And a etc.

4. I sent it home in a walnut shell,
      etc.
   I threshed it with my needle and thread,
      etc.

5. I winnowed it with my handkerchief,
      etc.
   I sent it to mill with a team of great rats,
      etc.

6. The carter brought a curly whip,
      etc.
   The whip did pop and the waggon did stop,
      etc.

The Fause Knight upon the Road

CHILD NO. 3

MOTHERWELL, in 1827, was the first to make this odd little song known to print. It is rooted in Scottish tradition, but has wandered as far as Nova Scotia, the Appalachians, Indiana, and may yet appear wherever Scots preserve memories from home. The tunes recovered seem at least distantly akin, but they are, as variants, noticeably diversified. Rhythmically, the basic pattern seems that of a reel, but it is interesting to see what sobriety a mountain soloist can impart to this intractable stuff. (See vt. 5.)

Motherwell printed his *text* in a confusing manner, in which Child follows him faithfully. The text may have been accommodated to a tune of the usual four-phrase type, like that given by Blaikie in Motherwell's musical appendix (vt. 1 here). In his stanza 1, Motherwell prints as the second and fourth lines what he abbreviates in stanza 2—and by implication throughout thereafter—as part of lines 1 and 3. This causes uncertainty as to where the division belongs, since lines 1 and 3 are either too short or alternatively too long. There may have been some phrasal repetition not noted in the first text, when it was sung, as in the Blaikie text given here with vt. 1. It may be observed that the Macmath version (vt. 8) rhythmically corresponds to Motherwell's text as first printed, which argues for printing it as long couplets.

The variant from North Carolina (vt. 7) has acquired—or has not lost—a second half; but yet seems related to the earlier Scottish tune in its general phrasal contours. A variant from Nova Scotia (here omitted) is quite clearly akin to the North Carolina tune, and also hints its connection with the Macmath tune. The Tennessee variant is striking in having an opening phrase which is not repeated, but which is built out of its last phrase. The first half of its refrain reminds us of the corresponding part of the North Carolina tune.

TUNES WITH TEXTS

1. [The False Knight]

Motherwell, 1827, App'x No. 32 and p. xxiv.

a M

O whare are ye gaun, quo' the false knight,
    And false false was his rede,
I'm gaun to the scule, says the pretty little boy,
    And still still he stude.

a. [The False Knight and the Wee Boy]

Moffat [1933], p. 24.

Same tune as No. 1 above. But, as printed by Moffat, probably from Motherwell, to the words below, the note-lengths are doubled, and the third and penultimate bars are composed of even quarter-notes. Also, the cadence of the second phrase is a half-note on A, followed by a quarter on B (if transposed to the pitch above).

1. "O where are ye gaun to, my wee lad?"
    (Quo' the False Knight on the road,)
"I'm gaun to the schule," said the bonnie, bonnie boy,
    (And still, still he stood.)

2. "And what is't ye have upon your back?"
    (Quo' the False Knight on the road).
"Atweel, it's my books," said the bonnie, bonnie boy,
    (And still, still he stood.)

3. "And what is that ye've in your arm?"
    (Quo' the False Knight on the road).
"Atweel, it's my peat," said the bonnie, bonnie boy,
    (And still, still he stood.)

4. "Wha owns thae sheep upon the hill?"
    (Quo' the False Knight on the road).
"They're mine and my mither's," said the bonnie, bonnie boy,
    (And still, still he stood.)

5. "How many o' them are mine, my lad?"
    (Quo' the False Knight on the road).
"A' they wi' blue tails," said the bonnie, bonnie boy,
    (And still, still he stood.)

6. "I wish that ye were on yonder tree,"
    (Quo' the False Knight on the road).
"Wi' a ladder under me," said the bonnie, bonnie boy,
    (And still, still he stood.)

7. "And the ladder to break below ye,"
    (Quo' the False Knight on the road).

"And you to fa' down," said the bonnie, bonnie boy,
    (And still, still he stood.)

8. "I wish ye were now in yonder sea,"
    (Quo' the False Knight on the road).
"Wi' a guid ship under me," said the bonnie, bonnie boy,
    (And still, still he stood.)

9. "And the ship for to break and sink wi' ye,"
 (Quo' the False Knight on the road).
"And ye to be drowned!" said the bonnie, bonnie boy,
 (And still, still he stood.)

5. [The False Knight upon the Road]

Sharp MSS., 3369/2466. Also in Sharp and Karpeles, 1932, I, p. 3(A); and, with piano accompaniment, in Sharp, 1918, p. 20. Sung by Mrs. T. G. Coates, Flag Pond, Tenn., September 1, 1916.

a M (– VI; inflected VII)

1932 gives F♮ (*i.e.*, transposed D♮) in the antepenultimate bar.

1. The knight met a child in the road.
 O where are you going to? said the knight
  in the road.
 I'm a-going to my school, said the child
  as he stood.
  He stood and he stood and it's well because
   he stood.
  I'm a-going to my school, said the child
   as he stood.

2. O what are you going there for?
 For to learn the Word of God.

3. O what have you got there?
 I have got my bread and cheese.

4. O won't you give me some?
 No, ne'er a bite nor crumb.

5. I wish you was on the sands.
 Yes, and a good staff in my hands.

6. I wish you was in the sea.
 Yes, and a good boat under me.

7. I think I hear a bell.
 Yes, and it's ringing you to hell.

7. "The False Knight upon the Road"

Emrich, LC/AAFS, Album XXI, rec. 104A-2. Sung by Mrs. Maud Long of Hot Springs, N.C.; recorded in Washington, D.C., 1947.

m I

Mrs. Long is the daughter of Mrs. Jane Gentry, and learned this ballad from her mother, one of Sharp's best contributors.

1. "Where are you going?" said the knight in the road.
 "I'm going to my school," said the child as he stood.
 He stood and he stood, he well thought on, he stood,
 "I'm going to my school," said the child as he stood.

2. "Oh, what do you study there?" said the knight in the road.
 "We learn the word of God," said the child as he stood.
 He stood and he stood, he well thought on, he stood,
 "We learn the word of God," said the child as he stood.

3. "Oh, what are you eating there?" said the knight in the road.
 "I'm eating bread and cheese," said the child as he stood.

4. "Oh, won't you give me some?" said the knight in the road.
 "No, nare a bite nor crumb," said the child as he stood.

5. "I wish you were in the sea," said the knight in the road.
 "A good boat under me," said the child as he stood.

6. "I wish you were in the sand," said the knight in the road.
 "A good staff in my hand," said the child as he stood.

7. "I wish you were in a well," said the knight in the road.
 "And you that deep in Hell," said the child as he stood.

8. [The Fause Knight upon the Road]

Child, 1882-98, V, p. 411; text, I, p. 485. Sung by Miss M. Macmath; learned from Jane Webster, Airds of Kells, Galloway.

a I/Ly (ending on VIII)

"O whare are ye gaun?"
 Says the false knight upon the road:
"I am gaun to the schule,"
 Says the wee boy, and still he stood.

"Wha's aught the sheep on yonder hill?"
"They are my papa's and mine."

"How many of them's mine?"
"A' them that has blue tails."

"I wish you were in yonder well:"
"And you were down in hell."

Lady Isabel and the Elf Knight

CHILD NO. 4

THIS, one of the most impressive of all ballads for the geographical sweep of its popularity and vital tenacity on traditional life, makes nevertheless no appearance in *our* musical records until the third decade of the last century; and Child's earliest *verbal* text is not much more venerable.

The earliest tunes to appear are Scottish, and they give no clear indication of the main melodic lines as they have since consolidated in a large number of variants collected mostly within the present century, in England and the U.S.A. These variants display a remarkable unity in their variety, and a variety in unity, at least on the English side. Hence, this ballad is worth close study by any who want to theorize on the irreducible essence of a tune. The characteristic Appalachian form is so extraordinarily favored by folk-singers as to deserve being taken for a hardy perennial of American traditional song. Much the same holds true of the English pattern, equally one of the melodic archetypes: cf., e.g., Child Nos. 73, 74, 75. The latter exhibits, however, a typical differentiation with each ballad to which it is habitually mated.

It would be easy to divide Group A into sub-classes. Yet familiarity will probably disclose a common denominator, and it seems unnecessary to multiply divisions. Taking the mid-cadence as a central point of reference, we find few variants resting there on the tonic. The great bulk of the English tradition, including the North Atlantic seaboard, comes to a mid-pause on the dominant, with a usual first-phrase cadence on the tonic.

Considering the frequency and English feeling of this familiar melodic pattern, it is at least a striking coincidence that a variant of it—though pausing on the third—appears in the tenth century, in the *Sanctus* of the Easter mass, *Lux et Origo*. Accident or not, the parallel may indicate how indigenous to the Western mind is this general conformation of phrasal contours.

For the American melodic tradition of this ballad not shared by England, but probably coming from Scotland, there is also early precedent, though not nearly so ancient as the other. So far as is known, the first written record of it appears in the Skene MS., dated in the first quarter of the seventeenth century, where it is called "Ladie Cassilles Lilt" (later becoming "The Gipsy Laddy"; cf. Child No. 200). The odd thing here is that only the second strain of the old tune has been used, and this fact accounts in part for the more recent lack of modal decisiveness, the elder's first two phrases seeming to establish a tonic on what subsequently becomes the lower dominant—that is, if we assume that the new Mixolydian is a false ending, the true tonic being a fourth higher. But in view of the fact that originally this was but the second, or downward, half of a complete arch which began as it ended, I prefer to regard the tune as having established its right, both historically and on grounds of accepted and current traditional use, to be considered a π^2 tune. Wherever it occurs, it is surprisingly consistent and steady. But it may be confused by the unwary with another old family almost as generally favored: that of "Boyne Water," which also will be frequently met in other connections (e.g., "Barbara Allen," Child No. 84, Group D). In fact, the two types occasionally get confused in traditional use, owing to their resemblance of phrasal contour over-all. But the "Boyne Water" tune is usually D/Æ, and its mid-cadence, a feminine one, is easily distinguishable from "Ladie Cassilis." Various distortions of the melodic idea of the latter will be visible at either end of Group B. Typically, however, the mid-cadence here, as also the first accented note, is on the dominant, and the first-phrase cadence—an unemphatic note—on the fourth. This is, of course, to accept the final as tonic, and the tune as an authentic π^2 tune.

(On this ballad-family, consult the very important monograph by Holger O. Nygard, The Ballad of *Heer Halewijn*. Folklore Fellows Communications No. 169. Vol. LXVII₂, Helsinki 1958.)

GROUP A

28a. [The Outlandish Knight]

Sharp MSS., 1405/1290. Also in Sharp, 4th series, 1908, No. 84; and Sharp, 1916, p. 29, with piano accompaniment. Sung by Joseph Laver (73), Bridgwater, August 14, 1907.

a D

1. An outlandish knight came from the North Lands,
   And he came wooing to me,
   He told me he'd take me to some foreign lands
   And there he would marry me.

2. Go fetch me some of your mother's gold
   And some of your father's fee
   And two of the best nags out of the stable
   Where there stood thirty and three.

9. Lay there, lay there you false hearted man,
   Lay there in the stead of me.
   There are six pretty maidens thou hast a [*sic*] drowned the
   But the seventh have drownded thee.

10. Now she mounted on her milk-white steed
    And led the dipple grey
    And she rode till she came to her own father's house
    Three hours before it was day.

30. [The Outlandish Knight]

Kidson, *JFSS*, II (1906), p. 282(2). Sung at Knaresbro',
Yorkshire.

a I

An outlandish Knight from the northlands,
And he came a-wooing to me;
He promis'd he'd take me unto the northlands,
And there he would marry me;
Oh! and there he would marry me.

40. [The Outlandish Knight]

Sharp MSS., 235/327. Also in Sharp, *JFSS*, IV (1910), p.
120(5). Sung by Harry Richards, Curry Rivell, July 29,
1904.

a M

An outlandish knight came from the North land
As he come a-wooing to me.
He said he would take me unto the North land
And there he would marry me.

3. She fetched him some of her mother's gold
   And some of her father's fee
   And two of the best nags out of the stable
   Where there stood thirty and three.

4. Now she mounted on her milk white steed
   And he on his dippled grey
   And they rode till they came to the sea side
   Three hours before it was day.

5. Duff off, duff off, your silken things
   And deliver them up to me
   For it looks too rich and too gay
   To rot all in the salt sea.

6. If I must take off my silken things
   Pray turn thy back unto me
   For it's not fitting that such a ruffian
   A naked woman should see.

7. Now he turned his back unto her
   And viewed the watery stream,
   She catched him round the middle so small
   And forced him into the stream.

8. He drooped high, he drooped low,
   Until he came to the side.
   Catch hold of my hand my pretty Polly
   And you shall be my bride.

Go fetch me some of your father's gold
And some of your mother's fee,
And out in the stable there stands thirty and three.

And she mount on her middle quite speed*
And he on his doublet† gray.
They rode till they came to some broad water's side
Three hours before it was day.

Unlight, unlight, you gay Lady
Unlight of your middle quite speed
Deliver it unto me
For I seems it looks too rich and too gay
To melder all in the salt sea.

Sharp's MS. note: "He sang the song complete once, but on repeating got fuddled in his words. As, however, the words followed
the usual versions I did not press him."
* i.e., milk-white steed
† i.e., dapple

56. [The Outlandish Knight]

Sharp MSS., 749/. Sung by Mrs. Glover, Huish, December
5, 1906.

D tonic: a M (final on II)

In Sharp's MS. the last note of the first phrase is a quarter but the
next two are eighth-notes.

Hold your tongue my pretty Polly
And tell no tales of me
Your cage shall be made of the glittering gold
And the bars of the best ivory*
And the bars of the best ivory

* Sharp's note: "*Ivory* should be *I'vry*."

61. "Pretty Polly"

Mackenzie, 1928, p. 391; text, pp. 7-8. Sung by Mrs. Levi
Langille, Marshville, Pictou County, Nova Scotia.

a I (final on II)

This variant seems to slip from its major mooring at the mid-
cadence and pass into the Dorian mode. Normally, the second half of
the tune would have run consistently a step lower; but the Dorian
instinct was too strong.

1. There was a lord in Ambertown
    Courted a lady fair,
    And all he wanted of this pretty fair maid
    Was to take her life away.

2. "Go get me some of your father's gold
    And some of your mother's fees,
    And two of the best horses in your father's stall
    Where there stands thirty and three."

3. So she mounted on her steed white milk,
    And he on his dappling grey,
    And they rode forward to the sea
    Two hours before it was day.

4. "Light off, light off thy steed white milk,
    And deliver it unto me,
    For six pretty maids I have drownded here,
    And the seventh one thou shalt be.

5. "Take off, take off thy bonny silk plaid,
    And deliver it unto me.
    Methinks they are too rich and gay
    To rot in the salt salt sea."

6. "If I must take off my bonny silk plaid,
    Likewise my golden stays,
    You must turn your back around to me
    And face yon willow tree."

7. He turned himself around about
    To face yon willow tree;
    She grasped him by the middle so small,
    And she tumbled him into the sea.

8. So he rolléd high and he rolléd low
    Till he rolléd to the seaside.
    "Stretch forth your hand, my pretty Polly,
    And I'll make you my bride."

9. "Lie there, lie there, you false-hearted man,
    Lie there instead of me,
    For six pretty maids thou has drownded here,
    But the seventh hath drownded thee!"

10. She mounted on her steed white milk,
    And she led her dappling grey,
    And she rode forward to her father's door
    An hour before it was day.

11. The old man he, it's being awoke,
    And heard all that was said.
    "What were you prittling and prattling, my
                                        pretty Polly,
    And keeping me awake all night long?"

12. "The old cat had got up to my littock so high,
    And I was afraid she was going to eat me,
    And I was calling for pretty Polly
    To go drive the old cat away."

13. "Don't prittle, don't prattle, my pretty Polly,
    Nor tell any tales on me.
    Your cage shall be made of the glittering gold
    Instead of the greenwood tree."

67. [Lady Isabel and the Elf Knight]

Sharp MSS., 3167/2301-2. Also in Campbell and Sharp,
1917, p. 3(A). Sung by Elizabeth Coit, Amherst, Mass.,
July 1916; learned from her aunt in South Byfield, Mass.

a Æ/D

1. O bring down some of your father's gold
   And more of your mother's money
   And two of the best horses in your father's stable
   That daily are thirty-three.

2. She brought down some of her father's gold
   And more of her mother's money
   And two of the best horses in her father's stable
   That daily are thirty-three.

3. He rode on the milk-white steed
   And she rode on the bay
   And together they came to the North of Scotland
   Three hours before it was day.

4. Light down, light down, my pretty colleen,
   I've something here to tell thee.
   Six kings' daughters lie drowned here
   And thou the seventh shall be.

5. O turn your back to the billowy waves,
   Your face to the leaves of the tree,
   For it ill beseems an outlandish knight
   Should view a stark lady.

6. He turned his back to the billowy waves,
   His face to the leaves of the tree,
   When quickly she threw both her arms round his neck
   And tossed him into the sea.

7. Lie there, lie there, thou false young man,
   Lie there instead of me.
   You promised to take me to the North of Scotland,
   And there you would marry me.

8. O give me hold of your little finger
   And hold of your lily white hand,
   And I'll make you the mistress* of all my estates
   And the ruler of all my land.

9. No, I won't give you hold of my little finger,
   Nor hold of my lily white hand,

And I won't be the mistress of all your estates
And the ruler of all your land.

10. She rode on the milk white steed,
    And by her went the bay,
    And together they came to her father's castle
    Three hours before it was day.

11. 'Twas then the† parrot spoke
    From his cage upon the wall:
    O what is the matter, my pretty colleen,
    Why did you not answer my call?

12. O hush, O hush, my pretty parrot,
    Don't tell any tales upon me,
    And your cage shall be of the beaten gold
    And your perch of the almond tree.

13. 'Twas then her father spoke
    From the chamber where he lay:
    O what is the matter my pretty parrot
    That you're calling so long before day.

14. O these rats, these rats are at my cage door;
    They're trying to take me away,
    So I am just calling my pretty colleen
    To drive these rats away.

* 1917: "ruler"
† 1917 adds "pretty."

81. (Unnamed)

Barry, Eckstorm, and Smyth, 1929, pp. 22(E)-23. Sung by
Mrs. Sarah Robinson Black, Southwest Harbor, Maine,
September 1928. Melody recorded by George Herzog.

p Æ (inflected VI)

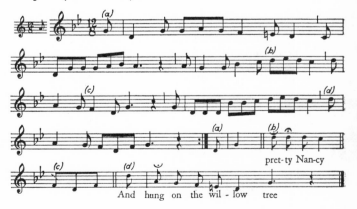

"Go get me some of your mother's gold,
    Some of your father's fee,
And we will ride side by side,
· · · · · · ·

She mounted on her milk-white steed,
    And led the dapple gray,
When she arrived at her father's house
    Three hours before it was day.

The parrot he began to talk
    And unto her did say:
"O Nancy, O Nancy, where have you been
    All on this long summer's day?"

"O parrot, O parrot, hold your tongue,
    Don't tell no tales of me,
Your cage shall be covered all over with gold,
    And hung on the willow tree."

The old folks heard the parrot talk
    And unto him did say:
"O parrot, O parrot, what makes you talk
    So long before it is day?"

"The old cat stands at my cage door
    And threatens [me to slay]*
I'm only calling the pretty Nancy
    To drive the pussy away."

* Sung, "my cage door."

83. [May Colvin]

Smith [1820-24], III, p. 92. Also in Eyre-Todd, *Ancient Scots Ballads*, n.d., p. 90; and Maver, 1866, No. 472, p. 236 (with one alteration at the beginning of the last phrase).

p Æ/D (or a Æ/D, ending on VIII)

The tune appears in *The Scots Musical Museum* with a version of "Cowdenknowes" (Child 217) called "Bonnie May" (No. 110). It is also virtually the same as "The Bonnie Mermaid" in Motherwell, 1827, App'x p. xxx, as Barry has observed in a MS. note. The tune is given by G. P. Jackson, *Spiritual Folk Songs of Early America*, 1937, p. 100, as from *Missouri Harmony*, 1820, with a text attributed to Isaac Watts, and with half a dozen other references, of which the most interesting is that to a copy of "Little Musgrave" (Child 81) collected by Sharp (ed. 1932, I, p. 182[P]; MSS., 4171/), a tune in the major. Smith's text is apparently from David Herd, 1776, I, 93-95, omitting the last five stanzas.

1. O! false Sir John a wooing came
    To a maid of beauty rare;
May Colvin was this Lady's name,
    Her Father's only heir.

2. He woo'd her butt, he woo'd her ben,
    He woo'd her in the ha',
Untill he got this Lady's consent
    To mount, and to ride awa.

3. He went down to her Father's bower,
    Where a' the steeds did stand,
And he's tane ane o' the best steeds
    That was in her Father's hand.

4. And he's got on, and she's got on,
    And fast as they could flee,
Untill they came to a lonesome part,
    A rock by the side of the sea.

5. "Loup aff the steed," says false Sir John;
    "Your bridal here you see;
For I have drowned seven young Ladies,
    The eight ane you shall be.

6. "Cast aff, cast aff, my May Colvin,
    All, and your silken gown;
For 'tis o'er good, and o'er costly,
    To rot in the salt sea foam.

7. "Cast aff, cast aff, my May Colvin,
    All, and your embroidered shune;
For they are o'er good, and o'er costly,
    To rot in the salt sea foam."

8. 'O, turn ye about, O false Sir John,
    And luik to the leaf o' the tree;
For it never became a gentleman
    A naked woman to see.'

9. He turn'd himself straight round about,
    To luik to the leaf o' the tree;
So swift as May Colvin was
    To throw him into the sea.

10. "O help! O help! my May Colvin;
    O help! or else I'll drown;
I'll tak ye hame to your Father's bower,
    And set you down safe and sound."

11. 'Nae help, nae help, you false Sir John;
    Nae help, tho' I pity thee,
Tho' seven knights daughters you have drown'd,
    But the eight shall not be me.'

12. So she went on her Father's steed,
    As swift as she could flee;
And she came hame to her Father's bow'r
    Afore the break o' day.

95. "The Knight and the Chief's Daughter"

Child MSS., XXI, Nos. 51-55; from British Museum Add. MS. 20,094, fols. 21-23. Sent by Miss M. Pigott Rogers to [?T. Crofton] Croker, in two letters, April 28 and December 7, ?1829; learned in childhood from an Irish nurse.

a I (inflected IV)

1. "Now steal me some of your father's gold,
   And some of your mother's fee,
   And steal the best steed in your father's stable
   Where there lie thirty three."

2. She stole him some of her father's gold,
   And some of her mother's fee,
   And she stole the best steed from her father's stable
   Where there lay thirty three.

3. And she rode on the milk white steed,
   And he on the barb so grey,
   Until they came to the green green wood
   Three hours before it was day.

4. "Alight, alight, my pretty Colleen,
   Alight immediately
   For six knight's daughters I drowned here,
   And thou, the seventh shall be."

5. "Oh hold your tongue, you false knight villain,
   Oh hold your tongue" said she,
   " 'Twas you that promised to marry me
   For some of my father's fee."

6. "Strip off, strip off your jewels so rare
   And give them all to me,
   I think them too rich and too costly by far
   To rot in the sand with thee."

7. "Oh turn away, thou false knight villain
   Oh turn away from me,
   Oh turn away with your back to the cliff
   And your face to the willow tree."

8. He turned about with his back to the cliff,
   And his face to the willow tree,
   So sudden she took him up in her arms,
   And threw him into the sea.

9. "Lie there, lie there, thou false knight villain,
   Lie there instead of me,
   'Twas you that promised to marry me
   For some of my father's fee."

10. "Oh take me by the arm my dear,
    And hold me by the hand,
    And you shall be my gay Lady
    And the queen of all Scotland."

11. "I'll not take you by the arm my dear,
    Nor hold you by the hand,
    And I won't be your gay lady
    And the queen of all Scotland."

12. And she rode on the milk white steed
    And led the barb so grey,
    Until she came back to her father's castle
    One hour before it was day.

13. And out then spoke her parrot so green
    From the cage wherein she lay,
    "Where have you now been my pretty Colleen
    This long long summer's day?"

14. "Oh hold your tongue, my favourite bird
    And tell no tales on me,
    Your cage I will make of the beaten gold,
    And hang in the willow tree."

15. Out then spoke her father dear
    From the chamber where he lay.
    "Oh what hath befallen my favourite bird
    That she calls so loud for day."

16. " 'T is nothing at all, good lord" she said
    'T is nothing at all indeed,
    It was only the cat came to my cage door,
    And I called my pretty Colleen."

GROUP B

98. "Pretty Polly"

Hudson, 1937, No. 11. Sung by Mrs. R. C. Jones, Oxford, Miss., c. 1923-30.

m Æ/D

Oh take some of your father's gold,
Likewise your mother's fee,
And two of your father's finest horses,
Where there stands thirty-three, three, three,
Where there stands thirty-three.

101. "Pretty Polly"

Barry, Eckstorm, and Smyth, 1929, p. xxvii. Text, Barry MSS., IV, No. 206. Sung by Milton H. Osborn, Vineland, N.J., February 17, 1907; learned from his older sister in Missouri.

a I/M

1. "Mount up, mount up, my pretty Polly,
   And come along with me,
   And I'll take thee to the far Scotland,
   And there I'll marry thee, thee, thee,
   And there I'll marry thee!"

2. Then they went to her father's stable,
   And viewed the stalls around,
   He chose out the dapple gray,
   And she the pony brown.

3. She mounted upon the little pony brown,
   And he on the dapple gray,
   And they rode and they rode thro' the merry
                                   green woods,
   Till they came to the side of the sea.

4. "Light off, light off, my pretty Polly,
   Light off, light off," said he,
   "For 6 King's daughters I've drownded here,
   And the seventh you shall be!"

5. "Take off these costly robes of silk,
   And fold them upon your knee,
   For it is a shame . . .
   To rot in the salt water sea!"

6. "Turn your face quite round about,
   With your face to the leaves on the tree . .
   (*Something about a naked woman follows—
   not recollected.*)

7. ·   ·   ·   ·   ·   ·   ·
   And she picked him up quite manfully,
   And threw him into the sea.

8. "Lie there, lie there you false-hearted wretch
   Lie there in the place of me!
   For 6 King's daughters you've drownded here,
   And the seventh has drownded thee!"

9. "O help me out, my pretty Polly,
   O help me out!" cried he,
   "And I'll take thee to the far Scotland,
   And there I'll marry thee!"

10. She mounted upon her little pony brown,
    And led the dapple gray.

    ·   ·   ·   ·   ·   ·
    ·   ·   ·   ·   ·   ·

    (*Then followed some lines, not recollected, in
    which the parrot asks Polly where she has been.*)

11. "O hold your tongue, my pretty parrot,
    And tell no lies on me,
    And I'll line your cage with the pure yellow gold,
    And hang it on a green willow tree!"

    (*Then followed some lines, not recollected, in
    which Polly's father asks the parrot what is
    the matter.*)

12. "The cat she came to my cage window door,
    And threatened to devour me,
    And I called up my pretty Polly
    To drive the cat away!"

106. [Lady Isabel and the Elf Knight]

Sharp MSS., 3142/?. Also in Sharp and Karpeles, 1932, I,
p. 6(B). Sung by Mrs. Bishop, Clay County, Ky., July 16,
1909. Collected by Olive Dame Campbell. Text not included in Sharp's MSS.

a π² (or p π¹)

1. Pull off that silk, my pretty Polly,
   Pull off that silk, said he,
   For it is too fine and too costly
   To rot in the briny, briny sea,
   To rot in the briny sea.

2. Turn your back, sweet Willie, said she,
   O turn your back unto me,
   For you are too bad a rebel
   For a naked woman to see.

3. She picked him up in her arms so strong
   And she threw him into the sea,
   Saying: If you have drowned six kings' daughters here,
   You may lay here in the room of me.

4. Stretch out your hand, O pretty Polly,
   Stretch out your hand for me,

   And help me out of the sea . . .

5. She picked up a rock and threw on him, saying:
   Lay there, lay there, you dirty, dirty dog,
   Lay there in the room of me.
   You're none too good nor too costly
   To rot in the briny, briny sea.

6. Hush up, hush up, my pretty parrot,
   Hush up, hush up, said she.
   You shall have a golden cage with an ivory lid
   Hung in the willow tree.

124. "The King's Seven Daughters"

Halpert, LC/AAFS, rec. 2954 B1. Sung by Mrs. Theodosia
Bonnett Long, Saltillo, Miss., 1939.

a π² (compass of sixth)

This variant has been transcribed from the phonograph record. An earlier performance appears in Arthur P. Hudson, *Folk Tunes from Mississippi*, 1937, No. 10, where it has a 3/4 meter but no other melodic differences. The words are mainly the same.

1. "Go bring me some of your father's gold,
    Likewise your mother's keys,
   And bring your father's best horses,
    Where they stand by thirty and three, three, three,
    Where they stand by thirty and three."

2. She got some of her father's gold,
    Likewise her mother's keys,
   And two of her father's best horses,
    Where they stood by thirty and three, three, three,
    Where they stood by thirty and three.

3. She mounted upon the milk-white steed,
    And led the dapple gray,
   She rode and she rode the livelong night,
    Till she come to the salt water sea, sea, sea,
    Till she come to the salt water sea.

4. "Light down, light down, my pretty fair maid,
    Light down in the cause of me,
   For six of the kings' daughters I've drownded here,
    And you the seventh shall be, be, be,
    And you the seventh shall be."

5. "Pull off that costly robe," he said,
    "And fold it on my knee,
   It cost too much of your father's gold,
    To rot in the salt water sea, sea, sea,
    To rot in the salt water sea."

6. "O turn your body around about,
    And view the leaves of the tree,
   You're too much of a gentleman,
    An undressed lady to see, see, see,
    An undressed lady to see."

7. He turned his body around about,
    And viewed the leaves of the tree.
   She caught him round his slender waist,
    And tripped him into the sea, sea, sea,
    And tripped him into the sea.

8. "O help me out, my pretty fair maid,
    O help me out," said he,
   "I'll take you to some far off land,
    And married we will be, be, be,
    And married we will be."

9. "Lie there, lie there, you false-hearted man,
    Lie there in the cause of me,
   For six of the kings' daughters you've drownded here,
    And you the seventh shall be, be, be,
    And you the seventh shall be."

10. She mounted upon the milk-white steed,
     And led the dapple grey,
    She rode till she came to her father's cot,
     Two hours before it was day, day, day,
     Two hours before it was day.

11. "Where have you been," my pretty Polly said,
     "O where have you been," said she,
    "I've cried, I've cried the livelong night,
     To be alone with thee, thee, thee,
     To be alone with thee."

12. "Hush up, hush up, my parrot dear,
     Don't tell no tales on me,
    A golden cage that you shall have,
     With doors of ivory, ry, ry,
     With doors of ivory."

127. "Six Kings' Daughters"

Cox, 1939, pp. 4-5. Sung by Frances Sanders, Morgantown, W.Va., June 1924.

a M (or p I)

1. He followed her up and he followed her down,
    To the bed chamber where she lay . . .

2. She mounted on her bonny, bonny, brown,
    And he on the dappled gray,
   And they rode till they came to the salt sea side,
    Four long hours before it was day, day, day,
    Four long hours before it was day.

3. "Six kings' daughters I have drowned here,
    And the seventh one you shall be . . ."

4. · . . . .
    And tumbled him into the sea, sea, sea,
    And tumbled him into the sea.

5. She mounted on her bonny brown,
    And she led the dappled gray,
   And she rode till she came to her father's own door,
    Three long hours before it was day, day, day,
    Three long hours before it was day.

6. · . . . .
    "Your cage shall be lined with my father's beaten gold
     And hung on a willow tree, tree, tree,
     And hung on a willow tree."

130. "The Outlandish Knight"

Flanders and Brown, 1931, pp. 190-92. Sung by Mr. Sharon Harrington, Bennington, Vt., September 12, 1930; learned from his mother. Recorded by George Brown. From *Vermont Folk-Songs and Ballads*, edited by Helen Hartness Flanders and George Brown; copyright 1931 by Arthur Wallace Peach.

a M (or p I)

1. He followed me up and he followed me down,
   And he followed [me] where I lie.
   He followed me til I had not a tongue
   To answer "yes" or "no."

2. "Go steal, go steal your mother's gold,
   Likewise your father's fees
   And go and steal two the very best of the steeds
   Where in there stands thirty and three."

3. So she went and she stole her mother's gold
   And likewise her father's fees,
   And she went and she stole the very best of steeds
   Where in there stood thirty and three.

4. Then she jumped onto the milk-white steed
   And she led Nelly Grey.
   She rode till she came to her lover's side
   Four long hours before it was day.

5. Then he jumped onto the milk-white steed
   And she rode Nelly Grey
   And they rode till they came to the broad seashore
   Three long hours before it was day.

6. "Get you down, get you down, my pretty Polly,
   For I've something to tell to thee;
   For six king's daughters I've drownded here
   And you the seventh shall be.

7. "Take off, take off these gay clothing
   And hang 'em on the willow tree.
   For they are too rich and too costly
   To rot with your body in the sea.

8. "Turn yourself around, turn yourself around,
   Around to the limbs of the tree.
       .   .   .   .
       .   .   .   .

9. .   .   .   .
       .   .   .   .
   And she grasped him around the middle so small
   And threw him into the sea.

10. "Lay there, lay there, you false-hearted one,
    Lay there in the room of me.
    For it's six king's daughters you have drownded here
    And the seventh has drownded thee."

11. Then she jumped onto the milk-white steed
    And she led Nelly Grey.
    She rode till she came to her father's barnyard
    Two hours before it was day.

12. Then up speaks the pretty parrot
    Who in his cage did lay.
    Saying, "Why are you calling for pretty Polly,
    So long before 'tis day?"

13. Then up speaks the good old man
    Who in his bed did lie,
    Saying, "Why are you calling for pretty Polly
    So long before it is day?"

14. "There's been a black cat to my cage door
    All for to devour me
    And I've been calling for pretty Polly
    All for to scat that cat away."

15. "Now hark your noise, my pretty parrot,
    And tell no tales on me,
    And your cage will be lined with a yellow beaten gold
    And hung in the willow tree."

135. [Lady Isabel and the Elf Knight]

Sharp MSS., 3612/. Also in Sharp and Karpeles, 1932, I, p. 13(I). Sung by May Ray, Harrogate, Tenn., April 29, 1917.

m M

In 1932, the sixth note is a D; but not in the MS. Sharp's MS. note indicates that the holds are equal to two quarters.

You go and get your father's gold,
Likewise your mother's fee,
And two of the best studs* in yonders Hall,
Where there stand thirty and three.

* 1932: "steeds"

Gil Brenton

CHILD NO. 5

THIS ballad, the non-Continental records of which are all Scottish, appears to have died out of tradition during the nineteenth century, although Motherwell speaks as if it were flourishing in his day. The scanty surviving records show no strong central current for either text or tune. It is unfortunate that the earliest tune, matched to the most interesting text, and going back in living memory beyond the middle of the eighteenth century, was set down by a confessedly inexpert hand, so that conjecture is inevitable as to the intention. Some melodic affinity between the extant tunes perhaps justifies a greater confidence in guessing. The records are dated at about fifty-year intervals, but not more than two generations need separate the first and the last.

Both the later records are in triple time and have an interlaced refrain, whereas the first is written in common time and shows no refrain in the text. The last has a characteristically Scottish feminine cadence, inescapable at the end, ambiguous in the other three phrases.

Mrs. Brown's tune is in a manuscript not recovered by Child. It was apparently mislaid for many years, but was recently found at Aldourie Castle, and the National Library of Scotland now houses a photocopy. Previous to that, an accurate copy in the hand of the antiquary Joseph Ritson, made from the original about 1792-94, was given by Dr. Rosenbach to the Harvard University Library. It contained the texts of fifteen ballads, with their tunes, taken down from Mrs. Brown's singing. The tunes were noted by her nephew, Robert Scott, "he being then but a meer novice in musick," to give some idea of the "lilts" to which she sang her ballads. The irregularities of the transcript must be Scott's: Ritson, who had no technical proficiency in music, copied with entire fidelity.

In this manuscript, it is noteworthy that only one ballad exhibits a refrain. The exceptional case is "The Two Sisters" (cf. Child no. 10, vt. 79). One other ballad, "Brown Robin" (Child No. 97), indicates a repetition of each stanza's first *two* lines— a very unusual proceeding, but hardly to be considered a refrain. In a gathering taken down from actual singing, we should expect a fair proportion of refrains, and we may reasonably surmise that not everything was copied into the record, so far as concerns the texts. The normal ballad-tune contains not fewer than four phrases, and the rule holds for Mrs. Brown's own tunes. It therefore seems quite possible that her ballads, which are written as rhyming couplets, were actually sung with refrains on the second and fourth lines of each stanza, though not so dictated. A further piece of evidence pointing in that direction will be seen in "Clerk Colven" (Child No. 42), where the tune is too long for a stanza of her text; and again there is no record of a refrain. In the present case, the only alternative is to sing two couplets to each repetition of the tune. But the experiment will prove an awkward expedient. The lines do not fall naturally into quatrains. As the manuscript is written, we are not helped by words written under the notes: the tune stands by itself, and the text follows after.

There are, however, other difficulties in the present case. The tune is written as six four-four bars. Six bars usually signify twelve accents. The text is in octosyllabic couplets, normally iambic. Instead of six and six accents, therefore, we should expect eight and eight. Even if we suppose a lost refrain, interlaced between each two lines of text, a six-bar tune is not easily accommodated in the straightforward British rhythmical tradition.

From the evidence of the manuscript as a whole, it appears that Mrs. Brown was in the habit of emphasizing certain notes with a trill or mordent—a "flourish," as they used to say. There are four trills in the present tune, each at about the place where a cadence might fall; but all except the third come on unaccented positions. When the tune is editorially justified, it is natural to make the last stress of each phrase coincide with the first beat of a bar; but one might alternatively shift each bar-line one beat ahead of its present position.

Judging by the Christie tune, with which this has perceptible similarities, it seems probable that Mrs. Brown's was really in triple time. Strictly sung, it would be in 3/4 throughout, and the time-values of the four notes preceding the first and last phrase-finals would be only half as long as they were set down. It was perhaps Mrs. Brown's deliberation at these points that threw the transcriber off his reckoning. The singer may also have shortened the mid-pause by a beat; but I have preferred to allow the phrase its full length. Other adjustments in our reading are self-explanatory.

Another way, perhaps easier but rejected after much deliberation, would be to accept the 4/4 signature and adjust to regular eight-beat phrases in common time. The other two tunes have swung this editor's decision toward the 3/4 timing.

TUNES WITH TEXTS

1. "Chil' Brenton"

Ritson-Tytler-Brown MS., pp. 22-30. Sung by Mrs. Brown, Falkland, Aberdeenshire; copied by Joseph Ritson, c. 1792-1794.

5. GIL BRENTON

1. Chil' Brenton has sent o'er the fame,
   Chil' Brenton's brought his lady hame;

2. An' seven score o' ships came her wi',
   The lady by the greenwood tree.

3. There was twal' and twal' wi' beer and wine,
   And twal' and twal' wi' muskadine,

4. And twal' and twal' wi' bouted flour,
   And twal' and twal' wi' the paramour,

5. And twal' and twal' wi' baken bread,
   And twal' and twal' wi' the gou'd sae red.

6. Sweet Willy was a widows son,
   And at her stirrup foot he did run.

7. An' she was dress'd i' the finest pa',
   But ay she loot the tears down fa';

8. And she was dress'd wi' the finest flow'rs,
   But ay she loot the tears down pour.

9. "O is there water i' your shee?
   Or does the wind blaw i' your glee?

10. Or are you mourning in your meed
    That e'er you left your mither gueed?

11. Or are you mourning i' your tide
    That e'er you was Chil' Brentons bride?"

12. "There is nae water i' my shee,
    Nor does the wind blaw i' my glee,

13. Nor am i mourning i' my tide
    That e'er i was Chil' Brentons bride;

14. But i am mourning i' my meed
    That e'er i left my mither gueed.

15. But, bonny boy, (now) tell to me
    What is the customs o' your country."

16. The customs o' it, my dame, he says,
    Will ill a gentle lady please.

17. Seven kings daughters has our king wedded,
    An' seven kings daughters has our king bedded,

18. But he's cutted the paps frae their breast-bane,
    An' sent them mourning hame again.

19. But whan you come to the palace-yate
    His mither a golden chair will set,

20. An' be you maid or be you nane,
    O sit you there till the day be dane;

21. And gin you're sure that you're a maid,
    Ye may gang safely to his bed;

22. But if o' that ye be nae sure,
    Then hire some virgin o' your bower.

23. O whan she came to the palace-yate
    His mither a golden chair did set,

24. An' was she maid or was she nane,
    She sat in it till the day was dane.

25. An' she's call'd on her bow'r-woman,
    That waiting was her bow'r within:

26. "Five hundred pounds i'll gi to thee
    An' sleep this night wi' the king for me."

27. Whan bells was rung and mess was sung,

28. And a' man unto bed was gone,
    Chil' Brenton and the bonny maid
    'Intill' ae chamber they were laid.

29. "O speak to me, blankets, and speak to me, sheets,
    And speak to me, cods, that under me sleeps,

30. Is this a maid 'at i ha' wedded?
    Is this a maid 'at i ha' bedded?"

31. "It's not a maid that you had wedded,
    But it's a maid 'at you ha' bedded;

32. Your lady lies in her bigly bow'r,
    An' for you she drees mony sharp show'r."

33. O he has ta'en him through the ha',
    And on his mother he did ca':

34. "I am the most unhappy man
    That ever was in christen'd lan';

35. I woo'd a maiden meek and mild,
    And i've marry'd a woman great wi' child."

36. "O stay, my son, into this ha',
    An' sport you wi' your merry men a',

37. And i'll gang to yon painted bow'r,
    An' see how't fares wi' yon base whore."

38. The auld queen she was stark and strang,
    She gar'd the door flee off the band;

39. The auld queen she was stark and steer,
    She gar'd the door lye i' the fleer:

40. "O is your bairn to laird or loon?
    Or is it to your fathers groom?"

41. "My bairn's nae to laird or loon,
    Nor is it to my fathers groom.

42. But hear me, mither, o' my knee,
    'Till my hard wierd i tell to thee.

43. O we were sisters, sisters seven,
    We was the fairest under heaven;

44. We had nae mair for our seven years wark
    But to shape and sew the kings son a sark.

45. It fell on a Saturdays afternoon,
    Whan a' our langsome wark was doone,

46. We kest the kavels us amang,
    To see which should to the green-wood gang.

47. Ohon! alas! for i was youngest,
    An' ay my wierd it was the hardest,

48. The cavel it on me did fa',
    Which was the cause of a' my woe;

49. For to the green-wood i must gae,
    To pu' the nut but an the slae,

50. To pu' the red rose and the thyme,
    To strew my mithers bow'r and mine.

51. I had nae pu'd a flow'r but ane,
    Till by there came a jolly hind-greem,

52. Wi' high-coll'd hose and laigh-coll'd sheen,
    An' he seem'd to be some king his son;

53. And be i maid or be i nane,
    He kept me there till the day was dane;

54. And be i maid or be i nae,
    He kept me there till the close o' day.

55. He gae me a lock o' yellow hair,
    An' bade me keep it for evermair;

56. He gae me a carket o' gude black beeds,
    An' bade me keep them against my needs;

57. He gae to me a gay gold ring,
    An' bade me keep it aboon a' thing;

58. He gae to me a little penknife,
    An' bade me keep it as my life."

59. "What did you wi' these tokens rare
    That ye got frae that young man there?"

60. "O bring that coffer unto me,
An' a' the tokens ye shall see."

61. And ay she ra[u]ked and she flang,
Till a' the tokens came till her han'.

62. "O stay here, daughter, your bow'r within,
Till i gae parly wi' my son."

63. O she has ta'en her through the ha',
An' on her son began to ca':

64. "What did you wi' that gay gold ring
I bade you keep aboon a' thing?

65. What did you wi' that little penknife
I bade ye keep while ye had life?

66. What did ye wi' that yallow hair
I bade ye keep for evermair?

67. What did ye wi' that gude black beeds
You should ha' kept against your needs?"

68. "I gae them till a lady gay
I met i' the green wood on a day;

69. And i would gie a' my ha's and tow'rs
I had that bright bird i' my bow'rs;

70. I would gie a' my fathers lan'
I had that lady by the han'."

71. "O, son, keep still your ha's and tow'rs,
You ha' that lady i' your bow'rs,

72. An' keep you still your fathers lan',
Youse get that lady by the han'."

73. Now or a month was come and gone
This lady bare a bonny young son,

74. An' 'twas well written on his breast-bane,
"Chil' Brenton is my fathers name."

2. "Lord Bengwill; or, Lord Bingwell"

Motherwell, 1827, App'x No. 5. Singer unknown. Collected by Andrew Blaikie, Paisley.

a I/M

It might be better to move all the bars forward one beat, so as to give a feminine ending on the second and fourth phrasal cadences. This would accord with the evidence of Christie's tune, following; and also, we surmise, with Mrs. Brown's.

Seven ladies liv'd in a bower,
    Hey down and ho down,
And aye the youngest was the flower,
    Hey down and ho down.

3. "Aye the Birks a-bowing; or, Lord Dingwall"

Christie, II, 1881, p. 10. Sung by his paternal grandfather; "arranged." Text "epitomized" from Buchan, 1828, I, p. 204.

a π⁴

The second strain is probably Christie's invention.

O we were sisters, sisters seven,
    A-bowing down, a-bowing down;
The fairest women under heav'n,
    And aye the birks a-bowing.
And we kiest kevels us amang,
    A-bowing down, a-bowing down,
Wha wou'd now to the greenwood gang,
    And aye the birks a-bowing. [etc.]

Earl Brand

CHILD NO. 7

THIS impressive ballad exhibits a marked formal cleavage in tradition, the more ancient-looking type having, among several distinguishing traits, an interlaced refrain, the other having none at all. It is fresh evidence of the probability that ballads in tetrameter couplets originally had such a refrain, that although the Abbotsford-Heber copy (Child A* in the abridged edition) lacks it, the copy taken with its tune conforms to the expected pattern.

Although placed late in his series, Child's F-text is actually one hundred and fifty years older, by the record, than any of the others. Had the compiler of Percy's Folio MS., whence it came, but exerted himself with equal diligence to get the proper tunes, he would have doubled and redoubled the debt of posterity, for we might then have had a purchase of utmost value on the earlier ballad-music. Nothing extant can fill this gap—not all the editions of Playford's *Dancing Master*, nor all the earlier instrumental and sophisticated versions of popular tunes.

None of the extant records of a tune is older than the first quarter of last century, and most of them are quite recent. Between the tunes of the two branches of the family there may earlier have been a closer connection: on one side, however, we have to generalize from a solitary instance. It does not appear that the single tune for the older-seeming branch is entitled to anything like the same veneration as its text: some of the records made in Aberdeenshire about the beginning of the present century have a much more antique look.

In the American tunes collected in the present century, there is sufficient evidence of continuity in tradition from the Scottish line of descent. But in the Appalachians, and spreading westward, a strong tendency is noticeable toward a reduction to the "Boyne Water" and "Lady Isabel" (Group B) or "Gypsy Laddie" type of tune. The variants here, however, show greater independence of the norm than heretofore.

The varieties, though presenting points of affiliation, are strongly enough marked to justify division into five groups, if only for convenience of study.

The first group—so-called for courtesy's sake—consists of two Northumbrian copies of about the middle of the last century, deriving from the same source. These are plagal, in one case π^1, in the other I/M: they have an interlaced refrain on the second and fourth phrases. Melodically, as will be obvious, there is

more than a trace of "Loch Lomond" in their later phrases.

Group B is again composed of a few closely related tunes, perhaps likewise deriving from a single (Scottish) source. The two later copies, in fact, may be editorial revisions of the R. A. Smith copy. All are plagal major, of the "progressive" [ABCD] type, and there is no refrain. It is odd that, whereas the tunes of Group A echoed "Loch Lomond" in all but the first phrase, the first phrase of Group B resembles that tune noticeably, but none of the others.

Group C, where the main extant record lies, is a most interesting study in the dissolution of a clear melodic pattern. Variants stretch in time from the early part of the last century (or before) to the present; and in space from Scotland to Newfoundland and the length of the Atlantic seaboard as far south as Georgia. So long as the tune remained in Scotland it was a quite stable, authentic major; but when it reached Western shores it began to experiment. A Maine copy is close enough to the norm, but the Newfoundland copy tries a new attack and never quite recovers. The Appalachian copies seem, as it were, to take this hint and venture on Mixolydian and pentatonic paths, finally going so far afield in melodic contour as to be almost unrecognizable. All, however, remain in the major galaxy.

Group D is a comparatively small gathering of Virginia variants with mid-cadence consistently on the flat seventh. All are authentic Dorian tunes. The group as a whole begins to display marks of the omnipresent "Gypsy Laddie" scheme, which appears much more clearly in the next group.

Group E is composed of variants that squint, having ambiguous finals which might be Mixolydian or plagal Ionian. These are rather distorted forms of the "Gypsy Laddie" tune, but still related to the preceding group.

Group F is composed of variants that, although carrying marks of kinship with the preceding and with one another, are generally speaking so aberrant as to deserve segregation. They come from areas as far asunder as New Brunswick, Indiana, and Tennessee, and are of various modalities which seem unnecessary to specify, since they relate so distantly. The Maine copy is suggestive of Motherwell's "Queen Eleanor's Confession" (156); a Kentucky variant strongly suggests the favorite tune of "The House Carpenter" (243).

TUNES WITH TEXTS

GROUP A

1b. [The Brave Earl Brand and the King of England's Daughter]

Bruce and Stokoe, 1882, pp. 31-33. Tune sung by Mrs. Andrews, Claremont Place, Newcastle; text recited by an old Northumberland fiddler.

p I/M

This and the preceding variant (as to tune) came from the same singer. The changes here in the third and fourth phrases may be editorial alterations.

1. O did you ever hear of the brave Earl Brand,
      Hey lillie, ho lillie lallie;
   He's courted the King's daughter o' fair England,
      I' the brave nights so early!

2. She was scarcely fifteen years that tide,
      Hey lillie, &c.
   When sae boldly she came to his bedside,
      I' the brave nights, &c.

3. "O, Earl Brand, how fain wad I see
   A pack of hounds let loose on the lea."

4. "O lady fair, I have no steed but one,
   But thou shalt ride, and I will run."

5. "O, Earl Brand, but my father has two,
   And thou shalt have the best o' tho'."

6. Now they have ridden o'er moss and moor,
   And they have met neither rich nor poor.

7. Till at last they met with old Carl Hood,
   He's aye for ill and never for good.

8. "Now, Earl Brand, an' ye love me,
   Slay this old Carl and gar him dee."

9. "O lady fair, but that would be sair,
   To slay an auld Carl that wears grey hair.

10. "My own lady fair, I'll not do that,
    I'll pay him his fee . . . . ."

11. "O, where have you ridden this lee lang day,
    And where have you stown this fair lady away?"

12. "I have not ridden this lee lang day,
    Nor yet have I stown this lady away.

13. "For she is, I trow, my sick sister,
    Whom I have been bringing fra' Winchester."

14. "If she's been sick and nigh to dead,
    What makes her wear the ribbon sae red?"

15. "If she's been sick and like to die,
    What makes her wear the gold sae high?"

16. When came the Carl to the lady's yett,
    He rudely, rudely rapped thereat.

17. "Now where is the lady of this hall?"
    "She's out with her maids a-playing at the ball."

18. "Ha, ha, ha! ye are all mista'en,
    Ye may count your maidens owre again.

19. "I met her far beyond the lea,
    With the young Earl Brand his leman to be."

20. His father of his best men armed fifteen—
    And they're ridden after them bidene.

21. The lady looked owre her left shoulder, then
    Says, "O, Earl Brand, we are both of us ta'en."

22. "If they come on me one by one,
    You may stand by me till the fights be done

23. "But if they come on me one and all,
    You may stand by and see me fall."

24. They came upon him one by one,
    Till fourteen battles he has won;

25. And fourteen men he has them slain,
    Each after each upon the plain.

26. But the fifteenth man behind stole round,
    And dealt him a deep and a deadly wound.

27. Though he was wounded to the deid,
    He set his lady on her steed.

28. They rode till they came to the river Doune,
    And there they lighted to wash his wound.

29. "O, Earl Brand, I see your heart's blood."
    "It's nothing but the glent and my scarlet hood."

30. They rode till they came to his mother's yett,
    So faintly and feebly he rapped thereat.

31. "O my son's slain, he is falling to swoon,
    And it's all for the sake of an English loon."

32. "O say not so, my dearest mother,
    But marry her to my youngest brother."

33. "To a maiden true he'll give his hand,
      Hey lillie, ho lillie lallie,
    To the king's daughter o' fair England,
    To a prize that was won by a slain brother's brand,
      I' the brave nights so early."

GROUP B

3. [The Douglas Tragedy]

Scott, 1833-34, III, pp. 1-3; text, pp. 6-9. Copy from Charles Kirkpatrick Sharpe of Hoddam Castle, Perthshire. Last three stanzas from a stall printing of c. 1792.

p I

R. Chambers, 1844, p. 17, gives Scott's text and a tune sharing traits of this and the R. A. Smith copy.

1. "Rise up, rise up, now, Lord Douglas," she says,
   "And put on your armour so bright;
Let it never be said that a daughter of thine
   Was married to a lord under night.

2. "Rise up, rise up, my seven bold sons,
   And put on your armour so bright,
And take better care of your youngest sister,
   For your eldest's awa' the last night."—

3. He's mounted her on a milk-white steed,
   And himself on a dapple grey,
With a bugelet horn hung down by his side,
   And lightly they rode away.

4. Lord William lookit o'er his left shoulder,
   To see what he could see,
And there he spy'd her seven brethren bold,
   Come riding over the lee.

5. "Light down, light down, Lady Marg'ret," he said,
   "And hold my steed in your hand,
Until that against your seven brethren bold,
   And your father, I mak a stand."

6. She held his steed in her milk-white hand,
   And never shed one tear,
Until that she saw her seven brethren fa',
   And her father hard fighting, who lov'd her so dear.

7. "O hold your hand, Lord William!" she said,
   "For your strokes they are wondrous sair;
True lovers I can get many a ane,
   But a father I can never get mair."

8. O, she's ta'en out her handkerchief,
   It was o' the holland sae fine,
And aye she dighted her father's bloody wounds,
   That were redder than the wine.

9. "O chuse, O chuse, Lady Marg'ret," he said,
   "O whether will ye gang or bide?"
"I'll gang, I'll gang, Lord William," she said,
   "For you have left me no other guide."

10. He's lifted her on a milk-white steed,
   And himself on a dapple grey,
With a bugelet horn hung down by his side,
   And slowly they baith rade away.

11. O they rade on, and on they rade,
   And a' by the light of the moon,
Until they came to yon wan water,
   And there they lighted down.

12. They lighted down to tak a drink
   Of the spring that ran sae clear;
And down the stream ran his gude heart's blood,
   And sair she 'gan to fear.

13. "Hold up, hold up, Lord William," she says,
   "For I fear that you are slain!"—
" 'Tis naething but the shadow of my scarlet cloak,
   That shines in the water sae plain."—

14. O they rade on, and on they rade,
   And a' by the light of the moon,
Until they cam to his mother's ha' door,
   And there they lighted down.

15. "Get up, get up, lady mother," he says,
   "Get up, and let me in!—
Get up, get up, lady mother," he says,
   "For this night my fair lady I've win.

16. "O mak my bed, lady mother," he says,
   "O mak it braid and deep!
And lay Lady Marg'ret close at my back,
   And the sounder I will sleep."—

17. Lord William was dead lang ere midnight,
   Lady Marg'ret lang ere day—
And all true lovers that go thegither,
   May they have mair luck than they!

18. Lord William was buried in St Marie's kirk,
   Lady Marg'ret in Marie's quire;
Out o' the lady's grave grew a bonny red rose,
   And out o' the knight's a brier.

19. And they twa met, and they twa plat,
   And fain they wad be near;
And a' the warld might ken right weel,
   They were twa lovers dear.

20. But bye and rade the Black Douglas,
   And wow but he was rough!
For he pull'd up the bonny brier,
   And flang'd in St Marie's Loch.

GROUP C

11. [Earl Brand]

Sharp MSS., 4182/3015. Also in Sharp and Karpeles, 1932,
I, pp. 21(E)-22. Sung by Mrs. Lizzie Gibson, Crozet, Va.,
April 26, 1918.

a M

In singing the first line of the song, the singer borrowed the first
note of the second phrase for the final syllable, "sleepers," and
slurred the sixteenth and dotted eighth in the same bar for "seven."

1. Wake you up, wake you up, you seven sleepers,
   And do take warning of me;
O do take care of your oldest daughter dear,
   For your youngest are going with me.

2. He mounted her up on his bonny, bonny brown,
   Himself on the dark apple grey;
   He grewn* his buckles down by his side,
   And away he went singing away.

3. Get you up, get you up, my seven sons bold,
   Get on your arms so bright,
   For it never shall be said that a daughter of mine
   Shall lie with a lord all night.

4. He rode, he rode that livelong day,
   Along with this lady so dear,
   Until she saw her seventh brother come
   And her father were walking so near.

5. Get you down, get you down, Lady Margaret, he cried,
   And hold my horse for a while,
   Until I can fight your seventh brother bold,
   And your father is walking so nigh.

6. She held, she held, she better, better held,
   And never shedded one tear
   Until she saw her seventh brother fall
   And her father she loved so dear.

7. Do you choose for to go, Lady Margaret, he cried,
   Do you choose for to go or to stay?
   O I'll go, I'll go, Lord Thomas, she cried,
   For you've left me without any guide.

8. He mounted her up on his bonny, bonny brown,
   Himself on the dark apple grey;
   He grewn* his buckles down by his side,
   And away he went bleeding away.

9. He rode, he rode that livelong night
   Till he came to his mother's stand.
   Get you down, get you down, Lady Margaret, he cried.
   So that we can rest for a while.

10. It's mother, mother, make my bed,
    And fix it smooth and wide,
    And lie my lady down by my side
    So that we can rest for a while.

11. Lord Thomas he died by midnight,
    Lady Margaret before it were day,
    And the old woman for the loss of her son,
    And there was several lives lost.

   * 1932: "drew"

GROUP D

23. [Earl Brand]

Wilkinson MSS., 1935-36, pp. 9-11(B). Sung by H. B.
Shiflett, Dyke, Va., April 16, 1936.

a D

1. Wake up, wake up, you seven sleepers,
   And it's to beware of me;
   Take care of your oldest daughter dear,
   For the youngest one's a going with me.

2. He mounted her up on a milk white steed,
   And himself on a difle grey.
   He drew his buckler down by his side,
   And away he went singing away.

3. Wake up, wake up, you seven sons dear,
   And put on your armor so bright;
   I will never have it said that a daughter of mine,
   Will be with a lord all night.

4. They rode, they rode, they better had a-rode,
   Along with his lady so gay;
   Until he saw her seven brothers bold,
   And her father a-walking so near.

5. Get you down, get you down, Lady Margaret: he said,
   And hold my stakes for awhile;
   Until I fight your seven brothers so bold,
   And your father a-walking so near.

6. She held, she held, she better had a-held,
   And she never shed one tear;
   Until she saw her seven brothers fall,
   And her father she loved so dear.

7. Stop your hand, stop your hand, Lord William: she cried,
   O stop your hand for awhile;
   A many sweethearts I once could have had,
   But a father dear I'll have no more.

8. You may choose, you may choose, Lady Margaret:
   he said,
   You may choose to go or stay;
   I'll go, I'll go, Lord William: she cried,
   For you left me without any guide.

9. He mounted her up on a milk white steed,
   And himself on a diple grey;
   He drew his buckler down by his side,
   And away went bleeding away.

10. He rode, he rode, he better had a-rode,
    Along with his lady so gay;
    Until he came to his own mother's stile,
    Where once he had loved so well.

11. O mother, O mother, make my bed,
    And make it soft and wide;

That I may lay my lady by my side,
That I may rest for awhile.

12. Lord William he died about midnight,
Lady Margaret, just before day;
The old woman died for the loss of her son,
And there was eleven lives lost.

GROUP E

25. "Lord Douglas"

Greig MSS., IV, p. 38; text, Bk. 708, p. 38. Also in Greig
and Keith, 1925, p. 7(2). Sung by Alexander Robb, New
Deer, Aberdeenshire, according to 1925, but unassigned
in MS.

a M

He's placed Lady Margret on a milk white steed,
Himself on a dapple gray,
His bugle horn down by his side,
An' slowly they both rode away.

GROUP F

37. "Sweet William and Fair Ellen"

Wells, NPMSS, VI, No. 1 (January 1935), pp. 2-3. Sung
by "Singing Willie" Nolan, Harlan County, Ky., 1920. Also
in Wells, 1950, pp. 147-49.

a π⁴

1. Sweet William rode up to Fair Ellen's gate
And he sounded on the ring.
:No one no readier than she was
To arise and let him in.:

2. He mounted her on a milk-white horse
And himself on an iron gray,
:He swung his bugle about his neck
And so went riding away.:

3. He rode till he came in three miles of town,
He turned himself all around;
:He looked and he saw some seven horsemen
Come travelling over the ground.:

4. Get you down, get you down, Fair Ellen, he said,
And take my steed in hand,
:Till I go back to yon little spring,
And I will fight them seven horsemen.:

5. She stood till she saw her six brothers fall,
And her old father she loved so dear;
:Slack your arm, slack your arm, Sweet William,
she said,
For your licks they are wonderful severe.:

6. Are you offended at what I have done,
Or at what's been said before?
:I wish myself in Old England's land,
And you was in the valley so low.:

7. I am not offended at what you have done,
Or at what's been said before,
:I wish myself in Old England's land,
And you was in the valley so low.:

8. She drew her handkerchief from her side,
And wiped Sweet William's wounds,
:The blood kept rolling down his cheeks,
As red as any wine.:

9. He mounted her on her milk-white horse
And himself on his iron grey,
:He swung his bugle around his neck
And so went riding away.:

10. He rode till he came to his mother's hall,
And sounded on the ring.
:Says, Sleeper, awake, Dear Mother, he says,
And arise and let me in.:

11. As she were getting up, a-slipping on her clothes,
To let Sweet William in,
:Bind up my head, sweet sister, he said,
For you never will bind it again.:

The Fair Flower of Northumberland

CHILD NO. 9

THIS libel on the Scottish race seems to have had a considerable popularity north of the Border, and six out of the seven recorded tunes for it are Scottish. Scots singers contrived to give it a twist that flattered their nation's sexual vanity; but the compliment still keeps an ugly side. The earliest English text may have been printed before 1600. It is not altogether impossible that the Scottish was the original form, made over by the English for their own purposes. At least, the Deloney text shows much less of a traditional cast and was probably not a little altered by his craftsman's hand. Besides the phraseology, the ingenious alteration of the last refrain line of almost every stanza is a suspicious circumstance, unlikely long to survive the insensitive chances of traditional rendition, and certainly calculated to tax the cooperative powers of a chorus such as Deloney so prettily pictures: "The King and Queene, and all the Nobility heedfully beheld these women, who for the most part were very faire and comely creatures, and were all attired alike from top to toe. Then (after due reuerence) the maidens in dulcet manner chanted out this Song, two of them singing the Ditty, and all the rest bearing the burden." (Quoted from the 10th edition, 1626, of *Iacke of Newberie*, reprinted by F. O. Mann in Deloney's *Works*, Oxford, 1912, p. 33. The book was registered as early as March 7, 1596-97.)

The ballad, perhaps, never had a very wide currency. By the opening of the twentieth century it had almost died out of oral tradition; and all its tunes thus far known belong to the nineteenth century. They all appear to have been cut from the same bolt and maintain the same tripping rhythm; but they nevertheless display a striking variety of melodic outline—so wide, in fact, that it is not easy to account for their appearance at so late a date and within so comparatively short a span of time. We should have expected more stability in a tradition in touch with recollection. The predominantly dactylic measure of Deloney's text at least seems to anticipate the invariably 6/8 rhythm of our much later extant tunes.

Such foreign parallels as Child was able to find are only partial and thematic, and it is not necessary to presume a very ancient history for the ballad. Nor is there anything in the character of the surviving tunes to imply a great age: they would not appear uncomfortable among the dance-tunes of Shakespeare's era and the seventeenth century.

The variants are all in a major tonality (I/Ly, I, π^1 and I/M) and all except vt. 5, which is mixed, are authentic. Two copies, numbered 1 and 2 (2 here omitted), have finals on the supertonic (as I believe) and mid-cadences above the octave. Two copies from Northumbria and Buchan in Scotland have a mid-cadence on the octave. The second strain of Christie's copy is doubtless his editorial invention (vt. 4). The copies (vts. 5 and 6) from a Sharpe MS. in the National Library of Scotland and Motherwell's from the Paisley region have their mid-cadence on the dominant. The Duncan copy (not reprinted) has too many echoes: e.g. "Todlin Hame," "My ain Fireside," "Whistle and I'll come to ye, my Lad." Christie, oddly, refers to his Appendix for another and different air to this ballad, but no such air is discoverable in that place. Probably he forgot his announced intention.

TUNES WITH TEXTS

1. [The Heiress of Northumberland]

Sharpe MS., p. 7. Also in Child, 1882-98, V, p. 411; text, I, pp. 207-8.

a I/Ly, ending on II

1. "Why, fair maid, have pity on me,"
     Waly's my love wi the life that she wan
 "For I am bound in prison strong,
     And under the heir o Northumberland."

2. "How can I have pity on thee,"
     Waly's my love, etc.
 "When thou hast a wife and children three,
     All dwelling at home in fair Scotland?"

3. Now he has sworn a solemn oath,
     And it was by eternity,
 That wife and children he had none,
     All dwelling at home in fair Scotland.

4. Now she's gone to her father's bedstock,
     Waly's my love, etc.
 And has stolen the key of the dungeon-lock,
     And she the great heir o Northumberland.

5. And she's gone to her father's chest,
     She has stolen away a suit of the best,
     Altho she was heir o Northumberland.

6. Now she's gone to her father's coffer,
     And has taen out gold nane kens how meickle,
     Altho she, etc.

7. She's gane to her father's stable,
     And taen out a steed baith lusty and able,
     For a' she was heir, etc.

8. The rade till they cam to Crafurdmoor,
     He bade her light down for an English whore,
     Altho she, etc.

9. The rade till the came to the water o Clyde,
He bade her light down, nae farer she should ride,
    "For now I am at hame in fair Scotland."

10. "Yonder view my castle," said he;
"There I hae a wife and children three,
    All dwelling at home," etc.

11. "O take me by the middle sae sma
And thro me oer your castle-wa,
    For I darena gang hame to Northumberland."

12. When she came to her father's yett,
She durst hardly rapp thereat,
    Altho she was, etc.

13. Out then spoke her stepmother sour,
She bad her pack off for an impudent whore,
    "For thou shalt not be heir o Northumberland."

14. Out then spock her bastard brother;
"She'll hae nae mair grace than God has gien her,
    And she shall be heir o Northumberland."

15. Out and spoke her father sae mild,
"She's no the first maid a false Scot has beguild,
    And she shall be," etc.

4. [The Flower o' Northumberland]

Christie, II, 1881, p. 46. Noted in Buchan. Text apparently refined out of Peter Buchan, *Ancient Ballads and Songs*, 1828, II, pp. 208ff.

a M

A maid pass'd by the prison door,
    (Maid's love whiles is easy won;)
She saw a prisoner standing there,
    And wishing to be in fair Scotland. [Etc.]

5. [The Flower of Northumberland]

Lady John Scott's Sharpe MS., NL Scotland MS. 843, fol. 17[r].

m I

There was a young lady was walking alone,
    Wat ye, my love, in the life that she wan!
She heard a poor prisoner making his moan;
    And she's the brave heir of Northumberland!

When they came to Scotland brig;
    Wat ye, my love, in the life that she wan!
"Light aff, light aff, from my black steed;
    And hie ye awa' to Northumberland."

6. [The Flower of Northumberland]

Motherwell, 1827, App'x No. 2; text, p. xv. Collected by Andrew Blaikie, Paisley.

a π[1]

When they came to Scotland brig,
    O my dear, my love that she wan;
Light off, ye hure, from my black steed,
    And hie ye awa to Northumberland.

The Two Sisters

CHILD NO. 10

THIS ballad is still in active traditional life, especially in those regions of the U.S.A. where the "play-party" dancing custom has persisted. In many variants the words of the refrain affirm the association; and in connection with the dance, the ballad has generally kept hold of an elaborate interlaced form of refrain, combined with the thrice repeated first line of the stanza —a scheme which is relatively ancient, and found also in company with other ballads, notably "The Three Ravens" (Child No. 26), "The Wedding of the Frog and the Mouse," "Sir Eglamore" (cf. Child no. 18), "The Friar in the Well" (Child no. 276), and the lately familiar "Mademoiselle from Armentières." The stanzaic pattern is at least as old as the sixteenth century,* but has not been found with the present song before the middle of the eighteenth.

Phillips Barry has claimed that the traditional Scandinavian air proves that the ballad came thence to Scotland; but the melodic parallel holds only with the "Binnorie" form of the ballad, and takes no account of the British form described above. Musically, the latter form—that of "The Three Ravens" —implies a double-strain melody, with the middle pause at the end of the second refrain-element; but a tendency to abbreviate this pattern sometimes appears. The bulk of recent examples proves that the two-strain pattern has become the prevailing one for this ballad, however it came about.

So far as the verbal texts provide a clue, the earlier scheme was simpler: an alternating refrain on the second and fourth phrases of the quatrain. The earliest texts (of mid-seventeenth-century English broadsides) are of this type, and it has kept its popularity in Scotland and Ireland. All the "Binnorie" group belong to it.

Group A, basically quatrains with refrain-lines on 2 and 4, contains a number of the older, Scottish, records. As a whole, the group moves between the modal boundaries of Æ and I/M, with variants anywhere within those limits. The tunes are almost always plagal. The mid-cadence and final are always feminine, but the cadence-notes of the first two phrases vary considerably.

Group B is large, and carries the bulk of recorded tradition. A few of its variants are English, but far more are American, ranging from the Eastern seaboard to Arkansas and Missouri. The typical tune is major, two-strained, and in 6/8 time. Most copies are mixed, a few authentic, a few plagal. Many are hexatonic, few pentatonic.

The order in setting forth here has been altered from normal practice in this work, in order to bring out what appears to be exceptional to our hypothetical principle, namely, that tunes do not usually pass over directly from major to minor. The opposite seems to be the fact in this case, and one can observe it in a succession of variants that put more and more emphasis on lower VI. The process becomes visible in vts. 42-47 [only the first shown here], where the cadence-note of the first phrase has moved up from the lower V of preceding variants. After tentative interest in lower VI, there appears to be a growing hesitation to decide on the cadence-note of the first refrain-element ("Bow down"), and thereafter on the final itself. Through vts. 48-52 there is genuine ambiguity. Because of preconditioning, we incline to classify as I/Ly with a final on lower VI; but a few have clearly gone over to the D/Æ side. Vts. 53-60 are mainly M/D tunes. Most of vts. 61-72 are irregular in one way or another, with the tune truncated or upset by loss of its full complement of phrases: there are 7-phrase, 6-phrase, 5- and 4-phrase variants, and increasing reluctance to end on the tonic, and a wide modal spread.

Group C is entirely Scottish, with "Edinburgh, Edinburgh" in the refrain, and containing some early variants, major modalities, and 3/4 timing. Group D reverts to quatrains, with swans lurking in the refrain, major modes, and has been found, infrequently, in Scotland, Ireland, and the U.S.A. There are also a few anomalies, or blends, here ignored.

TUNES WITH TEXTS

GROUP A

7. [Binnorie; or, The Cruel Sister]

Bruce and Stokoe, 1882, pp. 61-63. Also, with piano accompaniment, in Stokoe and Reay [1892], p. 8.

m Æ

The editors of 1882 remark with rash confidence: "The tune is a true Northumbrian melody, never before published; it differs from the Scottish tune, which is of modern date" (p. 63).

1. There were twa sisters sat in a bow'r,
   Binnorie, O Binnorie;
   There cam a knight to be their wooer,
   By the bonny mill-dams of Binnorie.

2. He courted the eldest wi' glove and ring,
   Binnorie, &c.
   But he lo'ed the youngest aboon a' thing.
   By the bonny, &c.

3. He courted the eldest wi' broach and knife,
   But he lo'ed the youngest aboon his life.

4. The eldest she was vexed sair,
   And sore envied her sister fair.

5. The eldest said to the youngest ane:
   "Will you go and see our father's ships come in."

6. She's ta'en her by the lily hand,
   And led her down to the river strand.

7. The youngest stude upon a stane,
   The eldest cam' and pushed her in.

8. She took her by the middle sma',
   And dashed her bonny back to the jaw.

9. "O sister, sister, reach your hand,
   And ye shall be heir of half my land."

10. "O sister, I'll not reach my hand,
    And I'll be heir of all your land.

11. "Shame fa' the hand that I should take,
    It's twinèd me, and my world's make."

12. "O sister, reach me but your glove,
    And sweet William shall be your love."

13. "Sink on, nor hope for hand or glove,
    And sweet William shall better be my love.

14. "Your cherry cheeks and your yellow hair
    Garr'd me gang maiden ever mair."

15. Sometimes she sunk, sometimes she swam,
    Until she cam to the miller's dam.

16. The miller's daughter was baking bread,
    And gaed for water as she had need.

17. "O father, father, draw your dam!
    There's either a mermaid or a milk-white swan."

18. The miller hasted and drew his dam,
    And there he found a drown'd woman.

19. Ye couldna see her yellow hair
    For gowd and pearls that were sae rare.

20. Ye couldna see her middle sma',
    Her gowden girdle was sae braw.

21. Ye couldna see her lily feet,
    Her gowden fringes were sae deep.

22. A famous harper passing by,
    The sweet pale face he chanced to spy;

23. And when he looked that lady on,
    He sighed and made a heavy moan.

24. "Sair will they be, whate'er they be,
    The hearts that live to weep for thee."

25. He made a harp o' her breast bone,
    Whose sounds would melt a heart of stone;

26. The strings he framed of her yellow hair
    Their notes made sad the listening ear.

27. He brought it to her father's ha',
    There was the court assembled a'.

28. He laid the harp upon a stane,
    And straight it began to play alane—

29. "O yonder sits my father, the king,
    And yonder sits my mother, the queen;

30. "And yonder stands my brother Hugh,
    And by him my William, sweet and true."

31. But the last tune that the harp played then
    Was—"Woe to my sister, false Helen!"

13.2. ["The Two Sisters"]

Sung by Mrs. Kelby, Aberdeen, ?1962. Collected and sent
to the Editor by Ewan MacColl and Peggy Seeger.

a I/Ly

1. I says to my dear sister, are ye comin for to walk?
   A-ee, a-O, and sae bonny O
   And it's I'll show you wonders before we go back
   And the swan it swims so bonny O.

2. Put your foot on like a marble stone
   A-ee, a-O, and so bonny O
   And it's I'll show you wonders before we go home
   And the swan it swims so bonny O.

3. But miller, O miller, come dry up your dam
   A-ee, -O, and so bonny O,
   For I see a maid all white like swan
   And the swan it swims so bonny O.

4. But the miller, he quickly, he dried the dam
   A-ee, -O, and so bonny O,
   And he took out the maid all white m'like swan
   And the swan its swims so bonny O.

5. He took out the maid and he hung her up to dry,
   A-ee, O, and sa' bonny O.
   And there was three fiddlers passing by
   And the swan it swims sae bonny O.

6. There was one of th'lm 'at took three lengths of her hair
   A-ee, O, and sae bonny O
There was another of th'lm took her breast bone
   And the swan it swims so bonny O.
There to make a fiddle-head to play a tune upon
   And the swan its swims so bonny O.

7. But those three fiddlers was play'n goin' along
   A-ee, O, and so bonny O,
Until they come to the castle so high
   And the swan its swims so bonny O.

8. But fiddlers sweet fiddlers and let them be goin
Out then it speaks her father the king
   A-ee, O, and sa bonny O.
An' out then it speaks her father says to Jean
   And the swan it swims so bonny O.

7. I'll neither loan you my hand nor my glove,
   But I will have your own true-love.

8. Down she sank and away she swum,
   She swum into the miller's mill pond.

9. Miller, O miller, yonder swims a swan,
   Miller, O miller, or a fair maiden one.

10. The miller came out with his fish hook,
    To fish the fair maid from the brook.

11. O miller, O miller, O loan me your hand,
    And you shall have my house and land.

12. O miller, O miller, here's five gold rings,
    If you will turn me home again.

13. And off her fingers he taken her rings,
    And he pushed her in the brook again.

14. The miller was hung at his own mill gate,
    For drowning of my sister Kate.

GROUP Ba

28. [The Two Sisters]

Wilkinson MSS., 1935-36, pp. 16-17(D). Sung by Mrs. F. S. Smith, Altavista, Va., October 20, 1935.

m I (inflected VII)

1. There was a Lord Mayor in our town,
      Bow down,
   There was a Lord Mayor in our town,
      Bow it's been to me.
   There was a Lord Mayor in our town,
   And he had daughters one, two, three.
         Love will be true, true to my love,
         Love will be true to you.

2. There was a young man went courting,
   And he did choose the youngest fair.

3. O Sister, O Sister, let's we walk out,
   And view the ships a-sailing about.

4. The oldest pushed the youngest in,
   And down she sunk and away she swim.

5. O Sister, O Sister, O loan me your hand,
   And you may have my house and land.

6. Sister, O Sister, O loan me your glove,
   And you may have my own true-love.

35. [The Two Sisters]

Wilkinson MSS., 1935-36, pp. 12(A)-13. Sung by Mrs. Jane Morris, Mrs. Lucy McAllister, and Alice Bruce, Harriston, Va., October 9, 1935.

p M (inflected VII)

1. There was an old woman in Northern 'try,
      Bow her down,
   There was an old woman in Northern 'try
      The bough has bent to me.
   There was an old woman in Northern 'try
   She had some daughters, two or three.
         Love will be true, true to my love,
         Love if my love will be true to me.

2. There went a young man a-courting there,
   He chose the youngest one was there.

3. He gave to her a beaver hat,
   The oldest one thought hard of that.

4. O sister, O sister, let's we walk out,
   To see the ships go (come) sailing about.

5. Across the brook they both did walk,
   The oldest pushed the youngest off.

6. O sister, O sister, lend me your hand,
   You may have my house and land.

7. I neither want your house nor land,
   For your true love I'm going to have.

8. Away she sunk and away she swum,
   She swum on down to the miller's mill-pond.

9. O miller, O miller, yonder swims a swan,
   A-swimming about in your mill-pond.

10. The miller ran out with his fish hook,
    To fish the swan out of the brook.

11. O brother (miller), O brother (miller), here's
                                    five gold rings,
    If you'll return me home again.

12. Off of her fingers he taken those rings,
    And pushed her in the brook again.

13. The miller was hung at his mill gate,
    For drowning of his sister Kate.

GROUP Bb

42. "The Two Sisters"

Smelser, *JAF*, XLIV (1931), pp. 295-96. Sung by Mrs. Anne Menefee, Missouri.

m π¹

This, with piano accompaniment, is included in Reed Smith and Rufty, *American Anthology of Old-World Ballads*, 1937, pp. 2-3. The variant, text and tune, has been recorded, with dulcimer accompaniment, by Andrew Rowan Summers for Columbia, Album M408, rec. 5-6 (WCO 26509-10).

Sister, dear sister, let's walk the seashore,
Bow ye down, bow ye down,
Sister, dear sister, let's walk the seashore.
Very true to you,
Sister, dear sister, let's walk the seashore,
And watch the ships as they sail o'er,
I'll be true to my love, if my love will be true to me.

As they were walking along the sea brim,
Bow ye down, bow ye down,
As they were walking along the sea brim,
Very true to you,
As they were walking along the sea brim,
The oldest pushed the youngest in.
I'll be true to my love, if my love will be true to me.

She bowed her head and away she swam,
Bow ye down, bow ye down,
She bowed her head and away she swam,
Very true to you,
She bowed her head and away she swam,
She swam unto the Miller's dam.
I'll be true to my love, if my love will be true to me.

The miller he threw out his grab hook,
Bow ye down, bow ye down,
The miller he threw out his grab hook.
Very true to you,
The miller he threw out his grab hook
And brought her safely from the brook.
I'll be true to my love, if my love will be true to me.

I'll give to thee a golden pen,
Bow ye down, bow ye down,
I'll give to thee a golden pen,
Very true to you,
I'll give to thee a golden pen
To push her in the brook again.
I'll be true to my love, if my love will be true to me.

She bowed her head and away she swam,
Bow ye down, bow ye down,
She bowed her head and away she swam,
Very true to you,
She bowed her head and away she swam,
She swam to her eternal home,
I'll be true to my love, if my love will be true to me.

GROUP BC

49. "There Was a Squire of High Degree"

Kidson, *JFSS*, I (1904), p. 253. Sung by Miss Carr Moseley; learned from old lady born c. 1800, who learned it from her mother.

Tonic G: m I, ending on *VI* (inflected *V*)

Kidson notes the resemblance to "Greensleeves" in the last two phrases; other readers will note phrases 5 and 6 as identical with "Armentières."

There was a Squire of high degree,
Bow down, Bow down,
There was a Squire of high degree
As the bough doth bend to me.
There was a Squire of high degree,
And he had daughters, one, two, three,
And I'll be true to my true love,
If my love will be true to me.

50. [The Two Sisters]

Sharp MSS., 3700/. Also in Sharp and Karpeles, 1932, I, p. 31(G). Sung by Violet Henry, Berea, Ky., May 21, 1917.

Tonic G: m I/Ly, ending on VI

A copy melodically identical is given by J. W. Raine, *The Land of Saddle-Bags*, 1924, p. 118. A third printing is in E. P. Richardson and S. Spaeth, *American Mountain Songs*, 1927, p. 27.

O sister, O sister, there swims a swan,
Bow-ey down,
O sister, O sister, there swims a swan,
Bow and balance to me,
O sister, O sister, there swims a swan,
O no, it's not, it's some fair one.
I'll be true to my love,
If my love'll be true to me.

GROUP B d

53. [The Two Sisters]

Wilkinson MSS., 1935-36, p. 23(H). Sung by Richard Chase, Chapel Hill, N.C., April 4, 1936.

ʔ a Æ/D, ending on IV (inflected III)

Sister, O sister, let's take a walk out,
Bow down, Bow down,
Sister, O sister, let's take a walk out,
And the bough has been to me.
Sister, O sister, let's take a walk out
To see those little ships sailing about.
Be true, true, be true to my love,
My love will be true to me.

55. [The Two Sisters]

Sharp MSS., 3518/2597. Also in Sharp and Karpeles, 1932, I, pp. 27(B)-28; Davis, 1929, p. 554(F); text pp. 99-100. Sung by Welsey Batten, Mount Fair, Va., September 22, 1916.

m D (inflected III)

The notes starred were occasionally sharpened to B♮ and F♯.

1. There lived an old lady in the north country,
   Bow down,
   There lived an old lady in the north country,
   The bough has been to me,
   There lived an old lady in the north country,
   She has daughters one, two, three,
   True to my love, love my love be true to thee.*

2. There came a young man a-courting there,
   And he made a† choice of the youngest there.

3. He made her a present of a beaver's hat,
   The oldest thought a heap of that.

4. O sister, O sister, just walk out
   To see those vessels a-sailing about.

5. The oldest pushed the youngest in.
   She did struggle and she did swim.

6. O sister, O sister, give me your hand,
   And I will give you my house and land.

7. I will not give to§ you my hand,
   But I will marry that young man.

8. The miller picked up his drab book (hook?),
   And then he fished her out of the brook.

* 1932: "me"
† 1932: "the"
§ 1932 omits "to."

9. The miller got her golden ring,
   The miller pushed her back again.

10. The miller was hung at his mill gate
    For drownding my poor sister Kate.

GROUP Bє

61. [The Barkshire Tragedy]

Broadwood and Maitland, 1893, pp. 118-19. Tune from G. K. Fortescue, Berkshire; text from Thomas Hughes, *The Scouring of the White Horse*, 1859, by permission of Messrs. J. B. Cramer & Co., Ltd., London.

p I

1. A varmer he lived in the West Countree,
   (With a hey down, bow down:)
   [A varmer he lived in the West Countree,]
   And he had daughters, one, two, and three,
   (And I'll be true to my love, if my love'll be true to me).

2. As they were walking by the river's brim
   (With a hey down, bow down:)
   The eldest pushed the youngest in,
   (And I'll be true to my love, if my love'll be true to me).

3. "O sister, O sister, pray gee me thy hand,
   (With a hey down, bow down:)
   And I'll gee thee both house and land,"
   (And I'll be true to my love, if my love'll be true to me).

4. "I'll neither gee thee hand nor glove,
   (With a hey down, bow down:)
   Unless thou'lt gee me thine own true love,"
   (And I'll be true to my love, if my love'll be true to me).

5. So down she sank, and away she swam,
   (With a hey down, bow down:)
   Until she came to the miller's dam,
   (And I'll be true to my love, if my love'll be true to me).

6. The miller's daughter stood by the door,
   (With a hey down, bow down:)
   As fair as any gilly-flower,
   (And I'll be true to my love, if my love'll be true to me).

7. "O vather, O vather, here swims a swan,
   (With a hey down, bow down:)
   Very much like a drownded gentlewoman,"
   (And I'll be true to my love, if my love'll be true to me).

8. The miller he fot his pole and hook,
   (With a hey down, bow down:)

And he fished the fair maid out of the brook,
(And I'll be true to my love, if my love'll be true to me).

9. "O miller, I'll gee thee guineas ten,
   (With a hey down, bow down:)
   If thou'lt fetch me back to my vather again,"
   (And I'll be true to my love, if my love'll be true to me).

10. The miller he took her guineas ten,
    (With a hey down, bow down:)
    And he pushed the fair maid in again,
    (And I'll be true to my love, if my love'll be true to me).

11. But the Crowner he came, and the Justice too,
    (With a hey down, bow down:)
    With a hue and a cry and a hullabaloo,
    (And I'll be true to my love, if my love'll be true to me).

12. They hanged the miller beside his own gate,
    (With a hey down, bow down:)
    For drowning the varmer's daughter Kate,
    (And I'll be true to my love, if my love'll be true to me).

13. The sister she fled beyond the seas,
    (With a hey down, bow down:)
    And died an old maid among black savagees,
    (And I'll be true to my love, if my love'll be true to me).

14. So I've ended my tale of the West Countree,
    (With a hey down, bow down:)
    And they calls it the Barkshire Tragedee,
    (And I'll be true to my love, if my love'll be true to me).

67. "The Two Sisters"

Halpert, LC/AAFS, Album 7, rec. 33A(544). Sung by Horton Barker, Chilhowie, Va., 1939.

p π¹

1. There was an old woman lived on the seashore,
   Bow and balance to me.
   There was an old woman lived on the seashore,
   Her number of daughters one, two, three, four,
   And I'll be true to my love if my love'll be
                                        true to me.

2. There was a young man came by to see them,
   And the oldest one got struck on him.

3. He bought the youngest a beaver hat,
   And the oldest one got mad at that.

4. "Oh, sister, oh, sister, let's walk the seashore,
   And see the ships as they sail o'er."

5. While these two sisters were walking the shore,
   The oldest pushed the youngest o'er.

6. "Oh, sister, oh, sister, please lend me your hand,
   And you may have Willie and all of his land."

7. "I never, I never will lend you my hand,
   But I'll have Willie and all of his land."

8. Sometime she sank and sometime she swam,
   Until she came to the old mill dam.

9. The miller he got his fishing hook,
   And fished the maiden out of the brook.

10. "Oh, miller, oh, miller, here's five gold rings,
    To push the maiden in again."

11. The miller received those five gold rings,
    And pushed the maiden in again.

12. The miller was hung at his own mill gate,
    For drowning little sister Kate.

GROUP C

79. [The Cruel Sister]

Ritson-Tytler-Brown MS., No. 15; text, pp. 99-102. Also in
Child, 1882-98, V, p. 411. Sung by Mrs. Brown, Falkland,
Aberdeenshire.

Mrs. Brown's tune, conjectural reading.

m M

There was twa sis-ters in ae bour
Ed-in-brough Ed-in-brough, There was twa sis-ters
in ae bour Stir-ling for aye There was
twa sis-ters in ae bour There came a knight to be their woo'r
Bon-ny St. John-ston stands up-on Tay

1. There was twa sisters in ae bow'r,
   Edinbrough, Edinbrough;
   There was twa sisters in ae bow'r,
   Stirling for ay;
   There was twa sisters in ae bow'r,
   There came a knight to be their wooer,
   Bonny Saint Johnston stands upon Tay.

2. He courted the eldest wi' glove and ring,
   But lov'd the youngest aboon a' thing.

3. He courted the eldest wi' broach and knife,
   But lov'd the youngest as his life,

4. The eldest she was vexed sair,
   And sair envy'd her sister fair.

5. Into the bow'r she could nae rest,
   Wi' grief and spite she almost brest.

6. Upon a morning fair and clear
   She cry'd upon her sister dear,

7. "O sister, go to yon sea strand,
   And see our fathers ships come in."

8. She's ta'en her by the milk-white hand,
   An' led her down to yon sea strand.

9. The youngest stood upon a stane,
   The eldest came and threw her in.

10. She took her by the middle sma',
    And dash'd her bonny back to the jaw.

11. "O sister, sister, take my hand,
    An' ise mak' you heir to a' my land.

12. O sister, sister, tak' my middle,
    An' yese get my goud and gouden girdle.

13. O sister, sister, save my life,
    An' i swear ise never be no mans wife."

14. "Foul fa' the hand that i should take,
    It twin'd me and my warlds make:

15. Your cherry cheeks and your yallow hair
    Gars me gang maiden for evermair."

16. Sometimes she sank, and sometimes swam,
    Til she came down yon bonny mill-dam.

17. O, out it came the millers son,
    And saw the fair maid swimming in.

18. "O father, haste and draw your dam,
    Here's either a mermaid or a swan."

19. The miller quickly drew his dam,
    And there he found a drown'd woman.

20. You could nae see her yallow hair,
    For goud and pearl that was sae rare.

21. You could nae see her middle sma',
    Her gouden girdle it was sae braw.

22. You could nae see her fingers white,
    For the gou'd rings that were sae gryte.

23. O, by there came a harper fine,
    That harped to the king at dine.

24. When he did look that lady upon,
    He sigh'd and made a heavy moan.

25. He's ta'en three locks o' her yallow hair,
    An' wi' them strung his harp sae fair.

26. The first tune he did play and sing
    Was Farewel to my father the king.

27. The next tune that he played seen
    Was Farewel to my mother the queen.

28. The last tune that he played then
    Was Woe to my sister fair Ellen.

81. [There Lived Twa Sisters]

Lady John Scott's Sharpe MS., NL Scotland MS. 843, fol. 11ᵛ. Text, Sharpe, 1824, repr. 1891, I, pp. 31-34. Sung by Sharpe's mother.

m I

1. There liv'd twa sisters in a bower,
     Hey Edinbruch, how Edinbruch,
   There liv'd twa sisters in a bower,
     Stirling for aye;
   The youngest o' them, O, she was a flower!
     Bonny Sanct Johnstoune that stands upon Tay.

2. There cam a squire frae the west,
     Hey Edinbruch, how Edinbruch,
   There cam a squire frae the west,
     Stirling for aye;
   He lo'ed them baith, but the youngest best,
     Bonny Sanct Johnstoune that stands upon Tay.

3. He gied the eldest a gay gold ring,
     Hey Edinbruch, how Edinbruch,
   He gied the eldest a gay gold ring,
     Stirling for aye;
   But he lo'ed the youngest aboon a' thing,
     Bonny Sanct Johnstoune that stands upon Tay.

4. "Oh, sister, sister, will ye go to the sea?
     Hey Edinbruch, how Edinbruch,
   Oh, sister, sister, will ye go to the sea?
     Stirling for aye;
   Our father's ships sail bonnilie,
     Bonny Sanct Johnstoune that stands upon Tay."

5. The youngest sat down upon a stane,
     Hey Edinbruch, how Edinbruch,
   The youngest sat down upon a stane,
     Stirling for aye;
   The eldest shot the youngest in,
     Bonny Sanct Johnstoune that stands upon Tay.

6. "Oh, sister, sister, lend me your hand,
     Hey Edinbruch, how Edinbruch,
   Oh, sister, sister, lend me your hand,
     Stirling for aye;
   And you shall hae my gouden fan,
     Bonny Sanct Johnstoune that stands upon Tay.

7. "Oh, sister, sister, save my life,
     Hey Edinbruch, how Edinbruch,

Oh, sister, sister, save my life,
     Stirling for aye;
And ye shall be the squire's wife,
     Bonny Sanct Johnstoune that stands upon Tay."

8. First she sank, and then she swam,
     Hey Edinbruch, how Edinbruch,
   First she sank, and then she swam,
     Stirling for aye;
   Until she cam to Tweed mill dam,
     Bonny Sanct Johnstoune that stands upon Tay.

9. The millar's daughter was baking bread,
     Hey Edinbruch, how Edinbruch,
   The millar's daughter was baking bread,
     Stirling for aye;
   She went for water, as she had need,
     Bonny Sanct Johnstoune that stands upon Tay.

10. "Oh, father, father, in our mill dam,
      Hey Edinbruch, how Edinbruch,
    Oh, father, father, in our mill dam,
      Stirling for aye;
    There's either a lady, or a milk-white swan,
      Bonny Sanct Johnstoune that stands upon Tay."

11. They could nae see her fingers small,
      Hey Edinbruch, how Edinbruch,
    They could nae see her fingers small,
      Stirling for aye;
    Wi' diamond rings they were cover'd all,
      Bonny Sanct Johnstoune that stands upon Tay.

12. They could nae see her yellow hair,
      Hey Edinbruch, how Edinbruch,
    They could nae see her yellow hair,
      Stirling for aye;
    Sae mony knotts and platts war there,
      Bonny Sanct Johnstoune that stands upon Tay.

13. They could nae see her lily feet,
      Hey Edinbruch, how Edinbruch,
    They could nae see her lilly feet,
      Stirling for aye;
    Her gowden fringes war sae deep,
      Bonny Sanct Johnstoune that stands upon Tay.

14. Bye there cam a fiddler fair,
      Hey Edinbruch, how Edinbruch,
    Bye there cam a fiddler fair,
      Stirling for aye;
    And he's taen three taits o' her yellow hair,
      Bonny Sanct Johnstoune that stands upon Tay.

*   *   *

GROUP D

83. "The Swan Swims so Bonny, O"

Kidson, *JFSS*, II (1906), p. 285. Sung by an Irishman in Liverpool. Also in Kidson and Moffat, 1926, p. 26.

p I/Ly

10. THE TWO SISTERS

1. The miller's daughter being dress'd in red,
    Hey ho, my Nanny, O,
   Oh, she went for some water to make her bread,
    Where the swan swims so bonny, O.

2. And there does sit my false sister Anne,
    Hey ho, my Nanny, O,
   Who drowned me for the sake of a man,
    Where the swan swims so bonny, O.

3. The miller's (or, farmer's) daughter being
                         dressed in red,
    Hey ho, my Nanny, O,

   She went for some water to make her bread,
    Where the swan swims so bonny, O.

4. They laid her on the bank to dry,
    Hey ho, my Nanny, O,
   There came a harper passing by,
    Where the swan swims so bonny, O.

5. He made a harp of her breast-bone,
    Hey ho, my Nanny, O,
   And the harp began to play alone,
    Where the swan swims so bonny, O.

6. He made harp-pins of her fingers so fair,
    Hey ho, my Nanny, O,
   He made his harp-strings of her golden hair,
    Where the swan swims so bonny, O.

Kidson and Moffat, 1926, give a fourteen-stanza text incorporating some of "The Swan Swims So Bonny, O," but constructed apparently by the editors themselves. In 1906, the first stanza, above, was printed with the notes. Since it duplicates stanza 3, perhaps the fragment actually began with 2.

The Cruel Brother

CHILD NO. 11

As LATE as the middle of the last century, we learn from editors Aytoun and Dixon of that period, this ballad was popular in Scotland and the west of England. Its central idea, the murderous pride of an offended brother, was familiar in Scandinavian analogues. Folk-singers, however, are not likely to cherish ballads in the literal truth of which they do not believe. The present narrative turns for motivation not so much on a permanent trait of human nature as on a system of manners; and it was natural that with the dying out of a family code which could rate the failure to ask a brother's consent to his sister's marriage as a mortal affront, the ballad would wither from tradition. In Cornwall and Scotland it lingered until the present century, and it has also been found in the Appalachians fairly recently. But latterly the text comes to imply, rather than for-getfulness, a deliberate neglect such as would rouse an already smoldering hatred to overt vengeance. I can grant little credence to Barry's suspicion of a veiled incest motive behind the murder (*BFSSNE*, vii, 8), not so much because of repugnance as because the "folk" would have felt no need to veil the fault, if that had been the point, and would formerly have found the motive of injured pride sufficient of itself.

Except between the Appalachian copies, it is hard to discern lines of connection among the extant tunes. But the refrain-patterns are at least homogeneous, and resemble one another in coming on lines 2 and 4 of the common quatrain. Baring-Gould's and Sharp's Cornish variants add to this an extra burden of three lines.

TUNES WITH TEXTS

1. "There waur three Ladies in a Ha'"

Harris MS., No. 13. Also in Child, 1882-98, V, p. 412; text, I, p. 147(C).

m M

The MS. is very inexpertly noted: the quarter-notes are written as halves, but most of the eighths as eighths, and the time-signature is 2/4. In the Child printing, the up-beat of the second phrase is given as G.

1. There waur three ladies in a ha,
   Hech hey an the lily gey
   By cam a knicht, an he wooed them a'.
   An the rose is aye the redder aye.

2. The first ane she was cled in green;
   "Will you fancy me, an be my queen?"

3. "You may seek me frae my father dear,
   An frae my mither, wha did me bear.

4. "You may seek me frae my sister Anne,
   But no, no, no frae my brither John."

5. The niest ane she was cled in yellow;
   "Will you fancy me, an be my marrow?"

6. "Ye may seek me frae my father dear,
   An frae my mither, wha did me bear.

7. "Ye may seek me frae my sister Anne,
   But no, no, no frae my brither John."

8. The niest ane she was cled in red:
   "Will ye fancy me, an be my bride?"

9. "Ye may seek me frae my father dear,
   An frae my mither wha did me bear.

10. "Ye may seek me frae my sister Anne,
    An dinna forget my brither John."

11. He socht her frae her father, the king,
    An he socht her frae her mither, the queen.

12. He socht her frae her sister Anne,
    But he forgot her brither John.

13. Her mither she put on her goun,
    An her sister Anne preened the ribbons doun.

14. Her father led her doon the close,
    An her brither John set her on her horse.

* * * * * * *

15. Up an spak our foremost man:
    "I think our bonnie bride's pale an wan."

* * * * * *

16. "What will ye leave to your father dear?"
    "My . . . . . an my . . . . . chair."

17. "What will ye leave to your mither dear?"
    "My silken screen I was wont to wear."

18. "What will ye leave to your sister Anne?"
    "My silken snood an my golden fan."

19. "What will you leave to your brither John?"
    "The gallows tree to hang him on."

4. [The Cruel Brother]

Sharp MSS., 3814/2802. Also in Sharp and Karpeles, 1932, I, p. 37(B). Sung by Mrs. Julie Williams, Hot Springs, N.C., July 27, 1917.

a I/M

The first landlord was dressed in white,
  I am the lil-i-no,
He asked her would she be his wife,
  And the roses smell so sweet I know.

[3. The next landlord was dressed in green.
  He asked his maid if she'd be his queen.

4. The next landlord was dressed in white.
  He asked his maid if she'd be his wife.

5. It's you may ask my old father dear,
  And you may ask my mother too.

6. It's I have asked your old father dear,
  And I have asked your mother too.

7. Your sister Anne I've asked her not,
  Your brother John and I had forgot.

8. Her old father dear was to lead her to the yard,
  Her mother too was to lead her to the step.

9. Her brother John was to help her up.
  As he holp her up he stabbed her deep.

10. Go ride me out on that green hill,
  And lay me down and let me bleed.

11. Go haul me up on that green hill,
  And lay me down till I make my will.

12. It's what will you will to your old father dear?
  This house and land that I have here.]

O what will you will to your mother dear?
  I-o the lil-i-you,
This robe of gold (or silk) that I have here,
  And the roses so sweet I know.

[14. Go tell her to take them to yonders stream,
  For my heart's blood is in every seam.

15. It's what will you will to your sister Anne?
  My new gold ring and my silver fan.

16. It's what will you will to your brother John's wife?
  In grief and sorrow the balance of her life.

17. It's what will you will to your brother John's son?
  It's God for to bless and to make him a man.

18. It's what will you will to your brother John?
  A rope and a gallows for to hang him on.]

6. "The Three Maids"

Halpert, LC/AAFS, rec. 2758 A2. Sung by Mrs. Polly Johnson (73), Wise, Va., 1939.

p I/Ly

*F♯ sometimes almost F♮

1. There was three maids a-playing ball
  I lily O
There was three maids a-playing ball
There come three lords for to court them all
  For the rose is sweet I know.

2. The foremost one was dressed in red
  [*Repeat as before, throughout*]
'And this is the one I make my wed'
  For the rose is sweet I know.

3. The middle one was dressed in green
  'And this is the one I make my queen'

4. The foremost [*sic*] one was dressed in white
  'O this is the one I make my wife'

5. Her brother John was standing by
  He wounded his sister with a knife

6. 'Ride on, ride on to yonder stile
  Till I get down and bleed awhile

7. 'Ride on, ride on to yonder hill
    Till I get down 'n' I make my will'

8. 'What do you will your sister Ann?'
    'My trunk of gold and silver pan'

9. 'What do you will your true-love dear?'
    'This snow-white horse that I rode here'

10. 'What do you will your mother dear?'
    'My snow-white dress that I wore here'

11. 'Tell her to wash it nice and clean
        I lily O
    Tell her to wash it nice and clean
    So my heart's blood can never be seen
        For the rose is sweet I know.'

9. "Flowers of the Valley"

Sharp MSS., 217/. Sung by Thomas Williams, St. Mawgan
East, Cornwall. Noted by Mr. W. Gilbert.

a M

There was a widow all forlorn
Nine brave boys from her body were borne [*sic*]
Flowers that were in the Valley
The harp the lute the fife the flute & the cymbal
Sweet goes the treble violin
Flowers that were in the Vally

Lord Randal

CHILD NO. 12

THIS ballad now known as "Lord Randal" has held with extraordinary tenacity to its stanzaic pattern, wherever and whenever it has been found—in Italy in the early seventeenth century or in the Appalachians in our own day: the first half of the stanza a question repeated with only a change of address; the second half an answer, addressed to the questioner, and a premonitory assertion of desperate illness. The name of the protagonist, meanwhile, has changed with kaleidoscopic variety: a page could be filled with his aliases. Of a number of rather strange trisyllabic appellatives, beginning with T and D—Tar(r)anty, Tyranty, Tyranting, Tyranna, Terencè, Teronto, Durango, Dorendo—it does not appear to have been suggested that they may probably have arisen from a perversion of one form of the preliminary question: "Oh, where have you been *to*, *Randal*, my son?"—*to* having slipped off the verb and adhered to the name, with consequent havoc in nomenclature.

In an interesting note (*JFSS*, III [1907], p. 44), Anne Gilchrist suggests a connection between this ballad and Piers Plowman's rimes of Randolf, Earl of Chester. The historical Ranulf, or Randall III, sixth Earl of Chester, who died in 1232, was divorced and left no heir, but was succeeded by his nephew John, whose wife was supposed to have tried to poison her husband. This Randall was also associated with minstrelsy in another sort, for which cf. Chappell, *Popular Music of the Olden Time*, earlier ed., p. 10.

Most of the divisions suggesting themselves within the large body of tunes are subdivisions rather than actual cleavages. Thus, for example, the group of tunes that identify themselves with more or less distinctness as variants of the well-known "Villikens and his Dinah" tune—an air that has had enormous vogue for the last hundred years and lent itself to a great variety of contexts—will be felt here rather as a family within the larger clan than as a separate class. What may be called the nursery branch of the ballad, however—the "Croodin Dow" variety in which the hero has retrogressed from young manhood into pre-adolescence—appears not to subscribe to the main melodic tradition; and the same may be said of the consciously comic rifacimento, "Billy Boy" (No. 12, Appendix), the stanzaic form of which is too closely modeled on the older pattern for its text to be unrelated. Such, incidentally, appears to be the destiny of too many fine old tragic ballads: they are not to be permitted a dignified demise, but we must madly play with our forefathers' relics and make a mock of their calamities. The high seriousness of the parents is the children's favorite joke. So it has been with "Earl Brand," "Young Beichan," "Lord Lovel," "Lady Alice," "The Mermaid," "Bessie Bell and Mary Gray," "Queen Jane," and "The Three Ravens," to name but the most familiar examples; and, in a different sort, Robin Hood dwindled to the relics and make a mock of their calamities. The high seriousness of the parents is the children's favorite joke. So it has been with "Earl Brand," "Young Beichan," "Lord Lovel," "Lady Alice," "The Mermaid," "Bessie Bell and Mary Gray," "Queen Jane," and "The Three Ravens," to name but the most familiar examples; and, in a different sort, Robin Hood dwindled to the stature of a custard-pie farce before he was finally tossed out for

daws to peck at. It is a fact—but what to do with it I know not—that all the recovered variants in which the name Henry is used instead of Randal (or its perversions) have a clear duple rhythm. Elsewhere the triple rhythm is the rule.

There is, in addition, a very small number of serious versions of "Lord Randal" which have either acquired a new increment of refrain or burden, or put on an entirely alien melodic dress. In *JAF*, XXIII (1910), pp. 440-45, Phillips Barry makes the confident statement that "Lord Randal" "is in all probability unique as being the only old ballad which has retained its original melody." This assertion appears to me to derive mainly from some transcendental source of information to which I have been denied access. But I am not disposed to cavil over his further declaration that "Lochaber No More," "King James's March to Ireland," "Limerick's Lamentation," and "Reeve's Maggot" are related tunes. Cf., on these, Moffat's *Minstrelsy of Ireland*, 1897, pp. 300, 352.

The main melodic tradition for the ballad lies in Group A, here subdivided into four main varieties. The oldest copy with the ballad text is that recovered by Burns in Ayrshire, and sent to Johnson's *Museum*. Melodically, it is one of the comeliest, and closely allied to "Lochaber No More." In kindred versions, this tune can be followed back, as Moffat, *loc. cit.*, has noted, to the latter part of the seventeenth century. Taking Burns's copy as representative of earlier—and richer—forms of the tradition, it will be observed that the tune is typically in the major area, in triple time, with a mid-cadence on the tonic, a first cadence on the supertonic, and considerable emphasis at the beginning on the mediant. As this pattern is passed on, its compass tends to shrink to the limits of a sixth or even a fifth (tonic to dominant), and the cadence of the first phrase shifts to the tonic, the mediant, and, infrequently, to other points.

Subgroup Ab is typically of the familiar "Villikens and his Dinah" pattern. With one exception, it stays within the ambit I/Ly to M. The exception is an Æ Irish variant printed by Petrie, which was obtained from Joyce, though Joyce himself later printed the same tune as a major (vts. 60, 61). With two Appalachian exceptions, all the tunes in this subgroup have a mid-cadence on the fifth, a first cadence on the tonic. The first stress is commonly on III or I. The variants are consistently in some form of triple time.

Group B, the "Henry" group, is mainly English, but copies have been found in the west of Scotland and in America. With the exception of two or three doubtful copies, all variants are in duple time. Most of the copies have a fifth or even a sixth phrase. All but two have a mid-cadence on the supertonic. The first cadence varies, but is on the fifth in the majority of cases.

Group C, the "Croodin' Doo," is of two varieties, to judge by the scanty evidence. One is Scottish and Æolian, with first and second cadences on the tonic. The other is English, and major (I, I/M, M) in tonality, with first and second cadences on the dominant, the whole tune being of the familiar "Lord Lovel" type.

TUNES WITH TEXTS

GROUP A a

1. [Lord Ronald my son]

Johnson [1792], repr. 1853, IV, No. 327, p. 337. Collected by Robert Burns, as sung in Ayrshire.

p I/M

This is the copy transmitted by Robert Burns as from Ayrshire tradition. It has been fairly frequently reprinted (e.g., R. A. Smith [1820-24], III, p. 58; R. Chambers, 1844, p. 21; G. F. Graham, *Songs of Scotland*, 1848 and subsequently [e.g., 1887, p. 47]; Maver, 1866, p. 18 [No. 35, with a second strain]); and it has received abundant but inconclusive annotation (e.g., especially, Graham, *loc.cit.*, and J. Glen, *Early Scottish Melodies*, 1900, pp. 87-89, 165). The gist of Glen's argument, which catches up previous discussion, is that "Lochaber" may be older than "Lord Ronald" and therefore that Burns may well be wrong in thinking the latter the original tune; and that both derive from "King James March to Irland" (*sic*), which he prints from the Blaikie MS. of 1692.

O where hae ye been Lord Ronald, my son?
O where hae ye been, Lord Ronald my son?
I hae been wi' my sweetheart, mother, make my bed soon,
For I'm weary wi' the hunting and fain wad lie down.

What got ye frae your sweetheart Lord Ronald, my son.
What got ye frae your sweetheart Lord Ronald, my son.
I hae got deadly poison, mother, make my bed soon;
For life is a burden that soon I'll lay down.

8. "Lorendo"

Chappell, 1939, p. 14. Sung by Charles Tillett, Wanchese, N.C., text, 1934; tune, 1935.

a π[1]

1. Where have you been, Lorendo, Lorendo, my son?
   Where have you been, Lorendo, my dear little one?
   I've been to see my sweetheart, mother, make my bed soon,
   I am sick to my heart and I wish to lie down.

2. What did you eat for supper, Lorendo, my son?
   What did you eat for supper, my dear little one?
   A dish of fried eels, mother, pray make my bed soon,
   I am sick to my heart and I wish to lie down.

3. What do you will your mother, Lorendo, my son?
   What do you will your mother, my dear little one?
   My house and plantation, mother, make my bed soon,
   I am sick to my heart and I wish to lie down.

4. What do you will your brother, Lorendo, my son?
   What do you will your brother, my dear little one?
   My horse, bridle, and saddle, mother, make my bed soon,
   I am sick to my heart and I wish to lie down.

5. What do you will your sister, Lorendo, my son?
   What do you will your sister, my dear little one?
   My gold watch and bracelet, mother, make my bed soon,
   I am sick to my heart and I wish to lie down.

6. What do you will your sweetheart, Lorendo, my son?
   What do you will your sweetheart, my dear little one?
   The keys of hell's gate, mother, pray make my bed soon,
   For she was the cause of my sad lying down.

14. [Lord Randal]

Sharp MSS., 3205/2350. Also in Sharp and Karpeles, 1932, I, p. 38(B). Sung by Mrs. Mary Sands, Allanstand, N.C., August 3, 1916.

a π[1]

This is transposed to E major in the 1932 printing.

1. What did you eat for your supper, Jimmy Randal my son?
   What did you eat for your supper, my own dearest one?
   Cold poison, cold poultry. Mother, make my bed soon,
   For I am sick-hearted and I want to lie down.

2. What will you will to your mother . . .
   My gold and my silver.

3. What will you will to your father . . .
   My mules and my wagons.

4. What will you will to your sister . . .
   My land and my houses.

5. What will you will to your brothers . . .
   My trunks and my clothing.

6. What will you will to your sweetheart . . .
   Two tushes bullrushes and them both parched brown,
   For she is the cause of my lying down.

24. "Lord Ronald"

Shuldham-Shaw, *JEFDSS*, VI (December 1949), p. 15.
Sung by James Laurenson, Fetlar, Shetland Islands, September 4, 1947.

p π¹

What had you for supper Lord Ronald my son,
What had you for supper, my jolly young man?
I had fishes for supper, go make my bed soon,
Sick at the heart, and fain would lie doon.

What leave to your mother, Lord Ronald, my son,
What leave to your mother, my jolly young man,
My watch and my chain, go make my bed soon,
Sick at the heart and fain would lie doon.

What leave to your sweetheart, Lord Ronald, my son
What leave to your sweetheart, my jolly young man.
A rope and a tree, and hanged she shall be
And all for the sake of poisoning me.

31. [Lord Ronald]

Campbell, II, [1818], p. 45. Also in Child, 1882-98, I, p. 160(D), as from Scott, 1803, p. 292. Sung by Sophia Scott, the daughter of Sir Walter Scott.

a D/M

1. "O where hae ye been, Lord Randal, my son?
   O where hae ye been, my handsome young man?"

"I hae been to the wild wood; mother, make my bed soon,
For I'm weary wi hunting, and fain wald lie down."

2. "Where gat ye your dinner, Lord Randal, my son?
   Where gat ye your dinner, my handsome young man?"
   "I din'd wi my true-love; mother, make my bed soon,
   For I'm weary wi hunting, and fain wald lie down."

3. "What gat ye to your dinner, Lord Randal, my son?
   What gat ye to your dinner, my handsome young man?"
   "I gat eels boild in broo; mother, make my bed soon,
   For I'm weary wi hunting, and fain wald lie down."

4. "What became of your bloodhounds, Lord Randal, my son?
   What became of your bloodhounds, my handsome young man?"
   "O they swelld and they died; mother, make my bed soon,
   For I'm weary wi hunting, and fain wald lie down."

5. "Oh I fear ye are poisond, Lord Randal, my son!
   O I fear ye are poisond, my handsome young man!"
   "O yes! I am poisond; mother, make my bed soon,
   For I'm sick at the heart, and I fain wald lie down."

33. "Lord Ronald, my Son"

Macmath MS. Also in Child, 1882-98, V, p. 413; text, I, pp. 499-500(P). From William Macmath of Edinburgh; learned from his aunt, Jane Webster, formerly of Airds of Kells, who learned it from a nursemaid at Airds, c. 1830.

m Æ/D

1. "Where hae ye been a' day, Lord Ronald, my son?
   Where hae ye been a'day, my handsome young one?"
   "I've been in the wood hunting; mother, make my bed soon,
   For I am weary, weary hunting, and fain would lie doun."

2. "O where did you dine, Lord Ronald, my son?
   O where did you dine, my handsome young one?"
   "I dined with my sweetheart; mother, make my bed soon,
   For I am weary, weary hunting, and fain would lie doun."

3. "What got you to dine on, Lord Ronald, my son?
   What got you to dine on, my handsome young one?"
   "I got eels boiled in water that in heather doth run,
   And I am weary, weary hunting, and fain would lie doun."

4. "What did she wi the broo o them, Lord Ronald, my son?
   What did she wi the broo o them, my handsome young one?"
   "She gave it to my hounds for to live upon,
   And I am weary, weary hunting, and fain would lie doun."

5. "Where are your hounds now, Lord Ronald, my son?
   Where are your hounds now, my handsome young one?"
   'They are a' swelled and bursted, and sae will I soon,
   And I am weary, weary hunting, and fain would lie doun."

6. "What will you leave your father, Lord Ronald, my son?
   What will you leave your father, my handsome young one?"
   "I'll leave him my lands for to live upon,
   And I am weary, weary hunting, and fain would lie doun."

7. "What will you leave your brother, Lord Ronald, my son?
   What will you leave your brother, my handsome young
   one?"
   "I'll leave him my gallant steed for to ride upon,
   And I am weary, weary hunting, and fain would lie doun."

8. "What will you leave your sister, Lord Ronald, my son?
   What will you leave your sister, my handsome young one?"
   "I'll leave her my gold watch for to look upon,
   And I am weary, weary hunting, and fain would lie doun."

9. "What will you leave your mother, Lord Ronald, my son?
   What will you leave your mother, my handsome young
   one?"
   "I'll leave her my Bible for to read upon,
   And I am weary, weary hunting, and fain would lie doun."

10. "What will you leave your sweetheart, Lord Ronald, my
    son?
    What will you leave your sweetheart, my handsome young
    one?"
    "I'll leave her the gallows-tree for to hang upon,
    It was her that poisoned me;" and so he fell doun.

GROUP A b

35.1. "Lord Ranald"

Archive, School of Scottish Studies, rec. No. 1960/196/A4.
Sung by Norman Kennedy, Aberdeen. Collected by John
MacInnes. Transcribed by Ailie Munro.

a I

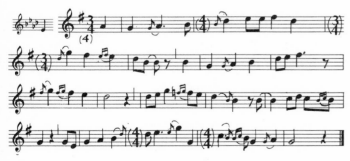

1. "Faur hae ye been all the day, Lord Ranald, my honey?
   Faur hae ye been all the day, my gentleman son?"
   "I've been tae dine wi my wife—mither, mak my bed,
   For I'm seik until the hert, an fain wid I lie doon."

2. "An fit gat ye there, Lord Ranald, my honey?
   An fit did she gie ye, my ain darlin son?"
   "Eels, believe it, poisont me—mither, mak my bed,
   For I'm seik until the hert, an fain wid I lie doon."

3. "An fit dae ye leave me, Lord Ranald, my honey?
   An fit dae ye leave me, my ain dear son?"
   "My blessin an my land—mither, mak my bed,
   For I'm seik until the hert, an fain wid I lie doon."

4. "An fit dae ye leave yee-er bairns, Lord Ranald, my honey,
   An fit dae ye leave them, my ainlie son?"
   "Let them gae beg through life—mither, mak my bed,
   For I'm seik unto the hert, an fain wid I lie doon."

5. "An fit dae ye lea' yee-er wife, Lord Ranald, my honey?
   An fit will ye leave her, my ain darlin son?"
   "A new rope tae hang her wi—mither, mak my bed,
   For I'm seik untae the hert, an fain wid I lie doon."

35.2. "Lord Randal"

Archive, School of Scottish Studies, rec. 1951/1/A3. Sung
by Ewan MacColl and his mother, Mrs. Miller. Collected
by Hamish Henderson and Alan Lomax. Transcribed by
Francis M. Collinson.

m I (inflected III and VII)

1. O whaur hae ye been, Lord Randal my son?
   O whaur hae ye been, my bonnie young man?
   I've been tae the wild wood, mither mak my bed sune
   For I'm weary wi' huntin' and I fain would lie doun.

2. Whaur gat ye your dinner, Lord Randal my son?
   Whaur gat ye your dinner, my bonnie young man?
   O I dined wi' my true love, mither mak my bed sune
   For I'm weary wi' huntin' and I fain would lie doun.

3. What gat ye for your dinner, Lord Randal my son?
   What gat ye for your dinner, my bonnie young man?
   I gat eels boiled in brew, mither mak my bed sune
   For I'm weary wi' huntin' and I fain would lie doun.

4. What happened tae your bloodhounds, Lord Randal my
      son?
   What happened tae your bloodhounds, my bonnie young
      man?
   O they swalled and they died, mither mak my bed sune
   For I'm weary wi' huntin' and I fain would lie doun.

5. I fear ye hae been poisoned, Lord Randal my son,
   I fear ye hae been poisoned, my bonnie young man.
   O I hae been poisoned, mither mak my bed sune
   For I'm sick at the heart and I fain would lie doun.

6. What will ye leave yer brither, Lord Randal my son?
   What will ye leave yer brither, my bonnie young man?
   My horse and my saddle, mither mak my bed sune
   For I'm weary wi' huntin' and I fain would lie doun.

7. What will ye leave yer sister, Lord Randal my son?
   What will ye leave yer sister, my bonnie young man?
   My gowd box and rings, mither mak my bed sune
   For I'm weary wi' huntin' and I fain would lie doun.

8. And what will ye leave yer true love, Lord Randal my son?
   And what will ye leave yer true love, my bonnie young
     man?
   That . . . that halter, that halter, that hangs on yon tree,
   And there let her hang for the poisonin o' me.

43. [Lord Ronald]

Greig MSS., III, p. 37. Also in Greig and Keith, 1925, p. 14(1c). Sung by A. Greig, Oldwhat, 1907.

a I/M

Oh whaur hae ye been to Lord Ronald my son?
Oh whaur hae ye been to my handsome young man?
I've been to the wild wood, mother mak' my bed soon;
For I'm weary, weary wand'ring and fain wad lie doon.

43.2. "Lord Donald"

Archive, School of Scottish Studies, rec. No. 1957/44/B2. Sung by Jeannie Robertson, Aberdeen. Collected by Hamish Henderson. Transcribed by James Porter.

a π¹

1. "Whaur hae ye been all the day,
   Lord Donald, my son?
   Whaur hae ye been all the day,
   My jolly young man?"

2. "Awa coortin, mither—
   Mak my bed soon,
   For I am seik at the hairt,
   An I fain wud lie doon."

3. "What will ye hae for your supper,
   Lord Donald, my son?
   What will ye hae for your supper,
   My jolly young man?"

4. "I hae had my supper—
   Mither, mak my bed soon,
   For I am seik at the hairt,
   An I fain wud lie doon."

5. "What had ye for supper,
   Lord Donald, my son?
   What had ye for supper,
   My jolly young man?"

6. "I had little smaa fishes—
   Mither, mak my bed soon,
   For I am seik at the hairt,
   An I fain wud lie doon."

7. "What like were the fishes,
   Lord Donald, my son?
   What like were the fishes,
   My gallant young man?"

8. "Black back an spreckled belly—
   Mither, mak my bed soon,
   For I am seik at the hairt,
   An I fain wud lie doon."

9. "Oh, I doubt you are poishoned,
   Lord Donald, my son—
   Oh, I doubt you are poishoned,
   My jolly young man.

10. "What will ye leave tae your father,
    Lord Donald, my son?
    What will ye leave tae your father,
    My jolly young man?"

11. "My houses an lands, mither—
    Mak my bed soon,
    For I am seik at the hairt,
    An I fain wud lie doon."

    . . .

12. "What will ye leave tae your true-love
    Lord Donald, my son?"

13. "The tow an the helter
    To hang on yon tree,
    An there for to hang
    For the poishonin o' me."

14. "What will ye leave tae your true-love,
    Lord Donald, my son?
    What will ye leave tae your true-love,
    My jolly young man?"

15. "The tow an the helter
   Tae hang on yon tree,
   An there for to hang
   For the poishonin o' me."

48. [Lord Randal]

Creighton and Senior, 1950, pp. 9-10. Sung by Ben Henneberry, Devil's Island, Nova Scotia.

a I

1. "O what is the matter Henery my son,
   O what is the matter my own dearest one,"
   I've been to my sweetheart mother, make my bed soon,
   I feel sick at the heart, and fain would lie down.

2. "What did she give you, Henery my son,
   O what did she give you, my own dearest one?"
   "She gave me golden fishes, mother, make my bed soon,
   I feel sick at heart and fain would lie down."

3. "What will you will your mother, Henery my son,
   What will you will your mother, my own dearest one?"
   "I will will you my money, mother, make my bed soon,
   I feel sick at the heart and I fain would lie down."

4. "What will you will your father, Henery my son,
   What will you will your father, my own dearest one?"
   "I will him my land and houses, mother, make my bed soon,
   I feel sick at heart and I fain would lie down."

5. "What will you will your sister, Henery my son,
   What will you will your sister, my own dearest one?"
   "I'll will her my sheep and cattle, mother, make my bed soon,
   I feel sick at heart and I fain would lie down."

6. "What will you will your brother, Henery my son,
   What will you will your brother, my own dearest one?"
   "I'll will him my horse and saddle, mother, make my bed
   soon,
   I feel sick at the heart and I fain would lie down."

7. "What will you will your sweetheart, Henery my son,
   What will you will your sweetheart, my own dearest one?"
   "I'll will her a rope to hang herself on yonder green tree,
   It was poison she gave me and she has you and me."

53. [Lord Randal]

Sharp MSS., 4198/. Also in Sharp and Karpeles, 1932, I,
p. 43(H). Sung by Mrs. Ada Maddox, Buena Vista, Va.,
April 30, 1918.

a M

Sharp's MS. note to the second bar: "Bars of this rhythm, which
occur constantly in this tune, were sung so that the first two notes
were given each rather more than their face value, i.e. the first note
was nearly a crotchet, the second nearly a minim. The whole melody
was sung quite slowly."

What for your supper? John Randolph, my son
What for your supper? my darling one.
Eel soup and vin'gar has made my bed soon, Mother,
I'm sick at the heart and want to lie down.

60. "Where were you all the day, my own pretty boy?"

Joyce, 1909, No. 812, pp. 394-95. Sung by Peggy Cudmore,
c. 1848.

a I

"Where were you all the day, my own pretty boy?
Where were you all the day, my truelove and joy?"
"I was fishing and fowling: mother, dress my bed soon;
There's a pain in my heart, and I want to lie down."

"What did you get for dinner, my own pretty boy?
What did you get for dinner, my truelove and joy?"
"Bread, mutton, and poison: mother, dress my bed soon;
There's a pain in my heart, and I want to lie down."

"What will you leave your mother, my own pretty boy?
What will you leave your mother, my truelove and joy?"
"A coach and four horses: mother, dress my bed soon;
There's a pain in my heart, and I want to lie down."

* * * * *

"What will you leave your married wife, my own pretty boy?
What will you leave your married wife, my truelove and joy?"
"A long rope to hang her: mother, dress my bed soon;
There's a pain in my heart, and I want to lie down."

61. "Where were you all the day, my own pretty boy"

Petrie, 1902-5, No. 330. From P. W. Joyce.

a Æ (inflected III)

It seems odd that this copy, so similar to Peggy Cudmore's in all but mode, also came from Dr. Joyce. We may perhaps suspect editorial revision by Petrie or Stanford.

GROUP A d

72. "Lord Ronald my Son"

Barry, Eckstorm, and Smyth, 1929, pp. 55(H)-56. Sung by Mrs. James McGill, Chamcook, New Brunswick, April 1928; learned from her mother in Galloway, Scotland. Melody recorded by George Herzog.

a M

1. "Whaur hae ye been a' day, Lord Ronald my son?
   Whaur hae ye been a' day, my jolly young man?"
   "I've been awa huntin', mither mak my bed sune,
   For I'm weary wi' huntin' an' fain wad lie doon."

2. "What'll ye hae tae yer supper, Lord Ronald my son?
   What'll ye hae tae yer supper, my jolly young man?"
   "I've gotten my supper, mither mak my bed sune,
   For I'm weary wi' huntin' an' fain wad lie doon."

3. "What did ye get tae yer supper, Lord Ronald my son?
   What did ye get tae yer supper, my jolly young man?"
   "A dish o' gold fishes, mither mak my bed sune,
   For I'm weary wi' huntin' an' fain wad lie doon."

4. "Where got ye the fishes, Lord Ronald my son?
   Where got ye the fishes, my jolly young man?"

"In my faither's black ditches, mither mak my bed sune,
For I'm weary wi' huntin' an' fain wad lie doon."

5. "They hae poisoned Lord Ronald, they hae poisoned my son,
   "They hae poisoned Lord Ronald, my jolly young man."
   "O my heart it is weary, mither mak my bed sune,
   For I'm weary wi' huntin' an' fain wad lie doon."

6. "What'll ye leave tae yer faither, Lord Ronald my son?
   What'll ye leave tae yer faither, my jolly young man?"
   "My lands an' my houses, mither mak my bed sune,
   For I'm weary wi' huntin' an' fain wad lie doon."

7. "What'll ye leave tae yer brother, Lord Ronald my son?
   What'll ye leave tae yer brother, my jolly young man?"
   "My horse an' my saddle, mither mak my bed sune,
   For I'm weary wi' huntin' an' fain wad lie doon."

8. "What'll ye leave tae yer sister, Lord Ronald my son?
   What'll ye leave tae yer sister, my jolly young man?"
   "My box of gold rings, mither mak my bed sune,
   For I'm weary wi' huntin' an' fain wad lie doon."

9. "What'll ye leave tae yer sweetheart, Lord Ronald my son?
   What'll ye leave tae yer sweetheart, my jolly young man?"
   "A rope for to hang her on yon gallows tree,
   For it's her this night that has poisonèd me."

GROUP B a

84. [Lord Rendal]

Sharp MSS., 755/. Sung by Mrs. Pike, Somerton; transmitted by Mrs. Snow, January 5, 1906.

p I

Where have you been to day Henery my son
Where have you been to day Henery my one
Courting mother courting mother make my bed soon
For I'm sick to my heart and I want to lie down.

GROUP B b

90. [Lord Rendal]

Sharp MSS., 350/. Also in Sharp, JFSS, II (1905), pp. 29 (2)-30, and Sharp, One Hundred English Folksongs, 1916, p. 44. Sung by Mrs. Perry, Langport, August 23, 1904.

a I

The original is in 2/4 time.

This is doubtless the set altered for use in *One Hundred English Folk Songs*, 1916, No. 18, p. 44.

1. "Where have you been to all the day, Henery my son?
   Where have you been to all the day? You're a pretty one."
   "Out in the green fields, mother,
   Out in the green fields, mother;
   Make my bed quick, I've a pain in my heart
       And I wants to lie down."

2. "What have you been eating of, Henery, my son?
   What have you been eating of? You're a pretty one."
   "Eels, mother,
   Eels, mother;
   Make my bed quick, I've a pain in my heart
       And I wants to lie down."

3. "What will you leave your father, Henery, my son?
   What will you leave your father? You're a pretty one."
   "Land and houses, mother,
   Land and houses, mother;
   Make my bed quick, I've a pain in my heart
       And I wants to lie down."

4. "What will you leave your mother, Henery, my son?
   What will you leave your mother? You're a pretty one."
   "Coals and horses, mother,
   Coals and horses, mother;
   Make my bed quick, I've a pain in my heart
       And I wants to lie down."

5. "What will you leave your brother, Henery, my son?
   What will you leave your brother? You're a pretty one."
   "Ham and chicken, mother,
   Ham and chicken, mother;
   Make my bed quick, I've a pain in my heart
       And I wants to lie down."

6. "What will you leave your sister, Henery, my son?
   What will you leave your sister? You're a pretty one."
   "A rope to hang her, mother,
   A rope to hang her, mother;
   Make my bed quick, I've a pain in my heart
       And I wants to lie down."

Only the first stanza appears in Sharp's MSS.

94. "Henry, My Son"

Eddy, 1939, p. 21(C). Sung by William Lavey, Canton, Ohio; learned from Russian Jewish children in Winnipeg.

a I/M (compass of sixth)

1. "Where have you been, Henry, my son,
       Where have you been, my beloved one?"
   "At sister's, at sister's,
       Make my bed for the pain at my side,
   For I want to lie down and die."

2. "What did she give you, Henry, my son,
       What did she give you, my beloved one?"
   "Poison to drink, poison to drink;
       Make my bed for the pain at my side,
   For I want to lie down and die."

3. "What will you give your father, Henry, my son,
       What will you give your father, my beloved one?"
   "Golden watches, golden watches;
       Make my bed for the pain at my side,
   For I want to lie down and die."

4. "What will you give your mother, Henry, my son,
       What will you give your mother, my beloved one?"
   "Gold and silver, gold and silver;
       Make my bed for the pain at my side,
   For I want to lie down and die."

5. "What will you give your brother, Henry, my son,
       What will you give your brother, my beloved one?"
   "Heavenly kisses, heavenly kisses;
       Make my bed for the pain at my side,
   For I want to lie down and die."

6. "What will you give your sister, Henry, my son,
       What will you give your sister, my beloved one?"
   "Knives to kill her, ropes to hang her;
       Make my bed for the pain at my side,
   For I want to lie down and die."

GROUP BC

97. "King Henry, my Son"

Nicholson, *JFSS*, III (1907), p. 43. Sung by Mr. Lattimer, Carlisle; learned as a boy in Cumberland.

p Æ

Lucy Broadwood, *English Traditional Songs and Carols*, 1908, pp. 96-99, prints an almost identical copy (with accompaniment) as from

Margaret Scott, Cumberland, who sang it, in a fuller version, before 1868.

Miss Broadwood refers to the cognate tune, "The trees they do grow high," collected by Vaughan Williams in Sussex (JFSS, II [1906], p. 206).

"Oh, where have you been wandering, King Henery, my son,
[Oh,] where have you been wandering, my pretty one?"
"I've been to my sweetheart's, mother, make my bed soon,
For I'm sick to the heart, and would fain lay me down."

"And what did your sweetheart give you, King Henery, my
son,
What did your sweetheart give you, my pretty one?"
"She fried me some paddocks, mother, make my bed soon,
For I'm sick at the heart, and would fain lay me down."

"And what will you leave your sweetheart, King Henery, my
son?
What will you leave your sweetheart, my pretty one?"
"My garter to hang her, mother, make my bed soon,
For I'm sick at the heart, and would fain lay me down."

GROUP C

98. "Willie Doo"

Moffat, [1933], p. 5.

a Æ

O where hae ye been a' the day,
(Willie Doo,* Willie Doo?)
I've been to see my stepmither,
(Die shall I now!)

What got ye frae your stepmither,
(Willie Doo, Willie Doo?)
She gaed to me a speckled trout,
(Die shall I now!)

Where got she you the speckled trout,
(Willie Doo, Willie Doo?)
'Twas caught amang the heather hills,
(Die shall I now!)

What gaed she you there for to drink,
(Willie Doo, Willie Doo?)
She brewed some deadly hemlock stocks,
(Die shall I now!)

They made his bed, then laid him down
Puir Willie, Willie Doo!
He turned his wee face to the wa',
Willie's died now!

* Doo: dove.

99. "The Wee Little Croodin' Doo"

Broadwood, *JFSS*, V (1915), p. 118(2). Sung by Henry Fowler Broadwood (b. 1811, d. 1893), Lyne, Sussex.

a I

"Where hae ye been the live-long day,
My wee little croodin' doo?"*
"I've been to see my step-mother,
Mammy, mak' my bed noo."

"And what did your step-mother give ye to eat,
My wee little croodin' doo?"
"She gave me a wee, wee blue fish.
Mammy, mak' my bed noo."

"And what did ye do with the bones of the fish,
My wee little croodin' doo?"
"I gave them to my wee, wee dog,
Mammy, mak' my bed noo."

"And what did your dog when he'd eat of the bones,
My wee little croodin' doo?"
"He stretched his wee leggies and died,
Mammy, as I do noo."

* Cooing dove.

Billie Boy

CHILD NO. 12, APPENDIX

WILLIAM STENHOUSE (*Illustrations of the Lyric Poetry and Music of Scotland*, 1839) and John Glen (*Early Scottish Melodies*, 1900) both ascribe the first appearance of this song to *The Bee*, May 1791, an Edinburgh magazine. The words are said to be by Hector Macneill. They are a sentimentalized version of an older song of which Stenhouse deprecatingly quotes two stanzas. Glen observes that Macneill's song appeared also in Napier's, G. Thomson's and Urbani's collections before it was printed in the sixth volume of the *Scots Musical Museum*, No. 502, 1803.

There can be little doubt in anyone's mind that the older song cited by Stenhouse is a spirited parody of "Lord Randal." The tune, as Glen rightly notices, is cut from the same cloth as "Muirland Willie," discussed by him at length elsewhere in his volume. It is clear that the records of the parody are of approximately equal age with those of the serious ballad (i.e., in English); and that the existence of the tune can be followed back in one form or another for a century earlier.

It seems likely that all the tune-families for the present ballad are at least distantly related, but they diverge in characteristic and vigorous ways. The Celtic form stands apart; the English shows two varieties hard to disentangle; and the American form is again characteristic, quite consistent, and very widely known.

The Celtic variants, although scarce, have been set first. They swing between Æolian and Dorian. Miss Gilchrist has pointed out the relation of one of them to "When Johnny comes marching home," calling attention also to analogy with "John Anderson, my Jo" and another tune in the *Museum*, "The Maid gaed to the Mill," No. 481. She also quotes a partial text of an earlier version from Herd's MSS. Cf. H. Hecht, *Songs from David Herd's Manuscripts*, 1904, p. 105.

The English and American variants, on the contrary, are without exception in major tonality (I, π^1, I/M). Three Somerset variants stand together with a Northumbrian capstan shanty as particularly related, both words and music, although varying considerably in contour. These form our group B. Group C comes half from Somerset, half from American singers, Appalachian and Canadian. All these variants have a mid-cadence on the fifth, and all have noticeable traits in common with one another, but again with considerable variety. Much the same may be said of Group D, which is, however, all English, all plagal major. Group E contains the main stream of tradition in America. Its melodic contour changes too seldom to be very interesting; but the last few variants display shifts of octave-emphasis and finally a tendency to level out in a lazier line, which point toward deterioration.

TUNES WITH TEXTS

GROUP A

2. "My Boy Tommy, O!"

O'Sullivan, *JIFSS*, XVIII (1921), p. 33. Sung by Bat Riordan, Kilnanare, County Kerry.

a Æ/D

As O'Sullivan remarks, this tune (like the preceding) appears related to "Muirland Willie," for which cf., e.g., A. Moffat, *Minstrelsy of Scotland*, n.d., p. 150. Moffat notes that "Muirland Willie" was printed in *Orpheus Caledonius*, 1725, and in *Musick for Allan Ramsay's Collection*, 1726, and that "Lord Frog," in *Apollo's Banquet*, London, 1669, "seems to be an early version."

1. "Where have you been all the day,
    My boy Tommy, O?
   Where have you been all the day,
    My bonny blue-eyed Tommy, O?"
   "I've been rolling in the hay,
    With a lassie young and gay."

"Wasn't she the young thing
  That lately left her mammy, O?"

2. "What did she give you to eat?
    My boy Tommy, O?
   What did she give you to eat,
    My bonny blue-eyed Tommy, O?"
   "She gave me bread, she gave me meat,
   And that's what she gave me to eat."
   "Wasn't she the young thing
    That lately left her mammy, O?"

3. "What did she give you to drink,
    My boy Tommy, O?
   What did she give you to drink,
    My bonny blue-eyed Tommy, O?"
   "She gave me wine as black as ink,
   And that's what she gave me to drink."
   "Wasn't she the young thing
    That lately left her mammy, O?"

4. "Can she mend and can she make,
    My boy Tommy, O?
   Can she mend and can she make,
    My bonny blue-eyed Tommy, O?"
   "She can mend and she can make,
   She can give and she can take."
   "Wasn't she the young thing
    That lately left her mammy, O?"

5. "Can she bake a corn-cake,
    My boy Tommy, O?
Can she bake a corn-cake,
    My bonny blue-eyed Tommy, O?"
"She can bake a corn-cake
Fit for any man to eat."
"Wasn't she the young thing
    That lately left her mammy, O?"

6. "Can she make a feather bed,
    My boy Tommy, O?
Can she make a feather bed,
    My bonny blue-eyed Tommy, O?"
"She can make a feather bed
Fit for any man to rest."
"Wasn't she the young thing
    That lately left her mammy, O?"

7. "What age is this young thing,
    My boy Tommy, O?
What age is this young thing,
    My bonny blue-eyed Tommy, O?"
"Twice two, twice four,
Twice seven and eleven more."
"Wasn't she the young thing
    That lately left her mammy, O?"

O'Sullivan's editorial note: "Noted some years ago from the singing of my friend Bat Riordan, of Kilnanare. Both words and air are undoubtedly of Scottish origin, and the song appears in Johnson's *Museum* (see *Popular Songs of Scotland*, Balmoral Edition, page 270). The air is probably an altered form of 'Muirland Willie.' I have not seen any other version in which the surprise concerning the lady's age is given, and this may be a piece of Irish humour. As regards the manner of singing this last verse, it may be remarked that in Kerry, as in other parts of Munster, the word *twice* is pronounced very nearly as disyllable, even in ordinary speech, thus: *two-ice*."

GROUP B

6. [Billy Boy]

Terry, 1921, Pt. I, pp. 2-3. A Northumbrian capstan shanty.

a I (inflected IV)

The timing of this variant seems debatable: if it is to conform to the prevailing pattern, the bar-lines of the first two phrases might better be moved forward three beats, with a 9/8 bar at the junction of the second and third phrases (bars 7 and 8 above).

Where hev ye been åål the day,
    Billy Boy, Billy Boy?
Where hev ye been åål the day, me Billy Boy?

I've been walkin' åål the day
With me charmin' Nancy Grey.
And me Nancy kittl'd me fancy
Oh me charmin' Billy Boy.

Is she fit to be yor wife
    Billy Boy, Billy Boy?
Is she fit to be yor wife, me Billy Boy?
    She's as fit to be me wife
    As the fork is to the knife
    And me Nancy, etc.

Can she cook a bit o' steak
    Billy Boy, Billy Boy?
Can she cook a bit o' steak, me Billy Boy?
    She can cook a bit o' steak,
    Aye, and myek a gairdle cake
    And me Nancy, etc.

Can she myek an Irish Stew
    Billy Boy, Billy Boy?
Can she myek an Irish Stew, me Billy Boy?
    She can myek an Irish Stew
    Aye, and "Singin' Hinnies" too.
    And me Nancy, etc.

GROUP D

15. [My boy Willy]

Sharp MSS., 2618/. Also, with piano accompaniment, in Sharp, 1912, IV, p. 6. Sung by John Bradley, Shiperton Union, August 22, 1911.

p I

MS. note by Sharp: "Time oscillated between compound time and compound 6/8."

O where have you been all the day my boy Willy
O where have you been all the day
O Willie wont you tell me now
I've been all the day courting of a lady gay
But she is too young to be taken from her mammy.

Can she brew and can she bake, my boy Willie (2)
Oh Willy wont you tell me now?
She can brew & she can bake, she can make a wedding cake
But she is too young to be taken from her mammy.

Can she knit & can she spin my boy Willie (2)
    Etc.
She can knit & she can spin, she can do most anything
But she is etc.

O how old is she now, my boy Willie (2)
    Etc.
Twice six, twice seven, twice twenty & eleven
But she is too young to be taken from her mammy.

GROUP E

20. "Billy Boy"

Creighton and Senior, 1950, pp. 246-47. Sung by Mrs.
Dennis Greenough, West Petpeswick, Nova Scotia.

a I/M

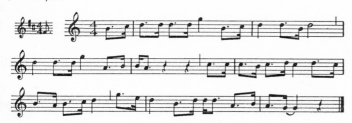

1. Where have you been all the day Billy Boy, Billy Boy,
Where are you going charming Billy?

I've been gone to seek a wife, she's the joy of my life,
She's a young thing and cannot leave her mammy.

2. Can she bake a cherry pie, Billy Boy, Billy Boy,
Can she bake a cherry pie, charming Billy?
She can bake a cherry pie, quick as a cat can wink her eye,
She's a young thing and cannot leave her mammy.

3. Can she make a feather bed, Billy Boy, Billy Boy,
Can she make a feather bed, charming Billy?
She can make a feather bed, with good pillows at the head,
But she's a young thing and cannot leave her mammy.

4. Is she fit to be your wife, Billy Boy, Billy Boy,
Is she fit to be your wife, charming Billy?
She's as fit to be my wife, as the fork is to the knife,
She's a young thing and cannot leave her mammy.

5. Can she knit, can she spin, Billy Boy, Billy Boy,
Can she knit and can she spin, charming Billy?
She can knit and she can spin, she can spin most anything,
She's a young thing and cannot leave her mammy.

6. How old is she, Billy Boy, Billy Boy,
How old is she, charming Billy?
She is one, she is two, twice eleven and twenty-two,
She's a young thing and cannot leave her mammy.

Edward

CHILD NO. 13

THIS ballad has mainly been confined in European traditional singing to the Scandinavian countries, to Finland, and to Scotland, whence it has traveled to take fresh root in the Appalachian regions. Archer Taylor has argued convincingly that the ballad passed from Britain to Scandinavia. (*"Edward" and "Sven i Rosengård,"* Chicago, 1931.) It appears to me that the most artistic and best-known version, first given to the world in Percy's *Reliques*, is a literary rehandling of the traditional song. (Cf. *SFQ*, IV [1940], pp. 1-13, 159-61.) None of the traditional variants except Motherwell's, which was possibly influenced by Percy, implicates the mother in the son's guilt.

Although Motherwell says he prints his text chiefly with the intention of introducing the traditional melody, he curiously fails to give us any tune, so that all but a very few recently recovered tunes for this ballad come from the Appalachians. Greig failed to find any in his region, but the gap has since been closed.

Three tunes associated particularly with other ballads are also employed traditionally with this one. All three have points in common and have been grouped together (B). Our last group (C) is composed of tunes having little or nothing in common with the other groups or with one another. They are probably vehicles borrowed for present use by individual singers. Those, however, from North Carolina, Virginia, and Texas may be related; and they bespeak kinship with the American branch of "Gypsy Davy" (Child No. 200). One from Arkansas appears to have "Camptown Races" as its nearest relative.

Group A, owing to fresh variants lately added, is no longer easy to rationalize. The chief normative factor is a mid-cadence on the dominant. But, in spite of occasional resemblances, the components are too variable to allow of any assurance about the group as a whole. The Scottish variants are also rhythmically and in stanza-pattern distinct from the norm.

Group B falls into three distinct patterns, none peculiar to this ballad. The first (vts. 7 to 10) is that of "Gypsy Laddie" (the Cassilis type: cf. Child No. 200). The final is ambiguous, and the variants, mostly pentatonic, may be taken as either authentic π^2 or plagal π^1. The second pattern is that of "Boyne Water"* (vts. 11 to 13). Again the final squints: the pentatonics may be either authentic π^3 or plagal π^2 with fallen closes. The third (C) type employs the "House Carpenter" (Child No. 243) idea at starting, in a plagal Mixolydian form. But it falls away rapidly, seduced by other memories.

Over-all, it is impossible to discover any single dominating melodic tradition for Child No. 13, and the groups A and C are especially vague. These facts may be taken as an indication that, however it may be with the transmission of texts, this ballad has not during its recorded life-time had a secure and continuous hold on the folk memory.

* Cf., e.g., 209, 213, 214, 233, for its use with other ballads.

TUNES WITH TEXTS

GROUP A

2. [Edward]

Flanders and Olney, 1953, pp. 100-1. Sung by Edith Ballenger Price, Newport, R.I., October 8, 1945; learned in Amherst, Mass., c. 1910. From *Ballads Migrant in New England*, edited by Helen Hartness Flanders and Marguerite Olney; copyright 1953 by Helen Hartness Flanders.

a π^4

The 1953 copy has been corrected in the first note of line 4—from A to G—by authority of Miss Olney.

1. "How came this blood on your shirt sleeve,
     O dear love, tell me, me, me?"
   "It is the blood of my old gray hound
   That traced that fox for me, me, me,
     that traced that fox for me."

2. "It does look too pale for the old gray hound,
     O dear love, tell me, me, me—
   It does look too pale for the old gray hound
   That traced that fox for thee, thee, thee,
     that traced that fox for thee."

3. "How came this blood on your shirt sleeve,
     O dear love, tell me, me, me?"
   "It is the blood of my old gray mare
   That ploughed that field for me, me, me,
     that ploughed that field for me."

4. "It does look too pale for the old gray mare,
     O dear love, tell me, me, me—
   It does look too pale for the old gray mare
   That ploughed that field for thee, thee, thee,
     that ploughed that field for thee."

5. "How came this blood on your shirt sleeve,
     O dear love, tell me, me, me?"
   "It is the blood of my brother-in-law
   That went away with me, me, me,
     that went away with me."

6. "And it's what did you fall out about,
     O dear love, tell me, me, me?"
   "About a little bit of bush
   That never would have growed to a tree, tree, tree,
     that never would have growed to a tree."

7. "And it's what will you do now, my love,
     O dear love, tell me, me, me?"
  "I'll set my foot into yonders ship
  And sail across the sea, sea, sea—
     and sail across the sea!"

8. "And it's when will you come back again,
     O dear love, tell me, me, me?"
  "When the sun sets into yonders sycamore tree
  And that will never be, be, be—
     and that will never be!"

8. "I'll go away in a bottomless boat,
     Yes, lady mother, etc.
  It's I'll go away in a bottomless boat,
     An a good scholar I'll come home."

9. "When will you be back again,
     Hey son Dauvit, etc.
  When will you be back again,
     Come promise, etc."

10. "When the sun an the moon shall meet in yon glen,
     Yes, lady mother, etc.
  When the sun an the moon shall meet in yon glen,
     An that will never be."

3.2. "Son David"

Archive, School of Scottish Studies, rec. No. 1954/102/A1.
Sung by Margaret Stewart, Aberdeen. Collected by Hamish
Henderson. Transcribed by Francis M. Collinson.

a D/Æ? or p I/M (—IV; ending on VI)

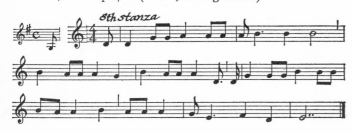

1. "What's the blood 'it's on your sword,
     Hey, son Dauvit, ho son Dauvit,
  What's the blood 'it's on your sword,
     It's promise, tell me true."

2. "That's the blood of my grey mare,
     Yes, lady mother, aye, lady mother,
  That's the blood of my grey mare,
     'Caise she would not rule by me."

3. "That blood is faur too clear,
     Hey, son Dauvit, etc.
  That blood is faur too clear,
     An promise, etc."

4. "Yes, lady mother, aye, lady mother,
  That's the blood of my haukin-hound,
     'Caise it would not rule by me."

5. "That blood is faur too clear,
     Hey, son Dauvit, etc.
  That blood is faur too clear,
     An promise, etc."

6. "That is the blood of my brother, John,
     Yes, lady mother, aye lady mother,
  That's the blood of my brother John,
     'Caise he would not rule by me."

7. "It was cast o'er a silly one,
     Yes, lady mother, etc.
  It was cast o'er a silly one
  When he drew his sword to me."

GROUP B

8. [Edward]

Sharp MSS., 4552/3185. Also in Sharp and Karpeles, 1932,
I, p. 53(J). Sung by Mrs. Mary Gibson, Marion, N.C.,
September 3, 1918.

a π²

1. What blood is that all on your shirt?
     O son, come tell to me.
  It is the blood of the old grey mare
  That ploughed the corn for me, O me,
  That ploughed the corn for me.

2. It is too red for the old grey mare.
     O son, etc.
  It is the blood of the old grey hound
  That run the deer for me, etc.

3. It is too red for the old grey hound.
  It is the blood of the little guinea-pig
  That eat the corn for me.

4. It is too red for the little guinea-pig.
  It is the blood of my oldest brother
  That travelled along with me.

5. What did you fall all* out about?
  About a little holly bush
  That might have made a tree.

6. What will you do when your father comes home?
  I'll set my foot in a bunkum boat
  And sail all on the sea.

7. What will you do with your pretty little wife?
I'll take her on a bunkum boat
And sail along with me.

8. What will you do with your oldest son?
I'll leave him here for you to raise
And dance around your knees.

9. What will you do with your oldest daughter?
I'll leave her here for you to raise
For to remember me.

* 1932 omits "all."

11. [Edward]

Sharp MSS., 3821/2804. Also in Sharp and Karpeles, 1932, I, p. 47(C). Sung by Strauder Medford, Balsam, N.C., July 31, 1917.

a π³

This is the "Boyne Water" type.

How came that blood on the point of your knife?
My son, come tell to me.
It is the blood of my old coon dog
That chased the fox for me, O me,
That chased the fox for me.

How came that blood, etc.
It is the blood of the olive bush
Which would have made a tree, etc.

How came that blood, etc.
It is the blood of my oldest brother
Who raised a row with me, etc.

O what are you going to do with your little children?
O son, come tell to me.

I'll leave them here to stand around you
And cry after me when I'm gone.

22. [Edward]

Davis, 1929, p. 558(D); text, p. 124. Sung by Mrs. Travers D. Moncure, Aylett, Va., September 13, 1917; learned from her mother, who learned it from *her* mother. Collected by John Stone.

a π¹ (compass of sixth)

The original copy is written straight through in 6/8 time.

"What is that on your sword so red?
Dear son, pray tell unto me."
"'Tis the blood of a gay gilleon.
Dear mother, pity me.
'Tis the blood of a gay gilleon.
Dear mother, pity me."

"No gilleon's blood was e'er so red.
Dear son, pray tell unto me."
"'Tis the blood of my dear brother.
O mother, pity me.
'Tis the blood of my dear brother.
O mother, pity me."

"What will you do when your father comes home?
Dear son, tell unto me."
"I'll get aboard of yonder ship
And sail away to sea.
I'll get aboard of yonder ship
And sail away to sea."

"When will you return, my son?
Dear son, pray tell unto me."
"When the sun and the moon set on yonder hill,
And that will never be.
When the sun and the moon set on yonder hill,
And that will never be."

Babylon

CHILD NO. 14

In the English language, this ballad has a recorded history of about a century and a half, and the musical record, as seldom happens, is nearly as old and good. The tradition appears to have held pretty consistently to LM quatrains, rhyming alternately,* with interlaced refrain as the general habit. The words of the refrain vary considerably, as is often true of refrains which are rather musical than meaningful.

It appears to me that there are at most two melodic families in the record for this ballad; but the divergence of copies is considerable. The rhythm seems originally to have been triple in both cases, and in both to have shifted gradually to duple time. It may be that such a shift has occurred much oftener in ballad melody than there is any likelihood of demonstrating. Kinloch's copy, virtually a π^3 tune, but literally D/M, may be allowed to head the larger group, composed of Dorian and Æolian variants, the Bute copy of which (vt. 6) is closer to the "Hind Horn" (Child No. 17) tradition than to the present.

Motherwell's copy, Mixolydian but lacking its fourth, may be related—though not proudly!—to the debased π^1 version found in Vermont, "Heckey-Hi Si-Bernio." From "bower" to "barn" is a decline in tradition: whether from a "rank robber" to a "bank robber" is the opposite, who shall say? These last two copies may by courtesy be allowed to stand as a separate group.

In spite of the strong Scottish infusion conspicuous in Appalachian tradition, this ballad seems not to have taken root there.

[* There is probably a corruption in stanzas 14-17 of Motherwell's version, where the rhyme of lines 1 and 3 disappears. The injury may have occurred by the dropping-out of the true line 3 in stanza 14, so that the actual rhymes come in different stanzas: $14^3 = 15^1$, $15^3 = 16^1$; then an interpolated and unnecessary line, 17^1, to make up the complement, where $16^3 = 17^3$ are the proper pair. The curious name, "Baby Lon," doubtless a perversion, is not yet accounted for, and awaits some lucky guess.]

TUNES WITH TEXTS

GROUP A

1. [The Duke of Perth's Three Daughters]

Kinloch, 1827, App'x. to p. 210; text, pp. 212-16. Sung in Mearnsshire.

m D/M

1. The Duke o' Perth had three daughters,
     Elizabeth, Margaret, and fair Marie;
   And Elizabeth's to the greenwud gane
     To pu' the rose and the fair lilie.

2. But she hadna pu'd a rose, a rose,
     A double rose, but barely three,
   Whan up and started a Loudon Lord,
     Wi' Loudon hose, and Loudon sheen.

3. "Will ye be called a robber's wife?
   Or will ye be stickit wi' my bloody knife?
   For pu'in the rose and the fair lilie,
   For pu'in them sae fair and free."

4. "Before I'll be called a robber's wife,
   I'll rather be stickit wi' your bloody knife,
   For pu'in the rose and the fair lilie,
   For pu'in them sae fair and free."

5. Then out he's tane his little penknife,
   And he's parted her and her sweet life,
   And thrown her o'er a bank o' brume,
   There never more for to be found.

6. The Duke o' Perth had three daughters,
     Elizabeth, Margaret, and fair Marie;
   And Margaret's to the greenwud gane
     To pu' the rose and the fair lilie.

7. But she hadna pu'd a rose, a rose,
     A double rose, but barely three,
   When up and started a Loudon Lord,
     Wi' Loudon hose, and Loudon sheen.

8. "Will ye be called a robber's wife?
   Or will ye be stickit wi' my bloody knife?
   For pu'in the rose and the fair lilie,
   For pu'in them sae fair and free."

9. "Before I'll be called a robber's wife,
   I'll rather be stickit wi' your bloody knife,
   For pu'in the rose and the fair lilie,
   For pu'in them sae fair and free."

10. Then out he's tane his little penknife,
    And he's parted her and her sweet life,
    For pu'in the rose and the fair lilie,
    For pu'in them sae fair and free.

11. The Duke o' Perth had three daughters,
      Elizabeth, Margaret, and fair Marie;
    And Mary's to the greenwud gane
      To pu' the rose and the fair lilie.

12. She hadna pu'd a rose, a rose,
    A double rose, but barely three,
When up and started a Loudon Lord,
    Wi' Loudon hose, and Loudon sheen.

13. "O will ye be called a robber's wife?
    Or will ye be stickit wi' my bloody knife?
For pu'in the rose and the fair lilie,
    For pu'in them sae fair and free."

14. "Before I'll be called a robber's wife,
    I'll rather be stickit wi' your bloody knife,
For pu'in the rose and the fair lilie,
    For pu'in them sae fair and free."

15. But just as he took out his knife,
    To tak' frae her, her ain sweet life,
Her brother John cam ryding bye,
    And this bloody robber he did espy.

16. But when he saw his sister fair,
    He kenn'd her by her yellow hair,
He call'd upon his pages three,
    To find this robber speedilie.

17. "My sisters twa that are dead and gane,
    For whom we made a heavy maene,
It's you that's twinn'd them o' their life,
    And wi' your cruel bloody knife.

18. Then for their life ye sair shall dree,
    Ye sall be hangit on a tree,
Or thrown into the poison'd lake,
    To feed the toads and rattle-snake."

3. "The Bonny Banks of Virgie-O"

Karpeles, 1934, II, pp. 78-82. Sung by Mr. and Mrs. Kenneth Monks, King's Cove, Bonavista Bay, Newfoundland, September 24, 1929. Text as collected by Miss Karpeles.

m D

1. Three young ladies went out for a walk;
       All a lee and a lonely O
   They met a robber on their way,
       On the bonny bonny banks of Vergeo.

2. He took the first one by the hand,
   And whipped her around till he made her stand.

3. O will you be a robber's wife?
   Or will you die by my penknife?

4. I will not be a robber's wife;
   I would rather die by your penknife.

5. He took the penknife in his hand,
   And it's there he took her own sweet life.

6. He took the second one by the hand,
   And whipped her around till he made her stand.

7. O will you be a robber's wife?
   Or will you die by my penknife?

8. I will not be a robber's wife;
   I would rather die by your penknife.

9. He took the penknife in his hand,
   And it's there he took her own sweet life.

10. He took the third one by the hand,
    And whipped her around till he made her stand.

11. O will you be a robber's wife?
    Or will you die by my penknife?

12. I will not be a robber's wife,
    Nor I will not die by your penknife.

13. If my brothers were here to-night
    You would not have killed my sisters fair (*or* bright).

14. Where are your brothers, pray now tell?
    One of them is a minister.

15. And where is the other, I pray now tell?
    He's out a-robbing like yourself.

16. The Lord have mercy on my poor soul,
    I've killed my sisters all but one.

17. Then he took his penknife in his hand,
    And then he took away his own sweet life.

GROUP B

7. [The Banks of Fordie]

Motherwell, 1827, App'x No. 26; text, p. xxii. Collected by Andrew Blaikie, Paisley.

a M (−IV)

There were three sisters liv'd in a bower,
    Fair Annet, and Margaret, and Marjorie,
And they went out to pu' a flower,
    And the dew draps off the hyndberry tree.

The long version that Motherwell admits as full text (18 stanzas), pp. 88-92, does not go so well to the tune above. It begins:

> There were three ladies lived in a bower,
>   Eh vow bonnie,
> And they went out to pull a flower,
>   On the bonnie banks o' Fordie.

The last six stanzas, to which the headnote makes reference, are as follows:

13. "I'll not be a rank robber's wife,
       Eh vow bonnie,
    Nor will I die by your wee penknife,
       On the bonnie banks o' Fordie.

14. "For I hae a brother in this wood,
       Eh vow bonnie,
    And gin ye kill me, it's he'll kill thee,
       On the bonnie banks o' Fordie."

15. "What's thy brother's name, come tell to me?
       Eh vow bonnie."
    "My brother's name is Baby Lon,
       On the bonnie banks o' Fordie."

16. "O sister, sister, what have I done,
       Eh vow bonnie,
    O have I done this ill to thee,
       On the bonnie banks o' Fordie?

17. "O since I've done this evil deed,
       Eh vow bonnie,
    Good sall never be seen o' me,
       On the bonnie banks o' Fordie."

18. He's taken out his wee penknife,
       Eh vow bonnie,
    And he's twyned himsel o' his ain sweet life,
       On the bonnie banks o' Fordie.

7.1. "The Banks o' Airdrie"

Sung by Mary Campbell, at Blairgowrie, Perthshire, August 1967 and April 1968. Learned a number of years earlier from Peggy Cameron, in whose family the song was well known. Collected and transcribed by Peter Shepheard, and sent by him to the Editor.

a I

[First verse forgotten. It tells of how three sisters meet the robber John.]

2. He took the first pretty sister by the hand
      Hey win sa bonnie
   He whirled her round an' he made her stand
      On the dewy banks o' Airdrie O

3. Will you be a rank robber's wife
      Hey win sa bonnie
   Or will you die by my penknife
      On the dewy banks o' Airdrie O

4. I won't be a rank robber's wife
      Hey win sa bonnie
   So I will die by your penknife
      On the dewy banks o' Airdrie O

5. He took the next pretty sister by the hand
   He whirled her round an' he made her stand
      [*Refrain lines sung with each verse.*]

6. Will you be a rank robber's wife
   Or will you die by my penknife

7. I won't be a rank robber's wife
   So I will die by your penknife

8. He took the third pretty sister by the hand
   He whirled her round an' he made her stand

9. Will you be a rank robber's wife
   Or will you die by my penknife

10. I have three brothers who pass this way
    If you kill me it's they'll kill you

11. Pray tell me your three brothers' names
    William, Peter, an' the other's named John

12. Pray tell me what's this I have done
       Hey win sa bonnie
    I've killed my three pretty sisters all but one
       On the dewy banks o' Airdrie O

"On singing the song again in April 1968, she sang the first refrain line: Hey win sa bonnie O (this was without any comment from myself)." [*Shepheard's MS. note.*]

Sheath and Knife

CHILD NO. 16

THIS ballad has been rarely found in British tradition, never outside Scotland. No new copy has appeared since the first half of the last century; and the only tune known is the plaintive one which Burns salvaged for Johnson's *Museum* in the last decade of the eighteenth century. Of this, a variant was published, with other words, in 1866.

Of the very appropriate tune there is a manuscript copy, with no differences except for holds on the second and third phrase-finals, in Nat. Lib. Scotland MS. 843, fol. 18ᵛ. This MS.

is of "Ballads, &c. from the Collection of the late Charles Kirkpatrick Sharpe, Esquire, of Hoddam. Arranged for The Right Honourable Lady John Scott." The words are taken from Jamieson, 1806. There is still another copy, marked "very old," in Lady John Scott's MS. (Nat. Lib. Scotland MS. 840). These copies may probably have been taken from Johnson and not directly from tradition. It might be mentioned that the haunting refrain appears in an almost identical form in Child 15 B, a ballad for which, unfortunately, no tune is known.

TUNES WITH TEXTS

1. [The broom blooms bonie]

Johnson, V [1796], No. 461, p. 474.

a I

It's whisper'd in parlour, it's whisper'd in ha',
  The broom blooms bonie, the broom blooms fair;
Lady Marget's wi' child amang our ladies a',
  And she dare na gae down to the broom nae mair.

One lady whisper'd unto another,
  The broom blooms bonie, the broom blooms fair;
Lady Marget's wi' child to Sir Richard her brother,
  And she dare na gae down to the broom nae mair.
      *   *   *   *   *
O when that you hear my loud loud cry,
  The broom blooms &c.
Then bend your bow and let your arrows fly,
  For I dare na gae down &c.

Hind Horn

CHILD NO. 17

ALL the tunes which have been recorded for this ballad are representatives of a single melodic idea. Save in one or two cases, there has been remarkably little variation, considering that together they span a century and an ocean. The same tune, in one guise or another (usually with greater variation), occurs with a number of alien texts, and especially with a song of which the English *textual* record is a good deal older than that of "Hind Horn"—namely, "The Bird Song," found among Restoration broadsides with the titles "The Woody Querristers," and "The Birds Lamentation," and directed to be sung to the tune of "The Bird-catchers Delight"—a tune which has not been identified, though the title would suit "Three Maids a-milking did Go," a well-known traditional song never so called. "The Bird Song" is known widely in America, especially in New England and the Southern Mountains, and has been given added currency through broadcasts and popular phonograph records, as "The Leather-winged Bat." The persistence of some of the seventeenth-century stanzas is startling, as can be seen from the old broadside text, e.g.:

> Then said the Leather-winged Batt,
> Mind but my tale, and I'le tell you what

> Is the cause that I do flye by night,
> Because I lost my hearts delight.

The favorite tune is also very widely known with a cowboy song, "Oh, bury me not on the lone prairie" (J. and A. Lomax, *Folk-Song U.S.A.*, 1947, p. 208, among numerous examples). Other permutations of the tune abound. Keith (*Last Leaves*, 1925, p. 20) finds it to be common in Scottish folk-song, declaring that "it is, no doubt, the original of the modern air, 'Logan Braes,' and often sung to the old words of 'Logan Banks.'" Greig's MSS. contain many variants of the tune.

Variants of this melodic family with the text of "Hind Horn" are, as so far noted, mainly confined to Scotland and the Northeastern seaboard of America, taking in Maine, New Brunswick, and Newfoundland. The tune is habitually D/Æ, plagal, and in duple time. Characteristically, the mid-cadence is on V, the cadence of the first phrase on lower VII. Nearly all variants are of the "progressive" type (ABCD), although the later phrases contain elements of the earlier. Second strains, where they occur, may be regarded as probably editorial.

TUNES WITH TEXTS

2. "The Beggar Man"

Karpeles, 1934, II, pp. 99-103. Sung by Jacob Courage, Frenchman's Cove, Garnish, Fortune Bay, Newfoundland, July 15, 1930; text from Collector's MS.

p I

A Nova Scotia variant (Creighton, version A), with a longer text (13 stanzas), is melodically almost identical with the present copy.

1. On board of a ship and away sailed he,
   He sailed right away to a far countrie.
   He looked at the ring, it was pale and dim;
   That showed that his love was false to him.

2. You put on my driving suit,
   And I'll put on your begging rig.
   Your driving suit it won't fit me,
   My begging suit it won't fit thee.

3. Let it be right or let it be wrong,
   The begging suit I will put on.
   When he came to Napoleon's gate,
   He lay on his staff in a weary state.

4. He saw his true love come skipping downstairs,
   Rings on her fingers, gold in her hair,
   And in her hand a glass of wine,
   To treat this little old beggar man.

5. He drink-ed and he drink-ed and he drink-ed so free,
   Into the tumbler the ring slipped he.
   Did you get it by the land, or did you get it by the sea,
   Or did you get it from a drowned man's hand?

6. I neither got it from land, I neither got it from sea,
   Nor neither did I get it from a drowned man's hand.
   But I got it from a true love was courting me so gay,
   And now I return it on her wedding day.

7. Then rings from her fingers she then pulled off
   And gold from her hair it all fell off,
   Saying: I'll follow my true love for ever, ever more,
   And beg my bread from door to door.

8. Between the kitchen and the hall
   The beggar man's suit he then let fall;
   He showed the best and the first of them all,
   He was the best little man in the hall.

4. "The Old Beggar Man"

Barry, Eckstorm, and Smyth, 1929, pp. 73(A)-75. Sung by Thomas Edward Nelson, Union Mills, New Brunswick, September 28, 1928; learned from his mother, who was born in Ireland. Melody recorded by George Herzog.

m Æ/D

1. "Whence came ye, or from what counteree?
   Whence came ye, or where were you born?"
   "In Ireland I was bred and born
   Until I became a hele and his horn.

2. "I gave my love a gay gold watch
   That she might rule in her own counteree,
   And she gave me a gay gold ring,
   And the virtue of this was above all things.

3. "'If this ring bees bright and true,
   Be sure your love is true to you;
   But if this ring bees pale and wan,
   Your true love's in love with some other man.'"

4. He set sail and off went he,
   Until that he came to a strange counteree;
   He looked at the ring, it was pale and wan,
   His true love was in love with some other one.

5. He set sail and back came he,
   Until that he came to his own counteree,
   And as he was riding along the plain,
   Who should he meet but an old beggar man.

6. "What news, what news, you old beggar man?
   What news, what news have you got for me?"
   "No news, no news," said the old beggar man,
   "But tomorrow is your true love's wedding day."

7. You lend me your begging rig,
   And I'll lend you my riding stage."
   "Your riding stage ain't fit for me,
   Nor my begging rig ain't fit for you."

8. "Whether it be right, or whether it be wrong,
   The begging rig they must go on.
   So come, tell to me as fast as you can
   What's to be done with the begging rig."

9. "As you go up to younder hill,
   You may walk as fast as 'tis your will,
   And when you come to yonder gate,
   You may lean upon your staff with trembling step.

10. "You may beg from Pitt, you may beg from Paul,
    You may beg from the highest to the lowest of them all;
    But from them all you need take none
    Until you come to the bride's own hand."

11. She came trembling down the stairs,
    Rings on her fingers and gold in her hair,
    A glass of wine all in her hand,
    Which she gave to the old beggar man.

12. He took the glass and drank the wine,
    And in the glass he slipped the ring.
    "O, where got you this, by sea or by land,
    Or did you get it off a drowned one's hand?"

13. "Neither got I it by sea or land,
    Neither did I get it off a drowned one's hand;
    I got it in my courting gay,
    And gave it to my love on her wedding day."

14. Rings from her fingers she did pull off,
    Gold from her hair she did let fall,
    Saying, "I'll go with you forevermore
    And beg my bread from door to door."

15. Between the kitchen and the hall
    The diner's coat he did let fall,
    All a-shining in gold amongst them all,
    And he was the fairest in the hall.

4.1. "The Old Beggarman"

Sung by Joseph R. Estey, Red Bank, New Brunswick, August 1963. Collected by Lee B. Haggerty and Henry Felt; sent by them to the Editor.

m D/Æ

1. Where were you bred and where were you born?
   In dear old Scotland, where I was bred and born.
   I am going for to leave you, so Love, do not mourn
   Until the day when I do return.

2. Here is a ring, I'll give it unto thee
   As a token of true friendship, given by me,
   And when this ring is faded and worn
   You'll know that your true-love's with another one.

3. For seven long years he sailed o'er the sea,
   He sailed and he sailed to a foreign country.
   He looked at the ring, it was faded and worn,
   He knew that his true-love was with another one.

4. And he turned, he sailed o'er the sea,
   He sailed and he sailed to his own country.
   The first one he met when he came to the land
   Was a poor old beggarman.

5. Old man, good man, old man, said he,
   What news, what news have you got for me?
   Bad news, bad news, the old man did say.
   Tomorrow is your true-love's wedding day.

6. Then give to me your rags and your shield
   And I'll give to you my coat and my steel.
   Your coat and your steel is far too good for me,
   While an old beggar's clothes is not fit for thee.

7. Let it be right, or let it be wrong,
   The old beggar's clothes I will put on,
   I will beg fróm the richest to the poorest in the land,
   Take nothing but the best from the young bride's hand.

8. So he begged from Peter, and he begged from Paul,
   He begged from the richest to the poorest of them all,
   He begged till he came to his own true-love's hall,
   He stood on the bridge, he leaned against the gate.

9. Down came the bride a-tripping down the stair,
   Rings on her fingers and jewelry in her hair.
   The glass of wine she held in her hand
   She gave it to the old beggarman.

10. Out of the tumbler he drank the wine,
    Back in the tumbler he dropped the ring.
    She said, Where did you get it? on sea or on land?
    Or did you steal it off some dead man's hand?

11. I did not get it on sea or on land,
    Neither did I take it off a dead man's hand.
    It's a token of true friendship when we used to court so gay
    And I have returned it all on your wedding day.

12. Rings from her fingers she did pull off,
    Trinkets from her hair she did let fall,
    Saying, Willie, I'll go with you for now and evermore
    Supposing that we beg fróm door to door.

13. O between the kitchen and the hall
    The old beggar's clothes he did let fall.
    His costly garments they shone far above them all,
    He was the finest-looking yóung man that stood in the hall.

14. It was early the next morning just at the break of day
    This couple hastened off to church and made no delay,
    It's now they're married, as you may understand,
    No more will he be called the old beggarman. (Last
        word spoken.)

21. "The Beggarman"

Greenleaf and Mansfield, 1933, pp. 12-14. Sung by Daniel
Endacott, Sally's Cove, Newfoundland, 1921.

m Æ

1. O, 'twas of a young couple they lived in this place,
       They was courting by each other, you may plainly see,
   Until strange news was come to him,
       That he would sail* in a far counteree.

2. When they was a-parting, she gived to him
       A gay gold ring . . .
   "When you looks at the ring and it's bright and clear,
       You know I am constant to my dear.

3. . . . .
       . . . .
   "And when you looks at your ring and 'tis pale and wan,
   You may know I'm engaged with some other young man."

4. Then he took a ship and away sailed he,
   He sailed till he came to a far counteree;
   He looked at his ring and 'twas bright and clear,
   He knowed she was constant to her dear.

5. And then he took a ship and away sailed he,
   He sailed till he came to the Turkish shore;
   He looked at his ring and 'twas pale and wan,
   He knowed she was engaged with some other young man.

6. Then he took a ship and back sailed he,
   He sailed till he came to his own counteree;
   As he was riding along one day,
   And who should he meet but an old beggarman?

7. "What news, beggarman, have you for me?"
   "Bad news, bad news, I have for thee;
   Bad news, bad news, I have for thee,
   For to-morrow is your true-love's wedding day."

8. "O, you'll give to me your bag and rig,
   And I'll give to you my riding steed."
   "My bag and rig is no good for thee,
   Nor your riding steed is no good for me."

9. O let it be so, or let it be not,
   The beggar's rig he then put on.
   "Beggarman, beggarman, come tell me with speed,
   What must I do with your bag and rig?"

10. "You'll walk as fast as is your will
    Until you come to yonder hill,
    And you'll walk as fast as is your rate,
    And you'll lean on your staff in wayward state,

11. "And you'll beg from Peter and you'll beg from Paul,
    You'll beg from the highest to the lowest of them all,
    And from none of them you'll receive nothing
    Until you receives it from the bride's own hand."

12. He walked as fast as was his will,
    Until he came to yonder hill,
    And he walked as fast as was his rate,
    And he leaned on his staff in wayward state.

13. He begged from Peter and he begged from Paul,
    He begged from the highest to the lowest of them all,
    And from none of them he received nothing
    Until he received it from the bride's own hand.

14. As she came trippling down the stairs
    With rings on her fingers, gold bobs on her hairs,
    And a glass of wine in her hand so small,
    And she gave it to the old beggarman.

15. Then out of the glass he drinks the wine,
    And into the glass he slipped a ring.
    "Did you get it by sea, or yet by land,
    Or did you get it from a drownded man's hand?"

16. "I neither got it by sea, nor yet by land,
    Nor yet did I get it from a drowned man's hand;
    But I got it in a courting way,
    And I give it to my true-love on her wedding day."

17. The rings from her fingers they fell on the floor,
    Gold bobs from her hair she throwed against the wall:
    "I will go with you forevermore,
    Supposing I beg my bread from door to door!"

18. Between the kitchen and the hall
    The beggar's rig he then let fall;
    For he shines the blackest among them all,
    He's the richest man that's in the hall.

   * Or, "was sailing."

22. [Hind Horn]

Creighton and Senior, 1950, p. 17(E). Sung by Ralph
Huskins, Cape Sable Island, Nova Scotia.

a M

I'll beg from Peter and I'll beg from Paul,
I'll beg from the highest to the lowest of them all
As for money I will take no toll
Unless it's received from the bride's own hand.

O the maid came tripping down the stairs
With rings on her fingers and jewels on her hair,
And a glass of wine all in her hand
For to treat this old beggar man.

He took the glass and he drank the wine,
And in the glass he slipped this ring,
"Oh where did you get it, from sea or land,
Or did you get it from some dead man's hand?"

"I neither got it from sea nor land,
Nor neither did I get it from some dead man,
This ring I received on my courting days,
I'll return it back to you on your wedding day."

The rings from her fingers she did pull off,
The jewels from her hair she did let fall,
Saying, "I'll go with you for ever ever more
If I have to beg my bread from door to door."

Between the kitchen and the hall
The beggar's rig he did let fall,
The gold upon him shone bright on them all,
He was the best looking man that was in the hall.

23. [Hind Horn]

Child, 1882-98, V, p. 413; text, I, pp. 503-4. Sung by Jane
Webster, Stewartry of Kirkcudbright, December 12, 1882,
and by Jessie Jane Macmath and Agnes Macmath, nieces of
Miss Webster, December 11, 1882; learned from an old
nurse. Noted by Minnie Macmath.

p I/M (ending on II)

1. She gave him a gay gold ring,
    Hey lillelu and how lo lan
   But he gave her a far better thing.
    With my hey down and a hey diddle downie.

2. He gave her a silver wan,
   With nine bright laverocks thereupon.

      *   *   *   *   *   *   *

3. Young Hynd Horn is come to the lan,
   There he met a beggar man.

4. "What news, what news do ye betide?"
   "Na news but Jeanie's the prince's bride."

5. "Wilt thou give me thy begging weed?
   And I'll give thee my good grey steed."

6. "Wilt thou give me thy auld grey hair?
   And I'll give ye mine that is thrice as fair."

7. The beggar he got on for to ride,
   But young Hynd Horn is bound for the bride.

8. First the news came to the ha,
   Then to the room mang the gentles a'.

9. "There stands a beggar at our gate,
   Asking a drink for young Hynd Horn's sake."

10. "I'll ga through nine fires hot
    To give him a drink for young Hynd Horn's sake."

11. She gave him the drink, and he dropt in the ring;
    The lady turned baith pale an wan.

12. "Oh got ye it by sea, or got it by lan?
    Or got ye it off some dead man's han?"

13. "I got it not by sea, nor I got it not by lan,
    But I got it off thy milk-white han."

14. "I'll cast off my dress of red,
    And I'll go with thee and beg my bread."

15. "I'll cast off my dress of brown,
    And follow you from city to town."

16. "I'll cast off my dress of green,
    For I am not ashamed with you to be seen."

17. "You need not cast off your dress of red,
    For I can support thee on both wine and bread.

18. "You need not cast off your dress of brown,
    For I can keep you a lady in any town.

19. "You need not cast off your dress of green,
    For I can maintain you as gay as a queen."

Sir Lionel

CHILD NO. 18

THE only orally transmitted form of this ballad that makes any effort to maintain a serious romantic tone is the one recorded by Christie, about 1850, from an old woman in Banffshire. Through her, Christie said, he could trace the song a hundred years further back. Still another century back (i.e., before 1650) lies the text of the Percy Folio—in its surviving state very defective, tuneless, and not known ever to have been sung. This version, also, is serious. All other versions that have yet been found, whether in Britain or America, are in varying degree farcical. About half a dozen English texts, or fragments of texts, were recorded during the nineteenth century. All of them have an interlaced refrain with alternating lines, close to the seventeenth-century one of "Blow thy horne, good hunter" and "As I am a gentle hunter," on the second and fourth lines of the quatrain. Two American variants on the same plan have been found in recent tradition. The resemblance of this refrain to a song of Henry VIII's time caught the notice of Child. (For it, cf. Chappell's *Popular Music*, first edition, I, 58.) There is little in the melody to suggest a popular ballad air, and the connection with the refrain of "Sir Lionel" is probably fortuitous.

In recent memory, a change of phrase and pattern has occurred. Instead of the staid refrain of the older versions, we find, both in England and America, a series of nonsense syllables, sometimes suggesting a hunting-horn, fitted into an ancient stanzaic pattern. The scheme is exemplified in a Wiltshire variant, published without its tune in 1923. The first stanza is:

> Bold Sir Rylas a-hunting went—
> I an dan dilly dan
> Bold Sir Rylas a-hunting went,
> Killy koko an.
> Bold Sir Rylas a-hunting went,
> To kill some game was his intent—
> I an dan dilly dan killy koko an.
> [Alfred Williams, *Folk Songs of the Upper Thames*, 1923, p. 118.]

This, with occasional shortening, is the nearly universal pattern of the stanza in current tradition. Obviously, there has been either a complete break with older tradition, or else the traditional antecedents of the modern form are not represented in Child. The latter alternative, I believe, is the true state of the case.

Child pointed out that the ballad of "Sir Lionel" had much in common with the old metrical romance of "Sir Eglamour of Artois," a version of which is also preserved in Percy's Folio MS. Both heroes battle with horrendous boars and giants on behalf of captive ladies; and although it is not maintained that the ballad is based on the romance, the two have obvious affinities. Early in the seventeenth century, a ballad of Sir Eglamore became popularly current, and circulated in broadside form. It was still in circulation and generally known, independent of print, at the end of that century. Its tune was preserved both in print and MS., and eventually found a place in D'Urfey's *Pills to Purge Melancholy*, 1719, vol. III, with the text given below (vt. 3). With its catchy tune, the stanza-form was that of the "Sir Rylas" copy just quoted. The tune itself is that which is sung, though with considerable variety within the basic form, to variants of "Bangum and the Boar." It is natural to conclude that two songs, originally distinct, have fallen together in the course of time in their traditional journeying.

The stanzaic pattern of "Eglamore" has been in frequent use since the sixteenth century and probably earlier. Usually the first line of the stanza is thrice repeated: D'Urfey compresses for narrative progress. We have met the pattern already with "The Twa Sisters" (Child No. 10), and shall meet it soon again with "The Three Ravens" (Child No. 26), and elsewhere later (e.g., Child No. 277). It seems to be more native to the dance and dancing-games than to ballads, and may derive from the medieval carol tradition. A number of familiar Elizabethan and seventeenth-century dance tunes conform to it, as "Trenchmore," "Confess" (in Playford's *The English Dancing Master*), and "The Frog's Wedding." The tunes belonging to the earlier (D'Urfey's) "Eglamore" type appear to favor a plagal major and triple time. The later, "Bangum," style is also major and plagal, but duple. Christie's tune (vt. 1) is not typical: it is Æolian, plagal, in duple rhythm, and related to a melodic family found in Scots tradition with a variety of ballad texts, e.g. Child Nos. 209, 212, 214-215, 240.

TUNES WITH TEXTS

GROUP A

1. [Isaac-a-Bell and Hugh the Græme]

Christie, I, 1876, pp. 110-11. Sung by an old woman in Buckie, Enzie, Banffshire, about 1850.

p Æ

As usual, the second strain is doubtless Christie's invention.
In this case, Christie states that the text is genuine.
The tune has numerous relations in that region. Cf., e.g., Greig and Keith, 1925, p. 133(2), "Geordie"; p. 136(1), "The Duke of Atholle's Nurse"; pp. 143-44, "Yarrow"; p. 194, "The Rantin' Laddie."

1. A knight had two sons o' sma' fame,
    Hey nien nanny,
   Isaac-a-Bell and Hugh the Græme,
    And the Norlan' flowers spring bonny;
   And to the youngest he did say,
    Hey nien nanny,
   "What occupation will you ha'e,
    When the Norlan' flowers spring bonny?

2. "Will you gae fee to pick a mill?
    Hey nien nanny;
   Or will you keep hogs on yon hill,
    While the Norlan' flowers spring bonny?"
   "I winna fee to pick a mill,
    Hey nien nanny;
   Nor will I keep hogs on yon hill,
    While the Norlan' flowers spring bonny.

3. "But it is said, as I do hear,
    Hey nien nanny,
   That war will last for seven year,
    And the Norlan' flowers spring bonny,
   With a giant and a boar,
    Hey nien nanny,
   That range into the wood o' Tore,
    And the Norlan' flowers spring bonny.

4. "You'll horse and armour to me provide,
    Hey nien nanny,
   That through Tore wood I may safely ride,
    When the Norlan' flowers spring bonny."
   The Knicht did horse and armour provide,
    Hey nien nanny,
   That through Tore wood Græme micht safely ride,
    When the Norlan' flowers spring bonny.

5. Then he rode through the wood o' Tore,
    Hey nien nanny;
   And up it started the grisly boar,
    When the Norlan' flowers spring bonny.
   The firsten bout that he did ride,
    Hey nien nanny,
   The boar he wounded in the left side,
    When the Norlan' flowers spring bonny.

6. The nexten bout at the boar he gaed,
    Hey nien nanny,
   He from the boar took aff his head,
    And the Norlan' flowers spring bonny.
   As he rode back through the wood o' Tore,
    Hey nien nanny,
   Up started the giant him before,
    And the Norlan' flowers spring bonny.

7. "Oh, cam' you through the wood o' Tore,
    Hey nien nanny;
   Or did you see my good wild boar,
    And the Norlan' flowers spring bonny?"
   "I cam' now through the wood o' Tore,
    Hey nien nanny;
   But woe be to your grisly boar,
    And the Norlan' flowers spring bonny.

8. "The firsten bout that I did ride,
    Hey nien nanny,
   I wounded your wild boar in the side,
    And the Norlan' flowers spring bonny.
   The nexten bout at him I gaed,
    Hey nien nanny,
   From your wild boar I took aff his head,
    And the Norlan' flowers spring bonny."

9. "Gin you have cut aff the head o' my boar,
    Hey nien nanny,
   It's your head shall be ta'en therefore,
    And the Norlan' flowers spring bonny.
   I'll gi'e you thirty days and three,
    Hey nien nanny,
   To heal your wounds, then come to me,
    While the Norlan' flowers spring bonny."

10. "It's after thirty days and three,
    Hey nien nanny;
   When my wounds heal, I'll come to thee,
    When the Norlan' flowers spring bonny."
   So Græme is back to the wood o' Tore,
    Hey nien nanny;
   And he's kill'd the giant, as he kill'd the boar,
    And the Norlan' flowers spring bonny.

2. "Wild Boar"

Halpert, LC/AAFS, rec. 2805B. Sung by Samuel Harmon, Maryville, Tenn., 1939; learned from his father.

1. Abram Bailey he'd three sons
    Blow your horn center*
   And he is through the wildwood gone
    Just like a jovial hunter.

2. As he marched down the greenwood side
    Blow your horn center
   A pretty girl O there he spied
    As he was a jovial hunter.

3. There is a wild boar all in this wood
    Blow your horn center
   He slew the lord and his forty men
    As he was a jovial hunter.

4. How can I this wild boar see?
    Blow your horn center
Wind up your horn and he'll come to you
    As you are a jovial hunter.

5. He wound his horn unto his mouth
    Blow your horn center
He blew East, North, West, and South
    As he was a jovial hunter.

6. The wild boar heard him unto his den
    Blow your horn center
He made the oak and ash then far to bend
    As he was a jovial hunter.

7. They fit three hours by the day
    Blow your horn center
And at length he this wild boar slay
    As he was a jovial hunter.

8. As he marched by the mouth of the wild boar's den
    Blow your horn center
He saw the bones of five hundred men
    As he was a jovial hunter.

9. He meets the old witch wife on the bridge
    Blow your horn center
Begone you rogue, you've killed my pig
    As you are a jovial hunter.

10. There is three things I crave of thee
    Blow your horn center
Your hawk, your hound, your gay lady
    As you are a jovial hunter.

11. These three things you'll not have of me
    Blow your horn center
Neither hawk nor hound nor gay lady
    As you are a jovial hunter.

12. He split the old witch wife to the chin
    Blow your horn center
And on his way he went ag'in
    Just like a jovial hunter.

* "Center" seems clearly the word sung, but I do not understand it. Scenter? Centaur? Or is it an adverb in the comparative degree? The text as a whole resembles Child's C.

GROUP B

3. [Sir Eglamore]

D'Urfey, 1719-20, III, pp. 293-94.

p I

Sir *Eglamore*, that valiant Knight,
    Fa la, lanky down dilly;
He took up his Sword, and he went to fight,
    Fa la, lanky down dilly:
And as he rode o'er Hill and Dale,
All Armed with a Coat of Male,
    Fa, la, la, la, la, la, lanky down dilly.

The last two phrases would normally divide evenly, but here the leading of the words has been respected.
    See the headnote above for other members of this branch of the tribe.

There leap'd a Dragon out of her Den,
That had slain God knows how many Men;
But when she saw Sir *Eglamore*,
Oh that you had but heard her roar!

Then the Trees began to shake,
Horse did Tremble, Man did quake;
The Birds betook them all to peeping,
Oh! 'twould have made one fall a weeping.

But all in vain it was to fear,
For now they fall to't, fight Dog, fight Bear;
And to't they go, and soundly fight,
A live-long day, from Morn till Night.

This Dragon had on a plaguy Hide,
That cou'd the sharpest steel abide;
No Sword cou'd enter her with cuts,
Which vex'd the Knight unto the Guts.

But as in Choler he did burn,
He watch'd the Dragon a great good turn;
For as a Yawning she did fall,
He thrust his Sword up Hilt and all.

Then like a Coward she did fly,
Unto her Den, which was hard by;
And there she lay all Night and roar'd,
The Knight was sorry for his Sword:
But riding away, he cries, I forsake it,
He that will fetch it, let him take it.

GROUP C

4. [Sir Lionel]

Kidson MSS. Printed in *JEFDSS*, III (1936), p. 46. From an unknown source (not in Kidson's hand).

m I (inflected IV)

1. Tom and Harry went to plough,
    Dillom down dillom
    As Tom and Harry went to plough,
    Quidly quo quam
    As Tom and Harry went to plough
    They saw a fair maid on a bough,
    Kambery quo, quoddle dam, quidly quo quam.

4. "If I should kill the boar [*sic*]," said he,
   "Wilt thou come down and marry me?"

5. "If thou shouldst kill the boar," said she,
   "I will come down and marry thee."

6. Then Brangywell pulled out his dart,
   And shot the wild boar through the heart.

7. The wild boar fetched out such a sound
   That all the oaks and ash fell down.

8. Then hand in hand they went to the den,
   And found the bones of twenty men.

Miss Gilchrist has a long and interesting note on this song, *JEFDSS*, III, pp. 46-49. She calls attention to the connection with "Duncan Gray," which she says was first printed in Oswald's *Caledonian Pocket Companion*, c. 1750.

2. "Why do ye, fair maid, sit so high
   That no young man can you come nigh?"

3. The fair maid unto them did say
   "If you can fetch me down you may."

4. There is a wild boar in the wood,
   If he comes out he'll suck your blood!"

*　*　*　*　*

5. The wild boar came with such a sound
   That rocks and hills and trees fell down.

5. "Brangywell"

Leather, 1912, pp. 203-4. Sung by Mrs. Mellor, Dilwyn, Herefordshire, 1905; noted by R. Hughes Rowlands.

p I

1. As Brangywell went forth to plough,
   Dillum, down dillum;
   As Brangywell went forth to plough,
   Kil-ly-co-quam;
   As Brangywell went forth to plough,
   He spied a lady on a bough,
   Kil-ly-do, cuddle-dame,
   Kil-ly-co-quam.

2. "What makes thee sit so high, lady,
   That no one can come nigh to thee?"

3. "There is a wild bear [*sic*] in the wood,
   If I come down he'll suck my blood."

10. "Old Bang 'em"

Davis, 1929, p. 559(B); text, pp. 127-28. Also in Smith and Rufty, 1937, p. 4. Sung by Evelyn Purcell of the Farmville Ballad Club, Albemarle County, Va., November 20, 1913; handed down from her great-grandfather, c. 1760.

p I

The third and fourth bars from the end may be mis-timed, as they upset the verbal rhythm.

1. Old Bang'em would a-hunting ride,
   Dillem, down, dillem.
   Old Bang'em would a-hunting ride,
   Dillem down.
   Old Bang'em would a-hunting ride,
   Sword and pistol by his side.
   Cubby, ki, cuddle down,
   Killi, quo, quam.

2. "There is a wild boar in this wood,"
   Dillem, down, dillem.
   "There is a wild boar in this wood,"
   Dillem down.
   "There is a wild boar in this wood
   Will eat your meat and suck your blood."
   Cubby, ki, cuddle down,
   Killi, quo, quam.

3. "Oh, how shall I this wild boar see?"
   Dillem, down, dillem.
   "Oh, how shall I this wild boar see?"
   Dillem down.
   "Oh, how shall I this wild boar see?"
   "Blow a blast and he'll come to thee."
   Cubby, ki, cuddle down,
   Killi, quo, quam.

4. Old Bang'em blew both loud and shrill,
The wild boar heard on Temple Hill.
    Cubby, ki, cuddle down,
        Killi, quo, quam.

5. The wild boar came with such a rush
He tore down hickory, oak and ash.
    Cubby, ki, cuddle down,
        Killi, quo, quam.

6. Old Bang'em drew his wooden knife
And swore that he would take his life.
    Cubby, ki, cuddle down,
        Killi, quo, quam.

7. "Old Bang'em, did you win or lose?"
He swore that he had won the shoes.
    Cubby, ki, cuddle down,
        Killi, quo, quam.

King Orfeo

CHILD NO. 19

THAT a tune should, in the middle of the twentieth century, be overheard along with this whisper out of the Middle Ages was as little to be supposed as that we should hear "the horns of Elfland faintly blowing." The Shetlands seem to have proved to be the last retreat, in traditional memory, of this very delightful product of medieval recreative imagination. Clearly, the fragments before us stem from the same root as the fuller fragment given by Child from a printing of 1880. (A text of 21 stanzas, from a number of *The Shetland Times*, of unspecified date but "written down from oral recital at Gloup . . . in 1865," was recovered by Mr. Patrick N. Shuldham-Shaw, to whom is owing also the first variant reprinted here.) In this version, King Orfeo has become a nondescript plural—a mere "noise of musicians," as it were—who are invited into a hall, enter,

and do their office as on a stage. The second variant makes connected sense, and so does Child's A. But there are several copies of the parallel medieval romance, the best being the Auchinleck MS. of the early fourteenth century, of which Child in his inimitable way gives a summary paraphrase. For its own sake, and to clarify the tale, this should be read without fail (Child I, p. 216).

The first tune falls in well enough with the melodic material recovered by Greig in the northeast of Scotland at the beginning of our century. Parallels can be found, e.g., in his *Last Leaves*, pp. 52, 56. The other tune dimly seems to reflect the first in a disconnected image. Compare its last phrase with the first and last of the other; its second with the other's second; and note the octave leap in the third phrase of both.

TUNE WITH TEXT

1. "King Orfeo"

Shuldham-Shaw, *JEFDSS*, V (December 1947), p. 77.
Sung by John Stickle, Baltasound, Unst, April 28, 1947.

p π⁴

Then they played the good old gab-ber reel, Scow an Earl

Will ye come in into our Ha',
Scowan Earl grey,
Yes we'll come in into your ha',
For yetter kangra norla

And we'll come in into your ha'
And we'll come in among ye a'

First they played the notes o noy
Then they played the notes o joy

Then they played the good old gabber reel
   Scowan Earl Grey.
Which might a made a sick heart heal,
   For gettar kangra norla.

2. "King Orfeo"

Archive, School of Scottish Studies, rec. No. 1955/145/6.
Sung by Kitty Anderson, Shetland. Collected by Francis M. Collinson.

a π⁴ (ending on V)

1. Der lived a king into da aist
   Sconner le groon
  Der lived a lady in da wast
   Whar yorten han groon varlee*

  [*Interlinear chorus as above in each verse.*]

2. Dis king he has a huntin geen
  An left his lady Isabel alane.

3. Oh, I wiss ye'd never geen away
  For at your hame it's dule an wae.

4. For the King o Faerie wi his dairt
  His pierced your lady ti da hert.

5. An eftir them the king is geen
  But when he cam it wis a grey stane

6. Dan he took oot his pipes to play
  But sair his hert wi dule an wae.

7. An first he played da notes o noy,
  An dan he played da notes o joy.

8. Noo he's geen in inta dir haa,
  An he's geen in among them aa.

9. Dan he took oot his pipes to play
  But sair his hert wi dule an wae.

10. Noo tell tae us what you will hae,
  What sall we gie you for you play?

11. What I will hae I will you tell
  An dat's me Lady Isabel.

12. Yees tak yir lady an yees gane hame
  An yees be king o'er aa yir ain.

* In rec. No. 1953/3 the singer gives two versions of the chorus, the second of which is also found in the *Shetland Folk Book*, II, ed. E. S. Reid Tait, 1947-51, p. 56:

Sconner le groon (?"The wood is green yearly") = Scan arlish groon (?"The wood is yearly green")
Whar yorten han groon varlee (?"Where the garden grows green yearly") = Whar yorten han gor arlish (?"Where the hart goes yearly"). Cf. also *JEFDSS*, V, 77.

The Cruel Mother

CHILD NO. 20

FOR the number of beautiful melodic variations on a basically constant rhythmic pattern this ballad is exceptional. The binding element in the rhythmical design appears to have been the interlaced refrain at the second and fourth lines. This has suffered in the main only slight variation, and, where variations occur, has been usually able to find metrical equivalents for the supplanted syllables. Expressed in 4/4 time, it can be felt in the lines

> Áll alóne and alóney
> and   Dówn by the gréenwoòd sídèy.

Such a scheme appears to have been a favorite of this ballad for the past two centuries. The melodic record is almost as long as the textual one in Britain, if we exclude a late seventeenth-century broadside text. Between the latter and the first traditional record there is a gap of nearly a century. But the broadside text is very good, in the sense of being unusually close to traditional style; in fact, stanzas 6 to 22 might be almost innocent of the broadside touch. (Cf. Child P.) The refrain of the broadside, however, differs from that of typical traditional variants, and would seem to imply a different tune. Although it comes likewise on the second and fourth phrases, the second is apparently a five-stress iambic line and the fourth a tetrameter. Though either might be compressed to a different metre in singing, neither has the characteristic feminine ending of the traditional variants. It may be noticed incidentally that this older refrain has some resemblance, verbally, to a familiar one (Group B) of the "Twa Sisters" (Child No. 10). There is no clue to the tune of the broadside, unfortunately: the printed direction is merely "to an excellent new tune"—a stereotyped phrase found on numberless broadsides, appealing to those in pursuit of the *dernier cri*.

Other favorite traditional ballads, usually Scottish, consistently exhibit the characteristic rhythmical features of this one in the second and fourth lines; e.g., "Binnorie" (No. 10), "Geordie" (No. 209), "Yarrow" (Nos. 214, 215). It is not surprising, therefore, to find further melodic kinship between those and the present ballad.

Beside the habitual refrain quoted above, there is another which has seldom appeared outside Scotland, with mention of flowers (e.g., vts. 1, 5, 15). The earliest traditional copy, Herd's (Child's A), without tune, has a unique refrain ("Oh and alelladay, oh and alelladay" and "Ten thousand times good night and be with you"). Two of Motherwell's copies have numerical refrains: ("Three, three, and three by three," and "Three, three, and thirty-three." Cf. the Virginia variants of Child No. 1).

From a reading of Child's texts by themselves, it might be supposed that the copies divide on the basis of whether the second and fourth lines contain three stresses or four. But an examination of the tunes shows that as the ballads are sung, there is no divergence: both kinds are treated as four-stressed. A few other refrains are unique or all but unique. Several variants are exceptional in one way or another, either by accretion of extraneous elements or by abrasion, by failure to achieve definition, or by confusion with other ballads.

Groups A-C below appear valid and defensible on internal grounds. The first contains some of the oldest copies, as well as recent ones that are Scottish, English, and American. Two-thirds of this group are plagal, the other third authentic without seriously deranging the cast of the melody. Modes are minor (Æ, D/Æ, π^4, D, M/D). There is not much consistency of cadence, although a mid-cadence on the lower fifth is favored.

Group B, containing good nineteenth- and twentieth-century copies, is (with a Dorian exception) Mixolydian, I/M, and M/D, that is, major in tonal cast. The favored mid-cadence is on the upper fifth; the first cadence on the tonic. Variants are all authentic.

Group C is again predominantly major (I/Ly, I, π^1, I/M), but plagal. Here again the cadences are less than consistent, but lower V is common for the first phrase. Mid-cadences are most frequently on II or V.

TUNES WITH TEXTS

GROUP A

1. [Fine Flowers in the Valley]

Johnson, [1792], IV, No. 320, p. 331. Also (in nearly identical notes) in Lady John Scott's Sharpe MS., NL Scotland MS. 843, fol. 19ᵛ; Smith, 1820-24, IV, p. 33; and Maver, 1866, No. 365, p. 183.

p Æ/D (but inflected VII)

According to Stenhouse (*Illustrations*, p. 308), Burns was the transmitter of this piece to Johnson's *Museum*.

The variants given are from the R. A. Smith copy. The sharp in the penultimate bar were better away.

1. She sat down below a thorn,
      Fine flowers in the valley
   And there she has her sweet babe born
      And the green leaves they grow rarely.

2. Smile na sae sweet, my bonie babe
      Fine flowers in the valley,
   And ye smile sae sweet, ye'll smile me dead,
      And the green leaves they grow rarely.

3. She's taen out her little penknife
      Fine flowers, &c.
   And twinn'd the sweet babe o' its life.
      And the green, &c.

4. She's howket a grave by the light o' the moon,
      Fine flowers, &c.
   And there she's buried her sweet babe in,
      And the green, &c.

5. As she was going to the church,
      Fine flowers, &c.
   She saw a sweet babe in the porch.
      And the green, &c.

6. O sweet babe and thou were mine,
      Fine flowers, &c.
   I wad cleed thee in the silk so fine.
      And the green, &c.

7. O mother dear, when I was thine,
      Fine flowers, &c.
   You did na prove to me sae kind.
      And the green, &c.

1. She laid herself back against a thorn,
      All aloney, aloney,
   And there she had two pretty babes born,
      Down by the greenwood sidey.

2. She had a penknife long and sharp,
      All aloney, aloney,
   And she pressèd it through their tender hearts
      Down by the greenwood sidey.

3. She diggèd a grave both wide and deep,
      All aloney, aloney,
   And she buried them under the marble stone,
      Down by the greenwood sidey.

4. As she was set in her Father's hall,
      All aloney, aloney,
   Oh! there she saw two pretty babes playing at ball,
      Down by the greenwood sidey.

5. "Oh! babes, Oh! babes if you were mine,
      All aloney, aloney,
   I would dress you up in the scarlet fine,"
      Down by the greenwood sidey.

6. "Oh! Mother, Oh! mother, we once were thine,
      All aloney, aloney,
   You did not dress us in the scarlet fine.
      Down by the greenwood sidey.

7. You digged a grave both wide and deep,
      All aloney, aloney,
   And you buried us under the marble stone."
      Down by the greenwood sidey.

4. [The Cruel Mother]

Hammond, *JFSS*, III (1907), p. 70(2). Sung by Mrs. Case, Sydling St. Nicholas, Dorset, September 1907.

p Æ

The outlines of this typical tune can be traced, in one meter or another, in scores of folk-tunes, from "How should I your true love know?" onward to the present time. For illustrations of its keeping a recognizable identity through changes of all sorts, cf. the above with Sharp's 5/4 version of "Searching for Lambs" (1916, No. 48, p. 108), and with the Scottish tunes for "Thomas the Rhymer" (*post*, No. 37). Cf. on the type, *Journal of the American Musicological Society*, III, No. 3 (1950), pp. 126-34.

5. "The Rose o' Malindie O"

Child, 1882-98, App'x. to V, p. 413, 20 Ja; text, I, p. 224. From Mrs. Harris "and others."

p Æ/D

1. She leant her back against a thorn,
      Hey for the Rose o' Malindie O
   And there she has twa bonnie babes born.
      Adoon by the green wood sidie O.

2. She's taen the ribbon frae her head,
   An hankit their necks till they waur dead.

3. She luikit outowre her castle wa,
   An saw twa nakit boys, playin at the ba.

4. "O bonnie boys, waur ye but mine,
   I wald feed ye wi flour-bread an wine."

5. "O fause mother, whan we waur thine,
   Ye didna feed us wi flour-bread an wine."

6. "O bonnie boys, gif ye waur mine,
   I wald clied ye wi silk sae fine."

7. "O fause mother, whan we waur thine,
   You didna clied us in silk sae fine.

8. "Ye tuik the ribbon aff your head,
   An' hankit our necks till we waur dead.

*   *   *   *   *   *

9. "Ye sall be seven years bird on the tree,
   Ye sall be seven years fish i the sea.

10. "Ye sall be seven years eel i the pule,
    An ye sall be seven years doon into hell."

11. "Welcome, welcome, bird on the tree,
    Welcome, welcome fish i the sea.

12. "Welcome, welcome, eel i the pule,
    But oh for gudesake, keep me frae hell!"

6. "Down by the Greenwood Side"

Barry, Eckstorm, and Smyth, 1929, p. xxii; and, with text, pp. 80-82. Sung by Mrs. Susie Carr Young, Brewer, Maine, c. 1925; learned from her grandmother, c. 1865. Melody recorded by George Herzog.

p D

The timing in the original copy is a queried 5/4, in bars double the length of the above, and notes half their value here.

1. There was a lady lived in York,
   It was all alone and alo-ne;
   She fell in love with her father's clerk,
   Down by the greenwood si-de.

2. She leaned her back against an oak,
   It was all alone and alo-ne;
   First it bent and then it broke,
   Down by the greenwood si-de.

3. She leaned her back against a thorn,
   It was all alone and alo-ne;
   And there those two pretty babes were born,
   Down by the greenwood si-de.

4. She took her penknife out of her pocket,
   It was all alone and alo-ne;
   She pierced those pretty babes to the heart,
   Down by the greenwood si-de.

5. She washed her penkife in the brook,
   It was all alone and alo-ne;
   The more she washed it the redder its look,
   Down by the greenwood si-de.

6. She wiped her penknife on the clay,
   It was all alone and alo-ne;
   And there she wiped the stains away,
   Down by the greenwood si-de.

7. She dug a grave both long and deep,
   It was all alone and alo-ne;
   She lay-ed those pretty babes in for to sleep,
   Down by the greenwood si-de.

8. When she returned to her father's farm,
   It was all alone and alo-ne;
   She spied those pretty babes arm in arm,
   Down by the greenwood si-de.

9. When she returned to her father's hall,
   It was all alone and alo-ne;
   She spied those pretty babes playing ball,
   Down by the greenwood si-de.

10. "Pretty babes! pretty babes, if thou art mine,"
    It was all alone and alo-ne;
    "I'll dress you up in satin so fine,"
    All down by the greenwood si-de.

15. "The Minister of New York's Daughter"

Greig MSS., III, p. 41. Also in Greig and Keith, 1925, p. 22(2). Singer unspecified; perhaps Mrs. Milne, October 1907?

a D/M

Welcome, welcome calling bells;
   Hey the rose & the linsie O;
But Guid keep me frae the torments o' hell;
   Doon by yon green wood sidie O.

19.1. "Cruel Mother"

Archive, School of Scottish Studies, rec. No. 1955/64/A1.
Sung by Duncan Burke, Perthshire. Collected by Hamish
Henderson and Peter Kennedy. Transcribed by Ailie
Munro.

m D

1. There were a lady—she proved unkind;
   She drownded her three babes in the draw-well,
   Sayin, Ba la looly nee.

2. Oh a year been gone and a year been past,
   Sayin, Ba la loo an a linny-oh,
   When she happent tae pass that draw-well
   Ba la loo an a linny-oh,

[Spoken] Now, we'll have to explain it. A year's gone,
from she done the murder, an she's passin the well,
here's the three little spirits jumps up out of the well,
ye see. She'd been married an done a lot of trouble since
that. . . . these little spirits comes up an they were sittin
jist on a baukin up above the well—night-time, ye see
an she spotted them. So then when she seen them, she
says:

[Sung]

3. "Oh, pretty little babes, oh if you were mine,
   I would dress you in silks so fine,
   I would dress you in silks so fine,
   Ba la loo an a linny-oh."

[Spoken]. . . . . so a little spirit got up—the oldest one
of the three—. . . . . got up and said:

[Sung]

4. "Oh dear mother, you didn't prove so kind
   When ye drownded us in this draw-well,
   Sayin, Ba la loo an the linny-oh.

5. "For seven year, you'll be a fish in the sea,
   And other seven as aul' horse-bones.

An for ever an for ever you'll be a porter in hell.
Sayin Bala loo an the linny-oh.

[Spoken] So that's your Ba la loo.

Q. And who did you hear it from?

A. My grannie, och. She was from Islay. She
   always maintained that the woman would be a
   porter in hell.

20. [The Cruel Mother]

Creighton and Senior, 1950, p. 20. Sung by John Roast,
Chezzetcook, Nova Scotia.

a Æ

She said "Pretty maids if you were mine
All alone and aloneyo,
I would dress you up in silks so fine
Down by the greenwood siding."

22. "There was a Lady lived in York"

Korson, 1949, pp. 38-39. Sung by Peter Cole, Greene
County, Pa., 1929. Recorded by Samuel P. Bayard.

a M

1. There was a lady lived in York,
      Tra la lee and a lidey O!
   She fell in love with her father's clerk,
      Down by the greenwood sidey O!

2. She leant herself against an oak,
    Tra la lee and a lidey O!
And first it bent, and then it broke,
    Down by the greenwood sidey O!

3. She leant herself against a tree,
    And there she had her misery.

4. She leant herself against a thorn,
    And there's where these two babes were born.

5. She pulled out her little penknife;
    She pierced them through their tender hearts.

6. She pulled out her white handkerchief;
    She bound them up both head and foot.

7. She buried them under a marble stone,
    And then returned to her merry maid's home.

8. As she sat in her father's hall,
    She saw these two babes playing ball.

9. Says she, Pretty babes, if you were mine,
    I'd dress you in the silk so fine.

10. Say, dear mother, when we were thine,
    You neither dressed us coarse nor fine.

11. But you pulled out your little penknife;
    You pierced it through our tender hearts.

12. Then you pulled out your white handkerchief;
    You bound us up both head and foot.

13. You buried us under a marble stone,
    And then returned to your merry maid's home.

14. Seven years to wash and wring,
    Seven more to card and spin.

15. Seven more to ring them bells,
        Tra la lee and a lidey O!
    Seven more to serve in hell,
        Down by the greenwood sidey O!

GROUP B

24. [The Cruel Mother]

Burne, 1886, p. 651; text, p. 540. Sung by Elizabeth Wharton and her brothers, Shropshire gypsies, July 13, 1885. Collected by James Smart.

a I/M

1. There was a lady, a lady of York,
        (Ri fol i diddle i gee wo!)
    She fell a-courting in her own father's park,
        Down by the greenwood side, O!

2. She leaned her back against the stile,*
        (Ri fol i diddle i gee wo!)
    There she had two pretty babes born,
        Down by the greenwood side, O!

3. And she had nothing to lap 'em in (etc.),
    But she had a penknife sharp and keen (etc.)

4. [She did not care if they felt the smart] (etc.),
    There she stabbed them right through the heart (etc.).

5. She wiped the penknife in the sludge,
    The more she wiped it, the more the blood showed.

6. As she was walking in her own father's park,
    She saw two pretty babes playing with a ball.

7. 'Pretty babes, pretty babes, if you were mine,
    I'd dress you up in silks so fine.'

8. 'Dear mother, dear mother [when we were thine],
    You dressed us not in silks so fine!'

9. 'Here we go to the heavens so high,
        (Ri fol i diddle i gee wo!)
    You'll go to bad when you do die!
        Down by the greenwood side, O!

    * Read "thorn."

31. [The Cruel Mother]

Sharp MSS., 1454/1333-34. Also in Sharp, [1916], p. 35. Sung by Mrs. Woodberry (80), Ash Priors, August 31, 1907. [The text of 1916 has been filled out.]

a M

There was a lady dwell in York
    Fal the dal the dido
She fell in love with her father's clerk
    Down by the green wood side O.

As she was walking home one day
    Fal the dal the dido
She met those babes all dressed in white
    Down by the green wood side O.

She said dear children where have you been
    Fal the dal the dido
. . . .
    Down by the green wood side O.

O yes Dear Mother we can tell
    Fal the dal the dido
For it's we to Heaven & you to Hell
    Down by the green wood side O.

6. She buried them under a marble stone
   And then she said she would go home.

7. As she was (going through) (a-going in)* her father's hall
   She spied those babes a-playing at a ball.

8. "Oh babes, oh babes if (you were) (thou wast) mine
   I would dress you up in silks so fine."

9. "Oh mother dear when we were thine
   You did not dress us up in silks so fine,

10. "You took your topknot from your head
   And tied us babies' hands and legs.

11. "Then you took your penknife (long) (keen) and sharp
   And pierced us babies' tender hearts.

12. "It's seven years to roll a stone
   And seven years to toll a bell.

13. "It's mother dear oh we can't tell
   Whether your portion is heaven or hell."

* The song was noted twice; parentheses mark the singer's changes.

GROUP C

45. [The Cruel Mother]

Creighton and Senior, 1950, pp. 19-20. Sung by Mrs. R. W. Duncan, Dartmouth, Nova Scotia.

p M (inflected VII)

1. There was a lady came from York
   All alone, alone and aloney,
   She fell in love with her father's clerk
   Down by the greenwood siding.

2. When nine months was gone and past
   Then she had two pretty babes born.

3. She leaned herself against a thorn
   There she had two pretty babes born.

4. Then she cut her topknot from her head
   And tied those babies' hands and legs.

5. She took her penknife keen and sharp
   And pierced those babies' tender hearts.

47. [The Cruel Mother]

Morris, 1950, pp. 251-52. Sung by Mrs. G. A. Griffin, Newberry, Fla., 1937; learned from her father.

a M

1. There was a lady lived in New York,
   All de lone and de loney;
   She fell in love with her father's clerk,
   All down by the greeny woodside ny;
   She fell in love with her father's clerk,
   All down by the greeny woodside ny.

2. She leant herself against the oak,
   All de lone and de loney;
   It was it leant and then it broke,
   All down by the greeny woodside ny;
   It was it leant and then it broke,
   All down by the greeny woodside ny.

3. She leaned herself against the thorn,
   All de lone and de loney;
   There she had two pretty babes borned,
   All down by the greeny woodside ny.
   There she had two pretty babes borned,
   All down by the greeny woodside ny.

4. She takened her hairstring offen her hair,
   All de lone and de loney;
   She tied them up both hands and feet,
   All down by the greeny woodside ny;
   She tied them up both hands and feet,
   All down by the greeny woodside ny.

5. She takened her pen knife outen her pocket,
   All de lone and de loney;
   She pierced it to their tender hearts,
   All down by the greeny woodside ny;
   And she buried them both at Marblestone,
   All down by the greeny woodside ny.

6. One even she was sitting in her father's hall,
   All de lone and de loney;
   She saw two pretty babes playing with a ball,
   All down by the greeny woodside ny;
   She saw two pretty babes playing with a ball,
   All down by the greeny woodside ny.

7. "O babes, O babes, if you was mine,
   All de lone and de loney;
   I'd dress you up in silks so fine,
   All down by the greeny woodside ny;
   I'd dress you up in silks so fine,
   All down by the greeny woodside ny.["]

8. "O Mother, O Mother, when we was yours,
   All de lone and de loney;
   You seemed to give us coarse nor fine,
   All down by the greeny woodside ny;
   You seemed to give us coarse nor fine,
   All down by the greeny woodside ny;

9. "You takened your hairstring offen your hair,
   All de lone and de loney;
   You tied us up both hands and feet,
   All down by the greeny woodside ny;
   You tied us up both hands and feet,
   All down by the greeny woodside ny.

10. "You takened your pen knife all outen your pocket,
    All de lone and de loney;
    You pierced it to our tender hearts,
    All down by the greeny woodside ny;
    You buried us both at Marblestone,
    All down by the greeny woodside ny."

The Maid and the Palmer

CHILD NO. 21

It was not to be expected that a traditional version of this ballad, which had barely survived in a fragmentary form in Scotland a century and a half ago, should have turned up in Ireland after the Second World War. But such is the case, and we have word of yet another variant in the same vicinity in the year 1970. The musical tradition is very unstable, and perhaps the tunes have been borrowed for the nonce, from material well worn in other connections. In the British Isles, the persons of the ballad are equally blurred and indistinct in identity. On the Continent, the Christ is more perceptible, but the Magdalen and the woman of Samaria are still confused. In the penances forecast, the ballad seems very probably to have crossed the sturdier tradition of "The Cruel Mother" (No. 20).

TUNES WITH TEXTS

1. "The Well below the Valley"

Ceol. A Journal of Irish Music, III, No. 12 (1969), p. 66.
Sung by John Reilly, Boyle, County Roscommon, Ireland.
Collected by Tom Munnelly.

a D

1. A gentleman was passing by,
   He asked a drink as he got dry,

   Refrain:

   At the well below the valley-o
   Green grows the lilly-o
   Right among the bushes-o

2. She said "My cup it overflows
   If I stoop down I might fall in".

3. "If your true love was passing by,
   You'd fill him a drink if he got dry".

4. She swore by grass, she swore by corn,
   That her true love was never born.

5. "I say, young maid, you're swearing wrong".

6. "If you're a man of noble fame,
   You'll tell me who's the father of them".

7. "There was two of them by your Uncle Dan".

8. "Another two by your brother John".

9. "Another by your father dear".

10. "Well if you're a man of noble fame
    You'll tell me what did happen to them".

11. "There was two of them buried by the stable door".

12. "Another two 'neath the kitchen floor",

13. "Another's buried by the well".

14. "Well if you're a man of noble fame
    You'll tell me what will happen mysel'."

15. "You'll be seven years a-ringing a bell",

16. "And seven years a-portin' in Hell".

17. "I'll be seven years a-ringing a bell,
    But the Lord above may save my soul from portin'
    in Hell".

2. "The Well below the Valley"

Sung by John Reilly, Boyle, County Roscommon, Ireland,
February 22, 1969. Recorded by Tom Munnelly, D. K. and
E. Wilgus, and sent by Mr. Munnelly to the Editor.

a I

1. A gentleman he was passing by.
   He axed a drink as he got dry
   At the well below the valley O.
     Green grows the lily O
     Right among the bushes O.

2. My cup it is an (in? on?) overflow
   And if I do stoop I may fall in
   At the well below the valley O.
     Green grows the lily O
     Right among the bushes O.

3. Well if your true love was passing by
   You'd fill him a drink if he got dry
   At the well below the valley O.
     Green grows the lily O
     Right among the bushes O.

4. She swore by grass and swore by corn
   That her true love was never born.
   I say, fair maiden, you've swore in wrong
   At the well below the valley O.
     Green grows the lily O
     Right among the bushes O.

5. Well if you're a man of that noble fame
   You'll tell to me the father o' them
   At the well below the valley O.
     Green grows the lily O
     Right among the bushes O.

6. Two o' them by your father dear
   At the well below the valley O.
     Green grows the lily O
     Right among the bushes O.

7. Two more o' them came by your uncle Dan
   At the well below the valley O.
     Green grows the lily O
     Right among the bushes O.

8. Another one by your brother John
   At the well below the valley O.
      Green grows the lily O
      Right among the bushes O.

9. Well if you're a man of the noble fame
   You'll tell to me what happened then
   At the well below the valley O.
      Green grows the lily O
      Right among the bushes O.

10. There was two o' them buried by the kitchen fire
    At the well below the valley O.
       Green grows the lily O
       Right among the bushes O.

11. Two more o' them buried by the stable door
    At the well below the valley O.
       Green grows the lily O
       Right among the bushes O.

12. The other was buried by the well
    At the well below the valley O.
       Green grows the lily O
       Right among the bushes O.

13. Well if you're a man of the noble fame
    You'll tell to me what will happen mysel'
    At the well below the valley O.
       Green grows the lily O
       Right among the bushes O.

14. You'll be seven long years a-ringin' a bell
    At the well below the valley O.
       Green grows the lily O
       Right among the bushes O.

15. You'll be seven more a-portin' in Hell
    At the well below the valley O.
       Green grows the lily O
       Right among the bushes O.

16. I'll be seven long years a-ringin' the bell
    But the Lord above might save my soul
    From portin' in Hell
    At the well below the valley O.
       Green grows the lily O
       Right among the bushes O.

Bonnie Annie

CHILD NO. 24

THE metre of this ballad is sufficiently uncommon among the Child ballads to attract our attention. There are not, I think, more than a dozen or so in clearly dactylic measure, and this one may be unique in its consistently feminine line-endings. The evidence of the tunes convinces one that the texts should be printed, probably in all variants, as tetrameter couplets with feminine rhymes. This looks like an Irish habit, but, if so, it seems surprising that the influence is not a great deal more often exerted in this form.

Neither Kinloch nor Motherwell, who provide us with our earliest texts, has preserved a tune for "Bonnie Annie." In fact, Baring-Gould, gathering songs in Devon and Cornwall toward the end of the last century, appears to have been the first collector to secure a tune, and he neglected to print it. (Three variants, under the name "The Undutiful Daughter," and an analogue from *The Baby's Opera*, are preserved in his MSS.) Consequently, all our records are of the present century or close to it. Neither is there anything in any one of them that sounds old. The texts are in much the same case, being, perhaps, for the most part pretty well saturated with nineteenth-century broadside influences. It must, I think, be acknowledged, that if Child, on the strength of the Jonah parallel, intended us to draw inferences of great age for this song, he was himself drawing a very long bow. "Captain Glen," a song popular in the last century and circulating in tradition as well as on broadsides, contains the same idea; but few would draw any inference of age from that fact. Superstitions flourish at sea.

With few exceptions, the tunes for this ballad are closely related. They are plagal, usually major or I/Ly, and habitually in genuine triple time. They are formally two phrases long, the first-phrase cadence usually balancing the final feminine cadence; e.g., *V III* and II I. All the Somerset copies save one conform to this pattern. Mrs. Hooper's (vt. 17) is more independent, and suggests five phrases; but it declares its allegiance in the last two cadences.

TUNES WITH TEXTS

2. [Banks of Green Willow]

Sharp MSS., 346/474. Also in Sharp, *JFSS*, II (1905), p. 34(4). Sung by Mrs. Overd, Langport, August 22, 1904.

p I/Ly

Go and get your father's good will
And get your mother's money,
And sail right over the ocean
Along with your Johnny.

She had not been sailing
Been sailing many days O.
Before she wanted some woman's help
And could not get any.

O hush your tongue, you silly girl,
O hush your tongue, you huzzy,
For I can do so much for thee
As any woman can for thee.

Go and get a silk napkin
And I'll tie thy head up softly
And I'll throw thee overboard,
Both thee and thy baby.

Look how my love's swimming along,
See how my love swager.
I'm afraid she'll swim to dry land
Which makes my heart quaver.

I'll buy my love a coffin,
And the gold shall shine yellow,
And she shall be buried
By the banks of green willow.

16. [Banks of Green Willow]

Sharp MSS., 567/. Sung by Mrs. Mary Anne Milton (80), Washford, August 17, 1905.

p I/Ly

I gainèd my fathers good will
Likewise my mother's money
And I roved off to sea
Along with young Johnny.

17. [Banks of Green Willow]

Sharp MSS., 103/94. Also in Sharp, *JFSS*, II (1905), p. 33(1). Sung by Mrs. White and Mrs. Louie Hooper, Hambridge, December 28, 1903.

p I

Contrary to the rest, this is clearly a five-phrase tune. Note also the textual influence of "Lady Isabel" (4).

Go home and get some of your father's gold
And some of your mother's money
And you shall go and board with me
For to be my dear honey, for to be my dear honey.

He had not sailed many miles,
Not many miles nor scarcely
Before he was troubled
With her and her baby, with her and her baby.

He tied a napkin round her head
And he tied it to the baby,
And then he throwed them overboard,
Both her and her baby, both her and her baby.

See how my love she will try to swim,
See how my love she will taver,
See how my love she will try to swim
To the banks of green willow, to the banks of green willow.

I will have the coffin made for my love
And I'll edge it all with yellow.
Then she shall be buried
On the banks of green willow, on the banks of green willow.

Willie's Lyke-Wake

CHILD NO. 25

OF THIS ballad, continental analogues are found in both northern and southern Europe, and the Danish records carry it up into the sixteenth century. But in English it has never (to my knowledge) been found outside Scotland, and no record of it is older than the nineteenth century. That, of course, is no reason for concluding that it did not exist in Scotland centuries before*; but it is perhaps allowable to infer a limited currency for a ballad that was not met by Herd, Scott, or Jamieson, to mention no lesser collectors. It has been recorded, however, by five collectors of the nineteenth century: Kinloch, Motherwell, Buchan, Christie, and Duncan (Greig).

Only four tunes have been noted, all of them so far apart and carrying such marks of alien affiliation as to confirm the suspicion that no steady oral tradition has been upholding the ballad since the record began. Conversely, the comparative steadiness of the text, especially in the refrain, might argue some control from print—*laxis effertur habenis*—and there is extant a broadside of 1810 to support the hypothesis. Nevertheless, Christie's second tune is furthest away from the melodic idea that the other three tunes seem as a group to be suggesting.

* Certainly the enterprising Willie could have given Barbara Allan's lover some pertinent lessons in survival, and seems to date from a happier era, vital, and not sicklied o'er with the introspective habit.

TUNES WITH TEXTS

2. "Among the Blue Flowers and the Yellow"

Duncan MS., No. 56 (*per* W. Walker). Also in Greig and Keith, 1925, p. 25. Sung by Mrs. Gillespie, Glasgow; learned in Buchan from her father's stepmother.

m I/M

Keith notes the coincidence here with "Loch Lomond," and with other folksongs, as "Be kind to your nainsel, John." It may be also noted that the scaffolding of the tune is the same as that of "Lord Lovel" and the English "Lady Isabel" type, to mention no more.

O Willie, my son, what makes ye sae sad,
    As the sun shines over the valley?—
I lie sairly sick for the love o a maid,
    Among the blue flowers an' the yellow.

O is she an heiress or lady fine,
    As the sun shines over the valley,
That she winna tak nae pity on thee,
    Amang the blue flowers an' the yellow?

*   *   *   *   *

Though a' your kin were aboot yon bower,
    As the sun shines over the valley,
Ye shall not be a maiden one single hour,
    Amang the blue flowers an' the yellow.

For maid ye cam here without a convoy,
    As the sun shines over the valley,
And ye shall return wi a horse and a boy,
    Amang the blue flowers an' the yellow.

Ye cam here a maiden sae meek and mild,
    As the sun shines over the valley,
But ye shall gae hame a wedded wife wi a child,
    Amang the blue flowers an' the yellow.

4. [Willie's Lyke-Wake]

Christie, I, 1876, p. 122. Text from Buchan, 1828, II, pp. 51-54, "with some changes from the way the Editor has heard it sung."

p Æ/D

With this tune, cf. "Johnie Cock (114) and "Trooper and Maid" (299).

Child prints this text as version E in I, p. 506. It is nearly the same as Peter Buchan's (1828, II, pp. 51-54).

1. If my love loves me, she lets me not know,
    This is a dowie chance;
   I wish that I the same could do,
    Tho' my love were in France, France,
    Tho' my love were in France.

2. O lang think I, and very lang,
    And lang think I, I trow;
   But langer and langer will I think,
    'Ore my love o' me rue, rue,
    'Ore my love o' me rue.

3. But I will write a broad letter,
    And write it sae perfite;
   That gin she winna o' me rue,
    I'll bid her come to my lyke, lyke,
    I'll bid her come to my lyke.

4. Then he has written a broad letter,
    And seal'd it wi' his hand,
   And sent it on to his true love,
    As fast as boy could gang, gang,
    As fast as boy could gang.

5. When she lookèd the letter upon,
    A light laugh then ga'e she;
   But ere she read it to an end,
    The tear blinded her e'e, e'e,
    The tear blinded her e'e.

6. "O saddle to me a steed, father,
    O saddle to me a steed;
   For word has come to me this night,
    That my true love is dead, dead,
    That my true love is dead.

7. The steeds are in the stable, daughter,
    The keys are casten by;
   Ye canna won the night, daughter,
    The morn ye'se won away, away,
    The morn ye'se won away.

8. She has cut aff her yellow locks,
    A little aboon her e'e;
   And she is on to Willie's lyke,
    As fast as gang could she, she,
    As fast as gang could she.

9. As she gaed ower yon high hill head,
    She saw a dowie light;
   It was the candles at Willie's lyke,
    And torches burning bright, bright,
    And torches burning bright.

10. Three o' Willie's eldest brothers
    Were making for him a bier;
   One half o' it was gude red gowd,
    The other silver clear, clear,
    The other silver clear.

11. Three o' Willie's eldest sisters
    Were making for him a sark;
   The one half o' it was cambric fine,
    The other needle wark, wark,
    The other needle wark.

12. Out spake the youngest o' his sisters,
    As she stood on the fleer;
   "How happy would our brother been,
    If ye'd been sooner here, here,
    If ye'd been sooner here."

13. She lifted up the green covering,
    And ga'e him kisses three;
   Then he look'd up into her face,
    The blythe blink in his e'e, e'e,
    The blythe blink in his e'e.

14. O then he started to his feet,
    And thus to her said he:
   "Fair Annie, since we're met again,
    Parted nae mair we'se be, be,
    Parted nae mair we'se be."

The Three Ravens

CHILD NO. 26

THE earliest text we possess of this moving elegy comes from Ravenscroft's *Melismata*, 1611, where it is given with the music, arranged for four voices. When Ritson reprinted it in 1790, he remarked that it was obviously much older than the date of first publication. No one who has studied it carefully will be likely to dispute the assertion. There exists a piece of collateral evidence which would move it back into the fifteenth century. That evidence is the now well-known "Corpus Christi" carol, still current, like the ballad, in oral tradition, and of which the oldest extant text was recorded in the first part of the sixteenth century. A good deal has been written by recent scholars about the occult significance of this carol, as to which the student may consult R. L. Greene, *Early English Carols*, 1935, pp. 221-22, 411-12, and the important references there given. For our immediate purpose it is sufficient to note general agreement that the piece is a pious adaptation of an earlier secular folk-song or ballad. My own persuasion is that some prior variant of "The Three Ravens" is that very antecedent. The disjointed introduction making use of birds without regard to the narrative proper; the comparable particularization of place; the knight with his grievous and bloody wounds; the devoted animals attending him, his steed (in a traditional variant), his hawks, his hounds:

> His hounds they lie down at his feete,
> So well they can their master keepe.
> [Ravenscroft]

> His hounds all standing at his feet,
> Licking his wounds that run so deep.
> [18th-19th century traditional]

> At that bed side there lies a hound,
> Which is licking the blood as it daily runs down.
> [Staffordshire variant of carol]

Then the appearance of the knight's love: in Ravenscroft's variant a fallow doe put figuratively for a woman, but perhaps originally—like the white hind of "Leesome Brand" (15) that was "of the woman kind," like the "Biche Blanche" of French folksong, like the hypothetical doe behind "Molly Bawn," and other similar ballad creatures—a case of metensomatosis; her weeping solicitude and tender action:

> She lift up his bloudy hed
> And kist his wounds that were so red:—

all these points of comparison appear too striking to be purely accidental.*

The best copies of the ballad, those that seem to maintain its early form, are themselves in the carol- or dancing-pattern which we have already more than once met, most notably in "The Two Sisters": a couplet with first line thrice repeated, and interlaced with elements of refrain. This seems, I repeat, to have been the original habit of the ballad in its English branch, and we shall note that the habit has persisted down to our own day, even when almost all else has disappeared, whether of ancient dignity or pathetic narrative, and when the air has suffered a strange transmutation.

The Scottish counterpart of the ballad appears to be responsible for sweeping away its former tenderness and suffusing it with an alien and reckless cynicism. It is the Scottish branch which is oftenest met in this country today, and it will doubtless before long have swallowed up all trace of the other in oral tradition—if it has not already effectually done so. It is noteworthy that, while both Motherwell and Chappell spoke in the early and middle part of the last century of the ballad's widespread contemporary currency in Scotland and England, neither Sharp nor Greig at the beginning of the present century ran across it in Britain. All Sharp's copies are Appalachian; but in debased forms it is widely known in America. Kittredge attributed this popularity to its vogue in the old minstrel shows. (*JAF*, XXXI [1918], p. 273, cited by H. M. Belden, *Ballads and Songs*, 1940, p. 31.)

It is of course regrettable that we have so few earlier traditional copies of the tune, but we must consider ourselves lucky to have one so early as 1611. Ravenscroft's is a very fine tune as it stands, but it can hardly be regarded as untouched tradition. It is probable that if we had an earlier traditional copy it would be in a triple time, as indeed are many of the later ones. The interests of harmony seem to have had some effect upon the Dorian modality of the original. No copy of the later seventeenth century has come down, but it may be observed that the phrasal pattern is one of the commonest country dance-tune forms to be found in Playford's collection, of which perhaps two-thirds of the total number are in 6/8 time. There is nothing to show for the eighteenth century; but the nineteenth, so far as it is represented by the scanty record, favors a common-time duple rhythm. When the Scottish influence becomes paramount, the melodic pattern loses its continuity and alien encroachments are everywhere apparent. The proper narrative element drops away, and nothing remains except the raucous fun of the crows. After the relatively dignified involvement with "Johnny comes marching home," and with "Bonnie Doon," there appear noticeable echoes of "Whisky Johnny," "Sweet Adeline," "Little Brown Jug," "Buffalo Gals," "Rig-a-jig." Most of these debased versions are plagal, and in the major galaxy (I/Ly, I/M, π^1, M). The older and better tradition is nearly always in a minor tonality (D, Æ/D), authentic or plagal. The shift to major is in keeping with the change of spirit.

---

* A connection between the two has been suggested before by J. A. Fuller-Maitland, with utmost brevity (*JFSS*, IV, p. 64). He refrains—wisely, no doubt—from drawing any inferences; and probably the question will never be carried as far as to certainty.

GROUP A

1. [The Three Ravens]

Ravenscroft, 1611, No. 20. Also in Ritson, 1790, pp. 155-56. Text, Child, 1882-98, I, p. 254.

m D (but inflected VII)

Cf. on this also Chappell, 1855, I, p. 59. In the lost lute MS. compiled by Robert Gordon of Straloch, 1627-29, there was a tune, "There wer three Ravns." (Cf. Dauney, *Ancient Scottish Melodies*, 1838, p. 368.) The early copy is unbarred.

To the present editor it seems likely that the tune is built out of plain chant material, perhaps not from a single chant, but from common phrases in the first or second mode. Compare, for example, the phrases of the *Agnus Dei* in the Mass *Orbis Factor* (XI in the Ordinary); or, with the tune's second half, the clauses of the great *Dies Irae*, beginning at "Quaerens me, sedisti lassus" and proceeding through the next five.

1. There were three rauens sat on a tree,
    Downe a downe, hay down, hay downe
  There were three rauens sat on a tree,
    With a downe
  There were three rauens sat on a tree,
  They were as blacke as they might be.
    With a downe derrie, derrie, derrie, downe, downe

2. The one of them said to his mate,
  'Where shall we our breakefast take?'

3. 'Downe in yonder greene field,
  There lies a knight slain vnder his shield.

4. 'His hounds they lie downe at his feete,
  So well they can their master keepe.

5. 'His haukes they flie so eagerly,
  There's no fowle dare him come nie.'

6. Downe there comes a fallow doe,
  As great with yong as she might goe.

7. She lift vp his bloudy hed,
  And kist his wounds that were so red.

8. She got him vp vpon her backe,
  And carried him to earthen lake.

9. She buried him before the prime,
  She was dead herselfe ere euen-song time.

10. God send euery gentleman,
  Such haukes, such hounds, and such a leman.

2. [The Three Ravens]

Motherwell, 1827, App'x No. 12; text, p. xviii. Collected by Andrew Blaikie, Paisley.

a Æ/D

Three ravens sat upon a tree,
  Hey down, hey derry day,
Three ravens sat upon a tree, hey down,
  Three ravens sat upon a tree
And they were black as black could be,
  And sing lay doo and la doo and day.

3. [The Three Ravens]

Kidson, 1891, pp. 17-18. Sung by John Holmes, Roundhay; learned from his mother in Derbyshire, c. 1825.

p Æ/D, ending on II (– VII)

The barring of each of the last three measures has been delayed by a note to conform to the verbal accent. Also the present editor has introduced the holds and shortened the written value of the notes over which they stand by a half-beat's length.

There were three ravens on a tree,
  A-down, a-down, a derry down,
There were three ravens on a tree,
  Heigh ho!
The middlemost raven said to me,
  "There lies a dead man at yon tree,"
  A-down, a-down, a derry down,
  Heigh ho!

There comes his lady full of woe,
    A-down, a-down, a derry down,
There comes his lady full of woe,
        Heigh ho!
There comes his lady full of woe,
[As great with child?] as she could go,
    A-down, a-down, a derry down,
        Heigh ho!

"Who's this that's killed my own true love,
    A-down, a-down, a derry down,
Who's this that's killed my own true love,
        Heigh ho!
I hope in heaven he'll never rest,
Nor e'er enjoy that blessed place."
    A-down, a-down, a derry down,
        Heigh ho!

GROUP B

7. [The Three Ravens]

Sharp MSS., 3808/2799. Sung by Mrs. Jane Gentry, Hot Springs, N.C., July 27, 1917.

m Æ/D

There was three crows sat on a tree
    O Billy MacGee MacGore,
There was three crows sat on a tree,
    O Billy MacGee MacGore,
There was three crows sat on a tree
And they were as black as crows could be,
    And they all flapped their wings and cried:
    Caw, caw, caw,
    And they all flapped their wings and cried:
    Billy MacGee MacGore.

Said one old crow unto his mate:
What will we do for grub to eat?

There is a dead horse on yonders plain,
Just by some cruel butcher's slain.

We'll perch ourselves on his back-bone,
And pick his eyes out one by one.

GROUP C

8. [The twa Corbies]

Campbell, II, [1818], pp. 26-27. Sung by Thomas Shortreed, Jedburgh; learned from his mother.

m M

The same, with insignificant differences, is in R. Chambers, 1844, p. 15; there given in 4/4 time.

As I cam' by yon auld house end
I saw twa corbies sittin thereon,
The tane unto the t'other did say,
"O whare sall we gae dine the day?"—

"Whare but by yon new fa'en birk,
There, there lies a new slain knight;
Nae mortal kens that he lies there
But his hawks and hounds, and his ladye fair.

"We'll sit upon his bonny breast bane,
And we'll pick out his bonny gray een;
We'll set our claws intil' his yellow hair
And big our bow'r,—its a' blawn bare.

My mother clekit me o' an egg,
And brought me up i' the feathers gray,
And bade me flee where'er I wad,
For winter wad be my dying day.

Now winter it is come and past,
And a' the birds are biggin' their nests,
But I'll flee high aboon them a'
And sing a sang for summer's sake.

Campbell's note: "This Edition of the words, and *Set* of the Air of 'The Twa Corbies,' was taken down by the present Editor from the singing of Mr. Thomas Shortreed of Jedburgh, as sung and recited by his mother, the lady mentioned in a preceding page of this work. The sweetly wild peculiarity of the melody, and correspondent imagery of this Scottish lyric, are very striking."

9. [The Twa Corbies]

Eyre-Todd, n.d., pp. 82-84. From "tradition." Text from Scott's *Minstrelsy*, with insignificant alteration.

a I/M (within a sixth)

This looks like a worn-down version of a very familiar type. Cf. the relatively recent "Buffalo Gals" and "Rig-a-jig."

As I was walking all alane
I heard twa corbies making mane,
The tane unto the tither say,
"Whare sall we gang and dine the day?"

"In behint yon auld fail dyke
I wot there lies a new-slain knight;
Naebody kens that he lies there
But his hawk, his hound, and his lady fair.

"His hound is to the hunting gane,
His hawk to fetch the muirfowl hame,
His lady's tane anither mate,
Sae we may mak' our dinner sweet.

"Ye'll sit on his white hause-bane,
And I'll pyke out his bonnie blue e'en;
Wi' ae lock o' his gowden hair
We'll theek our nest when it grows bare.

"Mony a ane for him mak's mane,
But nane shall ken whare he is gane;
O'er his white banes, when they are bare,
The wind sall blaw for evermair."

11. [The Three Ravens]

Creighton and Senior, 1950, p. 21. Sung by William Nelson, Kinsac, Nova Scotia.

p I/Ly

Three black crows sat on a tree
Ca beelya geelya gaw ye,
And they were black as crows could be
Ca beelya geelya gaw ye.

One black crow said unto his mate,
Ca beelya geelya gaw ye,
What shall we do for something to eat?
Ca beelya geelya gaw ye.

An old red horse in yonder lane,
Ca beelya geelya gaw ye,
Who very lately has been slain,
Ca beelya geelya gaw ye.

We'll pick his eyes out one by one,
Ca beelya geelya gaw ye,
And pick the meat from off his bones,*
Ca beelya geelya gaw ye.

* Or, "and eat its flesh until it's gone."

King Henry

CHILD NO. 32

Mrs. Brown of Falkland is again the sole preserver of this offshoot of Arthurian romance. Her tune has been saved in two manuscripts, the "Abbotsford" manuscript of Scottish songs in Scott's library, and William Tytler's manuscript at Aldourie Castle, long mislaid but lately recovered, of which a photostatic copy is now on deposit in the National Library of Scotland. Of the latter a careful copy had been made by the antiquary Joseph Ritson, who borrowed it for the purpose in the early 1790's.

Cf. the headnote to Child No. 5, for more on this transcript.

It should be noted here that the tune is wrongly attributed in the musical appendix in Child, V, 422 to "Lady Elspat" (Child no. 247). Tytler's MS. identifies it as "King Henry." The tune is Æolian—strictly D/Æ—and authentic. It will be found again with "Young Benjie" (Child No. 86) as printed in A. Campbell's *Albyn's Anthology*, and in variant forms has appeared elsewhere. Cf. the latter ballad for references.

TUNE WITH TEXT

[King Henry]

Ritson-Tytler-Brown MS., pp. 85-90. Sung by Mrs. Brown, Falkland, Aberdeenshire.

a Æ (+VI in grace note)

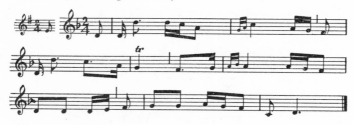

1. Lat never a man a wooing wend
   That lacketh thingis three,
   A routh o' gold, and open heart,
   An' fu' o' charity.

2. As this i speak o' king Henry,
   (For he lay burd alone,)
   And he's ta'en until a jelly hunts ha',
   Was seven miles frae a town.

3. He chase'd the deer now him before,
   An' the roe down by the den,
   Til the fattest buck in a' the flock,
   King Henry he has slain.

4. O he has ta'en him til his ha',
   To make him beerly cheer,
   An' in it came a griesly ghost,
   Stood stapping in the fleer.

5. Her head hat the reef-tree o' the house,
   An' her middle ye mat well span,
   He's thrown to her his gay mantle,
   Says, Lady, hap your lingcan.

6. Her teeth was a' like taether stakes,
   Her nose like club or mell;
   An' i ken nae thing she 'pear'd to be,
   But the fiend that wiends in hell.

7. "Some meat, some meat, ye king Henry,
   Some meat ye gie to me!"
   "An' what meat's i' this house, lady?
   An' fat have i to gie?"
   "O ye dee slay your berry-brown steed,
   An' you bring him here to me."

8. O whan he slew his berry-brown steed,
   Wow but his heart was sair!
   She eat him a' up, skin and been,
   Left naething but hide and hair.

9. "Mair meat, mair meat, ye king Henry,
   Mair meat ye gie to me!"
   "An' fat meat's i' this house, lady?
   An' what have i to gie?"
   "O ye do kill your good greyhounds,
   An' bring them a' to me."

10. O whan he slew his good greyhounds,
    Wow but his heart was sair!
    She eat them a' up, skin and bane,
    Left naething but hide and hair.

11. "Mair meat, mair meat, ye king Henry,
    Mair meat ye bring to me!"
    "An' what meat's i' this house, lady,
    That ye've nae welcome ti?"
    "O ye do fell your gay goss-hawks,
    An' you bring them a' to me."

12. O whan he fell'd his gay goss-hawks,
    Wow but his heart was sair!

She eat them a' up, bane by bane,
    Left naething but feathers bare.

13. "Some drink, some drink, ye king Henry,
    Some drink ye bring to me!"
"O what drink's i' this house, lady,
    That you're nae welcome ti?"
"O ye sew up your horses hide,
    An' bring in a drink to me."

14. "A bed, a bed now, king Henry,
    An' a bed you mak' to me!"
"O what bed's i' this house, lady,
    That you're nae welcome ti?"
"O ye man pu' the green heather,
    An' mak' a bed to me."

15. O pu'd has he the green green,
    An' made to her a bed,
An' up has he ta'en his gay mantle,
    And o'er it has he spred.

16. "Tak' aff your claiths now, king Henry,
    An' lye down me beside."
O god forbid, said king Henry,
    That ever the like betide!
That ever the fiend that wons in hell
    Should streak down by my side!

17. Whan night was gane and day was come,
    An' the sun shone through the ha',
The fairest lady that ever was seen,
    Lay atween him and the wa'.

18. O well is me! said king Henry,
    How lang will this last wi' me?
An' out it spake that fair lady,
    "Even til the day you dee.

19. For i've met wi' mony a gentle knight,
    That's gi'n me sic a fill,
But never before wi' a courteous knight
    That gae me a' my will."

Kempion

CHILD NO. 34

AGAIN Mrs. Brown is our only authority for a tune. The words of the first stanza are not written under the notes in the manuscript, and Robert Scott's* inexpert notation leaves one uncertain of the time-values of the *agréments* or graces of Mrs. Brown's singing. Instead of borrowing from the end of the previous bar for his upbeats at the beginning of a phrase, Scott sometimes writes a grace-note before the first beat, and sometimes an eighth note. In the face of uncertainty, it seems best to follow the manuscript reading here, since otherwise the reading is clear. The striking tune does not readily suggest any analogues.

* In this headnote as formerly printed, the name of Gordon, Mrs. Brown's father, was inadvertently substituted for that of Scott, her nephew.

TUNE WITH TEXT

[Kempion]

Ritson-Tytler-Brown MS., pp. 77-81. Sung by Mrs. Brown, Falkland, Aberdeenshire.

p π⁴

1. "Come here, come here, ye freely feed,
       An' lay your head low on my knee,
   The heaviest wierd i will you read,
       That ever was read til a lady.
2. O meikle dolour shall you drie,
       An' ay the sa't seas o'er ye swim,
   An' far mair dolour shall you drie,
       On East-muir-craigs, ere ye them clim'.
3. I wot yese be a weary wight,
       An' relieved shall you never be,
   Til Kempion the kingis son
       Come to the craig and thrice kiss thee."
4. O meikle dolour did she drie,
       An' ay the sa't seas o'er she swam,
   An' far mair dolour did she drie
       On East-muir-craigs ere she them clam':
5. An' ay she cry'd for Kempion,
       Gin he would but come til her hand.
   Now word has gane to Kempion
       That sic a beast was in his land;
   An' a be sure she would gae mad,
       Gin she got nae helping frae his hand.
6. Now, by my sooth, says Kempion,
       This fiery beast i'll gang and see.
   And by my sooth, says Segramour,
       My ae brother, i'll gang you wi'.
7. O biggit ha' they a bonny boat,
       An' they ha' set her to the sea
   An' Kempion and Segramour
       The fiery beast ha' gane to see.
   A mile afore they reach'd the shore,
       She gar'd the red fire flee.

8. "O Segramour, keep my boat afloat,
       An' lat her nae the land sae near,
   For the wicked beast shall sure gae mad,
       An' set fire to a' my land and mair."
9. "O out o' my sty i winna rise,
       And it is not for the awe o' thee,
   Til Kempion the kingis son,
       Come to the craig and thrice kiss me."
10. He's louted him o'er the East-muir-craig,
       An' he has gane her kisses ane;
    Awa' she gi'd, and again she came,
       The fieryest beast that ever was seen.
11. "O out o' my sty i winna rise,
       An' it is not for the awe o' thee,
    Till Kempion the kingis son
       Come to the craig and twice kiss me."
12. He's louted him o'er the East-muir-craig,
       An' he has gien her kisses twa;
    Awa' she gi'd and again she came
       The fieryest beast that ever you saw.
13. "O, out o' my sty i winna rise,
       An' it is not for the awe o' thee,
    Till Kempion the kingis son
       Come to the craig and thrice kiss me."
14. He's louted him o'er the East-muir-craigs,
       And he has gi'n her kisses three;
    Awa' she gi'd and again she came
       The bonnyest lady that ever could be.
15. An' by my sooth, says Kempion,
       My ain true love, (for this is she,)
    O was it wolf into the wood,
       Or was it fish into the sea,
    Or was it man, or vile woman,
       My ain true love, that misshap'd thee?
16. "It was not wolf into the wood,
       Nor was it fish into the sea,
    But it was my wicked step-mother
       An' wae and weary may she be!
17. O a heavier wierd light her upon,
    Than ever fell on vile woman,
    Her hairs' grow rough, and her teeths' grow lang,
    And on her four feet shall she gang;
18. Nane shall take pity her upon,
    But in wormes wood she shall ay won;
    An' relieved shall she never be
    Til Saint Mungo come o'er the sea."
    An' sighing said that weary wight,
       I fear that day i'll never see.

[96]

Thomas Rymer

CHILD NO. 37

THE single tune which has been preserved in two variants for this ballad may well be, as Scott calls it, "ancient." Scott, or his musical editor, writes as if a modern tune was also current in his day; but, if so, it has not been recorded, any more than recent texts that might accompany it. The tune which has survived is a member of a large family, in use with a number of ballads and songs in the south of England as well as the north, many of them very beautiful, and flowering in quite diverse ways both melodically and rhythmically. We have met it already in connection with Nos. 18, 20, and 26; Sharp's "Lord Bateman," and "Searching for Lambs," are also members of this clan, which can be followed back to the sixteenth century with ease, and doubtless a good deal further. Cf. *Journal of the Musicological Society*, III (1950), pp. 126, 132. A study of the variants will provide further evidence in support of the claim, made more fully elsewhere (e.g., "Young Beichan" [53]), that rhythmical developments in English folk-music have occurred through an instinctive tendency on the part of native singers to extend 3/4 into 4/4 time, 4/4 into 5/4 and finally into 6/4 or 3/2.

TUNES WITH TEXTS

1. [True Thomas; or, Thomas the Rhymer]

Scott, 1833, IV, opp. p. 116 ("The Ancient Tune"); text, pp. 117-21.

p Æ

1. True Thomas lay on Huntlie bank;
    A ferlie he spied wi' his ee;
And there he saw a ladye bright,
    Come riding down by the Eildon Tree.

2. Her shirt was o' the grass-green silk,
    Her mantle o' the velvet fyne;
At ilka tett of her horse's mane,
    Hung fifty siller bells and nine.

3. True Thomas, he pull'd aff his cap,
    And louted low down to his knee,
"All hail, thou mighty Queen of Heaven!
    For thy peer on earth I never did see."—

4. "O no, O no, Thomas," she said,
    "That name does not belang to me;
I am but the Queen of fair Elfland,
    That am hither come to visit thee.

5. "Harp and carp, Thomas," she said;
    "Harp and carp along wi' me;

And if ye dare to kiss my lips,
    Sure of your bodie I will be."—

6. "Betide me weal, betide me woe,
    That weird shall never daunton me."—
Syne he has kissed her rosy lips,
    All underneath the Eildon Tree.

7. "Now, ye maun go wi' me," she said;
    "True Thomas, ye maun go wi' me;
And ye maun serve me seven years,
    Thro' weal or woe as may chance to be."

2. She mounted on her milk-white steed;
    She's ta'en true Thomas up behind:
And aye, whene'er her bridle rung,
    The steed flew swifter than the wind.

9. O they rade on, and farther on;
    The steed gaed swifter than the wind;
Until they reach'd a desert wide,
    And living land was left behind.

10. "Light down, light down, now, true Thomas,
    And lean your head upon my knee;
Abide and rest a little space,
    And I will shew you ferlies three.

11. "O see ye not yon narrow road,
    So thick beset with thorns and briers?
That is the path of righteousness,
    Though after it but few enquires.

12. "And see ye not that braid braid road,
    That lies across that lily leven?
That is the path of wickedness,
    Though some call it the road to heaven.

13. "And see not ye that bonny road,
    That winds about the fernie brae?
    That is the road to fair Elfland,
    Where thou and I this night maun gae.

14. "But, Thomas, ye maun hold your tongue,
    Whatever ye may hear or see;
    For, if you speak word in Elflyn land,
    Ye'll ne'er get back to your ain countrie."

15. O they rade on, and farther on,
    And they waded through rivers aboon the knee,
    And they saw neither sun nor moon,
    But they heard the roaring of the sea.

16. It was mirk mirk night, and there was nae stern light,
    And they waded through red blude to the knee;
    For a' the blude that's shed on earth
    Rins through the springs o' that countrie.

17. Syne they came on to a garden green,
    And she pu'd an apple frae a tree—
    "Take this for thy wages, true Thomas;
    It will give thee the tongue that can never lie."—

18. "My tongue is mine ain," true Thomas said;
    "A gudely gift ye wad gie to me!

I neither dought to buy nor sell,
    At fair or tryst where I may be.

19. "I dought neither speak to prince or peer,
    Nor ask of grace from fair ladye."—
    "Now hold thy peace!" the lady said,
    "For as I say, so must it be."—

20. He has gotten a coat of the even cloth,
    And a pair of shoes of velvet green;
    And till seven years were gane and past,
    True Thomas on earth was never seen.

2. [Thomas the Rhymer]

Blaikie MS., NL Scotland MS. 1578, No. 63, p. 21.

p Æ/D

Tam Lin

CHILD NO. 39

THIS fine ballad has made infrequent appearances since Robert Burns sent his copy to the *Scots Musical Museum*, and seldom to the same tune. That is what we should expect, when a ballad rises to view at rare intervals; and in the present case the rule holds for at least a century after Burns. But in our own century a kinship between lately recovered Scottish variants and one recollected by Elinor Wylie (vt. 4 in the complete edition) from the singing of a nurse ("from the northern marshes"—presumably English) has emerged which is hard to gainsay, yet was certainly not transmitted from one to another. Two of them were published in *Scottish Studies*, vol. 9 (1965), pp. 23-26, by Hamish Henderson and Francis Collinson. A third is printed below (vt. 2.1). The editors just named print (p. 32) an analogous tune sung to "Little Sir Hugh" (Child No. 155), and a kindred one may be found with "Lady Jean" (Child No. 52). All show mutual resemblances of contour and metre. (Elinor Wylie did not preserve the nurse's words beyond the first stanza: those given with her tune are· probably a composite made out of the versions published by Child.)

The evidence of a singing and dancing tradition, of whatever sort, connected with Tam Lin, or Tamlene, or Thomalyn, or Thom of Lyn, or Thomlin, is frequent enough from the middle of the sixteenth century, but we are in darkness as to the nature of what was sung and danced about him. Some of it, however, must have belonged to the nursery branch of "Tommy a Lynn" or "Brian o' Lynn," which has also had a very wide vogue and often found its way into print. There seems to be no connection beyond the name. A version of the latter song may be found in Baring-Gould, *Songs of the West*, ed. Sharp, 1905, No. 41; and abundant references in the notes, App'x p. 13, to other occurrences. Cf. also I. and P. Opie, *The Oxford Dictionary of Nursery Rhymes*, 1951, pp. 413-14. In a Scottish medley of the early seventeenth century, printed by Forbes in 1666, but removed from the next edition of his work, certain musical notes are set down to the following words:

> The pypers drone was out of tune,
> sing young Thomlin, be merry,
> be merry, and twise so merry,
> with the light of the Moon,
> hey, hey down, down a down;

but the corresponding notes do not shape a tune, and it is not even certain that so much of the text is consecutive. Other than this, we have nothing in music until the end of the eighteenth century, when Burns, as said above, collected our best text of the ballad.

TUNES WITH TEXTS

2. [Tam Lin]

Johnson, V, [1796], No. 411, p. 423.

a Æ (but inflected VII)

The same, with dotted rhythm in the first two bars, and to other words, "O raging fortune's withering blast" (Burns's words), but with an air named "Tam Lin," appears in R. A. Smith, *The Scotish Minstrel*, (c. 1824), I, p. 2.

The time-values of the notes have been doubled in the present copy. The division of the stanzas has been readjusted in accordance with the rhyme. This is Child's A.

1. O I forbid you, maidens a'
   That wear gowd o[n] your hair,
   To come or gae by Carterhaugh,
   For young Tam Lin is there.

2. There's nane that gaes by Carterhaugh
   But they leave him a wad;
   Either their rings, or green mantles,
   Or else their maidenhead.

3. Janet has belted her green kirtle,
   A little aboon her knee,
   And she has broded her yellow hair
   A little aboon her bree;
   And she's awa to Carterhaugh
   As fast as she can hie[.]

4. When she came to Carterhaugh
   Tom-Lin was at the well,
   And there she fand his steed standing
   But away was himsel.

5. She had na pu'd a double rose
   A rose but only twa,
   Till up then started young Tam-Lin,
   Says, Lady, thou's pu' nae mae.

6. Why pu's thou the rose, Janet,
       And why breaks thou the wand!
   Or why comes thou to Carterhaugh
       Withoutten my command?

7. Carterhaugh it is my ain,
       My daddie gave it me;
   I'll come and gang by Carterhaugh
       And ask nae leave at thee.

8. Janet has kilted her green kirtle,
       A little aboon her knee,
   And she has snooded her yellow hair,
       A little aboon her bree,
   And she is to her father's ha,
       As fast as she can hie.

9. Four and twenty ladies fair,
       Were playing at the ba,
   And out then cam the fair Janet,
       Ance the flower amang them a',

10. Four and twenty ladies fair,
        Were playing at the chess,
    And out then cam the fair Janet,
        As green as onie glass.

11. Out then spak an auld grey knight,
        Lay o'er the castle wa',
    And says, Alas, fair Janet for thee,
        But we'll be blamed a'.

12. Haud your tongue, ye auld fac'd knight,
        Some ill death may ye die,
    Father my bairn on whom I will,
        I'll father nane on thee.

13. Out then spak her father dear,
        And he spak meek and mild,
    And ever alas, sweet Janet, he says,
        I think thou gaes wi' child.

14. If that I gae wi' child, father,
        Mysel maun bear the blame;
    There's ne'er a laird about your ha,
        Shall get the bairn's name.

15. If my Love were an earthly knight,
        As he's an elfin grey;
    I wad na gie my ain true-love
        For nae lord that ye hae.

16. The steed that my true-love rides on,
        Is lighter than the wind;
    Wi' siller he is shod before,
        Wi' burning gowd behind.

17. J[a]net has kilted her green kirtle
        A little aboon her knee;
    And she has snooded her yellow hair
        A little aboon her brie;
    And she's awa to Carterhaugh
        As fast as she can hie[.]

18. When she cam to Carterhaugh,
        Tam-Lin was at the well;
    And there she fand his steed standing,
        But away was himsel.

19. She had na pu'd a double rose,
        A rose but only twa,
    Till up then started young Tam-Lin,
        Says, Lady thou pu's nae mae.

20. Why pu's thou the rose Janet,
        Amang the groves sae green,
    And a' to kill the bonie babe
        That we gat us between.

21. O tell me, tell me, Tam-Lin she says,
        For's sake that died on tree,
    If e'er ye was in holy chapel,
        Or Christendom did see.

22. Roxbrugh he was my grandfather,
        Took me with him to bide
    And ance it fell upon a day
        That wae did me betide.

23. And ance it fell upon a day,
        A cauld day and a snell.
    When we were frae the hunting come
        That frae my horse I fell.
    The queen o' Fairies she caught me,
        In yon green hill to dwell[.]

24. And pleasant is the fairy-land;
        But, an eerie tale to tell!
    Ay at the end of seven years
        We pay a tiend to hell.
    I am sae fair and fu' o' flesh
        I'm fear'd it be mysel.

25. But the night is Halloween, lady,
        The morn is Hallowday;
    Then win me, win me, an ye will,
        For weel I wat ye may.

26. Just at the mirk and midnight hour
        The fairy folk will ride;
    And they that wad their truelove win,
        At Milescross they maun bide.

27. But how shall I thee ken Tam-Lin,
        Or how my true love know[,]
    Amang sae mony unco knights,
        The like I never saw[?]

28. O first let pass the black Lady,
        And syne let pass the brown;
    But quickly run to the milk white steed,
        Pu ye his rider down.

29. For I'll ride on the milk-white steed,
        And ay nearest the town.
    Because I was an earthly knight
        They gie me that renown.

30. My right hand will be glov'd lady,
    My left hand will be bare.
    Cockt up shall my bonnet be,
    And kaim'd down shall my hair,
    And thae's the takens I gie thee,
    Nae doubt I will be there.

31. They'll turn me in your arms lady,
    Into an esk and adder,
    But hald me fast and fear me not,
    I am your bairn's father.

32. They'll turn me to a bear sae grim,
    And then a lion bold,
    But hold me fast and fear me not,
    As ye shall love your child.

33. Again they'll turn me in your arms,
    To a red het gaud of airn.
    But hold me fast and fear me not,
    I'll do to you nae harm.

34. And last they'll turn me in your arms,
    Into the burning lead;
    Then throw me into well water,
    O throw me in wi' speed.

35. And then I'll be your ain true love,
    I'll turn a naked knight.
    Then cover me wi' your green mantle,
    And cover me out o' sight[.]

36. Gloomy, gloomy was the night,
    And eerie was the way,
    As fair Jenny in her green mantle
    To Milescross she did gae.

37. About the middle o' the night,
    She heard the bridles ring;
    This lady was as glad at that
    As any earthly thing.

38. First she let the black pass by,
    And syne she let the brown;
    But quickly she ran to the milk white steed,
    And pu'd the rider down.

39. Sae weel she minded what he did say
    And young Tam Lin did win;
    Syne cover'd him wi' her green mantle
    As blythe's a bird in spring.

40. Out then spak the queen o' fairies,
    Out of a bush o broom;
    Them that has gotten young Tam Lin,
    Has gotten a stately groom.

41. Out then spak the queen o' fairies,
    And an angry queen was she;
    Shame betide her ill-far'd face,
    And an ill death may she die,
    For she's ta'en awa the boniest knight
    In a' my companie[.]

42. But had I kend Tam Lin, she says,
    What now this night I see[,]
    I wad hae taen out thy twa grey een,
    And put it twa een o' tree.

2.1. "Tam Lin"

Archive, School of Scottish Studies, rec. No. SA 1967/140/
A1. Sung by Duncan Williamson, originally from Argyll;
learned as a boy from his grandmother. Collected by
Geordie MacIntyre and Helen Fullarton. Transcribed by
Ailie Munro.

a π⁴
Key is D♭ catch-note E♭

1. Margret stood in her high chamber;
   She'd sewn a silken seam.
   She lookèd east an she lookèd west,
   An she saw those woods grow green.

2. She lifted up her petticoat
   Beside a holland gown,
   An when she came to the pretty green woods,
   It was there that she let them down.

3. She had not pulled one nut, one nut,
   Nor scarcely bent one tree,
   When the highest lord in aa the country-side
   Came a-ridin throu the trees.

4. "Why do you pull those nuts, those nuts,
   Why do you bend those trees?"
   "Oh, oncet on time those nuts were mine,
   Without the leave of youse."

[lapse of memory]

[Spoken: There's something in between, and then there's
. . . he turns hissel intae a lion, an then "a fairy queen stole
me away when I was very young. . . ." An then he says . . .
first he'll turn to a lion, then he'll turn to a snake. . . . She
says—]

5. [Sung] "Oh now you've got the will of me,
   Come, tell me now your name,
   An when my baby it is born,
   I will call it the same."

6. "A fairy queen stole me away
   When I was very young."

[lapse of memory]

[Spoken: A grannie of mine used to sing it. She might have had the whole song, but I was young when I heard it. . . . He changes from a lion into a snake and from a snake into something else, an then to what he was before.]

3.1. "Tam Lin"

Telfer MS., No. 29, p. 14. Tune noted by William Oliver of Langraw, 1855.

a I/Ly (ending on the octave)

The Queen of Elfan's Nourice

CHILD NO. 40

WILLIAM WALKER supplied both Greig and Child with copies of the only surviving tune for this ballad, which he had learned from his mother. His note in the manuscript copy is: "Perhaps an improvised adaptation of a pibroch tune." He does not seem to have sent the words. The only text found in the Greig MSS. for the ballad is the one printed by Child from the Skene MS. (early nineteenth century). Greig and Keith, *Last Leaves*, do not print this ballad.

Another text was discovered in Wisconsin, with a stanzaic pattern that could not have been sung to the present tune (*JAF*, XX [1907], p. 155). It also derived from Scottish tradition, and the ballad does not seem to have been sung by "outlandish" folk, whether southron or others.

It may be noted that the tune appearing with the Wisconsin version in Evelyn K. Wells, *The Ballad Tree*, 1950, p. 141, is a happy borrowing from a Gaelic song on the theft of a child by the fairies. Cf. Alfred Moffat, *Minstrelsy of the Scottish Highlands*, n.d., pp. 24-25.

TUNE WITH TEXT

[The Queen of Elfan's Nourice]

Greig MSS., III, p. 183. Text, Greig MSS., Bk. 765, LV, pp. 8ff. Also, with variations below, in Child, 1882-98, V, p. 413. Noted by W. Walker, Aberdeen; learned from his mother.

a Æ/D

[I heard a coo low and a bonnie coo low
And a coo low doon in yon glen;
But lang lang will my young son greet
Ere his minnie bids him come hame.]

Two tunes in the Blaikie MS., Nos. 33 and 75 (the latter "John the little Scot"—Child 99), have the same final cadence as the above, and it is sometimes found in English tunes—e.g., "The Yeoman of Kent," in D'Urfey, *Pills*, 1719, I, p. 126. Cf. also the variant of "The Cruel Mother" from Mrs. Milne (Greig and Keith, 1925, No. 2, p. 22).

1. I heard a cow low, a bonnie cow low,
   An' a cow low down in yon glen,
Lang, lang will my young son greet
   Or his mither bid him come ben.

2. I heard a cow low, a bonnie cow low,
   An' a cow low down in yon fauld,
Lang, lang will my young son greet
   Or his mither take him frae cauld.

3. Waken, Queen of Elfan,
   An' hear your Nourice moan.
O moan ye for your meat,
   Or moan ye for your fee
Or moan ye for the ither bounties
   That ladies are wont to gie.

4. I moan na for my meat,
   Nor yet for my fee,
But I moan for Christened land,—
   It's there I fain would be.

5. O nurse my bairn, Nourice, she says,
   Till he stan' at your knee,
An' ye's win hame to Christen land,
   Whar fain it's ye wad be.

6. O keep my bairn, Nourice,
   Till he gang by the hauld,
An' ye's win hame to your young son
   Ye left in four nights auld.

7. O Nourice, lay your head
   Upo' my knee;
See ye na that narrow road
   Up by yon tree?

8. That's the road the righteous goes,
   And that's the road to heaven.
An' see ye na that braid road
   Down by yon sunny fell?
Yon's the road the wicked gae,
   An' that's the road to hell.

Hind Etin

CHILD NO. 41

MANY Continental texts of this ballad have survived, three Danish records as early as the sixteenth century. The rest are all of the nineteenth century; yet Child states that "the Norse forms of 'Agnes and the Merman' are conceded to have been derived from Germany"; and that the German ballad is somewhat nearer to the English—i.e. Scottish. The two surviving tunes have little in common except the last phrase, but perhaps that suffices to link them. Both come from the northeast of Scotland. Greig's tune (vt. 2) has kinship with several other Child ballads: Motherwell's "Lady Jean" (No. 52), Greig's "Child Waters" (No. 63), "Jellon Graeme" (No. 90)—but both these latter and the present are from the same singer. Cf. also the *Scots Musical Museum* version of "Tam Lin" (No. 39).

TUNES WITH TEXTS

1. [Young Akin]

Christie, II, 1881, p. 156. Sung in Banffshire. Words from Buchan's text, 1828, I, pp. 6-12; concluding stanzas as printed in Christie, 1881, II, p. 157.

a π³

Christie gives his copy in 2/4, with note-values half the present length.

1. Lady Margaret sits in her bower door
    Sewing at her silken seam;
   She heard a note in Elmond's-wood,
    And wish'd she there had been.

2. She loot the seam fa' frae her side,
    And the needle to her tae;
   And she is on to Elmond's-wood
    As fast as she cou'd gae.

3. She hadna pu'd a nut, a nut,
    Nor broken a branch but ane,
   Till by it came a young hind chiel,
    Says, Lady lat alane.

4. O why pu' ye the nut, the nut,
    Or why brake ye the tree;
   For I am forester o' this wood,
    Ye shou'd spier leave at me?

5. I'll ask leave at no living man,
    Nor yet will I at thee;
   My father is king o'er a' this realm,
    This wood belongs to me.

6. She hadna pu'd a nut, a nut,
    Nor broken a branch but three,
   Till by it came him young Akin,
    And gar'd her lat them be.

7. The highest tree in Elmond's-wood,
    He's pu'd it by the reet;
   And he has built for her a bower
    Near by a hallow seat.

8. He's built a bower, made it secure
    Wi' carbuncle and stane;
   Tho' travellers were never sae nigh
    Appearance it had nane.

9. He's kept her there in Elmond's-wood,
    For six lang years and one;
   Till six pretty sons to him she bear,
    And the seventh she's brought home.

10. It fell ance upon a day,
    This guid lord went from home;
   And he is to the hunting gane,
    Took wi' him his eldest son.

[stanza omitted]

12. A question I wou'd ask, father,
    Gin ye wou'dna angry be.
   Say on, say on, my bonny boy,
    Ye'se nae be quarrell'd by me.

13. I see my mither's cheeks aye weet,
    I never can see them dry;
   And I wonder what aileth my mither
    To mourn continually.

14. Your mither was a king's daughter,
    Sprung frae a high degree;
   And she might ha'e wed some worthy prince,
    Had she nae been stown by me;

15. I was her father's cup-bearer,
    Just at that fatal time;
   I catch'd her on a misty night,
    Whan summer was in prime;

16. My luve to her was most sincere,
    Her luve was great for me;
    But when she hardships doth endure,
    Her folly she does see.

17. I'll shoot the buntin' o' the bush,
    The linnet o' the tree,
    And bring them to my dear mither,
    See if she'll merrier be.

    [4 stanzas omitted]

22. He's ta'en his mither by the hand,
    His six brithers also,
    And they are on thro' Elmond's-wood,
    As fast as they cou'd go;

23. They wistna weel where they were gaen,
    Wi' the stratlins o' their feet;
    They wistna weel where they were gaen
    Till at her father's yate.

24. I hae nae money in my pocket,
    But royal rings hae three;
    I'll gie them you, my little young son,
    And ye'll walk there for me;

25. Ye'll gi'e the first to the proud porter,
    And he will lat you in;
    Ye'll gi'e the next to the butler boy,
    And he will show you ben;

26. Ye'll gi'e the third to the minstrel
    That plays before the king;
    He'll play success to the bonny boy,
    Came thro' the wood him lane.

27. He ga'e the first to the proud porter,
    And he open'd an' let him in;
    He ga'e the next to the butler boy,
    And he has shown him ben;

28. He ga'e the third to the minstrel
    That play'd before the king;
    And he play'd success to the bonny boy
    Came thro' the wood him lane.

29. Now when he came before the king,
    Fell low down on his knee;
    The king he turned round about,
    And the saut tear blinded his ee.

30. Win up, win up, my bonny boy,
    Gang frae my companie;
    Ye look sae like my dear daughter,
    My heart will birst in three.

31. If I look like your dear daughter,
    A wonder it is none;
    If I look like your dear daughter,—
    I am her eldest son.

32. Will ye tell me, ye little wee boy,
    Where may my Margaret be?
    She's just now standing at your yates,
    And my six brithers her wi'.

33. O where are all my porter boys
    That I pay meat and fee,
    To open my yates baith wide and braid?
    Let her come in to me.

34. When she came in before the king,
    Fell low down on her knee:
    Win up, win up, my daughter dear,
    This day ye'll dine wi' me.

35. Ae bit I canno' eat, father,
    Nor ae drop can I drink,
    Till I see my mither and sister dear
    For lang for them I think.

36. When she came before the queen,
    Fell low down on her knee:
    Win up, win up, my daughter dear,
    This day ye'se dine wi' me.

37. Ae bit I canno' eat, mither,
    Nor ae drop can I drink,
    Until I see my dear sister,
    For lang for her I think.

38. When that these two sisters met,
    She hail'd her courteouslie:
    Come ben, come ben, my sister dear,
    This day ye'se dine wi' me.

39. Ae bit I canno' eat, sister,
    Nor ae drop can I drink,
    Until I see my dear husband,
    For lang for him I think.

    [the rest is from Christie:]

    "O where are all my rangers bold,
        That I pay meat and fee,
    To search the forest far an' wide,
        And bring Akin to me?"
    Then out it speaks the little wee boy,—
        "Na, na, this manna be;
    Without ye grant a free pardon,
        I hope ye'll nae him see."

    "O here I grant a free pardon,
        Well seal'd by my own han';
    Ye may make search for young Akin,
        As soon as e'er you can."
    They search'd the country wide and braid,
        The forests far and near;
    And found him into Elmond's-wood,
        Tearing his yellow hair.

    ["]Win up, win up, now young Akin,
        Win' up and boun wi' me;
    We're messengers come from the court,
        The king wants you to see."
    "O lat him tak' frae me my head,
        Or hang me on a tree;
    For since I've lost my dear lady,
        Life's no pleasure to me."

"Your head will nae be touch'd, Akin,
  Nor hang'd upon a tree;
Your lady's in her father's court,
  And all he wants is thee."
When he came in before the king,
  He fell down on his knee:
"Win up, win up, now young Akin,
  This day ye'se dine wi' me."

But as they were at dinner set,
  The boy asked a boun;—
"I wish we were in the good church,
  For to get Christendoun;
We ha'e lived in guid green wood,
  This seven years and ane;
But a' this time since e'er I mind,
  Was never a church within."

"Your asking's nae sae great, my boy,
  But granted it shall be;
This day to guid church ye shall gang,
  And your mother shall gang you wi'."
Then out it speaks the parish priest,
  And a sweet smile gae he;—
"Come ben, come ben, my lily flower,
  Present your babes to me."

Charles, Vincent, Sam, and Dick,
  And likewise James and John;
They call'd the eldest Young Akin,
  Which was his father's name.
Then they staid in the royal court,
  And liv'd wi' mirth and glee;
And when her father was deceas'd,
  Heir of the crown was she.

2. [Hind Etin]

Greig MSS., IV, p. 92; text, Bk. 769, LIX, p. 10. Also in Greig and Keith, 1925, p. 31. Sung by Alexander Robb, New Deer, Aberdeenshire.

a Æ/D

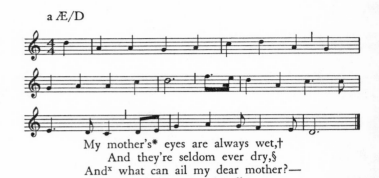

My mother's* eyes are always wet,†
  And they're seldom ever dry,§
And× what can ail my dear mother?—
  For she weeps continually.

Your mother was the fairest woman
  That ever my eyes did see,—

* Greig and Keith, 1925: "mithers's"
† Greig and Keith, 1925: "weet"
§ Greig and Keith, 1925: "An' they are seldom dry"
× Greig and Keith, 1925: "An' "

Clerk Colvill

CHILD NO. 42

IT is disappointing in the extreme that a fine ballad like "Clerk Colvill," whose analogues for upwards of four hundred years have covered the face of Europe from Iceland to Brittany, Spain, and Italy, and from Scotland to Bohemia, should yield, in the British musical record, but one solitary tune—and that through a cloudy glass. For it is again to Mrs. Brown and her nephew that we must resort; and this time they put us to no little trouble to divine a meaning. There are four copies (not to mention Spalding's reading in Child's Appendix) of Robert Scott's record of his aunt's tune: the Aldourie Castle original of William Tytler's Brown MS.; Ritson's transcript of that MS. in the Harvard Library; another in Sir Walter Scott's library at Abbotsford; and one (which I have not seen) in Glenriddell's hand in a copy of Herd's *Scottish Songs*, 1776, in the National Library of Scotland, after the Abbotsford MS. presumably.

The notes themselves look plausible; the problem is to fit them to the words. The first six bars obviously make provision for two lines of text, of equal length. The repeat would thus accommodate a full quatrain. But there are four bars left over, and these are to be repeated. If this be a second strain, to which the second and alternate stanzas are to be sung, it is very odd that it should be two bars shorter than the first: it has to carry the same length of text. There is no indication in the manuscript that the ballad possessed anything in the nature of a refrain, and it would be virtually impossible to eke out something to fill the extra *four* bars by repeating part of the quatrain for a refrain, even without the indicated repetition of the four bars. The only reasonable alternative appears to be the assumption of an unrecorded refrain or burden of different line-length, probably falling into two equal parts to follow the melodic scheme. Such a pattern would be by no means unprecedented, and is exemplified more than once in Greig's collection of tunes from the same region.

The prevailing iambic meter of the text suggests also a revision of Scott's barring, so as to provide up-beats for the phrase openings. Spalding's version, which takes unwarranted liberties with the record, is in Child, V, p. 414. Further discussion of the tune may be found in *CFQ*, I (1942), pp. 189-90, where it is noted that a tune in Greig for Child 237 (Greig and Keith, 1925, p. 189, tune 1b) parallels the first two (oddly Brahmsian) phrases. It may be admitted that the temptation to which Spalding succumbed, of changing the triple rhythm of the Scott record to a dotted one (6/8 or 6/4) corresponding to the iambic meter, is hard to resist. Yet it is equally hard to believe that Scott would have heard a succession of alternating halves and quarters (or quarters and eighths) as a sequence of notes of even length. And if he did not, he would not have written them so, for his notation is by no means illiterate. In this case, his notation makes reasonable sense, apart from suiting the words or not. Moreover, there is corroborative evidence in the large number of Christie's records from the same region which have a metrical pattern of a triple sort, where the meter of the words would suggest a dotted duple one.

TUNE WITH TEXT

[Clark Colven]

Ritson-Tytler-Brown MS., pp. 6-9. Sung by Mrs. Brown, Falkland, Aberdeenshire.

p π³

Conjectural reading

Original reading

1. Clark Colven and his gay lady,
      As they walk'd to yon garden green,
   A belt about her middle gimp,
      Which cost Clark Colven crowns fifteen.

2. "O hearken well now, my good lord,
      O hearken well to what i say;
   When ye gae to the walls o' Stream,
      Be sure ye touch nae well far'd may."

3. "O had your tongue, my gay lady,
      An' dinna deave me wi' your din;
   For i saw never a fair woman
      But wi' her body i cou'd sin."

4. He mounted on his berry-brown steed,
      An' merry merry rade he on,
   Till he came til the walls o' Stream,
      An' there he saw the mermaiden.

5. "Ye wash, ye wash, ye bonny may,
      And ay's ye wash your sark o' silk."
   "It's a for you, ye gentle knight,
      My skin is whiter than the milk."

6. He's taen her by the milk-white hand,
      And likewise by the grass-green sleeve,
   An' laid her down upon the green,
      Nor of his lady speer'd he leave.

7. Ohon! alas! says Clark Colven,
      An' ay sae sair's i mean my head.
   And merrily leugh the mermaiden:
      "O, even on, till ye be dead.   (Aside.)

8. But out ye tak' your little pen-knife,
      An' frae my sark ye shear a gare,
   Row that about your lovely head,
      And the pain you'll never feel nae mair."

9. Out has he taen his little pen-knife,
      An' frae her sark he's shorn a gare,
   Row'd that about his lovely head;
      But the pain increased mair and mair.

10. Ohon! alas! says Clark Colven,
      An' ay sae sair's i mean my head.
   An' merrily leugh the mermaiden:
      " 'Twill ay be war 'till ye be dead."

11. Then out he drew his trusty blade,
      An' thought wi' it to be her dead;
   But she became a fish again,
      And merrily sprang into the fleed.

12. He's mounted on his berry-brown steed,
      An' dowy, dowy rade he hame,
   'Till he came to his lady's bow'r door,
      An' heavily he lighted down.

13. "O mither, mither, mak' my bed,
      An', gentle lady, lay me down;
   O brither, brither, unbend my bow,
      'Twill never be bent by me again."

14. His mither she has made his bed,
      His gentle lady laid him down,
   His brother he has unbent his bow,
      'Twas never bent by him again.

The Broomfield Hill

CHILD NO. 43

THERE is no evidence to connect this song with any early song-title or burden mentioning the broom in lyrical fashion, as the "Brume, brume on hill" of *The Complaynt of Scotland*, c. 1549, and Wager's "The Longer thou Livest, the More Fool thou art," c. 1568, or "All flowers in brome" in W. Ballet's Lute Book, c. 1600. Setting aside poems and tales on the theme, some of which were recorded as far back as the twelfth century, there are Scandinavian, German, and Italian ballads, Danish copies of the mid-seventeenth century being the earliest that have survived. So far as the British record is known, it begins with broadsides of the earlier (?) eighteenth century (Child's F). The earliest traditional copies were picked up in Scotland in the latter part of the same century, and the ballad was apparently common among the Scots at the beginning of the nineteenth century. Since that time it has nearly died out in the north; but it has been found in the present century occasionally in the Midlands and frequently in the more southern counties, particularly Somerset. It has been discovered also in the United States, but here it is of the utmost rarity, and only one tune appears to have been recorded for any American variant.

Except in the Somerset region, the recorded tunes show considerable variation—so much, in fact, that it is very difficult to make out whether there is actual relationship or not. Between the two oldest Scottish records there seems to be almost nothing in common; but one of them (3) is clearly connected with most of the southwestern variants, and the other (13) is doubtfully related to the recent variants from the Aberdeen region. A third distinct pattern has been found in the south, in several variants (17); two distant variants of a fourth, in Norfolk and Dorset (20); and several copies, in scattered counties, which cannot be related with any confidence to the rest, but which seem standard folktunes. Most of the tunes are full of charm and interest.

(A) The largest group of related variants comes mostly from Sharp's Somerset collection (4), but one member of the group is perhaps the oldest of record and is Scottish (3). All these variants are in major tonality (I, I-M, I/M). The striking feature is the mid-cadence on the octave; but the first phrase ends almost as consistently on the tonic. All the tunes of this group are authentic.

(B) The second group is Scottish and too small to be very positive about (13). It affects a burden with nonsense syllables, and seems to prefer to end on the supertonic. If this analysis be correct, all variants are π^1 or I/M. Variants of the same tune occur with "Earl of Errol" (231) and "Our Goodman" (274).

(C) The third group is again Southern English (17), and major authentic; the first and mid-cadences are I and (usually) V.

(D) A fourth group contains only two tunes, from Norfolk (20) and Dorset. Both are plagal; one Dorian, with a mixed metre; the other Æ/D, in straight triple measure.

(E) Four tunes, from Lincolnshire, Dorset, Herefordshire, and Somersetshire, have been grouped together, somewhat doubtfully. Two, major and I-M, are plagal; two, Dorian and D-Æ, are authentic. All are in duple time, and may be related to Group A. (The Herefordshire text starts on the Group A pattern (23). They have noticeable connections with other songs, especially "The Bailiff's Daughter" (Child No. 105) and "The Mermaid" (Child No. 289).

(Appendix) A final group, from Maine, Newfoundland, Nova Scotia, and Ireland, have seemingly little to do with any of the rest, and go to a curious marine adaptation of the text.

TUNES WITH TEXTS

GROUP A

3. [Lord John]

Kinloch, 1827, pp. 195-98.

m M (inflected VII)

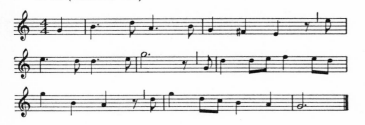

1. "I'll wager, I'll wager," says Lord John,
      A hundred merks and ten,
   That ye winna gae to the bonnie broom-fields,
      And a maid return again."—

2. "But I'll lay a wager wi' you, Lord John,
      A' your merks oure again,
   That I'll gae alane to the bonnie broom-fields,
      And a maid return again."

3. Then Lord John mounted his grey steed,
      And his hound wi' his bells sae bricht,
   And swiftly he rade to the bonny broom-fields,
      Wi' his hawks, like a lord or knicht.

4. "Now rest, now rest, my bonnie grey steed,
      My lady will soon be here;
   And I'll lay my head aneath this rose sae red,
      And the bonnie burn sae near."

5. But sound, sound, was the sleep he took,
      For he slept till it was noon;
   And his lady cam at day, left a taiken and away,
      Gaed as licht as a glint o' the moon.

6. She strawed the roses on the ground,
   Threw her mantle on the brier,
   And the belt around her middle sae jimp,
   As a taiken that she'd been there.

7. The rustling leaves flew round his head,
   And rous'd him frae his dream;
   He saw by the roses, and mantle sae green,
   That his love had been there and was gane.

8. "O whare was ye, my gude grey steed,
   That I coft ye sae dear;
   That ye didna waken your master,
   Whan ye ken'd that his love was here."—

9. "I pautit wi' my foot, master,
   Garr'd a' my bridles ring;
   And still I cried, Waken, gude master,
   For now is the hour and time."—

10. "Then whare was ye, my bonnie grey hound,
    That I coft ye sae dear,
    That ye didna waken your master,
    When ye ken'd that his love was here."—

11. "I pautit wi' my foot, master,
    Garr'd a' my bells to ring;
    And still I cried, Waken, gude master,
    For now is the hour and time."—

12. "But whare was ye, my hawks, my hawks,
    That I coft ye sae dear,
    That ye didna waken your master,
    When ye ken'd that his love was here."—

13. "O wyte na me, now, my master dear,
    I garr'd a' my young hawks sing,
    And still I cried, Waken, gude master,
    For now is the hour and time."—

14. "Then be it sae, my wager gane!
    'Twill skaith frae meikle ill;
    For gif I had found her in bonnie broom-fields,
    O' her heart's blude ye'd drunken your fill."

1. A squire, a squire, he lived in the wood,*
   He courted a lady gay,
   A little while and he passed a joke
   And a wager he did lay.

2. A wager, a wager I'll lay to any man,
   A thousand guineas to one
   That a maid won't go to the merry green woods
   And a maid return again.

3. O when she came to the merry green woods
   She found her love asleep
   With a knife in his hand and a sword by his side
   And a greyhound at his feet.

4. Three times she walked all round his head,
   Three times all round his feet,
   Three times she kissed his red rosy cheeks
   As he lay fast asleep.

5. And when she done all what she could
   She walked softly away;
   She hide herself in the merry green wood
   To hear what her love did say.

6. When he waked out from his dream,
   He looked up in the skies;
   He looked round and round and down on the ground
   And he wept most bitterly.

7. Up he called his serving man
   Whom he loved so dear:
   Why hasn't thou awakened me
   When my true love was here?

8. And with my voice I hallooed Master
   And with my bells I rung;
   Awake, awake and awake, Master,
   Your true love's been and gone.

9. I wish I had my true love here
   As free as I a got my will
   And every bird in the merry green wood
   For they should have their fill.

10. Sleep more in the night, master,
    And wake more in the day,
    And then you will see when your true love come
    And when she goes away.

   * Sharp, *JFSS*: "woods"

4. [Broomfield Wager]

Sharp MSS., 1212/1189-91. Also in Sharp, *JFSS*, IV (1910), p. 112(2). Sung by William Briffet, Bridgwater, January 19, 1907.

a I

10.1. "The Squire in the North Countree"

Vaughan Williams MSS., I, p. 265. Sung by Mr. Verrall, Horsham, Sussex, September 8, 1908.

a I

1. It's of a rich squire in the North country
   in the North country ridèd he
   and as he was a-riding all fitting for a joke
   saying a wager I will lay with thee.

2. What wager, what wager will you lay with me
   500 bright guineas to y[ou]r 10
   that you do not go a maiden to the bonny blooming fields
   and return back a fair maid again.

3. The wager was made and the money was paid down
   500 bright guineas to y[ou]r 10
   that you do not go a maiden to the bonny blooming fields
   and return back a fair maid again.

4. Then off ridèd he to the bonny blooming fields
   and he laid himself fast down asleep
   with (his) horse a-by his side and silver saddle too
   and his hounds laying down at his feet.

5. Then off ridèd she through the bonny blooming fields
   where she found her own true love fast asleep
   with his horse a-by his side and his silver saddle too
   and his hounds laying down at his feet.

6. 3 times she did walk round the crown of his hat
   3 times round the soles of his boots
   3 times she kissed his red and ruby lips
   as he laid on the ground fast asleep.

7. Then off from her finger she pulled a gold ring
   and placed it all on his right hand
   and twas to let him know his true love had been there
   and the wager she fairly had won.

8. When that he woke all out of his sleep
   unto his hound he did say
   Why have you not woken me out of my sleep
   when you saw my own true love standing by[?]

9. I howled and I hollowed and I shook your shirt collar
   crying awake O master awake
   I [howled and I hollowed and I shook your shirt collar]
   but no notice at all w[oul]d you take.

10. If I'd been awake instead of being asleep
    when my true love was standing by
    I'm sure I w[oul]d have murdered her or else I'd have
       my will of her
    and the small birds s[houl]d all have their fill.

13. "Leatherum thee thou and a'"

Greig MSS., I, p. 266. Also in Greig and Keith, 1925, p. 32(1). Sung by Alexander Robb, New Deer, Aberdeenshire, May 1906.

a π¹, ending on II

There was a knicht an' a lady bricht,
  Set trysts amang the broom,
The ane to come at twelve o'clock,
  An' the ither true at noon.
      Leatherum thee thou an' a'
      Madam aye wi' you,
      An' the seal o' me be abrachee,
      Fair maiden I'm for you.

17. [The Merry Broomfield]

Sharp MSS., 1457/. Sung by Mrs. Priscilla Cooper, Stafford Common, September 2, 1907.

a I

(a) was sometimes a B♭.

A wager a wager a wager I will lay
I'll bet you five and fifty pounds to your one O
That you don't ride a maid to the bonny bush abloom
And a maid to return safe home again

GROUP D

20. "The Squire who lived in the West"

Amherst, *JFSS*, IV (1911), p. 114(4). Sung by George
Turvey (77), an agricultural laborer, Foulden, Stoke Ferry,
Norfolk.

p Æ/D

1. 'Tis of a young Squire who lived in the West,
   And he courted a lady so fair;
   But my love unto you I never will request,
   For I mean to go merry and free.

2. "A wager, a wager, with you my pretty maid,
   Here's five hundred pounds to your ten,
   That a maid you shall go to yon merry, green broom,
   But a maid you shall no more return."

3. "A wager, a wager, with you kind sir,
   With your hundred pounds to my ten;
   That a maid I will go to yon merry, green broom,
   And a maid I will boldly return."

4. Now when that she came to this merry green broom,
   Found her true love was fast in a sleep,
   With a fine finished rose, and a new suit of clothes,
   And a bunch of green broom at his feet.

5. Then three times she went from the crown of his head,
   And three times from the sole of his feet,
   And three times she kissed his red, rosy cheeks
   As he layed fast in a sleep.

6. Then she took a gold ring from off her hand,
   And put that on his right thumb,
   And that was to let her true love to know
   That she had been there and was gone.

7. As soon as he had awoke from his sleep,
   Found his true love had been there and was gone;
   It was then he remembered upon the cost,
   When he thought of the wager he'd lost.

8. Then three times he called for his horse and his man,
   The horse that he'd once bought so dear;
   Saying, "Why didn't you wake me out of my sleep
   When my lady, my true love, was here?"

9. "Three times did I call to you, master,
   And three times did I blow with my horn;

But out of your sleep I could not awake,
Till your lady, your true love, was gone."

10. "Had I been awake when my true love was here,
    Of her I would had my will;
    If not the pretty birds in this merry green broom,
    With her blood they should all had their fill."

GROUP E

23. "A Wager, A Wager"

Vaughan Williams, *JFSS*, IV (1911), p. 114(5). Sung by
Mrs. Powell, near Weobley, Herefordshire, August 1910.

a D

Miss Broadwood calls attention to "The Pretty Ploughboy" (*JFSS*,
II, p. 146; IV, pp. 303-8; VIII, p. 268). Again, it is worth citing
"The Mermaid" from Calcott, "The Child's Own Singing Book,"
1843 (reprinted in John Goss, *Ballads of Britain*, 1937, p. 136), for
an interesting variant.

APPENDIX

27. [The Sea Captain; or, The Maid on the Shore]

Karpeles, 1934, I, pp. 30-31. Sung by Mrs. Joanie Ryan,
Stock Cove, Bonavista Bay, Newfoundland, September 18,
1918. Text according to collector's MS.

a M

43. THE BROOMFIELD HILL

1. 'Twas of a sea captain 'twas deep in love,
   He was deep in despair O;
   For I shall die, the sea captain, he cried,
   If we don't get this maid from the shore, shore,
   If we don't get this maid from the shore.

2. I have silver and I have gold,
   I have costly wear O,
   And I will buy a jolly ship's crew,
   If they'll row me this maid from the shore, shore,
   If they'll row me this maid from the shore.

3. With long persuaded they got her on boat, [*sic*]
   The seas rose calm and clear O.
   She sang so neat, so sweet and complete,
   She sent sailors and captain to sleep.

4. She robbed them of silver, she robbed them of gold,
   And robbed them of costly wear O;
   She took a broad sword instead of an oar,
   And paddled away from the shore.

5. When this man woke and found she was gone,
   He was like a man in despair O.
   He called up his men and commanded a boat
   To row me away for the shore.

6. And this man's not drunk,
   He's not deep in despair.
   She saluted the captain as well as the crew,
   Said: I am a maiden once more on the shore.

The Twa Magicians

CHILD NO. 44

ONLY two British texts of this interesting ballad appear to have been recorded, although it is claimed to be extant in recent memory both in Ireland and in northern Maine (cf. Barry, Eckstorm, and Smyth, *British Ballads from Maine*, 1929, p. 444). One of the texts is Scottish, of the first quarter of the last century; the other is English, found at Minehead in 1904. Although at first glance very different, it can, I believe, be demonstrated to fair conviction that the English text is remade from the Scottish. (Cf. the full edition of the present work, I, pp. 348-49.) Unfortunately, the Scots preserved no tune. The English tune seems to be basically a major analogue of the minor tune best known as "An old woman poor and blind"— a tune very popular in the early eighteenth century, employed for various broadside ballads, and in ballad operas, and printed with different texts at least thrice in D'Urfey's *Pills*, 1719-20, vols. V, 22, 29; VI, 124. See also Chappell's *Popular Music*, II, 551.

As to the subject-matter of the present ballad, Child has called it "a base-born cousin of a pretty ballad known over all Southern Europe, and elsewhere, and in especially graceful forms in France." (Child, I, 399.) It is fair to observe that "base-born" is a moral or aesthetic, rather than a historical, judgment. One might infer, at least, that a form of the ballad

in which magic was powerfully practiced was more primitive than one in which the necromancy was confined to the limits of poetic fancy, or wish-fulfillment, as in most of the Continental versions cited by Child. One may further notice that Child—though his placing this ballad next to two riddling ballads may be intended to suggest it—does not overtly comment that in its latter guise the ballad allies itself with those verbal contests in which the opponents match wits in proposing equal impossibilities, or in solving each other's challenging questions in order to gain, or evade, a desired, or unwelcome, mate.

It is very probable that a song familiar in the West of England, and known in Ireland and New England, collected by Cecil Sharp under the name "Hares on the Mountains," is a derivative of this ballad. Magic has been rationalized out of existence, and along with it has gone the narrative element. Instead of these, we have a series of conditional statements expressing the idea that no matter what form the girls might take, the men would pursue and find them out. All the variants that I have seen are in triple time and seem at least distantly related. Sharp gathered five copies of this song and four copies of the closely related "Sally, my Dear." Of the latter, only the concluding stanzas pertain to the radical idea.

TUNES WITH TEXTS

1. [The Two Magicians]

Sharp MSS., 276/383-84. Also, as "The Coal-Black Smith," in Sharp, *JFSS*, II (1905), p. 50; Sharp and Marson, 1904, pp. 38-39; and Sharp [1916], pp. 48-49. Sung by Mr. Sparks, a blacksmith, Minehead, August 8, 1904.

a I

O she looked out of the window
As white as any milk.
But he looked into the window
As black as any silk.
    Hulloa, hulloa, hulloa, hulloa,
    You coal-black smith!
    You have done me no harm.
    You never shall change my maiden name
    That I have kept so long.
    I'd rather die a maid,
    Yes, but then, she said,
    And be buried all in my grave
    Than I'd have such a nasty,
    Husky, dusky, musty, fusky
    Coal-black smith
    A maiden I will die.*

Then she became a duck
A duck all on the stream.
And he became a water-dog
And fetched her back again.
    Hulloa, &c.

* Sharp, *JFSS*: "My maiden name shall die."

Then she became a hare,
A hare upon the plain.
And he became a greyhound dog
And fetched her back again.
    Hulloa, &c.

Then she became a fly,
A fly all in the air.
And he became a spider
And fetched her to his lair.
    Hulloa, &c.

APPENDIX—GROUP A

2. [Hares on the Mountains]

Sharp MSS., 9/16. Also in Sharp and Marson, 1904, pp.
20-21; and Sharp [1916], pp. 142-43. Sung by Mrs. Louie
Hooper and Mrs. Lucy White, Hambridge, September
1903.

m I

The original is in F.

Young women they'll run like hares on the mountains,
Young women they'll run like hares on the mountains.
If I were but a young man, I'd soon go a-hunting,
    To my right fol diddle dero, To my right fol diddle dee.

Young women they sing like birds in the bushes,
Young women they sing like birds in the bushes.
If I was a young man, I'd go and bang the bushes,
    To my right fol diddle dero, To my right fol diddle dee.

Young women they'll swim like ducks in the water,
Young women they'll swim like ducks in the water.

If I was a young man, I'd go and swim all after,
    To my right fol diddle dero, To my right fol diddle dee.

GROUP B

12. "O Sally, my Dear"

Sharp MSS., 891/960. Also in Sharp and Marson, 3rd
series, 1906, pp. 60-61; and Sharp, [1916], pp. 144-45. Sung
by John Barnett, Bridgwater, April 16, 1906.

a Æ/D

The variants are from the 1916 edition.

With the music:

O Sally my dear shall I come up to see you
O Sally my dear shall I come up to see you
She laugh & reply I'm afraid you'll undo me
    Sing fal the diddle i-do Sing whack fal the diddle day.

6. If blackbirds was blackbirds as thrushes was thrushes
   If blackbirds was blackbirds as thrushes was thrushes
   How soon the young men would go beating the bushes.
       Sing fal the diddle i do, Sing whack fal the diddle day.

7. Should young women be hares and race round the mountain
   Should young women be hares and race round the mountain
   Young men (would) take guns and they'd soon go a-hunting
       Sing fal the diddle i do, Sing whack fal the diddle day.

8. Should young women be ducks and should swim round the
                                                        ocean
   Should young women be ducks and should swim round the
                                                        ocean
   Young men would turn drakes and soon follow after.
       Sing fal the diddle i do, Sing whack fal the diddle day.

King John and the Bishop

CHILD NO. 45

THE stuff of this ballad, as Child's introduction makes very clear, is out of the storehouse of tradition. On the other hand, Child's parallels—an impressive array—are almost wholly drawn from *tales* both popular and literary. The earlier we get in the English records, the less does the ballad resemble traditional verse. Neither is there any later traditional form which I have seen that has shaken clear of its broadside associations. Here, then, we have a ballad that may have started its career, as a ballad, in close connection with writing, and that was refashioned and reprinted for broadside dissemination at frequent intervals, probably from the time of Elizabeth down to the nineteenth century. So far as we know, it never took hold in Scotland (although Child mentions a Faroe version of the nineteenth century), and its strongest lease on life has been where it could renew its forces by contact with the mother press.

There seems, then, no hope of working back toward an "uncontaminated" traditional ballad, and in this case external form is no determinant of purity. The various seventeenth-century broadsides, however, are directed to be sung to three different tunes, depending on the copy. The names of the tunes are "The Shaking of the Sheets," "Chievy-Chase," and "The King and the Lord Abbot." At best, then, we may infer that the makers of various versions of the ballad had one or another of these specific tunes in mind to guide them in shaping their stanzas. There is no cheat about this, because the tunes are of easily distinguishable patterns, and the texts in each case do go to the tunes designated—albeit stumblingly. Seventeenth-century variants of all three tunes are extant.

An attempt to determine the relative age of these tunes from external evidence will not lead to positive conclusions, nor enable us to fix the priority of the textual tradition. It is true that a song of "The Hunttis of Chevet" is mentioned in c. 1549, and we may assume that that ballad was a good deal older. But the earliest extant text of it has a disconcerting way of shifting from CM to LM; we have no equally early record of the proper tune; and, anyway, it need not be inferred that the earlier copies of "The King and the Bishop" (or "Abbot") were sung to the tune—any tune—of "Chevy Chase." (The tune best known as "Chevy Chase," employed in vulgar balladry *ad nauseam* in the seventeenth and eighteenth centuries, seems previously to have been called by the name of "Flying Fame," and was therefore probably borrowed for the use that gave it its common title: but it held its accustomed shape with a most wearisome persistence, and provides us with no clue to the present purpose.)

"The Shaking of the Sheets" is likewise old, and references to it are common in the second half of the sixteenth century. As a ballad-tune it would appear to have had an earlier vogue than the other. Moreover, "The Shaking of the Sheets," besides the fact that there are two distinct tunes of that name, became modified in the course of years almost out of recognition. The earliest extant copy (c. 1600) may be the one in William Ballet's lutebook (in tablature), in Trinity College, Dublin.

The other tune known as "The Shaking of the Sheets," or "The Night-Peece," makes its first known appearance in Playford's *Dancing Master*, 1650. As it is there printed, it will accommodate ten lines of CM text. But its second part is printed out in a triple repetition, and the last of the three may have been simply to fill out the stave. When danced, there was no necessary limit to the number of repetitions; but as a song the tune has properly four phrases, or eight if each half is sung twice. This tune, it will be apparent, does not go to the form of our ballad which is directed to be sung to "The Shaking of the Sheets." Neither, by the same token, does it go to the broadside texts of "The Dance of Death," although Chappell, by forcing dactyls into an iambic rhythm and repeating the last line without authority, has arbitrarily compelled it to serve in that capacity. Both in the venturesome and unusual stanza-form and in the archaic character of the tune, the song belongs to the sixteenth century, if not before. To find it printed late in the seventeenth century is to infer Elizabethan copies of the same pattern and to suggest a reason for remodeling in a newer mode. This form of the ballad, then, entitled "The Old Abbot and King Olfrey," although in the least popular vein of any, may be with some confidence assigned to a date as early as that of the more "popular" types.

The third tune remains to be considered. This is "The King and the Lord Abbot," a tune which is indicated for singing with the form of the ballad chosen by Child as his B-text. The broadsides of this type are entitled "A *new* Ballad of King John and the Abbot of Canterbury." From the adjective Child infers an older ballad, now lost. We need not grant too much weight to the adjective, either way, since the broadside press was utterly unscrupulous in its claims. If an Elizabethan ballad was printed as "a new ballad," a Restoration reprint was quite likely to repeat the phrase. Nevertheless, Child's assumption is in this case perhaps supported by the name of the tune, which is hardly suggested by the accompanying text. "To its own tune" would be the ordinary direction if text and tune had grown up together. The ballads of type B have a different stanza-form from the others, a four-line dactylic (= anapaestic) tetrameter pattern rhyming in couplets, followed by an end-refrain of "Derry down, down hey, derry down." This scheme entails a different musical vehicle. Since the latter cannot be a variant of either "Chevy Chase" or "The Shaking of the Sheets," it is reasonable to identify it with the tune which appears in various forms almost as early as the B texts, is printed with a B text by D'Urfey, and is for the next two hundred years generally used and known as "The Abbot of Canterbury." In spite of a great deal of superficial change, this tune has kept its basic outline with noteworthy fidelity, and there is no reason to suppose its earlier forms were very different. If, then, our B-text is really a rewriting, it is justifiable to infer a parent text used with previous variants of the same tune, and therefore having the same textual pattern. How far back this tune might go is hard to guess, but it cries sib to "Greensleeves" and "Packington's Pound," both characteristically Elizabethan.

Child's A-text is taken from the Percy Folio. There is nothing but the date of the MS. (c. 1640) to put it before the broadsides, except its length and perhaps greater elegance. The style of it is certainly not more "popular" than that of B, and it sounds copied from earlier print or manuscript. There is no indication of a tune to go with it, but the fact is worth mentioning that as it stands—without any refrain—it is the only version that will sing at all to the second tune of "The Shaking of the Sheets." The latter appears in Playford's *Dancing Master*, 1650, as "The Night Piece," and is reprinted by Chappell, I, p. 84. It might be corroborative of this possibility that eight of the ballad's thirty-eight stanzas (or nine of thirty-seven, if a two-line stanza be attached to its predecessor) have an additional couplet, and, as Playford's printing of this tune demonstrates, these would be absorbed with perfect ease by the tune's expansibility—a fact not equally true of the other tunes for this ballad. If this tune is later than the other, as it sounds, and if this text was ever sung to it, we might take the folio copy as representing an intermediate stage in the ballad's development, between the types of "The old Abbot and King Olfrey" and

"The King and the Bishop" in CM. On the other hand, in the absence of definite evidence on the point, it appears almost equally credible that the actual singers of the folio text have been few indeed.

It is at any rate only in the "Derry Down" pattern that the ballad has been perpetuated in traditional singing. In this form it has been found in our own century in the Midlands, and in New England, the Mid-West, and Far West within the last decade. It is perhaps significant of the prevailing Scotch-Irish roots of Appalachian tradition that it does not occur in so large a collection as Sharp's. Thanks to frequent transfusions of printer's ink, its condition is still vigorous wherever it appears; and for its sturdy merit a long succeeding life is still to be hoped.

TUNES WITH TEXTS

1. [King John and the Abbot of Canterbury]

D'Urfey, 1719-20, IV, pp. 28-31.

m Minor, or D (inflected VII)

1. I'll tell you a Story, a Story anon,
Of a Noble Prince, and his Name was King *John*;
For he was a Prince, a Prince of great might,
He held up great Wrongs, and he put down great Right,
Derry down, down, hey derry down.

2. I'll tell you a Story, a Story so merry,
Concerning the Abbot of *Canterbury*;
And of his House-keeping and high Renown,
Which made him repair to fair *London* Town.
Derry down, &c.

3. How now, Brother Abbot! 'tis told unto me,
That thou keep'st a far better House than I;
And for thy House-keeping and high Renown,
I fear thou hast Treason against my Crown.
Derry down, &c.

4. I hope my Liege, that you owe me no Grudge,
For spending of my true gotten Goods;
If thou dost not answer me Questions Three,
Thy Head shall be taken from thy Body.
Derry down, &c.

5. When I am set on my Steed so high,
With my Crown of Gold upon my Head;
Amongst all my Nobility, with Joy and much Mirth,
Thou must tell me to One Penny what I am Worth.
Derry down, &c.

6. And the next Question you must not flout,
How long I shall be Riding the World about?
And the Third Question thou must not shrink,
But tell to me truly what I do think.
Derry down, &c.

7. O These are hard Questions for my shallow Wit,
For I cannot answer your Grace as yet;
But if you will give me Three days space,
I'll do my Endeavour to answer your Grace.
Derry down, &c.

8. O Three Days space I will thee give,
For that is the longest day thou hast to Live;
And if thou dost not answer these Questions right,
Thy Head shall be taken from thy Body quite.
Derry down, &c.

9. And as the Shepherd was going to his Fold,
He spy'd the old Abbot come riding along;
How now Master Abbot, you're welcome home,
What News have you brought from good King *John.*
Derry down, &c.

10. Sad News, sad News, I have thee to give,
For I have but Three Days space for to Live;
If I do not answer Him Questions Three,
My Head will be taken from my Body.
Derry down, &c.

11. When He is set on His Steed so high,
With His Crown of Gold upon His Head;
Amongst all His Nobility, with Joy and much Mirth,
I must tell Him to One Penny what He is worth.
Derry down, &c.

12. And the next Question I must not flout,
How long He shall be Riding the World about;
And the Third Question I must not shrink,
But tell to Him truly what he does Think.
Derry down, &c.

13. O Master did you never hear it yet,
That a Fool may learn a Wise Man Wit?
Lend me but your Horse and your Apparel,
I'll ride to fair *London* and answer the Quarrel.
Derry down, &c.

14. Now I am set on my Steed so high,
With my Crown of Gold upon my Head;
Amongst all my Nobility, with Joy and much Mirth,
Now tell me to One Penny what I am worth.
Derry down, &c.

15. For Thirty Pence our Saviour was Sold,
Amongst the false *Jews*, as you have been told;
And Nine and Twenty's the Worth of Thee,
For I think thou art One Penny worser than he.
Derry down, &c.

16. And the next Question thou maist not flout,
How long I shall be Riding the World about?
You must Rise with the Sun, and Ride with the same,
Until the next Morning he Rises again:
And then I am sure, You will make no doubt,
But in Twenty Four Hours you'll Ride it about.
Derry down, &c.

17. And the Third Question thou must not shrink,
But tell me truly what I do Think?
All that I can do, and 'twill make your Heart Merry,
For you think I'm the Abbot of *Canterbury*,
But I'm his poor Shepherd as you may see,
And am come to beg Pardon for he and for me.
Derry down, &c.

18. The King he turn'd him about, and did Smile,
Saying thou shalt be Abbot the other while;
O no my Grace, there is no such need,
For I can neither Write nor Read.
Derry down, &c.

19. Then Four Pounds a Week will I give unto thee,
For this merry true Jest thou hast told unto me;
And tell the old Abbot when thou comest home,
Thou hast brought him a Pardon from good King *John*:
Derry down, down, hey derry down.

4. "The Bishop of Canterbury; or, King John"

Robertson, UC/LC Folk-Record 4196 A. Sung by Warde H. Ford, Central Valley, Calif., December 25, 1938; learned from his mother, Mrs. J. C. Ford, Crandon, Wisc.

1. A story a story a story anon
I'll tell unto thee concerning King John
He had a great mind for to make himself merry
So he called for the Bishop of Canterbury
Lol li dol lay, lol li dol luddy, tri ol di dum day.

2. 'Good morning good morning' the old king did say
'I've called you to ask you questions three
And if you don't answer them all right
Your head shall be taken from your body quite'
Lol li dol lay, lol li dol luddy, tri ol di dum day.

p I/Ly

The first two phrases are repeated in stanzas 3 and 6 to accommodate the extra lines.

3. 'My first question is and that without doubt
How long I'll be trav'ling this whole world about
And the next question is when I set in state
With my gold crown upon my pate
And all the nobility joined in great mirth
You must tell to one penny just what I am worth'
Lol li dol lay, lol li dol luddy, tri ol di dum day.

4. 'And the last question is and when I do wink
You must tell to me presently what I do think
(Next two lines forgotten)
Lol li dol lay, lol li dol luddy, tri ol di dum day.

5. As the old Bishop was returning home
He met his young shepherd and him all alone
'Good morning good morning' the young man did say
'What news do you bring from the old king today?'
Lol li dol lay, lol li dol luddy, tri ol di dum day.

6. 'Oh very bad news' the old bishop did say
'The king has asked me questions three
And if I don't answer them all right
My head shall be taken from my body quite'
Lol li dol lay, lol li dol luddy, tri ol di dum day.

7. 'Well I'm sorry a man of such learning as thee
Can't go back and answer the king's questions three
But if you will lend me a suit of apparel
I'll go to King John and settle the quarrel'
Lol li dol lay, lol li dol luddy, tri ol di dum day.

8. 'A suit of apparel I freely will give
And ten thousand pounds as sure as you live'
And now the young shepherd has gone to King John
To settle the quarrel that he had begun
Lol li dol lay, lol li dol luddy, tri ol di dum day.

9. 'Good morning good morning' the young shepherd did say
'I've called to answer your questions three
Your first question is and that without doubt
How long you'll be trav'ling this whole world about
If you start with the sun and you travel the same
In twenty-four hours you'll come back again'
Lol li dol lay, lol li dol luddy, tri ol di dum day.

10. 'The next question is when you sit in state
With your gold crown upon your pate
And all the nobility joined in great worth (*sic*, for mirth)
I'm to tell to one penny just what you are worth'
Lol li dol lay, lol li dol luddy, tri ol di dum day.

11. 'For thirty gold pieces our dear Lord was sold
By those old Jews so brazen and bold
And for twenty-nine pieces I think you will do
For I'm sure he was one piece better than you'
Lol li dol lay, lol li dol luddy, tri ol di dum day.

12. 'The last question is and when you do wink
I'm to tell to you presently what you do think
And that I will do if 'twill make your heart merry
You think I'm the Bishop of Canterbury'
Lol li dol lay, lol li dol luddy, tri ol di dum day.

13. 'And that I am not as is very well known
I am his young shepherd and him all alone'
'Go tell the old Bishop, go tell him for me
That his young shepherd has outwitted me'
Lol li dol lay, lol li dol luddy, tri ol di dum day.

7. "King John"

Grainger MS., No. 138. Sung by Joseph Skinner, Barrow-on-Humber, July 27, 1906.

a Æ

1. An ancient story I'll tell you anon,
Of a notable King that was called King John,
Who reüled over England with main & with might,
Who did great wrong & maintained little right. Derry down.

2. An àbbot who lived at Canterburý,
Who for his housekeeping so rich & merry;
That for his housekeeping & wealth & renoun
King John bade him hasten to fair London town. Derry down.

3. "Sir àbbot," says John, "unto me it is told,
More state than the King thou hast dared to uphold;
For treason like this thou must forfeit thine head,
Unless thou can answer 2 questions instead." Derry down.

4. "The first, I will ask thee most plainly to show
How long round the world it'll take me to go,
& at the next question thou mayest not shrink
But tell me I pray thee, now what do I think." Derry down.

5. Then home rode the àbbot his fate to bewail,
& met his good shepherd & told him his tále.
"Don't trouble thý brains, my goodmaster," said he,
"For I'll go to King John & he'll think it is thee." Derry down.

6. In 3 weeks time his mule he bestrode,
& úp to the King as the àbbot he rode.
"Sir àbbot, yé're welcome, it's now quickly shown
How long roun' the world it'll take to go." Derry down.

7. "You must start with the sun when at morn he doth rise,
& travel with him all the day thro' the skies;
& then thou need not make any doubt
That in 24 hour thou'll ride it about." Derry down.

8. "Right well to my 1st question thou hast replied,
Now tell me my 2nd & home thou shalt hie."
"Yes, that I will do, it will make your grace merry;
You think I'm the abbot of Canterbury." Derry down.

9. "But I'm his poor shepherd, as plain you can see,
& I've come to beg pardon for him & for me."
"O ho! here is gold, get thee gone.
Tell the abbot he's pardoned by good King John."
Derry down. Down, derry down, Derry down.

APPENDIX

15. [The old Abbot and King Olfrey]

Playford, 1650, reprinted 1933, p. (3). Also in Chappell, I [1855], p. 85. Playford's title is "The Night Peece." See Chappell for other names.

p I

Chappell observes, *loc. cit.*, that the tune of "The Shaking of the Sheets" is mentioned as a country-dance in *Misogonus*, c. 1560. "The Dance and Song of Death" was entered in the Stationer's Register, 1568-69. Chappell finds "The Night Piece" often between 1650 and 1783, in which latter year it is printed in *The Vocal Enchantress*.

Captain Wedderburn's Courtship

CHILD NO. 46

FOR the theme of this ballad Child has cited ancient parallels in European and Eastern folk-tales. It is not clear, however, that any other people has made a song of it; and there is nothing to prove that the British ballad is very old. If it is so, it must have been thoroughly overhauled in quite modern times. Even in the earliest texts (Scottish, of the later eighteenth century), the talk of livery-men and butlers' bells ringing supper has certainly a very incongruous sound mixed with the lady's primitive riddling conditions. In view of the proven antiquity of these riddles and their independent use in folk-song (cf. the Appendix to this ballad), it seems possible that the whole extant narrative frame is a recent (and highly inartistic) concoction, on the analogy of Child 1 and 2, but in more modern dress. The early texts are in much too sound a condition to have been long independent of writing, and we may suppose that broadside-makers are the persons who would concern themselves with this kind of manufacture.

The old wine, at any rate, has had savor enough to keep the ballad in vogue, particularly in Scotland and Ireland, down to our own day. American copies have doubtless come from one or the other of those countries, as there appears to be no English tradition for this ballad. The melodic tradition shows a fairly distinct cleavage between Scottish and Irish variants, with the Irish perhaps slightly in the lead. But one or two of those with an Irish character have been found on Scottish soil, and the racial distinction as between these two countries in folk-song is notoriously blurred at many points.

Both lines are mainly in the major tonality, with a strong Mixolydian leaning. The Irish tradition is likely to fall into the "Come-all-ye" pattern of tune. Most of the tunes in the first two groups are authentic or, occasionally, mixed. All are in duple time (including examples of 6/8 and 12/8).

A very good recent version, with a tune on the order of our vt. 7, and I/M, is printed by H. Henderson and F. Collinson, in *Scottish Studies*, IX, 1965, pp. 14-17.

TUNES WITH TEXTS

GROUP A

7. [Captain Wedderburn's Courtship]

Greig MSS., I, p. 165; text, Bk. 726, XVI, pp. 85ff. Also in Greig and Keith, 1925, p. 36(1b). Sung by J. W. Spence, April 1906.

a M, ending on VIII

1. The Laird o' Roslin's daughter
Walked through the woods her lane
Met in wi' Captain Wedderburn
A servant to the king
He said unto his serving man
Were't not against the law
I wad tak' her to my ain bed
And lay her neist the wa'.

2. "I am walking here alane" she says,
"Amang my father's trees
And you must let me walk alane
Kind sir now if you please

The supper bell it will be rung
And I'll be missed awa'
Sae I winna lie in your bed
Either at stock or wa'.

3. He says "My pretty lady
I pray lend me your hand
And ye'll hae drums & trumpets
Always at your command
And fifty men to guard you wi'
That well their swords can draw
Sae we'se baith lie in ae bed
And ye'se lie neist the wa'."

4. "Haud awa frae me" she said
And pray let gae my hand
The supper bell it will be rung
I can nae langer stand
My father he will angry be
Gin I be missed awa
Sae I'll nae lie in your bed
Either at stock or wa'.

5. Then said the pretty lady
"I pray tell me your name"
"My name is Captain Wedderburn
A servant to the King
Tho your father and his men were here
O['] them I'd hae nae awe
But wad tak ye to my ain bed
And lay you neist the wa'."

6. "Oh haud awa frae me she says
I pray you let me be
I winna be in your bed
Till ye dress dishes three
Dishes three ye maun dress me
Gin I should eat them a'
Afore I lie in your bed
Either at stock or wa'.

7. It's ye maun get to my supper
A cherry without a stane
And ye maun get to my supper
A chicken without a bane
And ye maun get to my supper
A bird without a ga'
Or I winna lie in your bed
Either at stock or wa'."

8. It's when the cherry is in its bloom
I'm sure it has nae stane
And when the chicken is in its shell
I'm sure it has nae bane
The dove she is a gentle bird
She flies withoot a ga'.
Sae we'll baith lie in ae bed
And ye'll lie neist the wa'.

9. Oh haud your tongue young man she says
Nor that way me perplex
For ye maun tell me questions
And that is questions six
Questions six ye maun tell me
And that is three times twa
Afore I lie in your bed
Either at stock or wa'.

10. What's greener than the greenest grass?
What's higher than the trees?
What is worse than woman's wish?
What's deeper than the seas?
What bird sings first and
Whereupon first doth the dew down fa'
Tell me afore I lay me doon
Between you & the wa'.

11. Holly's greener than the grass
Heaven's higher than the trees
The devil's worse than woman's wish
Hell's deeper than the seas
The cock craws first on cedar tap
The dew doon first doth fa'.
So we'll baith be in ae bed
And ye'll lie neist the wa'.

12. Oh haud your tongue young man she says
And gie your pleadin over
And unless you find me ferlies
And that is ferlies four
Ferlies four ye maun find me
And that is twa & twa
Or I'll never lie in your bed
Either at stock or wa'.

13. It's ye maun get to me a plum
That in December grew
And ye maun get a silk mantle
That waft was ne'er ca'ed through
A sparrow's horn, a priest unborn
This night to join us twa
Or I'll nae lie in your bed
Either at stock or wa'.

14. My father he has winter fruit
That in December grew
My mother has an Indian gown
That waft was ne'er ca'ed through
A sparrow's horn is quickly found
There's ane on ilka claw
And twa upon the nib o' him
And ye shall get them a'.

15. The priest he's standing at the door
Just ready to come in
Nae man can say that he was born
Nae man unless he sin
A wild boar tore his mother's side
He oot o' it did fa'.
Sae we'll baith lie in ae bed
And ye'll lie neist the wa'.

16. Little thought this fair maid
That morning when she raise
That this wad be the hindmost
O' a' her maiden days.
But now there's no within the realm
I think a blyther twa
And they baith lie in ae bed
And she lies neist the wa'.

GROUP B

13. "Six Questions"

Mackenzie, 1928, p. 391; text, pp. 14-15. Sung by John Adamson, Westville, Pictou County, Nova Scotia. Text also in *JAF*, XXIII, 377, and Mackenzie, *The Quest of the Ballad*, 1919, pp. 108-110.

p I

1. The Duke of Merchant's daughter walked out one summer
day;
She met a bold sea captain by chance upon the way.
He says, "My pretty fair maid, if it wasn't for the law
I would have you in my bed this night, by either stock
or wa'."

2. She sighed and said, "Young man, O do not me perplex,
. . . .
You must answer me in questions six before that I gang awa,
Or before that I lie in your bed by either stock or wa'."

3. "O what is rounder than your ring? What's higher than the
trees?
Or what is worse than women's tongue? What's deeper
than the seas?
What bird sings first? What bird sings last? Or where does
the dew first fall?
Before that I lie in your bed by either stock or wall."

4. "The globe is rounder than your ring; sky's higher than the
trees;
The devil's worse than women's tongue; Hell's deeper than
the seas;
The roe sings first, the thirst sings last; on earth the dew
first falls,
Before that I lie in your bed by either stock or wall."

5. "You must get for me some winter fruit which in December
grew;
You must get for me a silken cloak that ne'er a waft went
through;
A sparrow's thorn, a priest new-born, before I gang awa,
Before that I lie in your bed by either stock or wa'."

6. "My father's got some winter fruit which in December
grew;
My mother's got a silken cloak that ne'er a waft went
through;
A sparrow's thorns they're easy found—there's one on every
claw;
So you and I lie in one bed, and you lie next the wa'."

7. "You must get for my wedding supper a chicken without a
bone;
You must get for my wedding supper a cherry without a
stone;
You must get for me a gentle bird, a bird without a gall,
Before that I lie in your bed by either stock or wall."

8. "O when the chicken's in the egg I'm sure it has no bone;
And when the cherry's in full bloom I'm sure it has no stone;
The dove it is a gentle bird—it flies without a gall,
Before that I lie in your bed by either stock or wall."

9. He took her by the lily-white hand and led her through
the hall;
He held her by the slender waist for fear that she would fall;
He led her on his bed of down without a doubt at all,
So he and she lies in one bed, and he lies next the wall.

14. [Captain Wedderburn]

Barry, Eckstorm, and Smyth, 1929, p. 96. Sung by Mrs.
James McGill, Chamcook, New Brunswick; learned in Scotland. Melody recorded by George Herzog.

a M

Herzog barred his copy in 12/8 time.

24. "Mr. Woodburn's Courtship"

Gardner and Chickering, 1939, pp. 139-40. Sung by Mrs.
Eliza Youngs, Greenville, Mich., 1934; learned from her
mother.

a Æ/D

1. A nobleman's fair daughter walked down a narrow lane;
She met with Mr. Woodburn, a keeper of the game.
He said unto his servants, "If it wasn't for the law,
This maid I'd have within my bed, and she would lie at
the wall."

2. "Get you gone, young man," she said, "and do not trouble
me;
Before you lie one night with me, you must get me dishes
three.
Three dishes you must get for me; suppose I eat them all,
Before you lie one night with me at either stock or wall."

3. "For my breakfast you must have a bird without a bone,
And for my dinner you must have cherries without a stone,
And for my supper you must have a bird without a gall,
Before you lie one night with me at either stock or wall."

4. "When the bird is in the egg, it really has no bone;
When cherries are in blossom, they really have no stone;
The dove she is a gentle bird, she flies without a gall;
So you and I in bed must lie, and you must lie at the wall."

5. "Get you gone, young man," she said, "and do not me perplex;
Before you lie one night with me, you must answer questions six.
Six questions you must answer me when I set forth them all
Before you lie one night with me at either stock or wall.

6. "What is rounder than a ring, what's higher than a tree?
What is worse than women, else what's deeper than the sea?
What bird sings best of three birds first, and where the dew does fall?
Before you lie one night with me at either stock or wall."

7. "The globe is rounder than the ring, heaven's higher than a tree.
The devil's worse than women, else hell's deeper than the sea.

The thrush sings best of three birds first, and there the dew does fall,
So you and I in bed must lie, and you must lie at the wall."

8. "Well, you must get me some winter fruit that in December grew.
You must get me a mantle that weft it ne'er went through.
You must get me a sparrow's horn, a priest unborn to join us one and all,
Before you lie one night with me at either stock or wall."

9. "My father has some winter fruit that in December grew,
And my mother has a mantle that weft it ne'er went through.
A sparrow's horn is easy got, there's one on every claw;
Melchesik he was a priest unborn, so you must lie at the wall.

10. .   .   .   .
.   .   .   .
Seeing she was so clever my heart she did enthrall,
I took her in my arms and rolled her from the wall."

Riddle Song

CHILD NO. 46, APPENDIX

ONE of the oldest songs in the language, this still keeps a strong hold on life. The earliest text of it that has come down is of about the same date as the earliest text of the first ballad in Child's canon—that is, of the mid-fifteenth century. In this earliest shape, the song lacks all extraneous circumstance, either of narrative frame (except the bare suggestion in "my sister sent me from oversea," &c.) or of refrain or burden. It is in long couplets, metrically so free and easy as to prove that their stress depended on the music which went with them. Doubtless, this was a dancing-song; it probably had a refrain or burden, not recorded, as do most of the later versions. Probably, again, the couplets were of seven stresses, i.e., ballad meter, as in the first version below. Unfortunately, the MS. (Sloane 2593) in which it occurs has no music. Whether it is anterior or posterior to the ballad (Child 46) of which it now forms a part is anyone's guess. My own guess is that it is of prior origin; but I do not know that I could produce very cogent arguments to support the conjecture. If it be, instead, a worn-down descendant of the ballad, it would be analogous to the "Scarborough Fair" variants of Child 2, which have little more of a narrative framework for the "tasks" than is to be found here.

There is nothing in the musical tradition, so far as we know it, to connect the ballad and the song. The earliest tune that I have found is in a manuscript of about the mid-seventeenth century, or a little later (?): here (vt. 1) it is clearly for dancing, and of a type not uncommon in that era. With one exception, later versions are all connected in one way or another; but fall into various subdivisions according to the refrain material with which at various points they have coalesced, or which they have discarded. At some period, the song picked up an acquaintance with another old ditty, "Go no more a-rushing" (vt. 16), a version of which is printed, from an old MS. of Byrd's pieces formerly in Rimbault's possession, in Chappell, I, p. 158. Chappell notes that that tune also occurs in the Fitzwilliam Virginal Book as "Tell me, Daphne" (set by Giles Farnaby, ed. 1899, II, p. 446).

Most of the variants, in both main classes, are of major tonality, although it happens that the oldest of record is a melodic minor. Several are in gapped scales, π^1, π^2, and I/Ly. All but one, a somewhat anomalous Æolian tune from Dorset (vt. 3), are authentic.

TUNES WITH TEXTS

GROUP A

1. [My Love gave me a cherry]

Edinburgh Univ. MS. DC.1.69, No. 2 (at back of MS.).

a Æ (Melodic minor)

With this tune compare the following in Playford, *The English Dancing Master*, 1650 (reprinted 1933): "Confesse" (p. 19); "Hearts Ease" (p. 54); "Jack Pudding" (p. 56); "Dissembling Love" (p. 59). These are dance-tunes in the same style, though not variants.

My Love gave me a Cherry a Cherry without a stone
My Love gave me a Chicken a Chicken without a Bone
My Love gave me a Ringe a Ringe wthout a rim
My Love gave me a Child wench a Child wench a
    [Child wench] a Child without mourninge.

2a. "I'll Give My Love an Apple"

Creighton and Senior, 1950, p. 163(A). Sung by Dennis Smith, Chezzetcook, Nova Scotia.

a Æ/D

1. I'll give my love an apple without e'er a core,
   I'll give my love a dwelling without e'er a door,
   I'll give my love a palace wherein she might be
   That she might unlock it without e'er a key.

2. How can there be an apple without e'er a core,
   How can there be a dwelling without e'er a door,
   How can there be a palace wherein she might be
   That she might unlock it without e'er a key?

3. My head is an apple without e'er a core,
   My mind is a dwelling without e'er a door,
   My heart is a palace wherein she might be
   That she might unlock it without e'er a key.

4. I'll give my love a cherry without e'er a stone,
   I'll give my love a chicken without e'er a bone,
   I'll give my love a baby and no crying.

5. How can there be a cherry without e'er a stone,
   How can there be a chicken without e'er a bone,
   How can there be a baby and no crying?

6. When the cherry's in blossom it has no stone,
   When the chicken's in the egg it has no bone,
   When the baby is a-getting there's no crying.

3. "I will give my love an apple"

Hammond, *JFSS*, III (1909), p. 114. Sung by Mr. J. Burrows, Sherborne, Dorset, July 1906. Also sung by Clive Carey on English Columbia, rec. WA 10686 (DB 335).

p Æ

Miss Gilchrist cites "Glenlogie" in Boulton, *Songs of the North,* n.d., I, pp. 2-4, as an analogous tune. Miss Broadwood presumes a Celtic origin and refers to a tune from County Antrim, published in *JIFSS*, I (1904), p. 58.

I will give my love an apple without e'er a core;
I will give my love a house without e'er a door;
I will give my love a palace wherein she may be,
And she may unlock it without e'er a key.

My head is the apple without e'er a core,
My mind is the house without e'er a door,
My heart is the palace wherein she may be,
And she may unlock it without e'er a key.

I will give my love a cherry without e'er a stone,
I will give my love a chick without e'er a bone,
I will give my love a ring, not a rent to be seen,
I will give my love children without any crying.

When the cherry's in blossom, there's never no stone,
When the chick's in the womb, there's never no bone,
And, when they're rinning running [the ring is running?],
                                  not a rent's to be seen,
And, when they're [love-making],* they're seldom crying.

   * *Sic* Hammond, *pudoris causa* for *a-getting?*

7. [The Riddle Song]

Sharp MSS., 3621/2688. Also in Sharp and Karpeles, 1932, II, p. 190(A). Sung by Mrs. Wilson, Pineville, Ky., May 2, 1917.

a π²

Sharp's MS. copy is in A major.
A variant nearly allied to this is sung by Burl Ives on Keynote, rec. No. 6315, Album K-3. Also, the copy printed by M. E. Henry, 1938, p. 141, is very close. It may likewise be mentioned that a variant of "The Wagoner's Lad," sung by Buell Kazee on Brunswick, rec. No. 213B (069), is basically the present tune in triple time.

I gave my love a cherry that* has no stones,
I gave my love a chicken that has no bones,
I gave my love a ring that has no end,
I gave my love a baby that's no cry-en.

How can there be a cherry that has no stones?
How can there be a chicken that has no bones?
How can there be a ring that has no end?
How can there be a baby that's no cry-en?

A cherry when it's blooming it has no stones,
A chicken when it's pipping it has no bones,
A ring when it's rolling it has no end,
A baby when it's sleeping there's no cry-en.

   * Sharp's MS. note: "It was difficult to hear whether Mrs. Wilson said 'it' or 'that.'"

GROUP C

14. [A Paradox]

Mason, 1878 [ed. of 1908], p. 23.

m I/Ly (– VI)

I have four brothers over the sea,
   Perry, merry, dictum, domine;
They each sent a present unto me,
   Perry, merry, dictum, domine.
      Partum quartum pare dissentum,
   Perry, merry, dictum, domine.

The first sent a chicken without any bone,
   Perry, &c.
The second a cherry without any stone,
   Perry, &c.
      Partum, &c.

The third sent a book that no man could read,
  Perry, &c.
The fourth sent a blanket without any thread,
  Perry, &c.
    Partum, &c.

How could there be a chicken without any bone?
  Perry, &c.
How could there be a cherry without any stone?
  Perry, &c.
    Partum, &c.

How could there be a book that no man could read?
  Perry, &c.
How could there be a blanket without any thread?
  Perry, &c.
    Partum, &c.

When the chicken is in the egg, it has no bone,
  Perry, &c.
When the cherry is in the blossom, it has no stone,
  Perry, &c.
    Partum, &c.

When the book is in the press, no man can it read,
  Perry, &c.
When the blanket is in the fleece, it has no thread,
  Perry, &c.
    Partum, &c.

Barrett's note: "This melody which is still to be heard in country places appears in Queen Elizabeth's Virginal Book with the same title, and probably was sung to the same words three hundred years ago."
  The Elizabethan tune is properly "Tell me, Daphne." Cf. Chappell, *Popular Music*, I, 1855, p. 158.

m Æ (inflected VII)

Go no more a rushing, maids, in May;
Go no more a rushing, maids, I pray;
Go no more a rushing, or you'll fall a blushing,
Bundle up your rushes and haste away.
You promised me a cherry without any stone,
You promised me a chicken without any bone,
You promised me a ring that has no rim at all,
And you promised me a bird without a gall.

How can there be a cherry without a stone?
How can there be a chicken without a bone?
How can there be a ring without a rim at all?
How can there be a bird that hasn't got a gall?
When the cherry's in the flower it has no stone;
When the chicken's in the egg it hasn't any bone;
When the ring it is a making it has no rim at all;
And the dove it is a bird without a gall.

16. [Go No More a-Rushing]

Barrett [1891], p. 62.

Proud Lady Margaret

CHILD NO. 47

This ballad appears not to have wandered often beyond the Scottish boundaries. Reed Smith announced it, by title only, as found in America, but his copy is not discovered. No American tune is as yet on the record.

The three extant tunes are of dates approximately fifty years apart, and seem to have no relation to one another. The first sounds as if drawn out of eighteenth-century hymnody, in keeping with the moralizing tone of the ballad as we have it. On the other hand, this may be no more than a pious influence acting on folk material. Such give-and-take between sacred and secular is, of course, not at all uncommon, especially in Scotland. The second tune is, according to Christie, a major variant of "The Laird abeen the Dee." The third sounds like a fragmentary recollection of the "Gilderoy" tune, worn down to a repeated double phrase.

It is again apparent that we have here no strong single tradition: nothing would indicate that these tunes had not been sharked up for a late text wherever they came conveniently to hand.

TUNES WITH TEXTS

1. "The Knicht o' Archerdale"

Harris Music MS., No. 1; text, Harris MS., fol. 7, No. 3. Also in Child, 1882-98, V, p. 414; text, I, pp. 430-31.

a Æ

1. There cam a knicht to Archerdale,
      His steed was winder sma,
   An there he spied a lady bricht,
      Luikin owre her castle wa.

2. "Ye dinna seem a gentle knicht,
      Though on horseback ye do ride;
   Ye seem to be some sutor's son,
      Your butes they are sae side."

3. "Ye dinna seem a lady gay,
      Though ye be bound wi pride;
   Else I'd gane bye your father's gate
      But either taunt or gibe."

4. He turned aboot his hie horse head,
      An awa he was boun to ride,
   But neatly wi her mouth she spak:
      Oh bide, fine squire, oh bide.

5. "Bide, oh bide, ye hindy squire,
      Tell me mair o your tale;
   Tell me some o that wondrous lied
      Ye've learnt in Archerdale.

6. "What gaes in a speal?" she said,
      "What in a horn green?
   An what gaes on a lady's head,
      Whan it is washen clean?"

7. "Ale gaes in a speal," he said,
      "Wine in a horn green;
   An silk gaes on a lady's head,
      Whan it is washen clean."

8. Aboot he turned his hie horse head,
      An awa he was boun to ride,
   When neatly wi her mouth she spak:
      Oh bide, fine squire, oh bide.

9. "Bide, oh bide, ye hindy squire,
      Tell me mair o your tale;
   Tell me some o that unco lied
      You've learnt in Archerdale.

10. "Ye are as like my ae brither
      As ever I did see;
   But he's been buried in yon kirkyaird
      It's mair than years is three."

11. "I am as like your ae brither
      As ever ye did see;
   But I canna get peace into my grave,
      A' for the pride o thee."

12. "Leave pride, Janet, leave pride, Janet,
    Leave pride an vanitie;
    If ye come the roads that I hae come,
    Sair warned will ye be.

13. "Ye come in by yonder kirk
    Wi the goud preens in your sleeve;
    When you're bracht hame to yon kirkyaird,
    You'll gie them a' thier leave.

14. "Ye come in to yonder kirk
    Wi the goud plaits in your hair;
    When you're bracht hame to yon kirkyaird,
    You will them a' forbear."

15. He got her in her mither's bour,
    Puttin goud plaits in her hair;
    He left her in her father's gairden,
    Mournin her sins sae sair.

The Two Brothers

CHILD NO. 49

This Scottish ballad was not known to the world until the beginning of the nineteenth century. It disappeared from Scotland for about a century, but has latterly reappeared in a number of melodically related variants there; and abundant copies have been found in America, along the Eastern Seaboard both South and North, in the Appalachians, and as far West as the Ozarks.

The American variants show clear marks of family relationship wherever they have been collected, although they are by no means always close variants. Rhythmically, a slight preference is shown for triple measure, but usually compound, as 6/8, 6/4, 3/2, and rarely simple 3/4.

The tunes in this case are separated quite strictly according to the middle cadence: the tonic, the supertonic,* the dominant, and the upper octave. Roughly speaking, all the tunes in Group A, and probably all but one in Group B, are in a major tonality; but Group C shows a drift toward minor tonality, and so does Group D. Mixolydian leanings appear in Groups C and D (and E). About a third of the total are genuinely hexatonic; five are pentatonic. Group B is consistently plagal; Group D, authentic; A and C are divided between plagal and authentic variants. No marked regional distinctions are discernible.

* Variant 13.1 rises from the second to the fourth.

TUNES WITH TEXTS

GROUP A

1. [The Two Brothers]

Sharp MSS., 3770/2781. Also in Sharp and Karpeles, 1932, I, pp. 73(I)-74. Sung by Mrs. Ollie Huff, Berea, Knox County, Ky., May 31, 1917.

p I

There's two little brothers going to school.
The oldest to the youngest called:
Come go with me to the green shady grove
And I'll wrestle you a fall.

They went to the green shady grove,
Where they wrestled up and down.
The oldest to the youngest said:
You've given me a deadly wound.

Rip my shirt from off my back,
Rip it from gore to gore,
And then tie up those bleeding wounds,
And they won't bleed no more.

He ripped his shirt off of his back,
Ripped it from gore to gore,
And then tied up those bleeding wounds,
And they did bleed no more.

When you go home tell mother dear,
If she isn't quarrelling about me,
Tell her I'm laid at the new church-yard,
Let be what church it may.

* * * * *

She mourned and she mourned,
She mourned for little Willie,
She nearly mourned him out of his grave
To come home and be with her.

4. [The Two Brothers]

Wilkinson MSS., 1935-36, p. 35(B). Sung by Mrs. Kit Williamson, Evington, Va., October 19, 1935.

p I (– VI)

Two brothers, dear brothers, walked out one day
To view the chestnut grove.
The youngest had a long, keen knife,
And he stoved it through the older one's heart.

GROUP B

11. [The Two Brothers]

Sharp MSS., 3688/2747. Also in Sharp and Karpeles, 1932, I, pp. 71(G)-72. Sung by Mrs. Delia Knuckles, Barbourville, Knox County, Ky., May 16, 1917.

p I

1. O brother, O brother, play ball with me,
   Or will you either throw a stone,
   Or will you go to yon shady grove
   And there we'll wrestle and throw?

2. I'll not play ball* with you,
   Or either will I throw a stone;
   But if you'll go to yon shady grove
   There we will wrestle and throw.

3. O brother, O brother, you've wounded me,
   You've wounded me so bad.
   Go and tear my shirt from off my back
   And tear it from gore to gore,
   And wrap it around my bleeding wound
   That it won't bleed no more.

4. He tore his shirt from off his back,
   And tore it from gore to gore.
   And wrapped it around his bleeding wound
   That it might bleed no more.

5. If you meet my father, as you turn round home,
   Enquiring for his son John,
   Go tell him I've gone to Langford's Town
   To bring those new books home.

6. If you meet my mother, as you turn round home,
   Enquiring for her son John,
   Go tell her I'm gone to the cottage gate
   To learn to sing and pray.

7. If you meet my true love, as you turn round home,
   Enquiring for her true love John,
   Go tell her I'm buried in the old churchyard,
   And it's for her sake I'm gone.

8. He met his father, as he turned round home,
   Enquiring for his son John.
   O father, O father, he's gone to Langford's Town
   To bring those new books home.

9. He met his mother, as he turned round home,
   Enquiring for her son John.
   O mother, O mother, he's gone to the cottage gate
   To learn to sing and pray.

10. He met his true love, as he turned round home,
    Enquiring for her true love John.
    O true love, O true love, he's buried in the old churchyard,
    And it's for your sake he's gone.

11. They buried his bible at his head,
    His testament at his feet,
    And on his breast his little hymn-book,
    That with them he might sleep.

* 1932: "play at ball"

13.1. "The Twa Brothers"

Archive, School of Scottish Studies, rec. No. 1958/25/B19. Sung by Jeannie Robertson, Aberdeenshire. Collected by Hamish Henderson. Transcribed by the Editor, after James Porter.

p D/Æ

1. There were twa brotheris at the schuil,
   An when they got awa,
   'It's will ye play at the stane-chuckin,
   Or will ye play the baa
   Or will ye gae up tae yon bonnie, green hill,
   An there we'll wrastle a faa?'

2. 'I willnae play at the stàne-chuckin,
   Or will I play at the baa,
   But I'll gae up tae yon bonnie, green hill,
   And there we'll wrastle a faa.'

3. They wrastl't up, they wrastl't down,
   Till John fell to the ground,
   But a dirk fell out of William's pooch,
   Gave John a deadly wound.

4. 'Oh, lift me, lift me on your back;
   Tak me to yon well sae fair,
   An wash the blood frae off my wound,
   That it may bleed nae mair.

5. He's liftit him upon his back,
   Taen him to yon well sae fair;
   He's washed the blood frae off his wound,
   But aye it bled the mair.

6. 'Oh, ye'll take off my holland sark,
   Rive it frae gair tae gair,
   Ye'll stuff it in the bloody wound,
   That it may bleed nae mair.'

7. For he's taen off his holland sark,
   Rived it frae gair tae gair;
   He's stuffed it in the bloody wound,
   But it bled mair an mair.

8. 'Oh lift me, lift me on your back;
   Tak me tae Kirkland fair,
   An dig a grave baith wide an deep
   And lay my body there.

9. 'Ye'll lay my arrows at my head,
   My bent bow at my feet,
   My sword an buckler by my side,
   As I wes wont tae sleep.'

19. [The Two Brothers]

Sharp MSS., 3972/2856. Also in Sharp and Karpeles, 1932,
I, pp. 69(F)-70; and, with piano accompaniment, in Sharp,
1918, p. 7. Sung by Mrs. Margaret Dunagan, St. Helen's,
Lee County, Ky., September 5, 1917.

p I

1. O brother, can you toss the stone,
   Or can you play the ball?
   I am too little, I am too young,
   Go, brother, let me alone.

2. His brother took his little penknife,
   He hung it up* by his side,
   He put it deeply deathly wound
   As it hung by his side.

3. O brother, take my holland shirt,
   And rip it from gore to gore;
   You tie it around my bleeding wound
   And still it'll bleed no more.

4. His brother took his holland shirt
   And ripped it from gore to gore;
   He tied it around his bleeding wound,
   But still it bled the more.

5. O brother, take me on your back,
   Carry me to Chesley Town;
   You dig me a deep and large, wide grave
   And lay me there so sound.

6. You put my bible at my head,
   My solberd (psalter?) at my feet,
   My little bow and arrow at my side,
   And sounder I will sleep.

7. His brother took him on his back,
   He carried him to Chesley Town;
   He dug him a deep and large, wide grave
   And laid him there so sound.

8. He put his bible at his head,
   His solberd at his feet,
   His little bow and arrow at his side,
   So sounder he will sleep.

9. O brother, as you go home at night
   And my mother asks for me,
   You tell her I'm along with some schoolboys,
   So merry I'll come home.

10. And if my true love asks for me,
    The truth to her you'll tell;
    You'll tell her I'm dead and in grave laid
    And buried in Chesley Town.

11. With my bible at my head,
    My solberd at my feet,
    My little bow and arrow at my side,
    And sounder I will sleep.

12. And as his brother went home at night,
    His mother asked for him.
    He told he's along with some schoolboys,
    So merry he'll come home.

13. And then his true love asked for him;
    The truth to her he told.
    He told he was dead and in grave laid
    And buried in Chesley Town.

14. With his bible at his head,
    His solberd at his feet,
    His little bow and arrow at his side,
    So sounder he will sleep.

15. And then his true love put on small hoppers
    And tied them with silver strings.
    She went hopping all over her true love's grave
    A twelve-months and a day.

16. She hopped the red fish out of the sea,
    The small birds out of their nests;
    She hopped her true love out of his grave,
    So he can't see no rest.

17. Go home, go home, you rambling reed;
    Don't weep nor mourn for me;
    If you do for twelve long years,
    No more you'll see of me.

* 1932: *del.* up

GROUP C

22. "The Dying Soldier"

E. C. and M. N. Kirkland, *SFQ*, II (1938), p. 66. Sung by
Miss Nanie McNew, Carlisle, Ky., July 25, 1937. Recorded
by Dr. Claudius Capps.

m I/Ly

This has typical affiliations with "Barbara Allen" (84; cf., e.g.,
Sharp and Karpeles, 1932, I, p. 191[I]). Cf. also "Lizie Wan" (51)
and "Edward" (13).

Oh, Willie, take my highland shirt,
Tear it from gore to gore,
And wrop it around my bleeding wounds,
And I will bleed no more.

Willie took his highland shirt,
Tore it from gore to gore,
And wropt it around his bleeding wounds;
He still bled more and more.

Oh, Willie, take me on your back
And carry me to the church door,
And lay me down on the cold ground
And I will bleed no more.

Willie took him on his back
And carried him to the church door,
And laid him down on the cold ground
And he bled more and more.

Oh, Willie, go dig my grave,
Dig it both wide and deep,
And place my prayer book by my side,
A marble stone at my head and feet.

25. [The Two Brothers]

Sharp MSS., 3563/2633. Also in Sharp and Karpeles, 1932,
I, p. 76(L). Sung by Mrs. James A. Maples, Bird's Creek,
Sevierville, Tenn., April 16, 1917.

a M (– VI)

Little Willie, can't* you throw a ball,
Nor even cast a stone?
No, I'm too small to throw a ball,
Or even cast a stone.

Little Willie had a new penknife
Which was both keen and sharp
He pierced little Johnnie to the side
And quickly touched his heart.

Go bury my Bible at my head,
My Testament at my feet,
And if any of them ask for me,
Pray tell them I'm asleep.

* 1932: "can"

29. "John and William"

McGill, 1917, pp. 54-58.

a D (– II; inflected VII)

This beautiful variant has relations with "Young Hunting" (68)
and "Lady Gay" (79).

1. O John and William walkèd out one day
   To view the iron band.
   Says John to William, "At any price
   We'd better turn home again."

2. "O no," says William, "That can never be
   That we'll return again,
   For I'm the one loves pretty Susanne
   And I will murder thee."

3. "What will you tell to my mother dear,
   When she askès for her son John?"
   "I left him at the cottage school
   His lessons for to learn."

4. "What will you tell to my father dear,
   When he askès for his son John?"
   "I left him in the high wild woods
   A-learnin' his hounds to run."

5. "What will you tell to my pretty Susanne
   When she askès for her true love John?"
   "I left him in the grave-lie deep,
   Never more to return."

6. She mourned the fish all out of the sea,
   The birds all out of the nest;
   She mourned her true love out of his grave
   Because that she could not rest.

7. "What do you want, my pretty Susanne,
    What do you want with me?"
    "A kiss or two from your pretty bright lips
    Is all that I ask of thee."

8. "Go home, go home, my pretty Susanne,
    Go home, go home," said he;
    "If you weep and mourn all the balance of your days
    You'll never more see me."

GROUP D

37. [The Two Brothers]

Wilkinson MSS., 1935-36, pp. 36-37(C). Sung by Mrs. Mary McAllister, Grottoes, Va., October 30, 1935.

a D

1. One evening two brothers was going from school;
    They fell into a play.
    The oldest said to the youngest one:
    Let's take a wrestle and fall.

2. The oldest threw the youngest down;
    He threwed him on the ground.
    And out of his pocket a pen-knife drew,
    And give him a deathly wound.

3. Pick me up, pick me up, all on your back,
    And carry me to yonder's church yard.
    And dig my grave both wide and deep
    And gently lie me down.

4. Take off, take off, your woolen shirt,
    And tear it from gore to gore.
    And wrap it around my bloody wound,
    So it won't bleed anymore.

5. He took off his woolen shirt.
    He tore it from gore to gore.
    He wrapt it around his bloody wound,
    But still it bled the more.

6. What must I tell your loving old father,
    This night when I go home?
    Tell him I'm in some lonely greenwoods
    A-learning young hounds to run.

7. What must I tell your loving old mother,
    This night when I go home?
    Tell her I'm at some college school
    My books to carry home.

8. What must I tell your loving little Susie,
    This night when I go home?
    Tell her I'm in some lonely church yard
    To never turn back (home) no more.

9. He picked him up all on his back,
    And carried him to yonder's church yard.
    He dug his grave both wide and deep
    And gently laid him down.

10. She took her banjo all in her arms,
    . . . .
    She charmed the fishes out of the sea,
    Young Johnny out of his grave.

Lizie Wan

CHILD NO. 51

This ballad, which might have been supposed to have died a hundred and fifty years ago, has surprisingly been recovered in late copies on both sides of the Atlantic. The theme is one not much affected in the last century. But the music gives evidence of a continuous and unbroken tradition, which would seem to indicate that where this ballad has been learned it has neither made a vague impression nor become confused. On the contrary, it may be much more generally known than appears from the record, and kept close from casual collectors—strangers at best.

There appears to be a definite, if unconscious, association in folk tradition between this ballad and "Edward." Such a connection is suggested both melodically and textually. The fact might lend some countenance to Barry's interpretation of "Edward" as a ballad on the incest-theme, although there is no hint of this on the surface of any text except, possibly, the (famous) Dalrymple-Percy version.

Perhaps all copies of the present ballad's tune should be classed as plagal majors, although the Vermont copies have the dropped ending (Mixolydian), and the Kentucky copy lacks the seventh (I/M). One copy only is of English record.

Melodic relations may be noted with "The Unquiet Grave" (78) and "Little Musgrave" (81).

TUNES WITH TEXTS

2. [Lizie Wan]

Sharp MSS., 3838/2810. Also in Sharp and Karpeles, 1932, I, p. 89. Sung by Benjamin J. Finlay, Manchester, Clay County, Ky., August 10, 1917.

p I/M

Compare "Edward" (13) in Sharp and Karpeles, 1932, I, p. 50(F), and "The Cruel Mother" (20), a Kentucky variant in *JFSS*, II, p. 109, from Esther White.

1. Fair Lucy sitting in her father's room,
   Lamenting and a-making her mourn;
   And in steps her brother James:
   O what's fair Lucy done?

2. It is time for you to weep,
   Lamenting and a-making your mourn.
   Here's a babe at my right side,
   And it is both mine and yourn.

3. O what will you do when your father comes home?
   Dear son, come tell to me.
   I'll set my foot into some little ship
   And I'll sail plumb over the sea.

4. O what will you do with your house and land?
   Dear son, come tell to me.
   I'll leave it here, my old, dear mother;
   Be kind to my children three.

5. O what will you do with your pretty, little wife?
   Dear son, come tell to me.
   She can set her foot in another little ship
   And follow after me.

6. Back home, back home will you return?
   Dear son, come tell to me.
   When the sun and moon sets in yon hill,
   And I hope that'll never be.

4. "Fair Lucy"

Flanders, *BFSSNE*, No. 7 (1934), p. 7(1). Sung by Mrs. Alice Slayton Sicily, North Calais, Vt., July 28, 1933. From *Bulletin of the Folk-Song Society of the Northeast*, No. 7 (1934), edited by Phillips Barry; copyright 1934 by the Folk-Song Society of the Northeast.

p I, ending on *V*; or a M

1. Fair Lucy was sitting in her own cabin door,
   Making her laments alone;
   Who should come by but her own mother dear,
   Saying, "What makes Fair Lucy mourn?"

2. "I have a cause for to grieve," she said,
   "And a reason for to mourn;
   For the babe that lies in the cradle asleep,
   Dear mother, it is his own."

3. Fair Lucy was sitting in her own cabin door,
   Making her laments alone;
   Who should come by but her own brother dear,
   Saying, "What makes Fair Lucy mourn?"

4. "I have a cause for to grieve," she said,
   "And a reason for to mourn;
   For the babe that lies in the cradle asleep,
   Dear brother, it is your own."

5. He took her by the lily-white hand
   And he led her into the woods;
   What he did there, I never can declare,
   But he spilt Fair Lucy's blood.

6. "O, what is that upon your frock,
   My son, come tell to me."
   "It is one drop of Fair Lucy's blood,
   And that you plainly can see."

7. "What will your father say to you,
   When he returns to me?"
   "I shall step my foot on board a ship,
   And my face he never shall see."

8. "What will you do with your three little babes,
   My son, come tell to me?"
   "I shall leave them here at my father's command,
   For to keep him companee."

9. "What will you do with your pretty little wife,
   My son, come tell to me?"
   "She shall step her foot on board a ship,
   And sail the ocean with me."

10. "What will you do with your houses and lands,
    My son, come tell to me?"
    "I shall leave them here at my father's command,
    For to set my children free."

11. "When will you return again,
    My son, come tell to me?"
    "When the sun and the moon set on yonders green hill,
    And I'm sure that never can be."

The King's Dochter Lady Jean

CHILD NO. 52

THIS is another ballad of which only a Scottish tradition is known. It is a little hard to see why Child did not rank it as a version of his No. 50 ("The Bonny Hind"), for it shows no more divergence from that ballad than do the versions of a number of others which he has united, e.g., "Lady Isabel" (4), "Leesome Brand" (15).

Three of the seven recorded tunes were collected by Greig at the beginning of the present century, and another related Scottish variant quite recently. Surprisingly, an American ver-

sion, perhaps a little too literary and reminiscent of other ballads (especially Child No. 39, both text and tune), has lately been recovered in upper New York State from a singer with a phenomenally rich repertory. Her tune's contour is an analogue of a favorite and ancient type which we have already met more than once, and of which many examples have been noted in *Journal of the American Musicological Society*, III (1950), dating from the twelfth century to now.

TUNES WITH TEXTS

GROUP A

1. [Lady Jean]

Motherwell, 1827, App'x No. 23; text, p. xxi. Noted by Andrew Blaikie, Paisley.

p Æ

This may be compared especially with C. K. Sharpe's copy of "The Cruel Mother" (20). Cf. also "The Sprig of Thyme" (Sharp, *One Hundred English Folksongs*, 1916, No. 34, p. 79).

The king's young daughter was sitting in her window
    Sewing at her fine silken seam,
She luikit out at her braw bower window
    And she saw the leaves growin' green, my love,
    And she saw the leaves growing green.

1.1. "Queen Jane"

Sung by Sara Cleveland, Brant Lake, N.Y., June 1965. Folk-Legacy LP, rec. No. FSA-33(A2). Collected and recorded by Sandy Paton.

p D/Æ

1. Queen Jane sat at her window one day
A-sewing a silken seam;
She looked out at the merry green woods
And saw the green nut tree,
And saw the green nut tree.

2. She dropped her thimble at her heel
And her needle at her toe,
And away she ran to the merry green woods
To gather nuts and so,
To gather nuts and so.

3. She scarce had reached the merry green woods,
Scarce had pulled nuts two or three,
When a proud forester came striding by,
Saying, "Fair maid, let those be."
Saying, "Fair maid, let those be.

4. "Why do you pull the nuts," he said,
"And why do you break the tree?
And why do you come to this merry green woods
Without the leave of me,
Without the leave of me?"

5. "Oh, I will pull the nuts," she said,
"And I will break the tree,
And I will come to this merry green woods;
I'll ask no leave of thee,
I'll ask no leave of thee."

6. He took her by the middle so small
And he gently laid her down,
And when he took what he longed for,
He raised her from the ground,
He raised her from the ground.

7. "Oh, woe to you, proud forester,
And an ill death may yours be.
Since I'm the King's youngest daughter," she cried,
"You will pay for wronging me,
You will pay for wronging me."

8. "If you're the King's youngest daughter," he said,
   "Then I'm his eldest son;
   And woe unto this unhappy hour
   And the wrong that I have done,
   And the wrong that I have done.

9. "The very first time I came from sea,
   O Jane, you were unborn;
   And I wish my gallant ship had sunk
   And I'd been left forlorn,
   And I'd been left forlorn.

10. "The very next time I came from sea
    You were on your nurse's knee;
    And the very next time I came from sea
    You were in this woods with me,
    You were in this woods with me.

11. "I wish I ne'er had seen your face,
    Or that you had ne'er seen mine;
    That we ne'er had met in this merry green woods
    And this wrong could be undone,
    And this wrong could be undone."

12. "I wish to God my babe was born
    And on its nurse's knee,
    And, as for me, I was dead and gone
    And the green grass growing over me,
    And the green grass growing over me."

GROUP B

3. [Fair Rosie Ann]

Greig MSS., III, p. 166; text, Bk. 742, XXXII, pp. 86ff.
Also in Greig and Keith, 1925, p. 39(a). Sung by Alexander Robb, New Deer, Aberdeenshire, March 1909.

a I

Keith notes the relation with "The Douglas Tragedy" (7). Cf.
also the English variants of "Lady Isabel and the Elf Knight" (4).

1. Fair Rosie Ann sat on her castle wa',
   Sewing at her satin seam,
   And she's awa to good greenwoods
   Some nuts for to pull & bring hame.

2. She hadna pulled a nut, a nut,
   A nut but barely three,
   When a young man entered into the wood,
   To ruin her fair bodie[.]

3. Oh cam' ye here to pull my nuts?
   Or cam' ye here to be my slave?
   Or cam' ye here, kind sir, she said,
   For to put me in my grave?

4. I came nae here to pull your nuts,
   Nor I came nae to be your slave,
   But your mantle or your maidenhead
   Some o' them I maun have[.]

5. It's if ye tak' my mantle, she said,
   My mother can caird & spin,
   But if ye tak' my maidenhead
   There's nae pardon for the sin.

* * * * *

6. Since ye've gotten your wills (*sic*) o' me,
   Your wills o' me ye've ta'en,
   Would you be so good, kind sir, she said,
   As to tell me your name?

7. My name, my name, fair maid, he said,
   My name I'll never deny,
   For I'm Lord Barnet's ae only son,
   And he never had another but I.

8. If ye be Lord Barnet's ae only son,
   There's little between thee & me,
   For I'm Lord Barnet's ae daughter,
   And he never had another but me.

9. Heel weel, heel weel, my sister dear,
   Heel weel, heel weel, on me;
   For I wish my ship she had been wrecked,
   And sunk to the bottom of the sea.

10. Fair Rosie Ann sat in good greenwoods,
    Lamentin' for what she had done,
    When her mother entered into the wood,
    Says, What ails thee, fair Rosie Ann?

11. As I cam' in by yon high high hill,
    And in by yon high castle wa',
    Oh heavy, heavy was the stone
    That on my foot did fa'.

12. O fair Rosie Ann, dry up your tears,
    And come awa hame wi' me,
    For your brother John is new come home,
    Is new come home from sea.

13. Haud your tongue, dear mother, she said,
    Oh haud your tongue frae me;
    For he may be made welcome by a' the hoose,
    But he'll never be made welcome by me.

Young Beichan

CHILD NO. 53

THIS ballad, whatever its earlier history may have been, has enjoyed in the last century, and apparently still enjoys, a popularity as great as almost any ballad in the record. It is a popularity which has been frequently fortified in its verbal text by the broadside press; but the remarkably wide spread of a vigorous and consistent musical tradition proves with equal clarity that there has been no interruption in oral transmission. For access to a printed tune can only have been possible in very recent years, and then hardly among the class of singers from whom ninety-nine per cent of our variants have been gathered. What has occurred, we may suppose, is that singers have continuously learned the song from other singers; but that, knowing it so, they have refreshed or revised their notions of the words from time to time by the sight of the printed ballad-sheets. Moreover, the occasional discovery, by collectors, of a good many manuscript collections of "song-ballets" among undeniably "folk" singers, provides further evidence of a practice which, while it can have done little to increase the poetic merit of these old things, must yet have done much to prevent the extremes of mutilation by dullness or forgetfulness, and must often have enabled them to survive at all. Thus, far from agreeing with Scott's Jenny Laidlaw that printing (or writing) would stop the singing of her ballads, we should rather conclude that it was one of the most potent aids in keeping them alive. Jenny was only expressing the usual distrust of the uninstructed for "book-learning." And what has been true for the nineteenth century must have been true for the eighteenth, seventeenth, and even sixteenth, though in ever lessening degree as literacy became more and more restricted. It is natural to suppose that anyone who loved to sing narrative songs, and who had experienced the annoyances of forgetfulness, would be glad to put himself beyond the reach of such annoyance by securing a record if he could. That he did not more often succeed is our misfortune as well as his. Of course, the breath of life itself lay in the music, which made him wish to keep the songs in mind and perpetuated oral transmission. He would not sing from book, but would merely resort to his copy upon need. Nevertheless, tradition, for at least the last three hundred years, is inextricably bound up with writing, whether printed or manuscript, and we must reckon this element a potent and positive force in our study, rather than the purely negative and deleterious influence it has been too generally accounted. All this is not to deny the vulgarity and relative inferiority of many of the texts so perpetuated: it is merely to insist that an inferior text is better than no text at all. No text at all, for one thing, must have meant, sooner or later, no tune at all; and the value of the music gathered from singing tradition with the merest orts of texts is beyond argument.

There is no extant tune for the present ballad earlier than the earliest verbal records—that is to say, than the second half of the eighteenth century. It is an interesting, and may be a significant, fact in the development of the musical tradition that the earliest tunes we have are in common time, and the vast majority of later ones in triple time. It is also a fact that most of the nineteenth-century records are in 3/4, and of the twentieth-century in 3/2, time; but this, probably, indicates no real difference in the singing—only a change in the conventions of notation. The change (if there was one) from duple to triple rhythm, however, would be significant, because it might confirm our hypothesis, already suggested, that five-time and three-time, when they take the pattern, as they generally do in the variants here to be seen, of ♩♩♩ ♩|♩♩♩ and ♩♩♩. ♩|♩♩♩., are traditional developments or extensions of common or duple time. The probable sequence is as follows, although some of the steps might be skipped:

♩|♩♩♩♩|♩♩♩ to ♩|♩♩♩. ♪|♩♩♩.

to ♩|♩♩♩ ♩|♩♩♩ to ♩|♩♩♩. ♩|♩♩♩.

(=♪♪♪♪. ♪|♪♪♪♪.) or to ♩♩♩|♩. ♩♩♩|♩.

(=♪♪♪|♩. ♪♪♪|♩.) Cf. *Western Folklore*, XI (October 1952), p. 245.

The identity of the tune has persisted with quite remarkable clarity through most of the variants noted. Apart from half a dozen cases that seem to have stronger affiliations elsewhere, there is hardly any question of membership in the large class, and the following groups comprise not distinct traditions but subdivisions according to where the mid-cadences lie. Of these, the group with mid-cadence on the fifth is nearly twice as large as its nearest competitor in popularity, with mid-cadence on the supertonic.

TUNES WITH TEXTS

GROUP Aa

1. "Lord Bakeman"

Flanders and Olney, 1953, pp. 54-57. Sung by Asa Davis, Milton, Vt., June 23, 1939; learned from his grandfather, Charles Atkins, of Duxbury, Vt. From *Ballads Migrant in New England*, edited by Helen Hartness Flanders and Marguerite Olney; copyright 1953 by Helen Hartness Flanders.

a I

The variants are from the later recording, in the H. H. Flanders Collection of New England Folk Songs, Middlebury College, Vermont, Vol. I. (LP phonographic disc)

1. In India lived a noble lord,
   Whose riches were beyond compare;
   He was the darling of his parents,
   And of his estate the only heir.

2. Oh, he had gold and he had silver,
   And he had houses of high degree,
   But he could never be contented,
   Until a voyage he had been to sea.

3. He sail-ed east, he sail-ed west,
   Until he came to the Turkish shore.
   There he was taken and put in prison,
   Where he could neither see nor hear.

4. For seven long months he lay lamenting,
   He lay lamenting in iron chains.
   There happened to be a brisk young lady,
   Who released him out of his iron bands.

5. The jailer had an only daughter,
   And a brisk young lady gay was she.
   As she was a-walking across the floor,
   She chanced Lord Bakeman to see.

6. She stole the keys of her father's prison,
   And vowed Lord Bakeman she would set **free.**
   She went into the prison door,
   And opened it without delay.

7. "Have you got gold, have you got silver?
   And have you houses of high degree?
   What will you give to the lady fair,
   If she from bondage will set you free?"

8. "Yes, I've got gold and I've got silver,
   And I have houses of high degree
   And I'll give them all to the lady fair,
   If she from bondage will set me free."

9. "I do not want your gold nor silver,
   Nor your houses of high degree.
   All I want for is to make me happy,
   And all I crave is your fair bodee.

10. "Let us make a bargain and make it strong,
    For seven long years it shall stand:
    You shall not marry no other woman,
    Nor I'll not marry no other man."

11. The seven long years had gone and passed.
    The seven long years were at an end.
    She pack-ed up all her rich gay clothing,
    Saying: "Now I'll go and seek a friend."

12. She sail-ed east, she sail-ed west,
    Until she came to the Indian shore.
    There she could never be contented
    Till for Lord Bakeman she did inquire.

13. She inquired for Lord Bakeman's palace
    At every corner of the street.
    She did inquire for Lord Bakeman's palace,
    Of every person she chanced to meet.

14. And when she came to Lord Bakeman's palace,
    She knocked so loud upon the ring,

There was no one so ready as the brisk young porter
To arise and let this fair lady in.

15. "Oh, is this Lord Bakeman's palace?
    And is the Lord himself within?"
    "Oh, yes, oh, yes," cries the brisk young porter.
    "He and his new bride have just entered in."

16. She wept, she wept, she wrung her hands,
    Crying, "Alas, I am undone.
    I wish I was in my native country,
    Across the seas there to remain.

17. "Tell him to send me an ounce of bread,
    And a bottle of his wine so strong,
    And ask him if he has forgot the lady
    Who released him out of his iron bands."

18. The porter went unto his master,
    He knelt so low upon one knee.
    "Arise, arise, my brisk young porter,
    And tell to me what the matter is."

19. "There is a lady stands at your gate
    And she doth weep most bitterly.
    I think she is the finest creature
    That ever I chanced my eyes to see.

20. "She's got more rings on her four fingers,
    And around her waist a diamond band;
    She's got more gold about her clothing
    Than your bride and all her kin.

21. "She wants you to send her an ounce of bread,
    And a bottle of your wine so strong,
    And ask you if you have forgot the lady
    Who released you out of your iron bands?"

22. He jumped into the middle of the floor,
    He smashed the table in pieces three.
    "You came here on a horse and saddle,
    You may ride home in a coach and three."

23. Then up spoke his new bride's mother,
    And she was a lady of high degree,
    " 'Tis you have married my only daughter,
    Why, she is none the worse for thee."

24. "But since my fair one has arrived,
    A second wedding there shall be.
    Your daughter came on a horse and saddle,
    She may ride home in a coach and three."

25. He took his fair lady by the hand;
    He led her over the marble stone.
    He changed her name from Susannah Fayer*
    To be the wife of Lord Bakeman.

26. He took her by the lily-white hand,
    He led her through from room to room,
    He changed her name from Susannah Freeman
    To be the wife of Lord Bakeman.

27. He took her by the lily-white hand,
    He led her across the marble stone,
    He changed her name from Susannah Freeman
    To be the wife of Lord Bakeman.

* For fair?

6. [Lord Bateman]

Creighton and Senior, 1950, pp. 28-29. Sung by Dennis Smith, Chezzetcook, Nova Scotia.

a M

The original timing is 6/4.

1. In India lived a noble lord,
His riches they were beyond compare,
But still he would not be contented
Until a voyage he had been to sea.

2. He sailèd east he sailèd west
Until he came to the Turkish shore,
There he was taken and put in prison
Where he could neither see nor hear.

3. The jailor had one only daughter
A nice young lady fair was she,
She stole the keys of her father's prison
And swore Lord Bateman she would set free.

4. "Let us make a bargain and make it strong,
For seven long years oh it shall stand,
You'll never wed with no other woman
Or me with any other man."

5. When seven long years was gone and past,
When seven long years was to an end,
She packed up all her rich clothing
Saying, "Now I'll go and seek my friend."

6. Then she sailèd East and she sailèd West
Enquired for Lord Bateman's palace.
Every person she chanced to meet
 . . . .

7. . . . .
She knocked upon the door,
There was none so ready as the brisk young porter
To rise and let this fair lady in.

8. "Oh is this Lord Bateman's palace,
And is the lord himself within?
And ask him if he knows the lady
That set him free from yon iron claws?"

9. "There is a lady at your door
And she does weep most bitterlee,
I think she is the finest lady
That ever my two eyes did see.

10. "She's got more gold on her four fingers
And around her waist a diamond chain,
She's got more gold about her clothing
Than your new bride and all her kin.

11. "She wants you to send her an ounce of bread
And a bottle of your wine so strong,
And ask her if she knows the lady
That let you free from yon iron strong."

12. He stamped his feet upon the floor
And broke the table in pieces three,
"Here's adieu to you my wedded bride
For this fair lady I must go see."

13. He took her by the lily white hand
And led her through from room to room,
And he changed her name for Susannah fair
And she's now called the wife of Lord Bateman.

9. [Lord Baykim]

Joyce, 1909, No. 617, p. 317. From the Forde Collection.

a M

It seems fairly certain that the timing of this copy should be triple, and not duple; and I have ventured to make the change.

12. "Lord Bateman"

Kidson, *JFSS*, I (1904), p. 240(1). Sung in Shropshire.

a M

Lord Bateman was a noble Lord,
A noble Lord of high degree.
He put his foot upon shipboard,
Some foreign country he would go see.

23. [Lord Bateman]

Sharp MSS., 663/. Sung by Mr. Jeffreys (86), **Cheddar**, September 16, 1905.

a M

Lord Bateman was a noble Lord
A noble Lord of high degree
He shipped himself on board a ship
Some foreign country he would go and see

30.2. "Lord Bateman"

Archive, School of Scottish Studies, rec. No. 1956/170/B4. Sung by the Rev. Campbell MacLean, Campbelltown, Argyllshire, as sung by his grandfather, Donald Mackenzie, of Scourie, in northwest Sutherland. Collected by Hamish Henderson. Transcribed by Francis M. Collinson.

a D

Lord Beichan was a noble lord,
A noble lord of high degree;
He sailed his ships upon the ocean,
Some foreign country he would go to see.

He sailèd east and he sailèd west,
Until he came to Turkey;
There he was taken and put to prison
Until his life was a misery.

34. [Lord Bateman]

Grainger MS., No. 170. Also in Grainger, *JFSS*, III (1909), p. 192. Sung by Joseph Taylor, Brigg, Lincolnshire, July 28, 1906.

a D

Lord Bateman was aden (an) noble Lord,
A noble Lord of sóme high dēgéree; (degree)
He shipped himsedelf (self) on board of a ship,
Sóm (some) foreign coúntéry he would go see.

He sailed east and he sailed west,
Until he came to péroud Turkey,
Where he was taken and put in prisun
Until his élife it é grēö (grew) quite weary.

And in this prisun there grēö (grew) a tree,
It grēö so large and it grēö so strong;
Where he was chēned (chained) around the middle
Until his è life it é was almost gone.

His jailor 'àd bùt one honly (only) daughter,
The fairest creature my two eyes did see;
She stole the keys of her father's prisun,
And said Lord Batemun she would set free.

37. [The Loving Ballad of Lord Bateman]

Cruikshank, 1839. Also in Child, 1882-98, I, pp. 476-77. According to Kidson (*JFSS*, I, p. 241), Cruikshank learned his tune from a street singer nicknamed "Tripe Skewer," who used to sing it outside a public house at Battle Bridge (King's Cross).

a I

1. Lord Bateman was a noble lord,
      A noble lord of high degree;
   He shipped himself all aboard of a ship,
      Some foreign country for to see.

2. He sailed east, he sailed west,
      Until he came to famed Turkey,
   Where he was taken and put to prison,
      Until his life was quite weary.

3. All in this prison there grew a tree,
      O there it grew so stout and strong!
   Where he was chained all by the middle,
      Until his life was almost gone.

4. This Turk he had one only daughter,
      The fairest my two eyes eer see;
   She steel the keys of her father's prison,
      And swore Lord Bateman she would let go free.

5. O she took him to her father's cellar,
      And gave to him the best of wine;
   And every health she drank unto him
      Was, 'I wish, Lord Bateman, as you was mine.'

6. 'O have you got houses, have you got land,
      And does Northumberland belong to thee?
   And what would you give to the fair young lady
      As out of prison would let you go free?'

7. 'O I've got houses and I've got land,
      And half Northumberland belongs to me;
   And I will give it all to the fair young lady
      As out of prison would let me go free.'

8. 'O in seven long years, I'll make a vow
      For seven long years, and keep it strong,
   That if you'll wed no other woman,
      O I will wed no other man.'

9. O she took him to her father's harbor,
      And gave to him a ship of fame,
   Saying, Farewell, farewell to you, Lord Bateman,
      I fear I never shall see you again.

10. Now seven long years is gone and past,
       And fourteen days, well known to me;
    She packed up all her gay clothing,
       And swore Lord Bateman she would go see.

11. O when she arrived at Lord Bateman's castle,
       How boldly then she rang the bell!
    'Who's there? who's there?' cries the proud young porter,
       'O come unto me pray quickly tell.'

12. 'O is this here Lord Bateman's castle,
       And is his lordship here within?'
    'O yes, O yes,' cries the proud young porter,
       'He's just now taking his young bride in.'

13. 'O bid him to send me a slice of bread,
       And a bottle of the very best wine,
    And not forgetting the fair young lady
       As did release him when close confine.'

14. O away and away went this proud young porter,
       O away and away and away went he,
    Until he come to Lord Bateman's chamber,
       When he went down on his bended knee.

15. 'What news, what news, my proud young porter?
       What news, what news? Come tell to me:'
    'O there is the fairest young lady
       As ever my two eyes did see.

16. 'She has got rings on every finger,
       And on one finger she has got three;
    With as much gay gold about her middle
       As would buy half Northumberlee.

17. 'O she bids you to send her a slice of bread,
       And a bottle of the very best wine,
    And not forgetting the fair young lady
       As did release you when close confine.'

18. Lord Bateman then in passion flew,
       And broke his sword in splinters three,
    Saying, 'I will give half of my father's land,
       If so be as Sophia has crossed the sea.'

19. Then up and spoke this young bride's mother,
       Who never was heard to speak so free;
    Saying, 'You'll not forget my only daughter,
       If so be as Sophia has crossed the sea.'

20. 'O it's true I made a bride of your daughter,
       But she's neither the better nor the worse for me;
    She came to me with a horse and saddle,
       But she may go home in a coach and three.'

21. Lord Bateman then prepared another marriage,
       With both their hearts so full of glee,
    Saying, 'I will roam no more to foreign countries,
       Now that Sophia has crossed the sea.'

The text has been decanted out of Cockney by the hand of Child.

45. [Lord Beichan and Susie Pye]

Kinloch, 1827, App'x to p. 260; text, pp. 260-70.

a M

1. Young Beichan was in London born,
   He was a man of hie degree;
   He past thro' monie kingdoms great,
   Until he cam unto Grand Turkie.

2. He view'd the fashions of that land,
   Their way of worship viewed he;
   But unto onie of their stocks
   He wadna sae much as bow a knee:

3. Which made him to be taken straight,
   And brought afore their hie jurie;
   The savage Moor did speak upricht,
   And made him meikle ill to dree.

4. In ilka shoulder they've bor'd a hole,
   And in ilka hole they've put a tree;
   They've made him to draw carts and wains,
   Till he was sick and like to dee.

5. But young Beichan was a Christian born,
   And still a Christian was he;
   Which made them put him in prison strang,
   And cauld and hunger sair to dree;
   And fed on nocht but bread and water,
   Until the day that he mot dee.

6. In this prison there grew a tree,
   And it was unco stout and strang;
   Where he was chained by the middle,
   Until his life was almaist gane.

7. The savage Moor had but ae dochter,
   And her name it was Susie Pye;
   And ilka day as she took the air,
   The prison door she passed bye.

8. But it fell ance upon a day,
   As she was walking, she hear him sing;
   She listen'd to his tale of woe,
   A happy day for young Beichan!

9. "My hounds they all go masterless,
   My hawks they flee frae tree to tree,
   My youngest brother will heir my lands,
   My native land I'll never see."

10. "O were I but the prison-keeper,
    As I'm a ladie o' hie degree,
    I soon wad set this youth at large,
    And send him to his ain countrie."

11. She went away into her chamber,
    All nicht she never clos'd her ee;
    And when the morning begoud to dawn,
    At the prison door alane was she.

12. She gied the keeper a piece of gowd,
    And monie pieces o' white monie,
    To tak her thro' the bolts and bars,
    The lord frae Scotland she lang'd to see:—
    She saw young Beichan at the stake,
    Which made her weep maist bitterlie.

13. "O hae ye got onie lands," she says,
    "Or castles in your ain countrie?
    It's what wad ye gie to the ladie fair
    Wha out o' prison wad set you free?"

14. "It's I hae houses, and I hae lands,
    Wi' monie castles fair to see,
    And I wad gie a' to that ladie gay,
    Wha out o' prison wad set me free."

15. The keeper syne brak aff his chains,
    And set Lord Beichan at libertie:—
    She fill'd his pockets baith wi' gowd,
    To tak him till his ain countrie.

16. She took him frae her father's prison,
    And gied to him the best o' wine;
    And a brave health she drank to him,—
    "I wish, Lord Beichan, ye were mine!

17. It's seven lang years I'll mak a vow,
    And seven lang years I'll keep it true;
    If ye'll wed wi' na ither woman,
    It's I will wed na man but you."

18. She's tane him to her father's port,
    And gien to him a ship o' fame,—
    "Farewell, farewell, my Scottish lord,
    I fear I'll ne'er see you again."

19. Lord Beichan turn'd him round about,
    And lowly, lowly, loutit he:—
    "Ere seven lang years come to an end,
    I'll tak you to mine ain countrie."

*   *   *   *   *

20. Then whan he cam to Glasgow town,
    A happy, happy man was he;
    The ladies a' around him thrang'd
    To see him come frae slaverie.

21. His mother she had died o' sorrow,
    And a' his brothers were dead but he;
    His lands they a' were lying waste,
    In ruins were his castles free.

22. Na porter there stood at his yett;
    Na human creature he could see;
    Except the screeching owls and bats,
    Had he to bear him companie.

23. But gowd will gar the castles grow,
    And he had gowd and jewels free;
And soon the pages around him thrang'd,
    To serve him on their bended knee.

24. His hall was hung wi' silk and satin,
    His table rung wi' mirth and glee;
He soon forgot the lady fair,
    That lows'd him out o' slaverie.

25. Lord Beichan courted a lady gay,
    To heir wi' him his lands sae free,
Ne'er thinking that a lady fair
    Was on her way frae Grand Turkie.

26. For Susie Pye could get na rest,
    Nor day nor nicht could happy be,
Still thinking on the Scottish Lord,
    Till she was sick and like to dee.

27. But she has builded a bonnie ship,
    Weel mann'd wi' seamen o' hie degree;
And secretly she stept on board,
    And bid adieu to her ain countrie.

28. But whan she cam to the Scottish shore,
    The bells were ringing sae merrilie;
It was Lord Beichan's wedding day,
    Wi' a lady fair o' hie degree.

29. But sic a vessel was never seen,
    The very masts were tapp'd wi' gold!
Her sails were made o' the satin fine,
    Maist beautiful for to behold.

30. But whan the lady cam on shore,
    Attended wi' her pages three,
Her shoon were of the beaten gowd,
    And she a lady of great beautie.

31. Then to the skipper she did say,
    "Can ye this answer gie to me—
Where are Lord Beichan's lands sae braid?
    He surely lives in this countrie."

32. Then up bespak the skipper bold,
    (For he could speak the Turkish tongue,)—
"Lord Beichan lives not far away,
    This is the day of his wedding."

33. "If ye will guide me to Beichan's yetts,
    I will ye well reward," said she,—
Then she and all her pages went,
    A very gallant companie.

34. When she cam to Lord Beichan's yetts,
    She tirl'd gently at the pin,
Sae ready was the proud porter
    To let the wedding guests come in.

35. "Is this Lord Beichan's house," she says,
    "Or is that noble Lord within?"
"Yes, he is gane into the hall,
    With his brave bride, and monie ane."

36. "Ye'll bid him send me a piece of bread,
    Bot and a cup of his best wine;
And bid him mind the lady's love
    That ance did lowse him out o' pyne."

37. Then in and cam the porter bold,
    I wat he gae three shouts and three,—
"The fairest lady stands at your yetts,
    That ever my twa een did see."

38. Then up bespak the bride's mither,
    I wat an angry woman was she,—
"You micht hae excepted our bonnie bride,
    Tho' she'd been three times as fair as she."

39. "My dame, your daughter's fair enough,
    And aye the fairer mot she be!
But the fairest time that e'er she was,
    She'll na compare wi' this ladie.

40. She has a gowd ring on ilka finger,
    And on her mid-finger she has three;
She has as meikle gowd upon her head,
    As wad buy an Earldom o' land to thee.

41. My lord, she begs some o' your bread,
    Bot and a cup o' your best wine,
And bids you mind the lady's love
    That ance did lowse ye out o' pyne."

42. Then up and started Lord Beichan,
    I wat he made the table flee,—
"I wad gie a' my yearlie rent
    'Twere Susie Pye come owre the sea."

43. Syne up bespak the bride's mother,—
    She was never heard to speak sae free,—
"Ye'll no forsake my ae dochter,
    Tho' Susie Pye has cross'd the sea?"

44. "Tak hame, tak hame, your dochter, madam,
    For she is ne'er the waur o' me;
She cam to me on horseback riding,
    And she sall gang hame in chariot free."

45. He's tane Susie Pye by the milk-white hand,
    And led her thro' his halls sae hie,—
"Ye're now Lord Beichan's lawful wife,
    And thrice ye're welcome unto me."

46. Lord Beichan prepar'd for another wedding,
    Wi' baith their hearts sae fu' o' glee;—
Says, "I'll range na mair in foreign lands,
    Sin Susie Pye has cross'd the sea.

47. Fy! gar a' our cooks mak ready;
    And fy! gar a' our pipers play;
And fy! gar trumpets gae thro' the toun,
    That Lord Beichan's wedded twice in a day!"

GROUP A♭

74. [Young Beichan]

Greig MSS., I, p. 28. Also in Greig and Keith, 1925, p. 43(c). Sung by J. D. Knowles, Buckie, 1904.

p M

Lord Bateman was a noble lord,
Likewise a lord of high degree.
He shipped himself in a ship of fame,
Some foreign country to go & see.

92. [Lord Bateman]

Sharp MSS., 695/772-76. Also in Sharp, 3rd series, 1906, pp. 28-31, with accompaniment; and Sharp, 1907, pp. 22-23. Sung by Henry Larcom(be), Haselbury Plucknett, December 26, 1905.

p Æ/D

This extraordinarily fine copy, it will be observed, is the only variant with minor tonality in this group.

1. Lord Bateman was a noble Lord,
   A noble lord of high degree,
   He shipped himself on a board a ship
   Some foreign country to go and see.

2. He sailèd East, he sailèd West,
   He sailèd into proud Turkey,
   Where he was taken and put in prison
   Until his life was quite weary.

3. And in this prison there growed a tree,
   It growed so stout, it growed so strong,
   He was chained up all by the middle,
   Until his life was almost gone.

4. This Turk he had one only daughter,
   The fairest creature that ever you see,
   She stole the keys of her father's prison
   And swore Lord Bateman she would set free.

5. Have you got lands, have you got livings,
   Or dost Northumberland belongs to thee?
   What will you give to a fair young lady
   If out of prison she'll set you free?

6. Yes, I've got lands and I've got livings
   And half Northumberland belong to me
   And I'll give it all to a fair young lady
   If out of prison she will set me free.

7. She took him to her father's cellar
   And give to him the best of wine,
   And every health that she drinked unto him.
   I wish, Lord Bateman, that you were mine.

8. Seven long years we will make a vow,
   And seven long years we will keep it strong.
   If you will wed with no other woman,
   I will never wed with no other man.

9. She took him to her father's harbour
   And give to him a ship of fame.
   Farewell, farewell, to you Lord Bateman,
   I'm afraid I never shall see you again.

10. Now seven long years is agone and past
    And fourteen days well known to me.
    She packèd up all her gay clothing
    And swore Lord Bateman she'd go and see.

11. And when she came to Lord Bateman's castle
    So boldly how she did ring the bell.
    Who's there, who's there? cried the young proud porter.
    Who's there, who's there? come quickly tell.

12. O is this called Lord Bateman's castle,
    O is his lordship here within?
    O yes, O yes, cries the young proud porter,
    He has just now taken his young bride in.

13. You tell him to send me a slice of bread
    And a bottle of the best of wine
    And not forgetting that fair young lady
    That did release him when he was close confined.

14. Away, away, went this proud young porter,
    Away, away, away went he,
    Until he came to Lord Bateman's chamber
    Down on his bended knees fell he.

15. What news, what news, my young proud porter,
    What news, what news hast thou brought to me?
    There is the fairest of all young ladies
    That ever my two eyes did see.

16. She have got rings on every finger,
    Round one of them she have got three.
    She have gold enough around her middle
    To buy Northumberland that belongs to thee.

17. She tells you to send her a slice of bread
    And a bottle of the best of wine
    And not forgetting that fair young lady
    That did release you when you were close confined.

18. Lord Bateman then in a passion flew,
    He broke his sword in splinters three,
    Saying: I will give you all my father's riches
    And if Sophia have acrossed the sea.

19. O then up spoke this young bride's mother
    Who was never heard to speak so free,
    Saying: You'll not forget my only daughter
    For if Sophia have acrossed the sea.

20. I only made a bride of your daughter,
    She's neither the better nor worse for me.
    She came to me over horse and saddle,
    She may go back in a coach and three.

21. Lord Bateman prepared for another marriage,
    So both their hearts so full of glee.
    I will range no more to foreign countries
    Now since Sophia have acrossed the sea.

94. "Young Becon"

Harris MS., No. "27" (=26). Also in Child, 1882-98, V, p. 415.

a I

The sixteenths in the penultimate bar are given in the MS. as eighths.

The Harris copy is one of the oldest in the record and quite unlike most of the rest. Mrs. Harris' daughter noted that her mother sang No. 106 to the tune of "Young Becon," but as given in the MS. her tune to No. 106 ("My husband built for me a Bowr") differs markedly.

GROUP AC

100. "Lord Bateman"

Kidson, 1891, pp. 33-36. Sung by Mrs. Holt, Alderhill, Meanwood.

p I

1. Lord Bateman was a noble Lord,
     A noble Lord of high degree;
   He put himself all on a ship,
       Some foreign countries he would go see.

2. He sailèd east and sailèd west,
     Until he came to fair Turkey,
   Where he was taken and put in prison,
       Until his life was quite weary.

3. And in this prison there grew a tree,
     It grew so stout and it grew so strong,
   Where he was chained by the middle,
       Until his life was almost gone.

4. The Turk he had an only daughter,
     The fairest creature ever my eyes did see;
   She stole the keys of her father's prison,
       And swore Lord Bateman she would set free!

5. "Have you got houses, have you got lands?
     Or does Northumberland belong to thee?
   What would you give to the fair young lady,
       That out of prison would set you free?"

6. "I have got houses, I have got lands,
     And half Northumberland belongs to me;
   I'll give it all to the fair young lady,
       That out of prison would set me free."

7. Oh, then she took him to her father's palace,
     And gave to him the best of wine,
   And every health she drank unto him—
       "I wish, Lord Bateman, that you were mine."

8. "Now, for seven long years, I'll make a vow,
     For seven long years, and keep it strong,
   If you will wed no other woman,
       That I will wed no other man."

9. Oh, then she took him to her father's harbour,
     And gave to him a ship of fame;
   "Farewell, farewell, my dear Lord Bateman,
       I'm afraid I shall never see you again."

10. Now, seven long years were gone and past,
      And fourteen long days well known to me
    She packed up her gay clothing,
        And Lord Bateman she would go see.

11. And then she came to Lord Bateman's castle,
      So boldly now she rang the bell;
    "Who's there?" cried the young porter,
        "Who's there—now come unto me tell?"

12. "Oh, is this Lord Bateman's castle,
      And is his Lordship here within;"
   "O yes, O yes," cried the proud young porter,
      "He's just taking his young bride in."

13. "Oh, then tell him to send me a slice of bread,
      And a bottle of the best wine;
   And not forgetting the fair young lady,
      That did release him when close confined."

14. Away, away, went that proud young porter,
      Away, away, and away went he,
   Until he came to Lord Bateman's door,
      Down on his bended knees fell he.

15. "What news, what news, my young porter,
      What news have you brought unto me?"
   "There is the fairest of all young ladies,
      That ever my two eyes did see.

16. "She has got rings on every finger,
      And round one of them she has got three;
   And such gay gold hanging round her middle,
      That would buy Northumberland for thee.

17. "She tells you to send her a slice of bread,
      And a bottle of the best wine;
   And not forgetting the fair young lady,
      That did release you when close confined."

18. Lord Bateman then in a passion flew,
      And broke his sword in splinters three,
   Saying, "I will give all my father's riches,
      If that Sophia has crossed the sea."

19. Then up spoke this bride's young mother,
      Who never was heard to speak so free—
   "You'll not forget my only daughter,
      If Sophia has crossed the sea."

20. "I own I made a bride of your daughter,
      She's neither the better nor worse for me;
   She came to me with a horse and saddle,
      She may go home in a coach and three."

21. Lord Bateman prepared another marriage,
      With both their hearts so full of glee;
   "I'll range no more in foreign countries,
      Now since Sophia has cross'd the sea."

101. "Lord Akeman"

Karpeles, 1934, II, pp. 88-92. Sung by William Holloway,
King's Cove, Bonavista Bay, Newfoundland, September 25,
1929. The text given according to the collector's MS.

m I; G tonic, ending on III

1. Lord Akeman was a noble lord,
   A noble lord of a high degree;
   He shipped himself on board of a vessel
   Foreign countries for to go see.

2. He sailed East and he sailed West
   Until he came to proud Turkey.
   'Twas there he was taken and put in prison
   Until his life was most weary.

3. By the side of the prison there grew a tree;
   It grew so mighty stout and long.
   He was tied to that right round his middle
   Until his life was almost gone.

4. The gaoler had one only daughter,
   One of the fairest creatures I have ever seen.
   She stole the keys of her father's prison,
   And said Lord Akeman she would set free.

5. Have you got houses, or have you got land?
   Or is any of Northumberland belongs to thee?
   What would you give to any fair maiden
   Who from this prison would set you free?

6. Yes, I've got houses and I got land,
   And half Northumberland belongs to me.
   I would give it all to any lady
   Who from this prison would set me free.

7. Seven long years you made a promise,
   Fourteen days he kept it strong;
   If you don't wed with no other woman,
   Sure I won't wed with no other man.

8. Seven long years have passed and over,
   And fourteen days being well known to her,
   She pack-ed up her 'mosquey' clothing,
   And she said Lord Akeman she'd go to see.

9. When she sees Lord Akeman's castle
   So merrily she rang the bell.
   Who's there, who's there? asked the proud young
                                          porter,
   I pray unto me tell.

10. Is Lord Akeman within? she says,
    Or is her ladyship within that hall?
    O yes, O yes, says the proud young porter,
    It's just after bringing a young bride in.

11. Go tell him to send me a slice of his best bread,
    And a bottle of his best wine,
    And not to forget the fair young maiden
    Who released him from his close combine.

12. Away ran the proud young porter,
    Down on his knees he fell to pray,
    Saying: I have seen one of the fairest creatures
    That ever my eyes would wish to see.

13. On every finger she has rings,
    And on one of them she has got three,
    And the golden robes around her middle
    I know Northumberland belongs to she.

14. Lord Akeman rose then in a passion
     And threw his sword in pieces three,
    Saying: I'll go no more to foreign countries
     Since young Sophia have a-crossed the sea.

15. Then up speaks the young bride's mother,
     Who was never known to speak so free,
    Saying: Are you going to leave my daughter
     Since young Sophia have a-crossed the sea?

16. I owe my bride I made out of your daughter,
     It's neither the better nor the worse for thee;
    She came to me in a horse and saddle,
     And I'll send her home in a coach and three.

105. "A Gentleman of the Courts of England"

Garrison, 1944, pp. 16-18. Sung by Mrs. Daisy Turner,
Marshall, Ark., April 1941.

a π²

This tune was originally noted in 4/4 time, but the note-values
are unchanged.

1. A gentleman of the courts of England,
    A gentleman of the high degree,
   He seemed to grow more discontented
    Till he taken a tantrum out on the sea.

2. He sailed east and he sailed west
    Until he came to the Turkish shore,
   And there he was caught and put in prison,
    No hope of freedom anymore.

3. The old jailer had a very nice daughter,
    A daughter of a high degree;
   She stole the keys of her father's prison
    And said Lord Bateman she'd set free.

4. Have you gold or have you silver?
    Have you money at a high degree?
   Could you afford to give it to a lady,
    One that would now set you free?

5. I have gold and I have silver,
    I have money at a high degree,
   And I can afford to give it to a lady,
    One that will now set me free.

6. She takened him down to her father's cellar,
    Drawed glasses of old port wine,
   And every health that she drank to him
    She'd cry, "Lord Bateman, I wish you were mine."

7. Seven long years had passed and over,
    Seven long years and two or three.
   She gathered up her gold and diamonds
    And said Lord Bateman she'd go see.

8. She rode and she rode till she came to his castle;
    She knocked so loud she made it ring,
   And none was so ready as his bold, bright porter
    To rise and see who wanted in.

9. Sir, is this Lord Bateman's castle,
    Or is he within?
   Oh yes, oh yes, he has just this day
    Gone and brought a new bride in.

10. Go tell him I want a slice of his bread,
     A bottle of his wine so strong;
    And tell him he must never forget the lady
     That freed him from his prison bond.

11. Sir, stands at your gate a fair damsel
     As ever my two eyes did see;
    She wears a gold ring on her little finger,
     And on her others two or three.

12. She said she wanted a slice of your bread
     And a bottle of your wine so strong,
    And to tell you you must never forget the lady
     Who freed you from your prison bond.

13. Up rose Lord Bateman from the table,
     And sliced his bread in pieces three,
    Saying, "Fare you well to the land of the living,
     Since my Susannah's crossed the sea.

14. "Sir, today I've married your daughter,
     And she is none the worse by me.
    She rode here a horse and saddle,
     And she may return in a coach with thee."

GROUP B

112. [Young Bekie]

Ritson-Tytler-Brown MS., pp. 38-47. Sung by Mrs. Brown,
Aberdeen.

Probably a I, ending on V

Note that this is the only CM variant in the "Beichan" album. But
Child's A copy, also from Mrs. Brown—the present is Child C with
slight verbal differences—is in LM, like all the rest.
    I cannot persuade myself that the final here is the true tonic. The
tune has none of the Mixolydian feeling.

1. Young Bekie was as brave a knight
       As ever sail'd the sea,
   An' he's ta'en him to the court of France
       To serve for meat and fee.

2. He had nae been in the French court
       A twelvemonth nor sae long
   Till he fell in love wi' the kings daughter,
       An' was thrown in prison strong.

3. The king he had but ae daughter,
       Burd Isbel was her name,
   An' she has to the prison-house gane
       To hear the prisoners moan.

4. "O gin a lady would borrow me,
       At her stirrup-foot i would run;
   Or gin a widow would borrow me,
       I'd swear to be her son;

5. Or gin a virgin would borrow me,
       I'd wed her wi' a ring,
   I'd gi' her ha's, i'd gi' her bow'rs,
       The bonny tow'r o' Lin."

6. O barefoot, barefoot gi'd she but,
       An' barefoot came she ben,
   It was nae for want o' hose and sheen,
       Nor time to put them on,

7. But a' for fear her father dear
       Had heard her making din;
   She's stown the keys o' the prison-house door
       An' latten the prisoner gang[.]

8. O whan she saw him young Bekie,
       Her heart was wond'rous sair,
   For the mice but and the bold rottens
       Had cutted his yallow hair.

9. She's gi'n him a shaver for his beard,
       A comber for his hair,
   Five hundred pound in his pocket,
       To spend and nae to spare.

10. She's gi'n him a steed was good in need,
        An' a sadle o' royal bone,
    A leash o' hounds of ae litter,
        An' Hector called one.

11. Atween this twa a vow was made,
        'Twas made full solemnly,
    That ere three years was come and gone
        Well marry'd they should be.

12. He had nae been in's ain country
        A twelvemonth till an end
    Till he's forc'd to marry a dukes daughter,
        Or than lose a' his land.

13. Ohon! alas! says young Bekie,
        I know no' what to dee,
    For i can no' win to burd Isbel,
        An' she kens nae to come to me.

14. It fell once upon a day,
        Burd Isbel fell asleep,
    An' up it starts the Belly-blind,
        An' stood at her bed-feet.

15. "O waken, waken, burd Isbel,
        How can you sleep sae soun',
    Whan this is Bekies marriage-day,
        An' the marriage going on?

16. Ye do ye to your mithers bow'r,
        Think neither sin nor shame,
    An' tak' ye twa o' your mithers Marys
        To keep you frae thinking lang.

17. Ye dress yoursel' i' the scarlet red,
        Your Marys in dainty green,
    An' ye put girdles about your middles
        Would buy an earldome.

18. Ye put nae money in your pocket,
        But barely guineas three,
    And that to gie to the proud porter,
        To bid him speak you wi'.

19. O ye gang down to yon sea-side,
        An' down by yon sea-strand,
    Sae bonny will the Holland boats
        Come rowing till your hand.

20. Ye set your milk-white foot on board,
        Cry Hail ye, dominee!
    And i shall be the steerer o't,
        To row you o'er the sea."

21. She's ta'en her to her mithers bow'r,
        Thought neither sin nor shame,
    An' she took twa o' her mithers Marys
        To keep her frae thinking lang.

22. She dress'd hersel i' the red scarlet,
        Her Marys in dainty green,
    An' they pat girdles about their middles
        Would buy an earldome.

23. An' they gi'd down to yon sea-side,
        An' down by yon sea-strand,
    Sae bonny did the Holland boats
        Come rowing to their hand.

24. She set her milk-white foot on board,
        Cry'd Hail ye, dominee!
    And the Belly-blind was the steerer o't
        To row her o'er the sea.

25. Whan she came to young Bekies yate,
        She heard the music play,
    Sae well she kent frae a' she heard
        It was his wedding-day.

26. She's pitten her hand in her pocket,
        Gi'n the porter guineas three:
    "Tak' ye that, ye proud porter,
        Bid the bride-groom speak to me."

27. O whan that he came up the stair,
    He fell low down on's knee,
He hail'd the king, and he hail'd the queen,
    An' he hail'd him young Bekie:

28. "O i've been porter at your yates
    This thirty years and three,
But there's three ladys at them now,
    Their like i ne'er did see.

29. There's ane of them dress'd in red scarlet,
    An' twa in dainty green,
An' they ha' girdles about their middles
    Would buy an earldome."

30. Then out it spake the bierly bride,
    Was a' gowd to the chin,
"Gin they be braw without, she says,
    Wese be as braw within.["]

31. It's nae to anger the king, he says,
    Nor yet to vex your grace,
But the blackest bit o' the sole o' her fit
    Is whiter nor your face.

32. Then up it starts him young Bekie,
    An' the tears was in his ee,
"I'll lay my life it's bird Isbel,
    Come o'er the sea to me."

33. O quickly ran he down the stair,
    An' whan he saw 'twas she,
He kindly took her in his arms,
    An' kiss'd her tenderly.

34. "O ha' you forgotten, young Bekie,
    The vow you made to me,
Whan i took you out o' prison strong,
    Whan you was condemn'd to dee?

35. I ga' you a steed was good in need,
    An' a sadle o' royal bone,
A leash o' hounds of ae litter,
    And Hector called one."

36. It was well kent what the lady said,
    That it was no a lee,
For at ilka word 'at the lady spake
    The hound fell at her knee.

37. "Take hame, take hame your daughter,
    A blessing gae her wi',
For i man marry my burd Isbel,
    That's come o'er the sea to me."

38. "Is this the custom o' your house,
    Or the fashion o' your lan',
To marry a maid in a May morning,
    An' send her hame at even?"

The Cherry-Tree Carol

CHILD NO. 54

THE musical tradition of this charming and deservedly popular carol, or religious ballad, does not begin to appear in the record until about the beginning of the nineteenth century. From then on, it has been continuous, and, apart from a few anomalies, fairly consistent.

The core of the musical tradition appears to be a rhythmical pattern basically as follows:

It seems altogether probable that all the variants in the central tradition originally belonged to this type, and that those in duple rhythm are alterations of it. To the same metrical (and melodic) pattern belongs the old favorite, "Love will find out the way," a tune still current, as Chappell informs us, in mid-nineteenth century tradition. (Cf. Chappell, *Popular Music*, I, [1855], p. 304.) The textual tradition allies the song with a small number of ballads which normally take the form of dac-tylic or hypersyllabic tetrameter couplets. These may be broken into quatrains, but the general absence of caesural pauses makes this a very arbitrary proceeding, and the violence is underlined by the music's failure to indicate any natural division until the mid-pause. Among the ballads in this group it is not unusual to find melodic parallels. (Cf. "Lamkin" [No. 93], "Death of Queen Jane" [No. 170].)

Among the members of this central melodic tradition there are no very significant subdivisions. The range is nearly always plagal. We should therefore expect the mid-pause to be ordinarily on the second degree; but, probably because the active range of many variants is narrow, mid-pauses on the fifth are the commonest. There is an overwhelming preference for the Ionian or the Mixolydian tonality, or hexatonic and pentatonic varieties which do not controvert those systems. A half-dozen variants make a refrain by repeating the second half of the stanza, to either a literal or an altered musical repetition. Half as many variants have a second strain, either for chorus or to carry new lines of text; and two add to this increment a burden as well.

TUNES WITH TEXTS

GROUP A a

1. "Joseph was an old man"

D. Gilbert MS. Pt. I, 1767-68, opp. p. 22.

p I

CONJECTURAL READING

On the proper timing of this tune, cf. especially Sir Richard R. Terry, *Gilbert and Sandys' Christmas Carols*, London, [1931], pp. xiv, 38; and Anne G. Gilchrist, *JFSS*, V, No. 18 (1914), p. 13(1). Terry adds an initial half-note and reduces to 3/2, keeping the time-values of the original as given by Sandys, 1833 (nearly identical with the copy above). Husk's copy is in duple time with values altered. The traditional course of the melody might justify the 3/4 reading suggested above. Cf. especially the Cornish copy that follows.

1. Joseph was an old man and an old man was he
   Joseph was etc.
   When he wedded mary in the Land of Gallilie

2. Joseph and mary walked through the orchards Good
   Joseph and etc.
   Where was Cherrys and berrys as Red as the blood

3. Joseph and mary walk'd through the orchards Green
   Joseph and etc.
   Where was Cherrys and berrys as good as might be Seen

4. O then bespake mary so meek and so mild
   O then etc.
   Pluck me a Cherry for I am with Child

5. O then bespake Joseph with words most reveild [p. 23]
   O then etc.
   Let him pluck thee a Cherry that brought thee with Child

6. O then bespake the babe in his mothers womb
   O then etc.
   Bow Down he [*sic*] tall trees to my mothers hand

7. Then Did bow down the highest branch to her hand
   Then did etc.
   O then bespake Joseph I have Done thee much wrong

8. Then mary pluck't a Cherry as red as the blood
   Then mary etc.
   And then She went home with her heavy Load

9. Mary took the babe upon her knee
   Mary took etc.
   Saying tell me my Dear Son what this world will be

10. I Shall be as Dead mother as the Stones in the wall
    I Shall etc.
    O the Stones in the Streets mother Shall morn [*sic*] for me all

11. Upon Easter Day mother my uprising Shall be
    Upon Easter etc.
    O the Sun and the moon mother Shall both rise with me.

3. [The Cherry Tree Carol]

Sharp MSS., 2821/. Also in Sharp, *JFSS*, V, No. 18 (1914),
p. 11. Sung by Mr. J. Thomas, Camborne, Cornwall, May
9, 1913.

p I

1. When Joseph was an old man,
   An old man was he,
   He wedded our Mary,
   The Queen of Galilee

2. And when he had a wedded her
   And at home had her brought
   Mary proved to be with child
   But Joseph knew her not.

3. Then Joseph and Mary
   Was a walking in the grove
   They saw cherries and berries
   As red as any rose

4. When Joseph and Mary
   Was in the garden green
   They saw cherries and berries
   That was fit to be seen.

5. And Mary said to Joseph
   In words meek and mild
   Pick me some cherries Joseph
   For I am with child

6. Then Joseph spoke to Mary
   In words so unkind
   Let him pick thee cherries Mary
   Who brought thee with child.

7. Then Jesus spoke unto the tree
   From within his mothers womb
   Bow down sweet cherry tree
   For my mother to have some

8. Then the highest branches bent as low
   As mother Mary's knee
   And she picked of the cherries
   By one two & three.

9. Then Mary had a young son
   Which she dandled on her knee
   And she said to her fair child
   What will this world be

10. This world he said is no other
    Than the stones in the street
    But the sun moon and stars
    Shall sail under thy feet.

11. And I must not be rocked
    In silver nor gold
    But in a wood cradle
    That rock on the ground

12. And I must not be clothed
    In purple nor poll
    But be clothed in fine linen
    The child is your own.

GROUP A d

16. [The Cherry-Tree Carol]

Sharp MSS., 4081/2918. Also in Sharp and Karpeles, 1932,
I, p. 92(C). Sung by William Wooton, Hindman, Knott
County, Ky., September 21, 1917.

p π[1]

Cf. another variant from the same singer (?) collected by Josephine
McGill (variant 20 in complete ed.).

1. When Joseph was a young man,
   A young man was he,
   He courted Virgin Mary,
   The Queen of Galilee,
   He courted Virgin Mary,
   The Queen of Galilee.

2. As Joseph and Mary
   Were walking one day,
   Here is apples and cherries
   Enough to behold.

3. Then Mary spoke to Joseph
   So neat (meek?) and so mild:
   Joseph, gather me some cherries,
   For I am with child.

4. Then Joseph flew in angry,
   In angry he flew:
   Let the father of the baby
   Gather cherries for you.

5. Lord Jesus spoke a few words
   All down unto them:
   Bow low down, low down, cherry tree,
   Let the mother have some.

6. The cherry tree bowed low down
   Low down to the ground,
   And Mary gathered cherries
   While Joseph stood around.

7. Then Joseph took Mary
   All on his right knee.
   He cried: O Lord, have mercy
   For what have I done.

8. And Joseph took Mary
   All on his left knee.
   Pray tell me, little baby,
   When your birthday will be?

9. On the fifth day of January
   My birthday will be,
   When the stars and the elements
   Doth tremble with fear.

The Carnal and the Crane

CHILD NO. 55

THE record for the singing tradition of this religious carol is meager. Only three tunes seem to have been collected, two of one type and one of another, all three between the years 1892 and 1912. The tunes from the West of England are plagal Æ/D.

Carol-tunes have been handed about and borrowed indiscriminately for different texts as freely as almost any others. Or it might be better to say that carols can scarcely be claimed to possess any proper tunes of their own. Nothing is clearer than the fact that, as they have been sung in the last century and a half, they do not form a separate and distinct category in folksong. Even the formal distinction which has been drawn between the carol and ballad, of stanza plus burden for the carol, internal refrain for the ballad, is not necessarily a differentiation from the musical point of view. In general, the rule has been that a good traditional tune is good enough to put to spiritual uses. In fact, folk-music, morally speaking, is virtually incorruptible. Folk-tunes have within them as their inalienable birthright such a gift of purity that they are a standing contradiction of the axiom, "Evil communications corrupt good manners." They associate unhesitatingly with the dirtiest companions, and come away unsoiled. In spite of Falstaff's allusion to "filthy tunes," there never has been such a phenomenon in folk-music, apart from momentary nonce-associations. This truth has been recognized by the pious and devout since time immemorial, and the continual give-and-take between sacred and secular ever since the record began is one of the reasons why the history of medieval music is so difficult to trace. Official edicts might force an artificial segregation from time to time, but in the long run they have had to yield before the stainless freshness of the traditional tunes, whether Ionian (*modus lascivus*) or not. For indeed, these do not have to become as little children: born "on a holy Thursday, their innocent faces clean," they are always fit for translation to the realms of light.

TUNES WITH TEXTS

GROUP A

1. "The Carnal and the Crane"

Vaughan Williams, *JFSS*, IV, No. 14 (1910), p. 22. Also in Leather, 1912, p. 188. Sung by Mr. Hirons (60), at Haven, Herefordshire, July 1909.

p Æ/D

This is a member of the "Lazarus" or "How should I your true-love know" family. The tune was also sung to the carol, "The man that lives" (cf. Leather, 1912, p. 195, tune 1).

1. As I walked out one morning.
   A little before it was day,
   I heard a conversation
   Between a carnal and a crane.

2. The carnal said unto the crane
   "If all the world should turn,
   But once we had a Father,
   But now we have a Son."

3. There was a star in all the East
   Shone out a shining throng,
   And shone into King Pharaoh's chamber,
   And where King Pharaoh lay.

4. The wise men they soon spied it,
   And soon King Pharaoh told
   That an earthly babe was born that night
   As no man on earth could destroy.

5. King Pharaoh sent for his armèd men.
   And ready then they be,
   For all children under two years old
   Shall be slainèd, they shall be.

6. Joseph and Mary
   Was weary of their rest,
   They travelled into Egypt
   Into the Holy Land.

7. "Go speed thy work," said Jesus,
   "Go fetch thy oxen-wain,
   And carry home thy corn again
   As which this day hath sown.

8. "If anyone should ask you
   Whether Jesus He has passed by,
   You can tell them Jesus He did pass by
   Just as your seeds were sown."

9. Then up came King Pharaoh
   With his armèd men so bold,
Enquiring of the husbandman
   Whether Jesus He has passed by.

10. "The truth it must be spoken,
   The truth it must be told,
I saw Jesus passing by
   Just as my seeds were sown."

11. King Pharaoh said to his armèd men
   "Your labour and mine's in vain,
It's full three quarters of a year
   Since these seeds were sown!"

2. "King Herod and the Cock"

Sharp MSS., 2585/. Also, harmonized, in Sharp, 1911, p. 2;
and in Sharp, [1913], p. 3. Sung by Ellen Plumb (85),
Armscote, April 13, 1911.

p Æ/D

There was a star in David's land
In David's land appear.
And in King Herod's chamber so high it did shine there.

The Wise Men soon spied it
And told the King anigh
That a Prince's Babe was born that night
No King shall e'er destroy.

If this be the truth King Herod said
That thou hast told to me
The roasted cock that lies in the list
Shall crow full senses three.

Oh, the cock soon thrustened and feathered well
By the works of God's own hand
And he did crow full senses three
In the dish where he did stand.

Dives and Lazarus

CHILD NO. 56

As CHILD's note informs us, something on the order of this ballad was in print in early Elizabethan times, and seventy-five years later was still matter for common allusion as "the merry ballad of Diverus and Lazarus." No early text survived, however, and Child had to resort to nineteenth-century reprintings of eighteenth-century broadsides for his copy. Unfortunately, the ballad also failed to give its name to a tune persisting with other texts.

Nevertheless, the melodies traditionally associated with the ballad in recent times belong to a family which is very widespread indeed, and demonstrably ancient. The members of it are both sacred and secular. Broadwood has a note on the tunes in *JFSS*, II, p. 119. Her list is in no sense complete, and could easily be augmented by reference to the collections of Joyce, Greig, and Sharp. Cf. also *Journal of the American Musicological Society*, III (1950), pp. 120-34.

The central tradition appears to lie with a group of authentic variants in major tonalities (I, I/M, M), most of them noted in Herefordshire about the beginning of the present century. Another, smaller, group was collected by Sharp in the West of England; Dorian or leaning toward it, also authentic. This second group is affiliated with other carol-texts as well: "The Twelve Apostles," "The Moon shines bright," "God made a trance," "The Seven Virgins." The first group has echoes of "The Bailiff's Daughter" (Child No. 105), "O Ponder Well," and "Lowlands of Holland."

Apart from these is another Lazarus ballad, or carol, or popular hymn, more didactic and less narrative, but not unknown to tradition on both sides of the Atlantic. Its words usually begin, "There was a man in ancient times," etc. The tunes are usually of the "Babe of Bethlehem" type, preferring some form of triple rhythm, and frequently having two strains. They can be read either as plagal tunes with dropped closes, or as authentic. Preferring the latter, we find a modal range from D/M to π^4. If, as appears, the Westminster "Lazarus" tune is of this family, we may add Æolian. Examples of the "Babe of Bethlehem" may be seen in Jackson, *Spiritual Folk-Songs of Early America*, 1937, p. 82; Davis, *Traditional Ballads of Virginia*, 1929, p. 566; Sharp and Karpeles, *English Folk Songs from the Southern Appalachians*, 1932, II, p. 29; Kirkland, *SFQ*, II, p. 67.

The tunes associated with this secondary text are included here (vt. 13), partly because they are sufficiently involved with the ballad proper to have been confused therewith, and partly for their impressive spread, interest, and associations.

TUNES WITH TEXTS

GROUP A

1. [Dives and Lazarus]

Andrews, *JFSS*, II, No. 7 (1905), p. 125. Also in Leather, 1912, p. 190 (1st tune). Sung by Mrs. Harris (80), a mole-catcher's widow, Eardisley, Herefordshire, 1905; learned from her father, a noted singer.

a I

1. As it fell out on a light dully day,*
        high holiday,
   When Diverus made a feast;
   And he invited all his friends,
        And grand gentry of the best.

2. Then Lazarus laid himself down and down
        Under Dives' wall:
   "Some meat! some drink! brother Diverus?
        For hunger, starve I shall!"

3. "Thou wert none of my brethren as I tell thee,
        Lie begging at my wall;
   No meat nor drink will I give thee,
        For hunger, starve thou shall!"

4. Then Diverus sent out his hungry dogs
        To worry poor Lazarus away.
   They hadn't the power to bite one bite,
        But they licked his sores away.

5. Then Lazarus, he laid himself down and down,
        And down at Diverus' gate:
   "Some meat! some drink! brother Diverus,
        For Jesus Christ His sake."

6. Then Diverus sent to his merry men
        To worry poor Lazarus away.
   They'd not the power to strike one stroke,
        But they flung their whips† away.

7. As it fell out, on a light dully day,*
   When Lazarus sickened and died;
   There came two Angels out of heaven,
   His soul for to guide.

8. "Arise! arise! brother Lazarus,
   And come along with we;
   There's a place provided in heaven,
   (For) To sit on an Angel's knee."

9. As it fell on a dark dully day,§
   When Dives sickened and died;
   There came two serpents out of hell,
   His soul for to guide.

10. "Arise! arise! brother Diverus,
    And come along with we;
    There is a place provided in hell,
    For to sit on a serpent's knee!

11. There is a place provided in hell
    For wicked men, like thee;
    .   .   .   ."
    .   .   .   .   .   .

12. "Who had they as many days to live
    As there is blades of grass,
    I would be good unto the poor
    As long as life would last!"

* (?) Bright holiday
† Pronounced "weeps"
§ (?) Dark holiday

11. Then Divus lifted up his eyes,
    And saw poor Lazarus blest,
    "A drop of water, brother Lazarus!
    For to quench my flaming thirst.

12. If I had as many years to live
    As there is blades of grass,
    I would make it in my will secure
    That the Devils should have no power!"

13. Oh, hell is dark, oh, hell is deep,
    Oh, hell is full of mice,
    It is a pity that any poor sinful soul
    Should depart from our Saviour Christ.

14. And now my carol's ended,
    No longer can I stay,
    God bless you all, both great and small,
    And God send you a happy New Year.

5. "Diverus and Lazarus"

Sharp MSS., 4867/3339. Sung by Thomas Taylor, Ross Workhouse, September 7, 1921.

a M

1. As it fell out upon one day
   Rich Diverus made a feast
   And he invited all his men
   And gentlemen of the best.

2. And Lazarus laid him down,
   Down at Diverus' gate.
   Some meat, some drink, brother Diverus,
   For Jesus Christ his sake.

3. And Lazrus laid him a-down,
   Down at Diverus door.
   No meat, no drink will I give to thee
   Nor bestow upon the poor.

4. And he sent out his hungry dogs
   To bite him as he lay.
   They had no power to bite at all,
   But they licked his sores away.

5. Then he sent out his merry men all
   To whip poor Lazarus away.
   They had no power to strike one stroke,
   But throw their whips away.

6. And it fell out upon one day
   Poor Lazarus sickened and died.
   There came two angels out of Heaven
   Therein his soul to guide.

3. [Dives and Lazarus]

Vaughan Williams, *JFSS*, IV No. 14 (1910), p. 47. Also in Leather, 1912, p. 190 (2nd tune). Sung by J. Evans, Dilwyn, Herefordshire, January 1907.

a I/M

Cf. "The Bailiff's Daughter" (No. 105).

1. [As it] fell out upon one day
      Rich Div'rus made a feast,
   And he invited all his friends
      And gentry of the best.

[etc., as in variant 1 above, according to *JFSS*, II, No. 7 (1905), p. 125, and after the "serpent's knee" verse, as follows:]

7. Saying: Rise up, rise up, brother Lazrus,
   And come along with me;
   For there's a place prepared in heaven
   For to sit on an angel's knee.

8. And it fell out upon one day
   Diverus sickened and died,
   And there came two angels out of hell
   Therein his soul to guide.

9. Saying: Rise up, rise up, brother Diverus,
   And come along with me,
   For there's a place prepared in hell
   From which thou canst not flee.

APPENDIX

13. "Lazarus"

Broadwood and Maitland, 1893, p. 102; text in *N & Q*,
Series 4, III, p. 76. From A. J. Hipkins, Westminster.

a Æ

Cf. the reference given by Miss Broadwood, *loc. cit.*, and on p. 35
of the same work. Vaughan Williams has composed an orchestral piece
on this melody: *Five Variants of "Dives and Lazarus."*

1. As it fell out upon one day,
   Rich Diverus he made a feast;
   And he invited all his friends,
   And gentry of the best.
   And it fell out upon one day,
   Poor Lazarus he was so poor,
   He came and laid him down and down,
   Ev'n down at Diverus' door.

2. So Lazarus laid him down and down,
   Ev'n down at Diverus' door;
   "Some meat, some drink, brother Diverus,
   Do bestow upon the poor."

"Thou art none of mine, brother Lazarus,
   Lying begging at my door,
No meat, no drink will I give thee,
   Nor bestow upon the poor."

3. Then Lazarus laid him down and down,
   Ev'n down at Diverus' wall;
   "Some meat, some drink, brother Diverus,
   Or surely starve I shall."
   "Thou art none of mine, brother Lazarus,
   Lying begging at my wall;
   No meat, no drink will I give thee,
   And therefore starve thou shall."

4. Then Lazarus laid him down and down,
   Ev'n down at Diverus' gate;
   "Some meat, some drink, brother Diverus,
   For Jesus Christ his sake."
   "Thou art none of mine, brother Lazarus,
   Lying begging at my gate,
   No meat, no drink will I give thee,
   For Jesus Christ his sake."

5. Then Diverus sent his merry men all,
   To whip poor Lazarus away;
   They had not power to whip one whip,
   But threw their whips away.
   Then Diverus sent out his hungry dogs,
   To bite poor Lazarus away;
   They had not power to bite one bite,
   But licked his sores away.

6. And it fell out upon one day,
   Poor Lazarus he sickened and died;
   There came two angels out of heaven,
   His soul thereto to guide.
   "Rise up, rise up, brother Lazarus,
   And come along with me,
   There is a place prepared in heaven,
   For to sit upon an angel's knee."

7. And it fell out upon one day,
   Rich Diverus sickened and died;
   There came two serpents out of hell
   His soul thereto to guide.
   "Rise up, rise up, brother Diverus,
   And come along with me;
   There is a place prepared in hell,
   For to sit upon a serpent's knee."

By permission of J. B. Cramer & Co., Ltd., London.

Sir Patrick Spens

CHILD NO. 58

CHILD failed to find sufficient evidence to convince him of the "historicity" of this very celebrated ballad, and none has since been produced to tip the scales decisively in either direction. Its own recorded history begins with Percy's preparations for the *Reliques*. It was one of the group of admirable ballads transmitted to him from Scotland, presumably by Sir David Dalrymple, Lord Hailes, clearly a man with a remarkable nose for excellence. (See *The Percy Letters*, Vol. IV, edited by A. F. Falconer, 1954, pp. 48, 50.) The ballad belongs to the Scots alone, and has come to America without English or Irish assistance. There is (I think) no record of its being sung traditionally in either England or Ireland. It was known widely in Scots tradition by the beginning of the nineteenth century, whenever it commenced its traditional career.

Child scouts Chambers' theory of Lady Wardlaw's authorship of this and other ballads, and points out that Chambers' arguments were demolished by Norval Clyne and J. H. Watkins. He neglects to mention, however, that even so well-informed a judge as David Laing, writing additional notes to Stenhouse's *Illustrations*, had previously remarked of "Sir Patrick Spens": "Very little evidence would be required to persuade me that we were not also [i.e. as well as for "Hardyknute"] indebted for it to Lady Wardlaw." (Johnson, *The Scots Musical Museum*, Stenhouse's notes, 1839, repr. 1853, IV, p. *320.) With this conjecture Rimbault, in 1850, registers hearty accord, declaring there was "every reason to believe" that Lady Wardlaw was the author (Rimbault, *Musical Illustrations of Bishop Percy's Reliques*, 1850, p. 5). But, on the contrary, the "very little evidence" that Laing desiderates will in all likelihood never be forthcoming.

The musical tradition commences at about the opening of the last century. The record is hardly homogeneous or consistent enough to suggest a strong and continuous oral tradition. It appears probable that Johnson, who first printed a tune for the ballad, was ignorant of any traditionally associated with it, and his setting is arbitrary and inappropriate. It has been perpetuated in a series of reprintings, but never, apparently, in oral tradition.

The central tradition appears to lie with a group of tunes of modal cast, predominantly Dorian in authentic forms, Mixolydian in plagal, and found during the last century and a half all the way from Moray to Tennessee.

TUNES WITH TEXTS

GROUP A

2. [Sir Patrick Spens]

Campbell, II, [1818], p. 63(2). Also in Thomson, IV, 1805, p. 193.

p M

Note that the first strain lacks the 4th, and the second strain the 7th.

The King sat in Dunfermline town,
Drinkin' the blude reid wine;
O quher sall I get a sailor bold,
To sail this schip o' mine?

Up ther spak an eldern knight,
Was sittin' at the King's right knee;
Sir Patrick Spence is the best Sailor,
That sails upon the Sea.

3. [Sir Patrick Spens]

Greig MSS., III, p. 164; text, Bk. 766, LVI, p. 20. Also in Greig and Keith, 1925, p. 47; text, p. 46(B). Sung by A. Robb, New Deer, Aberdeenshire.

a D

Oot then spak' an auld sailor

I saw the auld moon in the new moon's airms
I fear we'll have weather soon.

Even owre by Aberdour
Where the sea lies wide and deep,
And there there lies young Prince Patrick
And the King's son at his feet.

Hold, oh hold, my captain, he said,
And let your anchor doon.

[159]

5. [Sir Patrick Spens]

Harris MS., No. 3 [corrected]. Also in Child, 1882-98, V, p. 415; text, II, p. 28(J).

p I/M

The printed copy does not accord with the MS. Cf. also *CFQ*, I, 195.

1. Hie sits oor king in Dumfermline,
    Sits birlin at the wine;
   Says, Whare will I get a bonnie boy
    That will sail the saut seas fine?
   That will hie owre to Norraway,
    To bring my dear dochter hame?

2. Up it spak a bonnie boy,
    Sat by the king's ain knie:
   "Sir Patrick Spens is as gude a skipper
    As ever sailed the sea."

3. The king has wrote a broad letter,
    And signed it wi his hand,
   And sent it to Sir Patrick Spens,
    To read it gif he can.

4. The firsten line he luikit on,
    A licht lauchter gae he;
   But ere he read it to the end,
    The tear blindit his ee.

5. "O wha is this, or wha is that,
    Has tauld oor king o me?
   I wad hae gien him twice as muckle thank
    To latten that abee!

6. "But eat an drink, my merrie young men,
    Eat, an be weel forn;
   For blaw it wind, or blaw it weet,
    Oor gude ship sails the morn."

7. Up it spak his youngest son,
    Sat by Sir Patrick's knie:
   "I beg you bide at hame, father,
    An I pray be ruled by me.

8. "For I saw the new mune late yestreen,
    Wi the auld mune in her arms;
   An ever an alake, my father dear,
    It's a token o diedly storms."

9. "It's eat an drink, my merrie young men,
    Eat, an be weel forn;
   For blaw it wind, or blaw it weet,
    Oor gude ship sails the morn."

10. They hadna sailed a league, a league,
    A league but only three,
   When the whirlin wind an the ugly jaws
    Cam drivin to their knie.

11. They hadna sailed a league, a league,
    A league but only five,
   When the whirlin wind an the ugly jaws
    Their gude ship began to rive.

12. They hadna sailed a league, a league,
    A league but only nine,
   When the whirlin wind an the ugly jaws
    Cam drivin to their chin.

13. "O whaur will I get a bonnie boy
    Will tak the steer in hand,
   Till I mount up to oor tapmast,
    To luik oot for dry land?"

14. "O here am I, a bonnie boy,
    Will tak the steer in hand,
   Till you mount up to oor tapmast,
    To luik oot for dry land."

15. He's gaen up to the tapmast,
    To the tapmast sae hie;
   He luikit around on every side,
    But dry land he couldna see.

16. He luikit on his youngest son,
    An the tear blindit his ee;
   Says, I wish you had been in your mother's bowr,
    But there you'll never be.

17. "Pray for yoursels, my merrie young men,
    Pray for yoursels an me,
   For the first landen that we will land
    Will be in the boddam o the sea."

18. Then up it raise the mermaiden,
    Wi the comb an glass in her hand:
   "Here's a health to you, my merrie young men,
    For you never will see dry land."

19. O laith, laith waur oor gude Scots lords
    To weet their cork-heeled shoon;
   But lang, lang ere the play was played,
    Their yellow locks soomed aboun.

20. There was Saturday, an Sabbath day,
    An Monnonday at morn,
   That feather-beds an silken sheets
    Cam floatin to Kinghorn.

21. It's och, och owre to Aberdour,
    It's fifty faddoms deep;
   An there lie a' oor gude Scots lords,
    Wi Sir Patrick Spens at their feet.

22. O lang, lang will his lady sit,
    Wi the fan into her hand,
   Until she see her ain dear lord
    Come sailin to dry land.

23. O lang, lang will his lady sit,
     Wi the tear into her ee,
   Afore she see her ain dear lord
   Come hieing to Dundee.

24. O lang, lang will his lady sit,
     Wi the black shoon on her feet,
   Afore she see Sir Patrick Spens
   Come drivin up the street.

Sir Cawline

CHILD NO. 61

This ballad, based on materials common to medieval romance, and preserved in a fairly full but yet fragmentary form in the Percy Folio, has been demonstrably current in Scottish oral tradition within the past two centuries. The two Scottish copies were not regarded as of equal authenticity, either with each other, or with the Folio copy: Child thought Buchan's an obvious manufacture ("We may doubt whether [it] was ever sung or said"), and thought Mrs. Harris's "most likely . . . put together by some one who was imperfectly acquainted with the copy in the Reliques" (Child, II, p. 61)—the last being a literary remaking by Percy out of hints in the Folio ballad. Child's relegation of the Harris and Buchan copies to an appendix deserves to be examined for its latent implications.

Child admits that the Harris copy "undoubtedly has passed through a succession of mouths" (II, p. 60). We know that Mrs. Harris not only said it, but sang it, having learned it traditionally in her childhood, in Perthshire, about 1790, from her old nurse. For further evidence of life in tradition we have Christie's tune, sung to some form of text not preserved by him, but close enough to Buchan's to be recognizable as the same ballad. As usual, Christie merely prints an "epitomized" version of Buchan for text. We may grant, after the arguments of William Walker and Alexander Keith, that Buchan's inventions differed not in kind but only in degree and taste, from the textual revisions of other, more esteemed, preservers of traditional balladry: that is, the presence of a ballad in his collection corroborates its existence in contemporary tradition in his time and region.

If Child be correct in the hypothesis that the ballad was in its latter days a rifacimento of Percy's spurious version, we would seem to have in this noteworthy case of a very late commencement (or recommencement) of a traditional career. It would appear hence that the era of creative ballad-making had not by any means expired by the end of the sixteenth century, but was still vigorous in Percy's own day. For the Harris version is not in the least a mere abridged and imperfect recollection of the *Reliques* text. On the contrary, Percy's pathetic ending has been repudiated for a happy conclusion; and the ballad has been simplified to a single episode, the combat with the eldritch knight, just as we have seen the complexities of "Sir Lionel" (No. 18) reduced to the central incident of the boar-fight. It is nothing to the point that the stylistic quality of this recreation is inferior and cheap. What is significant is

that, granting Child's surmise, between 1765 and 1790 an anonymous ballad-maker, half-acquainted with a piece in a printed book, could without the aid of the broadside press (apparently) fashion a fresh ballad, fit it to a traditional tune (or make, or make over, such a tune) and then by singing give his piece such a lease on life that it would be learned by nurses through the usual channels of oral delivery and handed on by their charges for the next hundred years.

If Child was wrong in his hypothesis, as he may have been, and if the Harris and Buchan variants are the descendants of an older and more deeply-rooted tradition, then of course they should be promoted from the appendix and placed at least on a level with the Folio version. And in fact their right to that promotion is good on any showing. We have the historical evidence of their traditional circulation; we have none for the Folio text; and on intrinsic grounds no case could be made out that the style of the Folio text is even passable for oral tradition. It may be in a tolerable minstrel style; but what is minstrel style other than an earlier fashion of the broadside style? The general level of artistic merit of popular ballads goes *pari passu* with the cultural level of those who transmit them traditionally. This is not basically a question of literate knowledge but of sympathetic awareness. In general, the interest of persons with such qualities has since the days of easy access to books gone elsewhere. But in Scotland money was scarce and books were dear; and so it happened that the average level of traditional balladry remained comparatively high in Scotland for a longer time than it did in England. It is no accident that for nearly a third of the ballads in Child's collection, the north of Scotland, particularly Aberdeenshire, provided the best texts. And these texts, for the most part, date from the eighteenth and early nineteenth centuries, the period of most general interest in this form.

There is at any rate no great problem of decision here for the musical editor. The two tunes which have been recovered are indubitably traditional, whatever reservations one may have as to the accuracy of their notation. One tune was learned in the late eighteenth century; the other probably considerably later. They appear to have nothing in common. The Harris tune is M/D, and there are interesting parallels to it in an Appalachian tune for "Young Beichan" (No. 53) (Sharp and Karpeles, *Appalachians*, 1932, I, p. 86[*H*]; as well as Greig's tune for "Hughie Graham" (No. 191).

1. "Sir Colin"

Harris MS., No. 12 [corrected]. Also in Child, 1882-98, V, p. 415; text, II, p. 61. Sung by Mrs. Harris, as learned in Perthshire, c. 1790-1800.

a M/D

The MS. is unskillfully written, but only the last two bars require adjustment in timing.

This variant is close to one collected by Greig for "Hughie Graham" (No. 191), q.v. Basically, the tune is allied to the type of "Boyne Water."

1. The king luikit owre his castle wa,
   To his nobles ane an a';
   Says, Whare it is him Sir Colin,
   I dinna see him amang you a'?

2. Up it spak an eldern knicht,
   Aye an even up spak he:
   "Sir Colin's sick for your dochter Janet,
   He's very sick, an like to dee."

3. "Win up, win up, my dochter Janet,
   I wat ye are a match most fine;
   Tak the baken bread an wine sae ried,
   An to Sir Colin ye maun gieng."

4. Up she rase, that fair Janet,
   An I wat weel she was na sweer,
   An up they rase, her merrie maries,
   An they said a' they wad gae wi her.

5. "No, no," said fair Janet,
   "No, no such thing can be;
   For a thrang to gae to a sick man's bour,
   I think it wald be great folie.

6. "How is my knicht, all last nicht?"
   "Very sick an like to dee;
   But if I had a kiss o your sweet lips,
   I wald lie nae langer here."

7. She leant her doon on his bed-side,
   I wat she gae him kisses three;
   But wi sighen said that fair Janet,
   "As for your bride, I daurna be.

8. "Unless you watch the Orlange hill,
   An at that hill there grows a thorn;
   There neer cam a liven man frae it,
   Sin the first nicht that I was born."

9. "Oh I will watch the Orlange hill,
   Though I waur thinkin to be slain;
   But I will gie you some love tokens,
   In case we never meet again."

10. He gae her rings to her fingers,
    Sae did he ribbons to her hair;
    He gae her a broach to her briest-bane,
    For fear that they sud neer meet mair.

11. She put her hand in her pocket,
    An she took out a lang, lang wand;
    "As lang's ony man this wand sall keep,
    There sall not a drap o his blude be drawn."

12. Whan een was come, an een-bells rung,
    An a' man boun for bed,
    There beheld him Sir Colin,
    Fast to the Orlange hill he rade.

13. The wind blew trees oot at the rutes,
    Sae did it auld castles doon;
    'Twas eneuch to fricht ony Christian knicht,
    To be sae far frae ony toon.

14. He rade up, sae did he doon,
    He rade even through the loan,
    Till he spied a knicht, wi a ladie bricht,
    Wi a bent bow intil his han.

15. She cried afar, ere she cam naur,
    I warn ye, kind sir, I rede ye flee;
    That for the love you bear to me,
    I warn ye, kind sir, that ye flee.

16. They faucht up, sae did they doon,
    They faucht even through the loan,
    Till he cut aff the king's richt han,
    Was set aboot wi chains a' goud.

17. "Haud your hand now, Sir Colin,
    I wat you've dung my love richt sair;
    Noo for the love ye bear to me,
    See that ye ding my love nae mair."

18. He wooed, he wooed that fair Janet,
    He wooed her and he brocht her hame;
    He wooed, he wooed that fair Janet,
    An ca'd her Dear-Coft till her name.

Fair Annie

CHILD NO. 62

THIS ballad, running back into the mists through Scandinavian and German analogues, does not appear in the Scottish record until the second half of the eighteenth century. As Child points out, the story—a story is not a ballad, though where there is a story there may be a ballad—is told by Marie de France before the year 1200, in the *Lai del Freisne*. From Scotland the ballad appears not to have traveled South, but it has been brought West and is found both in New England and in the Southern mountains.

All the tunes which we have are very late. It is interesting that one of the earliest in the record (learned c. 1885) exhibits the rhythm balanced precariously between triple and duple, whereas most of the rest present a straightforward duple rhythm. There is no evidence, however, to show that a triple rhythm was the original.

TUNES WITH TEXTS

GROUP A

1. "Fair Annie"

Greig-Duncan MS. 785 (Walker transcript), from Duncan MS., No. 11. Also in Greig and Keith, 1925, p. 50(1a). Sung by Mrs. Gillespie in Glasgow, 1905; learned in Buchan fifty years earlier.

a I, ending on V

This tune seems clearly related to Christie's tune for "Sir Patrick Spens" (No. 58), which he gives arbitrarily to "Young Bekie" (Christie, I, p. 8). Technically, this copy is Mixolydian, but it lacks the feeling of that mode, and I prefer to call it Ionian, with a dominant ending.

> O learn, learn, fair Annie,
> O learn to lie your leen,
> For I am gaun owre the sea
> To woo an' to bring hame.

GROUP B

3. "Fair Annie"

Davis, 1929, p. 566; text, p. 177. Sung by Mrs. Martha E. Lethcoe, Damascus, Va., September 2, 1921. Collected by John Stone.

p π[1]

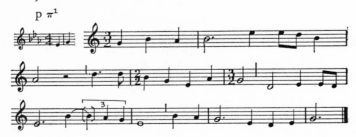

This copy has had to be drastically re-barred. The poignant tune seems related to the type appearing with "The False Lover" (No. 218) and elsewhere. Cf. Christie's "The Place where my love Johnny dwells" (I, p. 144).

1. "Comb back your hair, Fair Annie," he said,
    "Comb it back into your crown,
   For you shall look a fair maid's life
      When I bring my bridal home."

2. "How can I look a fair maid's life,
    A maid all in her bloom,
   When six fair sons I've had for you
      And another yet to come?"

3. On the back door he hung a silk towel,
    Hanging on a silver pin,
   For Fair Annie to wipe her eyes
      As she passed out and in.

4. Six months being gone and nine coming on,
    Fair Annie thought the time long;
   She took her spy glass in her hand
      And up her bower she ran.

5. She looked east, she looked west,
    She looked all under the sun,
   And she saw Lord Thomas
      Bringing his bridal home.

6. "You are welcome, Lord Thomas," she said,
    "You are welcomed home by me;
   You and your men, your merry men
      Are all as welcome as one."

7. She waited on them all day long
    With strong brew ale and wine;
   She taken herself of cold well water
      To keep her spirits mild.

8. She waited on them all day long,
    Fair Annie thought the time long;
   She takened her flute in her hand
      And up her bower she run.

9. She fluted east, she fluted west,
    She fluted loud and shrill;
   She wished her seven sons were seven grey hounds,
      And her a wolf on the hill.

10. "Come down stairs, Fair Annie," she says,
    "Come down stairs," says she.
    "Tell me the name of your father dear
    And I'll tell mine to thee."

11. "Prince Douglas was my father's name,
    Queen Chatten was my mother,
    King Henry was my brother dear,
    Queen Mary was my sister."

12. "If Prince Douglas was your father dear,
    Queen Chatten was your mother,
    King Henry was your brother dear,
    I'm sure I am your sister.

13. "I have seven ships sailing on the sea,
    All loaded to the brim;
    Six of them I'll give to you,
    If you'll have Lord Thomas hung;
    Six of them I'll give to you,
    And one will carry me home."

Child Waters

CHILD NO. 63

THIS beautiful and moving ballad, which Child was willing to give preeminence over all other ballads in any language, appears to have maintained its popular favor, at least in Scotland, well into the nineteenth century, and has been lately found in North Carolina and Arkansas. There is a gap of over a century between the oldest text and the next. Mrs. Brown's tune, unfortunately, was not recorded, although her text was taken down more than once. The two Scottish tunes, nearly a hundred years apart, seem to have but the most tenuous relationship, if any; and the Arkansas tune is again quite distinct.

It may be mentioned here that Mrs. Harris was a little girl when she learned her ballads from her nurse, through whom they are said to go back orally to the manse of the Reverend P. Duncan, about the year 1745. Mrs. Harris herself was born in Blairgowrie, Perthshire, in 1782; but the songs she taught her children were perhaps not set down until after the middle of the next century. There is, however, no reason to suppose that they are not in the main as she had learned them, due allowance being made for lack of skill in notation. The present tune has two obvious errors in the MS., quarters being written for the eighths in the sixth bar; but the extra beat in the ninth bar appears genuine, and may be left uncorrected. The irregularity in the next to last bar might be unintentional, but it too may stand. In both these cases the extra beat is given in the MS. to the bar following.

Greig's pentatonic tune, also in the Dorian area, has already appeared in a Dorian form in connection with "Young Akin" (Child No. 41), where it was given by the same singer. It may have a distant connection with the "Boyne Water" family.

TUNES WITH TEXTS

1. "Fair Margaret"

Harris MS., No. 7 (emended by Editor); text, No. 8, fol. 12b. Also in Child, 1882-98, V, p. 415; text, II, p. 91. Originally from Jannie Scott, an old nurse in Perthshire, c. 1790.

a D

In the tune as printed in Child's Appendix (V, p. 415), the verbal emphases are wrenched into conformity with a four-square barring throughout. The above reading follows the time-values of the MS.

1. "I beg you bide at hame, Margaret,
   An sew your silken seam;
   If ye waur in the wide Hielands,
   Ye wald be owre far frae hame."

2. "I winna bide at hame," she said,
   "Nor sew my silken seam;
   For if I waur in the wide Hielands,
   I wald no be owre far frae hame."

3. "My steed sall drink the blude-red wine,
   An you the water wan;
   I'll mak you sigh, an say, alace,
   That ever I loed a man!"

4. "Though your steed does drink the blude-red wine,
   An me the water wan,
   Yet will I sing, an merry be,
   That ever I loed a man."

5. "My hounds shall eat the bread o wheat,
   An you the bread o bran;
   I'll mak you sigh, an say, alace,
   That ever you loed Lord John!"

6. "Though your hounds do eat the bread o wheat,
   An me the bread o bran,
   Yet will I sing, an merrie be,
   That ever I loed Lord John."

7. He turned aboot his high horse head,
   An awa he was boun to ride;
   She kilted up her green clieden,
   An after him she gaed.

8. Whan they cam to that water
   Whilk a' man ca the Clyde,
   He turned aboot his high horse head,
   Said, Ladie, will you ride?

9. "I learnt it in my mother's bour,
   I wish I had learnt it weel,
   That I could swim this wan water
   As weel as fish or eel."

10. Whan at the middle o that water,
    She sat doon on a stone;
    He turned aboot his high horse head,
    Says, Ladie, will ye loup on?

11. "I learnt in my mother's bour,
    I wish I had learnt it better,
    That I culd swim this wan water
    As weel as eel or otter."

12. He has taen the narrow ford,
    An she has taen the wide;
    Lang, lang ere he was at the middle,
    She was sittin at the ither side.

13. . . . .
     Wi sighen said that Fair Margaret,
        Alace, I'm far frae hame!

14. "Hoo mony miles is't to your castle?
        Noo Lord John, tell to me;"
     "Hoo mony miles is't to my castle?
        It's thirty miles an three:"
     Wi sighen said that Fair Margaret,
        It'll never be gane by me!

15. But up it spak the wily bird,
        As it sat on the tree,
     "Rin on, rin on noo, Fair Margaret,
        It scarcely miles is three."

16. Whan they cam to the wide Hielands,
        An lichted on the green,
     Every an spak Erse to anither,
        But Margaret she spak nane.

17. Whan they waur at table set,
        An birlin at the best,
     Margaret set at a bye-table,
        An fain she wald hain rest.

18. "Oh mither, mither, mak my bed
        Wi clean blankets an sheets,
     An lay my futeboy at my feet,
        The sounder I may sleep."

19. She has made Lord John his bed,
        Wi clean blankets an sheets,
     An laid his futeboy at his feet,
        But neer a wink culd he sleep.

20. "Win up, win up noo, Fair Margaret,
        An see that my steed has meat;
     See that his corn is in his travisse,
        Nor lyin amang his feet."

21. Slowly, slowly rase she up,
        An slowly put she on,
     An slowly gaed she doon the stair,
        Aye makin a heavy moan.

        .   .   .   .

22. "An asken, an asken, gude Lord John,
        I pray you grant it me;
     For the warst bed in a' your hoose,
        To your young son an me."

23. "Your asken is but sma, Margaret,
        Sune grantet it shall be;
     For the best bed in a' my hoose
        Is owre little for thee."

24. "An asken, an asken, gude Lord John,
        I pray you grant it me;
     For the warst ale in a' your hoose,
        That ye wald gie to me."

25. "Your asken is but sma, Margaret,
        Sune grantet it sall be;
     For the best wine in a' my hoose
        Is owre little for thee.

26. "But cheer up your heart noo, Fair Margaret,
        For, be it as it may,
     Your kirken an your fair weddin
        Sall baith be on one day."

2. "Lord William and Lady Margaret"

Greig MSS., III, p. 166; text, Bk. 742, XXXII, p. 97. Also in Greig and Keith, 1925, p. 52. Sung by Alexander Robb, New Deer, Aberdeenshire.

a π³

The same singer used a variant of this tune for "Young Akin" (No. 41). The underlying pattern is that of "Boyne Water."

1. Lord William stood in his stable door,
        Says, I'll awa & ride;
     Lady Marit stood in her bower door,
        Says, I'll go by your side.

2. . . . .
     It's if ye go with me, he said,
        My horse-boy ye maun be.

3. He rade on & she gaed on,
        And she gaed by his side,
     Till they cam' till a wan water
        And a' man ca'd it Clyde.

4. He rade in & she wade in,
        Till it cam' till her knee,
     And sichin' said this fair ladie,
        This widin's nae for me.

5. But he rade in & she wade in,
        Till it cam' till her han',
     And the bairnie atween her sidies twa,
        For caul' was like to [tyne].

6. But in the middle o' Clyde's water
        There stan's a steadfast stone,
     And he turned his broon horse' heid aboot,
        And he's ta'en his lady on.

7. When he arrived at his father's ha',
        . . . .
        . . . .

8. There was 4 & 20 bonnie ladies
   Stood a' upon the green,
But the bonniest lady amon' them a'
   Took Willie's horse frae him.

9. There was 4 & 20 braw ladies
   Sat a' thegither at meat,   (*met*)
But the bonniest lady amo' them a'
   At a by-table was set.
But the bonniest lady amo' them a'
   A bit she couldna eat.   (*et*)

10. . . . .
   . . . . . .
   Go groom my horse, gae sup my horse,
   And rub him down sae fine[.]

11. He's nowise like a man, Willie,
   He's nowise like a man,
Your horse-boy's like a woman wi' bairn,
   Or else she's borne a son.

12. . . . .
   She thocht she heard a bairn's greet
   Likewise a lady's moan,
   . . . .

13. He gae the door wi' his fit,
   And keppit it wi' his knee,
Till iron bolts & steel staples
   On the fleer he gart them flee.

Fair Janet

CHILD NO. 64

THE tune of Child's A was preserved, along with the text, from the singing of an old woman in Perthshire. It appears to have been printed for the first time by G. F. Graham, in his *Songs of Scotland* (1848-49, I, p. 92), and has been reprinted thence a number of times. The leading-note at the opening of the fourth phrase may be editorial, in which case the tune, although lacking its fourth, would show strong Mixolydian inclinations. The triple time seems to have been heard by the earlier collectors far more frequently than of late.

TUNES WITH TEXTS

1. [Fair Janet]

Graham, 1848-49, I, p. 92. Also in Lady John Scott's Sharpe MS., NL Scotland MS. 843, fol. 10, in hand of Thomas Logorwood Hateby; and Eyre-Todd, n.d. |1894|, p. 74. Tune from C. K. Sharpe, as sung by an old woman in Perthshire. Text from Sharpe, 1823, p. 1; also in Child, 1882-98, II, p. 103.

a I/Ly (inflected VII)

1. "Ye maun gang to your father, Janet,
   Ye maun gang to him soon;
   Ye maun gang to your father, Janet,
   In case that his days are dune."

2. Janet's awa to her father,
   As fast as she could hie:
   "O what's your will wi me, father?
   O what's your will wi me?"

3. "My will wi you, Fair Janet," he said,
   "It is both bed and board;
   Some say that ye loe Sweet Willie,
   But ye maun wed a French lord."

4. "A French lord maun I wed, father?
   A French lord maun I wed?
   Then, by my sooth," quo Fair Janet,
   "He's neer enter my bed."

5. Janet's awa to her chamber,
   As fast as she could go;
   Wha's the first ane that tapped there,
   But Sweet Willie her jo?

6. "O we maun part this love, Willie,
   That has been lang between;
   There's a French lord coming oer the sea,
   To wed me wi a ring;
   There's a French lord coming oer the sea,
   To wed and tak me hame."

7. "If we maun part this love, Janet,
   It causeth mickle woe;
   If we maun part this love, Janet,
   It makes me into mourning go."

8. "But ye maun gang to your three sisters,
   Meg, Marion, and Jean;
   Tell them to come to Fair Janet,
   In case that her days are dune."

9. Willie's awa to his three sisters,
   Meg, Marion, and Jean:
   "O haste, and gang to Fair Janet,
   I fear that her days are dune."

10. Some drew to them their silken hose,
    Some drew to them their shoon,
    Some drew to them their silk manteils,
    Their coverings to put on,
    And they're awa to Fair Janet,
    By the hie light o the moon.

* * * * * *

11. "O I have born this babe, Willie,
    Wi mickle toil and pain;
    Take hame, take hame, your babe, Willie,
    For nurse I dare be nane."

12. He's tane his young son in his arms,
    And kisst him cheek and chin,
    And he's awa to his mother's bower,
    By the hie light o the moon.

13. "O open, open, mother," he says,
    "O open, and let me in;
    The rain rains on my yellow hair,
    And the dew drops oer my chin,
    And I hae my young son in my arms,
    I fear that his days are dune."

14. With her fingers lang and sma
    She lifted up the pin,
    And with her arms lang and sma
    Received the baby in.

15. "Gae back, gae back now, Sweet Willie,
    And comfort your fair lady;
    For where ye had but ae nourice,
    Your young son shall hae three."

16. Willie he was scarce awa,
    And the lady put to bed,
    Whan in and came her father dear:
    "Make haste, and busk the bride."

17. "There's a sair pain in my head, father,
    There's a sair pain in my side;
    And ill, O ill, am I, father,
    This day for to be a bride."

18. "O ye maun busk this bonny bride,
    And put a gay mantle on;
    For she shall wed this auld French lord,
    Gin she should die the morn."

19. Some put on the gay green robes,
    And some put on the brown;
    But Janet put on the scarlet robes,
    To shine foremost throw the town.

20. And some they mounted the black steed,
    And some mounted the brown;
    But Janet mounted the milk-white steed,
    To ride foremost throw the town.

21. "O wha will guide your horse, Janet?
    O wha will guide him best?"
    "O wha but Willie, my true-love?
    He kens I loe him best."

22. And when they cam to Marie's kirk,
    To tye the haly ban,
    Fair Janet's cheek looked pale and wan,
    And her colour gaed an cam.

23. When dinner it was past and done,
    And dancing to begin,
    "O we'll go take the bride's maidens,
    And we'll go fill the ring."

24. O ben than cam the auld French lord,
    Saying, Bride, will ye dance with me?
    "Awa, awa, ye auld French lord,
    Your face I downa see."

25. O ben than cam now Sweet Willie,
    He cam with ane advance:
    "O I'll go tak the bride's maidens,
    And we'll go tak a dance."

26. "I've seen ither days wi you, Willie,
    And so has mony mae,
    Ye would hae danced wi me mysel,
    Let a' my maidens gae."

27. O ben than cam now Sweet Willie,
    Saying, Bride, will ye dance wi me?
    "Aye, by my sooth, and that I will,
    Gin my back should break in three."

28. She had nae turned her throw the dance,
    Throw the dance but thrice,
    Whan she fell doun at Willie's feet,
    And up did never rise.

29. Willie's taen the key of his coffer,
    And gien it to his man:
    "Gae hame, and tell my mother dear
    My horse he has me slain;
    Bid her be kind to my young son,
    For father he has nane."

30. The tane was buried in Marie's kirk,
    And the tither in Marie's quire;
    Out of the tane there grew a birk,
    And the tither a bonny brier.

Lady Maisry

CHILD NO. 65

THE English records of the last fifty years present the most consistent picture of a melodic tradition for "Lady Maisry." Nevertheless, they cover a wide modal ambit (from major to Æolian), and carry echoes of familiar songs—"The Sprig of Thyme," "The Bailiff's Daughter," "The Wife of Usher's Well"—and carol-tunes. They prefer the authentic range, with a favorite mid-cadence on the dominant, and first-phrase cadence on the tonic. All are in duple time.

In contrast, the two earliest records, which are Scottish, are unrelated to each other and to the English or American tunes, but agree in a somewhat uncomfortable choice of triple time. Mrs. Brown's tune is a surprise after the mid-cadence; and it is just possible that an inexpert copyist, her nephew or another,

when writing the tune over fair, started on a new stave a note above the true one at the beginning of the fourth—or perhaps even the third—phrase, and kept it up consistently to the end. If so, the tune was Dorian. As it stands in the MS., the first half is Æ/P, but the second half has an inflected second and sixth, and the last two phrases seem to modulate to a new anchorage—unless we think of it as a timid Phrygian, with the second inflected. On the other hand, it may be that all that is wrong is an omission of a sharp on the second note in the fifth bar—in which case the tune is Æolian, with an unimportant accidental on lower VI.

The American tune, from Kentucky, here printed, belongs to the "Gypsy Laddie" clan.

TUNES WITH TEXTS

1. "Lady Maisery"

Ritson-Tytler-Brown MS., p. 91. Sung by Mrs. Brown, Falkland, Aberdeenshire; copied by Joseph Ritson, c. 1792-94.

a Bimodal? (Æ—P)

1st half lacks II (Æ/P); 2nd half inflected II and VI and lacks IV, V

Cf. the headnote, above, on the modality of this tune.

1. The young lords o' the north country
     Have all a wooing gane,
   To win the love o' lady Maisery,
     But of them she would ha' nane.

2. O they have courted lady Maisery
     Wi' broaches and wi' rings,
   An' they ha' courted her lady Maisery
     Wi' a' kin' kind o' things.

3. An' they ha' sought her lady Maisery
     Frae father and frae mother,
   An' they have sought her lady Maisery
     Frae sister and frae brother.

4. And they ha' follow'd her lady Maisery
     Through cha'mer and through ha'
   But a' that they could say to her,
     Her answer still was na'.

5. ["]O had your tongues, young men, she says,
     An' think nae mair o' me,
   For i've gi'n my love to an English lord,
     An' i have nae mair to gi."

6. Her fathers kitchy boy hard that,
     Ane ill deid may he dee!

7. "O is my father and mother well,
     But and my brothers three?
   Gin my sister lady Mais'ry be well,
     There's naething can ail me."

8. "Your father and your mother is well,
     Likewise your brothers three;
   Your sister lady Maisery is well,
     So big wi' bairn gangs she."

9. "Gin this be true you tell to me,
     My malison light on thee!
   But gin it be a lie you tell,
     You shall be hanged hi'."

10. He's done him to his sisters bow'r
     Wi' meikle deil and care,
    An' there he saw her lady Maisery
     Keming her yallow hair.

11. ["]O wha is aught that bairn, he says,
     That ye sae big are wi'?
    An' gin you winna own the truth,
     This moment you shall die.["]

12. She turn'd her right and round about,
     An' the kem fell frae her hand,
    A trembling seiz'd her fair body,
     An' her rosy cheek grew wan.

13. "O, pardon me, my brother dear,
     An' the truth i'll own to thee;
    My bairn it is to lord William,
     And now he is betrothed to me."

14. "O, could na ye gotten dukes or lords
     Into your own country,
    That ye drew up wi' an English dog,
     To bring this shame on me?

15. But ye man gie up the English blood,
     The moment your babe is born,
    For gin you keep by'm an hour longer
     Your life shall be forborn."

16. "I will gie up this English blood
     Till my young babe be born,

GROUP C

GROUP C

But the never a day nor hour langer,
 Though my life should be forborn."

17. "O, whare is a' my merry young men,
 Whom i gie meat and fee,
To pu' the thistle and the thorn,
 To burn this vile whore wi'?"

18. "O, whare will i get a bonny boy,
 To help me in my need?
To run with haste to lord William,
 An' bid him come wi' speed?"

19. O, out it spake a bonny boy,
 Stood by her brothers side,
"O, i would run your errand, lady,
 O'er all the world wide.

20. Aft have i run your errands, lady,
 Wi' sa't tears on my cheek;
Aft have i run your errands, lady,
 Whan blawn baith win' and weet."

21. O, whan he came to broken brigs,
 He bent his bow and swam,
An' whan he came to green grass growing,
 He took off his sheen and ran.

22. And (whan) he came to lord Williams yates,
 He bade na to chap or ca',
But set his bent bow till his breast,
 An' lightly lap the wa';
And or the porter was at the gate,
 The boy was in the ha'.

23. "O is my biggins broken, boy?
 Or is my towers won?
Or is my lady lighter yet,
 Of a dear daughter or son?"

24. ["]Your biggins is no brunt, my lord,
 Nor is your towers won,
But the fairest lady in a' the land
 For you this day man burn."

25. "O, saddle to me the black, the black,
 Or saddle to me the brown,
O, saddle to me the swiftest steed
 That e'er rode frae a town."

26. Or he was near a mile awa'
 She hear'd his wild horse sneeze:
"Mend up the fire, my false brother,
 It's nae come to my knees."

27. And whan he lighted at the yate,
 She hard his bridle ring:
"Mend up the fire, my false brother,
 It's far yet frae my chin.

28. Mend up the fire to me, she says,
 Mend up the fire to me,
For i see him coming hard and fast
 Will soon men' 't up to thee.

29. O, gin my hands had been loose, Willie,
 So hard as they are bound,
I would have turn'd me frae the gleed,
 An' casten out your young son."

30. "O i'll gar burn for thee, Mais'ry,
 Your sister and your brother;
An' i'll gar burn for thee, Mais'ry,
 Your father and your mother;

31. And i'll gar burn for thee, Mais'ry,
 The chief of all your kin;
An' the last bonfire that i come to,
 Mysel' i will cast in."

8. [Lady Maisry]

Sharp MSS., 912/986. Also in Sharp and Marson, 3rd series, 1906, p. 56; and Sharp, 1916, p. 26. Sung by John Barnett, Bridgwater, April 18, 1906.

p Æ

1. She called to her little page boy
 Who was her brother's son,
She told him as quick as he could go
 To bring the lord safe home.

2. Now the first mile he would walk,
 And the second he would run,
And when he came to a broken bridge
 He would bend his breast and swim.

3. When he came to the new castle,
 The lord was sot to meat.
If you knew as much as me
 How little would you eat.

4. Is my bower falling, falling down,
 Or is my tower down,
Or is my gay lady put to bed
 With a daughter or a son?

5. O no, your bower is not a-falling down
 Neither your tower down,
Neither is your gay lady put to bed
 With a daughter or a son.

6. O no your bower is not falling down,
 Neither my tower down,
But we are afraid before you return
 Your lady will be dead and gone.

7. Now when he came to the new castle
 He heard a big bell toll,
And there he saw eight noble noble men
 A-bearing of a pall.

8. Lay down, lay down that gentle, gentle corpse
 As it lay fast asleep,
Lay down, lay down that gentle, gentle corpse
 That I wish to kiss so sweet.

9. Six times he kissed her red ruby lips,
 Nine times he kissed her chin,

Ten times he kissed her snowy white breast
Which love did enter in.

10. The lady was buried on that Sunday
Before the prayer was end,
And the lord he died on Sunday next
Before the prayer begun.

Sharp makes numerous verbal alterations in the printed copy to render the text more acceptable, and introduces the following stanza between nos. 6 and 7:

Come saddle, saddle my milk white steed,
Come saddle my pony too,
That I may neither eat nor drink
Till I come to the old castell.

GROUP D

12. [Lady Maisry]

Sharp MSS., 3898/2835 (in no signature). Also in Sharp and Karpeles, 1932, I, p. 99(B). Sung by Mrs. Dan Bishop, Teges, Clay County, Ky., August 21, 1917.

a D/M

This belongs to the "Gypsy Laddy" tribe. Cf. No. 200.

1. Down stepped her old father dear,
He stepped over the floor.
It's how do you do, Lady Margrie, said he,
Since you became a whore?

2. O dear father, I am no whore,
Nor never expect to be;
But I have a child by an English lord,
And I hope he'll marry me.

3. Down stepped her old mother dear,
She stepped over the floor.
It's how do you do, Lady Margrie, said she,
Since you became a whore?

4. O dear mother, I am no whore,
Nor never expect to be;
But I have a child by an English lord,
And I hope he'll* marry me.

5. Down stepped her oldest brother dear,
He stepped over the floor.
It's how do you do, Lady Margrie, said he,
Since you became a whore? (or, How do you do
to-day?)

6. Very bad, very bad, dear brother,
As you can plainly see,

For my father and mother is both gathering wood
To burn my poor body.

7. I wish I had some pretty little one,
One errand for to run.
I'd run to my young lord's house
And tell him I said to come,
And to come quickly,
For my father and mother are both gathering wood
To burn my poor body.

8. Down stepped her brother's eldest son,
And stepped down over the floor,
And says: Many a mile that I have run,
And one for you I'll go.

9. I wish him well, for ever well,
And here send him a ring,
In hopes that he may mourn after me
But come to my burying.

10. I wish him well, for ever well,
And here I send him a glove,
In hopes that he might mourn after me,
But seek him another true love.

11. He run and he run till he came to the broad water,
He pitched in and swum;
He swum to the other side
And took to his heels and run.

12. He run to the young lord's gate,
And tingled on the bell;
And no one was so ready to rise and let him in
As the young lord himself.

13. What news, what news, my pretty little page,
What news have you brought to me?
.   .   .   .

14. Go saddle unto me the make-speed horse,
Go saddle unto me the brown,
Go saddle unto me the fastest horse
That ever run on ground.

15. .   .   .   .
He got his pistols and sword and bugle,
And threw his bugle around his neck.

16. As he was going round them lone fields
And a-going in full speed,
The ring bursted off his finger
And his nose broke out for to bleed.

17. O dear mother, I value not† one straw,
For my young lord is coming,
I hear his bugle blow.
.   .   .   .   .   .

* 1932: he will
† 1932: value you not

Young Hunting

CHILD NO. 68

THIS Scottish ballad, if it ever had any currency in England, seems to have left no trace there, but to have passed directly to America, where it has enjoyed a great vogue in our own century—at least in the Appalachians.

The musical tradition, for which evidence remains from the late eighteenth and early nineteenth centuries as well as from recent dates, is perplexed and hard to make out. The records tend to fall into small groups of obviously related tunes, individual members of which strongly suggest, in one way or another, a connection with other groups. Thus it is possible, if we had a fuller body of evidence, that a continuous tradition uniting the whole mass could be deduced. It is noteworthy that three out of the four early records are in triple rhythm, whereas the modern records show a fairly strong tendency toward some kind of duple rhythm. If we choose to treat the recent 3/4 (sc. 6/4) and 6/8 examples as duple, and those of mixed 3/2 2/2 time as actually duple with holds, the statement can be made absolute.

An interesting point arises in connection with the small group of variants the texts of which commence with the sound of a distant horn, and the mixed feelings of the girl when she hears it. The tunes associated with these texts are members of the "Lady Isabel" family in its English branch. (Cf. *ante*, Child No. 4.) Now in the later variants of "Lady Isabel," there is no mention of a horn. But in earlier texts, as Child A, and in some continental analogues, the horn plays a very important part: in fact, its music has such supernatural force that the heroine is won by it alone to run away with the knight who blows it.

No other British ballad, I believe, makes such use of a horn, except "The Elfin Knight." The present occurrence, therefore, may be an intrusion from the other ballad, and may have drawn the characteristic tune over with it; or the tune may have brought the horn into "Young Hunting," from versions of "Lady Isabel" no longer sung. It is also worth notice that both ballads, besides sharing the theme of a sweetheart's killing her lover (though for very different reasons), make particular use of a talking bird. In "Young Hunting" this bird is taken by Wimberly to be a relic of belief in metempsychosis, the bird being the soul of the dead lover. It plays a significant role in the narrative. In "Lady Isabel," its function is quite superfluous to the plot, and appears to be an importation. There may be here a borrowing in the other direction, underlined by the usual promise in both ballads of a cage of beaten gold as a reward for silence. At any rate, there is sufficient evidence of a crossing of the two ballads in tradition.* It is a fact of less significance that the characteristic American tune of "Lady Isabel" is also found in some variants of "Young Hunting," because that tune appears in so many other connections as well.

The variants assembled run predominantly to the Ionian and Mixolydian modes, or to corresponding hexatonic forms. The middle cadences of the B group fall often on the 2nd; of the C group on the 5th; and of the D groups on the 4th and 5th.

---

* This point is discussed in *The Ballad as Song*, 1969, pp. 53-54 and mentioned in a table of mutual borrowings among the Child ballads, compiled by T. P. Coffin, *JAF*, LXII (1949), p. 158.

TUNES WITH TEXTS

GROUP A

2. [Young Hunting]

Sharp MSS., 3108/. Also in Sharp and Karpeles, 1932, I, p. 107(F). Sharp originally heard it from Mrs. Campbell, who learned it from Mrs. Hall. It was sung by Mrs. Hall, Kensington, Walker County, Ga., in April 1914.

Probably on C, a I (—II, ending on I)
If on A, p Æ (—IV, ending on *VII*)

1. Come in, come in, loving Henry, said she,
And stay all night with me;
For it's been almost one quarter of a year
Since I spake one word unto thee.

2. I can't come in, Lady Margaret, said he,
Nor stay all night with thee,
For the girl that I left in the Arkansas land
Will think long of my return.

3. Then stooping over the great high fence
And kissing all so sweet,
She had a penknife in her hand
And she plunged it into the deep.

4. Some taken him by his lily-white hands,
Some taken him by his feet,
And they carried him to the broad water side
And plunged him into the deep.

5. Lay there, lay there, loving Henry, said she,
Till the meat drops off your bones,
And the girl you left in the Arkansas land
Will think long of your return.

6. Come in, come in, pretty parrot, said she,
And sing all on my knee;
Your cage shall be made of ivory beaten gold
And the doors of ivory.

7. I can't come in, Lady Margaret, said he,
Nor sing all on your knee,
For you are the girl that killed loving Henry,
And surely you might kill me.

8. I wish I had a bow and arrow,
   And it all in its prime,
   I'd shoot yon yonders pretty little bird
   That sits on that tall pine.

9. Who cares I for your bow and arrow,
   And it all in its prime,
   I fly away to some lonesome valley
   And 'light on some high pine.

The text is missing in the Sharp MSS.

4. "Earl Richard"

Motherwell, 1827, App'x., No. 11 (2nd set). Also in Chambers, 1844, p. 9.

p Æ/D

GROUP B

6. "Earl Richard"

Motherwell, 1827, App'x., No. 8; text, App'x., p. xvii.

a I, ending on VIII.

Earl Richard is a hunting gone
   As hard as he could ride,
His hunting horn about his neck
   And his broad sword by his side.

13. [Young Hunting]

Sharp MSS., 4470/. Also in Sharp and Karpeles, 1932, I, p. 112(K). Sung by Mrs. Frances Richards, at St. Peter's School, Callaway, Va., August 17, 1918.

p π¹

You needn't ride East, you needn't ride West,
You needn't ride under the sun,
For there's ne'er a doctor in old Scotland
Can cure what I have done.

GROUP Da

27. [Young Hunting]

Sharp MSS., 4265/3065. Also in Sharp and Karpeles, 1932, I, p. 112(J). Sung by Mrs. Dol Small, at Nellysford, Va., May 22, 1918.

m I

This belongs to the English type of "Lady Isabel" (No. 4).

1. Last Friday night Lady Margaret she lie
   A-sleeping very sad.
   She heard a sound of a bugle horn,
   Which made her heart very glad.

2. She thought it were her brother John
   Returning from his king,
   Although it were her Henery
   Returning from his wild hunting.

3. Get down, get down, O Henery,
   And stay all night with me,
   And the very best of lodging I have here,
   I'll give it all to thee.

4. I shan't get down, I won't get down
   And stay all night with thee,
   For I've a lady in the merry green land
   I love far better than thee.

5. I wish I had my string and bow,
   And my arrow too.
   I'd pierce it to your heart so free
   That you'd be seen no more.

   Then up spoke a little par-ri-ot
   That sits on yonder tree:

How can you murder your own true love
That you and I have seen.

7. Come down, come down, little par-ri-ot,
   And set on my right knee.
   I'll buy you a cage of yellow gold
   And hang it on yonders tree.

8. I shan't come down, I won't come down
   And set on your right knee,
   For the sooner you'd murder your own true love,
   The sooner you'd murder me.

GROUP D♭

34. "The ladie stude in her bour-door"

Harris MS., No. 5. Also in Child, 1882-98, V, p. 416; text,
II, p. 147(C). From Mrs. Harris, Perthshire.

If tonic G, p M; if tonic C, a I, ending on V

Although technically Mixolydian, this has no feeling of that mode,
and is probably authentic Ionian, with a dominant ending.

1. The ladie stude in her bour-door,
   In her bour-door as she stude,
   She thocht she heard a bridle ring,
   That did her bodie gude.

2. She thocht it had been her father dear,
   Come ridin owre the sand;
   But it was her true-love Riedan,
   Come hiean to her hand.

3. "You're welcome, you're welcome, Young Riedan,"
                                        she said,
   "To coal an cannel-licht;
   You're welcome, you're welcome, Young Riedan,
   To sleep in my bour this nicht."

4. "I thank you for your coal, madame,
   An for your cannel tae;
   There's a fairer maid at Clyde's Water,
   I love better than you."

5. "A fairer maid than me, Riedan?
   A fairer maid than me?
   A fairer maid than ten o me
   You shurely neer did see."

6. He leant him owre his saddle-bow,
   To gie her a kiss sae sweet;
   She keppit him on a little penknife,
   An gae him a wound sae deep.

7. "Oh hide! oh hide! my bourswoman,
   Oh hide this deed on me!
   An the silks that waur shappit for me at Yule
   At Pasch sall be sewed for thee."

8. They saidled Young Riedan, they bridled Young
                                            Riedan,
   The way he was wont to ride;
   Wi a huntin-horn aboot his neck,
   An a sharp sword by his side.

9. An they are on to Clyde's Water
   An they rade it up an doon,
   An the deepest linn in a' Clyde's Water
   They flang him Young Riedan [in].

10. "Lie you there, you Young Riedan,
    Your bed it is fu wan;
    The [maid] you hae at Clyde's Water,
    For you she will think lang."

11. Up it spak the wily bird,
    As it sat on the tree:
    "Oh wae betide you, ill woman,
    An an ill death may you dee!
    For he had neer anither love,
    Anither love but thee."

12. "Come doon, come doon, my pretty parrot,
    An pickle wheat aff my glue;
    An your cage sall be o the beaten goud,
    Whan it's of the willow tree."

13. "I winna come doon, I sanna come doon,
    To siccan a traitor as thee:
    For as you did to Young Riedan,
    Sae wald you do to mee."

14. Come doon, come doon, my pretty parrot,
    An pickle wheat aff my hand;
    An your cage sall be o the beaten goud,
    Whan it's o the willow wand."

15. "I winna come doon, I sanna come doon,
    To siccan a traitor as thee;
    You wald thraw my head aff my hase-bane,
    An fling it in the sea."

16. It fell upon a Lammas-tide
    The king's court cam ridin bye:
    "Oh whare is it him Young Riedan?
    It's fain I wald him see."

17. "Oh I hae no seen Young Riedan
    Sin three lang weeks the morn;
    It bodes me sair, and driels me mair,
    Clyde's Water's him forlorn."

18. Up it spak the wily bird,
    As it sat on the tree;
    . . . .
    . . . .

19. "Leave aff, leave aff your day-seekin,
    An ye maun seek by nicht;
    Aboon the place Young Riedan lies,
    The cannels burn bricht."

20. They gae up their day-seekin,
    An they did seek by nicht;
    An owre the place Young Riedan lay,
    The cannels burnt bricht.

21. The firsten grip his mother got
    Was o his yellow hair;
    An was na that a dowie grip,
    To get her ae son there!

22. The nexten grip his mother got
    Was o his milk-white hand;
    An wasna that a dowie grip,
    To bring sae far to land!

23. White, white waur his wounds washen,
    As white as ony lawn;
    But sune's the traitor stude afore,
    Then oot the red blude sprang.

. . . .

24. Fire wadna tak on her bourswoman,
    Niether on cheek nor chin;
    But it took fast on thae twa hands
    That flang young Riedan in.

25. "Come oot, come oot, my bourswoman,
    Come oot, lat me win in;
    For as I did the deed mysell,
    Sae man I drie the pine."

37. [Young Hunting]

Sharp MSS., 4600/3219. Also in Sharp and Karpeles, 1932,
I, p. 113(L). Sung by Mrs. Virginia Bennett, Burnsville,
N.C., September 13, 1918.

m M (—VI)

1. Get down, get down, loving Henry, said she,
   And stay all night with me;
   And your bed shall be made of the purest yellow
                                                gold,
   And the pillows of ivory.

2. I can't get down, Lady Margaret, said he,
   Or stay all night with thee,
   For the girl that I left in the Arkansas land
   Will longingly look for me.

3. She leaned her hand against the fence,
   Just to speak a word or two,
   And with a little knife that she held in her hand,
   She pierced him through and through.

4. O live, O live, loving Henry, said she,
   One hour and a half or three,
   And all the doctors that live in this land
   Shall come to attend thee.

5. How can I live, Lady Margaret, said he,
   One hour and a half or three,
   When don't you see my own heart's blood
   Is trinkling to my knees?

6. She called the young maids of the town,
   Saying: Keep this a secret for me,
   And these gold rings that you see on my hands
   Shall all belong to thee.

7. Some took him up by the head
   And others by the feet;
   They carried him away to the broad water side
   And plunged him into the deep.

8. Lie there, lie there, loving Henry, said she,
   Till the flesh all rots from the bones,
   And the girl that you left in the Arkansas land
   Will think you're long coming home.

9. Fly down, fly down, pretty parrot, said she,
   And rest upon my knee,
   And your cage shall be made of the purest yellow
                                                gold
   And the doors of ivory.

10. I can't fly down, Lady Margaret, said he,
    Or rest upon your knee,
    For you've just murdered your own true love,
    And I fear that you might murder me.

GROUP E

41. [Young Hunting]

Sharp MSS., 3595/2655. Sung by Miss May Ray, at Lincoln
Memorial University, Harrogate, Tenn., April 25, 1917.

68. YOUNG HUNTING

a M/D

1. Come in, come in, loving Henry, she said,
   Come and stay hours one, two, three,
   For it has been most three long years
   Since I spent one hour with thee.

2. I can't come in and I won't come in
   And stay hours one, two, three,
   For there's a little girl in the old eastern land
   That I love much better than thee.

3. Then bending over her pillow side
   To take the kisses one, two, three,
   She held in her hand a little white knife
   Which wasn't any more to be.

4. She clasped one hand in his yellow hair,
   The other by the feet,
   And she plunged him into cold well water
   Which was both cold and deep.

5. Help me out, help me out, my own true love,
   Help me out, help me out, cried he,
   For there's not a girl in the old eastern land,
   That I love any better than thee.

6. Lie there, lie there, loving Henry, she cried,
   Lie there till the flesh rots from your bones
   And there's a little girl in the old eastern land
   Will long for your return.

7. Fly down, fly down, pretty parrot bird,
   Fly down and light on my right knee;
   I'll make you a cage of yellow beaten gold
   And doors of an oak tree.

8. I can't fly down and I won't fly down
   And light on your right knee,
   For you have murdered your own true love,
   And I'm sure you would murder me.

9. O if I had a bow and arrow
   And it all fixed on springs,
   I would let it slip at your cold red breast
   As you sit on yonders limb.

10. O if you had a bow and arrow
    And it all fixed on springs,
    As you would let it slip at my cold red breast
    I would light on another limb.

Clerk Saunders

CHILD NO. 69

THE few tunes that have been saved for this admirable ballad are Scottish, and seem all to have been recorded while it still had a fairly vigorous currency; and although they have marked differences, are clearly all of the same rise. The rhythmic pattern is characteristically

and the melodic contour tends to the A B B A type, with the A's concave and the B's convex; that is, down-up and up-down. No two agree in the middle cadence; none agree in modality. The Motherwell tune is most artfully contrived in the way it handles the second and fourth phrases. The ballad seems not to have left Scotland under its own momentum.

TUNES WITH TEXTS

1. "Clerk Saunders"

Kinloch, 1827, App'x. to p. 233; text, p. 233.

p Æ (inflected VII)

1. It was a sad and a rainy nicht,
   As ever rain'd frae toun to toun,
   Clerk Saunders and his lady gay,
   They were in the fields sae broun.

2. "A bed, a bed," Clerk Saunders cried,
   "A bed, a bed, let me lie doun;
   For I am sae weet, and sae wearie,
   That I canna gae, nor ride frae toun."

3. "A bed, a bed," his lady cried,
   "A bed, a bed, ye'll ne'er get nane;
   . . . .
   . . . .

4. For I hae seven bauld brethren,
   Bauld are they, and very rude,
   And if they find ye in bouer wi' me,
   They winna care to spill your blude."

5. "Ye'll tak a lang claith in your hand,
   Ye'll haud it up afore your een;
   That ye may swear, and save your aith,
   That ye saw na Sandy sin yestreen.

6. And ye'll tak me in your arms twa,
   Ye'll carry me into your bed,
   That ye may swear, and save your aith,
   That in your bou'r floor I never gaed."

7. She's tane a lang claith in her hand,
   She's hauden't up afore her een,
   That she might swear, and save her aith,
   That she saw na Sandy sin yestreen.

8. She has tane him in her arms twa,
   And carried him into her bed,
   That she might swear, and save her aith,
   That on her bou'r floor he never gaed.

9. Then in there cam her firsten brother,
   Bauldly he cam steppin in:—
   "Come here, come here, see what I see,
   We hae only but ae sister alive,
   And a knave is in bou'r her wi'!"

10. Then in and cam her second brother—
    Says, "Twa lovers are ill to twin:"
    And in and cam her thirden brother.—
    "O brother, dear, I say the same."

11. Then in and cam her fourthen brother,—
    "It's a sin to kill a sleepin man:"
    And in and cam her fifthen brother,—
    "O brother, dear, I say the same."

12. Then in and cam her sixthen brother,—
    "I wat he's ne'er be steer'd by me:"
    But in and cam her seventhen brother,—
    "I bear the hand that sall gar him dee."

13. Then out he drew a nut-brown sword,
    I wat he stript it to the stroe,
    And thro' and thro' Clerk Saunder's body,
    I wat he garr'd cauld iron go.

14. Then they lay there in ither's arms
    Until the day began to daw;
    Then kindly to him she did say,—
    "It's time, my dear, ye were awa.

15. "Ye are the sleepiest young man," she said,
    "That ever my twa een did see,
    Ye've lain a' nicht into my arms,
    I'm sure it is a shame to be."

16. She turn'd the blankets to the foot,
    And turn'd the sheets unto the wa',
    And there she saw his bluidy wound,
    . . . .

17. "O wae be to my seventhen brother!
    I wat an ill death mot he dee,
    He's kill'd Clerk Saunders, an earl's son,
    I wat he's kill'd him unto me."

18. Then in and cam her father dear,
    Cannie cam he steppin in,—
    Says, "Haud your tongue, my dochter dear,
    What need you mak sic heavy meane.

19. We'll carry Clerk Saunders to his grave,
    And syne come back and comfort thee:"—
    "O comfort weel your seven sons, father,
    For man sall never comfort me;
    Ye'll marrie me wi' the Queen o' Heaven,
    For man sall never enjoy me!"

2. [Clerk Saunders]

Motherwell, 1827, App'x., No. 16; text, App'x., p. xix.

And they lay still and sleeped sound
Until the day began to daw,
And kindly to him she did say,
It is time true love ye were awa'.

Lord Thomas and Fair Eleanor

CHILD NO. 73

THE recent popularity of this ballad is attested by the very large number of variants that have been recorded—probably, after "Barbara Allen," the largest number for any ballad in the canon. It is regrettable that the evidence is almost entirely modern, for we might otherwise have found in this abundance a most useful opportunity to study modal and rhythmic change. But very few of the tunes were set down even as early as the first part of the last century, and they are shared in common by other songs than our ballad. The music confirms the impression gained from the texts that the Scottish and English traditions were distinct before the records began. The Scottish was regarded by Child as the more truly popular of the two: it is unquestionably more artistic. The English textual record is more than a hundred years older than the Scottish, and it is clear that its traditional descent is in a direct line from seventeenth-century broadsides. These broadsides, of which there are alternative forms, were directed to be sung, some to "Chevy Chase" (but to which tune of that name is not determined), some to the tune of "Lord Thomas and Fair Ellinor." The latter tune is indicated for the copies with this same title; the former for those copies named "The Unfortunate Forrester, or Fair Elener's Tragedy." No copy of the proper tune has come down from the seventeenth, the eighteenth, or even the first half of the nineteenth, century with its own text, though the one printed by Sandys in 1833 (vt. 95), and reprinted with modification by Chappell and Rimbault, is entitled "Lord Thomas." The next in date are two variants collected by Petrie from County Mayo, about the mid-century, without words. It will hardly be doubted, however, with a tradition so solidly established and so widespread as the later variants prove it to be, that this tune has been long associated with the English form of the ballad. Whether it is actually the same as that sung to the early broadsides there is nothing to show.

The tune first associated with the Scottish ballad in the *Scots Musical Museum* at the end of the eighteenth century, reappearing in various nineteenth-century publications, had already been printed, without words, in Oswald's *Caledonian Pocket Companion*, under the title "The Old Bard." Christie gives this tune as from Aberdeen and Banffshire tradition, but in a form suspiciously close to Johnson's; and the fact that he also records a different tune from the same region might suggest that the first derived from the book. It may therefore be argued that the tune of "The Old Bard" was arbitrarily mated with the Scottish text soon after that text first emerged to public view in the *Reliques*, and has no early traditional association with the ballad. Christie's other tune, recorded from an identified singer, has already appeared with "Captain Wedderburn's Courtship" (Child No. 46), with the spirit of which it is undeniably more in keeping; and in the absence of any further evidence of its continuance in the Scottish tradition for the present ballad, we may guess that it was borrowed for the nonce from the other. There is, therefore, no firm anchorage for any musical tradition for "Lord Thomas and Fair Annie" among Scottish folk-singers.

The English tradition is very close to the musical tradition of "Lady Isabel and the Elf Knight" (Child No. 4). There is, in fact, no positive evidence for assigning the common tune originally to one ballad rather than to the other: it is doubtless accidental that the nineteenth-century variants with the "Lady Isabel" text are of more frequent record than those with "Lord Thomas."

The "Lord Thomas" tunes are normally four-phrase tunes, and perhaps predominantly of the non-reverting type, although those that do not revert make frequent use of parts of the previous phrasal material, so that personal feeling will largely determine our typing. Those variants that have five phrases usually repeat the fourth phrase as a refrain; and those with six similarly repeat the last two phrases. There are few double-strain variants. The normal metre is 6/8, exceptions being fewer than one-twelfth of the total. The exceptions are all in common time, or can be so regarded, allowing for occasional irregularities.

TUNES WITH TEXTS

GROUP A

1. [Lord Thomas and Fair Annet]

Johnson, VI, [1803], No. 535, p. 553 (repr. 1853). Also in *Caledonian Musical Repository*, 1809, p. 202; Smith, [1820-24], VI, p. 58; Rimbault, 1850, p. 112; Maver, 1866, No. 392, p. 196; Ritson, ed. of 1869, II, p. 524; Eyre-Todd, n.d. |1894|, p. 122.

p I (inflected VII)

John Glen, 1900, p. 224, traces Johnson's tune, after Stenhouse, to "The Old Bard," in Oswald's *Caledonian Pocket Companion*, Vol. XII, p. 10. He doubts that it is Scottish.

1. Lord Thomas and fair Annet
   Sat a' day on a hill.
   Whan night was come and the sun was set,
   They had not talk'd their fill.

2. Lord Thomas said a word in jest,
   Fair Annet took it ill;
   A! I will never wed a wife
   Against my ain friends will.

3. Gif ye will never wed a wife,
   A wife will ne'er wed yee.
   Sae he is hame to tell his mither,
   And knel'd upon his knee:

4. O rede, O rede, mither, he says,
   A gude rede gie to me.
   O sall I tak the nut-browne bride,
   And let fair Annet be?

5. The nut-browne bride has gowd and gear,
   Fair Annet she's gat nane,
   And the little bewtie fair Annet has,
   O it will soon be gane.

6. And he has to his brither gane,
   Now, brither, rede ye me,
   A! sall I marrie the nut-browne bride,
   And let fair Annet be?

7. The nut-browne bride has oxen, brother,
   The nut-browne bride has kye,
   I wad hae ye marrie the nut-browne bride,
   And cast fair Annet by.

8. Her oxen may dye i' the house, Billie,
   And her kye into the byre,
   And I sall hae naething to mysell
   But a fat fadge by the fyre.

9. And he has till his sister gane:
   Now, sister, rede ye me,
   O sall I marrie the nut-browne bride,
   And set fair Annet free?

10. I'se rede ye tak fair Annet, Thomas,
    And let the browne bride alane,
    Lest ye sould sigh, and say, Alas
    What is this we brought hame?

11. No, I will tak my mither's counsel,
    And marrie me out o' hand,
    And I will tak the nut-browne bride,
    Fair Annet may leave the land.

12. Up then rose fair Annet's father
    Twa hours or it were day,
    And he is gane into the bower
    Wherein fair Annet lay.

13. Rise up, rise up, fair Annet, he says,
    Put on your silken sheene,
    Let us gae to St. Marie's kirk,
    And see that rich wedden.

14. My maids, gae to my dressing-room,
    And dress to me my hair,
    Whair-ere ye laid a plait before,
    See ye lay ten times mair.

15. My maids, gae to my dressing-room
    And dress to me my smock,
    The one half is o' the holland fine,
    The other o' needle-work.

16. The horse fair Annet rade upon,
    He amblit like the wind,
    Wi' siller he was shod before,
    Wi' burning gowd behind.

17. Four-and-twenty siller bells
    Were a' tied till his mane,
    Wi' yae tift o' the norland wind,
    They tinkled ane by ane.

18. Four-and-twenty gay gude knights
    Rade by fair Annet's side,
    And four-and-twenty fair ladies,
    As gin she had bin a bride.

19. And whan she cam to Marie's kirke,
    She sat on Marie's stean,
    The cleading that fair Annet had on
    It skinkled in their een.

20. And whan she cam into the kirke,
    She skimmer'd like the sun,
    The belt that was aboute her waist
    Was a' wi' pearles bedone.

21. She sat her by the nut-browne bride,
    And her een they wer sae clear,
    Lord Thomas he clean forgat the bride,
    When fair Annet drew near.

22. He had a rose into his hand,
    He gae it kisses three,
    And reaching by the nut-browne bride,
    Laid it on fair Annet's knee.

23. Up then spak the nut-browne bride,
    She spak wi' meikle spite,
    And whair gat ye that rose-water
    That does mak yee sae white?

24. O I did get the rose-water
    Whair ye wull neir get nane,
    For I did get that very rose-water
    Into my mither's wame.

25. The bride she drew a long bodkin
    Frae out her gay head-gear,
    And strake fair Annet unto the heart,
    That word spak never mair.

26. Lord Thomas saw fair Annet wax pale,
    And marvelit what mote bee;
    But whan he saw her dear heart's blude,
    A' wood wroth wexed hee.

27. He drew his dagger that was sae sharp,
    That was sae sharp and meet,
    And drave it into the nut-browne bride,
    That fell deid at his feit.

28. Now stay for me, dear Annet, he said,
    Now stay, my dear, he cryd;
    Then strake the dagger until his heart,
    And fell deid by hir side.

29. Lord Thomas was bury'd without kirk-wa',
    Fair Annet within the quiere;
    And o' the tane thair grew a birk,
    The other a bonny briere.

30. And ay they grew, and ay they threw,
    As they wad fain be neare,
    And by this ye may ken right weil,
    They wer twa luvers deare.

Johnson's text follows Percy's in *Reliques*, Vol. III, Bk. III, No. 4, with slight change, mainly in spelling.

GROUP Ba

8. "Lord Thomas' Wedding"

Broadwood, *JFSS*, V, No. 19 (1915), p. 130. Sung by Mrs. Joiner, at Chiswell Green, Hertfordshire, September 7, 1914.

a M

1. She dressed herself all in her best,
   And merry men all in green,
   And ev'ry town that she rode through
   They took her to be some queen.

2. She rode till she came to Lord Thomas his bower,
   And jingling at the ring,
   Who was more ready than Lord Thomas
   To let Fair Ellinor in?

3. He took her by the lily-white hand
   And led her across the hall,
   There were four and twenty gay ladies,
   But she was the {fairest} of all.
                    {gayest}

4. "This is your bride, Lord Thomas?" she said,
   "I think she looks wonderful brown,
   When you might have had as fair a young woman
   That} ever trod England's ground."
   As }

5. The brown girl, having penknife in her hand
   And keeping it clean and sharp,
   She put the handle in her hand
   And pricked Fair Ellinor's heart.

6. "Oh, what is the matter?" Lord Thomas he said,
   "What! can't you plainly see?
   What! can't you see my own heart's blood
   Comes trinkling down my knee?"

7. Lord Thomas, he keeping a sword by his side,
   He keeping it long and small,
   He cut his bride's head right off her shoulders
   And dashed it against the wall.

8. "Oh, dig me a grave, dear mother," he said,
   "And dig it both deep and wide,
   And lay Fair Ellen at my right side
   And the brown girl at my feet."

9. Lord Thomas he put the sword in the ground,
   The point at his own heart;
   There was never three lovers that met together
   That ever so quickly [did] part.

21. "The Brown Girl"

Sung by Horton Barker, Chilhowie, Va., 1939. LC/AAFS, Album 7, rec. No. 33B. Collected by Herbert Halpert.

a π²

1. "Lord Thomas, Lord Thomas, take my advice,
   Go bring the brown girl home,
   For she has land and a house of her own;
   Fair Ellender she has none."

2. He called it to his waiting maids,
   By one, by two, by three.
   "Go bridle, go saddle my milky white steed;
   Fair Ellender I must see."

3. He rode and he rode till he came to her gate,
   So loudly he tingled the rein.*
   And none was so ready as fair Ellender herself
   As she rose to let him in.

4. "I've come to ask you to my wedding to-day."
   "Bad news, Lord Thomas," says she,
   "For I your bride I thought I would be.
   Bad news, Lord Thomas," says she.

5. She called it to her father and mother
   To make them both as one.
   "Shall I go to Lord Thomas's wedding
   Or tarry at home alone?"

6. She dressed herself so fine in silk,
   Her very maids in green;
   And every city that she rode through,
   They took her to be some queen.

7. She rode and she rode till she came to his gate.
   So loudly she tingled the rein.
   And none was so ready as Lord Thomas himself
   As he rose to let her in.

8. He took her by the lily-white hand;
   He led her through the hall;
   He sot her down at the head of the table
   Among the quality all.

9. "Lord Thomas," says she, "is this your bride?
   I'm sure she looks very brown.
   You might have married as fair a young lady
   As ever the sun shone on."

10. The brown girl had a penknife in her hand,
    It keen and very sharp.
    Between the long ribs and the short,
    She pierced Fair Ellender to the heart.

11. He took the brown girl by the hand;
    He led her through the hall;
    And with his sword he cut her head off,
    And kicked it against the wall.

12. He placed the handle against the ground,
    The point against his breast,
    Saying, "Here's the death of three true lovers.
    God send their souls to rest.

13. "I want my grave dug long and wide,
    And dig it very deep.
    I want Fair Ellender in my arms,
    The brown girl at my feet."

* ring

He took the brown girl by the hand,
And led her through the hall
He took his sword, cut off her head,
And kicked it against the wall.

GROUP Bb

91. [Lord Thomas and Fair Ellinor]

Sharp MSS., 4382/. Also in Sharp and Karpeles, 1932, I, p. 128(Z). Sung by Mrs. Molly E. Bowyer, Villamont, Va., June 10, 1918.

p I

95. [Lord Thomas and Fair Elinor]

Sandys, 1833, App'x., No. 18. From tradition.

p Ly

This tune is revised into major and reprinted by Rimbault, 1850, p. 94, and Chappell, I, p. 145. It is reprinted and re-barred by Terry, *Gilbert and Sandys' Christmas Carols*, [1931], pp. xviii and 48, with new words for the occasion. Chappell identifies the tune with "Who list to lead a soldier's life?" in Playford's *English Dancing Master*. Rimbault prints it for "Robin Hood rescuing the Widow's Sons," in Gutch, *Robin Hode*, 1847, II, p. 438. Sandys naturalizes the E at each occurrence.

Lord Thomas he was a bold forester,
   And a chaser of the king's deer,
Fair Ellinor was a fine woman,
   And Lord Thomas he loved her dear.

71. [Lord Thomas and Fair Ellinor]

Sharp MSS., 4757/. Also in Sharp and Karpeles, 1932, I, p. 131(Ee). Sung by Mrs. Mary Blankenshipp, Price's Creek, Burnsville, N.C., October 5, 1918.

a M

Lord Thomas, Lord Thomas, is this your wife?
I think she's very brown,
When you might have married as fair a young lady
As ever the sun shined on.

97. "Lord Thomas and Fair Eleanor"

Flanders and Brown, 1931, p. 209. Also in Flanders, 1934, p. 68. Sung by Josiah Kennison, Townshend, Vt., 1930; learned in childhood. Recorded by George Brown. From *Vermont Folk-Songs & Ballads*, edited by Helen Hartness Flanders and George Brown; copyright 1931 by Arthur Wallace Peach.

p I/M

1. Lord Thomas, he was a noble lord,
   The keeper of King's deer.
   Fair Eleanor, she was a lady most bright,
   Lord Thomas, he loved her dear.
   Fair Eleanor, she was a lady most bright,
   Lord Thomas, he loved her dear.

2. "Advise us both, dear mother," he says,
   "Advise us both as one.
   Had I best marry Fair Ellen, my dear,
   Or bring the Brown Girl home."

3. "The Brown Girl, she has houses and land,
   Fair Eleanor, she has none.
   Therefore, I charge you with my best care,
   To bring the Brown Girl home?"

4. He call-ed up his merry men all,
   And dressed them all in white.
   And every city that he rode through,
   They took him to be some knight.

5. He rode 'til he came to Fair Eleanor's gate,
   He knocked a-loud on the ring.
   There was none so ready as Fair Ellen herself,
   To rise and let him in.

6. "Oh, what is the news, Lord Thomas," she says,
   "What news have you brought unto me?"
   "I have come to invite you to my wedding."
   "Well, that is sad news to me!"

7. "Advise us both, dear mother," she says,
   "Advise us both as one.
   Had I best go to Lord Thomas's wedding,
   Or had I best stay at home?"

8. "There will be many of your friends there,
   And many that 'air' your foes.
   Therefore, I charge you with my best care,
   To Lord Thomas's wedding, don't go."

9. "There will be many of my friends there,
   And many that are my foes.
   May it bring me life or bring me death,
   To Lord Thomas's wedding I'll go."

10. She call-ed up her merry maids all,
    And dressed them all in green.
    And every city that she rode through,
    They took her to be some queen.

11. She rode 'til she came to Lord Thomas's gate,
    She knocked a-loud on the ring.
    There was none so ready as Lord Thomas himself,
    To rise and let her in.

12. He took her by her lily-white hand,
    And led her across the floor.
    And seated her in a rocking chair,
    Among the ladies there.

13. "Oh, who is that, Lord Thomas?" she says,
    "Methinks she looks wonderful brown.

You might have had as fair a lady,
As ever the sun shone on."

14. "Despise her not," Lord Thomas, he says,
    "Despise her not unto me.
    I have more regard for your little finger,
    Than I have for her whole body."

15. The Brown Girl held a knife in her hand,
    A knife that was pierce and sharp.
    She pierced it into Fair Eleanor's side,
    And touched her tender heart.

16. "Oh, what is the matter?" Lord Thomas, he says,
    "Methinks you look wonderful pale.
    The blood that once flowed in your cherry cheeks,
    Methinks is beginning to fail."

17. "Oh, 'air' you blind, Lord Thomas?" she says,
    "Or can't you very well see?
    The blood that once flowed in my cherry cheeks,
    Is a-trinkling down my knees."

18. Lord Thomas held a knife in his hand,
    A knife that was pierce and sharp.
    He cut the head of the Brown Girl off,
    And kicked it against the wall.

19. He placed the handle up on the floor,
    And the point against his heart.
    There were never three lovers that ever met,
    So quick and forever to part.

20. "Go dig my grave," Lord Thomas, he says,
    "Go dig it both wide and deep.
    And bury Fair Eleanor at my side,
    And the Brown Girl at my feet."

21. They dug his grave as Lord Thomas had said,
    They dug it both wide and deep.
    And they buried Fair Eleanor at his side,
    And the Brown Girl at his feet.
    And they buried Fair Eleanor at his side,
    And the Brown Girl at his feet.

103. [Lord Thomas and Fair Ellinor]

Sharp MSS., 3440/2533. Also in Sharp and Karpeles, 1932,
I, p. 115(A). Sung by Mrs. Hester House, Hot Springs,
N.C., September 14, 1916.

1. Lord Thomas he was a brave young man,
   The keeping of bachelor's hall.
   Come riddle to me, my mother dear,
   Come riddle to me as one.

2. Or shall I marry fair Ellendry now,
   Or bring you the brown girl home?
   Or shall I marry fair Ellendry now,
   Or bring the brown girl home?

3. The brown girl she has house and land,
   Fair Ellendry she has none.
   My request is to you, my son,
   Go bring the brown girl home.

4. Fair Ellendry dressed herself in white,
   And trimmed her merry maidens green,
   And every town that she rode through
   They took her to be some queen.

5. She rode up to Lord Thomas's hall,
   And tingled on the ring;
   No one so ordel but Lord Thomas himself
   For to rise and let her come in.

6. He took her by the lily-white hand,
   He led her through the hall,
   He sat her down at the head of the table
   Amongst those ladies all.

7. Is this your bride?—fair Ellendry she says—
   What makes her so wonderful brown?
   When you could have married as fair a lady one
   As ever the sun shined on.

8. Go hold your tongue, you pretty little miss,
   And tell no tales on me,
   For I love your little finger nail
   Better than her whole body.

9. The brown girl had a little penknife
   Which just had lately been ground,
   She pierced it through fair Ellendry's side,
   The blood come tumbling down.

10. He took her by her little hand,
    He led her in the room;
    He took his sword and cut her head off
    And kicked it against the wall.

11. He put the handle against the wall,
    The point against his breast.
    Here is the ending of three dear lovers.
    Pray take their souls to rest.

12. Go dig my grave both wide and deep
    And paint my coffin black,
    And bury fair Ellendry in my arms,
    The brown girl at my back.

13. They dug his grave both wide and deep
    And painted his coffin black,
    And buried the brown girl in his arms
    And fair Ellendry at his back.

115. "Lord Thomas and Fair Eleanor"

Kidson, 1891, p. 40. From the Whitby district, forwarded by a relative of Mr. Kidson.

p I

1. Lord Thomas he was a bold forester,
   And a chaser of the king's deer;
   Fair Eleanor was a fine woman,
   And Lord Thomas loved her dear.

2. "Come, riddle my riddle, dear mother," he said,
   "And riddle us both in one;
   Whether I shall marry with sweet Eleanor,
   And let the brown girl alone?"

3. "The brown girl she has got houses and land,
   Fair Eleanor she has got none;
   Therefore, I charge thee on my blessing,
   Bring me the brown girl home."

4. And as it befel on a holiday,
   As many more do beside,
   Lord Thomas went to fair Eleanor,
   That should have been his bride.

   .   .   .   .

5. "What news, what news, Lord Thomas?" she said,
   "What news hast thou brought to me?"
   "I am come to bid thee to my wedding,
   And that's sad news for thee."

6. "O, God forbid! Lord Thomas," she said,
   "That such a thing should ever be done;
   I thought to have been thy bride myself,
   And thou been the bridegroom."

   .   .   .   .

7. She clothed herself in gallant attire,
   And her merry men in green;
   And as she rode through every place,
   They took her to be some queen.

8. When she came to Lord Thomas's gate,
   She knocked at the ring;
   And who was so ready as Lord Thomas,
   To let fair Eleanor in.

   .   .   .   .

9. "Is this your bride?" fair Eleanor said,
   "Methinks she looks wondrous brown;
   Thou might'st have had as fair a woman,
   As ever trod upon the ground."

10. "Despise her not," Lord Thomas he said,
    "Despise her not unto me;
For better I love thy little finger,
    Than all her whole body."

11. This brown girl had a little penknife,
    Which was both keen and sharp,
And betwixt the short ribs and the long,
    She prick'd fair Eleanor to the heart.

12. "O Christ, now save me," Lord Thomas he said,
    "Methinks thou looks wondrous wan;
Thou us'd to look as good a colour,
    As ever the sun shone on."

13. "O, art thou blind, Lord Thomas?" she said,
    "Or canst thou not very well see;
O, dost thou not see my own heart's blood,
    Runs trickling down my knee."

. . . .

14. Lord Thomas he had a sword by his side,
    As he walked about the hall;
He cut his bride's head from her shoulders,
    And flung it against the wall.

15. He set his sword upon the ground,
    And the point against his heart;
There never was three lovers, sure,
    That sooner did depart.

GROUP BC

136. "Lord Thomas and Fair Ellinor"

Creighton and Senior, 1950, p. 40. Sung by Mrs. Annie C. Wallace, Halifax, N.S.

p D/Æ

1. Lord Thomas he was a warrior bold
    And wore a broadsword by his side,
Fair Ellinor she was a fair woman
    He wanted her for his bride,
    He wanted her for his bride.

2. "Come riddle my riddle dear mother," she said,
    "Come riddle my riddle for me,
Oh say will I go to Lord Thomas' wedding
    Or will I bide home with thee,
    Or will I bide home with thee?"

3. "Where five will be your friends," she said,
    "Twenty will be your foe,
So if you will my blessing win
    To Lord Thomas' wedding don't go,
    To Lord Thomas' wedding don't go."

4. She dressed herself in scarlet red
    Her merry maids all in green,
And as she rode all through the town
    They took her to be some queen,
    They took her to be some queen.

5. When she got to Lord Thomas' bower
    She loudly knocked at the ring,
There was none so ready as Lord Thomas
    To let fair Ellinor in,
    To let fair Ellinor in.

6. He took her by the lily white hand
    And he led her through the hall
And set her down on the noble chair
    Among her ladies all,
    Among her ladies all.

7. "Is this your bride Lord Thomas?" she says,
    "I think she looks wondrous brown,
When you might have had as fair a lady
    As ever the sun shone on,
    As ever the sun shone on."

8. The brown girl took a small penknife
    Which was both keen and sharp,
And 'twixt the long ribs and the short
    She pierced fair Ellinor's heart,
    She pierced fair Ellinor's heart.

9. Lord Thomas he had a sword by his side
    Which was not sharp at all,
He cut the brown girl's head right off
    And dashed it against the wall,
    And dashed it against the wall.

10. "Oh dig my grave," Lord Thomas he cried,
    "Dig it both wide and deep.
And lay fair Ellinor by my side
    And the brown girl at my feet,
    And the brown girl at my feet."

11. There were never three lovers more quicklier met
    Than quicklier parted were they.

143. [Sweet William and Fair Annie]

Greig and Keith, 1925, p. 57(2); from Duncan MS., No. 251. Sung by Alexander Mackay, Alford, 1874.

73 · LORD THOMAS AND FAIR ELEANOR

Lord Thomas he was a very fine man,
   Went out to hunt his career;
Fair Ellen she was the fairest woman
   That ever the sun shone on, on, on,
   That ever the sun shone on.

Fair Margaret and Sweet William

CHILD NO. 74

THE record of this ballad's existence in a form approximating what we know is carried back as far as 1611 by the chance quotation of a few lines in *The Knight of the Burning Pestle*. The first full texts, however, are on broadsides of the latter end of the seventeenth century. In one form or another, the ballad has been common since that time. It was lifted into literary prominence early in the eighteenth century by being "rewritten," as Child says, "in what used to be called an elegant style"; and in such a form was long attributed to David Malloch, or Mallet, who unjustifiably claimed the authorship of it. A print of c. 1711 was probably occasioned by somebody's invention of a fresh tune, not in the least folkish in character; and to another tune it was engraved on a single-sheet of c. 1727, appearing thereafter in *The Village Opera* and Watts's *Musical Miscellany*, both of 1729. Neither was this tune in a very popular style, and it has not been perpetuated in tradition, so far as is known. But Mallet's version of the ballad appeared in Thomson's *Orpheus Caledonius*, 1725, to a somewhat decorated form of the tune generally known as "Montrose's Lilt," which seems previously to have been used with the ballad, because the 1711 printing mentions this as an alternative tune. "Montrose's Lilt," under a variety of names, is a tune with a long and interesting history which can be traced back almost as far as Beaumont and Fletcher's farce, and forward to the nineteenth century; but there is no evidence to reassure us of its association with our ballad before 1711; and, unless it gave something to the traditional tune recorded in the nineteenth century by Robert Chambers and Christie—which is but barely possible—it passed to other uses before that century dawned.

The main melodic tradition for this ballad, as the present century has received it, is a strong, quite various, and interesting branch of the great family which we have for convenience identified with "Lady Isabel." This branch, however, is in the main easily separable from that of the ballad immediately preceding, thereby justifying Child's discrimination of the texts. Greig, or rather, perhaps, his editor, Keith, regarded "Lord Thomas" and "Fair Margaret" as basically one ballad: the difference in the main melodic streams of the two shows that tradition has distinguished between them. The overwhelming preponderance, in No. 73, of 6/8 variants, and, in No. 74, of duple-time variants other than 6/8, is in itself sufficient demonstration of the fact, and a closer comparison of the examples to be quoted will leave no doubt. On the whole, the present ballad gives the impression of greater freshness and variety in its handling of the melodic idea, doubtless because the 6/8 rhythm is more of a strait jacket than the suppler 4/4 or its metrical counterparts. Also, the present ballad tends to use more of the melodic idea than did the other: it goes far to suggest, in its various phases, a fairly definite image of a double-strain tune of the pattern (probably) A B C D/E F C D, of which the second strain is the enduring portion which is so commonly met. Why the other elements of the tune should be less abraded here than elsewhere I cannot conjecture: in spite of its age the song appears to be less *zersungen*. At any rate, the peculiar shape of the "Lady Isabel" tune in both of its 4/4 branches ("Boyne Water" being the other) is explained when it is seen as the second strain of a fuller tune: its first two phrases relatively high, its last two low, naturally suggesting the second half of a complete arc. (That it is so old as to have inherited the tradition of primitive, and animal, chants, which also gravitate, seems quite unlikely.)

TUNES WITH TEXTS

1. [William and Margaret]

Thomson, [1725], p. 49; ed. of 1733, I, p. 109. Also in Rimbault, 1850, p. 118.

m I/M

This tune is surely a variant of that called "The Lowlands of Holland" to which Burns set his "Of a' the airts." "The Lowlands" has connections also with "Bonny Bee Hom" (No. 92, q.v.); with its own words it is No. 115 in the *Scots Musical Museum*, II, [1788], p. 118. As "Miss Admiral Gordon's Strathspey," it is attributed to William Marshall. Cf. Stenhouse's note to *SMM*, No. 115 (*Illustrations*, ed. 1853, IV, p. 115) and Glen, *Early Scottish Melodies*, 1900, pp. 95-99, where the matter is further perplexed.

The broadside, of c. 1711 ("William and Margaret"), from which Thomson printed, directs as follows: "N.B. This Ballad will sing to the Tunes of Montrose's Lilt, Rothe's Lament, or the Isle of Kell." The present tune is also earlier known as "Montrose's Lilt," as Lucy Broadwood observed (*JFSS*, III, No. 11, [1907], p. 66). Various forms of it appear in the 17th century, e.g. in John Gamble's MS., c. 1659, and Blaikie's lyra-viol MS., c. 1692, versions reprinted by Glen, 1900, p. 31, with further information and a reference to Chappell, I, [1855], pp. 378-81. This song is *SMM*, No. 452, which Stenhouse (*Illustrations*, p. 400) asserts to be the ancient tune of "Chevy Chase," on no discoverable authority. But for "The Isle of Kell," cf. *post*, No. 162.

The variant readings above are differences in the 1725 edition from that of 1733.

11. "Lady Margaret"

Jean Ritchie, Riverside LP rec., RLP 12-620 (A8). As sung
by the Ritchie family, Viper, Ky.

a π²

1. Sweet William arose one May morning
   And dressed himself in blue.
   We want you to tell us something about
   That long love between Lady Marg'ret and you.

2. Well I know nothin' about Miss Lady Marget's love;
   I know that she don't love me.
   But tomorrow morning at eight o'clock
   Lady Marget my bride shall see.
        But tomorrow morning at eight o'clock
        Lady Marget my bride shall see.

3. Lady Marget was standin' in her own hall door,
   A-combin' down her hair;
   O who could she spy but Sweet William and his bride
   And the lawyers a-riding by.

4. O she threw down her iv'ry comb
   'N bound her hair in silk,
   And she stepped out of her own hall door
   To never return any more.
        O she stepped out of her own hall door
        To never return any more.

5. Well the day being past and the night coming on,
   When most all men was asleep,
   Sweet William espied Miss Lady Marget's ghost
   A-standin' at his own bed feet.

6. "O how do you like the bed?" she asked him,
   "Or how do you like your sheet?
   Or how do you like that pretty, fair miss
   That's a-lyin' in your arms asleep?"

7. "Very well, very well do I like the bed,
   Much better do I like the sheet,
   But the best one of all is the pretty, fair maid
   That's a-standin' at my own bed feet.
        But the best of all is the pretty, fair maid
        That's a-standin' at my own bed feet."

8. The night bein' past and day comin' on,
   When most all men was at work,
   Sweet William he said he was troubled in his head
   From a dream that he dreamed last night.

9. "Such dreams, such dreams they are no good,
   Such dreams they are no good.
   I dreamed my hall was filled with wild swine,
   And my true love was swimming in blood.
        I dreamed my hall was filled with wild swine,
        And my true love was swimming in blood."

10. He called his comrades to his side;
    He counted one, two, three.
    And the last one of them he asked of his bride
    Lady Marget he might go and see.

11. He rode till he come to Miss Lady Marget's hall,
    Tingled all on the ring.
    No one so ready as Lady Marget's brother
    To rise and welcome him in.
        No one so ready as Lady Marget's brother
        To rise and welcome him in.

12. "O is she in her garden," he asked him,
    "Or is she in her hall,
    Or is she in the upper parlor
    Amongst those ladies all?"

13. "She neither is in her garden," he answered,
    "She neither is in the hall,
    But yonder she lies in her cold coffin
    That's a-sitting by the side of the wall.
        But yonder she lies in her cold coffin
        That's a-sitting by the side of the wall."

14. "Hang up, hang up them milk-white sheets
    That's made of linen so fine,
    Today they shall hang o'er my Lady Marget's corpse,
    And tomorrow they shall hang over mine.

15. "Yes, hold up, hold up those milk-white sheets
    Made of linen so fine.
    May I go and kiss them cold clay lips,
    For they oft-times have kissed mine?
        May I go and kiss them cold clay lips,
        For they oft-times have kissed mine?"

16. Well first he kissed her on the cheek,
    And then he kissed her chin,
    And then he kissed them cold clay lips
    Which crushed his heart within.

17. Lady Marget was buried in the new church yard,
    Sweet William was buried near by her,
    And out of her grave there sprung a red rose,
    And out of his a brier.
        And out of her grave there sprung a red rose,
        And out of his a brier.

18. Well they grew and grew to the new church top,
    'N they could not grow no higher,
    And they wound and they tied in a true lover's knot
    For all young people to admire.

Yes they wound and they tied in a true lover's knot
For all young people to admire.

GROUP cb

47. [Fair Margaret and Sweet William]

Sharp MSS., 4596/3215. Also in Sharp and Karpeles, 1932,
I, p. 145(P). Sung by Mrs. Virginia Bennett, Burnsville,
N.C., September 13, 1918.

a π¹

1. Sweet William arose one morning in May
   And dressed himself in blue.
   Pray tell us this long, long love, said they,
   Between Lady Margaret* and you.

2. I know no harm of Lady Margaret,
   And she knows none of me;
   This day before twelve o'clock shall come
   Lady Margaret my bride shall see.

3. Lady Margaret was standing in her own hall door,
   Combing her long yellow hair;
   Sweet William came along with his bride;
   She was ne'er seen again there.

4. I dreamed a dream last night, mother,
   I know it was no good.
   I dreamed my hall was filled with white swine
   And washed away in blood.

5. Is Lady Margaret at home,
   Or is she at her bower,
   Or is she in her own dining-room
   Among her merry maids all?

6. Yes, Lady Margaret's at home,
   But she's not in her bower;
   Lady Margaret is dead and in her coffin
   That stands against yonders cold wall.

7. Throw down, throw down those white winding sheets,
   My soul doth her entwine.
   O may I kiss Lady Margaret's sweet lips,
   For I know she will never kiss mine.

* 1932: Margret

64. [Fair Margaret and Sweet William]

Kidson, *JFSS*, II, No. 9 (1906), p. 289. Sung by Kate
Thompson, Knaresbro', Yorkshire. Learned c. 1850.

p I

This version is sung by A. L. Lloyd, Riverside LP rec., RLP 12-
623 (B2), ed. K. S. Goldstein.

1. There sat two lovers on yon hill,
   See on yon hill so high,
   They sat together for a long summer's eve,
   And they never could tell their mind,
   And they never could tell their mind.

2. Miss Margaret sat in her bedroom,
   Combing out her long brown hair;
   Who should she spy but her own true love,
   Riding by with a lady fair.

3. She had a pen-knife in her hand,
   And it was long and sharp;
   She made no more of the use of it,
   But she rammed it to her heart.

4. The day being spent, the night coming on,
   When all was fast asleep;
   Miss Margaret appeared at twelve o'clock,
   And stood at his bed-feet,

5. Saying "How do you like your soft feather-bed?
   How do you like your sleep?"
   "Very well I like my soft feather-bed,
   Very well I like my sleep,
   But much better I like this pretty fair maid,
   That lies in my arms asleep."

       *   *   *   *   *   *   *

6. "Oh, can I see Miss Margaret alive?
   Or can I see her dead?
   Or can I kiss those clay-cold lips,
   That once were cherry-red?"

7. "You cannot see Miss Margaret alive,
   But you can see her dead;
   And you can kiss those clay-cold lips,
   That once were cherry-red."

GROUP cc

68. [Fair Margaret and Sweet William]

Karpeles, 1934, II, p. 95; text, Karpeles MSS., p. 4746. Sung
by Mrs. May McCabe, North River, Conception Bay,
Newfoundland, October 17, 1929.

74. FAIR MARGARET AND SWEET WILLIAM

p D

1. Lady Margaret was sitting in her bower one day
   And Knight William was sitting on her knee.
   My father he will think it deep, deep disgrace,
   Young William, if I wed with thee.

2. You'd better mind what you're saying, Lady Margaret,
       he said,
   You'd better mind what you're saying to me,
   For before three days they are to an end,
   A rakish wedding you may see.

3. Lady Margaret was sitting in her bower next day,
   A-combing her yellow hair,
   And who should she spy there a-riding up close by,
   But Knight William and his lady fair.

4. She threw away her ivory tooth-comb,
   She tossed back her yellow hair,
   And out of her bower this fair lady ran
   And she was never more seen there.

5. Young William he woke in the middle of the night,
   And unto his lady did say;
   Saying: I must go to see Lady Margaret, says he,
   By the lief of you, lady.

6. For I dreamed a dream, a terrible dream,
   I'm afraid it's not for our good.
   I dreamed that my love was entangled with a swan
   And my bride's bed flowing with blood.

7. I dreamed that I saw Lady Margaret, he said,
   A-standing at my bed-feet,
   Saying: The lily and the rose they are covered up
       with clothes,
   And I am in my cold winding-sheet.

8. He rode till he came to Lady Margaret's bower,
   Where so loudly he knocked at the ring,
   And none was so ready as her youngest brother there,
   He came down in deep mourning.

9. What mourn you, what mourn you? Knight William he
       said,
   What mourn you so deeply unto me.
   O we are in mourning for our sister there,
   Who died for loving of thee.

10. O who might eat some of her cake, he did say,
    Or who might drink some of her wine,
    Or who might ever live till this time tomorrow night
    He'll drink some of mine.

11. Lady Margaret she died in the middle of the night,
    And so did Knight William, the Squire.
    And out of Lady Margaret there sprang a rose
    And out of young William a briar.

12. And now our love-wars are all at an end,
    And all things must be forgot,
    For the branch and the briar they both grew up
        together
    And they tied in a true lovers knot.

Lord Lovel

CHILD NO. 75

No LIGHT is thrown upon the beginnings of this too too insipid ballad by the musical tradition. Its great popularity for at least a hundred years is powerful testimony to the life-giving energy of a memorable tune. For the narrative is of the slightest, and there is no sign in any known version that it has lost much in its passage. The textual tradition is, like the melodic one, unusually compact and consistent. But it is impossible to believe that there is enough nutriment in the story alone to win friends on every hand. Though it dallies with the innocence of love, it could hardly have struck most singers as silly sooth, unless for the reason that it was so strange to common experience. But the tune has been remembered almost note for note by multitudes, we must suppose; and this lack of deviation proves that it was everywhere learned without effort, if not all but involuntarily. There is no obvious bond of sympathy between tripping melody and lachrymose text, but the first effectually removes the curse from the second, so that it can be sung without much loss of self-possession. Cf. to the same effect Reed Smith, *South Carolina Ballads*, 1928, p. 12. Whether or not it was born of the eighteenth century, this union of text and tune prettily symbolizes a sentimentality too concerned with itself as interesting spectacle ever to be pulled under by the tide of genuine emotion. "Oh, Harry," Mackenzie's wife is said to have exclaimed, "You have feeling only on paper!" A word might be due here to those whose sensibilities are offended by the foregoing remarks. I remember to have heard it said that the great diva, Mme. Tetrazzini, once declared that the most beautiful vocables in the English language were the words "cellar door." Perhaps Poe had something similar in mind when he built his poem of "The Raven" about the word "Nevermore." Unquestionably, given the proper time, circumstances, and old associations, it is possible to be truly moved (as was Goldsmith when his old dairymaid sung him into tears with the ballad of "Barbara Allen") by the unaffected naiveté of a simple song. Let me not to the marriage of true minds admit impediments. But in the present case, it is worth noticing that what has become the most famous contemporary version, sung with superb natural artistry (vt. 32.1), stops short of the second death, the burial, and the rose-and-briar eschatological reunion.

The tune is again a member of the "Lady Isabel" family, but closer by far to the "Lord Thomas" line than to "Fair Margaret." Its typical form here is reiterated in so many variants that there is no room for doubt. It is a tune of major tonality, not infrequently pentatonic, lacking IV and VII, but most often hexatonic, lacking VII. The scarcity of clear Mixolydian variants suggests plainly that the hexatonic tunes point toward the Ionian alternative; and of such I/M tunes there are more than thirty —nearly half the total here collected. The tune is characteristically in 6/8 time, with occasional 4/4 or irregular variants; and habitually in five phrases, the fifth phrase either a mere repetition of the fourth or melodically new, to repeated words, and generally with a bridge, half a bar long, after the short fourth line. The mid-pause falls so consistently on the fifth that we must regard the exceptions as rather uncharacteristic; similarly, the first cadence comes almost as regularly on the tonic. The first accented note is frequently the tonic, rising a major third in the middle of the bar; and the middle cadence is typically reached by a drop from the octave. The third phrase generally contains a fall from octave to tonic, these being normally the first and last accents in the phrase. There are very few ballads of which abundant variants have been recorded, about which it is possible to be anywhere nearly so specific in describing the melodic type.

There is nothing archaic in the look of this typical melody, but for all that it may not have been born yesterday: in more than one variant its features reveal blood-kinship with Elizabethan ancestors, notably "Tomorrow is St. Valentine's Day" ("Who List to lead a Soldier's Life").

The examples to be cited come from Scotland, England, Ireland, The Isle of Man, the Atlantic Littoral from New Brunswick to South Carolina, and inland to Michigan, the Ozarks, and Mississippi. Most of them appear to me to be related, although some, it may be, are far from the norm, and on the very periphery of relationship. None is of older record than the Irish variant from the Hudson MS., of about 1840 (vt. 53), and most are of the present century.

TUNES WITH TEXTS

GROUP A a

8. "Lord Lovell"

Scarborough, 1937, p. 389(B); text, p. 101. Sung by Clara Callahan, Salada, N.C., c. 1932.

m π¹

1. Lord Lovel stood at his castle gate
   A-combing his milk-white steed,
   When up came Lady Nancy Belle
   To wish her lover good speed, good speed,
   To wish her lover good speed.

2. Oh, where are you going, Lord Lovel? she said;
   Oh, where are you going? cried she;
   I'm going away, Lady Nancy Belle,
   Strange countries for to see, see, see,
   Strange countries for to see.

3. How long will you be gone, Lord Lovel? she said;
   How long will you be gone? cried she;
   In a year or two or three at the most
   I'll return to my Lady Nancy-cy-cy,
   I'll return to my Lady Nancy.

[193]

4. He had not been gone but a year and a day
   Strange countries for to see,
When a strange thought came into his head,
   He'd go see his Lady Nancy-cy-cy,
   He'd go see his Lady Nancy.

5. He rode and he rode on his milk-white steed
   Till he came to London Town,
And there he heard the church bells ringing,
   And the people all mourning around, round, round,
   And the people all mourning around.

6. And who is dead? Lord Lovel he said,
   And who is dead? said he;
An old woman said, Some lady is dead
   And they call her Lady Nancy-cy-cy
   And they call her Lady Nancy.

7. He ordered the grave to be opened wide,
   And the shroud to be turned around,
And then he kissed her clay-cold lips
   Till the tears came trickling down, down, down,
   Till the tears came trickling down.

8. Lady Nancy she died as it might be today,
   Lord Lovel he died as tomorrow;
Lady Nancy died of pure, pure grief,
   Lord Lovel died of sorrow—sorrow,
   Lord Lovel died of sorrow.

9. The one was buried in the lower church,
   The other buried in the higher;
From one sprang a gallant red rose,
   From the other a gilliflower, flower,
   From the other a gilliflower.

10. And there they grew and turned and twined
    Till they gained the church top,
And there they grew and turned and twined
    And tied in a true lover's knot, knot,
    And tied in a true lover's knot.

1. Lord Lovell, he stood at his garden gate,
   A-combing his milk-white steed,
When along came Lady Nancy Bell,
   A-wishing her lover good speed, speed, speed,
   A-wishing her lover good speed.

2. "Oh, where are you going, Lord Lovell?" she cried,
   "Oh, where are you going?" said she.
"I'm going, my dear Lady Nancy Bell,
   Foreign countries for to see."

3. "When will you be back, Lord Lovell?" she cried.
   "When will you be back?" said she.
"In a year or two, or three at most,
   I'll be back to my Lady Nancy."

4. He had been gone a year and a day,
   Foreign countries for to see,
When languishing thoughts came into his head,
   Lady Nancy Bell he'd go see.

5. So he rode and he rode on his milk-white steed,
   Till he came to London town,
And then he see such a mournful sight,
   And the people all gathered around.

6. "Oh, what is the matter?" Lord Lovell he cried,
   "Oh, what is the matter?" said he.
"Oh, a lady is dead, and her lover is gone,
   And they call her the Lady Nancy."

7. He ordered the grave to be opened wide,
   The shroud to be turned down low,
And as he kissed her clay-cold lips,
   The tears began to flow.

8. Lady Nancy, she died the same as to-day,
   Lord Lovell he died as to-morrow.
Lady Nancy she died of pure grief,
   Lord Lovell he died of sorrow.

9. They buried them both by the castle wall
   In a grave that was close by the spire,
And out of her breast there grew a red rose,
   And out of Lord Lovell's a brier.

10. They grew, and they grew to the castle top,
    And then they could grow no higher.
They twined themselves in a true lover's knot,
    For all true lovers to admire.

23. "Lord Lovell"

Barry MSS., II, No. 75A₂; also IV, No. 312. Also in Barry, *JAF*, XVIII (1905), p. 292. Sung by Miss Caroline T. Graves, of Connecticut, May 22, 1905; transcribed by Miss Ina L. McDavitt.

m I/M

32.1. "Lord Lovat"

Archive, School of Scottish Studies, rec. No. 1953/247/ B8(B1). Sung by Jeannie Robertson, Aberdeen. Learned in Aberdeen "about 35 years ago" from a very old woman named Cameron, from Perthshire. Collected by Hamish Henderson. Transcribed by Francis M. Collinson.

a I

He ordered the grave to be opened wide
And the shroud to be turned down
That he may kiss the lily white lips
Till the tears came trinkaling down down down
Till the tears came trinkaling down

1. Lord Lovat he stands at his stable-door;
   He was brushing his milk steed down,
   When who passed by but Lady Nancy Bell;
   She was wishing her lover good speed. (bis)

2. "Where are you going, Lord Lovat?" she said;
   "Come promise, tell me true."
   "Over the sea, strange countries to see;
   Lady Nancy Bell, I'll come an see you." (bis)

3. He was away a year or two,
   But he scarcely had been three,
   When a mightiful dream cam into his head:
   "Lady Nancy Bell, I'll come an see you." (bis)

4. He passed down by the village church,
   An down to Mary's hall,
   An the ladies were all weeping forth. (bis)

5. "Who is dead?" Lord Lovat he said;
   "Come promise, tell me true."
   "Lady Nancy Bell died for her true-lover's sake,
   And Lord Lovat, that was his name." (bis)

6. He ordered the coffin to be opened up,
   And the white sheet rolled down;
   He kissed her on the cold-clay lips,
   An the tears came trinklin' down. (bis)

46. "Lord Lovell"

Eddy, 1939, p. 40(C). Sung by Mrs. Anna E. Housley (91), Canton, Ohio.

a I

1. Lord Lovell he rode on his milk-white horse
   Till he reached to London town,
   And there he heard St. Pancrum's bell,
   And the people all mourning around.
   And there he heard St. Pancrum's bell,
   And the people all mourning around.

2. "Oh, what is the matter?" Lord Lovell he said,
   "Oh, what is the matter?" said he;
   "The Lord Lady's dead," the women replied,
   "And some call her Lady Nancy."

3. He ordered her grave to be opened wide,
   And her shroud to be turned down,
   And there he kissed her clay-cold lips
   Till the tears came trembling down.

4. Lady Nancy she died with a pure, pure green,
   Lord Lovell he died with a sorrow;
   Lady Nancy was laid in St. Pancrum's church,
   Lord Lovell was laid in the choir.

5. Out of her bosom there grew a red rose,
   And out of his bosom a brier;
   It grew and it grew to the church steeple top,
   And then it could grow no higher.

6. So there they entwined the true lovers' may,
   For all the true lovers to admire,
   And ever since then the roses are red,
   And sharp indeed is the brier.

42. [Lord Lovell]

Sharp MSS., 1246/. Sung by Bill Bailey, Cannington, Somerset, January 24, 1907.

a I

53. "Lady Annisbel"

Hudson MS., No. 336, c. 1840. Also in Barry, *JAF*, XXIV (1911), p. 347.

a M

GROUP Ab

57. "Lord Lovell"

McDonald, 1939, p. 23. Sung by John Martin, Flood, Mo.

p π[1]

1. Lord Lovell he stood at the castle gate,
   A-combing his milk-white steed,
   When along come Lady Nancy Bell,
   A-wishing her lover good speed, speed, speed,
   A-wishing her lover good speed.

2. Oh, where are you going, Lord Lovell? says she,
   Oh, where are you going, says she.
   I am going, my dear Lady Nancy Bell,
   Strange countries for to see, see, see,
   Strange countries for to see.

3. When will you get back, Lord Lovell? she says,
   When will you get back? says she.
   In a year or two or three at the most,
   I'll return to my Lady Nancy, cy, cy,
   I'll return to my Lady Nancy.

4. He'd not been gone but a year and a day,
   Strange countries for to see,
   When languishing thoughts came into his head,
   Lady Nancy Bell he would see, see, see,
   Lady Nancy Bell he would see.

5. He rode and he rode on his milk-white steed
   Till he came to London town,
   And there he heard St. Varney's bell,
   And the people all mourning around, round, round,
   And the people all mourning around.

6. Is anybody dead? Lord Lovell he said,
   Is anybody dead? says he.
   A lady is dead, the people all said,
   And they called her Lady Nancy, cy -cy, -cy,
   And they called her Lady Nancy.

7. He ordered the grave to be opened forthwith,
   The shroud was folded down,
   And there he kissed her clay-cold lips
   Till the tears came a-trickling down, down, down,
   Till the tears came a-trickling down.

8. Lady Nancy she died as it might be today,
   Lord Lovell he died tomorrow,
   Lady Nancy she died of pure, pure grief,
   Lord Lovell he died of sorrow, -row, -row,
   Lord Lovell he died of sorrow.

9. Lord Lovell was buried in the greenchurchyard,
   Lady Nancy was buried in the choir,
   And out of his grave grew a red rose,
   And out of hers a briar, briar, briar
   And out of hers a briar.

10. They grew and they grew to the top of the church,
    Till they could not grow no higher,
    They twined in a true lover's knot,
    For all true lovers to admire, -mire, -mire,
    For all lovers to admire.

The Lass of Roch Royal

CHILD NO. 76

"The Lass of Roch Royal" must have been circulating freely before the middle of the eighteenth century, because Child's A-text, from a manuscript of the second quarter of that century, is in a state obviously disordered by traditional transmission. Of the early music of the ballad we know nothing. The tune published in the *Scots Musical Museum* in 1787 does not inspire confidence in its authenticity, although—perhaps *faute de mieux*—it has been frequently reprinted. According to Stenhouse's note it is a "very ancient Gallowegian melody"—a statement which has no support from MS. or print, so far as I have been able to discover. On the other hand, it has some resemblance to a tune now generally known as "The Miller of Dee," which in one form or another was in circulation early in the eighteenth century—and undoubtedly earlier—and which appears with various texts in D'Urfey's *Pills* (e.g., 1719-20, V, 22, 29, 46; VI, 124. Cf. also Chappell, *Popular Music*, II, pp. 666-

68; and Margaret Dean-Smith, *A Guide to English Folk Song Collections*, 1954, p. 120). As Johnson prints it, it is a modern minor tune in two strains, but it falls easily back into the Æolian mode.

The two tunes collected by Greig from recent Scottish tradition and a third lately added have nothing in common with the former, but may be related to each other. Apart from the tunes classed as D, only one of which has a text indubitably related to this ballad, there is no distinct melodic tradition in America for "The Lass of Roch Royal." The familiar lines,

> Who will shoe your pretty little foot,
> And who will glove your hand, &c.,

are something of a commonplace in balladry and are found in a number of other connections.

TUNES WITH TEXTS

GROUP A

1. [Oh open the door, Lord Gregory]

Johnson, I, [1787], No. 5, p. 5. Also, with changes, in Urbani, 1792, p. 1; Thomson, 1822, 1st Set, p. 38; Graham, 1848-49, I, p. 54; Maver, 1866, No. 87, p. 44; Eyre-Todd, n.d. |1894|, p. 36.

m Æ (inflected VII)

Oh open the door, Lord Gregory,
  Oh open and let me in;
The rain rains on my scarlet robes,
  The dew drops o'er my chin.
If you are the lass that I lov'd once,
  As I true* you are not she,
Come give me some of the tokens
  That past between you and me.

Ah wae be to you Gregory!
  An ill death may you die!
You will not be the death of one,
  But you'll be the death of three.

Oh don't you mind, Lord Gregory,
  'Twas down at yon burn side
We chang'd the ring off our fingers
  And I put mine on thine.

* *Sic*, for "trow."

GROUP B

4.1. "Lord Gregory"

Archive, School of Scottish Studies, rec. No. 1954/105/A4. Sung by Jock McEvoy, Glasgow. Collected by Hamish Henderson. Transcribed by Francis M. Collinson.

m M (inflected III)

1. "Go back from these windows, and likewise this hall,
   Lest dapping in the sea, you should find your downfall."

2. "I am a king's daughter, and I come from ? Cappa Quin
   In search of Lord Gregory, and I can't find him."

3. "The rain beats on my yellow locks, and the dew wets me still;
   My babe is cold in my arms; Lord Gregory, let me in."

4. "Lord Gregory is not here, and henceforth can't be seen;
   He has gone to bonnie Scotland to bring home his new queen."

5. "Oh remember, Lord Gregory, on that night in ? Cappa Quin
   When we both changed pocket-handkerchiefs, and that against my will.

6. For yours was pure linen, love, and mine but coarse cloth;
   Yours cost a guinea, love, and mine cost one groat."

7. "Go back from these windows, and likewise this hall,
   Lest dapping in the sea, you should find your downfall."

8. "Do ye remember, Lord Gregory, on that night in my father's hall,
   When you stole away my fond heart, and that was worst of all?"

9. "Go back from these windows, and likewise this hall,
   Lest dapping in the sea, you should find your downfall."

10. "A curse on you, father, and my curse has been swore
    For I dreamt the Maid of ? Arran came rapping at my door."

11. "Oh, lie down, you foolish one; oh lie down and sleep,
    For 'tis long ago my weary locks were wetting in the deep."

12. "Oh, saddle me my black horse, the brown and the bay;
    Go, saddle me the best horse in my stable this day.

13. "If I range over valleys, and over mountains wild,
    Till I find the Maid of ? Arran, and I'll lie down by her side."

GROUP C

5. "The Lass of Lochroyan"

Sung by Jean Ritchie, Cambridge, Mass., July 20, 1955.
Transcribed by Editor. Also on Folkways LP rec., FW
2301, ed. K. S. Goldstein.

a M

1. "O who will shoe my bonny feet
   And who will glove my hand
   And who will kiss my rosy cheeks
   Till you come home again?"

   "Your pa will shoe your bonny feet,
   Your ma will glove your hand,
   And I will kiss your rosy cheeks
   When I come back again."

2. "And who will build a bonny ship
   And set her on the sea,
   That I may go and seek my love,
   My own love Gregory?"

   O up and spoke her father dear
   And a wealthy man was he
   And he has built a bonny ship
   And set her on the sea.

3. O he has built a bonny ship
   And set her on the sea
   The mast was of a beaten gold
   As fine as it could be.

   She had not sailed but twenty leagues
   But twenty leagues and three
   When she met with a rank robber
   And all of his company.

4. "Are you the Queen of Heaven," they cried,
   "Come to pardon all our sins?
   Are you the Mary Magdalene
   That was born at Bethlehem?"

   "I'm not the Queen of Heaven," she said,
   "Come to pardon all your sins,
   Nor am I the Mary Magdalene
   That was born at Bethlehem.

5. "But I am the lass of Lochroyan
   That's sailin' on the sea
   To see if I can find my love,
   My own love Gregory."

   "O see ye not yon bonny bar
   All covered o'er with thyme?
   And when you sail it around and about,
   Lord Gregory is within."

6. "Now row the boat, my mariners,
   And bring me to the land,
   For it's now I see my true love's cástel
   Close by the salt sea strand."

   She sailed it around and sailed it around
   And loud and loud cried she:
   "Now break, now break your fairy charms
   And set my true-love free."

7. She has taken her young son in her arms
   And to the door she's gone
   And long she's knocked and loud she's called
   But answer she got none.

"O open the door, Lord Gregory,
O open and let me in.
The rain drops from my cold cold cheeks,
The rain drops from my chin.

8. "This shoe is frozen to my foot,
The glove unto my hand,
The wet drops from my frozen heart [?]
And I can scarcely stand."

Up then and spoke his ill mother
As mean as she could be,
"You're not the lass of Lochroyan
She's far out o'er the sea.

9. "Away, away, you ill woman,
You don't come here for good.
You're just some witch that strolls about
Or mermaid of the flood."

"Now open the door, Lord Gregory,
O open the door, I pray,
For thy young son is in my arms
And we'll be dead or it be day."

10. "Ye lie, ye lie, ye ill woman,
So loud I hear ye lie,
For Annie of the Lochroyan
Is far out o'er the sea."

Fair Annie turned her round and about,
"Well, since this all is so,
May never a woman that has borne a son
Have a heart so full of woe."

11. When the cock had crowed and the day had dawned
And the sun began to peep,
Up then arose Lord Gregory
And sore, sore did he weep.

"O I have dreamt a dream, Mother,
The thought it grieves me great
That fair Annie of the Lochroyan
Lay dead at my bed-feet."

12. "If it be for the Lass of the Lochroyan
You may call off this moan:
She stood last night at your bower window
But I have sent her home."

O he's gone down unto the shore
To see what he could see
And there he saw fair Annie's bark
Come roarin'* o'er the sea.

13. "O Annie, O Annie, love," he cried,
"O Annie, O Annie, my dear."
But all the loud that he could cry
Fair Annie she could not hear.

The wind blew loud and the waves dashed high,
They dashed the boat on shore.
Fair Annie's corpse was in the foam
That árose never more.

14. Then first he kissed her cold, cold cheeks,
And then he kissed her chin
And then he kissed her pale pale lips,
There was no breath within.

"O woe betide my ill mother,
And an ill death may she die!
She has not been the death of one,
She has been the death of three."

Then he took out a little dart,
That hung down by his side
And pierced it through and through his heart
And then fell down and died.

* For "rowin' "?

GROUP D

16. "Georgie Jeems"

Randolph, I, 1946, p. 120(G). Sung by Mrs. Irene Carlisle, Fayetteville, Ark., December 9, 1941. Learned from her grandmother, c. 1912.

a I

1. Oh who will shoe my narrow, narrow foot,
   And who will glove my hand,
   And who will wrap my narrow, narrow waist
   With a new-made London band?

2. Oh who will comb my yellow, yellow hair,
   With a new-made silver comb,
   And who will father my pretty little babe
   Till Georgie Jeems comes home?

3. Fair Annie she stood at her true love's door,
   And tirled the drawling-pin,
   Rise up, rise up, young Georgie Jeems.
   And let your true love in.

4. Then up rose his false, false lady,
   Says who's a-wanting in?

5. Oh don't you remember, young Georgie Jeems,
   When we two sat to dine,
   You taken the ring from off my hand
   And changed your ring for mine.

6. And yours was good and very, very good,
   But not so good as mine,
   For yours was of the good red gold
   But mine the diamonds fine.

Sweet William's Ghost

CHILD NO. 77

For this apparently old and—in some of its variants—movingly beautiful ballad, no clear musical tradition can be delineated. The melodic records are few and, except for a handful of Newfoundland variants, distant from one another. Mrs. Harris's tune, which presumably goes back in Perthshire tradition to the middle of the eighteenth century, has every appearance of authenticity, and is certainly to be preferred to the often reprinted tune in the *Scots Musical Museum*. The latter has already appeared with "Fair Margaret and Sweet William," No. 74, but there also without an assured right.

The Newfoundland tunes of Group B are good, and may even have some obscure relationship with Mrs. Harris's tune. Affiliations with other families, however, are more easily perceived. "Lord Lovel" is not far distant, and there may be a connection with "The Daemon Lover" (No. 243). The tunes of Group D from Newfoundland are related to the local tradition of "Fair Margaret and Sweet William" (No. 74).

The tune lately recovered in Scotland (vt. 12) stands by itself.

TUNES WITH TEXTS

GROUP A

1. "There cam' a Ghost"

Harris MS. Also in Child, 1882-98, V, p. 416.

a D/M (possibly on C, I/Ly)

This style of close is so favored in British, especially Scottish, folksong as perhaps to establish the final as tonic.
The MS. is noted in bars of 4/2, quick time.

> There cam a Ghost to Margit's door,
> Wi mony a grievous groan,
> An lang it tirled [at the pin]
> But answer made it none.

GROUP B

3. [Sweet William's Ghost]

Karpeles, 1934, I, p. 3; text, Karpeles MSS., p. 4804. Sung by Michael Carrol, Placentia, Newfoundland, July 5, 1930.

m I/Ly

A text from another singer is given with this tune in the printed version.

1. Lady Margaret was sitting in her own loyal bower
   It was built of lime and stone,
   Lady Margaret was sitting in her own loyal bower,
   When she heard a dead man's moan.

2. Now is it my father the king, she cries,
   Or is it my brother John,
   Or is it my own Willie, she said,
   From Scotland here have come.

3. No, 'tis not the king, he replied,
   It is not your brother John,
   But it is your own dear Willie
   From Scotland here have come.

4. Did you bring to me any token of love,
   Did you bring to me a ring,
   Did you bring to me any token at all
   That a true love ought to bring?

5. No, I've brought to you no token at all,
   I've brought to you no ring,
   But I've [brought] to you my winding-sheet
   That my body lies mouldering in.

6. Now in crossing over the frozen plain
   On a cold and stormy night,
   In crossing the plains of a cold winter's night
   In a dead man's company.

7. Now when they came to the old churchyard
   Where the graves were mossy green,
   Saying: Here is my place of residence
   For me to take a sleep.

8. Is there any room at your head? she said,
   Or any at your feet,
   Or any room about you
   For me to take a sleep?

9. No, my father is at my head, he said,
My mother is at my feet,
And there's three little devils
For my soul to take.

10. One of them is for my drunkenness,
And the other is for my pride,
And the other is for deluding of fair pretty maids
And staying out late in the night.

GROUP D

9. [Sweet William's Ghost]

Karpeles MSS., No. 5187; text, p. 4727. Sung by Mrs.
Emma Boone, North River, Conception Bay, Newfoundland, October 15, 1929.

p D/Æ

1. Lady Margaret was sitting in her lonely bower,
Build-ed with lime and stone,
Lady Margaret was sitting in her lonely bower
And she heard of a dismal moan.

2. Is this my father, the king, she cries,
Or is it my brother John,
Or is it my true love, Knight William,
From Scotland he has come.

3. It's not your father, the king, he cries,
Nor yet your brother John,
But it is your true love, Knight William,
From Scotland he has come.

4. Do you bring me any apparel, she said,
Or do you bring me a ring,
Or do you bring me any token at all
That a true love ought to bring?

5. I brought to you no apparel, he said,
I've brought to you no ring,
All I brought to you is my cold winding-sheet
That my poor body lies in.

6. There's one requestin I'll ask of thee,
I hope you will grant to me,
That is my faith and a troth,
Lady Margaret, I'll leave and pledge with thee.*

7. Your faith and a troth I'll not bring to you,
Or any such a thing,
Until you'll take me to yonder church
And wed me with a ring.

8. O God forbid, Lady Margaret, he said,
That ever that should be†
That the dead should arise and marry the quick
And banish away from thee.

9. She took her petticoats in her hands
And they above her knees,
And it's over the hills of a cold winter's night
In a dead man's company.

10. Until they came to a mossy green bank
Where the graves been grassy green§
There's my home, Lady Margaret, he said,
And the place I do dwell in.#

11. Have you any room at your bed's head,
Or any at your feet
Or have you any room at all
That I lay down to sleep?

12. My father he's at my bed's head,
And my mother is at my feet,
And there's three hell hounds all around me
Waiting my poor soul to keep.

13. One of them's for my drunkenness
And the other's for my pride,
And the other's for deluding a fair pretty maid
And staying out late by night.

14. She took her hand all from her side
And struck him all on the breast.
Here is my faith and a troth, Knight William,
God grant your soul to rest.

15. I thank you, Lady Margaret, he said,
I thank thee kinderly,
If ever the dead is allowed to pray for the quick,
I must be allowed to pray for thee.‡

The words of Mrs. Boone's son, John McCabe, varied as follows:
* I leaved in pledge with thee.
† That any such thing should be
§ They walked over hills and grassy plains
Till they came to a grassy grave
And the place where I'm to rest.
‡ If the living is allowed to pray for the dead,
I hope you'll pray for me.

GROUP E

12. "Sweet William's Ghost"

Archive, School of Scottish Studies, rec. No. 1952/42/B29.
Sung by Mrs. Elizabeth ("Betsy") Whyte, Killin, Perth-
shire; learned from her mother. Collected by Hamish
Henderson. Transcribed by Francis M. Collinson.

m I/M

For my mouth it is full of mould Maggie
My breath it is wonderful strong
And if I was to kiss your sweet ruby lips
Your time wouldnae be long
Gie me yer faith in mould Maggie
An' let me pass right on my way
My aiths that are true you'll never get
Nor nothing of the kind
To you tell me so many scores deid
Since his twa met the streen
There's three score deid and three score burned
And three score went awa
There was none of them dead they'd go to heaven
Oh none but barely three
There was one of them I tore his shepherd man
That payed his service free
There another of them my ship carpenter
That was daily on the sea
There another of them my pretty babe
Which died after nor see'd.
For the cocks may craw in thonder ha'
When poor Johnnie must awa.

The Unquiet Grave

CHILD NO. 78

NONE of the extant texts of this ballad is older than the early nineteenth century. In view, however, of the stanza with which, in its many variants, it nearly always commences, there is a special interest in a moralizing carol of about the end of the fifteenth century which has a similar opening formula, and which we may reasonably conjecture to have been based on some secular folk-song. The carol remained unprinted until 1935, when R. L. Greene gave it (without citing the parallel) in his *Early English Carols*, p. 127 (No. 170) from Ashmole MS. 1379, p. 32. It commences:

> There blows a colde wynd todaye, todaye,
> The wynd blows cold todaye;
> Cryst sufferyd hi*s* passyon for manys saluacyon,
> To kype the cold wynd awaye.

The last line serves as the refrain of each stanza. The carol is so completely made over in the moralizing vein that no trace of original narrative remains. It seems evident, however, that the unnecessary repetition of *todaye* in the first line is a substitution for something no longer appropriate, and a love-song of some sort would be most likely to be so remade. If the original line was "There blows a cold wynd todaye, *my love*," or "The wynd blows cold todaye, my love," it would be hard to resist speculating on a possible connection with the present ballad. The second line would be altered to mere repetition because the moralist intended to make the cold wind a figurative wind, upon which

the whole point of his carol was to turn, and had no particular use for the raindrops. But nothing useful can at present be added.* There are certainly other old songs which make their burdens or refrains out of the wind and the rain, from "Blow, northern wind" and "Western wind, when wilt thou blow" to "The rain it raineth every day." Incidentally, the plaintive and beautiful Æolian air of "Western wind" (cf. Chappell, *Popular Music*, I, [1855], p. 58) would be particularly appropriate for "The Unquiet Grave," and is, in fact, not improbably an ancient ballad tune. (Cf. "Go from my Window," and "Walsingham" [Chappell, I, pp. 121-23, 140-42].)

Almost all the variants that have been recorded are in the major or Mixolydian mode, and are clearly members of the same family. Most of the major tunes are plagal, and are the melodic counterparts of the Mixolydian tunes. Where the Mixolydian tunes end their first phrase on the tonic and their second on the dominant, the major tunes end the first phrase on the lower dominant (i.e., Mixolydian tonic) and pause at the mid-cadence on the second (Mixolydian dominant). The Mixolydian minor seventh then becomes the major fourth. If the tune is really ancient, it would be a temptation to suppose that the Mixolydian form is the earlier.

* The reader may consult an article on this song by Ruth Harvey in *JEFDSS*, IV, No. 2 (1941), pp. 49-66.

TUNES WITH TEXTS

GROUP A a

10. "Cold Blows the Wind"

Sharp MSS., 1640/1492. Sung by Mrs. Elizabeth Swetherd (65), Tewkesbury, April 11, 1908.

p I

1. Cold blows the wind on my true love,
   Cold blows the drops of rain.
   I never, never had but one true love,
   In the greenwoods he was slain.

2. I will do as much for my true love
   As any other girl.

   I'll sit and weep all over his grave
   For one twelvemonth and one day.

3. When a twelvemonth and a day is past
   This young man he arose:
   Why do you sit and weep all over my grave
   Where I can't take sweet repose.

4. One kiss, one kiss from your cold clay lips,
   One kiss is all I crave.
   If I can have one kiss from your cold clay lips
   I'll return back from your grave.

5. My breast it is as cold as clay
   My breath is earthly strong,
   So if you have a kiss from my cold clay lips
   Your days they won't be long.

6. Go fetch me a letter from the deserts so deep
   And blood from out of the stone;
   Go fetch me milk from a fair maid's breast,
   But a fair maid never had known.

7. How can I fetch your letter from the deserts so deep
   Or blood from out of a stone,
   Or how fetch milk from a fair maid's breast
   That a fair maid never had known.

GROUP AC

27. "How Cold the Winds do Blow"

Broadwood, *JFSS*, I, No. 4 (1902), p. 192(2). Also in Broadwood, 1908, p. 52. Sung by Mrs. Rugman, Dunsfold, Surrey, in 1896.

p I

1. "How cold the winds do blow, dear love!
   And a few small drops of rain!
   I never, never had but one true love,
   In the greenwood he was slain.

2. I'll do as much for my true love
   As any young girl may:
   I'll sit and mourn upon his grave
   For twelve months and a day."

3. When twelve months and a day were up
   Then he began to speak:
   "O, who is it sits upon my grave
   And will not let me sleep?"

4. "It's I, it's I, your own true love,
   Your own true love!" said she;
   "One single sweet kiss from your clay-cold lips!
   That's all I want from thee!"

5. "My lips they are as cold as [any] clay,
   My breath is heavy and strong,
   If you were to kiss my clay-cold lips
   Your life it won't be long.

6. It's down in yonder garden, love,
   Where we were used to walk,
   There's finest flowers that ever grew
   All withered to the stalk.

7. They're withered and dried up, dear love,
   Never to return any day,
   So it's you, and I, and all must die,
   When Christ calls us away."

GROUP Ad

35. "Cold Blows the Wind"

Sharp MSS., 131/205. Also in Sharp, *JFSS*, II, No. 6 (1905), with other words; and Sharp, 1916, p. 56. Sung by Mrs. William Rea, Hambridge, Somerset, April 4, 1904.

a I

I'll do so much for my sweetheart
As any young man may;
I'll sit and mourn all on her grave
A twelve month and a day.

The twelve months and the day was past,
The ghost began to speak:
What makes you sit all on my grave
And will not let me sleep?

There is one thing more I want sweetheart
There is one thing more I crave,
And that is a kiss from your lily-white lips
And then I'll go from your grave.

My lips are cold as clay sweetheart,
My breath smell heavy and strong
And if you kiss my lily-white lips
Your time will not be long.

36. [The Unquiet Grave]

Greenleaf and Mansfield, 1933, p. 23(A). Sung by Mrs. Rosie White, Sandy Cove, Newfoundland, in 1929.

a M

The editors compare this copy with Barry's of "The Two Brothers" (No. 49) in *British Ballads from Maine*, 1929, p. 99; and call attention to the parallel with three of Sharp's copies of that ballad, 1932, I, No. 12, B, C, D: *vide ante*, Vol. I, pp. 393(21), 388(10), 396(31), 394(24).

1. There been falling drops of dew, sweetheart,
   And heavy falls of rain;
   I've only had but one sweetheart,
   On the green fields he was slain.

2. I would do so much for my sweetheart
   As any young maid may;
   I'll sit and mourn upon his grave
   For a twelvemonth and a day.

3. When the twelvemonth and a day been up
   This young man rose and spoke:
   "What keeps you mourning upon my grave?
   You will not let me sleep.

4. "Why do you weep, why do you mourn?
    What do you want of me?"
  "One kiss, one kiss from your lily-white lips
    That's all I want of thee."

5. "My lily-white lips are cold as clay,
    And my breath smells vile and strong;
  If you takes one kiss from my lily-white lips,
    Your time it won't be long."

6. "Down yonder meadow where the grass grows green,
    Where you and I used to walk,
  The prettiest flowers that ever we had seen
    It is withered unto the stalk.

7. "It is withered unto the stalk, sweetheart,
    And the leaves will never return;
  But since I have lost my own sweetheart
    What shall I do but mourn?"

8. "Mourn not for me, my own true love,
    Mourn not for me, I pray,
  So I must leave you and all the whole world,
    And go into my grave."

GROUP B

41. "Cold Blows the Wind"

Burne, [1886], p. 651; text, p. 542. Also in Broadwood and Maitland, 1893, p. 34. Sung by Jane Butler, Edgmond, between 1870 and 1880.

p Æ (inflected VII)

This variant belongs to the far-flung tribe of "Lazarus" or "Geordie" tunes, already met in several connections, and to reappear in others. Cf., e.g., in Broadwood and Maitland, 1893, pp. 68 and 102, and "Gilderoy," in D'Urfey's *Pills*, 1719, V, p. 39; and an article by the present editor in *Journal of the American Musicological Society*, III (1950), pp. 120-34.

We are informed that the above singer employed only the second strain after the first stanza had been sung.

1. 'Cold blows the wind over my true love,
    Cold blow the drops of rain;
  I never never had but one true love,
    And in Camvīle he was slain.'

2. 'I'll do as much for my true love
    As any young girl may,
  I'll sit and weep down by his grave
    For twelve months and one day.'

3. But when twelve months were come and gone,
    This young man he arose.
  'What makes you weep down by my grave?
    I can't take my repose.'

4. 'One kiss, one kiss, of your lily-white lips,
    One kiss is all I crave;
  One kiss, one kiss, of your lily-white lips,
    And return back to your grave!'

5. 'My lips they are as cold as my clay,
    My breath is heavy and strong,
  If thou wast to kiss my lily-white lips
    Thy days would not be long!'

6. 'O don't you remember the garden-grove
    Where we was used to walk?
  Pluck the finest flower of them all,
    'Twill wither to a stalk!'

7. 'Go fetch me a nut from a dungeon deep,
    And water from a stone,
  And white milk from a maiden's breast
    [That babe bare never none].'

8. ['Go dig me a grave both long, wide, and deep,
    (*As quickly as you may*),
  I will lie down in it and take one sleep,
    For a twelvemonth and one day!
  I will lie down in it and take one sleep
    For a twelvemonth and one day!']

The Wife of Usher's Well

CHILD NO. 79

This admirable ballad has had a widespread currency in recent tradition in the Appalachian region. I am unable to trace the dominant melodic tradition (Group C) back into the nineteenth century, or back across the Atlantic ocean. The ballad appears to have all but died out in Scotland and England, and, so far as I know, has not been recorded in Ireland. The one musical record which antedates the opening of the present century—a Scottish variant (vt. 1) printed in 1833—has no perceptible relation with later records; nor have the two recorded English variants (vt. 3) (themselves representing a distinct line) any resemblance to the Scottish or to the American branches.

The Appalachian tradition is very attractive and consistent. Indeed, it is one of the most memorably beautiful of all our melodic *Gestalten*. It runs predominantly to the pentatonic scale in its fourth mode (lacking II and VI), seldom leaving the authentic range. Almost without exception, the tunes are four-phrase, usually of the progressive kind (ABCD), but with a final cadence that repeats the first, and sufficiently homogeneous to make use of earlier material in the later phrases. Nearly half the variants cadence at the mid-pause on the dominant, and almost all end their first phrase on the tonic. A second group, almost as large as the first, has the mid-pause on the flat seventh. The flat seventh and the fifth appear to be felt as almost equivalent, or indifferent, choices, which do not affect the pentatonic character of the tune. A few variants recall other well-known types—e.g., "Lady Isabel," "Lord Lovel," "Barbara Allen," "The Daemon Lover." The two English variants (vt. 3) also have a familiar ring, but, being from separate counties, may continue a fairly widespread earlier tradition.

TUNES WITH TEXTS

GROUP A

1. "The Wife of Usher's Well"

Scott, 1833-34, III, opp. p. 262; text, p. 258.

p π^1

There might be some family connection between this and the family of "Harlaw" (No. 163; cf. especially Greig and Keith, 1925, p. 105[d]).

1. There lived a wife at Usher's Well,
    And a wealthy wife was she,
  She had three stout and stalwart sons,
    And sent them o'er the sea.

2. They hadna been a week from her,
    A week but barely ane,
  When word came to the carline wife,
    That her three sons were gane.

3. They hadna been a week from her,
    A week but barely three,
  When word came to the carline wife,
    That her sons she'd never see.

4. "I wish the wind may never cease,
    Nor fishes in the flood,
  Till my three sons come hame to me,
    In earthly flesh and blood!"—

5. It fell about the Martinmas,
    When nights are lang and mirk,
  The carline wife's three sons came hame,
    And their hats were o' the birk.

6. It neither grew in syke nor ditch,
    Nor yet in ony sheugh;
  But at the gates o' Paradise,
    That birk grew fair eneugh.

*   *   *   *   *   *

7. "Blow up the fire, my maidens!
    Bring water from the well!
  For a' my house shall feast this night,
    Since my three sons are well."—

8. And she has made to them a bed,
    She's made it large and wide;
  And she's ta'en her mantle her about,
    Sat down at the bed-side.

*   *   *   *   *   *

9. Up then crew the red red cock,
    And up and crew the gray;
  The eldest to the youngest said,
    " 'Tis time we were away."—

10. The cock he hadna craw'd but once,
    And clapp'd his wings at a',
  Whan the youngest to the eldest said,
    "Brother, we must awa.—

11. "The cock doth craw, the day doth daw,
     The channerin' worm doth chide;
 Gin we be mist out o' our place,
     A sair pain we maun bide.

12. "Fare ye weel, my mother dear!
     Fareweel to barn and byre!
 And fare ye weel, the bonny lass,
     That kindles my mother's fire."

*   *   *   *   *   *

GROUP B

3. "There Was a Lady in Merry Scotland"

Leather, 1912, p. 198. Sung by Mrs. Loveridge, Dilwyn, 1908. Noted by R. Vaughan Williams from phonograph recording.

p I

1. There lived a lady in merry Scotaland,
     And she had sons all three;
 And she sent them out into merry Eng-e-land,
     For to learn some English deeds.

2. They had not been in a-merry Eng-e-land
     For twelve months and one day,
 When the news came back to their own dear mother
     That their bodies were in cold clay.

3. "I will not believe in a man," she said,
     "Nor in Christ in eternity,
 Till they send me back my own three sons,
     And the same as they went from me."

4. And God put life all in their bodies,
     Their bodies all in their chest,
 And sent them back to their own dear mother,
     For in heaven they could take no rest.

5. As soon as they reached to their own mother's gates,
     So loud at the bell they ring,
 There was none so ready as their own dear mother,
     For to loose the children in.

6. The cloth was spread, the meat put on;
     "No meat, Lord, can we take,
 Since it's so long and many a day,
     Since we have been here before."

7. The bed was made, the sheets put on;
     "No bed, Lord, can we take,
 It's been so long and many a day,
     Since we have been here before."

8. Then Christ did call for the roasted cock,
     That was feathered with His only (holy?) hands;
 He crowed three times all in the dish,
     In the place where he did stand.

9. "Then farewell stick and farewell stone,
     Farewell to the maidens all.
 Farewell to the nurse that gave us our suck";
     And down the tears did fall.

GROUP CA

5. [The Wife of Usher's Well]

Sharp MSS., 3616/2678, in different barring, starting after first note. Also in Sharp and Karpeles, 1932, I, p. 156(J). Sung by Mrs. Minnie Pope, Clear Creek, Wasioto, Bell County, Ky., May 1, 1917.

a Æ/D

There was a lady, a lady gay,
 Three babes, she has three.
 She sent them off to the foreign country
 For to learn both grammaree.

And on old Christmas times was drawing near
 While the nights was dark and cold,
 She fixed a table in her dining-room
 And on it put cakes and wine.

She fixed a bed in her parlour
 And on it put a linen sheet.
 Come eat, come sleep, my three little babes,
 Come eat, come sleep with me.

Mother, says the oldest one,
 I cannot eat or sleep with you.
 My Saviour's here and I must go,
 A marble stone is at my head
 And the green grass growing at my feet,
 I cannot eat nor sleep with you.

20. [The Wife of Usher's Well]

Sharp MSS., 3193/2340. Also in Sharp and Karpeles, 1932,
I, p. 153(D). Sung by Mrs. Dora Shelton, Allanstand, N.C.,
August 1, 1916.

a π⁴

1. Pretty Polly hadn't been married but a very short
time
When she had her three little babes;
She sent them away to the North Country
To learn their grammary.

2. She dreamed a dream when the nights were long,
When the nights were long and cold,
She dreamed she saw her three little babes
Come walking down to the home.

3. She spread a table with a milk-white cloth
And on it she put bread and wine.
Come and eat, come and eat, my three little babes,
Come and eat and drink of wine.

4. Take it off, take it off, dear mother, said they,
For we hain't got long to stay,
For yonder stands our Saviour dear
Where we must shortly be.

5. She spread a bed in the backside room
And on it she put three sheets,
And one of the sheets was a golden sheet
And under hit they must sleep.

6. Take it off, take it off, dear mother, said they,
For we hain't got long to stay,
For it was the pride of your own heart
That caused us under the clay.

7. We was buried on yonder old Blue Knob,
We was buried side by side;
Cold clods at our head, green grass at our feet,
We was wropped in a winding-sheet.

GROUP CC

30. "Lady Gay"

Buell Kazee, Brunswick recording, No. 212.

a π⁴

1. There was a lady and a lady gay
Of children she had three.
She sent them away to the North Country
To learn their grammarie.

2. They had not been there very long,
Scarcely six months and a day,
Till Death, cold Death came hasting along
And stole those babes away.

3. It was just about Old Christmas time,
The nights being cold and clear:
She looked and she saw her three little babes
Come running home to her.

4. She set a table both long and wide,
And on it she put bread and wine.
"Come eat, come drink, my three little babes,
Come eat, come drink of mine."

5. "We want none of your bread, Mother,
Neither do we want your wine.
For yonder stands our Savior dear,
And to Him we must resign.

6. "Green grass grows over our heads, Mother;
Cold clay is under our feet;
And every tear you shed for us,
It wets our winding sheet."

43. [The Wife of Usher's Well]

Sharp MSS., 3901/. Also in Sharp and Karpeles, 1932, I,
p. 157(L), revised. Sung by George W. Gibson, Oneida,
Ky., August 21, 1917.

a D/Æ

There was a lady and a lady gay,
And children she had three
O she sent them off to the Northern
School
For to learn their grammaree.

GROUP Ea

48. "The Three Little Babes"

Davis, 1929, p. 576(J); text, p. 287. Sung by Mrs. James Sprouse, Lawyers, Va., March 20, 1915. Collected by Juliet Fauntleroy.

a π¹

There was a lady, lady gay,
    Who had babies one, two, three;
She sent those babes to the north countrie
    To learn their grammaree.

They hadn't been there but a month and a day
    Before swift death came on,·
Before swift death came on
    And taken those babes away.

"There is a King who lives in Heaven
    Who used to wear a crown;
Pray send me back those three little babes
    Tonight or in the morning soon."

"Come in, come in, my three little babes,
    And eat this bread and wine."
"O mother, I cannot eat your bread,
    I cannot drink your wine."

GROUP Eb

54. "Lady Gray [sic]"

Brown MSS., 16 a. From I. G. Greer.

p π¹

Little Musgrave and Lady Barnard

CHILD NO. 81

THIS ballad is one of those quoted in Beaumont and Fletcher's *Knight of the Burning Pestle* (c. 1611), and it was entered in the Stationers' Register in 1630. The Gosson broadside printed by Child is little later, the Percy Folio text is of about the same date, and the A-text is of 1658. There has also survived a Scottish text earlier than any of these in the Panmure MS., as yet unprinted.* None of these early texts, so far as I have learned, either preserves or names a tune. They are in ordinary ballad-quatrains, single or double, and without refrain; except that the A-text has an interpolated "Hay downe" after the first line. In this feature it is like the scrap quoted in *The Knight*, except that the latter has an extra "down." These may probably be an abbreviated indication of a fuller refrain such as is found at the same place in several of the Robin Hood ballads. Some of the latter add a similar indication after the fourth line. One may conjecture that the refrain as actually sung in these cases was of the "Three Ravens" pattern, appearing as the second, fourth, and seventh and eighth phrases of an eight-phrase tune. This is a normal form for country dances in the seventeenth century; and ballad-tunes adapted to dancing, usually in 6/8 time, were likely to be so extended. On the other hand, the tune of "Arthur-a-Bland," used with some of the Robin Hood ballads, had only this single interpolated phrase after the second line and may be the one here intended.

The earliest tunes actually reported as from tradition are of a far later date, being Motherwell's of 1827 and Chappell's of c. 1858. (Rimbault, in 1850, follows Motherwell with editorial alteration.) These are both variants of the same tune. All the other records are of the present century, and all except one are from this side of the Atlantic. It would almost seem as if this particular brand of *crime passionel* had come to strike the traditional singer across the water as too extreme, although there are certainly brutalities enough of a more sordid variety among the nineteenth-century broadsides.

At any rate, "Little Musgrave" has flourished in our own day all up and down the Atlantic seaboard. The melodic tradition divides pretty distinctly into two main branches, one confined to the North, the other centering chiefly in the South, but reaching North occasionally (as far even as Newfoundland) and West to Ohio and Michigan. The latter form would appear to be the more deeply rooted, and to it the Motherwell and Chappell tunes probably belong. It is by no means steady or consistent in its habits; and after dividing it into ten varieties, I am not very sure that all are properly classified. The central tradition is strongly major.

The members of the New England branch (Group B) seem all to be built out of the Scottish tune familiarly known in the late nineteenth and present centuries as "Drumdelgie." This tune has been a favorite with northern woodsmen, and is found with a variety of recent semi-popular texts. It is found with "Little Musgrave" in its complete eight-phrase state, and in all stages of dilapidation down to a two-phrase remnant. It is always in 6/8 rhythm, is plagal, or authentic with ending on the octave above, and has a mid-pause either on the tonic, the octave, or the fourth or fifth. Nearly all variants are majors. For the most part, the variants preserve the marks of their identity quite distinctly, no matter how worn down they may be.

---

*Now National Library of Scotland MS. 9450 (Panmure MS. 11). "Litel Musgray" was printed from this MS. (Robert Edwards' Commonplace Book), in *The Ninth of May*, vol. 4, pp. 24-26, a private, limited printing, transcribed and annotated by Helena M. Shire (Rampant Lions Press, Cambridge, England, 1973).

TUNES WITH TEXTS

GROUP A b

6. "Lord Orland's Wife"

Kittredge, *JAF*, XXX (1917), p. 309. Sung by Hilliard Smith, Carr Creek, Knott County, Ky., 1916. Collected by Loraine Wyman.

a π^1, ending on the octave.

1. The first came in was a gay ladye;
   The next came in was a girl;
   The third came in was Lord Orland's wife,
   The fairest of them all.

2. Little Mathew Grew was standing by;
   She placed her eyes on him:
   "Go up with me, Little Mathew Grew,
   This livelong night we'll spend."

3. "I can tell by the ring that's on your finger
   You are Lord Orland's wife."
   "But if I am Lord Orland's wife,
   Lord Orland is not at home."

4. The little footpage was standing by,
   Heard all that she did say:
   "Your husband sure will hear these words
   Before the break of day."

5. He had sixteen miles to go,
   And ten of them he run;
   He run till he came to the broken bridge,
   He smote his breast and swum.

6. He ran till he came to Lord Orland's hall,
   He ran till he came to the gate,

He rattled those bells and he rung:
"Awake, Lord Orland, awake!"

7. "What's the matter, what's the matter, little footpage?
   What's the news you bring to me?"
   "Little Mathew Grew's in bed with your wife;
   It's as true as anything can be."

8. "If this be a lie," Lord Orland he said,
   "That you have brought to me,
   I'll build a scaffold on the king's highway,
   And hanged you shall be."

9. "If this be a lie I bring to you,
   Which you're taking it to be,
   You need not build a scaffold on the king's highway,
   But hang me to a tree."

.   .   .   .

10. At first they fell to hugging and kissing,
    At last they fell to sleep;
    All on the next morn when they awoke,
    Lord Orland stood at their bed feet.

11. "O how do you like my curtains fine?
    O how do you like my sheets?
    O how do you like my gay ladye,
    That lies in your arms asleep?"

12. "Very well I like your curtains fine,
    Very well I like your sheets;
    Much better I like your gay ladye,
    That lies in my arms and sleeps."

13. "Get up, get up, little Mathew Grew,
    And prove your words to be true.
    I'll never have it for to say
    A naked man I slew."

14. The first lick struck little Mathew Grew struck,
    Which caused an awful wound;
    The next lick struck Lord Orland struck,
    And laid him on the ground.

15. "O how do you like my curtains fine?
    O how do you like my sheets?
    O how do you like little Mathew Grew,
    That lies on the ground and sleeps?"

16. "Very well I like your curtains fine,
    Very well I like your sheets;
    Much better I like little Mathew Grew,
    That lies on the ground and sleeps."

15. "Lyttle Musgrave"

Ritchie, 1955, p. 135. Learned from singing of Uncle Jason
Ritchie, Ball Fork, Troublesome Creek, Ky.

p π¹ (or a π¹, ending on the octave)

1. One day, one day, one fine holiday,
   As many there be in the year,
   We all went down to the preacher's house
   Some glorious words to hear.

2. Lyttle Musgrave stood by the church house door,
   The priest was at private mass,
   But he had more mind of the fair women
   Than he had for Our Lady's grace.

3. The first came in was a-clad in green,
   The next was a-clad in pall,
   And then came in Lord Arnol's wife
   She's the fairest one of them all.

4. She cast an eye on Lyttle Musgrave
   As bright as the summer sun,
   And then bethought this Lyttle Musgrave,
   This lady's heart have I won.

5. Quoth she, I have loved the Lyttle Musgrave
   Full long and many a day.
   Quoth he, I have loved you, fair lady,
   Yet never one word durst I say.

6. I have a bower in the Buckelsfordberry,
   It's dainty and it's nice,
   If you'll go in a thither my Lyttle Musgrave,
   You can sleep in my arms all night.

7. I cannot go in a thither, said Lyttle Musgrave,
   I cannot for my life,
   For I know by the rings on your fingers
   You are Lord Arnol's wife.

8. But if I am Lord Arnol's wife,
   Lord Arnol is not at home;
   He has gone to the academie
   Some language for to learn.

9. Quoth he, I thank thee, fair lady,
   For this kindness thou showest to me,
   And whether it be to my weal or my woe
   This night I will lodge with thee.

10. All this was heard by a lyttle foot page
    By his lady's coach as he ran,
    Says he, I am my lady's foot page,
    I will be Lord Arnol's man.

11. Then he cast off his hose and shoes
    Set down his feet and ran,
    And where the bridges were broken down
    He smote his breast and swam.

12. Awake, awake now, Lord Arnol,
    As thou art a man of life,
    Lyttle Musgrave is in the Buckelsfordberry
    Along with your wedded wife.

13. If this be true, my lyttle foot page,
    This thing thou tellest to me,
    Then all the land in Buckelsfordberry
    I freely will give it to thee.

14. But if it be a lie, thou lyttle foot page,
    This thing thou tellest to me,
    On the highest tree in the Buckelsfordberry
    Then it's hanged you shall be.

15. He called up his merry men all,
    Come saddle up my steed,
    This night I am away to the Buckelsfordberry
    For I never had greater need.

16. Some men whistled and some they sung,
    And some of them did say,
    Whenever Lord Arnol's horn doth blow,
    Away Musgrave away.

17. I think I hear the noisy cock,
    I think I hear the jay,
    I think I hear Lord Arnol's horn
    Away Musgrave away.

18. Lie still, lie still, my Lyttle Musgrave,
    Lie still with me till morn,
    Tis but my father's shepherd boy
    A-calling his sheep with his horn.

19. He hugged her up all in his arms
    And soon they fell asleep,
    And when they awoke at the early dawn
    Lord Arnol stood at their bedfeet.

20. O it's how do you like my coverlid,
    And it's how do you like my sheet?
    And it's how do you like my fair lady
    That lies in your arms and sleeps?

21. O I like your handsome coverlid,
    Likewise your silken sheet,
    But best of all your fair lady
    That lies in my arms and sleeps.

22. Arise, arise now, Lyttle Musgrave,
    And dress soon as you can.
    It shall not be said in my countree
    I killed a naked man.

23. I cannot arise, said Lyttle Musgrave,
    I cannot for my life,
    For you have two broadswords by your side
    And me with nary a knife.

24. I have two broadswords by my side,
    They both ring sweet and clear,

You take the best, I'll keep the worst,
Let's end the matter here.

25. O the very first lick Lyttle Musgrave struck
    He wounded Lord Arnol sore;
    The very first lick Lord Arnol struck
    Musgrave lay dead in his gore.

26. Then up and spoke this fair lady
    In bed where as she lay,
    Although you are dead, my Lyttle Musgrave,
    Yet for your soul I will pray.

27. Lord Arnol stepped up to the bedside
    Whereon these lovers had lain,
    He took his sword in his right hand
    And split her head in twain.

GROUP Ad

27. [Little Musgrave and Lady Barnard]

Sharp MSS., 3686/2742. Also in Sharp and Karpeles, 1932,
I, p. 175(J). Sung by Mrs. Delie Knuckles, Barbourville,
Ky., May 16, 1917.

a π² (or p π¹)

1. There was four and twenty ladies there
   A-dancing at the ball.
   The first came in was a lily-white robe,
   The next came pink and blue,
   The third came in was Lord Banner's wife,
   The flower of the view.

2. This little MacGroves a-being there,
   All dressed in oil of green,
   He looked at her, she looked at him,
   The like was never seen.

3. She said to him: My sweet MacGroves,
   Go home with me to-night;
   There's waiting-boys plenty there,
   And I'll ride by your side.

4. O no, O no, I dare not go,
   I dare not for my life;

I know you by the ring you wear
You are Lord Banner's wife.

5. O if I am Lord Banner's wife,
Lord Banner's hain't at home;
Lord Banner he's Redemption gone,
He's on Queen Anna's throne.

6. This little foot-page a-being there,
Determined Lord Banner should know.
He turned his course to Lord Banner's hall
And dingled on the ring.

7. What news, what news, my little foot-page?
What news are you bringing to me?
Is any of my fine brick castles blown down,
Or any of my men false been?

8. There's none of your fine brick castles blown down,
Nor none of your men false been,
But little MacGroves in fair Scotland
In bed with your lady.

9. O if this be a lie your telling to me,
As O I take it to be,
I'll build me a gallows in fair Scotland,
And hanged you shall be.

10. If this be a lie I'm telling to you,
As O you take it to be,
You need not build no gallows at all,
Just hang me on a tree.

11. In calling all his merry men,
By one, by two, by threes,
Saying: Let's all go to fair Scotland
This young MacGroves to slay.

12. Then one of Lord Banner's foremost men
Who wished MacGroves no ill,
He drew his horn and he blew it loud,
He blew it loud and thrill.

13. What's this I hear, says little MacGroves,
It blew so loud and clear.
I think it's Lord Banner's horn.
O him how do I fear.

14. Lie down, lie down, my sweet MacGroves,
And keep me from the cold;
It's nothing but my father's horn
Calling the sheep to the fold.

15. They lay and slept, they slumbered and slept,
So sweetly they did sleep;
But when they woke who did they spy,
Lord Banner's at their feet.

16. Says: How do you like my own bedside?
Or how do you like my sheet?
Or how do you like my gay young wife
Lies in your arms asleep?

17. Very well I like your own bedside,
Much better I like your sheet,
But the best of all's your gay young wife
Lies in my arms asleep.

18. Rise up, rise up, you young MacGroves,
Rise up, draw on your clothes.
It shall never be said in the fair Scotland
I slain a naked man.

19. O no, O no, I dare not rise,
I dare not for my life,
For you have two big, new, keen swords,
I have ne'er a knife.

20. O if I have two new, keen swords,
They cost deep in purse,
And you can take the best of them
And I will take the worst.

21. You can strike the very first blow,
But strike it like a man;
And I will strike the second blow;
I'll kill you if I can.

22. The very first lick that MacGroves struck,
He wounded Lord Banner full sore;
The second lick Lord Banner struck,
MacGroves he spoke no more.

23. Rise up, rise up, my gay young wife,
Rise up, draw on your clothes,
And tell to me which you like best,
I or this young MacGroves.

24. If you lay struggling in your blood
As MacGroves he does now,
I'd kiss the lips of sweet MacGroves,
But I never would kiss yours.

GROUP A i

55. "Lord Arnold"

Barry Dict. Cyl., No. 84, ctg. 1. Sung by Frank Tracy,
Brewer, Me., June 10, 1934. Transcribed by Editor.

p D

I thought I heard Lord Arnold's horn
I thought I heard his fold (?)

. . . .

Driving his flock to wold,
. . . . driving to wold.
[*Remainder undeciphered.*]

GROUP B

66. "Lord Banner"

Barry, Eckstorm, and Smyth, 1929, p. 186(I). Sung by
Mrs. D. J. Libby, St. Stephen, New Brunswick, March 1929.
Tune recorded by D. A. Nesbitt.

a I, ending on the octave

1. Four and twenty gay ladies,
   Obeying at a ball,
   Lord Banner's lady she was there,
   The gayest of them all,
   And young Magrue from Scotland too,
   As bright as the rising sun;
   He looked at her, she winked at him,
   The likes was never known.

2. "Oh, will you take a ride with me,
   Oh, will you take a ride?
   You will have servants to wait on you
   And a fair lady by your side."
   "To take a ride I dare not do it,
   Oh, not for all my life;
   For by the ring you wear on your finger
   You are Lord Banner's wife."

3. "Oh, what if I am Lord Banner's wife,
   Sure he is not at home;
   He has gone to fair England
   To take King Henry's throne."
   One of his foot-pages standing near
   Heard what had been said and done.
   He said, "My master shall have the news
   Before the rising sun."

4. He ran till he came to the river's side,
   There he jumped in and he swam,
   He swam till he came to the other side,
   He took to his heels and he run.

He ran till he came to the cottage door,
He rapped both loud and shrill;
There is none so ready as Lord Banner
To let this fair page in.

5. Saying, "Is there any of my castles down,
   Or any of my towers three,
   Or has there anything happenèd
   To my fair Lady?"
   "Oh, no, there's none of your castles down,
   Or none of your towers three,
   But young Magrue from Scotland
   Is in bed with your fair Lady."

6. "If that is a lie you tell to me,
   As I suppose it to be,
   I will rig a gallows
   And hangèd you shall be."
   "If this be a lie I tell to you,
   As you suppose it to be,
   You need not rig any gallows,
   You can hang me on a tree."

7. Then he called down his Army Men,
   By one, by two, by three,
   Saying, "We will go over to fair Scotland
   Those fancies for to see."
   "Oh, what is that," said young Magrue,
   "That sounds so loud in my ear?
   It is Lord Banner's bugle
   That sounds so loud and clear."

8. "Lay down, lay down and keep me warm,
   Pray keep me from the cold;
   It is Lord Banner's shepherd boy
   Driving the sheep to the fold."
   He huddled her and he cuddled her
   And they both fell fast asleep,
   And early the next morning
   Lord Banner stood at their feet,

9. Saying: "How do you like my blankets fine,
   And how do you like my sheets,
   And how do you like my false lady
   That lays in your arms and sleeps?"
   "It's well I like your blankets fine,
   And well I like your sheets,
   But best of all your fair lady
   That lays in my arms and sleeps."

10. "Rise up, rise up and put on your clothes
    As quick as ever you can,
    For they never shall say in fair Scotland
    I fought with a naked man."
    "To put on my clothes I dare not do it,
    Not for all my life;
    For by your side you have two broadswords
    And I not a single knife."

11. "If by my side I have two broadswords,
    They cost me deep in purse,
    But you may take the best one
    And I will take the worst;
    And you may strike the very first blow
    And strike it like a man,

And I will strike the second
And kill you if I can."

12. Magrue he struck the very first blow,
    He wounded Lord Banner sore;
    Lord Banner struck the second
    And left him in his gore.
    He caught his fair lady by the waist,
    He gave her kisses three,
    Saying, "Which of us do you like the best,
    Young Magrue or me?"

13. "It's well I like your rosy cheeks
    And your dimpled chin;

Far better I like young Magrue
Than you or any of your kin."
He caught her by the hair of the head,
He split her brains in twain,
He threw her on the floor
Where she never rose again.

14. He put the hilt of the sword
    Unto the floor, the point was to his breast;
    There never was three lovers
    So quickly sent to their rest.

Child Maurice

CHILD NO. 83

"Child [or Gil] Morice" received a large share of the literary limelight about the middle of the eighteenth century, when Home's tragedy, *Douglas*, based on the ballad, made northern patriots ask, "Whaur's yer Wully Shakespere noo?" The ballad was also the foundation of a now forgotten poem, "Owen of Carron," by John Langhorne. Thomas Gray, without losing his head over its literary progeny, or his admiration for Shakespeare, thought the ballad "divine." What text he had secured to make him so exclaim is not clear; but it may most easily have been one or other of the two printed by Foulis at Glasgow, the second one in 1755. This latter was reproduced, with "improvements," in Percy's *Reliques* a decade later, and in the meantime it had appeared with music in R. Bremner's *Thirty Scots Songs*, of uncertain date. (Glen dates this work 1757; the Harvard copy, formerly owned by Alfred Moffat, is dated in pencil 1749.) It is said to have been the opinion of Burns's friend Riddell that the piece was modern; and Burns himself attributed the air to William McGibbon. Stenhouse, who mentions those facts in his notes to the *Scots Musical Museum* (ed. 1853, IV, pp. 192ff.), confidently denies their accuracy. He declares that he had talked to Lord Woodhouselee on the subject, and that the latter, who had known McGibbon well, was of the opinion (like Stenhouse himself) that the air was one of the most ancient of Scottish melodies. Stenhouse further asserts that the piece was in none of McGibbon's published works. It is, however, in McGibbon's *Select Collection of Scots Tunes*, n.d., Bk. IV, p. 106. (Glen dates this work 1768, on what ground I do not know: the Harvard Library copy, formerly owned by Alfred Moffat, is dated in pencil, 1742-1755, but this may be by confusion with McGibbon's earlier collections with similar titles.) According to Glen, the tune is also in Oswald's twelfth book of the *Caledonian Pocket Companion* (without a text), and in Peacock's *Fifty Favorite Scotch Airs*, 1762, neither of which has been accessible to me. Fairly certain it is that wherever a tune has been recorded with the ballad, from that day to the present, it has been some form of the one appearing in the mid-eighteenth-century collections.

No outward evidence is forthcoming to carry the tune's record any farther back. It is of the text that Motherwell speaks when he says in 1827 that he "can distinctly trace this ballad as existing in its present shape at least a century ago." In a form equally authentic the text is carried back still another century in the Percy Folio MS. This is a respectable age, in the record alone, apart from whatever calculation we may make of the ballad's prehistoric existence. The geographical range is narrow, and there is little evidence that "Child Maurice" has often traveled traditionally outside its northern home. No problem of continental affiliations has arisen, and the ballad, I believe, has very rarely appeared in tradition on this side of the Atlantic (Greenleaf and Mansfield, *Ballads and Sea Songs of Newfoundland*, 1933, p. 25). With one exception, the tune-variants all come from Scotland, and the exception stems from the same root: Hipkins, d. before 1905, took down his copy (*JFSS*, II, No. 7 [1905], p. 110) from his grandmother's singing; she was Mrs. Grant (1770-1838) and probably learned the song as a child from her mother, Mary Fraser, of Inverness (and Edinburgh).

I can offer no conjectures on the real age of the tune. Its modal identity is debatable in over half of the extant examples, two of the variants appearing to end on the fifth above, two on the lower dominant. The modal differentiation is from I/Ly to π^4. It is clear that every one of the Scottish copies down to Motherwell was from a single original, for not one of them differs from the earliest by a note, except in the matter of key. That is to say, none is taken directly from tradition, unless the first. The nineteenth century, except Motherwell and Christie, followed the same example. But Greig's variants, indisputably authentic, prove at least that a genuine melodic tradition had developed out of the same material. It is noteworthy, however, that no dependable copy of the tune is of more than four phrases, whereas the earliest copy, reprinted again and again, has six phrases with a repetition of the last two to take an eight-line stanza. We may conjecture that the repeat was arbitrarily imposed to accommodate the double quatrain. For the fifth and sixth phrases are themselves a repetition (with slight initial variation in five) of the third and fourth. This is not the way of two-strain melodies. The double quatrains could, of course, be separated at will; and in fact they are printed in both forms in the early copies. But the favorite text began with a six-line stanza. If that was to be reconciled, either of two means could be used: the second half of every succeeding quatrain could be repeated to the tune to make six lines, or the last two phrases of the tune could be sung twice in order to get ahead with the text. The ballad was long, and the latter alternative was preferred. The only other extended pattern is Christie's tune, which is confessedly "arranged." Christie's fifth phrase repeats the third, his sixth repeats the fourth, but alters the ending to close on the real tonic (probably an editorial change). He then adds a full second strain, cobbled out of ideas in the first; and thus swallows twelve lines at a time. Here, as almost always in Christie, we have every right to discard the second strain.

There are variants in 3/4 at either end of the series, but the duple is, in my judgment, the basic rhythm. Here, as frequently elsewhere, triple rhythm is not genuinely triple: it is, like five-time in British folksong, an alternating even-odd or odd-even rhythm. The word-accent imposes this alternation and the music solves it by the compromise of one-two-one, one-two-one, or by one-one-two, one-one-two. In the second case the first beat is divided, so that the next accented syllable can come on the second beat of the bar, as may be seen in variant five of the series. Otherwise, and more often, the third beat is divided in order to carry a stressed and an unstressed syllable, as in the first variant. So we have a rhythm fundamentally duple, though uneven.

In one of its forms, as Keith has noted, the tune is habitually associated with "Sir James the Rose" (Child No. 213). This, in turn, is apparently related to the "Boyne Water" pattern. I am aware of no other analogies.

1. "Gill Morice"

Johnson, III, [1790], No. 203, p. 212 (repr. 1853). Also in McGibbon, n.d., IV, p. 106; Bremner, [1757], p. 30; *Dale's Collection*, n.d., I, p. 29; Ritson, 1794, II, p. 157; Smith, [1820-24], III, p. 106; Rimbault, 1850, p. 96; *British Orpheus*, n.d., p. 343; Maver, 1866, No. 280, p. 140; and Eyre-Todd, n.d. |1894|, p. 86.

a I/Ly, ending on V

The variant readings (a) and (b) are in the Rimbault copy; (x) and (y) appear in Eyre-Todd. The tune is given in various keys by the several editors.

1. Gill Morice was an earle's son,
    His name it waxed wide,
  It was na for his great riches,
    Nor yet his mickle pride;
  But it was for a lady gay,
    That liv'd on Carron side.

2. Where will I get a bonny boy,
    That will win hose and shoon,
  That will gae to Lord Barnard's ha',
    And bid his lady cum.
  Ye maun rin this errant, Willie,
    And ye may rin wi' pride;
  When other boys gae on their feet,
    On horseback ye sall ride.

3. Oh no! oh no! my master dear!
    I dare na for my life;
  I'll nae gae to the bauld baron's
    For to tryst furth his wife.
  My bird Willie, my boy Willie,
    My dear Willie, he said,
  How can ye strive against the stream,
    For I sall be obey'd.

4. But, oh my master dear, he cry'd,
    In green wood ye're your lain;
  Gi' o'er sic thoughts, I wou'd ye red,
    For fear ye shou'd be ta'en.
  Haste, haste, I say, gae to the ha',
    Bid her come here wi' speed;
  If ye refuse my high command,
    I'll gar thy body bleed.

5. Gae bid her tak this gay mantel,
    'Tis a' goud but the hem;
  Bid her cum to the good green wood,
    And bring nane but her lain;
  And there it is, a silken sark;
    Her ain hand sew'd the sleeve;
  And bid her cum to Gill Morice;
    Speer nae bauld baron's leave.

6. I will gae your black errand,
    Tho' it be to thy cost;
  Sen ye by me will nae be warn'd,
    In it ye sall find frost.
  The baron he's a man of might,
    He ne'er could 'bide a taunt,
  As ye will see before it's night,
    How sma' ye'll hae to vaunt.

7. Now, sen I maun your errand rin,
    Sae sair against my will,
  I'se make a vow, and keep it true,
    It sal be done for ill.
  And when he came to broken brigg,
    He bent his bow and swam;
  And when he came to grass growing,
    Set down his feet and ran. &c. &c. &c.

4. "Babe Norice"

Motherwell, 1827, App'x., No. 6; text, App'x., p. xvi. From A. Blaikie, Paisley, c. 1825.

p D/Æ, ending on V

Babe Norice is to the Greenwud gane,
  He's awa wi the wind;
His horse is siller shod afore
  In the burning gowd ahind.

5. "Gill Morice"

Greig MSS., III, p. 205. Also in Greig and Keith, 1925, p. 67(2). Sung by Alexander Robb, New Deer, Aberdeenshire.

a π⁴, ending on the octave.

Gill Morice was an Earl's son.
His name it waxed wide;
It was not for his riches great
Nor for his muckle pride.

7. "Gill Morice"

Greig-Duncan MS. 785 (Walker transcript); from Duncan MS., No. 334. Also in Greig and Keith, 1925, p. 67(1); text, p. 64. G. F. Duncan learned it from his parents in Buchan, c. 1850.

p π⁴

As Keith notes, this form of the tune is found with "Sir James the Rose" (Child No. 213).

1. Gill Morice was an earl's son,
   His name it waxèd wide;
   It wasna for his great riches,
   Nor for his muckle pride.

2. His face was fair, lang was his hair,
   In the wild wood where he stayed,
   But his fame was by a lady fair
   That lived on Carron-side.

3. "Where will I get a bonnie boy
   That will win hose an' shoon,
   That will go to Lord Bernard's ha',
   An' bid his lady come?

4. "O ye maun rin for me, Willie,
   An' ye maun rin wi pride;
   When other boys rin on their feet,
   On horseback ye shall ride."

5. "O no, O no, my master dear,
   I dare not for my life:
   I'll not go to the bauld baron's
   For to tryst forth his wife."

6. "My bird Willie, my boy Willie,
   My dear Willie," he said,
   "How can ye strive against the stream?
   For I shall be obeyed."

7. "But O, my master dear," he cried,
   "In greenwood ye're your lane,
   Gie ower sic thoughts, I would you pray,
   For fear ye should be taen."

8. "O haste, haste, I say, go to the ha',
   An' bid her come wi speed.
   If ye refuse my high command,
   I'll gar your body bleed.

9. "O bid her take this gay manteel,
   It's a' gowd but the hem,
   Bid her to the greenwood here,
   An' bring nane but her lane.

10. "An' there it is, a silken sark,
    Her ain hand sewed the sleeve;
    Bid her to the greenwood here,
    Spier nae bauld baron's leave."

11. "Yes, I will go your black errand,
    Though it be to my cost,
    Since ye by me will not be warned,
    In it ye shall find frost.

12. "The baron he's a man o might,
    An' ne'er could bide a taunt,
    As ye shall see before it's night
    How sma' ye hae to vaunt.

13. "Now since I maun your errand rin,
    Sair, sair against my will,
    I'll make a vow an' keep it true,
    It shall be done for ill."

14. An' when he cam to the broken brig,
    He bent his bow an' swam,
    An' when he cam to grass growin,
    Set down his foot an' ran.

15. An' when he cam to Bernard's ha',
    Would neither chap nor ca',
    He set his bent bow to his breast
    An' lightly leapt the wa'.

16. He would tell no man his errand,
    Though twa stood at the gate,
    But straight into the ha' he cam,
    Where great folk sat at meat.

17. "Hail, hail, my gentle sire an' dame,
    My message winna wait:
    Dame, ye maun to the greenwood gang,
    Before that it be late.

18. "Ye're bidden take this gay manteel,
    It's a' gowd but the hem:
    Ye maun go to the greenwood there
    E'en by yoursel alane.

19. "There it is, a silken sark,
    Your ain hand sewed the sleeve;
    Ye maun come speak to Gill Morice,
    Spier nae bauld baron's leave."

20. The lady stampit wi her foot,
    An' winket wi her e'e,
    But all that she could say or do,
    Forbidden he would not be.

21. But all that she could say or do,
    Forbidden he would not be;
    "It's surely to my bower woman,
    It ne'er could be to me."

22. Then up an' spake the wily nurse
    (The bairn upon her knee),
    "If it be come from Gill Morice,
    O dearly it's welcome to me."

23. "Ye lee, ye lee, ye filthy nurse,
    Sae loud's I hear ye lee:
    I've brought it to Lord B[e]rnard's lady,
    I trow ye be not she."

24. Then up an' spake the bauld baron,
    An angry man was he:
    He's taen the table wi his foot,
    In flinders gart it flee:

25. "Gae bring a robe o yon clothing
    That hangs upon the pin,
    An' I will to the greenwood gae,
    An' speak wi your leman."

26. "O bide at hame now, my good lord,
    I warn you, bide at hame,
    Nor wyte a man wi violence
    That ne'er wyte you wi nane."

27. Gill Morice sits in yon greenwood,
    He whistled an' he sang;
    "O what mean a' those folk comin?
    My mother tarries lang."

28. When the baron cam to the greenwood,
    Wi muckle dool an' care,
    It's there he saw brave Gill Morice
    A-kaimin his yellow hair.

29. "No wonder now, Gill Morice brave,
    My lady loes ye weel;
    The fairest part o my body
    Is blacker than your heel.

30. "Yet ne'ertheless now, Gill Morice,
    For a' thy great beauty,
    Ye'll rue the day that ye were born,
    That head shall go wi me."

31. Now he has drawn his trusty brand,
    An' slait it on the strae,
    An' through Gill Morice' fair body
    He gart cauld iron gae.

32. An' he has taen Gill Morice' head
    An' set it on a spear,
    The meanest man in a' his train
    He got the head to bear.

33. An' he has taen Gill Morice up,
    Laid him across his steed,
    An' brought him to his painted bower,
    An' laid him on a bed.

34. The lady sat on castle wa',
    Beheld baith dale an' down,
    An' there she saw Gill Morice' head
    Come trailin to the town.

35. "Far mair I loe that bloody head
    But an' that bloody hair,
    Than Lord Bernard an' a' his lands,
    As they lie here an' there."

36. An' she has taen Gill Morice up,
    An' kissed baith mouth an' chin:
    "I aince was fu' o Gill Morice
    As hip is o the stane.

37. "I got thee in my father's ha',
    Wi' muckle grief an' shame,
    An' brought thee up in greenwood
    Under the heavy rain.

38. "Oft have I by thy cradle sat,
    An' seen thee soundly sleep,
    An' now I'll go about thy grave
    The saut tears for to weep."

39. An' she has kissed his bloody cheek,
    An' syne his bloody chin:
    "Better I loe my Gill Morice
    Than a' my kith an' kin."

40. "Awa, awa, ye ill woman,
    An ill death may ye dee;
    Gin I had kent he was your son,
    He'd ne'er been slain by me."

41. "Upbraid me not, Lord Bernard,
    Upbraid me not for shame,
    Wi that same sword O pierce my heart,
    An' put me out o' pain.

42. "Since nothing but Gill Morice' head
    Thy jealous rage could quell,
    Let that same hand now take her life
    That ne'er to you did ill.

43. "To me nae after days or nights
    Will e'er be saft or kind;
    I'll fill the air wi heavy sighs
    An' greet till I am blind."

44. "Enough o blood by me's been spilt,
    Seek not your death from me;
    I'd rather it had been mysel
    Than either him or thee.

45. "Wi wae sae wae I hear your plaint,
    Sair, sair I rue the deed,
That e'er this cursed hand o mine
    Did gar his body bleed.

46. "Dry up your tears, my winsome dame,
    Ye ne'er can heal the wound;
Ye saw his head upon my spear,
    His heart's blood on the ground.

47. "I curse the hand that did the deed,
    The heart that thought the ill,
The feet that bare me wi such speed
    The comely youth to kill.

48. "I'll aye lament for Gill Morice
    As gin he were my ain;
I'll ne'er forget the dreary day
    On which the youth was slain."

Bonny Barbara Allan

CHILD NO. 84

This little song of a spineless lover who gives up the ghost without a struggle, and of his spirited beloved who repents too late, has paradoxically shown a stronger will-to-live than perhaps any other ballad in the canon. It is still universally known. By one of those odd cycles of history, even as our first knowledge of its existence comes from Pepys' happy record of hearing an actress sing it (January 2, 1666), so in our own day it has again been brought back to the stage and has acquired a fresh vogue in the singing—unco strange to folksong, be it confessed—of Maxine Sullivan and other popular entertainers. Dissemination by phonograph and radio is a new kind of oral circulation, which is likely to have an effect on folk-tunes comparable to that of the broadside press on folk-texts.

The number of recorded variants of "Barbara Allan" is somewhat unsteadying. They appear to me to fall into four distinguishable types, of which the first and third seem to have a good deal in common. The first class is quite consistently major, heptatonic, and fairly equally divided between authentic and plagal examples. It is mainly English, and many variants lean to 5/4 time, especially Sharp's tunes from Somerset. Its first-phrase final is likely to fall on the tonic. The authentic tunes move in the first phrase from tonic to dominant and back, rising in the second phrase to the octave, but falling back for the middle cadence from VII to V, with feminine ending. The melodic curve of the third phrase imitates that of the second, and that of the fourth follows the first; but there is seldom an exact repetition, the pattern remaining ABCD. The plagal cases prefer a middle cadence rising from lower seventh to the second degree, but there is some variety here, and also in the first-phrase cadence.

The second class is mainly confined to Scotland. It moves between the Dorian and Æolian modes, and generally favors common time, with a dotted metre somewhere before the second stress (that is, the third beat). It shows little consistency in its first-phrase cadence, but prefers a rising inflection at the middle cadence, typically from the lower dominant to the tonic, or lower flat seventh to tonic, with feminine ending. The final cadence is typically identical with the middle cadence. Melodic affiliates are found with a number of other ballads, notably, "Binorie" (No. 10), "The Cruel Mother" (No. 20), "Geordie" (No. 209), "Yarrow" (No. 215), and "Tifty's Annie" (No. 233). All of these have the characteristic feminine ending at the second and fourth lines, an effect to which the proper names conduce.

The third class centers in the pentatonic scale which lacks its fourth and seventh (π^1) and is composed, with few exceptions, of plagal tunes. Its most consistent features are a somewhat chaconne-like rhythm, with a held note at the second stress of the phrase, and a middle cadence, with feminine ending, that rises from the major third to the fifth. The query is answered in the final cadence. Most of the first-phrase finals are on the tonic. The metre may appear as 3/4, 5/4, or 3/2.

The fourth class is composed entirely of American variants, and belongs to the ubiquitous "Boyne Water" family. Rhythmically, its variants are indifferently in duple or some form of triple time. Its modality is by no means easy to decide, and is perennially debatable. The tune may be described in either of two ways, with almost equal propriety: as a π^3 melody with its first half referring entirely to the upper dominant as if tonic (hence quasi-π^4 in that half); or as a π^4 plagal tune with a fallen close on the lower fourth, taking the true tonic to be the final of the mid-cadence. But since the tune was originally the second half of "Boyne Water," we are perhaps historically justified in taking our final as the true tonic, and designating the mode as π^3. A good many variants show the sixth and are therefore D/M. The middle cadence commonly falls either the distance of a fourth or of a minor third, that is, from the octave or flat seventh to the dominant, when the tune is taken as π^3 or D/M. The cadence of the first phrase may fall either on the subdominant or on the dominant.

It may be noticed that, in the parallel case of the "Gypsy Laddie" tune, to feel the final—a fourth below the other possible tonic—as the true tonic is harder than to do so here, where the final is a fifth below. Compare Group B of Child No. 4.

There is a comparatively small number of anomalous variants, in particular two or three Somersetshire instances of the tune Sharp found with "The Cruel Mother." One South Carolina version presents the "Gypsy Laddie" tune in its full length—a rare phenomenon. For the rest, the persistence with which these four varieties manifest their underlying identities under innumerable superficial changes is striking support for the hypothesis that while a ballad is in a continuously flourishing state, its tune does not drift into unrecognizable forms, even over long stretches of time.

It is pertinent to observe, as it seems not to have been observed, that tradition has gradually but surely transformed the character of the heroine. In the earliest of our texts (on broadsides), unexplained obduracy was her characterizing trait, as reflected in the song-title "Barbara Allen's Cruelty." It has been a main effect of transmission to rationalize and minimize this quality. The popular sensibility has been unable to stomach her stony-heartedness, and has gone to work on motivation. In the black-letter broadside of Pepys's day, she had stopped the funeral procession to look at her victim:

> With scornful eye she looked downe,
> Her cheeke with laughter swellin.

Only later is she suddenly struck with remorse. But the popular mind has recoiled from such coldness. Fifty years later, in the earliest Scottish text, that of Ramsay's *Tea Table Miscellany*, she is not cold but filled with vindictive resentment. She leaves the death-bed with a sigh of reluctance, and goes home to forecast her imminent death. Thereafter, in many American copies, occur verses like the following:

> The more she looked, the more she grieved,
> She busted out to crying.
> "I might have saved this young man's life
> And kept him from hard dying."

Sometimes self-reproach changes to self-exculpation:

> "O mother dear, you caused all this;
> You would not let me have him."

Little by little, and partly through simple abridgment and condensation—as by omission of her anticipative refusal to soften, before she leaves her dwelling—a kindlier, more sympathetic image has replaced the cruel one that gave original point to the object-lesson. If, as Phillips Barry believed, Barbara was once a "real person," a historic character, she has unquestionably mellowed with age.

* On this ballad and its tunes, see the following articles: "All This for a Song," in B. H. Bronson, *The Ballad as Song*, 1969, pp. 224-42; Charles Seeger, "Versions and Variants of the Tunes of 'Barbara Allen,'" in *Selected Reports*: Publications of the Institute of Ethnomusicology of the University of California at Los Angeles, 1966, pp. 120-67; Mieczyslaw Kolinski, "'Barbara Allen': Tonal versus Melodic Structure," Pts. I and II, in *Ethnomusicology*, XII (1968), pp. 208-18, and XIII (1969), pp. 1-73.

TUNES WITH TEXTS

GROUP A

2. "Barbara Allen"

Sharp MSS., 179/. Also in Sharp, *JFSS*, II, No. 6 (1905), p. 16(2). Sung by Mrs. Jane Wheeler, Langport Union, April 12, 1904.

a I/Ly

'Twas in the merry month of May
When flowers were all a budding
A young man on his death-bed lay
For the sake of Barb'ra Allen

12. [Barbara Allen]

Sharp MSS., 901/973. Sung by Jim and Francis Gray, Enmore, April 17, 1906.

a I

1. In Scotland I was born and bred,
   In Scotland I was dwelling,
   When a young man on his death-bed lay
   For the sake of barb'rous Allen.

2. He sent his servant to her house,
   To the place where she was dwelling,
   Saying: You must come to my master's house
   If your name is barbarous Allen.

3. So slowly she put on her clothes,
   So slowly she came to him,
   And when she came to his bedside,
   She says: Young man, you're dying.

4. A dying man, O don't say so,
   For one kiss from you will cure me.
   One kiss from me you never shall have
   While your poor heart is breaking.

5. If you look up at my bed head
   You will see my watch a-hanging.
   Here is my gold ring and my gold chains
   I give it to Barbrous Allen.

6. And if you look down at my bed's foot
   You will see my bowl a-standing
   And in it is the blood that I have shed
   For the sake of Barbrous Allen.

7. As I was walking down the fields
   And heard some birds a-singing,
   And as they sung they seemed to say:
   Hard-hearted Barbrous Allen.

8. As I was walking down the lane
   And heard some bells a-tolling,
   And as they tolled they seemed to say:
   Hard-hearted Barbrous Allen.

9. As I was walking up the groves
   And met his corpse a-coming:
   Stop, stop, said she and steam (?) awhile
   That I may gaze all on you.

10. The more she gaze the more she smile
    Till she burst out a-laughing,
    And her parents cried out: Fie for shame,
    Hard-hearted Barbrous Allen.

11. Come mother, make up my bed,
    Make it both long and narrow,
    My true love died for me yesterday
    And I will die for him to-morrow.

12. And he was buried in diamond stone,
    And she was buried in cold harber,
    And out of him sprung roses red
    And out of her sweet briar.

13. It grew and grew so very high
    Till it could grow no higher,
    And around the top growed a true lover's knot
    And around it twined sweet briar.

14. [Barbara Allen]

Chappell, II, [1859], p. 538. Also in Rimbault, 1850, p. 98, with slight differences; Moffat and Kidson, 1901, p. 132; Smith, *MQ*, II (1916), p. 128(B); and doubtless frequently elsewhere.

a I

"A common traditional tune, well known in the northern counties of England." [*Rimbault*]

1. In Scarlet Town, where I was born,
   There was a fair maid dwellin',
   Made ev'ry youth cry, Well-a-day!
   Her name was Barbara Allen.

2. All in the merry month of May,
   When green buds they were swellin',
   Young Jemmy Grove on his death-bed lay,
   For love of Barbara Allen.

3. He sent his man unto her then,
   To the town where she was dwellin';
   You must come to my master dear,
   Giff your name be Barbara Allen.

4. For death is printed on his face,
   And o'er his heart is stealin';
   Then haste away to comfort him,
   O lovely Barbara Allen.

5. Though death be printed on his face,
   And o'er his heart is stealin',
   Yet little better shall he be
   For bonny Barbara Allen.

6. So slowly, slowly, she came up,
   And slowly she came nigh him;
   And all she said, when there she came,
   Young man, I think you're dying.

7. He turn'd his face unto her straight,
   With deadly sorrow sighing;
   O lovely maid, come pity me,
   I'm on my death-bed lying.

8. If on your death-bed you do lie,
   What needs the tale you're tellin';
   I cannot keep you from your death;
   Farewell, said Barbara Allen.

9. He turn'd his face unto the wall,
   As deadly pangs he fell in:
   Adieu! adieu! adieu to you all,
   Adieu to Barbara Allen.

10. As she was walking o'er the fields,
    She heard the bell a knellin';
    And every stroke did seem to say,
    Unworthy Barbara Allen.

11. She turn'd her body round about,
    And spied the corps a coming;

Lay down, lay down the corpse, she said,
That I may look upon him.

12. With scornful eye she looked down,
    Her cheek with laughter swellin';
    Whilst all her friends cried out amain,
    Unworthy Barbara Allen.

13. When he was dead, and laid in grave,
    Her heart was struck with sorrow,
    O mother, mother, make my bed,
    For I shall die to-morrow.

14. Hard-hearted creature him to slight,
    Who loved me so dearly:
    O that I had been more kind to him
    When he was alive and near me!

15. She, on her death-bed as she lay,
    Begg'd to be buried by him;
    And sore repented of the day,
    That she did e'er deny him.

16. Farewell, she said, ye virgins all,
    And shun the fault I fell in:
    Henceforth take warning by the fall
    Of cruel Barbara Allen.

Chappell's text follows Percy's, *Reliques*, III, Bk. II, No. 5.

28. [Barbara Allen]

Broadwood, *JFSS*, I, No. 5 (1904), p. 265(1). Noted by Mrs. Grahame, St. Leonard's-on-Sea, from the daughters of a Kentish squire, the last of whom died in 1865.

p I

In Scarlet Town where I was born
There was a fair maid dwellin'
Made ev'ry heart cry "Well-a-day!"
Her name was Barb'ra Allen.
All in the merry month of May,
When green buds they were swellin',
Young Jemmy Grove on his death-bed lay,
For the love of Barb'ra Allen.

30. "Barb'ra Allyn"

Sung by Elizabeth Cronin, Macroom, Cork, Ireland. Gordon-Pickow Collector Ltd. Eds., LP rec., LP 1201 (A8), coll. and ed. Jean Ritchie.

p I, ending on II

It was early early in the summer-time
When the flowers were freshly springing,
A young man came from the North Country,
Fell in love with Barb'ra Allyn,
Fell in love with Barb'ra Allyn,
A young man came from the North Country,
Fell in love with Barb'ra Allyn.

He fell sick and very very bad
And [? more inclined to] dying.
He rode till he [?'ruv] to the old house [? room]
To the place where she was dwelling,
To the place where she was dwelling,
He rode till he [?'ruv] to the old house [? room]
To the place where she was dwelling.

Very slowly she got up
And slowly she came to him
The first word she spoke when she came there
Was, "Young man, I fear you're dying,
Young man, I fear you're dying,"
The first word she spoke when she came there
Was, "Young man, I fear you're dying."

"Dying, dying doesn't matter at all," he said,
"One kiss from you would cure me."
"One kiss from me you ne'er shall see,
If I thought your heart was breaking,
If I thought your heart was breaking,
One kiss from me you ne'er shall see,
If I thought your heart was breaking."

33. "Barbara Allen"

Kidson, 1891, p. 37. Benjamin Holgate learned it from an English girl in Ghent, c. 1850.

p I

According to Kidson, the variant ending was used in the West Riding.

In Reading town, where I was born,
There was a fair maid dwelling,
Made every youth cry, "Well-a-day!"—
Her name was Barbara Allen.
Etc., etc.

38. "Barbara Ellen"

Creighton and Senior, 1950, p. 54(E). Sung by Mrs. Dennis Greenough, West Petpeswick, N.S.

p I

O early in the month of May,
The birds were sweetly singing,
A young man on his death bed lay
For the love of Barbara Ellen.

He turned his back unto the wall.

Out of her sprung a red rose bush
And out of his a briar,
Then they grew up to the high church wall
Till they could grow no higher,
And back they returned in a true lover's knot,
Red roses and sweet briar.

GROUP B

40. [Bonny Barbara Allan]

Johnson, III, [1790], No. 221, p. 230 (repr. 1853). Also in Ritson, 1794, II, p. 196; Smith, [1820-24], II, p. 80; Thomson, [1822-23], III, p. 35; Graham, 1848-49, II, p. 16; Rimbault, 1850, p. 99; Maver, 1866, No. 66, p. 33; and in Eyre-Todd, n.d. |1894|, p. 188.

a D/Æ, ending on the octave

This tune may make an earlier appearance in Oswald's *A Curious Collection of Scots Tunes*, [1740], p. 3, and in his *Caledonian Pocket Companion*, II, [c. 1745], p. 27, which I have been unable to compare. Cf. also Johnson, V, [1796], No. 420, p. 433 (repr. 1853), "Young Jamie pride of a' the plain," where a form of the tune is named "The carlin of the glen."

1. It was in and about the Martinmas time,
   When the green leaves were a falling,
   That Sir John Graham in the west countrie
   Fell in love with Barbara Allan.

2. He sent his man down thro' the town,
    To the place where she was dwelling;
  O haste and come to my master dear,
    Gin ye be Barbara Allan.

3. O hooly, hooly rose she up,
    To the place where he was lying,
  And when she drew the curtin by,
    Young man, I think youre dying.

4. O its I'm sick, and very very sick,
    And 'tis a' for Barbara Allan.
  O the better for me ye's never be,
    Tho' your heart's blood were a spilling.

5. O dinna ye mind, young man, said she,
    When ye the cups was fillin
  That ye made the healths gae round and round,
    And slighted Barbara Allan.

6. He turn'd his face unto the wa',
    And death was with him dealing,
  Adieu, adieu, my dear friends a',
    And be kind to Barbara Allan.

7. And slowly, slowly raise she up,
    And slowly, slowly left him;
  And sighing, said, she cou'd not stay,
    Since death of life had reft him.

8. She had nae gane a mile but twa,
    When she heard the deid-bell knelling,
  And ev'ry jow that the deid-bell geid,
    It cry'd, woe to Barbara Allan!

9. O mother, mother, mak my bed,
    O make it saft and narrow;
  Since my love died for me to-day,
    I'll die for him to-morrow.

Johnson's text follows Ramsay's (Child's A).

GROUP C

52. "Barbary Allen"

Campbell, *BTFLS*, III (1937), p. 92.

p π¹

It seems probable that the last three bars contain errors of transcription which may be safely emended as above.

He sent his servant down to say
In the place where she was dwelling,
Oh, come, oh come to my master's bed,
If your name be Barbary Allen.

60. [Barbara Allen]

Wilkinson MSS., 1935-36, p. 69(A). Sung by Mrs. Jane Morris, Harriston, Va., October 16, 1935.

m π¹

1. 'Twas in the merry month of May,
  The green buds they were a-swelling,
  Young Jimmy mourned on his death bed,
  For the love of Barb'ra Allen.

2. He sent his men unto her then,
  In the town where she was dwelling,
  You must go to my master,
  If your name be Barb'ra Allen.

3. So slowly she put on her clothes,
  So slowly came anigh him,
  The word she said when she got there:
  Young man I think you're dying.

4. He turned his back onto her then,
  And death was on him dealt;
  Adieu, adieu, to my friends all,
  Fare well to Barb'ra Allen.

5. So many miles she went from there,
  She heard the bells a-knelling,

44. [Barbara Allan]

Greig MSS., III, p. 48. Also in Greig and Keith, 1925, p. 69(1b). Sung by J. Quirrie, September 1906; learned from his mother.

a D, ending on the octave

And every stroke did seem to say:
Hard hearted (horns on) Barb'ra Allen.

6. She turned her body round and about,
She spied the corpse a-coming,
Sit down, sit down, the body: says she
That I may look upon it.

7. So scornful she did look at him,
His cheeks were not a-swelling,
Her friends were crying out for shame,
Hard Hearted Barb'ra Allen.

8. Young Jimmy died, it might be today,
And Allen died tomorrow,
Young Jimmy died for pure, pure love,
Young Allen died for sorrow.

And every tone it seemed to say
Hard hearted Barb'ra Allen.

7. Oh she went raging thru the town,
She saw the corpse a-coming.
Set down, set down, those corpse: she said,
And let me gaze upon him.

8. The more she looked the worse she cried,
The farther she got from him.
Said: If I had a been more kind to you
When I were closer to you.

9. Young Jimmy was buried in the new church-yard,
Barb'ra Allen was buried in the choir.
Out of young Jimmy's grave, there sprung a red rose,
Out of Barb'ra Allen's grave a green brier.

10. They growed, they growed to the church steeple top,
Till they could grow no higher.
They linked and tied in a true-lover's knot,
The rose wrapped around the brier.

63. [Barbara Allen]

Wilkinson MSS., 1935-36, p. 73(C). Sung by R. H. Mace,
Grottoes, Va., October 30, 1935.

a π¹

1. It was in the merry month of May
When green buds they were swelling.
A young man on his death-bed lay
For the love of Barb'ra Allen.

2. He sent the message thru' the town
Where this young girl was dwelling.
You must unto my master go
If your name be Barb'ra Allen.

3. Oh slowly, slowly, she got up
And slowly she went to him.
And when she came to his bed-side,
Young man I believe you're dying.

4. Oh do you remember in yonder's town?
In yonder's town a-drinking?
You passed your glasses all around
And slighted Barb'ra Allen.

5. He turned his pale face to the wall
And sorrow was his leaving.
Adieu, adieu to the pretty girls all
Adieu to Miss Barb'ra Allen.

6. Oh she went walking thru the town,
She heard the church bell tolling.

78. "Barbara Ellen"

Sharp MSS., 3932/. Also in Sharp and Karpeles, 1932, I,
p. 195(N). Sung by John Lewis, Pine Mountain, Harlan
County, Ky., August 29, 1917.

p π¹, ending on V

Early early in the spring
The green buds they were swellin
Sweet William on his death-bed lay
For love of Barbra Ellen.

79. [Babie Allan]

Harris MS., No. 14. Also in Child, 1882-98, V, p. 416.

p π¹, with ending on VI (if final tonic, a π⁴, but unlikely)

In the MS. the notes are double the length of the above.
This tune recalls parts of Christie's "The Place where my Love
Johnnie Dwells" (*Traditional Ballad Airs*, I, 1876, p. 144; Child
No. 219).

It fell aboot the Martmas time
When green leaves they war fallin';
That Sir John Graham o'th North Kintrie
Fell in love wi Bawbie Allan.

Sweet William died choked up in love
I'll die for him in sorrow
Sweet William died choked up in love
I'll die for him in sorrow

83. "Barbra Ellen"

Sharp MSS., 1343/. Sung by Mrs. Emma Callow (73),
April 9, 1907.

p I/Ly

El — len   Barbra El - len   Her name was Bar - bra El-len

"Aunt Maria is an old coloured woman, aged 85, who was a slave belonging to Mr. Coleman who freed her after the war and gave her the log cabin in which she now lives, which used to be the overseer's house. I found her sitting in front of her cabin smoking a pipe. We sang her The Sinnerman which delighted her beyond anything and made her dub me 'A soldier of Christ!' She sang very beautifully in a wonderfully musical way and with clear & perfect intonation." [*Sharp's MS. note*].

GROUP D

142. "Barbry Ellen"

Ritchie, 1955, p. 184. Also in Ritchie, 1953, p. 53. As sung by the Ritchie family, Viper, Ky. Copyright Broadcast Music, Inc.

a π³

Jean Ritchie sings this inimitably on Westminster LP recording, WLP 6037(A8), 1956.

1. In Scarlet Town where I was born
   There was a fair maid dwellin
   Made every youth cry well-a-day
   And her name was Barbry Ellen.

2. All in the merry month of May
   When the green buds they were swellin,
   Young William Green on his deathbed lay
   For love of Barbry Ellen.

3. He sent his servant to the town
   To her own father's dwellin,
   Sayin Master's sick and he bids you to come
   If your name be Barbry Ellen.

94. "Barbara Allen"

Kidson, 1891, p. 38(2). From the Northallerton district, Yorkshire.

p π¹

In Scotland I was born and bred,
   O, there it was my dwelling;
I courted there a pretty maid,
   O, her name was Barbara Allen.

I courted her in summer time,
   I courted her in winter;
For six long years I courted her,
   A-thinking I should win her.

· · · · · · · ·

4. So slowlye, slowlye, she got up
   And slowlye she came nigh him,
   And all she said when she got there,
   Young man I believe you're dying.

5. O yes I'm sick and I'm very sick
   And I never will be any better,
   Until I gain the love of one
   The love of Barbry Ellen.

6. O yes you're sick and you're very sick
   And you never will be any better,
   For you never will gain the love of one
   The love of Barbry Ellen.

137. [Barbara Allen]

Sharp MSS., 4271/. Also in Sharp and Karpeles, 1932, I, p. 195(P). Sung by Aunt Maria Tomes, Nellysford, Va., May 22, 1918.

p M (—VI)

7. O don't you remember in yonders town,
   In yonders town a-drinkin?
   You drunk the health of the ladies all round,
   And you slighted Barbry Ellen.

8. O yes, I remember in yonders town,
   In yonders town a-drinkin;
   I gave my health to the ladies all round,
   But my heart to Barbry Ellen.

9. He turned his pale face to the wall,
   For death was on him dwellin,
   Farewell, farewell you good neighbors all,
   Be kind to Barbry Ellen.

10. As she was going across the field
    She heard the death-bells knellin;
    And every stroke they seemed to say,
    Hard-hearted Barbry Ellen.

11. As she was going through the woods
    She saw the pale corpse comin;
    Lay down, lay down that corpse of clay
    That I may look upon him.

12. The more she looked, the more she grieved
    At last she burst out a-cryin,
    O take him away, O take him away,
    For I myself am dyin.

13. O Mother, O Mother, go make my bed,
    Go make it both long and narrow,
    Sweet William has died for the love of me,
    And I shall die of sorrow.

14. O Father, O Father, go dig my grave,
    Go dig it both long and narrow,
    Sweet William has died for me today,
    And I'll die for him tomorrow.

15. O she was buried in the old church-yard,
    Sweet William was buried a-nigh her
    And out of his grave sprung a red, red rose,
    Out of Barbry's grew a greenbriar.

16. They grew and they grew up the old church tower
    Till they couldn't grow any higher,
    And there they tied a true-lovers knot,
    Red rose around greenbriar.

2. I courted her for seven long years;
   I could nae court her langer, O,
   But I fell sick and very ill
   And I sent for Barbru Allan, O,
   And I sent for Barbru Allan, O.

3. It's when she came tae my bed-side
   She says, "Young man, You're dying, O."
   "O dying," I said, "it cannot be,
   One kiss from you wull cure me, O."
   "One kiss from me you'll never get,
   Long's your hard heart's a-breakin, O,
   Long's your hard heart's a-breakin, O."

4. "O turn my back untae the wa'
   And my face frae Barbru Allan,
   It's adieu to me and adieu to you,
   Be kind tae Barbru Allan, O,
   Be kind tae Barbru Allan, O.

5. "But look ye up at my bed-heid
   And you'll see what you'll see hangin there,
   A guinea gold watch and a silver chain,
   Gae that tae Barbru Allan, O,
   Gae that tae Barbru Allan, O.

6. "But look ye doun at my bed-fet
   And you'll see what you'll see stan'in there,
   A china basin fu' o' tears
   Was shed for Barbru Allan, O."

7. She was not one mile frae the toun
   She heard the deid bells tollin, O,
   And every toll they seemed to say,
   Hard-hearted Barbru Allan, O,
   Hard-hearted Barbru Allan, O.

8. "O Mother, Mother, make my bed,
   And make it long and narrow,
   My true love died for me today,
   And I'll die for him tomorrow."

156. "Barbru Allan"

Sung by Jimmy Stewart, Forfar, Scotland, n.d. Gordon-Pickow Collector Ltd. Eds., LP rec., LP 1201(A7), coll. and ed. Jean Ritchie.

a π³

1. (In) London I was bred and born,
   (In) Scotland was my dwellin, O,
   I fell in love with a nice young girl
   And her name was Barbru Allan, O,
   And her name was Barbru Allan, O.

167. [Barbara Allan]

Christie, I, 1876, p. 283.

a Æ (basically π⁴)

With this tune, printed in an appendix, Christie gives no text.

George Collins (Lady Alice)

CHILD NO. 85

So FAR as the music of this little song is concerned, the variants are all relatively close to one another and all stay within the ambit of π^1, the pentatonic lacking its fourth and seventh. This comprises the Lydian, Ionian, and Mixolydian modes and hexatonic forms lying between. The favored cluster-point for our ballad is probably the hexatonic pattern lacking the seventh, in the plagal range. It is an odd fact of probably little significance that in roughly a quarter of the total number of variants recorded the sixth is also lacking. This lack does not affect the modality. The metre is usually triple (or compound duple). The range is often narrow, and, apart from phrasal upbeats on the lower dominant, stays within the tonic and fifth or sixth.

The tune belongs to one of the commonest families in the register, and in one variety or another is found with many of the most familiar of our songs. Americans all know "My Bonnie lies over the Ocean," a very typical example which is actually found with the present ballad; and many know Ophelia's song of "Tomorrow is St. Valentine's Day." Although there is, I believe, no actual record of the latter tune with Shakespeare's words and contemporary with Shakespeare, the stage tradition for it is strong and there is good reason to suppose it unbroken. At any rate, the tune of "A Souldiers Life" which appears in the first (1650) and succeeding editions of Playford's *English Dancing Master* is a form of the same tune, and by this title it is carried back into the late sixteenth century. (Cf. Chappell, I, [1855], p. 144.)

Whether the ballad text is anywhere nearly so old as the tune is another matter. If the argument of Barbara M. Cra'ster in *JFSS*, IV, No. 15 (1910), p. 106, which points out a possible relationship with "Clerk Colvill" (No. 42), were to be accepted as proved—and its plausibility makes a strong appeal—we should be able to credit the little song with a high antiquity. "But oh! how fallen! how changed!" Already by the end of the eighteenth century in some quarters it had been reduced to the level of a nursery burlesque. But it is still sung widely in America as a serious ballad. The hero is usually called George Collins, as in the English versions which point to a connection with Colvill or Colven by involving him with a water-sprite; but in one version he is simply George, a hobo dying in an empty box-car. His true-love, however, has not lost all trace of her former brightness: she inhabits a "hall" and sews her silken seam so fine. In fact, by the time she reaches him, George himself has been shrouded in fine linen, which the attendants are enjoined to lay back, that he may receive the last kisses. Still, the box-car is a far cry from the milieu of the Knight of Staufenberg, of whom the tale is told in 1310.

Two interesting articles on this ballad are: S. P. Bayard, "The 'Johnny Collins' Version of 'Lady Alice'," *JAF*, LVIII (1945), pp. 73-103; and Harbison Parker, "The 'Clerk Colvill' Mermaid," *JAF*, LX (1947), pp. 265-85. Also to be consulted is T. P. Coffin's discussion, in *The British Traditional Ballad in North America*, 1950, pp. 90-92.

TUNES WITH TEXTS

2. "George Collins"

Davis, 1929, p. 582(E); text, p. 350. Sung by Mrs. Dan Maxie (*née* Holland), Altavista, Va., March 2, 1914. Collected by Juliet Fauntleroy.

p I (—VI)

1. George Collins drove home one cold winter night,
    George Collins drove home so fine,
    George Collins drove home one cold winter night,
    And was taken sick and died.

2. Sweet little Nellie in yonder hall,
    Sewing her silk so fine;
    But when she heard that George was dead,
    She laid her silk aside.

3. She followed him up, she followed him around,
    She followed him to his grave,
    And there she fell on her bended knees,
    She wept, she mourned, she prayed.

4. "Oh daughter, Oh daughter, what makes you weep so?
    There's more young boys than George."
    "Oh mother, Oh mother, he has my heart,
    And now he's dead and gone.

5. "Set down the coffin, unscrew the lid,
    Lay back the linen so fine,
    And let me kiss his clay-cold lips,
    For I'm sure he will never kiss mine.

6. "Don't you see that lonely little dove
    A-sitting on yonder pine?
    He's mourning for his own true love,
    And why not I for mine?"

18. "Georgie Collins"

Chappell, 1939, p. 33. Sung by Mrs. John Squire Chappell, Tyner, N.C., 1938.

1. Georgie Collins came home one cold winter night,
    Georgie Collins came home so bright,
    Georgie Collins came home one cold winter night,
    He was taken sick and died.

2. There was a fair lady in yonders town
    Who was clothed in silk so fine,
    But when she heard that Georgie was dead
    She laid it down and cried.

3. Dear daughter, dear daughter, what makes you do so?
   There's plenty of men besides George.
   O mama, mama, he's got my heart
   And now I'm left alone.

4. Lay down the coffin, take off the lid,
   Place back the linen so fine
   And let me kiss his clay cold lips,
   I'm sure he'll never kiss mine.

5. She followed him up, she followed him down,
   She followed him to his grave,
   And there she knelt on her bending knee,
   She wept, she mourned, she cried.

24. "George Collins"

Guyer and Gardiner, *JFSS*, III, No. 13 (1909), p. 301(3).
Sung by Henry Stansbridge (58), Lyndhurst, Hampshire,
September 27, 1906.

This version is sung by A. L. Lloyd on Riverside RLP 12-623(A4),
ed. K. S. Goldstein.
   Miss Broadwood finds a relationship between this and "The
Wealthy Farmer's Son" (*English Traditional Songs and Carols*,
1908, p. 26).

George Collins walked out one May morning,
When may was all in bloom,
There he espied a fair pretty maid
A-washing her marble stone.

26. "Giles Collins"

Morris, 1950, p. 291. Sung by Mrs. Lucy Holt Harrison,
Gainesville, Fla., 1950; traditional in family.

1. Giles Collins said to his mother one day,
   "Oh! Mother come bind up my head,
   And make me a pot of water-gruel,
   For tomorrow I shall be dead, dead, dead, dead, dead,
   For tomorrow I shall be dead."

2. His mother she made him the water-gruel
   And stirred it around with a spoon;
   Giles Collins drank that water-gruel,
   And he was dead before noon, noon, noon, noon, noon,
   And he was dead before noon.

3. "Oh! what bear ye, ye six strong men
   Upon your shoulders high?"
   "We bear the body of Giles Collins,
   Who for love of you did die, die, die, die, die,
   Who for love of you did die."

4. "Set him down, set him down, ye six strong men,
   Upon the grass so green,
   And tomorrow before the clock strikes seven,
   My body shall be with his'n, his'n, his'n, his'n, his'n;
   My body shall be with his'n."

5. Lady Anne sat in her window,
   A-sewing her scarf and coif, (pronounced *keef*)
   She said she had seen the prettiest corpse
   She had ever seen in her life, life, life, life, life;
                                   (pronounced *leef*)
   She had ever seen in her life.

6. They buried Giles Collins in the east,
   Lady Anne in the west;
   A lily grew on Giles Collins' grave
   And touched Lady Anne's breast, breast, breast, breast, breast,
   And touched Lady Anne's breast.

From *Folksongs of Florida* by Alton C. Morris. Published by the University of Florida Press. Used by permission.

29. "George Collins"

Davis, 1929, p. 582 (D, II); text, p. 349. Sung by Mrs. Lester, Roanoke, Va., November 30, 1923. Collected by Alfreda M. Peel.

1. George Collins rode home one cold winter night,
   George Collins rode home so fine,
   George Collins rode home one cold winter night,
   He was taken sick and died.

2. Oh, see Miss Mae in yonder hall,
   Sewing her silks so fine;
   But when she heard poor George was sick,
   She laid her silks aside.

3. She followed him up, she followed him down,
   She followed him to his grave;

She fell upon her bended knees,
   She wept, she prayed, she mourned.

4. "Oh daughter, oh daughter, why do you weep so?
   There are more young men than George."
   "Oh mother, oh mother, he won my heart,
   And now he's dead and gone.

5. "Set down the casket, unscrew the lid,
   Lay back the linen so fine;
   For I want to kiss his dear sweet lips,
   I am sure he will never kiss mine.

6. "See that dove in yonder grove,
   Flying from pine to pine,
   Mourning for his own true love,
   As I mourn for mine."

34. "George Collins"

Guyer and Gardiner, *JFSS*, III, No. 13, pp. 299(1); texts, pp. 299(A) and 300(B). First text sung by Henry Gaylor (76), Minstead, New Forest, Hampshire, September 27, 1906. Second text sung by Philip Gaylor.

(A.)

1. George Collins walked out one May morning,
   When may was all in bloom,
   'Twas then he beheld a fair, pretty maid,
   She was washing her marble stone.

2. She whooped, she holloed, she highered her voice
   And she held up her lily-white hand.
   "Come hither to me, George Collins," said she,
   "For thy life shall not last you long."

3. George Collins rode home to his father's own gate,
   And loudly he did ring.
   "Come rise, my dear father, and let me in,
   Come, rise, my dear mother, and make my bed.

4. · · · · · · · · · ·
   · · · · · · · · ·
   All for to trouble my dear sister
   For a napkin to bind round my head.

5. For, if I chance to die this night,
   As I suppose I shall,
   Bury me under that marble stone
   That's against fair Helen's hall."

6. Fair Helen doth sit in her room so fine,
   Working her silken skein;
   Then she saw the finest corpse a-coming
   As ever the sun shined on.

7. She said unto her Irish maid:
   "Whose corpse is this so fine?"
   "This is George Collins' corpse a-coming,
   That once was a true lover of thine."

8. "You go upstairs and fetch me the sheet
   That's wove with a silver twine
   And hang that over George Collins' head,
   To-morrow it shall hang over mine."

9. This news was carried to fair London town,
   And wrote all on fair London gate;
   Six pretty maids died all of one night,
   And all for George Collins' sake.

(B.)

1. George Collins walked out one May morning,
   When may was all in bloom,
   And there he beheld a fair pretty maid,
   She was washing her marble stone,

2. She whooped, she holloed, she highered her voice,
   And held up her lily-white hand,
   "Come hither to me, George Collins," said she,
   "And thy life shall not last thee long."

3. He put his foot to the broad water side,
   And over the lea sprung he,
   He embraced her around her middle so small,
   And kissed her red, rosy cheeks.

4. George Collins rode home to his father's own gate
   And loudly did he ring.
   · · · · · · · · · · ·

5. "Arise, my dear father, and let me in,
   Arise, my dear mother, and make my bed,
   Arise, my dear sister, and get me a napkin,
   A napkin to bind round my head.

6. "For, if I should chance to die this night,
   As I suppose I shall,
   You bury me under the marble stone,
   That joins the fair Eleanor's hall."

7. Fair Eleanor sat in her room so fine,
   A-working the silver twine,
   She saw the fairest corpse a-coming
   As ever the sun shone on.

8. She said unto her servant maid,
   "Whose corpse is this so fine?"
   "This is George Collins' corpse a-coming,
   And an old true lovyer of thine."

9. "Come, put him down, my six pretty lads,
   And open his coffin so fine;
   That I might kiss his lily-white lips,
   For ten thousand times he has kissed mine."

10. Those news was carried to London town
   And wrote on London gate,
   That six pretty maidens died all of that night,
   And all for George Collins' sake.

A pivotal text on account of its suggestion of the supernatural and its probable connection with "Clerk Colvil" (No. 42).

Young Benjie

CHILD NO. 86

THIS ballad has not been found in tradition for the last century, so far as I am aware, and never outside Scotland, although the superstition it commemorates can hardly have been confined to that country.*

Only once has a tune been recorded with the ballad, but that tune seems to have had some currency in Scott's time, for it has been noted with several other ballads: Mrs. Brown's "King Henry" (No. 32), Christie's "Love Robbie" (No. 97), and Kinloch's "Geordie" (No. 209). The last case is interesting, because the melodic tradition of "Geordie" is quite stable, and the present tune has been modified in its close to conform to the "Geor-die" pattern. The singer, however, seems to have had a clearer recollection of the present tune than of the proper tune for the other ballad. To be sure, the initial octave leap, later repeated, is striking enough to make a deep impression on the memory. It may be mentioned here that the same tune, appearing in Child, V, p. 422, as from the Abbotsford MS. of Scottish Songs, with "Lady Elspat," is in all probability a mistaken association. See the latter ballad (No. 247) in the complete collection.

* There is rumor of its being known in Ireland. Cf. Barry, Eckstorm, and Smyth, *British Ballads from Maine*, 1929, p. 453.

TUNE WITH TEXT

1. "Young Benjie"

Campbell, I, [1816], p. 34; text, Scott, 1803, III, p. 251 (Child A). Sent by John Leyden.

a π⁴

1. Of a' the maids o fair Scotland
   The fairest was Marjorie,
   And Young Benjie was her ae true-love,
   And a dear true-love was he.

2. And wow! but they were lovers dear,
   And loved fu constantlie;
   But ay the mair, when they fell out,
   The sairer was their plea.

3. And they hae quarrelled on a day,
   Till Marjorie's heart grew wae,
   And she said she'd chuse another luve,
   And let Young Benjie gae.

4. And he was stout, and proud-hearted,
   And thought o't bitterlie,
   And he's gaen by the wan moon-light
   To meet his Marjorie.

5. 'O open, open, my true-love,
   O open, and let me in!'
   'I dare na open, Young Benjie,
   My three brothers are within.'

6. 'Ye lied, ye lied, ye bonny burd,
   Sae loud's I hear ye lie;
   As I came by the Lowden banks,
   They bade gude een to me.

7. 'But fare ye weel, my ae fause love,
   That I hae loved sae lang!
   It sets ye chuse another love,
   And let Young Benjie gang.'

8. Then Marjorie turned her round about,
   The tear blinding her ee:
   'I darena, darena let thee in,
   But I'll come down to thee.'

9. Then saft she smiled, and said to him,
   O what ill hae I done?
   He took her in his armis twa,
   And threw her oer the linn.

10. The stream was strang, the maid was stout,
    And laith, laith to be dang,
    But ere she wan the Lowden banks
    Her fair colour was wan.

11. Then up bespak her eldest brother,
    'O see na ye what I see?'
    And out then spak her second brother,
    'It's our sister Marjorie!'

12. Out then spak her eldest brother,
    'O how shall we her ken?'
    And out then spak her youngest brother,
    'There's a honey-mark on her chin.'

13. Then they've taen up the comely corpse,
    And laid it on the grund:
    'O wha has killed our ae sister,
    And how can he be found?

14. 'The night it is her low lykewake,
    The mourn her burial day,
    And we maun watch at mirk midnight,
    And hear what she will say.'

15. Wi doors ajar, and candle-light,
        And torches burning clear,
    The streikit corpse, till still midnight,
        They waked, but naething hear.

16. About the middle o the night
        The cocks began to craw,
    And at the dead hour o the night
        The corpse began to thraw.

17. 'O wha has done the wrang, sister,
        Or dared the deadly sin?
    Wha was sae stout, and feared nae dout,
        As thraw ye oer the linn?'

18. 'Young Benjie was the first ae man
        I laed my love upon;
    He was sae stout and proud-hearted,
        He threw me oer the linn.'

19. 'Sall we Young Benjie head, sister?
        Sall we Young Benjie hang?
    Or sall we pike out his twa gray een,
        And punish him ere he gang?'

20. 'Ye mauna Benjie head, brothers,
        Ye mauna Benjie hang.
    But ye maun pike out his twa gray een,
        And punish him ere he gang.

21. 'Tie a green gravat round his neck,
        And lead him out and in,
    And the best ae servant about your house
        To wait Young Benjie on.

22. 'And ay, at every seven year's end,
        Ye'll tak him to the linn;
    For that's the penance he maun drie,
        To scug his deadly sin.'

Young Johnstone

CHILD NO. 88

APART from textual reprints, this ballad seems to have faded from traditional hearing after Motherwell's day for about a century. The tune that he preserved was printed again by Robert Chambers in 1844, but has not since been found in tradition. David Herd's *text* (1769 and 1776) was repeated by Joseph Ritson in 1794, without a tune. The tune was supplied in a reprint of Ritson in 1869 by the editor, "J.A." (?Joseph Anderson), but again with Herd's text, and without traditional authority. It has not again been found with this ballad; but Greig and Duncan found it sung constantly with "Young Allan" (Child No. 245) half a century later in Aberdeenshire. The only other tune in the 19th-century record is quite distinct from the rest; it was taken from a Banffshire woman by Christie and published in 1876. Christie did not preserve her text, but adopted Buchan's of 1828.

It is never safe to assert that a ballad is extinct. Two versions of this one were gathered from singers in Nova Scotia early in the present century, and latterly it has re-surfaced in the homeland in a fresh pair of variants with mutually related tunes but disparate texts. These last tunes do not appear to connect with any of the preceding; but, oddly, they do show a clear resemblance to that of one of the few surviving Robin Hood ballads (Child No. 132, vt. 8), collected in Maine but apparently brought from Wales to Nova Scotia two or three generations ago. Since only one of the two Nova Scotia tunes of "Young Johnstone" was saved, it is impossible to say whether or not they were alike. The one that we have is an attractive example of a common type.

It would appear, then, that we have no ground for determining that our ballad, in its recorded lifetime, has ever had a melodic tradition of its own.

A word may be said on the text of this ballad. Child waxes a shade indignant against the titular hero: "Awake or waking," he says, sceptical of apology, "Young Johnstone's first instinct is as duly to stab as a bulldog's is to bite." But possibly a protest should be lodged against this civilized viewpoint, as indicating a fundamental misapprehension. It seems probable that the makers of this song were more concerned with telling a tale of tragic error than they were with depicting the psychology of a rash and headstrong ruffian. On grounds of probability alone, a man who had been dismissed with curses by his own flesh and blood for killing the brother of his sweetheart, might lie down with a certain nervousness in that sweetheart's house, and be over-hasty to strike when someone came quickly and stealthily (softly at the least) into the room where he lay. To be sure, Herd's version makes much of the lady's hospitality (of course a deceptive ruse) to the four-and-twenty knights who were on her husband's track, and says nothing about the latter's being asleep. In this case, his stabbing may have been out of nervous suspicion.

Apology, says Child, "may go for what it is worth"; but surely it may go far. Johnstone's original crime arose from family pride, which was once respected, even honored; and his remorse when he finds out his mistake should plead his honest meaning. Our trouble lies rather in the fact that the technique of balladry encourages abruptness, makes transition difficult and out of place, and renders explanation ridiculous. Had the ballad not (in its traditional ordonnance) encountered the dilemma of, on the one horn, Johnstone's having to stab his love in his first alarm and, on the other, her having to assure him that the coast was clear *before* he stabbed her, because later she could hardly urge him either to rise up or to lie still, indignation would have been forestalled.

TUNES WITH TEXTS

GROUP A

2. [Willie and the Young Cornel]

Motherwell, 1827, App'x., No. 18; text, App'x., p. xx. Also in Chambers, 1844, p. 19.

p I/M (but should have been a Æ/D)

The alternate upbeat is the Chambers reading. Cf. the head-note above. Chambers is a re-working of Motherwell and Finlay.

> As Willie and the young Col'nel
> Were drinking at the wine,
> O will ye marry my sister, says Will,
> And I will marry thine.

This stanza from Motherwell's Appendix does not correspond with any in his MS., but seems closest to Jeanie Nicol's text, which is Child's C.

GROUP B

4. "Johnson and the Colonel"

Mackenzie, 1928, p. 393; text, p. 41. Sung by John Henderson, Tatamagouch, N.S.

m M (but inflected VII)

1. As Johnson and the young Colonel
   Together were drinking wine,
   Says Johnson to the young Colonel,
   "If you'll marry my sister, I'll marry thine."

2. "No, I'll not marry your sister,
   Nor shall you marry mine,
   For I will keep her for a miss
   As I go through the town."

3. Young Johnson has drawn his broad bright sword
   Which hung low down to the ground,
   And he has given the young Colonel
   A deep and deadly wound.

4. Then mounting on his milk-white steed,
   He swiftly rode away
   Until he came to his sister's house
   Long, long ere the break of day.

5. "Alight, alight, young Johnson," she said,
   "And take a silent sleep,
   For you have crossed wide wide waters,
   Which are both wide and deep."

6. "I cannot light, I cannot light,
   Nor neither sleep can I,
   For I have killed the young Colonel,
   And for it I did fly."

7. "O have you killed the young Colonel?
   O woe be unto thee!
   To-morrow's morn at eight o'clock
   It's hangéd you shall be."

8. "O hold your tongue, you cruel woman,
   O hold your tongue," said he,
   "How can I trust to a strange lady
   If I cannot trust to thee?"

9. He's mounted on his nimble steed
   And swiftly rode away,
   Until he came to his own true love
   Long, long ere break of day.

10. "Alight, alight, young Johnson," she said,
    "And take a silent sleep,
    For you have crossed the stormy waters,
    Which are both wide and deep."

11. "I can't alight, I cannot stop,
    Nor either sleep can I,
    For I have killed the young Colonel
    And for it I must fly."

12. "O have you killed my brother?" she said,
    "O what shall now be done?
    But come into my chamber,
    I'll secure you from all harm."

13. She's lockéd up his hawks
    And she's lockéd up his hounds,

And she's lockéd up the nimble steed
That bore him from the ground.

14. She's lockéd one, she's lockéd two,
    She's lockéd three or four,
    And then she stood for his life-guard
    Behind the entry door.

15. On looking east and looking west
    She happened for to see
    Four and twenty of the King's Life Guards
    Come riding merrily.

16. "O did you see young Johnson?" they said,
    "Or did he pass by this way?
    For he has killed the young Colonel,
    And for it he did fly."

17. "What color was his hawk?" she said,
    "And what color was his hound?
    And what color was his nimble steed
    That bore him from the ground?"

18. "A dark gray was his hawk," they said,
    "And a light gray was his hound,
    And a milk-white was the nimble steed
    That bore him from the ground."

19. "Then ride away, O ride away,
    And quickly ride, I pray;
    Or I fear he'll be out of London Town
    Long, long ere the dawn of day."

20. She went into his chamber
    For to tell him what she had done,
    And he has pierced his lovely dear
    That ne'er did him any wrong.

21. Young Johnson being in a silent sleep
    And dreaming they were near,
    He has drawn his bright broad shining sword
    And pierced his lovely dear.

22. "What cause for this, dear Johnson?" she said,
    "O what is this you've done?
    For you have pierced your dearest dear
    That ne'er did you any wrong."

23. "O can you live? O can you live?
    Can you live but one single half hour?
    And all the doctors in London Town
    Shall be within your bower."

24. "I cannot live, I cannot live!
    O how can I live?" said she,
    "For don't you see my very heart's blood
    Come trickling down from my knee?

25. "O ride away, you ride away,
    And quickly get over the plain,
    And never let it once enter your mind
    That your own true love you've slain."

6. "Young Johnstone"

Sung by Maggie Stewart, Springfield, Fife, March 15, 1968. Learned from her father, Hendry Johnson. Collected, transcribed, and sent to the Editor by Peter Shepheard.

a π²

1. Oh Johnstone an' the young Cornel
   Sat down to drinkin' wine
   If it's you will marry my sister
   Then I will marry thine

2. Oh no oh no said the young Cornel
   Oh that shall never be
   For I will never marry your sister
   Until the day I dee

3. For Johnstone had a sharp penknife
   That hung down by his side
   He rammed it in the Cornel's heart
   And a word he never cried

4. For Johnson had a gey swift steed
   An' a gey swift steed had he
   He mounted on his gey swift steed
   An' rode swiftly o'er the lea

5. Came five an' twenty belted knights
   An' belted knights were they
   They lighted at bold Johnson's door
   An' rapped upon the lee

6. Come out come out oh Johnson he cried
   Come out come out to me
   For you have done a cowardly deed
   An' a cowardly death you'll dee

7. Come Johnson's sweetheart to the door
   Alight you gentlemen
   Alight alight an' have some bread
   An' ye shall have some wine

8. Oh thank you for your bread lady
   An' thank you for your wine
   I'd rather have twenty o' Johnson's lives
   Your fair bodie was mine

The Lowlands of Holland

CHILD NO. 92, APPENDIX

THE lyric lament with which "Bonny Bee Hom" opens is a commonplace of popular poetry. Lacking a stable narrative core, it passes from ballad to ballad like the similarly floating stanzas about shoeing the foot and gloving the hand. (Cf. No. 76.) Properly, however, it occurs after, not before the tragedy; and we may regard the reverse order here as less primitive. The change, however, entails further modification in order to resuscitate the narrative: hence the device of overhearing, which makes possible a new farewell with the giving of magic gifts. (We recall that a new scene was made possible when Polonius, having said good-bye to Laertes, found that "occasion smile[d] upon a second leave.") The gifts themselves belong to the days of high and chivalric romance, and promise a tale of adventure. But the hope is disappointed: the perils of the voyage are omitted; even the purpose of it, to which the hero was deeply sworn, is left untold; nor do we learn what befell in the twelve-month that followed in Bee Hom. It could not very well have been a martial enterprise, for the hero bequeathed his riches there, as in peace, to the very young, the old, and the blind. Buchan's version, to be sure, supplies some of the gaps, but by the merest rationalization. There is thus no story in the ballad except the minimum of situation latent in the two features mentioned. Dim recollections of other ballads, feebly connected in the wrong order, would produce this result with the aid of a very little cheap mortar; and it can scarcely be felt that we have here the clear evidence of an old and independent line. The last stanza of Mrs. Brown's text, with its broadside piety, is certainly of the newest vintage. I do not remember that any one has yet thought it worth while to suggest that Bee Hom (in Buchan, *Bahome*) might be a corruption of Bahama.

It is on the whole a relief to turn to the "modern" ballad of the impressed sailor which has supplanted the other in popular favor, and which, going back at least to the middle of the eighteenth century, is still sung widely in England, in Ireland, and occasionally in America. Even though we may readily allow that this song is likely to have had its rise after Sidney's day— and in its press-gang form long after—there is perhaps as good reason for regarding it as a traditional ballad as there is for so regarding "Bonny Bee Hom." It has been revamped and modernized more than once by the broadside press; but all the while, for at least 200 years, it has gone on its way as a piece transmitted by *singing*, and the singing has been independent of print. During that time the hero, as is usual in songs that continue to live, has notably descended in the social scale, from the commander accompanied by "seven score good mariners" to the bridegroom impressed as a common seaman. In its later form it has the makings of a more gripping story.

The melodic tradition seems to take two main forms, and one of these branches early into two distinguishable patterns. Both of the latter appear to find their prototypes in the Skene MS. (early seventeenth century), in tunes named, respectively, "My love shoe winns not her away" and "Alace I lie my alon, I'm lik to die awld." The latter we have already met in connection with Child No. 74. It became associated in the latter half of the eighteenth century, possibly before, with "The Lowlands of Holland," and, under the title "Miss Admiral Gordon's Strathspey," was attributed to William Marshal and was later adopted by Burns for his universally known song, "Of a' the airts." The first tune, "My love" etc., was published in Oswald's *Collection of Curious Scots Tunes*, [1742] (according to John Glen, *Early Scottish Melodies*, 1900, where it is reprinted, p. 98) as "The Lowlands of Holland," and appeared again, with the words, in Ritson's *Scotish Songs*, 1794, I, p. 133. Glen is violently opposed to the idea that there is any connection between the tune "Alace I lie my alon" and "Miss Admiral Gordon's Strathspey," and firmly believes that Marshal composed the latter and that it was then borrowed, presumably by N. Gow and Urbani, for "The Lowlands." He argues that the Skene MS. was not published and that Marshal could not have seen it; that it is nonsense to think that tunes came floating down unwritten for generations; and avers that people in the eighteenth century could make tunes as well as people in the seventeenth. But since at the same moment he believes the Oswald tune of "The Lowlands" to be "evidently" the same as the Skene tune, "My love shoe winns not her away," it is hard to know where first to take hold, and it will be best perhaps to let him have it out with himself. "Alace I lie my alon" is assuredly cognate with "The Lowlands" as it appears in the *Scots Musical Museum*. Beautiful Irish variants of the same musical family, which seems characteristically Celtic, have been found in the present century.

The other main type is apparently confined to the southwesterly parts of England. It is always in 3/4 time and in plagal major forms.

TUNES WITH TEXTS

GROUP A a

1. "Abroad as I was Walking"

Ford, *JFSS*, V, No. 19 (1915), p. 170. Sung by Mr. Bodding, an agricultural laborer, at Elstead, Surrey, in 1907.

Lucy Broadwood calls this a variant of the Hammond copy of "The Prentice Boy" from Dorset.

Abroad as I was walking
Down by the river side,
'Twas there I beheld a fair damsèl,
She was to have been my bride.
She was to have been my bride, my boys,
Most charming to behold,
Oh the heav'ns above protect and keep
Those jolly sailors bold!

p I

(a)

I built my love a galliant ship,
A ship of noble fame,
It would take a hundred and sixty men
For to box her over the main.
To box her over the main, my boys
Most charming to behold—
Oh, I never, never had but one true love
And he got drowned at sea.

No ribands shall go round my waist
Nor comb go through my hair,
No fire-light nor no candle bright
Shall show my beauty fair,
Nor never will I married be
But single will I die,
Since the raging seas and the stormy winds
Parted my true love and I.

2. My love lies in the saut sea,
    And I am on the side,
Enough to break a young thing's heart
    Wha lately was a bride:
Wha lately was a bonie bride
    And pleasure in her e'e;
But the lowlands of Holland
    Hae twinn'd my love and me.

3. New Holland is a barren place,
    In it there grows no grain;
Nor any habitation
    Wherein for to remain:
But the sugar canes are plenty,
    And the wine draps frae the tree;
And the lowlands of Holland
    Hae twinn'd my love and me.

4. My love he built a bonie ship
    And set her to the sea,
Wi' seven score brave mariners
    To bear her companie:
Threescore gaed to the bottom,
    And threescore died at sea;
And the lowlands of Holland
    Hae twinn'd my love and me.

5. My love has built another ship
    And set her to the main,
He had but twenty mariners
    And all to bring her hame:
The stormy winds did roar again,
    The raging waves did rout,
And my love and his bonie ship
    Turn'd widdershins about.

6. There shall nae mantle cross my back
    Nor kame gae in my hair,
Neither shall coal nor candle light
    Shine in my bower mair;
Nor shall I chuse anither love
    Until the day I die,
Since the lowlands of Holland
    Hae twinn'd my love and me.

GROUP Ab

6. "The Lowlands of Holland"

Johnson, II, [1788], No. 115, p. 118 (repr. 1853). Also in
Urbani, n. d., II, p. 48; and in Maver, 1866, No. 77, p. 39.

m I

Cf. the headnote above, and further under *ante*, No. 74.

1. The love that I have chosen
    I'll therewith be content,
The saut sea shall be frozen
    Before that I repent;
Repent it shall I never
    Until the day I die,
But the lowlands of Holland
    Hae twinn'd my love and me.

7. "The Lowlands of Holland"

Ritson, 1794, I, p. 133; from Oswald, *A Collection of Curious Scots Tunes*, [1742]. Also in Glen, 1900, p. 98. Text from Herd, 1776, II, p. 2.

p I (virtually I/M)

On this tune see the headnote.

My love has built a bonny ship, and set her on the sea,
With seven score good mariners to bear her company;
There's three score is sunk, and three score dead at sea,
And the lowlands of Holland has twin'd my love and me.

My love he built another ship, and set her on the main,
And nane but twenty mariners for to bring her hame,
But the weary wind began to rise, and the sea began to rout,
My love then and his bonny ship turn'd withershins about.

There shall neither coif come on my head, nor comb come in
  my hair;
There shall neither coal nor candle light shine in my bower mair,
Nor will I love another one, until the day I die,
For I never lov'd a love but one, and he's drown'd in the sea.

O had your tongue my daughter dear, be still and be content,
There are mair lads in Galloway, ye need nae sair lament.
O! there is nane in Galloway, there's nane at a' for me,
For I never lov'd a love but ane, and he's drown'd in the sea.

GROUP A d

10. "Lowlands of Holland"

Hughes, II, 1915, p. 70. From County Derry.

a D

Last night I was a-married and on my marriage bed,
Up came a bold sea captain and stood at my bed head
Saying "Arise, arise you married-a-man and come along with me
To the low lowlands of Holland to fight your enemy."

She held her love in her arms still thinking he might stay,
When the captain gave another shout he was forced to go away.
It's many's a blithe young married-a-man this night must go
  with me
To the low lowlands of Holland to fight the enemy.

Oh! Holland is a wondrous place and in it grows much green,
It's a wild inhabitation for my love to be in.
There the sugar cane grows plentiful and fruit on every tree
But the low lowlands of Holland are between my love and me.

Nor shoe nor stocking I put on nor a comb go in my hair,
And neither coal nor candle light shine in my chamber fair.
Nor will I wed with any young man until the day I die,
Since the low lowlands of Holland are between my love and me.

Copyright 1915 by Boosey & Co., Ltd. Renewed 1942. Reprinted by permission of Boosey & Hawkes, Inc.

GROUP B

16. "The Lowlands of Germany"

Hammond, *JFSS*, VII, No. 27 (1923), p. 63(1). Sung by
William Bartlett, Wimborne, 1905.

p I

Oh, the very first night I was married, I was laid down on my
  bed,
The cruel captain he* said to me, as he stood by my bedside
  (bed's head);
Crying "Arise, my bride (brisk) and bonny lad (man), You
  must go along with me
To the Lowlands of Germany, For to face our enemy."

"Then I put my love on shipboard, and a lofty ship was she,
With fourscore jolly sailor boys for to bear my love company.
†And a score of them was drownded and I (they) kills the other
  three,
And one of them was my true love, that was killed in Germany.

Now no scarf then shall go round my neck; no, nor comb go
  thro' my hair,
Nor firelight, no, nor candlelight shall ever in my room appear,
Nor never will I get married, no, until the day I die,
For I never had but one true love; he was killed in Germany."

Now says the mother to the daughter, "What makes you so
  lament?
Isn't there lads enough in our town that will give you your
  heart's content?"
"Yes mother dear, there's lads enough, but there's nary one
  for me,
Since the stormy winds and raging seas parted my true love
  and me."

* Also: "came to me, and stood."
† "There was four score got wounded, And four score got slain."
[*Such's Broadside.*]

Lamkin

CHILD NO. 93

Miss Gilchrist, in a valuable study of this ballad (*JEFDSS*, I, No. 1 [1932], pp. 1-17), distinguishes between two traditions, the Scottish and the Northumbrian. The Scottish, she believes, has been carried into the Appalachians, and the Northumbrian has circulated in England and been brought to the northern parts of America. Both kinds are habitually in triple-time; but she believes the Scottish tradition favours the gapped scales, and the English the heptatonic. If so, the difference would be what we should expect to find. Herd's text is directed to be sung to the tune of "Gil Morrice" (1776, I, p. 145); but no clear variant of that tune has been traditionally collected with the Lamkin words. There is possibly enough resemblance of a typical kind to make one tune suggest the other; but the two do not appear to coalesce in tradition.

The divisions which have been settled upon below cannot claim such distinctness as Miss Gilchrist's. With two exceptions (Miss Eddy's rather anomalous Ohio version and the suspicious R. A. Smith copy), all of Group A are in triple time. The first two subgroups are hexatonic and pentatonic variants in major tonalities, and properly plagal. Subgroup Ac is composed, with one exception from Michigan, of Appalachian variants with ambiguous finals, either authentic Mixolydian or dropped Ionian on the lower dominant, and mainly pentatonic. Ah contains minor variants, one (I believe) hitherto unpublished. This ballad is habitually in tetrameter couplets, dactylic (or anapaestic); and its tunes sometimes recall the "Cherry Tree" and "A Virgin Unspotted," carols with similar metrical schemes.

Miss Gilchrist makes a successful distinction between versions of which the protagonist is a skilled mason disappointed of his pay and seeking revenge, and versions from which this motivation is absent and wherein the villain, no longer a mason, embarks on his crime for other reasons or for none at all. It appears highly probable, on Miss Gilchrist's showing, that the song was of Scottish origin, and that the secondary variety is a north-country offshoot arising from the loss of the first stanza, wherein —and there only—Lamkin's trade and ground of resentment are set forth. With this loss, deterioration at once begins to eat into the ballad from this side and that.

TUNES WITH TEXTS

GROUP Aa

2. "False Lamkin"

Sharp MSS., 2654/. Also in Sharp, 1916, p. 62. Sung by Yarrow Gill (72), Ely Union, Cambridge, September 11, 1911.

p I/M (but major in variants)

This is printed also in *JFSS*, V, No. 18 (1914), p. 83, and in Sharp, *Folk Songs of England*, 1908-12, IV (*Folk Songs from Various Counties*), p. 38. Vaughan Williams refers to "Glencoe" (*JFSS*, II, No. 8 [1905], p. 171) and Kidson refers the latter song to Petrie, No. 677.

1. The Lord says to the Lady
   Before he went out
   Beware of false Lamkin
   He's a walking about.

2. What care I for false Lamkin
   Or any of his kin
   When the doors are all bolted
   And the windows close pinned.

3. At the back kinchin window
   False Lamkin crep in
   And he pricked of the elder babes
   With a bright silver pin

4. O Nurse maid, O nurse maid
   How sound you do sleep
   Cant you hear of those elder babes
   A crying and weep.

5. How durst I go down
   In the dead of the night
   When there's no fire a kindled
   (And) no candle a light

6. As she was a going down
   And thinking no harm
   False Lamkin he caught her
   Right tight in his arm

7. O spare my life O spare my life
   For my life is so sweet
   You shall have as many bright guineas
   As stones in the street.

8. O spare my life, O spare my life
   Till one of the clock
   You shall have my daughter Bessie
   She's the flower of the flock.

9. Fetch me your daughter Bessie
   She will do me some good
   She will hold the silver basin
   To catch her own heart's blood.

10. Pretty Bessie being up
    At the window so high
    Saw her own dearest Father
    Come riding close by.

11. Dear Father, dear father
    Dont blame not of me
    It was False Lamkin
    Murdered Baby & she

12. Here's blood in the Kinchin
    Here's blood in the Hall
    Here's blood in the Parlour
    Where the Lady did fall

13. False Lamkin shall be hanged
    On the Gallus so high
    While his body shall be burned
    In the fire close by.

GROUP A b

5a. "Bolakins"

Sung by Mrs. Lena Turbyfill, Elk Park, N.C., 1939. LC/AAFS, Album 7, rec. No. 596(34A). Collected by Herbert Halpert.

p π¹

Bo - la - Kins was a ver-y fine We'll— stick her little

The above is only the underlying norm of the tune. It was never so sung, the phrases being altered perpetually throughout.

1. Bolakins was a very fine mason
   As ever laid stone.
   He built a fine castle
   And the pay he got none.

2. "Where is the gentleman?
       Is he at home?"
   "He's gone down to Marion
       For to visit his son."

3. "Where is the lady?
       Is she at home?"
   "She's upstairs sleeping,"
       Said the foster to him.

4. "How will we get her down
       Such a dark night as this?"
   "We'll stick her little baby
       Full of needles and pins."
   They stuck her little baby
       Full of needles and pins.

5. The foster she rocked,
       And Bolakins he sung,
   While blood and tears
       From the cradle did run.

6. Down come our lady,
       Not thinking any harm.
   Old Bolakins,
       He took her in his arms.

7. "Bolakins, Bolakins,
       Spare my life one day.
   I'll give you many marigolds
       As my horse can carry away.

8. "Bolakins, Bolakins,
       Spare my life one hour.
   I'll give you daughter Bessie,
       My own blooming flower."

9. "You better keep your daughter Bessie
       For to run through the flood,
   And scour a silver basin
       For to catch your heart's blood."

10. Daughter Bessie climbed up
        In the window so high,
    And saw her father
        Come riding hard by.

11. "Oh, father, oh, father,
        Can you blame me?
    Old Bolakins
        Has killed your lady.

12. "Oh, father, oh, father,
        Can you blame me?
    Old Bolakins
        Has killed your baby."

13. They hung old Bolakins
        To the sea-gallows tree
    And tied the foster
        To the stake of stand-by.

8. "False Lambkin"

Eddy, 1939, p. 59. Also in Tolman and Eddy, *JAF*, XXXV (1922), p. 344. Sung by Miss Jane Goon, Perrysville, Ohio.

Tonic G, p I/M (—VI), ending on II

1. False Lambkin was a mason,
       As good as ever laid stone;
   He built Lord Arnold's castle,
       And the Lord paid him none.

2. False Lambkin he swore
       That revenged he would be
   On Lord Arnold's castle,
       Or on his family.

3. Said the Lord to his Lady,
       "I'm going from home,
   And what would you do
       If false Lambkin should come?"

4. "Oh, I fear not false Lambkin,
      Nor men of his kin;
   For I'll keep my doors fastened,
      And my windows pinned in."

5. So she kept her doors fastened,
      And her windows pinned in,
   All except one kitchen window
      Where Lambkin came in.

6. "Oh, where is Lord Arnold?
      Is he not at home?"
   "No, he's gone to old Ireland
      To see his dear son."

7. "Oh, where is his lady,
      Has she gone along?"
   "No, she's up in her chamber
      Where no man can get in."

8. "Oh, what shall I do
      That I may get in?"
   "You must pierce this little babe's heart
      With your silver bodkin."

9. So he pierced the little babe's heart
      Till the blood did spin
   Out into the cradle;
      So falsely she did sing:

10. "Oh, hushy-by baby,
       Oh, what aileth thee?
    Come down, loving mistress,
       Oh, come down and see."

11. "Oh, how can I come down
       So late in the night,
    When there's no moon a-shining,
       Nor stars to give light?"

12. "Oh, you've seven bright lanterns,
       As bright as the sun;
    Come down, loving mistress,
       Oh, come down by one."

13. She had not advanced
       But steps two or three,
    Till she spied false Lambkin
       A-standing close by.

14. "Oh, spare me, false Lambkin,
       And I will go back
    And get all the money
       You can carry in your sack."

15. "I want none of your money,
       Nor nothing that I know
    That will spare this bright sword
       From your neck white as snow."

16. "Oh, spare me, false Lambkin,
       Oh, spare me one hour,
    And I'll call down daughter Betsy,
       The queen of the bower."

17. "Go, call down daughter Betsy,
       So neat and so clean,
    To hold the silver basin
       To catch your blood in."

18. "Daughter Betsy, stay up
       In your chamber so high,
    Till you see your dear father
       In a ship sailing nigh."

19. Daughter Betsy stayed up
       In her chamber so high,
    Till she saw her dear father
       In a ship sailing nigh.

20. When Lord Arnold came to the castle
       And opened the door,
    He saw his companion
       Lying dead on the floor.

21. False Lambkin was hung
       On the gallows so high,
    And the false nurse was burnt
       To a stake standing by.

GROUP AC

12. [Lamkin]

Sharp MSS., 3998/2880. Also in Sharp and Karpeles, 1932, I, p. 204(C). Sung by Mrs. Francis Carter, Beattyville, Lee County, Ky., September 8, 1917.

p π^1, ending on V (or a π^2)

1. Old Lamkin was as good a mason
      As ever laid a stone.
   He built the finest castle,
      But payment he had none.

2. Then at such an hour
      The king rode from home,
   Saying: Beware of old Lamkin,
      He'll be here at noon.

3. What cares I for Lamkin,
      Or any other man?
   My doors are all locked
      And my windows pinned down.

4. At twelve o'clock at night
      Old Lamkin come,
   And no one so ready
      As the false nurse to let him in.

5. How could we get her downstairs
On such a dark night?
Why, we'll stick her little baby
Full of needles and pins.

6. What a pity, what a pity,
Cried old Lamkin.
No pity, no pity,
Cried the false nurse to him.

7. Pretty Betsy coming downstairs
Not thinking any harm,
And there stood old Lamkin
To catch her in his arms.

8. O spare my life, Lamkin,
O spare it, I pray.
You shall have as much gay gold
As my horse can carry away.

9. What cares I for your gay gold,
Or any other thing?
I have got my desire,
That's all I do crave.

10. O spare my life, Lamkin,
O spare it, I pray.
You shall have my daughter Betsy,
My own blooming flower.

11. Keep your daughter Betsy
To wade through the blood
And scour the silver basin
That catched your own heart's blood.

GROUP A h

27. "Lambkin"

Blaikie MS., NL Scotland MS. 1578, No. 105, p. 33.

m Æ

29. [Long Lankin, or Young Lambkin]

Vaughan Williams, *JFSS*, II, No. 7 (1905), p. 111. From Miss Chidell, as sung by Mrs. Chidell, Bournemouth, 1902.

p Æ/D (—VII)

1. Said my Lord to his Lady, as he mounted his horse
"Beware of Long Lankin that lives in the moss!"

2. Said my Lord unto my Lady, as he went away,
"Beware of Long Lankin that lives in the clay!"

3. "Let the doors be all bolted, the windows all pinned,
And leave not a loophole for Long Lankin to creep in!"

4. So he mounted his horse, and he rode away,
And he was in London before the break of day.

5. And the doors were all bolted, the windows all pinned,
All but one little loophole, where Long Lankin crept in.

6. "Where is the Lord of this house?" said Long Lankin.
"He's away in fair London," said the false nurse to him.

7. "Where is the Lady of this house?" said Long Lankin.
"She's up in her chamber," said the false nurse to him.

8. "Where is the little Lord of this house?" said Long Lankin.
"He's asleep in this cradle," said the false nurse to him.

9. "Then we'll prick him all over and over with a pin,
And we'll make my Lady come down to him!"

10. So they pricked him all over and over with a pin,
And the nurse held the bason for the blood to flow in.

11. "Oh nurse how you slumber! O nurse how you sleep!
You leave my little son Johnson to cry and to weep!"

12. "Oh nurse! how you slumber! O nurse! how you snore!
You leave my little son Johnson to cry and to roar!"

13. "I've tried him with milk, and I've tried him with pap,
Come down, my fair Lady, and nurse him in your lap."

14. "I've tried him with onions, I've tried him with pears,
Come down, my fair lady, and nurse him in your chairs."

15. "How can I come down? tis so late at night,
There's no candle burning, or moon to give light."

16. "You have three silver mantles, as light as the sun,
Come down, my fair Lady, all by the light of one!"

17. So my Lady came down the stairs, fearing no harm,
Long Lankin stood ready, to catch her in his arm.

18. "Oh spare me Long Lankin! Oh, spare me till twelve
o'clock!
You shall have as much gold as you can carry on your
back!"

19. "Oh, spare me, Long Lankin! Oh, spare me one hour!
You shall have my daughter Betsy, she is a fair flower!"

20. "Where is your daughter Betsy? She may do some good;
She can hold the bason to catch your life's blood."

.   .   .   .   .   .

21. Lady Betsy sat up at her window so high,
She saw her dear father from London riding by.

22. "Oh father! Oh father! Don't lay the blame on me!
'Twas the false nurse and Lankin that killed your fair
Lady!"

.   .   .   .   .   .

23. So Long Lankin was hung on a gibbet so high,
The false nurse was burnt at a stake close by.

The Maid Freed from the Gallows

CHILD NO. 95

THIS ballad has been greatly loved in many parts of the world. It seems justifiable to make a broad division between two great groups on the basis of scene, although probably the second is but a decapitated form of the first. Along the Mediterranean coast and around the Baltic the ballad has been current in a form in which pirates or sea-marauders carry off a girl who appeals in vain for ransom to the various members of her family in turn, and finally to her lover with success. In the second group the maritime elements are absent. A prisoner, condemned to die, makes a similar series of appeals. This is the British form, and also the prevailing form in Eastern Europe. The earliest British text is of about 1770. The English variants frequently have a burden, or chorus, and are especially suited for a game-song with accompanying action. Among the negroes the ballad is still sung and said in the form of a *cante-fable*. The suggestion that the precious object, the loss of which involves the death-penalty, once had a sexual significance, seems entirely plausible.

In spite of very considerable superficial variation, it may be permissible to class all the British or British-descended tune-variants as members of one large musical family. This will, however, have to be subdivided into several types, the mid-cadence being a factor of importance, though not always compelling. Plagal forms predominate, and the melodic tradition has remained almost wholly within the Ionian galaxy. One group has affiliations with the "Giles Collins" pattern, another with that of "Lord Lovel," and a third with that of "Young Hunting." The burdens generally repeat the air in a varied form. English variants favor a "prickly bush" burden, which has been lost in America. Motherwell's text (Child B) is unique in having a "bonny broom" burden. That burden belongs especially to "The Broom of Cowdenknowes" (Child No. 217), and we may guess that the burden brought along its own melody in this case. The oldest record of a tune is the Irish one in the Hudson MS. (c. 1840), without words.

The ballad has been subjected to careful and prolonged analysis by Erich Pohl in a monograph, "Die Deutsche Volksballade von der 'Losgekauften'," published as No. 105 of *Folklore Fellows Communications*, Vol. XXXVIII 2, Helsinki, 1934, pp. 1-361. Again, in an outstanding study by Eleanor R. Long, *"The Maid" and "The Hangman,"* University of California, Folklore Studies:21. 1971.

Miss Broadwood (*JFSS*, V, No. 19 [1915], pp. 237-39) finds a melodic relationship between a Westphalian form of the ballad ("O Schipmann," reprinted from *Die Lieder des Zupfgeigenhansl*, Hofmeister, Leipzig, 1912) and a Keswick game-song, "Arise, Daughter Ellen," proceeding on a narrative formula parallel with our ballad. Cf. also Miss Gilchrist's interesting article on "The Prickly Bush," (*JFSS*, V, No. 19 [1915], pp. 228-37); and Paul G. Brewster (*SFQ*, V [1941], pp. 25-28) on a Rumanian analogue. It is worth noting that there is a Polish ballad in Bystroń, *Pieśni Ludowe*, 1927, I, p. 61(P), with a tune remarkably close to the best known of Cecil Sharp's Somerset variants (variant 49 below), as follows:

TUNES WITH TEXTS

GROUP Aa

1. "Oh, Stop Your Hand, Lord Judge"

Hudson MS., No. 355, c. 1840. Reprinted in Barry, *JAF*, XXIV (1911), p. 337.

a M

2. [The Maid Freed from the Gallows]

Sharp MSS., 4467/. Sung by David Webb, Burnsville, N.C., September 22, 1918; learned from a Negro.

m π¹

Mister Hangman, Mister Hangman, please slack
          up on your rope
Just for a little while;
I think I see my poor old father's face,
He has come for so many miles.

And I'm *not* come to see you hanged
All on the gallows-tree!"

Chorus: Oh! the Prickly Bush, etc., etc.

GROUP Ab

17. "The Prickly Bush"

Broadwood and Maitland, 1893, p. 112. Sung by Heywood
Sumner, Somerset.

p I

4. "The Prickly Bush"

Hammond, *JFSS*, V, No. 19 (1915), p. 230(2). Sung by
H. Way, Bridport, Dorset, May 1906.

a I/M (compass of a sixth)

"O hangman, hold thy hand,
And hold it for a while,
I think I see my own dear mother
Coming over yonder stile!
Oh! have you brought me gold?
Or can you set me free?
Or be you come to see me hanged
All on the gallows-tree?"
"Oh, I a'n't brought you gold,
Nor I can't set you free,
But I am come to see you hanged
All on the gallows-tree."

Chorus: Oh! the Prickly Bush
      That pricks my heart most sore!
      If ever I get out of the Prickly Bush
      I'll never get in no more!

*The verses run thus, until she has seen her father,
brother and sister likewise arrive, and then:*

"O hangman, hold thy hand,
And hold it for a while;
I think I see my own sweetheart
Coming over yonder stile!
Oh! have you brought me gold?
Or can you set me free?
Or be you come to see me hanged
All on the gallows-tree?"
"Oh! I have brought you gold,
And I can set you free,

This version is sung by A. L. Lloyd, Riverside LP rec., RLP 12-
623 (A2), ed. K. S. Goldstein.

"O hangman, hold thy hand," he cried,
    "O hold thy hand awhile;
For I can see my own dear father
    Coming over yonder stile.

"O father, have you brought me gold?
    Or will you set me free?
Or be you come to see me hung,
    All on this high gallows tree?"

"No, I have not brought thee gold,
    And I will not set thee free;
But I am come to see thee hung,
    All on this high gallows tree."

Chorus:

"Oh the prickly bush, the prickly bush,
    It pricked my heart full sore;
If ever I get out of the prickly bush,
    I'll never get in any more."

*Above repeated 3 times more, with substitution of
"mother," "brother," and "sister" for "father." Then
the 1st 2 verses are repeated with "sweetheart" in this
place, and for the third verse the following is sung:*

"Yes, I have brought thee gold," she cried,
    "And I will set thee free;
And I am come, but not to see thee hung,
    All on this high gallows tree."
      "Oh the prickly bush," &c.

By permission of J. B. Cramer & Co. Ltd., London.

GROUP AC

23. [The Hangman's Tree]

Smith, 1928, p. 144(A). Also in Sandburg, 1927, p. 72. Sung by an axeman in West Virginia in 1902.

m π¹

1. "Slack your rope, hangs-a-man,
    O slack it for a while;
   I think I see my father coming,
    Riding many a mile.

2. "O father have you brought me gold?
    Or have you paid my fee?
   Or have you come to see me hanging
    On the gallows-tree?"

3. "I have not brought you gold;
    I have not paid your fee;
   But I have come to see you hanging
    On the gallows-tree."

4. "Slack your rope, hangs-a-man,
    O slack it for a while;
   I think I see my mother coming,
    Riding many a mile.

5. "O mother have you brought me gold?
    Or have you paid my fee?
   Or have you come to see me hanging
    On the gallows-tree?"

6. "I have not brought you gold;
    I have not paid your fee;
   But I have come to see you hanging
    On the gallows-tree."

And so on for brother, sister, aunt, uncle, cousin, etc.

"Slack your rope, hangs-a-man,
 O slack it for a while;
I think I see my truelove coming
 Riding many a mile.

"O truelove have you brought me gold?
 Or have you paid my fee?
Or have you come to see me hanging
 On the gallows-tree?"

"Yes I have brought you gold;
 Yes, I have paid your fee;
Nor have I come to see you hanging
 On the gallows-tree."

GROUP Ae

33. [The Maid Freed from the Gallows]

Sharp MSS., 3497/2582. Also in Sharp and Karpeles, 1932, I, p. 208(B). Sung by Mrs. Sarah Buckner, Black Mountain, N.C., September 19, 1916.

p I—M (inflected VII)

Hold up your hand, O Joshuay, she cried,
Wait a little while and see;
I think I hear my own father dear
Come a-rambling over the sea.

O father dear,* have you any gold for me?
Any silver to pay my fee?
For I have stoled a golden cup
And hanging it will be.

No, daughter, no, I have no gold for thee
Nor silver to pay your fee;
For I have come for to see you hang
All on that willow tree.

. . . .
. . . .
. . . .

Yes, true love, I have some gold for you
And silver to pay your fee,
For I have come for to pay your fee
And take you home with me.

* Omitted in 1932.

GROUP Af

39.1. "Hold Up Your Hand"

Sung by Frank Proffitt, Reese, N.C., September 1961. Collected by Sandy Paton and sent by him to the Editor.

p M (inflected VII)

7. Hold up your hand, Old Joshuway, she said
     Wait a while and see
   I thought I see my own true love
     Come crossing over the sea.

8. Do you have any money for me
     Or gold for to pay my fee?
   For I have stole a silvery cup
     And hangeth I'm a-goin to be.

9. Yes, I have some money for you,
     And gold for to pay your fee
   I've just come to save your neck
     From yonders gallows tree.

49. "The Briary Bush"

Sharp MSS., 2030/1902. Also in Sharp, 5th series, 1909, p. 54; and in Sharp, 1916, p. 42. Sung by Mrs. Overd, Langport, January 4, 1909.

a I

Cf. the Polish analogue cited in the headnote above.

1. Hold up your hand, Old Joshuway, she said
     Wait a while and see
   I thought I see my dear old father
     Come a-crossing over the sea.

2. Do you have any money for me?
     Gold for to pay my fee?
   I've just stole a silvery cup
     And hangeth I'm a-goin to be.

3. I don't have no money for you,
     Or gold to pay your fee.
   I've just come to see you hanged
     On yonders gallows tree.

4. Hold up your hand, Old Joshuway, she said,
     Wait a while and see.
   I thought I see my dear old mother
     Come a-crossing over the sea.

5. Do you have any money for me?
     Gold to pay my fee?
   For I have stole a silvery cup
     And hangeth I'm a-goin to be.

6. I don't have any money for you
     Nor gold to pay your fee.
   I've just come to see you hanged
     On yonders gallows tree.

O hangman hold (stay) thy hand
And hold (stay) it for a while
For I fancy I see my father
A-coming across the yonder stile.

O father have you got my gold
And can you set me free
Or are you come to see me hung
All on the gallus tree?

No I have not brought thee gold
And I can't set thee free
But I have come to see thee hung
All on the gallus tree.

O the briary bush
That pricks my heart so sore
If I once get out of the briary bush
I'll never get in it any more.

*Same with mother, brother, sister,
and then finally:*

O hangman stay thy hand
And hold it for a while
For I fancy I see my true love
Coming across them yonder stile.

O true love have you got my gold
And can you set me free
Or are you come to see me hung
All on this gallus tree?

Yes my dear I brought thee gold
And I can set thee free
And I've not come to see thee
Hung on the gallus tree.

O the briary bush, etc.

GROUP A g

61. "Hangman"

Randolph, I, 1946, p. 145(D). Sung by Mrs. May Kennedy McCord, Springfield, Mo., May 16, 1938. Learned in Galena, Mo., c. 1897.

m Æ

"Say, paw"

Hangman, hangman, slack up your rope,
Slack it for a while,
I look over yonder an' I see my paw a-comin',
He's walked for many a mile,
Say paw, say paw, have you brung me any gold,
Any gold for to pay my fee.
No, my son, I have not any gold,
You must hang on th' gallows tree.

* * * * * *

Usual repetition, then final verse.

Hangman, hangman, slack up your rope,
Slack it for a while,
I look over yonder an' I see my true love comin',
She's walked for many a mile.
Say love, say love, have you brung me any gold,
Any gold for to pay my fee?
Yes, I have brung you yeller yeller gold,
To take you home with me.

Johnie Scot

CHILD NO. 99

THIS agreeable piece of Scottish self-congratulation has for the most part naturally been resident north of the border, though it has found its way, in congenial company, to American shores. There is no need to consider the ballad, as we have it, to be much older than the eighteenth century. Sharpe called attention to a story attaching the incident of the swordplay to an actual person of Charles II's day, and Child, who reports a similar story from Brittany perhaps centuries earlier, seems to think that that in turn may be based on something earlier still. Oral tradition, of course, although tenacious of the past, dies unless continually renovated. If the ballad ever existed in an English form, none is now known; and at any rate it got a new start in Scotland and acquired a great vogue. Judging from the consistent reappearance of certain features and phrases which smack little of tradition, there may well have been stall copies formerly in circulation, entitled "McNaughton's Valour." (See Child's note under copy Db, and Motherwell's headnote.) Such a detail is the lady's

My breast-plate's o the sturdy steel,
Instead of the beaten gold.

In the United States, tradition has preferred that Johnie should meet his lady first in the greenwood, rather than at court.

All variants of the ballad are in CM quatrains without refrain; but one of Motherwell's copies (Child Da) repeated the second half of the stanza when sung. Motherwell, we learn from a letter written before Oct. 8, 1825, sent C. K. Sharpe a couple of tunes for this ballad: one noted down by Andrew Blaikie from a woman in Paisley (possibly Mrs. Storie), and a different one got by Blaikie in the "South Country." Blaikie, it will be recalled, was responsible for the musical appendix in Motherwell's *Minstrelsy*, 1827.

Probably all the surviving tunes of this ballad stem from the same root, but there is a wide divergence between some of them. Modal variation extends from I/Ly to Æolian. The norm seems to be in the Dorian vicinity. Rhythms are duple, in 4/4, 2/2, and 6/8 varieties, and also triple. Plagal variants seem to lie mostly at either end of the modal range for this ballad, authentic tunes in the middle.

TUNES WITH TEXTS

10. "Jack the little Scot"

Ritson-Tytler-Brown MS., p. 14. Also in Child, 1882-98, V, p. 418(A). Sung by Mrs. Brown, Falkland, Aberdeenshire; copied by Joseph Ritson, c. July 17, 1794.

a Æ

* *Original ending:*

    This tune has a bi-modal feeling, the first half seeming to be p I/Ly.
    The Abbotsford copy printed in Child, V, p. 418(A), is nearly identical, and comes from the same source.

1. Johny was as brave a knight
     As ever sail'd the sea,
   And he is to the English court,
     To serve for meat and fee.
2. He had nae been in fair England
     But yet a little while,
   Until the king his ae daughter
     To Johny grows wi' chil'.
3. O, word's come to the king himsel',
     In his chair where he sat,

That his ae daughter was wi' bairn
  To Jack the little Scot.
4. "Gin this be true 'at i do hear,
     As i trust well it be,
   Ye put her into prison strong,
     And starve her 'till she dee."
5. O Johny's on to fair Scotland,
     I wot he went wi' speed,
   And he has left the king his court,
     I wot good was his need.
6. O, it fell once upon a day,
     That Johny he thought lang,
   An' he's doen him to the good green wood,
     As fast as he cou'd gang.
7. "O whare'll i get a bonny boy
     To run my errand seen,
   That will gang unto fair England,
     An' haste him back again?"
8. O up it starts a bonny boy,
     Gold yellow was his hair,
   I wish his mother meickle joy,
     His bonny love meickle mair.
9. "O here am i a bonny boy,
     Will run your errand soon,
   I will gang unto fair England,
     An' come right soon again."
10. O whan he came to broken brigs
     He bent his bow and swam,
   And whan he came to the green grass grow'n,
     He slack'd his sheen and ran.
11. Whan he came to yon high castle,
     He ran it round about,
   And there he saw the king's daughter
     At the window looking out.

12. "O here's a sark o' silk, lady,
    Your ain hand sew'd the sleeve,
    You're bidden come to fair Scotland,
    Speer nane o' your parents leave.
13. Ha', tak' this sark o' silk, lady,
    Your ain hand sew'd the gare,
    You're bidden come to good green wood,
    Love Johny waits you there."
14. She's turn'd her right and round about,
    The tear was in her ee:
    "How can i come to my true love,
    Except i had wings to flee?
15. Here am i kept wi' bars and bolts,
    Most grievous to behold,
    My breast-plate's o' the sturdy steel
    Instead o' the beaten gold.
16. But tak' this purse, my bonny boy,
    Ye well deserve a fee,
    An' bear this letter to my love,
    And tell him what you see."
17. Then quickly ran the bonny boy
    Again to Scotland fair,
    And soon he reach't Pitnachton's tow'rs,
    And soon found Johny there.
18. He pat the letter in his hand,
    An' taul' him what he saw,
    But ere he half the letter read,
    He leet the tears down fa'.
19. "O, i'll gae back to fair England,
    Tho' death shou'd me betide,
    An' i'll relieve the damesel
    That lay last by my side."
20. Then out it spake his father dear,
    "My son, you are to blame;
    An' gin you're catch'd in English ground,
    I fear you'll ne'er win hame."
21. Then out it spake a valiant knight,
    Johnys best friend was he,
    "I can command five hundred men,
    An' his surety i will be."
22. The firstin town that they came till,
    They gar'd the bells be rung;
    The nextin town that they came till,
    They gar'd the mess be sung;
23. The thirdin town that they came till,
    They gar'd the drums beat round,
    The king but and his nobles a'
    Was startled at the sound.
24. Whan they came till the kings palace,
    They rode it round about,
    An' there they saw the king himsel'
    At the window looking out.
25. "Is this the duke of Albany,
    Or James the Scotish king?
    Or are you some great foreign lord,
    That's come a visiting?"
26. "I'm no the duke of Albany,
    Nor yet the Scotish king,
    But i'm a valiant Scotish knight,
    Pitnachton is my name."
27. "O, if Pitnachton be your name,
    As i trust well it be,
    The morn, ere i taste meat or drink,
    You shall be hanged hi'."

28. Then out it spake the valiant knight
    That came brave Johny wi',
    "Behold five hundred bowmen bold,
    Will die or set him free."
29. Then out it spake the king again,
    An' a scornfu' laugh leugh he:
    "I have an Italian i' my house,
    Will fight you three by three."
30. O, grant me a boon, brave Johny cried,
    Bring out your Italian here,
    Then if he falls beneath my sword,
    I've won your daughter dear.
31. Then out it came this Italian,
    And a gurious ghost was he,
    Upo' the point o' Johnys sword
    This Italian did dee.
32. Out has he drawn his lang lang bran',
    Struck it across the plain:
    "Is there any more o' your English dogs
    That you want for to be slain?"
33. A clerk, a clerk, then cried the king,
    To write her tocher-free.
    A priest, a priest, says love Johny,
    To marry my love and me.

11. "Johnie Scot"

Macmath MS., p. 114. Also in Child, V, 1882-98, p. 418(O); text, II, p. 396(O). Sung by Miss Jane Webster, Kircudbrightshire, 1882; learned from Miss Jane Hannay, Newton Stewart. Collected by Miss M. Macmath.

1. Out then spak his auld faither,
   And a blythe auld man was he,
   Saying, I'll send five hunner o my brisk young men,
   To bear Johnie companie.

2. And when they were on saddle set,
   They were a pleasant sight for to see,
   For there was na ae married man
   In a' Johnie's companie.

3. And when they were on saddle set,
   They were a pleasant sight to behold,
   For the hair that hung down Johnie's back
   Was like the links of gold.

4. And when they came to Newcastle,
   They reined their horses about;
   Wha did he see but his ain Jeanie,
   At a window looking out!

5. "Come doun, come doun, Jeanie," he says,
   "Come doun, come doun to me;"
   "I canna come doun, Johnie," she says,
   "For King Edward has bolted me."

6. "My stockings are o the heavy iron,
   I feel them very cold;
   And my breast-plate's o the sturdy steel,
   Instead of beaten gold."

     .   .   .   .   .

7. .   .   .   .   .   .
   "I'll make it heir o a' my lands,
   And her my gay lady."

8. "There is an Italian in this court;
   This day he has slain knights three;
   And before tomorrow at eight o'clock
   The Italian will slay thee."

12. "Johnie Scot"

Sharp MSS., 3868/2826. Also in Sharp and Karpeles, 1932, I, p. 216(B). Sung by Mrs. Nancy Alice Hensley, Oneida, Ky., August 17, 1917.

p π^4

1. In the merry green woods a-hunting,
   In the merry green woods so wide,
   There Johnie Scot met with King Henry's oldest* daughter,
   And talked with her a while,
   There Johnie Scot met with King Henry's oldest* daughter,
   And talked with her a while.

2. The news unto old Ingram's (house)
   Old Ingram being gone;
   The news into† the kitchen house;
   O that's the worst of all.

3. She wrote young Johnie a letter
   That seemed to make him smile;
   Before he read it one half way through,
   He wept like any child.

4. I'll go fight for that lady fair
   That lay last by my side.
   Up spoke his old father who was sitting in his chair,
   Saying: If you do to old King Henry go,
   You'll never come back here.

5. Up spoke his oldest brother,
   An angry man was he:
   Here's me and five hundred of my life-guards
   Will bear you§ company.

6. They all mounted horse-back,
   And as they went on the road,
   The hair hung down young Johnie's back,
   Looked like the links of gold.

7. They rode on to Solver Town,
   They rode it all around.
   No one could see but his own true love
   In a windows looking down#.

8. Come down, come down, my own true love,
   Come low-lie unto me;
   Where I will swear before I go,
   I'll ride in your company.

9. I can't come down, I can't come down,
   I can't come unto you.
   My stockings once they was of silk,
   My shoe-buckles of gold;
   But now my feet's in some hard iron band.
   O lor! my feet they're cold.

10. They went a-fighting at two o'clock in the morning,
    They fit till two past noon,
    A-sweating blood lap in the ground
    Like dew upon the grass.
    He killed old King Henry and all his life-guards
    And got his love at last.

* 1932: only
† 1932: unto
§ 1932: your
# 1932: round

Willie o Winsbury

CHILD NO. 100

CHILD leaves us guessing as to his opinion of the antiquity of this ballad when, as his sole comment upon the question, he writes, "It was hardly an English (or Scots) ballad-maker of the sixteenth century that made this ballad." (Child, II, p. 399.) Whoever invented it, it would seem peculiarly the stuff of sentimental old wives' daydreams, and, though far from silly sooth, easily appropriated by free maids and knitters in the sun. But we learn that it is even today one of the best loved songs of Newfoundland, and it seems to have been sung with as great relish by men as by women. Certainly male vanity suffers no injury by it. There is one primitive touch in the ballad to which Child might have been expected to call attention. It is hardly to be doubted that the persistent recurrence (A, B, C, F, G) of the father's injunction to his daughter to put off her gown "upon the stone" in order that he may determine the fact of her pregnancy is a relic of belief in the magical properties of stone, and a dim reference to some chastity-test based upon it.

Even from Child's record of texts it is possible to distinguish three, and perhaps four, sorts of melodic pattern. One is marked by the addition of "O" at the end of each second and fourth line (Child A and F). Another is straight CM. A third has a repetition of the last line, introduced by a bridge, or repeated last syllable, as typically in "Lord Lovel." And a fourth, connected with the broadside tradition, is strongly anapaestic, and would naturally go to a 6/8 metre—from which, however, the rest are not precluded.

There are, in fact, four clearly marked patterns among the variant tunes noted, but they do not precisely correspond to Child's texts. The one to which I have given first place is identified only by its title, which is a line occurring toward the end of the ballad. This is Scottish; and a Manx copy may be distantly related. The next type is allied to it modally, being another variant, possibly only borrowed for the nonce, of the favorite family of "Binorie" tunes, also, of course, Scottish. The third style is of the first pentatonic mode (—IV, VII). The fourth is by far the most popular, and much more widely current, being found in England, New England, and Newfoundland, as well as Scotland. In one form or another, it is connected with sea-songs like "The Mermaid" and "The Greenland Fishery," but also is cousin to the ubiquitous "Lord Lovel" type. It is in fact a very typical folk pattern. As Keith notes (p. 77), Greig got seven variants of his tune, all very much alike.

TUNES WITH TEXTS

GROUP A

1. [O will ye marry my daughter Janet]

Blaikie MS., NL Scotland MS. 1578, No. 42, p. 15.

a Æ/D

GROUP B

3. "Lord Thomas of Winesberrie"

Kinloch, 1827, App'x. to p. 89; text, p. 92.

p Æ/D

1. It fell upon a time, when the proud king of France
Went a hunting for five months and more,
That his dochter fell in love with Thomas of Winesberrie,
From Scotland newly come o'er.

2. Whan her father cam hame frae hunting the deer,
And his dochter before him cam,
Her belly it was big, and her twa sides round,
And her fair colour was wan.

3. "What ails thee, what ails thee, my dochter Janet,
What maks thee to look sae wan?
Ye've either been sick, and very, very sick,
Or else ye hae lain wi' a man."

4. "Ye're welcome, ye're welcome, dear father," she says,
"Ye're welcome hame to your ain,
For I hae been sick, and very, very sick,
Thinking lang for your coming hame."

5. "O pardon, O pardon, dear father," she says,
"A pardon ye'll grant me."
"Na pardon, na pardon, my dochter," he says,
"Na pardon I'll grant thee.

6. "O is it to a man of micht,
Or to a man of mean?
Or is it to onie of thae rank robbers,
That I sent hame frae Spain?"

7. "It is not to a man of micht,
Nor to a man of mean;
But it is to Thomas o' Winesberrie,
And for him I suffer pain."

8. "If it be to Thomas o' Winesberrie,
As I trust well it be,

Before I either eat or drink,
   Hie hangit sall he be."

9. Whan this bonnie boy was brought afore the king,
   His claithing was o' the silk,
   His fine yellow hair hang dangling doun,
   And his skin was like the milk.

10. "Na wonder, na wonder, Lord Thomas," he says,
   "My dochter fell in love wi' thee,
   For if I war a woman, as I am a man,
   My bed-fellow ye shou'd be!

11. "Then will ye marry my dochter Janet,
   To be heir to a' my land;
   O will ye marry my dochter Janet,
   Wi' the truth o' your richt hand?"

12. "I will marry your dochter Janet,
   Wi' the truth o' my richt hand;
   I'll hae nane o' your gowd, nor yet o' your gear,
   I've eneuch in fair Scotland.

13. "But I will marry your dochter Janet,—
   I care na for your land,
   For she's be a queen, and I a king,
   Whan we come to fair Scotland."

GROUP C

4. [Thomas o' Winsbury]

Greig MSS., I, p. 128 (a and b). Also in Greig and Keith, 1925, p. 77. Tune and two stanzas of text from J. Beattie, Whitehill, April 1906; tune without text from A. [?] Barron.

p π[1]

It's ye will wed my daughter Janet,
   By the faith o your right hand, O,
Ye'll hae pairt o my gowd, ye'll hae pairt o my gear,
   An' the third pairt o my land, O.

It's I will wed your daughter Janet,
   By the faith o my right hand, O,
I'll hae nane o your gowd, I'll hae nane o your gear,
   I've eneuch into fair Scotland, O.

GROUP D

10. "Tom the Barber," or "John (Tom) Barbary"

Hammond, *JFSS*, III, No. 11 (1907), p. 72. Sung by W. Bartlett, Wimborne, Dorset, September 1906.

a I

1. Oh! it's of a merchant's daughter dear;
   She was dressed all in green;
   Oh! and she looked over her father's castle wall,
   For to see the ships sail in,
   For to see the ships sail in.

2. "Oh! what's the matter with you, fair maid?
   You do look so pale and wan.
   I'm sure you've had some sore sickness,"
   *   *   *   *   *   *   *

3. Then he called down all his merry, merry men
   Oh! by one, by two, by three.
   Oh! Tom the Barber used to come first,
   But the hinder one comes he.

4. Down then came Tom the Barber bold
   All dressed all in silk.
   Oh! his eyes did change like the morning sun,
   And his hands so white as milk.

5. "Oh! will you wed my daughter dear,
   And take her by the hand?
   And you shall dine and sup along with me,
   And be heir to all my land."

6. "Oh! yes, I'll wed your daughter dear,
   And take her by the hand,
   And I will dine and sup along with thee,
   And be heir of all thy land.

7. Now I have estate in fair Scotland,
   I have gold and silver so free,
   But where that you have got one guinea,
   There I have got thirty and three."

22. [Willie o Winsbury]

Macmath MS. Also in Child, 1882-98, V, p. 418(J); text, II, p. 514(J). From William Macmath of Edinburgh. Learned September 13, 1886, from his aunt, Miss Jane Webster, who learned it 50 years earlier in Kirkcudbright-shire, from the singing of Samuel Galloway.

a M

1. There was a lass in the North Countrie,
   And her clothing it was the green,
   And she's looked ower her father's castle-wa,
   For to see her father's ships sail in, in,
   For to see her father's ships on sea.

2. "What aileth thee, dear daughter?" he said,
   "What makes thee so pale and wan?
   I'm afraid you've got some sore sickness,
   Or have lain wi some young man, man,
   Or have lain wi some young man."

3. "O I have got no sore sickness,
   Nor I've lain with no young man;
   But the thing that grieves me to the heart
   Is my true-love is staying too long."
   That my true-love, etc.

4. "O is he a lord, or a duke, or a knight,
   Or a man of birth or fame?
   Or is he one of my own servant-men,
   That is lately come from Spain?"

5. "He's neither a lord, nor a duke, nor a knight,
   Nor a man of birth or fame;
   But he is one of your own servant-men,
   That is lately come from Spain."

6. "O call him down, the Spanish dog,
   O call him down to me,
   For before eight o'clock next morning
   Hanged he shall be, be,
   Aye, hanged on a tree."

7. "It's oh forbid, dear father," she said,
   "That anything there should be,
   For if that you hang John Barborough,
   You'll get nae mair good o me."

8. He's called down his merry men all,
   By one and by two and by three;
   John Barborough was to be the first,
   But the last man down came he.

   .   .   .   .

9. .   .   .   .

   .   .   .   .
   For every pound that he laid down,
   John Barborough laid down three.

The Bailiff's Daughter of Islington

CHILD NO. 105

THE musical tradition of this greatly loved ballad has not suffered any sharp breaks, to judge by the extant records. Compared one with another, the tune-variants might appear very unlike; but there is a distinct family resemblance about the group as a whole, in the general layout and rhythmical character of all but one of the variants noted, which permits their being classed together. There are also relationships with "The Gypsy Laddie" (No. 200) and with the so-called "Lazarus" pattern (cf. No. 56).

Chappell found the earliest record of the ballad's tune in *The Jovial Crew* (1731), where it was called "The Baily's Daughter of Islington." Rimbault discovered the same tune under the title "The Jolly Pinder" in a lute MS. of presumably earlier date. (Cf. J. M. Gutch, *Robin Hode*, 1847, II, p. 434. How much earlier I cannot say; but the tune as Rimbault and Chappell give it [Chappell, I, (1855) p. 203] is in the harmonic minor; and a more primitive variant of it is that in the Greig-Duncan MSS., which was learned from tradition in the 1830's

or '40's in Quilquox, Scotland.) Here the tune is plagal Æolian. In general, the plagal variants favor the Æolian galaxy and the authentic variants the Ionian, but by no means exclusively so.

The Restoration broadside copies of the ballad are directed to be sung "To a North Countrey Tune, or, I have a good old mother [*or* woman, *or* wife] at home." Chappell appears to take this tune to be the same as "The Jolly Pinder" or the tune in *The Jovial Crew*; but I know of no evidence to prove the assumption. Presumably, the tune named is suggested as an alternative to the "North Countrey Tune," and has therefore no previous association with "The Bailiff's Daughter." Whether the tune of the ballad which is now familiar was regarded as a North Country tune I cannot say; but one might have expected the phrase "To its own tune" if the association were the primary one. We are thus left with the uncharacteristic ballad-opera printing as the earliest certain record of a connection between the tune and some form of the text.

TUNES WITH TEXTS

GROUP A a

1. "The Bailiff's Daughter of Islington"

Broadwood, rev. ed., |1890|, p. 10. Arranged by A. H. Birch Reynardson.

p I

1. There was a youth and a well bred youth,
   And he was a squire's son,
   And he fell in love with the bailiff's daughter dear,
   That liv'd in fair Islington.

2. As soon as his father came for to know
   His fond and foolish mind,
   He sent him away up to fair London town
   As apprentice there to bind.

3. And when he had served his seven long years,
   His true love he ne'er had seen;
   Whilst he had shed many a tear for her,
   She little had thought of him.

4. As he was a riding out one day,
   The weather being fine and dry,

He thought he saw his own true love,
   As he was a riding by.

5. She stepped up to his horse's head,
   Took hold of his bridle rein;
   And she said "Kind sir will you let me ride a mile
   Just to ease my weary, weary pain?"

6. He said "Fair maid, where came you from?
   Oh where were you bred and born?"
   "In fair Islington, kind sir," said she,
   "Where I have had many a scorn."

7. "Pray did you know the bailiff's daughter dear,
   That lived in fair Islington?"
   "Yes, kind sir, I knew her very well,
   But she hath been dead so long agone."

8. "Then I'll saddle up my milk white steed,
   And take my arrow and bow;
   And I'll go down to some foreign country
   Where no one doth me know!"

9. "Oh no! kind sir, { she is not dead! / do not do so! }
   For she is by your side!
   And here she doth stand at your fair horses head
   All ready to be your bride!"

10. "Oh farewell to father, farewell to mother!
    Farewell to friend and foe!
    For now I'll enjoy my own true love,
    Who I thought was dead so long ago!"

GROUP Ab

8. "The Bailiff's Daughter of Isling-town"

Fox, *JIFSS*, I (1904), p. 46; text, III (1905-06), p. 31.
Sung by Ann Carter, County Galway, 1904.

p Æ/D

1. There was a youth, and a well-bred youth,
   A squire's only son;
   He fell in love with a bailiff's daughter,
   That lived near Isling-town.
   [That lived near Isling-town.]

2. When his parents came to hear
   Of his foolish courtship fond in mind,
   They sent him away to fair London town,
   An apprentice did him bind.

3. To study in the books and to learn in the law
   No comforts could he find:
   "Alas! and oh woe! I shall never see her more,
   She still runs in my mind."

4. When three long months were past and gone,
   School-maids got leave to play;
   The bailiff's daughter from Isling-town
   Cunningly stole away.

5. She sat herself down by a clear river-side;
   Her true love came riding by:
   "One word, one word, kind sir," she said,
   "To relieve a troubled mind.
   One penny, one penny, kind sir," she said,
   "To relieve a distressed mind."

6. "Where were you born?" says the well-
   bred youth;
   "Where were you born or from?"
   "In Isling-town, kind sir," said she,
   "Where I suffered many a wrong."

7. "Oh, if you are from Isling-town,
   I am sure you can't but know
   The Bailiff's daughter, is she dead or alive?
   Come, tell me, if you know?"

8. "She is not alive, but she is dead,
   And in her grave so low;
   She is not alive, but she is dead,
   These three long months and more."

9. "Well, take from me my milk-white steed,
   My saddle and my bow,
   And I will away to some foreign countree,
   Where no one will me know."

10. "She is not dead, but she is alive,
    And standing by your horse's side;
    She is not dead, but she is alive,
    Ready for to be your bride."

11. "Fly away grief and welcome joy
    Ten thousand times to me,
    Since I have got my own true love
    I thought I never would see."

"The ballad is now printed by request of a few antiquarian members of the Society. From several quaint phrases this version, found in Ulster, is believed to be much older in origin than those known in England. It is evidently one of the soldiers' songs, which were brought over by the Devonshire men quartered in English garrisons. The ballad was taught to an old woman by her grandmother, who was a native of Newry." [*Note by C. Milligan Fox.*]

11. [The Bailiff's Daughter]

Karpeles MSS., No. 5309; text, p. 4858. Sung by Mrs. Alice Sims, Pass Island, Newfoundland, July 24, 1930.

m D/Æ

1. It's of a youth and a well belov-ed youth,
   It's of a squire's son,
   Where he courted Bailey's own daughter dear,
   As she lived in sweet Islinkington.

2. As he was going up the street
   And she came riding down,
   Where she took her horse all by the bridle side
   And she swung herself right round.

3. Where are you going, my fair pretty maid,
   Where are you going, cried he
   I am in search of the Bailey's daughter dear
   As she lived in sweet Islinkington.

4. The Bailey's daughter of Islinkington,
   She's dead and don't you know,
   The Bailey's daughter of Islinkington,
   She's been dead, sir, this long time ago.

5. If Bailey's daughter is now dead,
   I'll sell my milkwhite steed,
   And I'll go to some foreign country
   Where no one shall never, never know.

6. The Bailey's daughter is not dead,
   She still remains alive
   And here she is all by the bridle side
   All ready to make you her bride.

7. How glad was he when he heard of this,
   How glad was he to stand,
   And how well he knew it was Bailey's daughter dear
   With the private mark she had on her hand.

18. "Bailiff's Daughter"

Creighton and Senior, 1950, p. 61(C). Also in Creighton and Senior, *JEFDSS*, VI, No. 3 (1951), p. 89. Sung by Thomas Young, West Petpeswick, N.S., September 7, 1933.

a D

1. It's of a youth and a well bred youth
   It was a squire's son,
   He fell in love with a bailiff's daughter
   That lived near Waterford town.

2. O when his parents came to know
   That he was so foolish inclined
   They bound him a prentice in Camertown
   And told him his business to mind.

3. For to mind his books and study them,
   And leave his true love behind,
   "Alas in this world may I never see you more
   But she'll still run in my mind."

4. O it happened to be in the summer time
   And all things were blooming and gay,
   She sat herself down on a bank that was green
   And her true lover came riding that way.

5. "O where were you bred? O where where you born?"
   The squire to her did say,
   "In Waterford town I was born, kind sir,
   Where I suffered a many's the day."

6. "O if you were born in Waterford town
   You cannot help but know
   Of the bailiff's daughter of Waterford town
   Whether she's alive or no?"

7. "She is not alive, for she is dead
   A many a long month ago,
   She is not alive for she is dead
   And in her grave I know."

8. "O come saddle to me a milk-white steed,
   O come saddle for me," cried he,

"Come saddle for me a milk-white steed
That I never expected for to see."

24. [The Bailiff's Daughter of Islington]

Rimbault, 1850, p. 100(2). From "Northern tradition" (England).

a I

There is a rumor, supported by Lucy Broadwood and Frank Kidson in *JFSS*, VII, No. 27, pp. 35-36, that Rimbault composed this tune. Miss Gilchrist thinks it more probably a modernized form of "Mother, mother, make my bed" (*JFSS*, III, No. 13, p. 304, and V, No. 19, p. 135). It is at any rate made out of traditional formulae.

There was a youthe and a well-beloved youthe,
   And he was a squire's son:
O he loved the bayliffe's daughter deare,
   That lived in Islington.

32. [Bailiff's Daughter of Islington]

Sharp MSS., 1438/1321. Sung by Mrs. Eliza Woodberry (79), Ash Priors, August 22, 1907.

a M

1. It's of a young youth and a kind young youth
   He was a squire's son,
   He courted the bailiff's daughter
   She lives in Asle-un-town.

2. And seven long years was over
   I thought to myself a soldier
   O for to see if ever I could
   Forget my love or no.

3. My father overheard me
   These very words did say
   My daughter he has broked his heart
   For the sake of you he died.

4. Don't tell me, don't tell me,
   It's more than I can bear,
   For if she's in her silent grave
   I wish that I was there.

5. As she was walking along
   Walking along the highway
   She sat herself down by the banks of green moss
   And her true love came riding by.

6. And she tooked hold of the horse's head
   Likewise, the bridle rein.
   Kind sir, you give to me 'tis one penny
   To rest my weary limbs.

7. If I give to thee 'tis one penny
   Pray tell to me where you were born
   In Asle-un-Town, kind sire, said she,
   [Where] there's many that do me scorn.

8. Stay one moment or two with me,
   One moment or two I pray
   For 'tis she standing near by your own horse's side
   Waiting for to be your bride.

9. Farewell then grief and sorrow too
   Ten thousand joys and more
   For now I've got my own heart's delight
   She's a girl I always adore.

The Famous Flower of Serving-Men

CHILD NO. 106

CHILD appears to regard all extant copies of the text of this ballad (i.e., to the end of the last century) as deriving ultimately, either through oral channels or print, from the Restoration broadsides. The latter, modified more or less, appeared in various publications (e.g. *A Collection of Old Ballads*, 1723, Percy's *Reliques*, 1765, Ritson's *Select Collection of English Songs,* 1783, Kinloch's *Ancient Scottish Ballads*, 1827), in the eighteenth and early nineteenth centuries. Child felt that the connection between this ballad and the analogous Scandinavian "Maid and the Stable Boy" was tenuous at best, though he thought that the English broadside might "reasonably be believed to be formed upon a predecessor in the popular style."

The Restoration copies give a variety of possibilities for tunes: "To a dainty tune, or Flora Farewel, Summer-Time, or Love's Tide." It is to be presumed that the three named tunes are alternative choices, not alternative names for a single tune. Although Rimbault and Chappell settled upon certain extant tunes as those intended by these designations, their identifications are not better than conjecture once or twice removed from a telling fact. Only one of the possibilities suggested has a stated connection with this ballad, and that only by reason of its asserted secondary title; but the tune in question is a form of the well-known Irish Elizabethan air, "Callino Casturame," not elsewhere than by Rimbault associated with the ballad. None of the hypotheses proposed by the foregoing brings us near to a traditional anchorage for a tune.

The later, nineteenth-century, tunes are associated with texts of a lament of the Border Widow, to which Scott gave currency in his *Minstrelsy of the Scottish Border*, III (1803), p. 83. This piece blends inextricably with parts of the "Famous Flower," as well as echoing other traditional songs. It appeared in musical collections throughout the last century, and might be thought to have superseded or supplanted the earlier song.

But in the present century there has been a re-emergence into traditional currency of the ballad in its earlier guise, and with tunes now closely, now distantly related, but offering at least the shadow of a melodic family. These later variants have been recovered on both sides of the Atlantic: in Scotland, in southern England, in Nova Scotia, and in New England. This evidence of tradition may even provide a bridge to the oldest surviving example of the oral line, in the visible relationship of the Harris and Duncan tunes (vts. 1 and 2). The Harris copy, learned about 1790, was not in print until 1898. The singer of the Duncan copy, an old sea-captain who died soon after 1900 at the age of 80, had learned his version from his own father, presumably in youth. Nearly all the tunes attaching themselves to this clan—all so far recorded except the New Hampshire variant (4)—are in major tonalities.

TUNES WITH TEXTS

GROUP A

1. "My Husband built for me a Bower"

Harris MS., No. 24. Also in Child, 1882-98, V, p. 418.

a I

My father was as brave a lord
As ever Europe did afford;
My mother was a lady bright,
My husband was a valiant knight;
My mother was a lady bright,
My husband was a valiant knight.

2. "Sweet William"

Greig and Keith, 1925, p. 85; from Duncan MS., No. 161. Sung by George Innes, Portgordon, who learned it from his father.

m I/M

1. Come, all ye ladies great and small,
   Give ear unto me, one and all,
   And I will let you understand
   What I have suffered in this land.

2. My father was as brave a lord
   As ever Europe did afford;
   My mother was a lady gay,
   Decked in glories of rich array;

3. And I myself a lady fair,
   My father's chief and only heir;
   And when my good old father died,
   Then I was made a young nice bride.

4. My love he built to me a bower,
   Decked with many a fragrant flower,
   A brighter bower did you never see
   Than what my true love built for me.

5. But there came thieves late in the night,
   They broke my bower and slew my knight;
   And after that my knight was slain,
   No longer could I there remain.

6. My servants all from me did fly,
In the midst of my extremity,
And left me by myself alone,
With a heart as cold as lead or stone.

7. But though my heart was full of care,
Heaven would not suffer me to despair,
So then in haste I changed my name.
From Fair Ellen to Sweet William.

8. Then on a day it chancèd so,
That I to the King's court did go,
All that I of his grace did crave
That I a servant's place might have.

9. "Keep up, young man," the King replied,
"Your suit it shall not be denied;
But first tell me what you can do,
You shall be suited thereunto.

10. "Will you be taster of my wine,
To wait upon me when I dine?
Or will you be my chamberline,
To make my bed both soft and fine?"

11. Sweet William with a smiling face
Said to the King, "If it please your Grace
To show such favour unto me,
Your chamberline I fain would be."

12. The King did all his nobles call,
And askèd counsel of them all,
Unto which they did all agree,
Sweet William the King's chamberline to be.

13. Now on a day it did happen so
That the King did a-hunting go;
He carried with him all his train
Sweet William did at home remain.

14. Then finding that the house was clear,
He took a flute that he had there,
And on it he played melodious,
Which made an old man's heart rejoice.

15. "I had my company fair and free,
Continually to visit me,
But now at last I have not one
Since I've become a servant man."

16. Now when the King from hunting came,
He called upon the good old man:
"What news? what news?" the King did say,
"What news hast thou for me to-day?"

17. "Brave news!" the old man he did say;
"Sweet William is a lady gay."
And when the King the truth had found,
His joys did more and more abound.

18. And then, for fear of any strife,
He took Sweet William for his wife:

The like before was never seen,
A servant man become a queen.

3. [The Famous Flower of Serving-Men]

Creighton and Senior, 1950, p. 62. From Mrs. R. W. Duncan, Dartmouth.

a I/Ly

The tune has been re-barred. The two 5/4 bars of the original copy begin two beats earlier.

1. I was by birth a lady fair,
My father's chief and only heir,
But when my good old father died
Then I was made a young knight's bride.

2. Although I got married unto this knight,
Although my mother owed me great spite,
She could not done me a greater harm
Than to slay the knight that lay on my arm.

3. She sent nine robbers that very same night,
She sent nine robbers to rob my knight,
She could not done me a greater harm
That to slay the knight that hung on my arm.

4. I dressed his wounds all alone alone
I laid him out all alone, alone,
They never left a thing for to lay him on
But the bloody sheets that they slew him on.

5. I dug his grave all alone, alone,
And buried him there all alone, alone,
I went unto the king one day
And there for services I did call.

6. "O can I be your kitchen cook,
Or can I be your stable boy,
Or can I be at your service all
For to wait on nobles when they shall call?"

7. "No you shan't be my kitchen cook,
No you shan't be my stable boy
But you shall be at my service all
To wait on noblemen when they do call."

8. . . . .
. . . .
"The very same words I heard him say,
Once I was a rich lady gay."

9. "If this be the lie you have told to me
   You shall be hung on the gallows tree,
   But if it be the truth you've told me
   I will pay you your wages and set you free."

10. Then he gave to me a gay gold ring
    For Willie to be crowned a king,
    For it don't look fit and it ain't a fit thing
    For a servant man to be crowned a queen.

3.2. "The Famous Flower of Serving Men"

Archive, School of Scottish Studies, rec. No. 1954/103/A1.
Sung by Jeannie Robertson, Aberdeen; learned from her
mother. Collected by Hamish Henderson. Transcribed by
Francis M. Collinson.

m π¹

My father built me a dandy bow'r
Wi' some fine roses and some fine flow'rs.
But my stepmother showed me her spite
For she sent that robber for to slain that knight.

For to rob my bow'r and to slain that knight
And they could not do me a greater harm
Than to kill the baby
That lay in my arms.

And they left me nothing
For to roll it in
But the bloody sheets
That my love lay in.

She laid her haid down upon a block
And she cut off her golden locks,
And she changed her name from young Elleanor fair,
She changed it to young Willie Dare.

Spoken: My mother said when she cut her hair off, she dressed

herself up as a young man and went to look for work. So she
came to a castle and in this castle was a young man, the master
of it. So when the butler took in the news to him that there was
a fine-looking young man at the door looking for work, and
wanted to be a stable boy, he said if he was fine looking as that,
he would be able to serve out the wine amongst his guests. So he
said fetch him in to see him. So when he saw him he had a
feeling it was not a young man . . . he had a feeling it was a
woman dressed up as a young man—so he give him the job of
serving out his wine to his guests. So as the weeks rolled on, he
knew then . . . as the weeks rolled on . . . that it was not a young
man but a young woman. So one day he told his housekeeper
to take her and dress her in silks as white as milk. And, of
course, she did that and she was found to be the finest looking
woman around the place for hundred of miles around. So he
married her . . . he fell in love with her and married her.

4. "Sweet William"

Flanders and Olney, 1953, p. 127. Sung by Mrs. Belle Richards, Colebrook, N.H., April 25, 1942. Collected by Marguerite Olney. From *Ballads Migrant in New England*,
edited by Helen Hartness Flanders and Marguerite Olney;
coypyright 1953 by Helen Hartness Flanders.

a Æ (inflected III)

1. My father was a noble knight.
   My mother was a lady bright,
   And I myself a lady gay,
   But now I wait as a servant boy.

2. My father built me a lovely bower.
   It was as fine as any flower.
   'Twas covered all o'er with the beautifulest green.
   O such a bower scarce ere was seen.

3. My father matched me with a knight.
   My stepmother owed me a dreadful spite.
   She sent four robbers all in the night
   To rob my bower and slay my knight.

4. 'Twas all alone they did him kill,
   And all alone they left him still.
   There was nothing left to wrap him in
   But the bloody sheet where my love was slain.

5. 'Twas all alone I dug his grave
   And all alone in it him I laid.
   While Christ was priest and I was clerk
   I laid my love in the clay-cold earth.

6. I saddled my horse and away did ride,
   With sword and pistols by my side;
   I cut off my hair and changed my name
   From Ellen Fair to Sweet William.

7. I rode till I came to the king's high hall
   And for my supper I did call.
   I gave the porter a gay, gold ring
   To carry my message unto the king.

8. The king came down and thus did say,
   "What can you do, young man, I pray?
   If you can do what I want you to,
   I'll hire you for a year or two."

9. " 'Tis I can be your kitchen cook
   Or I can be your stableman
   Or I can be waiter all in your hall
   And wait on the nobles as they call."

10. " 'Tis you shan't be my kitchen cook
    Nor you shan't be my stableman,
    But you shall be waiter all in my hall
    And wait on the nobles as they call."

11. The king being gone one day from home,
    There was no one there but the good old man.
    Sometimes she sighed, sometimes she sang,
    Sometimes the tears down her cheeks did run.

12. The king came home and thus did say,
    "What news, what news, old man, I pray?"
    "Good news, good news, my king," said he,
    "Sweet William is a lady gay."

13. "Go bring me down a suit of silk—
    It shall be white as any milk.
    I'll dress her up in the silk so fine.
    And make her rule over all that's mine."

4.1. "The Flower of Serving Men"

Pursley, *Folk Music Journal*, I, No. 3 (1967), pp. 147-48.
Sung by Albert Dee (58), Bartley, Hampshire, December
17, 1908. Noted by J. F. Guyer.

a I

1. My father he built me a shady bower,
   And covered it over with shamrock flowers,
   The finest bower that ever I see,
   My aged father he built for me.

2. My father he married me to a noble knight.
   My mother she owed me a dreadful spite;
   She sent nine robbers all in one night,
   To rob my bower and slay my knight.

3. How could she have done me a bigger harm,
   To murder my babies all in my arms?
   Left nothing at all for to wrap them in,
   But the bloody sheets that my love died in.

4. All alone, all alone then I will wash them,
   All alone, all alone I will bury them,
   Cut off my hair and I'll change my name,
   From Fair Eleanor to Sweet William.

5. I will saddle my horse and away I'll ride,
   And until I come to some fair king's side,
   And one of those servants I'll give a ring,
   That I might dissolve a gracious thing.

6. "It's do you want either horse or groom,
   Or do you want any stableman,
   Do you want a manservant all in your hall,
   To wait on the nobles when they do call?"

7. "It's we don't want neither horse nor groom,
   Nor we don't want ne'er a stableman,
   But we wants a manservant all in our hall,
   To wait on the nobles when they do call."

8. Then by and bye this young lord went out,
   . . . .
   Left no one at all but this gay old man,
   To keep company with Sweet William.

9. And when she found she was all alone,
   Took down her fiddle and played a tune,
   "Once my love was a rich, noble knight,
   And me myself was a lady bright."

10. Oh, then by and bye this young lord came home,
    "What news, what news, oh, my gay old man?"
    "Good news, good news, oh, my lord," said he,
    "Your servantman is a gay lady."

11. "Go and fetch me down, then, a pair of stays,
    That I might lace up her slender waist;
    Go and fetch me down that gay gownd of green,
    That I might dress her up like my queen."

12. "Oh, no! Oh, no! Oh, my lord," said she,
    "Pay me my wages and I'll go free,
    For I never heard tell of a stranger thing,
    As a servantman to become a queen."

The Knight and the Shepherd's Daughter

CHILD NO. 110

It is a valuable indication of the need to be sceptical about texts recited or printed without their tunes that, of Child's texts, A-L, only A, H, K, and L—that is, one-third—have any hint of refrain; while *every* copy collected *with* its tune has strong elements of refrain, ranging from a repeated last line to interlaced refrain and burden. The favorite pattern is a four-phrase tune; but the fifth phrase frequently extends beyond the normal four-pulse length and tends to become two phrases; and in several variants has become a four-phrase chorus or burden. A solitary instance occurs of refrain after the first and last lines, without any such element after the second, and without any repeated lines. This procedure is only paralleled, so far as I recall, in a Dorsetshire tune for "Robin Hood and the Bishop of Hereford" (Child No. 144).

The burden-texts appear to be borrowed from other songs. Such is Child's K, with its familiar "We'll go no more a roving, &c." In all probability that text was sung to the "Jolly Beggar" tune as given in the *The Scots Musical Museum*, No. 266, with its distinctive additional last phrase (cf. Child No. 279). Baring-Gould's "Blow away ye morning breezes" goes also with the "Baffled Knight" (No. 112), and is associated with sea songs as well.

The extant tunes range from Ionian to Æolian, the English rather favoring the former, the Scottish the latter, modal areas. The only American examples known to me were collected by Barry in New England. I am willing to suppose, on account of rhythm chiefly, that all the tunes of Group A have an ultimate tribal relationship. But there is plenty of variety. The first two subgroups appear to have the most substantial claims to traditional circulation, and it is striking that national boundaries are overstepped in both.

TUNES WITH TEXTS

GROUP Aa

2. [Earl Richard]

Sharp MSS., 456/571. Also in Sharp and Marson, 2nd series, 1905, p. 2; and Sharp, 1916, p. 6. Sung by John Swain, Donyatt, December 26, 1904.

p I (IV possibly inflected)

1. There was a little shepherd maid
   Keep sheep all on the hill
   And then comed a young man
   And sweared he'd have his will.
       Line twine the willow dee.

2. Now you've a-layed me down young man
   Pray help me up again,
   Now you've had your will of me
   Pray tell to me your name.

3. O some do call me Jack, fair maid,
   O some do call me John.
   But when I'm in the fair King's court
   My name is Sweet William.

4. So the king called up his merry men all,
   By one, by two, by three,
   Sweet William used to be the fore one of all
   But long behind came he.

5. But he brought up full fifty pound,
   Brought up all in a glove.
   Take this, take this, fair maid and go
   And seek for some other true love.

6. So I don't want none of thy gold
   Nor any of your fees
   But I will have thy whole body
   The king has given to me.

7. So the dog shall eat the flour thee sowed (?)
   And thou shalt eat the bran.
   I'll make thee rue the day and hour
   That ever thou wast born.

4. [Earl Richard]

Sharp MSS., 1589/1439. Also in Sharp, *JFSS*, V, No. 18 (1914), p. 88(2). Sung by Alfred Emery (78), Othery, Somerset, April 4, 1908.

a M (inflected III)

Miss Broadwood compares this with "The Greenland Whale Fishery" (*JFSS*, II, No. 9 [1906], p. 243).

1. It's [o]f a farmer's daughter dear
   Keeping sheep all on the plain.
   Who should ride by but Knight William
   And he got drunk by wine.
      [Right fol lol, the diddle al the dee.]

2. He onlighted off his horse
   And gentley laid her down
   And when he had his will of her
   He rosed her up again.

3. Now since you've had your will of me
   Pray tell to me your name
   For when this dear little baby's born
   I might call it the same.

4. Sometimes they call me Jack, say he,
   Sometimes they call me John,
   But when I come to the King's high court
   They call me Knight William.

5. He put his foot all in the stirrup,
   Away then he did ride;
   She tied a handkerchief all round her waist
   And followed the horse's side.

6. She run till she came to the riverside
   She fall on her belly and swim
   And when she came to the other side
   She took to her heels and run.

7. She run till she came to the King's high court
   She loudly knock-ed and she ring;
   None was so ready as the King himself
   To let this fair maid in.

8. Good morning to you, kind sir, said she,
   Good morning fair maid, said he.
   Have you got a knight all in your house
   This day have a-robbed me.

9. Have he robbed you of any of your gold
   Or any of your store?
   Have he robbed you of your gold ring
   Which you wear on your little finger?

10. He ain't robbed me of any of my gold
    Nor any of my store,
    But he's robbed me of my maidenhead
    That grieves my heart so sore.

11. And if he is a married man
    A-hanged he shall be,
    And if he is a single man
    His body I'll give to thee.

12. The King called up all his men,
    By one, by two, by three,
    Knight William used to be the fore best man
    But all behind comes he.

13. A-cursed be that very hour
    That I got drunk by wine
    To have the farmer's daughter here
    To be a true love of mine.

14. If I am a farmer's daughter
    Pray leave to me alone,
    If you make me a lady of one thousand land
    I can make thee lord of ten.

15. And then to church they both did went
    And they small things were doned.
    She appeared like a Duke's daughter
    And he like a squire's son.

GROUP Ab

8. [The Knight and the Shepherd's Daughter]

Kidson, 1891, p. 20. Sung by Benjamin Holgate, Leeds.

p D (inflected VII)

1. There was a shepherd's daughter
     Who sat upon yon hill,
   There came a young man riding by,
     Who swore he'd have his will.
   Fol lol lay, Fol lol di diddle lol di day.

2. There was a shepherd's daughter,
     Who kept sheep on yon hill;
   There came a young man riding by,
     Who swore he'd have his will.
       Fol lol lay, etc.

3. He took her by the lilly white hand,
     And by her silken sleeve;
   .   .   .   .
       Fol lol lay, etc.

4. .   .   .   .
     Or tell to me your name,
       Fol lol lay, etc.

5. "Oh, some they call me Jack, sweetheart,
     And some they call me Will;
   But when I ride the king's high-gate,
     [My] name is sweet William."
       Fol lol lay, etc.

11. "Earl Richard," or "Shepherd's Daughter"

Sharp MSS., 2663/. Also in Sharp, *JFSS*, V, No. 18 (1914), p. 90(4). Sung by Robert Feast (67), at Ely Union, Cambridge, September 11, 1911. Learned from his grandfather, an old Waterloo soldier.

p Æ/D

He took her round the middle so small
He laid her on the ground
After he had his will of her
He picked her up again
So a-lay, lay a lay right down

14. [The Knight and the Shepherd's Daughter]

Greig MSS., I, p. 154. Also in Greig and Keith, 1952, p. 89(1a). Sung by Alexander Robb, New Deer, March 1906.

p Æ/D

Sometimes they call me Jockie
An' sometimes they call me Jim,
When I'm in the king's high court,
Guilielmi is my name.
Hey O the merry gold
In the dowrin, In the dancin'
Hey O the merry gold
In the dowrin' ae.

GROUP AC

16. [The Shepherd's Daughter]

Kinloch, 1827, App'x. to p. 25; text, p. 25.

a D/Æ, ending on V

The same tune is to be found associated with Child Nos. 231, 236, 251.

1. There was a shepherd's dochter,
    Kept sheep on yonder hill;
   There cam a knicht o' courage bricht,
    And he wad hae his will.*

2. He has tane her by the milk-white hand,
    Gien her a gown o' green;—
   "Tak ye that, fair may," he said,
    "Na mair o' me'll be seen."

3. "Sin ye hae tane your wills o' me,
    Your wills o' me ye've tane;
   Sin ye hae tane your wills o' me,
    Pray tell to me your name."

4. "O, some they ca' me Jack, ladie,
    And ithers ca' me John,
   But whan I am in the King's court,
    Sweet William is my name."

5. She has kilted up her green claithing,
    A little below the knee,
   And she has gane to the king's court,
    As fast as she could hie.

6. And whan she cam unto the king,
    She knelt low on her knee;—
   "There is a man into your court,
    This day has robbed me."

7. "Has he robbed ye o' your gowd,
    Or of your white money,
   Or robbed ye o' the flow'ry branch,
    The flow'r of your bodie."

8. "He has na robb'd me of my gowd,
    Nor of my white money;
   But he's robb'd me o' the flow'ry branch,
    The flow'r of my bodie."

9. "O gin he be a bondsman,
    High hangit sall he be;
   But gin he be a freeman,
    He sall weel provide for thee."

10. The king has call'd on his nobles all,
    By therty and by three;
   Sweet William should hae been the foremost,
    But the hindmost man was he.

11. "Do ye mind yon Shepherd's dochter,
    Ye met on yonder hill,
   Whan a' her flocks were feeding round,
    Of her ye took your will."

12. Then he's tane out a purse o' gowd,
    Tied up intil a glove;—
   "Sae, tak ye that, fair may," he says,
    "And choice for you a love."

13. O he's tane out three hundred pund,
    Tied up intil a purse—
"See, tak ye that, fair may," he says,
"And that will pay the nurse."

14. "I'll neither have your gowd," she says,
    "Nor yet your white money,
But I will hae the king's grant,
    That he has granted me."

15. He has tane her on a milk-white steed,
    Himself upon anither,
And to his castle they hae rode,
    Like sister and like brither.

16. O ilka nettle that they cam to—
    "O weill mote you grow,
For monie a day, my minnie and me
    Hae pilkit at your pow."

17. O ilka mill that they cam to—
    "O weill mote you clap,
For monie a day, my minnie and me
    Hae buckled up our lap.

18. "You're the king o' England's ae brither,
    I trust weill that ye be;
I'm the Earl o' Stamford's ae dochter,
    He has na mae but me."

19. O saw ye ere sic a near marriage,
    Atween the ane and the ither,—
The Earl o' Stamford's ae dochter,
    And the king o' England's brither.

*Kinloch says the song has "the very common chorus of *Diddle, diddle*, &c. accompanying each verse in singing" (p. 14).

17.1. "I am the forester o' this land"

Archive, School of Scottish Studies, rec. No. 1952/26/A1. Sung by John Strachan, Fyvie, Aberdeenshire. Collected by Hamish Henderson. Transcribed by Donna Etherington.

m I (ending on *V*)

I am the forester o this land
As ye may plainly see,
An' it's the mantle o' your maidenheid
That I maun hae fae thee.

Chorus:

Wi ma roo rum rurrity rye rum rurrity
right ma wurrity an

He has taen her by the mulk-white haun,
An by the lea-lands-leave;
He's laid her doon. . . .

The Baffled Knight

CHILD NO. 112

FROM the days of the troubadours this gay song appears to have remained a favorite. It has been made over again and again by the broadside men—and others—following the manner of the day. But successive refurbishings have not entirely absorbed the old, and a variety of tunes has survived in the record. Those current in the seventeenth century seem to have been tossed aside in the eighteenth, although the earliest is probably only semi-popular in its printed form, and may have been known in a simpler guise. By the end of the seventeenth century another pattern had been adopted, echoed more than once or twice in Playford's dancing-tunes, and found continually in other connections down to the present. It is related to the ubiquitous family of "Boyne Water," and also, apparently, to the "Bonny Broom" (cf. No. 217). This fashion, too, was discarded by our song, except for rare traces, and was superseded by the one most current today in England, a jolly plagal tune in common or quick time, and almost always in a major tonality. It has been met as a capstan shanty. It consistently shows a burden or chorus of stanza-length, with a text about the winds that blow. The more recent of the Scottish variants seem to have stayed within hailing distance of their English cousins.

(On the theme of this ballad, our closest approach to a *bona fide* pastourelle, the reader should consult William Powell Jones, *The Pastourelle*, 1934, and his bibliographical references.)

TUNES WITH TEXTS

1. "The Over Courteous Knight"

Ritson, 1790, p. 160. From Ravenscroft, *Deuteromelia*, 1609 (Child's A text). Also in D'Urfey, 1719-20, III, p. 37.

m M (inflected VII)

1. Yonder comes a courteous Knight,
    Lustely raking ouer the lay,
  He was well ware of a bonny lasse,
    As she came wandring ouer the way.
        Then she sang downe a downe, hey downe derry,
        Then she, &c.

2. Ioue you speed fayre Lady, he said,
    Among the leaues that be so greene;
  If I were a king and wore a crowne,
    Full soone faire Lady shouldst thou be a queen.
        Then she sang, downe, &c.

3. Also Ioue saue you faire Lady,
    Among the Roses that be so red;
  If I haue not my will of you,
    Full soone faire Lady shall I be dead.
        Then she sang, &c.

4. Then he lookt East, then hee lookt West,
    Hee lookt North, so did he South;
  He could not finde a priuy place,
    For all lay in the Diuels mouth.
        Then she sang, &c.

5. If you will carry me, gentle sir,
    A mayde vnto my fathers hall,
  Then you shall haue your will of me,
    Vnder purple and vnder paule.
        Then she sang, &c.

6. He set her vp vpon a Steed,
    And him selfe vpon another:
  And all the day he rode her by,
    As though they had been sister and brother.
        Then she sang, &c.

7. When she came to her fathers hall,
    It was well walled round about;
  She yode in at the wicket gate
    And shut the foure ear'd foole without.
        Then she sang, &c.

8. You had me (quoth she) abroad in the field,
    Among the corne, amidst the hay;
  Where you might had your will of mee,
    For, in good faith sir, I neuer said nay.
        Then she sang, &c.

9. Ye had me also amid the field,
    Among the rushes that were so browne;
  Where you might had your will of me,
    But you had not the face to lay me downe.
        Then she sang, &c.

10. He pulled out his nut-browne sword,
    And wipt the rust off with his sleeue;
  And said, Ioues curse come to his heart,
    That any woman would believe.
        Then she sang, &c.

11. When you haue your owne true loue,
    A mile or twaine out of the towne,
    Spare not for her gay clothing,
    But lay her body flat on the ground.
        Then she sang, &c.

GROUP D

4. [There was a silly Shepherd Swain]

Johnson, V, [1796], No. 477, p. 490 (repr. 1853).

p π⁴

1. There was a silly shepherd swain,
    Kept sheep upon a hill,
   He laid his pipe and crook aside,
    And there he slept his fill.
   He laid his pipe and crook aside,
    And there he slept his fill.

2. He looked east, he looked west,
    Then gave an under-look,
   And there he spied a lady fair,
    Swimming in a brook,
        And there, &c.

3. He rais'd his head frae his green bed,
    And then approach'd the maid,
   Put on your claiths, my dear, he says,
    And be ye not afraid.
        Put on, &c.

4. 'Tis fitter for a lady fair,
    To sew her silken seam,
   Than to get up in a May morning,
    And strive against the stream.
        Than to get, &c.

5. If you'll not touch my mantle,
    And let my claiths alane;
   Then I'll give you as much money,
    As you can carry hame.
        Then I'll, &c.

6. O! I'll not touch your mantle,
    And I'll let your claiths alane;
   But I'll tak you out of the clear water,
    My dear, to be my ain,
        But I'll tak, &c.

7. And when she out of the water came,
    He took her in his arms;
   Put on your claiths, my dear, he says,
    And hide those lovely charms.
        Put on your, &c.

8. He mounted her on a milk-white steed,
    Himself upon anither;
   And all along the way they rode,
    Like sister and like brither.
        And all along, &c.

9. When she came to her father's yate,
    She tirled at the pin;
   And ready stood the porter there,
    To let this fair maid in.
        And ready, &c.

10. And when the gate was opened,
    So nimbly's she whipt in;
   Pough! you're a fool without, she says,
    And I'm a maid within.
        Pough! you're, &c.

11. Then fare ye well, my modest boy,
    I thank you for your care;
   But had you done what you should do,
    I ne'er had left you there.
        But had you, &c.

12. Oh! I'll cast aff my hose and shoon,
    And let my feet gae bare,
   And gin I meet a bonny lass,
    Hang me, if her I spare.
        And gin I, &c.

13. In that do as you please, she says,
    But you shall never more
   Have the same opportunity;
    With that she shut the door.
        Have the, &c.

14. There is a gude auld proverb,
    I've often heard it told,
   He that would not when he might,
    He should not when he would.
        He that, &c.

GROUP F

6. "Blow the Winds, I-Ho!"

Bruce and Stokoe, 1882, p. 81. Also in Stokoe and Reay,
n.d. [1893?], p. 112.

a Æ

16. "Blow away the Morning Dew"

Sharp and Marson, 1st series, 1904, p. 16. Also in Sharp, 1916, p. 46. Composite tune, from the singing of Mrs. Lucy White, Hambridge, and Mrs. Price, Compton Martin.

p I

There was a shepherd's son,
  He kept sheep on yonder hill;
He laid his pipe and his crook aside,
  And there he slept his fill.

And blow the winds, I-ho!
  Sing, blow the winds, I-ho!
Clear away the morning dew,
  And blow the winds, I-ho!

There was a farmer's son
  Kept sheep all on the hill;
And he walked out one May morning
  To see what he could kill.

And sing Blow away the morning Dew,
  The Dew and the Dew,
Blow away the morning Dew
  How sweet the Winds do blow.

The Great Silkie of Sule Skerry

CHILD NO. 113

CHILD owed the belated recovery of this extraordinary ballad to his friend and co-worker, William Macmath, who spotted it in the *Proceedings* of the Scottish Society of Antiquaries for 1852. A correspondent of Karl Blind (*Contemporary Review*, XL [1881], p. 404) quoted a stanza that appears below (5), and in the same form. The ballad was awkwardly introduced as the last item in Child's second volume, in order to clear the way for the group of woodland ballads that fills the first half of Volume III. Child remarks that it properly belongs after No. 40, among the ballads of shape-changers and mortals who traffic with folk of the Other-world.

The ballad was not again recovered until the summer of 1938, when the distinguished authority on Swedish folksong in Finland, Dr. Otto Andersson, cruising about the Orkneys, came upon a singer who remembered the tune. His essay should be consulted for the circumstances of the find.

This solitary musical example is an authentic Mixolydian variant of the air particularly associated with "Hind Horn" (No. 17), but met as well in a good many other British and American connections.

TUNE WITH TEXT

[The Grey Selchie of Sule Skerry]

Andersson, *Budkavlen*, XXVI (1947), p. 115, with text contributed by Miss Gilchrist. Tune and text of fifth stanza sung by John Sinclair, Orkney Islands, summer of 1938. Also in Collinson and Dillon, 1952, p. 48; and in Thomson, 1954, p. 204. Reprinted in Andersson, *Budkavlen*, XXXIII (1954), p. 39, with a slightly different text taken from an Orkney newspaper, *The Orcadian*, June 11, 1934.

a M

1. In Norway land there lived a maid.
   "Hush, ba, loo lillie," this maid began,
   "I know not where my baby's father is,
   whether by land or sea does he travel in."

2. It happened on a certain day,
   when this fair lady fell fast asleep,
   that in cam' a good grey selchie
   and set him down at her bed feet.

3. Saying "Awak', awak' my pretty fair maid,
   for oh, how sound as thou dost sleep,
   an' I'll tell thee where thy baby's father is,
   he's sittin' close at thy bed feet."

4. "I pray come tell to me thy name,
   Oh, tell me where does thy dwelling be?"
   "My name is good Hein Mailer,
   I earn my livin' oot o' the sea."

5. "I am a man upon the land,
   I am a selchie in the sea,
   an' whin I'm far from every strand,
   my dwelling is [in] Shool Skerry."

6. "Alas, alas this woeful fate,
   this weary fate that's been laid on me,
   that a man should come from the Wast o' Hoy
   to the Norway lands to have a bairn wi' me."

7. "My dear, I'll wed thee with a ring,
   with a ring, my dear, will I wed with thee."
   "Thoo may go wed thee weddens wi' whom thoo wilt,
   for I'm sure thoo'll never wed none wi' me."

8. "Thoo will nurse my little wee son
   for seven long years upon thy knee;
   an' at the end o' seven long years
   I'll come back and pay the nursing fee."

9. She's nursed her little wee son
   for seven long years upon her knee,
   an' at the end o' seven long years
   he came back wi' gold and white monie.

10. He says, "My dear, I'll wed thee wi' ring,
    wi' a ring, my dear, I'll wed wi' thee."
    "Thoo mat go wed thee weddens wi' whom thoo wilt,
    for I'm sure thoo'll never wed none wi' me."

11. "But I'll put a gold chain around his neck,
    an' a gey good gold chain it'll be,
    that if ever he comes to the Norway lands,
    thoo may bae a gey good guess on he."

12. "An thoo will get a gunner good,
    an' a gey good gunner it will be,
    an' he'll gae out a May morning
    an' shoot the son an' the grey selchie."

13. Oh, she has got a gunner good,
    an' a gey good gunner it was he.
    An' he gaed oot on a May morning
    an' he shot the son an' the grey selchie.

"When the gunner returned and showed the Norway woman the gold chain which he found round the neck of the young seal she realised that her son had perished, and gave expression to her sorrow in the last verse."

14. "Alas, alas, this woeful fate,
    this weary fate that's been laid on me."
    An' ance or twice she sobbed and sighed,
    an' her tender heart did brak in three.

Johnie Cock

CHILD NO. 114

ALTHOUGH Percy received a copy (Child A) of this very fine ballad in 1780, he did not introduce it into the fourth edition of the *Reliques*, and it was left for Scott to publish it for the first time. Scott published a conflated text and it is significant that his version has no refrain line. Scott was not interested in it as song. Nothing could be more distinct than the consistent refrain-pattern in the musical tradition. Only two copies lack a repetition of the fourth line of each quatrain as refrain, and both of these seem to have been inexactly set down. Of Child's texts, A to M, eight have the repetition.

This consistency of five-phrase tunes would suggest a single melodic tradition for the ballad. But modally, at any rate, the tunes subdivide into two classes, one in the Ionian galaxy, the other in the Dorian and Æolian. The first sort has relatives, in one or two of its forms, among the tunes found with Child No.

110, No. 236, and perhaps No. 78; the second is doubtless allied to the "Lazarus" tribe, and perhaps is made use of by "Trooper and Maid" (No. 299). In both its branches it is a sturdy and invigorating thing. The ballad's tradition appears not to have taken root south of the Border, in spite of melodic affiliates; but it was found in Ireland in the middle of the last century. Mrs. Harris's copy, in the first group, is perhaps of earliest record (learned c. 1790). The ballad has survived in Aberdeenshire down to our own day and living traditional singers continue to provide us with fresh variants. In Aberdeenshire, early in the present century, Greig collected seven records, all of which are of the second modal group.

The Palmer, or auld carl, in this ballad reminds one of Carl Hood in "Earl Brand" (No. 7).

TUNES WITH TEXTS

GROUP Aa

1. "Johnie of Breadislee"

Motherwell, 1827, App'x., No. 22; text, App'x., p. xxi. Also in Blaikie MS., NL Scotland MS. 1578, No. 127, p. 39; and Chambers, 1844, p. 13. From A. Blaikie, Paisley.

p π¹

Variants a, b, and c are the readings of the Blaikie MS. It appears to be a bar short in the fourth phrase.

> Johnie rose up in a May mornin,
> Called for water to wash his hands—
> Gar loose to me the gude gray dogs
> That are bound wi' iron bands.

3a. "What news, what news my gay old man?"

Hudson MS., No. 704, c. 1840. From Edward Clements.

p M

4. "Johnnie Brod"

Harris MS., No. 18; text, fol. 25. Also in Child, 1882-98, V, p. 419; text, III, p. 8(G). From Mrs. Amelia Harris; learned from an old nurse during childhood in Perthshire, late eighteenth century. Noted by her daughter.

p I/M

As Keith has observed, a variant of this tune is given by Kinloch (1827) for Child No. 110 ("The Shepherd's Dochter").

> 1. Johnnie Brad, on a May mornin,
> Called for water to wash his hands,
> An there he spied his twa blude-hounds,
> Waur bound in iron bands, bands,
> Waur bound in iron bands.
>
> 2. Johnnie's taen his gude bent bow,
> Bot an his arrows kene,
> An strippit himsel o the scarlet red,
> An put on the licht Lincoln green.
>
> 3. Up it spak Johnnie's mither,
> An' a wae, wae woman was she:
> I beg you bide at hame, Johnnie,
> I pray be ruled by me.
>
> 4. Baken bread ye sall nae lack,
> An wine you sall lack nane;
> Oh, Johnnie, for my benison,
> I beg you bide at hame!
>
> 5. He has made a solemn aith,
> Atween the sun an the mune,

That he wald gae to the gude green wood,
  The dun deer to ding doon.

6. He luiket east, he luiket wast,
   An in below the sun,
   An there he spied the dun deer,
   Aneath a bush o brume.

7. The firsten shot that Johnnie shot,
   He wounded her in the side;
   The nexten shot that Johnnie shot,
   I wat he laid her pride.

8. He's eaten o the venison,
   An drunken o the blude,
   Until he fell as sound asleep
   As though he had been dead.

9. Bye there cam a silly auld man,
   And a silly auld man was he,
   An he's on to the Seven Foresters,
   As fast as he can flee.

10. "As I cam in by yonder haugh,
    An in among the scroggs,
    The bonniest boy that ere I saw
    Lay sleepin atween his dogs."

. . . .

11. The firsten shot that Johnnie shot,
    He shot them a' but ane,
    An he flang him owre a milk-white steed,
    Bade him bear tidings hame.

The text here printed is from Child. In the tune MS., where the title
is "Johnnie Brod," the first stanza is as follows:

Johnnie Brod in a May mornin',
  Got water for his hands,
An' he ca'd on his twa bluid hounds,
  Waur bound wi iron bands, bands,
  Waur bound wi iron bands.

GROUP Ab

9. "Johnnie o' Braidisleys"

Greig and Keith, 1925, p. 95(b); text, p. 93. From Duncan
MS., No. 242. Sung by Alexander Mackay, Alford;
learned c. 1860.

p D/Æ

1. Johnnie arose on a May mornin,
   Called for water to wash his hands,
   Says, "Gae lowse to me thae twa greyhounds
   That lie bound in iron bands,
   That lie bound in iron bands."

2. When Johnnie's mother she heard o this,
   Her hands wi dool she wrang,

Says, "Johnnie, for your venison
  To the green woods dinna gang.

3. "We hae plenty o the white bread,
   An' plenty o the good red wine,
   So, Johnnie, for your venison
   To the greenwood dinna gang."

4. But Johnnie has breskit his good benbow,
   His arrows one by one,
   An' he is on to the gay green woods
   For to pull the dun deer doon.

5. As he gaed doon through Merrimoss,
   An doon amon yon scroggs,
   Twas there he spied a dun deer lie
   At the back o a bush o broom.

6. Johnnie shot, an' the dun deer lap,
   He had wounded her in the side,
   An' atween the water an' the wood,
   An' the greyhounds laid her pride.

7. Johnnie has handled the deer so weel,
   Taen oot her liver an' lungs,
   An' he has fed the dogs wi them
   As though they'd been yearl's sons.

8. They ate so much o the raw venison,
   An' they drank so much o the blood,
   That Johnnie an' his twa greyhounds
   Fell asleep as gin they'd been dead.

9. By there cam a silly aul man,
   Some ill death may he dee;
   An' he is on to the seven foresters
   For to tell what he did see.

10. "What news, what news, ye silly aul man,
    What news hae ye to gie?"—
    "Nae news, nae news," said the silly aul man,
    "But what my twa een did see.

11. "As I cam doon through Merriemoss,
    An' doon amon yon scroggs,
    An' the bonniest youth that ever I saw
    Lay a-sleepin atween twa dogs.

12. "The coat he bore upon his back
    Was o the Linkum twine,
    An' the stock he wore aroon his neck
    It was pearl an' precious stone.

13. "The buttons he wore upon his coat
    They were o the gold so good,
    An' the twa greyhounds that he lay atween,
    An' their mouths were a' dyed wi blood."

14. Twas oot then spak the first forester,
    An angry man was he,
    Says, "An this be Johnnie o Braidisleys,
    My faith, we'll gar him dee."

15. Twas oot then spak the second forester,
    His sister's son was he,
    Says, "An this be Johnnie o Braidisleys,
    We'd better lat him be."

16. Twas oot then spak the seventh forester,
    He was forester ower them a',
    Says, "An this be Johnnie o Braidisleys,
    An' to him an' we'll gang."

17. The first shots that the foresters fired,
    An' they wounded him in the knee,
    An' the second shots that the foresters fired,
    An' the red blood blinded his ee'.

18. As Johnnie awakened oot o his sleep,
    An angry man was he,
    Says, "Ye micht hae waukened me oot o my sleep,
    Ere the red blood blinded my e'e.

19. "Gin my bow prove true, as she used to do,
    An' my courage do not fail,
    I'll mak ye dearly rue that day
    Ye cam to the Dinspeerhill."

20. He planted his back against an oak,
    His foot against a stone,
    An' he has shot the seven foresters,
    He has shot them a' but one.

21. He has broken three o that one's ribs,
    Likewise his collar bone,

An' he laid him twa faul' ower his steed,
    Bade him carry the tidings home.

22. "Noo whaur will I get a bonnie little bird
    That wad sing as I will say,
    That will fly on to my mother's bower,
    An' tell them to tak Johnnie away?"

23. The starling flew to his mother's bower,
    It whistlèd an' sang,
    An' aye the owercome o its sang
    Was, Johnnie tarries lang!

24. Some o them pu'd o the hawthorn's bush,
    An' some o the hollin tree,
    An' mony, mony were the men
    At the fetchin o young Johnnie.

25. Noo Johnnie's good benbow is broke,
    An' his twa greyhounds they're slain;
    Noo Johnnie sleeps in Merriemoss,
    An' his huntin days are done.

26. But woe be to yon silly aul man,
    An ill death may he dee,
    An' the highest tree in Merriemoss
    Shall be his gallows tree.

Robin Hood's Death

CHILD NO. 120

FOR the Percy Folio text of this ballad, Child A, there is no trace of a refrain, nor any clue to the proper tune, by name or note. Child Ba, nearly a century and a half later (1786), is directed to be sung to the tune of "Robin Hood's last farewell, etc." There is no extant Robin Hood ballad that bears this title, and no tune has survived with the text; so that we are still in the dark. Child Ba has a refrain interpolated as the second and last lines of the stanza: "Down a down a down a down," and "Hey, etc." The latter abbreviation would seem to indicate a repetition of the second line; but the line is given at the end of the ballad as "Hey down a derry derry down." As Child notes after Ritson, however, the last two stanzas are apparently adopted from "Robin Hood and the Valiant Knight" (No. 153), so that this latter form of the refrain may be incorrect for the present ballad. Moreover, the Bb form of the ballad, in other respects textually very close, quite lacks any refrain, as well as any indication of a named tune.

Rimbault says (Gutch, *Robin Hood*, 1847, II, p. 435), on no authority, but obviously on the sole evidence of the refrain, that this ballad, like Nos. 135, 136, 141, and 145, was sung to the tune of the "Three Ravens," which he quotes from Ravenscroft's *Melismata*, 1611, declaring, again upon his own authority, that the tune "is there adapted to" the "Three Ravens" text. This we need not believe unless we choose; but adaptation in one direction or the other there would have to be, for the tune would not fit any extant form of "Robin Hood's Death" without some textual modification. At the least, the further refrain element "with a down," would need to be added after the (proper) second line of the quatrain. Rimbault goes on to remark that this tune is traditionally still current (i.e., c. 1850) in most counties of England, and that he has eight different versions of it; but he does not claim that any of these has been found with this or any other Robin Hood ballad; and it is probable that the texts were in most or all cases some form of the "Three Ravens" ballad. We have, therefore, no very secure ground for associating the tune with the present ballad. For "The Three Ravens," see Child No. 26.

Thus we reach the present century without any reliable musical record. In 1913, Miss Martha Davis contributed a version of the ballad, with a tune, current in her family for three generations, apparently reaching back to the eighteenth century in American oral tradition. Though found in Virginia, it went back through Maryland to a Pennsylvania settlement of Scotch-Irish.

The tune is interesting, and valuable at any rate as the sole recorded traditional air for this ballad. It is a two-strain melody, a Æ/P, if its final be tonic, but possibly p D/Æ, with its tonic a fourth above the final. Confirmation of its genuine association with Robin Hood comes in the fact that a variant was picked up recently in Kentucky to a text of No. 125, q. v. Furthermore, it may well be a form of "Arthur a Bland," which itself is the proper early tune of No. 126 and found with a considerable number of other Robin Hood ballads.

TUNE WITH TEXT

"Robin Hood's Death"

Davis, 1929, p. 586; text, p. 390. Contributed by Martha M. Davis, Harrisonburg, Rockingham County, Va., April 8, 1913. Text dictated by her grandmother in 1882.

a Æ/P (or p D/Æ, ending on *V*)

1. As Robin Hood and Little John
   Walked by a bank of broom,
   Said Robin in a mournful voice,
   "I fear approaching doom.

2. "And since the day that we did meet,
   Much mirth and joy we saw;
   To many a poor man have we given
   Since we became outlaw.

3. "But now, alas! these days are o'er,
   For I am taken ill;
   I must away to Kirkley Hall
   To try physician's skill."

4. "Fare thee well," said Little John,
   "O master dear, farewell;
   And when I see your face once more,
   Good news I hope you'll tell."

5. He is away to Kirkley Hall
   As fast as he could hie,
   But ere that he could reach that length
   He was nigh like to die.

6. And when he came to Kirkley Hall,
   He knocked and made great noise;
   His cousin flew to let him in,
   Full well she knew his voice.

7. "Will you sit down, dear cousin?" she said,
   "And drink some wine with me?"
   "I will neither eat nor drink
   Until I blooded be."

   .   .   .   .

8. When he perceived their treachery,
   Away he strove to fly

Out of the window, but could not,
   It was so very high.

9. Then he picked up his bugle horn
   That hung down by his knee;
He tried with all his might and main
   If he could blow blasts three.

10. Then Little John heard his master's call
   As he sat under a tree.
"I think," said he, "my master's ill,
   He blows so wearily."

11. Then he is away to Kirkley Hall,
   Its doors broke open wide,
And when he came to Robin Hood
   He knelt down by his side.

12. "What shall I do, dear master?" he said,
   "That you avenged may be?
Shall I burn cursed Kirkley Hall
   And all its nunnery?"

13. "O nay, O nay," said Robin Hood,
   "I ne'er in all my life
Burned any kirk nor any nun,
   Nor widow, child, nor wife.

14. "Nor shall it now be said of me
   In this my dying hour
Upon the head of Christian folks
   Destruction I did pour.

15. "Now bring me here my much-loved bow.
   One arrow I'll let fly,
And whereso'er that arrow lights,
   There let my body lie.

16. "Let green grass grow upon my grave,
   By my side my bow so good,
At my head a stone that all may read,
   'Here lies bold Robin Hood.'"

17. Underneath this little stone
   Lies Robert, Earl of Huntingdon.

Robin Hood and Little John

CHILD NO. 125

THE earliest copies of this ballad which are now extant are of the eighteenth century, although Thackeray's press is known to have printed it, late in the seventeenth, and doubtless it derives from early materials. The indicated tune is "Arthur a Bland," for which see the next ballad (No. 126).

Child has argued that the present ballad is that which must have been meant in references to "Robin Hood and the Stranger," to which "Robin Hood and the Tanner," "Robin Hood and the Beggar," "Robin Hood and the Bishop" (Nos. 126, 133, and 143) are all directed to be sung. Three other ballads of Robin Hood are to be sung to the tune of "Robin Hood and the Beggar," which therefore is to be equated as to tune; and two others to "Arthur a Bland," the named tune of this present ballad. All the ballads so qualified are alike in having mid-rhyme in line three of the stanza. Child's reason for thinking that the present ballad would be called "Robin Hood and the Stranger" is that in it Robin's antagonist is eleven times called "the stranger." In this feature it is exactly matched by "Robin Hood newly revived" (No. 128). Child thinks, however, that since the last-named ballad does not have the middle rhyme, there is "a slightly superior probability to the supposition that ['Robin Hood and Little John'], or rather some older version of it (for the one we have is in a rank seventeenth-century style), had the secondary title of 'Robin Hood and the Stranger' " (1882-98, III, p. 133). By supposing an older version Child seems inadvertently to have overturned his own argument, for the middle rhyme need not—and in his opinion (cf. *sub* No. 122, his last paragraph of headnote, p. 116)

would not—have been a feature of the earlier version. The tune of "Robin Hood newly revived," he grants in a footnote, was likewise "Arthur a Bland." Moreover, not only No. 128, but Nos. 130, 150, and possibly 129, were all to be sung to the same tune, yet 130 and 150 have the middle rhyme, whilst 128 and 129 lack it. And, contrariwise, 137, 151, 152, and 153, none of which goes to this tune, have still the middle rhyme. There is no evidence, then, in either text or tune, to tilt the scales in favor of Child's supposition that the present ballad rather than "Robin Hood newly revived," is "Robin Hood and the Stranger." Ritson gave his judgment in favor of the other (No. 128); and Child has scrupulously acknowledged that it (No. 128) is found in the 1663 garland along with "Robin Hood and the Bishop," "Robin Hood and the Butcher" and the other ballads of the group first mentioned above, but that "Robin Hood and Little John" is not among them—a fact which might finally tip the balance in favor of No. 128.

Very recently, a copy of this ballad was recovered in Kentucky from an oral source, where it could be followed back in family tradition for two generations. The text is somewhat disconcertingly close to the eighteenth-century form. The tune is, as has been remarked, a variant of that found in Virginia with "Robin Hood's Death" (No. 120). Its second strain would seem to be related to the "Jolly Pinder" or "Bailiff's Daughter" tune which Rimbault has produced from the Gostling MS. (Gutch, *Robin Hood*, 1847, II, p. 434). This is reassuring evidence of its traditional authenticity.

TUNES WITH TEXTS

1. "Robin Hood and Little John"

Archive, School of Scottish Studies. Sung by John Strachan, Aberdeenshire. Also on Caedmon rec. No. TC 1146(A4). Collected by Hamish Henderson for the School of Scottish Studies. Transcribed by Francis M. Collinson, 1963.

a I

When Robin Hood was about twenty years old,
  He happened to meet little John.
A jolly brisk blade, just fit for the trade,
  And he was a sturdy young man.

They happened to meet on Nottingham Bridge,
  And neither of them would give way.
Till brave Robin Hood, in right merry mood—
  "I'll show ye right Nottingham play."

Robin laid on so thick and so strong,
  He made little John to admire;
And every knock, it made his bones smoke
  As if he had been in a fire.

2. "Robin Hood and Little John"

Sung by Mrs. Mariana Schaupp, of Ohio, 1941; learned in 1914 from a schoolteacher, who had in turn learned it c. 1865. LC/AAFS, rec. No. 6081(A). Also in E. C. and M. N. Kirkland, *SFQ*, II (1938), p. 72.

a P/Æ

The catch-signature indicates the pitch at which the tune was printed in the *Quarterly*. I have transcribed afresh from tape, and failed to hear the raised seventh in the second, third, and penultimate bars.

1. When Robin Hood was about eighteen years old,
He chanced to meet Little John,
A jolly brisk blade, just fit for his trade,
For he was a sturdy young man.
Although he was Little, his limbs they were large;
His stature was seven feet high.
Wherever he came, he soon quickened his name,
And he presently caused them to fly.

2. One day these two met on a long narrow bridge,
And neither of them would give way,
When Robin stepped up to the stranger and said,
"I'll show you brave Nottingham play."
"You speak like a coward," the stranger he said,
"As there with your long bow you stand,
I vow and protest you may shoot at my breast
While I have but a staff in my hand."

3. "The name of a coward," said Robin, "I scorn,
And so my long bow I lay by.
And then for your sake a staff I will take,
The faith of your manhood to try."
Then Robin he stepped out into a grove,
And pulled up a staff of green oak,
And this being done straight back he did come
And thus to the stranger he spoke.

4. "Behold thou my staff; it is lusty and tough;
On this long narrow bridge let us play;
Then he who falls in, the other shall win
The battle, and then we'll away."
Then Robin hit the stranger a crack on the crown
Which was a most terrible stroke[1]
And then[2] so enraged they more [?][3] engaged
And they laid on the blows most severe.

5. The stranger hit Robin a crack on the[4] crown,
That[5] was a most horrible[6] stroke.
The very next blow laid Robin below
And tumbled him into the brook.
"Oh where are you now?" the stranger he cried.
With a hearty laugh in reply,
"Oh, faith in the flood," quoth[7] bold Robin Hood,
"And floating away with the tide."

6. Then Robin, he waded all out of the deep
And he[8] pulled himself up by a thorn;
And[9] just at the last he blew a loud blast
So merrily on his bugle horn.
The hills they did echo, the vales they did[10] ring,
Which caused his gay men to appear,

All dressed in green, most fair to be seen;
Straight up to the master they steer.

7. "What aileth thee, Master?" quoth William Stutely.
"You seem to be wet to the skin."
"No matter," said he, "this fellow you see,
In fighting hath tumbled me in."
"We'll pluck out his eyes, and duck him likewise."
Then seized they the stranger right there.
"Nay, let him go free," quoth bold Robin Hood,
"For he's a brave fellow. Forbear!"

8. "Cheer up, jolly blade, and don't be afraid
Of all[11] these gay men that you see.
There are fourscore and nine, and if you will be mine
You may wear of my own livery."
A brace of fat deer[12] was quickly brought in,
Good ale and strong liquor likewise;
The feast was so good all in the greenwood
Where this jolly babe was baptized.

The footnotes below record different readings in *SFQ* from an earlier singing by Mrs. Schaupp (1937).
[1] Which caused the blood to appear
[2] thus
[3] closely
[4] his
[5] Which
[6] terrible
[7] cries
[8] Omitted in *SFQ*
[9] Then
[10] valleys did
[11] Omitted in *SFQ*
[12] doe

3. "Robin Hood and Little John"

Gardiner MSS., No. Gar/Hp. 722. Sung by Moses Mills (82), Preston Candover, Hampshire, July 1907. Noted by Charles Gamblin.

p I/M (–VI)

Then Robin he went to a tree cutter's tree,*
To choose him a staff of ground oak,
And when he had done away he did run,
And the stranger so merrily spoke.

We measured our staffs and at it we went,
To pass a three hours or more,
And every bang it made the groves ring,
And we played the game over so sure.

* "In the typed copy of the text this has been amended to 'thicket of trees.'" [*Purslow's note.*]

Robin Hood and the Tanner

CHILD NO. 126

ALL the early broadsides of this ballad are directed to be sung to "Robin and the Stranger." If, by that title, "Robin Hood and Little John" (No. 125) be meant, as Child argues, the tune indicated is "Arthur a Bland," which can only be the present ballad! If, as Ritson judged, No. 128, or "Robin Hood newly revived" be intended, the tune indicated is only "a delightful new tune." In any case, and by any name, the characteristic refrain line coming after line one, and the internal rhyme in line three of each stanza, relate it to the group of ballads already mentioned under No. 125. The tune which fits this peculiar pattern was known in the eighteenth century as "Arthur a Bland," so that we rest here on firm ground. The earliest printing of this tune which Chappell succeeded in finding was in the ballad-opera *The Jovial Crew*, 1731. From this source both he and Rimbault reprinted it (see variant 1); perhaps Ritson (*Robin Hood*, 1795, II, p. 37) as well.

The most striking feature of the tune is the extra phrase between the first and (normal) second phrase. It seems to be carrying us to the middle cadence, and we are surprised to find ourselves mistaken, for folktunes are not given to tricks of this kind. The tune is quite complete without it, and its absence would never be missed. In fact, without the interpolated phrase the tune is seen to belong to one of the most favorite of British types. A simpler form of it is seen in the "Jolly Pinder" tune of Rimbault, where phrase three repeats phrase one instead of going on independent adventures. "Goddesses" in Playford's *English Dancing Master* is another form, as is "Fayne wold I wed" in the Fitzwilliam Book. Many other names could be added; but it is clear already that "Arthur a Bland" is made out of folk-stuff. It seems much more probable that the refrain phrase was a happy fancy that caught on than that the tune was originally of this shape. Catch on it did, and was by far the most popular of the Robin Hood tunes so far as we have record, being used for no fewer than ten of the extant ballads: Nos. 122, 125, 126, 128, 131, 133, 142, 143, 146, 150.

The other records are of the present century, though in each case pointing back deep into the nineteenth. Cecil Sharp has put on display a version of great interest for students of variation (*English Folk-Song: Some Conclusions*, 1907, pp. 21-22).

TUNES WITH TEXTS

1. "Arthur a Bland"

The Jovial Crew, 1731, p. 2. Also in Gutch, 1874, II, p. 433 (Rimbault); and Chappell [1855-59], II, p. 392. The text is from Child, 1882-98, III, p. 137.

m Minor

1. In Nottingham there lives a jolly tanner,
    With a hey down down a down down
  His name is Arthur a Bland;
  There is nere a squire in Nottinghamshire
  Dare bid bold Arthur stand.

2. With a long pike-staff upon his shoulder,
    So well he can clear his way;
  By two and by three he makes them to flee,
  For he hath no list to stay.

3. And as he went forth, in a summer's morning,
    Into the forrest of merry Sherwood,
  To view the red deer, that range here and there,
  There met he with bold Robin Hood.

4. As soon as bold Robin Hood did him espy,
    He thought some sport he would make;
  Therefore out of hand he bid him to stand,
  And thus to him he spake:

5. Why, what art thou, thou bold fellow,
    That ranges so boldly here?
  In sooth, to be brief, thou lookst like a thief,
  That comes to steal our king's deer.

6. For I am a keeper in this forrest;
    The king puts me in trust
  To look to his deer, that range here and there,
  Therefore stay thee I must.

7. 'If thou beest a keeper in this forrest,
    And hast such a great command,
  Yet thou must have more partakers in store,
  Before thou make me to stand.'

8. 'Nay, I have no more partakers in store,
    Or any that I do need;
  But I have a staff of another oke graff,
  I know it will do the deed.'

9. 'For thy sword and thy bow I care not a straw,
    Nor all thine arrows to boot;
  If I get a knop upon thy bare scop,
  Thou canst as well shite as shoote.'

10. 'Speak cleanly, good fellow,' said jolly Robin,
    'And give better terms to me;
  Else I'le thee correct for thy neglect,
  And make thee more mannerly.'

11. 'Marry gep with a wenion!' quoth Arthur a Bland,
    'Art thou such a goodly man?
  I care not a fig for thy looking so big;
  Mend thou thyself where thou can.'

12. Then Robin Hood he unbuckled his belt,
    He laid down his bow so long;

He took up a staff of another oke graff,
   That was both stiff and strong.

13. 'I'le yield to thy weapon,' said jolly Robin,
   'Since thou wilt not yield to mine;
For I have a staff of another oke graff,
   Not half a foot longer then thine.

14. 'But let me measure,' said jolly Robin,
   'Before we begin our fray;
For I'le not have mine to be longer then thine,
   For that will be called foul play.'

15. 'I pass not for length,' bold Arthur reply'd,
   'My staff is of oke so free;
Eight foot and a half, it will knock down a calf,
   And I hope it will knock down thee.'

16. Then Robin Hood could no longer forbear;
   He gave him such a knock,
Quickly and soon the blood came down,
   Before it was ten a clock.

17. Then Arthur he soon recovered himself,
   And gave him such a knock on the crown,
That on every hair of bold Robin Hoods head,
   The blood came trickling down.

18. Then Robin Hood raged like a wild bore,
   As soon as he saw his own blood;
Then Bland was in hast, he laid on so fast,
   As though he had been staking of wood.

19. And about, and about, and about they went,
   Like two wild bores in a chase;
Striving to aim each other to maim,
   Leg, arm, or any other place.

20. And knock for knock they lustily dealt,
   Which held for two hours and more;
That all the wood rang at every bang,
   They ply'd their work so sore.

21. 'Hold thy hand, hold thy hand,' said Robin Hood,
   'And let our quarrel fall;
For here we may thresh our bones into mesh,
   And get no coyn at all.

22. 'And in the forrest of merry Sherwood
   Hereafter thou shalt be free:'
'God-a-mercy for naught, my freedom I bought,
   I may thank my good staff, and not thee.'

23. 'What tradesman art thou?' said jolly Robin,
   'Good fellow, I prethee me show:
And also me tell in what place thou dost dwel,
   For both these fain would I know.'

24. 'I am a tanner,' bold Arthur reply'd,
   'In Nottingham long have I wrought;
And if thou'lt come there, I vow and do swear
   I will tan thy hide for naught.'

25. 'God a mercy, good fellow,' said jolly Robin,
   'Since thou art so kind to me;
And if thou wilt tan my hide for naught,
   I will do as much for thee.

26. 'But if thou'lt forsake thy tanners trade,
   And live in green wood with me,

My name's Robin Hood, I swear by the rood
   I will give thee both gold and fee.'

27. 'If thou be Robin Hood,' bold Arthur reply'd,
   'As I think well thou art,
Then here's my hand, my name's Arthur a Bland,
   We two will never depart.

28. 'But tell me, O tell me, where is Little John?
   Of him fain would I hear;
For we are alide by the mothers side,
   And he is my kinsman near.'

29. Then Robin Hood blew on the beaugle horn,
   He blew full lowd and shrill,
But quickly anon appeared Little John,
   Come tripping down a green hill.

30. 'O what is the matter?' then said Little John,
   'Master, I pray you tell;
Why do you stand with your staff in your hand?
   I fear all is not well.'

31. 'O man, I do stand, and he makes me to stand,
   The tanner that stands thee beside;
He is a bonny blade, and master of his trade,
   For soundly he hath tand my hide.'

32. 'He is to be commended,' then said Little John,
   'If such a feat he can do;
If he be so stout, we will have a bout,
   And he shall tan my hide too.'

33. 'Hold thy hand, hold thy hand,' said Robin Hood,
   'For as I do understand,
He's a yeoman good, and of thine own blood,
   For his name is Arthur a Bland.'

34. Then Little John threw his staff away,
   As far as he could it fling,
And ran out of hand to Arthur a Bland,
   And about his neck did cling.

35. With loving respect, there was no neglect,
   They were neither nice nor coy,
Each other did face, with a lovely grace,
   And both did weep for joy.

36. Then Robin Hood took them both by the hand,
   And danc'd round about the oke tree;
'For three merry men, and three merry men,
   And three merry men we be.

37. 'And ever hereafter, as long as I live,
   We three will be all one;
The wood shall ring, and the old wife sing,
   Of Robin Hood, Arthur, and John.'

2. "Robin Hood"

Sharp MSS., 632/683. Also in Sharp and Marson, 2nd series, 1905, p. 34; Sharp, 1907, p. 21; Sharp, 1916, p. 8; and Sharp, Selected Ed., [1920], I, p. 8. Sung by Henry Larcombe (82), Haselbury-Plucknett, Somerset, September 2 and 3, 1905.

a D

7. Then at it they went for bang for bang
   And the space of two hours or more
   Every blow made the grove for to ring
   And they played our game so sure
   Aye [etc.]

5. "Robin Hood and the Tanner"

Gardiner MSS., No. Gar/Hp. 1221. Sung by James Buckland, Micheldever, Hampshire, September 1908.

a M (inflected VII)

1. Bold Arden walked forth one summer morning
   For to view the merry green woods
   For to hunt for the deer that run here & there
   And there he espied bold Robin Hood
   Aye & there he espied bold Robin Hood.

2. What a fellow art thou? quoth bold Robin Hood
   And what business hast thou here?
   I'll tell thee now brief thou dost look like a thief
   And thou come for to steal the king's deer
   Aye and thou etc.

3. I am the keeper of this Parish
   And the king hath a put me in trust
   And therefore I pray thee must pray take thy way
   Or else upstanding [?] I must,
   Aye etc.

4. And thou must be more in particular of store
   Before thou canst make me stand
   For I have a staff he's made of ground graff [?]
   And I warrant he shall do my deed
   Aye etc.

5. And I have another said bold Robin Hood
   He's made of an oaken tree
   He's eight feet and a half & would knock down a calf
   And why shouldn't a knock down thee
   Aye [etc.]

6. Let us measure our staffs said bold Robin Hood
   Before we do begin a way
   For if mine should be half a foot longer than thine
   Then that will be counted foul play
   Aye [etc.]

1. 'Twas of a bold tanner in old Devonshire,
   His name was Arthur O'Brann,
   There was not a man in all Devonshire,
   Could make the bold Arthur to stand,
   Ay! Could make the bold Arthur to stand.

2. Bold Arthur walked out one fine Summer's morn,
   A-viewing the merry green woods,
   To search of a deer as runs here and there,
   And he thought he spied bold Robin Hood.

3. Good Morning, young fellow! says bold Robin Hood,
   What business hast thou here?
   I'll tell thee in brief thee looks like a thief,
   And thee has come to steal the King's deer.

4. I'll have a fat doe before I do go,
   Or else it shall cause me a fall,
   For I have a staff made out of green graft,
   And I think he'll do for you all.

5. And I have another, says bold Robin Hood,
   Made out of a bonny oak tree,
   He's three feet and a half and he'll knock down a calf,
   And why shouldn't he knock down thee?

6. Let's measure our sticks, says bold Robin Hood,
   Before we begins our play,
   And if mine is a half a foot longer than thine,
   Oh! that shall be counted fair play.

7. They measured their sticks and at it they went,
   For upwards an hour or more,
   I'm sure every blow made the ground to ring,
   They played their game so sure.

8. Hold on, hold on, says bold Robin Hood,
   I pray let our courage to fall,
   Before that we break our bones all to smash,
   And gain no coin at all.

9. Bold Robin pulled out his long bugle horn,
   And blew it both loud and shrill,
   And thereupon he spied Little John,
   Come tripping down over the hill.

10. Oh! what is the matter, said Little Johnnie,
    I pray thee, bold Robin, me tell,
    There's something the matter, said little Johnnie,
    For I see that thee doesn't look well.

11. Oh! here I stands, my staff in my hand,
    My bold tanner stands by my side,
    He's a bonny brisk man and he's fit for his [*sic*] gang,
    And so well he has tanned my hide.

12. If he is a tanner so true,
    And have tanned they hide so well,
    There's not the least doubt but he'll have another bout,
    And so well he shall tan my hide.

13. Oh! no, oh! no, says bold Robin Hood,
    For he's a hero so bold,
    He's a bonny old blade and he's fit for his trade,
    And by no man he shan't be controlled.

The Bold Pedlar and Robin Hood

CHILD NO. 132

THIS ballad was regarded by Child as a traditional variation of "Robin Hood Revived" (No. 128). I confess, this seems to me a very hasty assertion. The names Young Gamwell and Gamble Gold may be allowed a resemblance, especially if some version of the earlier ballad gave Gamwell the epithet of *bold*; and the two men's reasons for leaving home (murder), and their relation to Robin Hood (cousins) are alike. But with this the parallel concludes. Child himself finds more stanzas reminiscent of No. 136. The conduct of the present narrative is as far from that of No. 128 as it is from any one of the ballads dealing with Robin's meeting his match in a hand-to-hand encounter and thereupon enlisting his adversary in his band. The opponent in No. 128 is a bowman with nothing of the pedlar about him. And so on. Coupled with other differences, it seems not insignificant that No. 128 is formally of the "Arthur a Bland" pattern, while No. 132 not only is in tetrameter quatrains (LM), but also has a two-line refrain or burden. That one ballad may have borrowed from two stanzas of the other might be admitted without prejudice to the dichotomy.

"Robin Hood and the Pedlar," at any rate, has survived in tradition more successfully than most—or, at least, in the *record* of tradition. Copies are available from Derbyshire for the mid-nineteenth century, from Sussex for the latter part of it, and from Vermont, Maine, and Nova Scotia in recent tradition. All these copies conform to the tetrameter quatrain pattern; but fall apart in the matter of refrains. The Derbyshire copies conform to the earlier shape, having a two-phrase end-refrain. The later copies all lack the burden, and all seem related more closely in melodic pattern. The Derbyshire tunes were also used with No. 164.

TUNES WITH TEXTS

GROUP A a

3. "Bold Robin Hood and the Pedlar"

Flanders and Olney, 1953, p. 68. Also in Flanders, III, 1963, p. 101. Sung by Mrs. Belle Richards, Colebrook, N.H., November 20, 1940; learned from her father, who came from Canada. From *Ballads Migrant in New England*, edited by Helen Hartness Flanders and Marguerite Olney; copyright 1953 by Helen Hartness Flanders.

a I, ending on II

The tune has been re-barred by the present editor.

1. "What have you got, you pedlar trim?
   What have you got, pray tell to me?"
   "It's seven suits of the gay green silk,
   Beside my bow-strings two or three."

2. "If you've seven suits of the gay green silk,
   Besides your bow-strings two or three;
   Upon my word," said Little John,
   "One half of them belong to me."

3. The pedlar then took off his pack,
   And laid it down most manfully,
   Saying, "The man that can drive me two feet from this,
   The pack and all I will give to thee."

4. Then Little John he drew his sword.
   The noble pedlar held his hand.
   They swaggered swords till the sweat did drop,
   Saying, "Noble pedlar, stay your hand."

5. Then Robin Hood, he drew his sword.
   The noble pedlar held his hand.
   They swaggered swords till the blood did drop,
   Saying, "Noble pedlar, stay your hand."

6. "What is your name, you pedlar trim?
   What is your name, pray tell to me?"
   "Not one bit of it—of my name you'll get
   Till both of yours you tell to me."

7. "My name is Bold Robin Hood,
   The other Little John so free,
   And now it lies within your breast
   To tell us what your name can be."

8. "My name is Bold Gammon gay,
   And I came far beyond the sea;
   For killing a man in my father's court
   I was banished from my own country."

9. "Your name it is Bold Gammon gay,
   And you came far beyond the sea;
   And if we are two sister's sons;
   What nearer kindred need we be?"

GROUP B a

6. "Robin Hood and the Pedlar"

Sharp MSS., 1669/1509. Also in Sharp, *JFSS*, V, No. 18 (1914), p. 94. Sung by Job Francis (71), Shipley, April 21, 1908.

a M

GROUP B b

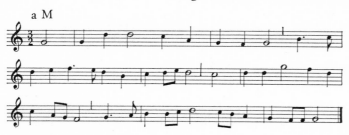

This melody is very near perfection in its modal kind.

1. Twas of a pedlar stout and bold
   As fine a pedlar as ever was seen
   He threw his pack all on his back
   And away went pedlar right over the lea.

2. The first he met two troublesome men
   Two troublesome men he there met him
   What have you on your pack cried Robin Hood
   What have you on your pack come tell to me.

3. I've several sorts of the gay green silks
   Silken bow-strings by one two three
   There's not a man in fair Nottingham
   That can take one half of this pack from me.

4. The[n] Little John drew out his sword
   The pedlar by his pack did stand
   They heaved about till they both did sweat
   He now cries pedlar pray hold your hand.

5. Bold Robin Hood was standing by
   To see them fight so heartily.
   When I find a man of smaller skill
   Could whop the pedlar & likewise you.

6. Go you try master says Little John
   Go you try master do all you can
   Go you try master without delay
   For the pedlar this night has well whopped me.

7. What is your name cries bold Robin Hood
   What is your name come tell to me
   My name to you I'll never tell
   Till both your names you tell to me.

8. For one of us is bold Robin Hood
   The other is Little John so free
   So now it lays in my good will
   Will you tell me your name or no?

9. I'm Gamble Gold from the merry green woods
   I'm Gamble Gold from over the dee
   For killing a man in my father's land
   From my native country I was forced to flee.

10. If you're Gamble Gold from the merry green woods
    If you're Gamble Gold from over the dee
    It's you and I are two sister's sons
    And here are cousins as ever can be.

11. So they sheathed their swords without delay
    Into the tavern they went straightway
    Into the tavern they all did dine
    Where they cracked their bottles & drinked their wine.

8. "Robin Hood and the Pedlar"

Sung by Mrs. Carrie Grover, Gorham, Me., 1941, LC/
AAFS, rec. No. 4697(A1). Also in Grover, n.d., p. 78.
Collected by Mrs. Sidney Robertson Cowell.

a π³

1. 'Tis of a pedlar, a pedlar trim,
   A pedlar trim he seemed to be,
   He strapped his pack all on his back,
   And he went linkin' o'er the lea.

2. He met two men, two troublesome men,
   Two troublesome men they seemed to be,
   And one of them was bold Robin Hood,
   And the other Little John so free.

3. What have you there? cries bold Robin Hood,
   What have you there, pray tell to me?
   I have six bolts of the gay green silk
   And silken bowstrings two or three.

4. If you have six bolts of the gay green silk
   And silken bowstrings two or three,
   Then, by my faith, cried bold Robin Hood,
   The half of them belong to me.

5. The pedlar he took off his pack,
   He hung it low down by his knee,
   Saying, The man who beats me three feet from that,
   The pack and all, it shall go free.

6. Bold Robin Hood drew his nut-brown sword,
   The pedlar he drew out his brand,
   They fought until they both did sweat:
   Oh pedlar, pedlar, stay your hand.

7. O fight him, Master, cried Little John,
   O fight him, Master, and do not flee!
   Now by my faith, cried the pedlar trim,
   'Tis not to either he or thee.

8. What is your name? cried bold Robin Hood,
   What is your name, pray tell to me?
   No, not one word, cried the pedlar trim,
   Till both your names you tell to me.

9. The one of us is bold Robin Hood,
   The other Little John so free.
   Oh, now I have it at my good will
   Whether my name I'll tell to thee.

10. I am Gamble Gold of the Gay Green Woods,
    Far far beyond the raging sea.
    I killed a man on my father's land,
    And was forced to leave my own countery.

11. If you're Gamble Gold of the Gay Green Woods,
    Far far beyond the raging sea,
    Then you and I are sisters' sons,
    What nearer cousins can we be?

12. They sheathed their swords with friendly words,
    And so like brothers did agree,
    Then unto an ale-house in the town,
    Where they cracked bottles merrily.

GROUP BC

11. "The Bold Pedlar and Robin Hood"

Broadwood, *JFSS*, I, No. 4 (1902), p. 144. Also in Broadwood, 1908, p. 4. Sung by Henry Burstow, Horsham, Sussex, 1893.

a D

1. There chanced to be a Pedlar bold,
   A Pedlar bold he chanced to be.
   He put his pack all on his back,
   And so merrily trudgèd o'er the lea.

2. By chance he met two troublesome men,
   Two troublesome men they chanced to be,
   The one of them was bold Robin Hood,
   And the other was little John so free.

3. "O Pedlar, Pedlar, what is in thy pack?
   Come speedily and tell to me."
   "I've several suits of the gay green silks,
   And silken bowstrings by two or three."

4. "If you have several suits of the gay green silk,
   And silken bowstrings two or three,
   Then, by my body," cries little John,
   "One half your pack shall belong to me."

5. "O nay, O nay," said the Pedlar bold,
   "O nay, O nay, that never can be,
   For there's never a man from fair Nottingham
   Can take one half my pack from me."

6. Then the Pedlar he pulled off his pack,
   And put it a little below his knee,
   Saying, "If you do move me one perch from this,
   My pack and all shall gang with thee."

7. Then little John he drew his sword,
   The Pedlar by his pack did stand,
   They fought until they both did sweat,
   Till he cried, "Pedlar, pray hold your hand."

8. Then Robin Hood he was standing by,
   And he did laugh most heartily,
   Saying, "I could find a man of smaller scale,
   Could thrash the Pedlar and also thee."

9. "Go you try, master," says little John,
   "Go you try, master, most speedily,
   For by my body," says little John,
   "I am sure this night you will know me."

10. Then Robin Hood he drew his sword,
    And the Pedlar by his pack did stand;
    They fought till the blood in streams did flow,
    Till he cried, "Pedlar, pray hold your hand.

11. "O Pedlar, Pedlar, what is thy name?
    Come speedily and tell to me."
    "Come, my name I ne'er will tell
    Till both your names you have told to me."

12. "The one of us is bold Robin Hood,
    And the other little John so free."
    "Now," says the Pedlar, "it lays to my good will,
    Whether my name I choose to tell to thee.

13. "I am Gamble Gold of the gay green woods,
    And travelled far beyond the sea,
    For killing a man in my father's land
    And from my country was forced to flee."

14. "If you are Gamble Gold of the gay green woods,
    And travelled far beyond the sea,
    You are my mother's own sister's son,
    What nearer cousins can we be?"

15. They sheathed their swords, with friendly words,
    So merrily they did agree,
    They went to a tavern and there they dined,
    And cracked bottles most merrily.

12. "Pedlar Bold"

Creighton, [1933], p. 12. Sung by Ben Henneberry, Devil's
Island, N.S. Tune as in 1966 edition.

a D/Æ

1. There chanced to be a pedlar bold,
   A pedlar bold there chanced to be,
   He put his pack upon his back
   And so merrily trudged o'er the lee.
   By chance he met with two troublesome men,
   Two troublesome men they chanced to be,
   One of their names was bold Robin Hood
   And the other Little John so free.

2. "Pedlar, pedlar, what's in thy pack?
   Come speedilie and tell to me."
   "I have several suits of the gay, green silk,
   And silken bow-strings one, two, and three."
   "If you have several suits of the gay, green silk,
   And silken bow-strings one, two and three,
   Then by my body," cried Little John,
   "Half your pack belongs to me."

3. The pedlar then took his pack
   And placed little below his knee,
   And demanded, "Moves me one perch from this
   The pack and all shall gang to thee."
   Little John he pulled forth the sword
   And the pedlar by his pack did stand,
   They swaggered swords till the sweat did flow
   And he cried, "Pedlar, pray hold your hand."

4. Robin Hood, he being standing by,
   He did laugh most heartilie,
   "I could find a man of smaller scale
   Could whip the pedlar and also thee."
   "Go try, master," cried Little John,
   "Go try, go try most speedilie,
   There is not a man in fair Nottingham
   Can beat the pedlar and also me."

5. Bold Robin Hood he drew forth his sword
   And the pedlar by his pack did stand,

Where they swaggered swords till the blood did flow,
When he cried, "Pedlar, pray hold your hand.
Oh pedlar, pedlar, what is thy name?
Come speedilie and tell to me."
"The devil a one of ye my name shall know
Before both your names ye have told to me."

6. "One of our names is bold Robin Hood,
   The other one Little John so free."
   "Now," said the pedlar, "it's my good will
   Whether my name I should tell to thee.
   I am Gamble Gold of the gay green woods,
   I have travelled far and o'er the sea,
   And for killing of a man in my father's court
   From my country I was forced to flee."

7. "If you're Gamble Gold of the gay, green woods
   And have travelled far and o'er the sea,
   You are my mother's own sister's son,
   What nearer cousins then can we be?"
   They sheathed the swords with friendly words,
   So merrilie they did agree,
   They went to a tavern and did they dine
   And cracked a bottle most merrilie.

8. Then these three they took hold of hand,
   Merrilie danced round the green tree.
   You drink water while your money lasts,
   There's a time you'll die, lads, as well as me.

Robin Hood's Progress to Nottingham

CHILD NO. 139

THE tune indicated for this ballad in all copies that mention a tune is "Bold Robin Hood." The stanzaic pattern is uncommon, but it occurs in Nos. 141, 147, and 153, in recent copies of 144, and in a MS. copy of 110 as well.

The ballad must have been popular, as it has contributed a tune's name for both No. 147 (i.e., "Robin Hood was a tall young man") and No. 153 ("Robin Hood and the Fifteen Foresters"). Child is less careful than usual when he says that "Robin Hood and Queen Katherine" (145) may be the ballad meant by "Bold Robin Hood." His reasons are that "this conjunction of words occurs several times in R. H. and Queen Katherine" and that No. 139, to be sung to "Bold Robin Hood," has the same burden (1882-98, III, p. 198). On the latter point he is inaccurate. He refers presumably to the broadsides of his B class in No. 145. But very few of the ballads fail to attach the epithet "bold" more than once. It would be easy to point to half a dozen—and probably more—Robin Hood ballads where the conjunction "bold Robin Hood" occurs as often, or nearly so, as in "Robin Hood and Queen Katherine" (five

times); and the disposition of the refrain is quite different in these two (i.e., 139 and 145). If the name refers to an extant ballad, perhaps the likeliest is "Robin Hood's Golden Prize" (No. 147). That ballad has the same stanza pattern, and the phrase "bold Robin Hood" occurs in the first line and a sufficient number of times else (five in all, if we allow "bold Robin" for one). It is typical that the tune-name for that ballad is the first line of the broadside texts of the present one! From that fact, Child argued the priority of the present ballad; and in the Pepys text collated here (e) by Child an extra "bold Robin Hood" occurs, to make up five: so it might be held at a pinch that, as sometimes happens, the ballad names its own tune.

At any rate, we shall hardly argue it back to life. No tune is known by the name of "Bold Robin Hood," and even the resourceful Rimbault fails, I believe, to identify one.

Versions of the ballad, with tunes, have been recently recovered from tradition in Nova Scotia by Helen Creighton. They have a "derry down" last phrase, the fifth; but the refrain line coming after line one is absent.

TUNES WITH TEXTS

1. **"Robin Hood's Progress to Nottingham"**
Creighton [1933], p. 15. Sung by Ben Henneberry, Devil's Island, N.S.

a I

Robin Hood he bent his noble good bow
And his broad arrow let fly,

Till fourteen of those fifteen foresters
Dead on the ground did lie.
Chorus.
Hi down, hi derry derry down.

Ten men they came from brave Nottingame
To take up Robin Hood,
Some lost arms and some lost legs
And more they lost their blood.
Chorus.

Ten men they came from brave Nottingham
To take up Robin Hood,
But he picked up his noble good bow
And he's off to the merry greenwood.
Chorus.

Robin Hood Rescuing Three Squires

CHILD NO. 140

THIS ballad has had a vogue which is not yet quite extinct. All the copies found are in CM, without refrain. There are many eighteenth-century printings of a text, but no tune has been recorded as of so early a date. Ritson, in 1795, noted the fact that his friend Edward Williams, a Welsh bard, had told him that the song was well known in South Wales by the name of *Marchog glas* ("Green Knight"), but nobody (I believe) has captured a copy, either text or tune. Rimbault remarks (Gutch, *Robin Hood*, 1847, II, p. 439) of Child's C type that in Staffordshire and Derbyshire it was sung in his day to "Robin Hood and the Curtall Friar's" tune, which he gives not from tradition but from an early MS. (cf. *sub* No. 123). But Rimbault also gives a traditional tune for Child's type B, from the "borders of Staffordshire," collected by himself in 1845 from an old man who remembered little of the words. The tune, as he says, is a variant of "Lord Thomas and Fair Eleanor" (No. 73).

More recently the ballad has been collected by Percy Grainger and Vaughan Williams, in attractive forms; and, still later, it has been surprised in North Carolina and Maine.

TUNES WITH TEXTS

GROUP A

3. "Robin Hood and the Three Squires"

Vaughan Williams, *JFSS*, III, No. 13 (1909), p. 268. Sung by Mrs. Goodyear (75), Axford by Basingstoke, Hampshire, January 1909. Collected by G. B. Gardiner.

a M

Miss Ann Gilchrist cites an analogous major version, from Yorkshire, used with Child No. 4 (*ante*, Vol. I, p. 77, variant 94). Others of that family could be added with ease.

1. Bold Robin Hood rangèd the forest all round,
    The forest all round rangèd he,
    And the first that he met was a gay lady,
    Come weeping along the highway.

2. "Oh, why do you weep, my gay lady?
    Oh, why do you weep?" said he.
    "Oh, why do you weep, my gay lady?
    I pray thee come tell unto me.

3. "Oh, do you weep for gold or fame,
    Or do you weep for me
    Or do you weep for anything else
    Belonging to anybody?"

4. "I don't weep for gold or fame,
    Nor I don't weep for thee;
    Nor I don't weep for anything else
    Belonging to anybody."

5. "Then why do you weep, my gay lady?
    Why do you weep?" said he.
    "Oh, why do you weep, my gay lady?
    I pray thee come tell unto me."

6. "Oh, I do weep for my three sons,
    For they are condemned to die."
    "Oh, what have they done?" said bold Robin Hood,
    "Oh, what have they done?" said he.

7. "What parish church have they robbed?" said bold Robin Hood,
    "Or what parish priest have they slain?
    Did they ever force a maid against her will,
    Or with other men's wives have they lain?"

8. "Oh, what have they done," said bold Robin Hood,
    "Oh, what have they done?" said he.
    "They have stole sixteen of the king's white deer,
    To-morrow they are condemned to die."

9. "Go your way home, my gay lady,
    Go your way home," said he.
    "Oh, go your way home, my gay lady,
    To-morrow I set them quite free."

10. "What men are all those?" said bold Robin Hood,
    "What men are all those?" said he.
    "They are all of them mine and none of them thine,
    They are come for the squires all three."

11. "Go and take them, go and take them," says the master sheriff,
    "Go and take them all," said he;
    "Never no more in fair Nottingham town
    Shall borrow three more of me."

GROUP B

5.1. "Robin Hood and the Widow's Three Sons"

Gardiner MSS., No. Gar/Hp. 1283. Sung by Mrs. Cole, Oakley, Hampshire, September 1908.

p I

1. Bold Robin he marched the forest along,
   As hard as he could ride (hie?),
   Until he met with an old beggar man,
   And he kept drawing so nigh.

2. "What news, what news, my old beggar man,
   What news, come tell unto me?"
   "There's weeping and wailing in Nottingham town,
   For the loss of the squires all three."

3. "Change clothing, change clothing, my old beggar man,
   I'll give you fifteen shillings to boot,
   For there's none other man in Nottingham town,
   That can borrow three more of me."

4. "What are you weeping for, my gay lady?
   Either for gold or fee,
   Or are you a-weeping for your maidenhead,
   It is gone many years from thee."

5. "I'm not a-weeping for gold," she said,
   And I'm not a-weeping for fee,
   And I'm not a-weeping for my maidenhead,
   It's been gone many years from me;

6. I am a-weeping for my three sons,
   They are all condemned to die."

7. "What parish church have they robbed,
   What parish priest have they slain,
   Or have they forced young maidens against their own will,
   Or with other men's wives have they lain?"

8. "No parish church have they not robbed,
   Nor no parish priest have they slain,
   Nor no young maidens have they forced against their will,
   Nor with other men's wives have they lain;

8. They have killed three of the King's fallow deers,
   And they're all condemned to die,
   In Nottingham town they are all chained and bound,
   And in Nottingham prison they lie."

9. "What will you give me in gold," he cried,
   "Or what will you give me in fee,
   If I will go to Nottingham town,
   Get your three sons freedom to-day?"

10. "I will give you all my gold,
    And a part of my fee,
    If you will go to Nottingham town,
    And get my three sons freedom I pray."

11. Bold Robin he marched the forest along,
    As hard as he could hie,
    And then he was 'ware of an old beggar man,
    As he kept drawing so nigh.

12. "What news, what news, my old beggar man,
    What news come tell unto me?"
    "There's weeping and wailing in Nottingham town,
    For the loss of the squires all three."

13. "Change clothing, change clothing, my old beggar man,
    I'll give you fifteen shillings to boot,
    And now you can drink both brandy or ale,
    Until I see you again."

14. He give three bugles with his bugle horn,
    And as loud as he could blow,
    And eight score and ten of bold Robin Hood's men,
    Came trippling over the plain.

15. Bold Robin he went up the scaffold so high,
    As hard as he could hie,
    Saying "I'll be Jack Ketch to-day. . . ."

16. "Take thou (them?) along, take thou (them?) along, my
       brave beggar man,
    Take thou along I'll grant them to thee,
    There's not another in Nottingham town,
    Can buy three more of me."

17. Bold Robin Hood marched the forest along,
    As hard as he could go,
    With his eight score and ten of bold Robin Hood's men,
    And his three squires all in a row.

7. "Robin Hood's Men"

Vaughan Williams MSS., I, p. 129. Sung by Mr. Flint,
Lyne, Surrey, on 20 August 1907.

a D

Three hundred and ten of bold Robin Hood's men
Came trippeling over the hill, came trippeling over the hill
"Whose men are all they?" the gentleman said.
"Those men are all mine, there's not a one thine
They come for the squires all three,
They come for the squires all three."

Robin Hood Rescuing Will Stutly

CHILD NO. 141

This ballad has the same stanza-pattern in the early copies as that of No. 139, q.v. The tune indication, however, is "Robin Hood and Queen Katherine" (No. 145). None of the three types of the latter ballad would sing to a tune that would carry the present text as it stands, and the direction would seem to be a reckless one. Rimbault's mating of the ballad to the "Three Ravens" tune (Gutch, *Robin Hood*, 1847, II, p. 435) is therefore equally ill-considered.

This is one of three Robin Hood ballads that was recovered from Martha Davis's grandmother in 1882, and deposited in the Virginia archive in 1913. It is noteworthy that her first line is "As Robin Hood in the green wood stood," which is—minus

As—the same as the named tune of "Robin Hood and Allen a Dale" (No. 138). Unless, however, the repeated last line of the latter were omitted, that ballad could not be sung to this tune. But, since the last phrase of the tune here apparently ends on the second degree, it is possible that the tune originally did repeat the last phrase, with a final cadence on the tonic. Sharp found other examples of tunes which by dint of repeating many stanzas with a circular inconclusive ending had lost their true conclusions. In any case, the Davis tune is of a different pattern from the ones quoted by Child: it is CM as it stands. It suggests a tune in D'Urfey, *Wit and Mirth: Or Pills to Purge Melancholy*, 1719, I, p. 126 ("In Kent I hear").

TUNE WITH TEXT

"The Rescue of Will Stutly"

Davis, 1929, p. 587; text, p. 397. Contributed by Martha M. Davis, Harrisonburg, Rockingham County, Va., April 8, 1913. Dictated by her grandmother in 1882; from Scots-Irish family tradition.

If C tonic, a I/Ly
If D tonic, a M/D

1. As Robin Hood in the green wood stood
   Under a green wood tree,
   Sad tidings came to him with speed,
   Tidings for certainty.

2. That Stutly he surprised was,
   In Aiken* prison lay.
   Three varlets whom the king had hired
   Did basely him betray.

3. When Robin Hood these news did hear,
   He grievèd was full sore,
   And likewise his brave bowmen bold,
   Who all together swore

4. That Stutly he should rescued be,
   Unto the woods again
   Return with them to hunt the deer,
   Or in his cause be slain.

5. "Will send one forth the news to hear
   From yonder palmer there,
   Whose cell is near the castle wall;
   Some news he may declare."

6. Then stepped forth a brisk young man,
   Of courage stout and bold,
   And straight unto the palmer went,
   Saying, "Ye palmer old,

7. "Tell me, if you can rightly tell,
   When must Will Stutly die,
   Who is of Robin Hood's brave men
   That here in prison lie?"

8. "Alas, alas," the palmer said,
   "That ever woe is me,
   This day Will Stutly must be hung
   Upon yon gallows tree.

9. "But did his noble master know,
   He soon would succor send;
   A few of his brave bowmen bold
   Would save him from this end."

10. "That is true," the young man said,
    "He soon would set him free;
    So fare thee well, thou good old man,
    With many thanks to thee."

11. Then Robin dressed himself in red,
    His merry men all in green,
    With swords and buckles and long bows
    Most glorious to be seen.

12. Not long from jail the young man went,
    The gates were open wide,
    When from the castle Stutly came,
    Guarded on every side.

13. Not far from castle they had gone,
    When appeared Little John,
    And straight unto the sheriff went
    And said to him, "Anon,

14. "Mr. Sheriff, with your leave,
    I'll speak with him a while."
    "No," said the sheriff, "you'll me seize;
    Thou art an outlaw vile.

15. "I'll not consent," the sheriff said,
    "But hangèd he shall be,
    And so shall his vile master be
    When in my custody."

16. Then in haste did Little John
    Away cut Stutly's bands,
    And from a man he twisted soon
    The sword out of his hands.

17. Saying, "Will, take you this sword a while,
    You can it better sway,
    And now defend thy life from harm
    For aid will come straight way."

18. And then they turned them back to back
    And fought with valor good,
    Until at length approachèd near
    The valiant Robin Hood.

19. Then quick an arrow Robin sent
    Which near the sheriff flew,
    And quickly made him for to run,
    And all his coward crew.

20. "O stay a while," said Will Stutly,
    "And do not from us start;
    O stay and hang up Robin Hood
    Before you do depart.

21. "Thanks, O thanks, my master dear,
    We'll in the green woods meet,
    Where we will make our bow strings twang
    Music for us most sweet."

* "Aiken," Davis shrewdly suggests, is a corruption of *eke in*. Presumably, "In" is subsequent, for *An(d)*.

Robin Hood and the Bishop of Hereford

CHILD NO. 144

THE early copies of this ballad have neither refrain nor tune name. They are all in CM. Luckily, the ballad has survived in tradition. Four records of a tune are known. The first was printed by Rimbault (Gutch, *Robin Hood*, 1847, II, p. 441) from a broadside printed for Daniel Wright, and later by Chappell (*Popular Music* [1855-59], II, p. 395), presumably from the same broadside (early eighteenth century?) with insignificant differences. The next was printed by Moffat and Kidson, 1901, p. 143, from a British Museum half-sheet en-

graved by T. Straight, c. 1780. It is the same tune, with slight differences. These have no refrains or provisions therefor.

The latest two copies were collected in the first decade of the present century in Dorset and Hampshire. The latter, found by Gardiner in 1906, shows clear affiliation with the engraved copy of c. 1780; but it was never learned from that print. Hammond's Dorset copy diverges much further. But the words of both look like oral abridgments of the Aldermary versions of Ritson's day, as reproduced in Child's Aa-d.

TUNES WITH TEXTS

GROUP A

2.1. "Robin Hood and the Bishop of Hereford"

Gardiner MSS., No. 797. Sung by Mrs. Goodyear (74), Axford, Hampshire, August 1907. Noted by Charles Gamblin.

a I/M, ending on the upper octave

1. Robin dressed himself in a shepherd's long cloak,
     And six of his men also;
   They watched the bishop so narrowly,
     For fear he another way should go.

2. Presently the bishop came riding by,
     And about the fire they did throw.
   "And why did you kill the king's white deer,
     When your company is so few?"

3. Then Robin put his back up against an oak
     And his foot against a thorn;
   And out underneath the shepherd's long cloak
     Pulled out a long bugle horn.

4. He put the little end to his mouth
     And a very loud blast blew he;
   A hundred and ten of bold Robin Hood's men
     Came tripping down the green hill.

5. "Oh, cut off his head, master," says Little John
     "And we'll haul him into his grave."
   And we made the bishop dance in his boots, till he sweat
     And glad for to get off free.

GROUP B

3. "Robin Hood and the Bishop of Hereford"

Hammond, *JFSS*, III, No. 11 (1907), p. 61. Also in Sharp, 1908-12, I, p. 4. Sung by George Stone, Wareham, Dorset, November 1906; learned sixty years before.

a I

1. Some will talk of bold Robin Hood,
     Derry derry down!
   And some of the barons so bold;
   But I'll tell you how they served the Bishop,
     When they robbed him of his gold.
       Derry down! Hey! derry derry down!

2. Robin Hood he dressed himself in shepherd's attire
     And six of his men also,
   And, when the Bishop he did come by,
     They round the fire did go.

3. "Oh! we are shepherds," said bold Robin Hood,
     "And keep sheep all the year,
   And we are resolved to make merry to-day,
     And to eat of our King's fat deer."

4. "You are a brave fellow," said the old Bishop,
     "And the King of your doings shall know,
   Therefore make haste and come along with me
     And before the King you shall go."

5. Robin Hood set his back against an oak
   And his foot against a thorn,
   And out underneath his shepherd's cloak
   Pulled out his bugle-horn.

6. He put the small end to his mouth,
   And a loud blast he did blow.
   Six score and ten of bold Robin's men
   Came tripping along in a row.

7. "Oh! what is the matter?" said Little John,
   "Oh! why do you blow so hastily?"
   "Oh! the Bishop of Hereford he has come by,
   And a pardon he shall have."

8. "Here's the Bishop," said bold Robin Hood,
   "No pardon I shall have."
   "Cut off his head, Master," says Little John,
   "And bundle him into his grave."

9. "Oh! pardon me, Oh! pardon me," says the Bishop,
   "Oh! pardon me I pray.
   If I had a-known it had been you,
   I'd a-gone some other way."

10. Robin Hood he took the Bishop by the hand,
    And led him to merry Barnsdale,
    And made him sup with him that night,
    And drink wine, beer, and ale.

11. "Call in the reckoning," the old Bishop said,
    "For I'm sure 'tis going very high."
    "Give me your purse, Master" said Little John,
    "I'll tell you by and bye."

12. Little John he took the Bishop's cloak,
    And spread it on the ground,
    And out of the Bishop's portmanteau
    He pulled five hundred pound.

13. "There's money enough, master" said Little John,
    "'Tis a comely sight to see.
    It makes me in charity with the Bishop;
    In his heart he don't love me."

14. Little John he took the Bishop by the hand,
    And he caused the music to play,
    And he made the old Bishop dance till he sweat.
    And he was glad to get so away.

Sir Hugh, or, The Jew's Daughter

CHILD NO. 155

THE connection of this ballad with the legend of Hugh of Lincoln seems deep-rooted and genuine, but the main tradition of the ballad nevertheless appears to be Scottish, passing thence to Ireland and the U.S.A.

Of Child's twenty-one variants, the only one with a refrain (a repeated last line) is that from Motherwell's Appendix, which alone has a tune. Among the variants with tunes—Scots, Irish, Nova Scotian, and U.S.—refrains of some kind occur more often than not.

The unsuitable rainy opening occurs in the earliest text to reach print, Percy's in 1765 (Child B): and again in Child's G, H, I, J, K, L, M, N, O, S. But it is not found in A (Mrs. Brown), nor in C (Paton-Percy, 1768), D (Herd MSS.), E (Motherwell, 1827). Perhaps it came in through contamination with "The Unquiet Grave" (Child No. 78), also concerned with a revenant and with mourning for the dead. There are also apparent crossings with "The Twa Brothers" (Child No. 49) at the beginning and end; and with "Lamkin" (Child No. 93)—cf. Linkim, Lincoln, Lankin—in the blood-letting passage.

It seems quite probable that the ballad has its roots in a story of ritualistic murder by Jews. There is in the earliest chronicles no reference to a miracle of Our Lady: the corpse is not resuscitated in any way, but itself performs miracles. There is no mention of a woman among the Jews, but the mother of the boy figures prominently. If this story were taken up by superstitious Protestants, there would be no tendency for accretions to grow upon it of the religious sort, and the miracles of the corpse would naturally drop out. In folk-story (although not in "Lamkin") the evil-doer is frequently a woman or witch, and it is natural for such a figure to appear as villainess. The ballad first comes to light in Scotland, the stronghold of Protestantism. The event seems, from the name Hugh, to have been originally localized at Lincoln, but already when it appears in the eighteenth century the name is beginning to be blurred out of recognition. Child A mentions "merry Lincoln" four times; D "merry Linkim"; but B and C have dissolved this to "Mirryland toun"; and E further to Scottish "Maitland town." F (Irish) does not localize, nor N (American-Irish), nor P and R (both fragments). G, H, I, J, M, O (all English and American) carry back to "Scotland" and Scotland is echoed by Shropshire K's "Merry-Cock land." (J, though placing the action in Scotland, mentions Lincoln in stanza ten.) Scottish Q has "Lincolnshire." This would indicate a Scottish tradition with original proper attribution to Lincoln, fading out; carried thence into England, where a sense of its Scottishness would throw back localization upon Scotland. The ballad appears to have no continental history, though there are widespread legends on the theme, and verses (early) in Anglo-Norman and English.

The ballad-makers certainly worked at a considerable remove from any dependence on chronicle or pious legend, and seem to have kept nothing more than the nucleus: that Hugh of Lincoln was murdered by a Jew, thrown into a well, sought by his mother, and discovered, "for murder, though it have no tongue, will speak/ With most miraculous organ." The event is alleged to have occurred in 1255. In 1290, Edward I officially expelled the Jews from England; and they were not readmitted till Cromwell's era.

Except for Percy, 1765, the best Scottish texts are very much alike, and thus point either to a strong and continuous tradition or one controlled by recent dissemination or narrow distribution. The Percy text seems already sufficiently corrupted or sophisticated for it to have gone some way in popular handling: e.g., stanzas 1, 2, 6, 10, 11, 12, and the general abridgment. But some of this could have been done by Lord Hailes or his donor.

The musical tradition cannot be taken very far back, and for the most part it is fairly homogeneous, keeping to the I-π^1-I/M region, and using the "Lady Isabel" B, or "Lord Lovel," style of tune. (See *ante*, Child No. 4, and CHILD No. 75.) This, however, allows for a good deal of variety, and runs all the way from "St. Valentine's Day" to "Cowdenknowes."

Departures from the main current of tradition occur among the earlier records, and also in the Irish line. The tune given in Johnson's *Museum* (variant 1 below) is, as printed, a six-phrase one. Glen is "doubtful if it ever appeared in any collection prior to the Museum"; he considers it, he says, "of the mongrel species, compounded from 'The Mason's Anthem, Merrily danced the Quaker,' &c." (Glen, *Early Scottish Melodies*, 1900, p. 237). To me it appears that the first two phrases would properly be repeated (ABAB) to form an eight-phrase tune. As it stands, the last two verbal lines are repeated to fill out the last four phrases (CDEB) of the tune—a way not followed in any other copy of this ballad. The tune is plagal and virtually I/M, but with the leading-note introduced twice as a passing note. It is not certain that this tune is of stuff quite alien from the main melodic stream.

The central singing tradition of the ballad (C) is represented in variants from Somerset, New York, Southern Pennsylvania, Ohio, Indiana, Missouri, and most strongly in the Appalachian region. Here it takes the "Lord Lovel" pattern, or that of "Lady Isabel" B, with a 6/8 metre. All examples are in the major area, and all except a couple of disordered copies are five-phrase, the last phrase repeating. But not Somerset and Indiana.

Of the total number of tunes now in hand, the greater proportion seems to be built of familiar melodic stock. The geographical range is unusually extensive, although—perhaps through the chances of collecting—the great majority is Appalachian. Dates of record run from 1803 to the present, but not many examples were collected before the present century. The Scottish tunes recorded in the early nineteenth century seem somewhat apart, as do the English one of the same time and Irish tunes of the late nineteenth and early twentieth century.

Within the largest groups, A and C, there is much variety of form, crystallizing into fairly well-marked sub-groups at certain points, with distinct affiliations among other ballads. Duple rhythm with 6/8 metre is by far the most favored measure. There is a nearly even division between plagal and authentic tunes. It is impossible to discern any *Ur*-pattern from which others have developed. The Kentucky and Tennessee variants are fairly homogeneous, favoring π^1 plagal, and 4/4 or 2/2 metre. The largest homogeneous group is Appalachian chiefly, but runs into Pennsylvania, Indiana, New York, Ohio, and is found once in Somerset. It is 6/8, with mid-cadence on V, is always authentic, mostly major, but with I/Ly, π^1, I/M forms; and almost universally repeats the last line to make a five-phrase tune.

GROUP Aa

1. [The rain rins down &c.]

Johnson, VI [1803], No. 582, p. 602 (repr. 1853). Also, with editorial changes, in Krehbiel, *N. Y. Tribune*, August 17, 1902, Pt. II, p. 2, col. 1.

p I (–VII, except in grace-note)

1. The rain rins down thro' Mirry-land toune,
   Sae does it down the Pa:
   Sae does the lads of Mirry-land town,
   When they play at the ba.
   Sae does the lads of Mirry-land town
   When they play at the ba.

2. Then out and cam the Jew's dochter,
   Said, will ye com in and dine!
   I winnae cum in, I winnae cum in,
   Without my play feres nine.

3. She pow'd an apple reid and white,
   To intice the young thing in:
   She pow'd an apple white and reid,
   And that the sweet bairn did win.

4. And she has taine out a little pen-knife,
   And low down by her gair,
   She has twin'd the young thing o' his life,
   A word he ne'er spake mair.

5. And out and cam the thick thick bluid,
   And out and cam the thin;
   And out and cam the bonny herts bluid;
   Thair was nae life left in.

6. She laid him on a dressing borde,
   And drest him like a swine,
   And laughing said, gae now and play
   With your sweet play-feres nine.

7. She row'd him in a cake of lead,
   Bade him ly still and sleep.
   She cast him in a deep draw-well,
   Was fifty fathom deep.

8. When bells wer rung, and mass was sung,
   And every lady went hame:
   Than ilk lady had her young son,
   But Lady Helen had nane.

9. She row'd her mantil her about,
   And sair sair gan she weep:

And she ran into the Jewis castle,
   When they wer all asleep.

10. My bonny Sir Hew, my pretty Sir Hew,
    I pray thee to me speak:
    "O lady rinn to the deep draw-well
    "Gin ye your son wad seek."

11. Lady Helen ran to the deep draw well,
    And knelt upon her knee,
    My bonny Sir Hew, and ye be here,
    I pray thee speak to me.

12. The lead is wondrous heavy, mither,
    The well is wondrous deep,
    A keen pen-knife sticks in my hert,
    A word I downae speak.

13. Gae hame, gae hame, my mother dear,
    Fetch me my winding-sheet,
    And at the back o' Mirry-land toune,
    Its there we twa sall meet.

GROUP Ab

4. "Little Sir Hugh"

Sharp MSS., 701/787. Also in Sharp and Marson, 3rd series, 1906, p. 39; Sharp, 1907, p. 75; Sharp, 1916, p. 22; Sharp, *JFSS*, V, No. 20 (1916), p. 255; and Sharp, Selected Ed. [1920], I, p. 22. Sung by Mrs. Joseph Ree, Hambridge, Somerset, December 26, 1905.

p I/M

1. Do rain, do rain in American corn
   Do rain both great and small
   When all the boys came out to play
   They played all with their ball.

2. They tossed their ball so high so low
   They tossed their ball so low
   They tossed it over in the Jew's garden
   When all the fine Jews below.

3. The first that came out was a Jew's daughter
   Was dressèd all in green
   Come in, come in, my little Sir Hugh
   Shall have your ball again.

4. I cannot come there, I will not come there
   Without my playmates all
   For if my mother should chance to know
   'Twould cause my blood to flow.

5. The first she offered him was a fig
   The next a finer thing

The third a cherry as red as blood
And that enticed him in.

6. She set him down in a chair of gold
And gave him sugar sweet
She laid him on a dresser board
And stabbed him like a sheep.

7. And when the school was over
His mother came out for to call
With a little rod under her apron
To beat her son withal.

8. Go home, go home my heavy mother
Prepare a winding-sheet
And if my father should ask of me
You tell him I'm fast asleep.

9. My head is so heavy I cannot get up
My grave it is so deep
Besides a penknife struck into my heart,
So up I cannot get.

Many editorial changes were made in the printed versions of the text.

5. "Little Harry Hughes and the Duke's Daughter"

Newell, 1883, p. 76. Also in Newell, *JFSS*, IV, No. 14 (1910), p. 36; and Smith, *MQ*, II (1916), p. 123(A). Sung by some New York children.

p I

1. It was on a May, on a midsummer's day,
When it rained, it did rain small;
And little Harry Hughes and his playfellows all
Went out to play the ball.

2. He knocked it up, and he knocked it down,
He knocked it o'er and o'er;
The very first kick little Harry gave the ball,
He broke the duke's windows all.

3. She came down, the youngest duke's daughter,
She was dressed in green;
"Come back, come back, my pretty little boy,
And play the ball again."

4. "I won't come back, and I daren't come back,
Without my playfellows all;
And if my mother she should come in,
She'd make it the bloody ball."

5. She took an apple out of her pocket,
And rolled it along the plain;

Little Harry Hughes picked up the apple,
And sorely rued the day.

6. She takes him by the lily-white hand,
And leads him from hall to hall,
Until she came to a little dark room,
That none could hear him call.

7. She sat herself on a golden chair,
Him on another close by;
And there's where she pulled out her little penknife
That was both sharp and fine.

8. Little Harry Hughes had to pray for his soul,
For his days were at an end;
She stuck her penknife in little Harry's heart,
And first the blood came very thick, and then
came very thin.

9. She rolled him in a quire of tin,
That was in so many a fold;
She rolled him from that to a little draw-well
That was fifty fathoms deep.

10. "Lie there, lie there, little Harry," she cried,
"And God forbid you to swim,
If you be a disgrace to me,
Or to any of my friends."

11. The day passed by, and the night came on,
And every scholar was home,
And every mother had her own child,
But poor Harry's mother had none.

12. She walked up and down the street,
With a little sally-rod in her hand;
And God directed her to the little draw-well,
That was fifty fathoms deep.

13. "If you be there, little Harry," she said,
"And God forbid you to be,
Speak one word to your own dear mother,
That is looking all over for thee."

14. "This I am, dear mother," he cried,
"And lying in great pain,
With a little penknife lying close to my heart,
And the duke's daughter she has me slain.

15. "Give my blessing to my schoolfellows all,
And tell them to be at the church,
And make my grave both large and deep,
And my coffin of hazel and green birch.

16. "Put my Bible at my head,
My busker at my feet,
My little prayer-book at my right side,
And sound will be my sleep."

10b. "Sir Hugh"

Sung by Mr. Dol Small (81), Nellysford, Va., September 10, 1950. LC/AAFS, rec. No. 10,003(A1). Collected by Maud Karpeles and Sidney Robertson Cowell.

a M (–IV, VI) (compass of a sixth)

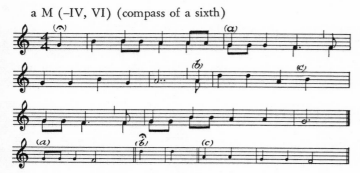

p π¹ (–VI)

1. She tossed it high, she tossed it low,
   She tossed it in yonders hall,
   Saying, Come along, my little boy Hugh,
   And get your silken ball.

2. I can't come in and I won't come in
   To get my silken ball,
   For if my master knew it all
   He'd let my life's blood fall.

3. She took him by his lily-white hand,
   She led him through the hall,
   And in that silver basin clear
   She let his life's blood fall.

4. She wound him up in a lily-white sheet,
   Three or four times four,
   And tossed him into her draw-well,
   'Twere both deep and cold.

5. The day had passed and the even had come,
   Scholars going home,
   Every mother had her son,
   Little Hugh's had none.

6. She broke a switch all off that birch,
   Through the town she run:
   I'm going to meet my little boy Hugh,
   I'm sure for to whip him home.

7. She ran till she came to the old Jews' gate
   The old Jews all so asleep.
   She heard a voice in that draw-well
   'Twere both cold and deep.

8. Cheer up, dear Mother, it's here I've lain,
   It's here I've lain so long,
   With a little pen-knife pierced through my heart,
   The stream did run so strong.

9. O take me out of this draw-well,
   Make me a coffin of birch;
   O take me out of this draw-well
   Bury me at yonders church.

GROUP A d

21. "Sir Hugh"

Sharp MSS., 3585/2648. Also in Sharp and Karpeles, 1932,
I, p. 223(C). Sung by W. M. Maples, Sevierville, Sevier
County, Tenn., April 20, 1917.

1. As I walked out one holiday
   The drops of dew did fall,
   And every scholar in the school
   Was out a-playing ball, ball,
   Was out a-playing ball.

2. They tossed the ball to and fro,
   In the Jews's garden it did go,
   There was no one ready to get it out,
   There stood little son Hugh.

3. The Jews's daughter come stepping along
   With some apples in her hand,
   Saying: Little son Hugh, come go with me
   And I will give you them.

4. I cannot go, I will not go,
   I cannot go at all,
   For if my mamma she knew it,
   The red blood she'd make fall.

5. She took him by the lily-white hand,
   She drug him from hall to hall,
   And took him to a great stone wall
   Where none could hear his call.

6. She set him down in a little arm-chair
   And pierced his heart within.
   She had a little silver bowl,
   His heart blood she let in.

7. She took him into the Jews's garden,
   The Jews was all asleep,
   And she threw him into a great deep well
   Was fifty fathoms deep.

8. His mother then she started out
   With a birch-rod in her hand,
   Walked the streets through and through.
   If I find little son Hugh,
   I'd avowed she'd whip him home.

9. When she come to the Jews's gate,
   The Jews was all asleep;
   She walked on to a great deep well
   Was fifty fathoms deep.

10. Saying: Little son Hugh, if you be,
    As I suppose you to be.
    Dear mother, I am here
    And stand in the need of thee.

11. With a little penknife pierced through my heart
And the red blood running so free.
Mother, O mother, dig my grave,
Dig it long, wide and deep.

12. And bury my bible at my head,
My prayer book at my feet.
And if any of the scholars ask for me,
Pray tell them I'm asleep.

25. "Little Sir Hugh"

Sharp MSS., 2085/1946. Sung by Sister Emma (about 70), at Clewer, February 27, 1909.

a I/M

1. Yesterday was a high holiday
Of all the days in the year
And all the little schoolfellows went out to play
But Sir William was not there

2. His mother she went to the Jew's wife's house
And knocked loud at the ring
O little Sir William if you are here
Come let your mother in

3. He is not here the Jew's wife said
He is not here today
He's with his little schoolfellows out on the green
Keeping this high holiday.

4. His mother she went to the Boyne Water
That flows so dark & deep.
O little Sir William if you are here
O pity your mother's weep.

5. O how can I pity your weep mother
And I so full of pain
For the little pen knife sticks close to my heart
And the Jew's wife has me slain

6. Go home go home my mother dear
And prepare me a winding sheet
For tomorrow morning before it is day
Your body and mine shall meet.

7. And lay my prayer book at my head
And my grammar at my feet
That all the little schoolfellows as they pass by
May read them for my sake.

28. "The Jew's Daughter"

Rinker, *JAF*, XXXIX (1926), p. 213. From Mrs. Samantha E. Rinker, Huntingdon County, Pa.; learned from her mother, c. 1872.

a I/Ly

1. It rained, it hailed, it snowed, it blowed,
It stormed all over the land;
And all the boys from our town
Came out to toss their ball, ball, ball,
Came out to toss their ball.

2. First they tossed it too high,
And then again too low,
And over into the Jew's garden it went,
Where no one dared to go, go, go,
Where no one dared to go.

3. Out came the Jew's daughter,
Dressed up in silk so fine,
She said, "Come in, my pretty little boy,
And toss your ball with me, me, me,
And toss your ball with me."

4. "I can't come in, nor I shan't come in,
Unless my playmates do,
For if I come in I'll never get out,
I'll never get out any more, more, more,
I'll never get out any more."

5. First a mellow apple,
And then a gay gold ring,
And next a cherry as red as blood,
To coax this little boy in, in, in,
To coax this little boy in.

6. She took him by the lily-white hand,
And into the cellar she ran;
And called for a bowl as yellow as gold,
To catch his heart's blood in, in, in,
To catch his heart's blood in.

7. "O place my prayer book at my head,
My hymn book at my feet,
And when my mother calls for me,
Tell her I am asleep, sleep, sleep,
Tell her I am asleep."

Queen Eleanor's Confession

CHILD NO. 156

This ballad first appeared in broadsides of the last quarter of the seventeenth century, "to a pleasant new tune." It was included in the collection of 1723 and in Percy's *Reliques*, 1765 and all subsequent editions. The oral circulation of it in Scotland seems to have followed in the wake of the *Reliques*. Child thinks that print lies behind all his recited copies; but that oral currency may be presumed behind the earliest printed copies. Such an assumption is very plausible: it is just the little roughnesses of narrative, arising from oral transmission, that Percy was usually at pains to smooth out; and his adjustments are still reflected in Motherwell's later traditional copy. Motherwell, at any rate, secured the sole surviving traditional tune, through Andrew Blaikie's good offices, and Rimbault reprinted it in 1850, with insignificant alterations and the remark that he had often heard it in Derbyshire and Staffordshire. Rimbault was followed by Chappell, who places it in the reign of Queen Elizabeth, doubtless on textual considerations. It is a sturdy English-sounding tune, like the first strain of the "British Grenadiers." Motherwell notes that "in singing, the two last lines of each stanza are repeated"; but, oddly, in his appendix the repetition is not indicated (1827, p. 1, and App'x., p. xxii, No. xxvii). Neither is it marked in Rimbault. All the other versions of the ballad are CM quatrains, without refrain.

TUNE WITH TEXT

"Earl Marshall"

Motherwell, 1827, App'x., No. 27; text, p. 1. Also in Rimbault, 1850, p. 65; and Chappell, [1855-59], I, p. 174. Andrew Blaikie, Paisley.

p I

1. Queene Eleanor was a sick woman,
   And sick just like to die;
   And she has sent for two fryars of France
   To come to her speedilie.
   And she has sent, &c.

2. The king called downe his nobles all,
   By one, by two, by three:
   "Earl Marshall I'll go shrive the queene,
   And thou shalt wend with mee."

3. "A boone, a boone," quoth Earl Marshall,
   And fell on his bended knee;
   "That whatsoever the queene may say,
   No harm thereof may bee."

4. "O you'll put on a gray friar's gowne,
   And I'll put on another;
   And we will away to fair London town,
   Like friars both together."

5. "O no, O no, my liege, my king,
   Such things can never bee;
   For if the Queene hears word of this,
   Hanged she'll cause me to bee."

6. "I swear by the sun, I swear by the moon,
   And by the stars so hie,
   And by my sceptre, and my crowne,
   The Earl Marshall shall not die."

7. The King's put on a gray friar's gowne,
   The Earl Marshall's put on another,
   And they are away to fair London towne,
   Like fryars both together.

8. When that they came to fair London towne,
   And came into Whitehall,
   The bells did ring and the quiristers sing,
   And the torches did light them all.

9. And when they came before the Queene,
   They kneeled down on their knee;
   "What matter! what matter! our gracious Queene,
   You've sent so speedilie?"

10. "Oh, if you are two fryars of France
    Its you that I wished to see;
    But if you are two English lords
    You shall hang on the gallowes tree."

11. "Oh, we are not two English lords,
    But two fryars of France we bee,
    And we sang the Song of Solomon,
    As we came over the sea."

12. "Oh, the first vile sin I did commit,
    Tell it I will to thee:
    I fell in love with the Earl Marshall,
    As he brought me over the sea."

13. "Oh, that was a great sin," quoth the king,
    "But pardon'd it must bee."
    "Amen! Amen!" said the Earl Marshall,
    With a heavie heart spake hee.

14. "Oh the next sin that I did commit,
    I will to you unfolde:
    Earl Marshalle had my virgin dower
    Beneath this cloth of golde."

15. "Oh, that was a vile sin," said the King,
    "May God forgive it thee."
    "Amen! Amen!" groaned the Earl Marshall,
    And a very frightened man was hee.

16. "Oh, the next sin that I did commit,
    Tell it I will to thee:
    I poisoned a lady of noble blood
    For the sake of King Henrie."

17. "Oh, that was a great sin," said the King,
    "But pardoned it shall bee."
    "Amen! Amen!" said the Earl Marshall,
    And still a frightened man was hee.

18. "Oh, the next sin that ever I did,
    Tell it I will to thee:
    I have kept strong poison this seven long years
    To poison King Henrie."

19. "Oh, that was a great sin," said the King,
    "But pardoned it must bee."
    "Amen! Amen!" said the Earl Marshall,
    And still a frightened man was hee.

20. "Oh, dont you see two little boys
    Playing at the football;
    Oh, yonder is the Earl Marshall's son,
    And I like him best of all.

21. "Oh, dont you see yon other little boy
    Playing at the football;
    Oh, that one is King Henrie's son,
    And I like him worst of all.

22. "His head is like a black bull's head—
    His feet are like a bear"—
    "What matter! what matter!" cried the King,
    "He's my son and my only heir!"

23. The King plucked off his fryar's gowne,
    And stood in his scarlet soe red:
    The Queen she turned herself in bed,
    And cryed that she was betrayde.

24. The King lookt o'er his left shoulder,
    And a grim look looked he:
    "Earl Marshall," he said, "but for my oath,
    Thou hadst swung on the gallowes tree."

Gude Wallace

CHILD NO. 157

REFERENCES in the fifteenth and seventeenth centuries inform us that there were wandering ballads on the subject of Wallace in early days (cf. Child, 1882-98, III, p. 266). But there is no evidence that the present ballad has its roots in any of these. Judging by the close correspondence of the versions which Child has assembled, the subject took a new and late start, and Child asserts that Blind Harry's *Wallace* is "clearly" the parent of this second crop. Child's G and H, which add a second episode out of the same original, are, as he says, "plainly a late piece of work, very possibly of this century, much later than the other [i.e., A-F], which itself need not be very old" (*ibid.*). Now, the first recorded appearance of the older part is in a chapbook of about 1745; and why may we not suppose that the reinvention was an offshoot of Jacobite enthusiasm in the first half of the eighteenth century? Certainly it has been carried out by some one steeped in the traditional style—and of such persons eighteenth-century Scotland had store.

Only two musical records have been found, one recovered by Robert Burns, the other of approximately the same era but set down a little later by C. K. Sharpe. The two have nothing in common—further evidence that the ballad had no rooted singing tradition. Burns's is the more homely tune; and Sharpe's seems to have been crossed with "The White Cockade" (cf. Johnson's *Museum*, III, [1790], No. 272).

TUNES WITH TEXTS

1. "Gude Wallace"

Johnson, V, [1796], No. 484, p. 498 (repr. 1853). From Robert Burns; traditional.

p D/Æ

1. O for my ain king, quo gude Wallace,
    The rightfu' king of fair Scotland.
   Between me and my soverign blude
    I think I see some ill seed sawn.

2. Wallace out over yon river he lap,
    And he has lighted low down on yon plain,
   And he was aware of a gay ladie,
    As she was at the well washing.

3. What tydins, what tydins, fair lady, he says,
    What tydins hast thou to tell unto me
   What tydins, what tydins, fair lady, he says,
    What tydins hae ye in the south Countrie.

4. Low down in yon wee Ostler house,
    There is fyfteen Englishmen,
   And they are seekin for gude Wallace,
    It's him to take and him to hang.

5. There's nocht in my purse, quo gude Wallace,
    There's nocht, not even a bare pennie,
   But I will down to yon wee Ostler house
    Thir fyfteen Englishmen to see.

6. And when he cam to yon wee Ostler house,
    He bad bendicite be there;

7. Where was ye born, auld crookit Carl,
    Where was ye born in what countrie,
   I am a true Scot born and bred,
    And an auld crookit carl just sic as ye see.

8. I wad gie fifteen shillings to onie crookit carl,
    To onie crookit carl just sic as ye,
   If ye will get me gude Wallace,
    For he is the man I wad very fain see.

9. He hit the proud Captain alang the chafft blade,
    That never a bit o' meal he ate mair;
   And he sticket the rest at the table where they sat,
    And he left them a' lyin sprawlin there.

10. Get up, get up, gudewife, he says,
     And get to me some dinner in haste;
    For it will soon be three lang days
     Sin I a bit o' meat did taste.

11. The dinner was na weel readie,
     Nor was it on the table set,
    Till other fyfteen Englishmen
     Were a' lighted about the yett.

12. Come out, come out, now gude Wallace
     This is the day that thou maun die;
    I lippen nae sae little to God, he says,
     Altho' I be but ill wordie.

[301]

13. The gudewife had an auld gudeman,
 By gude Wallace he stiffly stood,
 Till ten o' the fyfteen, Englishmen,
 Before the door lay in their blude.

14. The other five to the greenwood ran,
 And he hang'd these five upon a green,
 And on the morn wi' his merry men a'
 He sat at dine in Lochmaben town.

2. "Gude Wallace"

C. K. Sharpe MS. (Macmath transcript, p. 32). Also in Child, 1882-98, V, p. 419; text, V, p. 242.

a P/Æ (or if C tonic, a I/Ly, ending on III)

The Battle of Otterburn

CHILD NO. 161

THE Battle of Otterburn, fought (probably) August 19, 1338, was a Scottish victory. Child declares that "it would be against the nature of things that there should not have been a ballad as early as 1400" on the event (1882-98, III, p. 293). Allusions in *The Complaynt of Scotland*, 1549, indicate that a Scottish ballad on the subject was current in the sixteenth century. The earliest surviving text, however, is of about 1550; and its narrative is from the English point of view. It is likely, Child thinks, to have been modernized from an early predecessor. But this, too, would probably be an English ballad; and of the late eighteenth century Scottish versions and fragments, B-E, Child infers that they have borrowed from the English where correspondences occur. If, as seems altogether probable, "Chevy Chase" (No. 162) celebrates the same battle in later and more romantic fashion, there is no extant ballad from the Scots point of view that can stand comparison with the English. It seems peculiarly unjust that the English should have stolen the bays as well as a victory which they did not win. But justice is a commodity even scarcer in the ballad-world than in history.

Possibly on the musical side the palm may rest with the Scots. We have no knowledge of what the tunes may have been like that went to the earliest texts, known or unknown; and, speaking of "Otterburn" as distinct from "Chevy Chase," there is

in fact no record or hint of an English tune at all. The musical record is thus a blank until the Scottish forms of the ballad emerge toward the end of the eighteenth and early nineteenth century. (And by that time the English ballad seems to have vanished forever from tradition—had in fact departed a hundred and fifty years previously.)

The two musical records which have been preserved are both of about the end of the first quarter of the nineteenth century. There may be a very distant relationship between them, appearing now chiefly in the rhythm; but the tunes are distinct. It is important to note that, contrary to the English tradition, which is consistently CM, the Scottish appears—if we may generalize on so scanty a record—greatly to prefer LM. The present tunes reflect this preference. Of the two, Sharpe's has to our ears the more archaic and plaintive character. Scott's is a form of the tune most generally associated with the famous "Lines" of the Marquis of Montrose, "My dear and only love." Chappell, probably too hastily, has claimed the tune as English. The earliest appearance of any form of it is that in the Skene MS., c. 1627, entitled "Alace I lie my alon, I'm lik to die awld" (transcribed in Dauney, *Ancient Scotish Melodies*, 1838, No. 28, p. 227).

TUNES WITH TEXTS

1. "The Battle of Otterburn"

C. K. Sharpe MS. (Macmath transcript, p. 32). Also in Child, 1882-98, V, p. 419; text, V, p. 243.

m M/D

Cf. the MacColl version of "Hughie the Graeme" (No. 191).

1. It was about the Lammes time,
    When moorland men do win their hay,
  Brave Earl Douglass, in armer bright,
    Marchd to the Border without delay.

2. He hes tean wi him the Lindseys light,
    And sae hes he the Gordons gay,
  And the Earl of Fife, without all strife,
    And Sir Heugh Montgomery upon a day.

3. The hae brunt Northumberland,
    And sae have [the] Northumbershire,
  And fair Cluddendale they hae brunt it hale,
    And he's left it all in fire fair.

4. Ay till the came to Earl Percy's castle,
    Earl Percey's castle that stands sae high:
  "Come dowen, come dowen, thou proud Percey,
    Come down and talk one hour with me.

5. "Come down, come down, thou proud Percey,
    Come down and talk one hour with me;
  For I hae burnt thy heritage,
    And sae will I thy building high."

6. "If ye hae brunt my heritage,
    O dule, O dule, and woe is me!
  But will ye stay at the Otter burn
    Untill I gather my men to me?"

7. "O I will stay at the Otter burn
    The space of days two or three,
  And if ye do not meet me there,
    I will talk of thy coardie."

8. O he hes staid at the Otter burn
    The space of days two or three;
  He sent his page unto his tent-door,
    For to see what ferleys he could see.

9. "O yonder comes yon gallent knight,
    With all bonny banners high;
  It wad do ony living good
    For to see the bonny coulers fly."

10. "If the tale be true," Earl Douglass says,
    "The tidings ye have told to me,

The fairest maid in Otterburn
    Thy bedfellow sure shall she be.

11. "If the tale be false," Earl Douglass says,
    "The tidings that ye tell to me,
The highest tree in Otterburn,
    On it high hangëd shall ye be."

12. Earl Douglass went to his tent-door,
    To see what ferleys he could see;
His little page came him behind,
    And ran him through the fair body.

13. "If I had a little time," he says,
    "To set in order my matters high,
Ye Gordons gay, to you I say,
    See that ye let not my men away.

14. "Ye Linseys light, both wise and wight,
    Be sure ye carry my coulers high;
Ye Gordons gay, again I say,
    See that ye let not my men away.

15. "Sir Heugh Montgomery, my sistir's son,
    I give you the vangaurd over all;
Let it neer be said into old England
    That so little made a true Scot fall.

16. "O lay me dowen by yon brecken-bush,
    That grows upon yon liley lea;
Let it neer be said into old England
    That so little made a true Scot die."

17. At last those two stout knights did meet,
    And O but they were wonderous keen!
The foght with sowards of the temperd steel,
    Till the drops of blood ran them betwen.

18. "O yeald thee, Percie," Montgomery crys,
    "O yeald ye, or I'll lay the low;"
"To whome should I yeald? to whom should I yeald?
    To whom should I yeald, since it most be so?"

19. "O yeald ye to yon breckan-bush,
    That grows upon yon lilley lea;
And if ye will not yeald to this,
    In truth, Earl Percey, I'll gar ye die."

20. "I will not yeald to a breckan-bush,
    Nor yet will I yeald to a brier;
But fain wad I yeald to Earl Douglass,
    Or Sir Heugh Montgomery, if he were here."

21. O then this lord begun to faint,
    And let his soward drop to the ground;
Sir Heugh Montgomery, a courtious knight,
    He bravely took him by the hand.

22. This deed was done at the Otter burn,
    Betwen the sunshine and the day;
Brave Earl Douglass there was slain,
    And they carried Percie captive away.

The text is given from Child.

The Hunting of the Cheviot

CHILD NO. 162

It was this ballad, rather than the preceding, which, Child thinks, evoked the familiar praise of Sir Philip Sidney. Since Sidney called it only "the olde song of Percy and Duglas," it could, as Child admits, have been either; Child gives his vote for the present ballad on grounds of superior merit alone. Our earliest text is the one written down about the middle of the sixteenth century by Richard Sheale, a minstrel from Tamworth. Child supposes that Sidney knew a much older form of it than this, for reasons which I cannot follow. Sheale's version, he writes, "if heard by Sidney, could not have seemed to him a song of an uncivil age, meaning the age of Percy and Douglas, two hundred years before his day. It would give no such impression even now, if chanted to an audience three hundred years later than Sidney" (1882-98, III, p. 305). Elsewhere, Child points out that the grammatical forms of this text are older than those of "Otterburn" (c. 1550), the plural of nouns often keeping a syllabic ending—e.g. *lordes, bowys*; and it is incontrovertible—not to dispute about the reaction of an audience of today—that the ballad seemed so antiquated to the men of the early seventeenth century that it was thoroughly overhauled by the broadside poets, not for its content, but to modernize its old-fashioned style; and in the later form it was everywhere perpetuated with enthusiasm. One can easily suppose that Sidney himself might have felt something antiquated, quite apart from the spelling, about a stanza such as Sheale's forty-seventh:

> Ther was neu*er* a freake wone foot wolde fle,
> but still in stour dyd stand,
> Heawyng on yche othar, whyll*e* the myghte dre,
> w*ith* many a balfull brande.—

Speaking as the courtly, modern author of his own poetry, might he not refer to such verse as "being so evill apparrelled in the dust and cobwebbes of that uncivill age," especially if he had only heard it sung "by some blinde crouder, with no rougher voyce then rude stile?" Generally speaking, the language of a ballad transmitted by word of mouth keeps rough pace with the language of the transmitters; and it seems unlikely that any street-singer of Sidney's day would have proved more of an antiquary than Sheale, a quarter of a century earlier. I must therefore demur at supposing that Sidney had any opportunity to attend an older form of "Chevy Chase" than what has actually, by a miracle, been saved to us, from such a crowder as he describes, and of his own day.

In connection with this ballad, the names of three tunes appear early in the record, though it is not till the beginning of the eighteenth century, so far as I have learned, that words and a tune appear together. Child's collated copies, presumably the earliest and best, indicate the tune of "Flying Fame." Other ballads to be sung to this tune prove that it was in favor as early as 1600; and, with few exceptions, they are in CM.

Chappell remarks (*Popular Music* [1855-59], I, p. 196) that the earlier printed copies of the ballad of "Chevy Chase" direct it to be sung to "In Pescod Time." This tune is preserved in several Elizabethan instrumental MSS., and under that name. I have not seen the copies of the ballad, however, to which Chappell refers, and cannot vouch for the connection alleged.

But Rimbault says (*Musical Illustrations*, 1850, p. 15) that the earliest copy he has seen, printed by T. Passenger on London Bridge, is directed to be sung to this tune; so that the reference appears sufficiently definite. The earliest copies of "The Lady's Fall," a ballad much favored in the seventeenth century, are also to the tune of "Peascod Time," and this ballad seems to have supplanted the older name of the tune with its own name. But neither have I seen any copies of "Chevy Chase" to be sung to the tune of "The Lady's Fall."

Already, by the middle of the seventeenth century, a tune called "Chevy Chase" was being indicated for other ballads; but if there were more than one tune commonly associated with the ballad, any such would serve, and we cannot safely conclude that a single tune had superseded all rivals. It is, however, fairly clear that the *ballad* of "Peascod Time" (which was in *England's Helicon*, 1600) was no longer in circulation, and that its tune was going about under other names, if at all. By the eighteenth century, and throughout its length, "Chevy Chase" was one of the most popular tunes in use for ballads in CM, and copies of the tune under that name, in ballad-operas, etc., are usually found to be one and the same familiar air.

Not always, however. As Chappell remarks (*op.cit.*, I, p. 200), the single-sheets with music, printed about the beginning of the eighteenth century, carry the tune of the "Children in the Wood," which is the same as that of "O Ponder well" in *The Beggar's Opera*, and which is used also in various other ballad operas: *Penelope*, 1728; R. Fabian's *Trick for Trick*, 1735; *The Plot*, 1735. This, too, has Elizabethan roots. Cf. Chappell, *loc.cit.*

Lastly, some later broadsides direct the ballad to be sung to "Rogero," which appears in Elizabethan records perhaps earlier than all the rest, at least by name (Chappell, *op.cit.*, I, pp. 93-94; Rimbault, *op.cit.*, pp. 37-38 and 108). This is the tune, says Rimbault, to which *all* the black letter copies of the "Children" are directed to be sung. Whether these were originally the same tune I cannot decide.

According to Bruce and Stokoe, *Northumbrian Minstrelsy*, 1882, p. 2, the tune of "Ponder Well," or "The Children in the Wood," "is the tune which has been identified with and sung and played to Chevy Chase by all Northumberland minstrels and pipers without exception from time immemorial." Cf. also W. G. Whittaker, "The Folk-music of North-eastern England," in his *Collected Essays*, 1940, p. 36, where he prints the "magnificent melody," calls it "the national anthem of Northumberland," and praises its "simple grandeur and ruggedness" as summarizing the Northumbrian character.

To me it appears that the "Ponder Well" tune is a first cousin of "Peascod Time," with the rhythm stretched in folk fashion. I have not been able to find any early copy of the tune of "Flying Fame" and cannot justly challenge Rimbault's and Chappell's identification of it with the common tune of "Chevy Chase" printed, e.g., by Ritson, 1783, III, pt. 4, sig. I 2ᵛ, "God prosper long our noble king" with the tune-title "Flying Fame." The earliest copy I have seen is of the later seventeenth century in a MS. in the Edinburgh University Library, where it is called "Chevy Chase." The MS. in which it is found has only three traditional tunes, written at the back; the rest is filled with pieces by William Lawes, J. Wilson, and others; so that the MS. is not peculiarly Scottish in character. The Scottish tradition for this ballad, as for the preceding one, appears involved with the tune of Montrose's "Lines." That familiar but variable tune has been printed with the words of Montrose, in Johnson's *Museum*, in the notes to which Stenhouse calls it "the ancient tune of 'Chevy Chase'" (*Museum*, 1853, IV, p. 400); in Maver, *Genuine Scottish Melodies*, 1866; in Eyre-Todd's *Ancient Scots Ballads* [1894], with the words of "Otterbourne," and in Dale's *Collection* [1794]; also R. Bremner, *Second Set of Scots Songs* [1757], and Oswald's *Collection of Scottish Airs*, c. 1760. Bruce and Stokoe print the tune with "Derwentwater's Farewell," with a note on p. 73. It may be that originally these tunes were more closely related; or it may be that the rhythm has worked an associative influence. According to J. C. Dick, *Songs of Burns*, 1903, p. 483, a black letter broadside of the Scottish form of "Chevy Chase" in the Pepysian Library is to be sung to the "Isle of Kell," which is another tune in kindred rhythm, associated with "Hardyknute," as well. It is clear that, whatever the relations, there is a persistent Scottish tendency toward a slow triple rhythm for this ballad's tunes, either:

or else:

One line of the English tradition appears to have followed a triple rhythm of the following type:

Another has taken the 6/8 path, a scheme mainly compound duple, long and short alternating.

The ballad seems not to have flourished outside Britain. From a MS. of c. 1790, coming from Newburyport, Mass., Barry recovered an unusual copy, with affiliations unrecognizable by the present editor; but in this case it was the tune, not the words, that was valued and saved. Nevertheless, the ballad has been found traditionally circulating in this country, and was also printed as a broadside. Cf. Davis, *Traditional Ballads of Virginia*, 1929, pp. 416-18, with references; and Barry, Eckstorm, and Smyth, *British Ballads from Maine*, 1929, pp. 243-48, with a valuable note saying that the "tune" (whichever it was) was a favorite in eighteenth-century New England. Lately, in *More Traditional Ballads of Virginia*, 1960, Davis has printed the tune of the Virginia copy. It appears to me to be a traditional reshaping of "Peascod Time"; but I suspect that 6/8 rather than 2/4 was what the singer may have sung. The difference would be slight.

TUNES WITH TEXTS

GROUP A

1. ["Chevy-chase"]

Ritson, 1783, III, Pt. 4, sig. I 2ᵛ ("Flying Fame").

God prosper long our noble king,
Our lives and safeties all,
A woefull hunting once there did
In Chevy-chase befall.

3. "Chevy Chase"

Edinburgh University Library, MS. Dc. 1.69, p. 4. From the time of Charles II.

O prosper longe our noble Kinge,
Our lives & safetyes all
A woefull Hunting once ther did
In Chevy chase befall.

GROUP B

4. "The More Modern Ballad of Chevy Chace"

Rimbault, 1850, p. 56. From a Virginal book of the time of Elizabeth in Rimbault's possession.

God prosper long our noble king,
Our lives and safetyes all;
A woful hunting once there did
In Chevy Chase befall.

5. "The Battle of Chevy Chase"

Davis, 1960, p. 242. Sung by Miss Martha M. Davis, Harrisonburg, Va., in whose family it is traditional. The text was written down for Miss Davis by her uncle living in California, so far as he could recall it from his mother's singing; and was contributed to the Virginia Archive on January 8, 1914. Tune noted by Eunice Kettering in 1931.

p I/M (-VI)

1. God prosper long our noble king,
   Our lives and safeties all,
   A woeful hunting once there did
   In Chevy Chase befall.

2. Earl Percy of Northumberland
   A vow to God did make
   His pleasure in the Scottish woods
   Two summer days to take,

3. The chiefest harts in Chevy Chase
   To kill and bear away.
   The child may rue that was unborn
   The hunting of that day.

A forgotten verse which tells about the men who were his followers.

4. To chase the dear with hound and horn
   Earl Percy took his way;
   Like tidings to Earl Douglas came
   In Scotland where he lay,

5. Who sent Earl Percy present word
   He would prevent his sport;
   The English Earl not fearing this
   Did to the woods resort.

6. And long before the noon they had
   A hundred fat bucks slain,
   And having dined the drovers went
   To rouse them up again.

7. Earl Percy to the quarry went
   To view the nimble deer.
   He says, "Earl Douglas promisèd
   This day to meet me here.

8. "And if I thought he would not come,
   No longer would I stay,
   For we now have plenty killed
   For us to bear away."

Just then Douglas and his clansmen come into view.

9. Earl Douglas on a milk-white steed,
   Most like a baron bold,
   Rode foremost of his company;
   His armor shone like gold.

Another verse missing, hot words and a challenge from Douglas that they two fight it out, while the men looked on. They fought with swords. At last Douglas saw that Percy was weakening.

10. "Yield, yield, Earl Percy," Douglas said,
    "For faith I will thee bring,
    And thou shalt high renownèd be
    By James our Scottish King."

11. "Nay, nay, Earl Douglas," Percy said,
    "Thy proffer do I scorn,
    I would not yield to any Scot
    That ever yet was born."

They fought on until Percy fell dead. Then an arrow from an English bow struck Douglas. The song says,

12. With such vehement force and might
    It did his body gore,
    The spear went through the other side
    A good cloth yard or more.

Then the fighting became general—a hand to hand fight—neither side would yield until night came when there were only a few left. These deeds of valor of the men with their names were given in the song, but I cannot recall any more of the verse.

GROUP C

6. "Chevy Chase"

Bruce and Stokoe, 1882, p. 3. From Northumbrian tradition.

a I/M

7. "Chevy Chace"

Kidson, 1891, p. 19. From William Cheetham, of Horsforth.

a I/Ly

God prosper long our noble king,
Our lives, and safeties all;
A noble hunting did there once
In Chevy Chace befall.

To drive the deer with hound and horn,
Earl Percy took his way:
The child may rue that is unborn
The hunting of that day.
Etc. etc.

GROUP F

10. "Chevy Chase"

Barry, *JAF*, XVIII (1905), p. 294. From the Perkins MS., c. 1790, Newburyport, Mass.

a I

The Battle of Harlaw

CHILD NO. 163

THE dependable singing tradition of this ballad is confined to the last century and the present, and, as is natural, is narrowly circumscribed in locality. The musical records are surprisingly close to one another; the chief variation lying in the elaboration of the refrain or burden, which varies from one to four phrases in length, but always comes at the end of the stanza and makes play with kindred vocables. The textual record, as we have it, is also confined to the last two centuries.

There is, however, evidence enough that the Scots have long sung about this battle, which occurred in July 1411.[1] Such a song, "The battel of the Hayrlau," is mentioned in *The Complaynt of Scotland*, 1549; and again in the macaronic *Polemo-Middinia*, ascribed to Drummond of Hawthornden:

Interea ante alios dux piperlarius heros

Praecedens, magnamque gestans cum burdine pipam,
Incipit *Harlai* cunctis sonare *Batellum*.

At about the date when these verses were probably written, was set down in the lute-book of Sir Wm. Mure of Rowallan a piece called "Battel of Harlaw" (transcribed and reprinted in Dauney, *Ancient Scotish Melodies*, 1838, p. 349). Dauney regards this as the "march, or rather pibroch," which the piper would have played (*ibid.*, p. 139n.), but I must confess my own skepticism. To me it looks more like a lute accompaniment or obbligato to a tune not recorded in the MS.

[1] Cf. William Mackay, "The Battle of Harlaw: Its true Place in History," *Transactions of the Gaelic Society of Inverness*, XXX (1919-22), pp. 267-85.

TUNES WITH TEXTS

GROUP A a

1. "Battle o' the Harlaw"

Lady John Scott's MS., NL Scotland MS. 840.

m I

1. As I cam in by Garioch's land
   An down by Netherha
   There was fifty thousand hieland men
   A marching to Harlaw.
   Wi' a drie arie dredie drum dree drie

2. As I cam on & farther on
   And down by Balquhaim
   Oh there I met Sir James the Ross
   Wi' him Sir John the Grahame
   Wi' a drie &c.

3. Oh cam ye frae the hielands man
   Oh cam ye a' the way
   Saw ye McDonald and his men
   As they cam frae the Skye

4. Yes we cam frae the hielands man
   An we cam a' the way
   An' we saw McDonnell & his men
   As they cam in frae Skye.

5. Oh was you near McDonells men
   Did ye their numbers see
   Come tell to me John hielandman
   What might their numbers be

6. Yes, we were near & near eneuch
   An' we their numbers saw
   There was fifty thousand hielandman
   A marching to Harlaw.

7. Gin that be true, said James the Ross
   We'll no come muckle speed
   We'll cry upon our merry men
   An' turn our horses head.

8. Oh na, Oh na, says John the Graeme
   That thing maun never be
   The gallant Grahames were never beat
   We'll try what we can die.

9. As I cam on & farther on
   An down & by Harlaw
   They fell fu close on ilka side
   Sic fun you never saw.

10. They fell sic close on ilka side
    Sic fun ye never saw.
    For ilka sword gaid clash for clash
    At the Battle o' Harlaw.

11. The Hielandmen wi' their lang swords
    They laid on us fu sair
    An they drave back our merry men
    Their Armsbredgth & mair

12. Brave Forbes to his brother did say
    O' brither dinna ye see
    They beat us back on ilka side
    And we'll be bound to flee

13. Oh no, oh no, my brother dear
    That thing maun never be.
    You'll tak your guid sword in your hand
    An ye'll gang in wi' me.

14. Then back to back the brothers have
    Gaed in amang the throng
    An' they swept down the Hielandmen
    Wi' swords baith sharp & long.

15. The first ae stroke that Forbes straik
    He garred McDonnell well
    An' the next ae straik that Forbes straik
    The brave McDonnell fell.

16. An' sic cam a pitturichie
    I'm sure you never saw
    As was amang the Hielandmen
    When they saw McDonnell fa.

17. And when they saw that he was dead
    They turned & ran awa
    An' they buried him [in] Syate's Den
    A large mile frae Harlaw

18. Some rade, some ran, & some did gang
    Some went & some .   .   .
    But Forbes an' his merry men
    They slew them on the road

19. On Monday at morning
    The Battle it began
    On Saturday at gloamin
    Ye'll sure kent wha had won

20. An sic a weary burying
    I'm sure ye never saw
    As was the Sunday after that
    On the muirs aneath Harlaw

21. If anybody speir at ye
    For them ye took awa
    Ye may tell them plain & very plain
    There sleepin at Harlaw

GROUP AC

11. "The Battle of Harlaw"

Greig MSS., I, p. 161; text, Bk. 734, XXIV, p. 9. Sung by
J. W. Spence, Rosecroft, Fyvie, April 1906.

m I/M

1. As I cam in by Denniedeer
   An doon by Netherha
   There was fifty thousand Hielandmen
   A' marchin' to Harlaw.
       Wi my dirrum doo dirrum doo
         daddie dirrum dey.

2. As I cam on and farther on
   And doon and by Balquhain
   It's there I met Sir James the Rose
   And wi' him Sir John the Graham

3. Oh cam ye frae the Highlands man
   Oh cam ye a' the wey?
   Saw ye McDonald and his men
   As they came in frae Skye.

4. Yes we cam frae the Highlands man
   An' we cam a' the wey.
   And we saw McDonald & his men
   As they cam in frae Skye.

5. Oh was ye near McDonald's men
   Did ye their numbers see
   Come tell me Johnnie Hielandman
   What micht their numbers be

6. Yes we was near & near eneuch
   And we their numbers saw
   There was fifty thousand Hielandmen
   A marchin' to Harlaw.

7. Gin that be true says Sir James the Rose
   Will come nae muckle speed
   We'll cry upon our merry men
   An' turn oor horses head

8. Oh na, oh na, says John the Graham
   That thing can never be
   The gallant Grahams were never beat
   We'll try what we can dee.

9. As I cam on and farther on
   And doon and by Harlaw
   They fell fu close on ilka side
   Sic strokes ye never saw.

10. They fell fu' close on ilka side
    Sic strokes ye never saw
    For ilka sword gaed clash for clash
    At the battle o' Harlaw.

11. The Hielandmen wi' their lang swords
    They laid on us fu' sair
    And they drove back oor merry men
    Three acres breadth and mair

12. Brave Forbes to his brother said
    Oh brither don't ye see
    They've beat us back on ilka side
    And we'll be forced to flee.

13. Oh na, oh na, my brother said
    That thing can never be
    You'll tak your sword into your hand
    And ye'll come on wi' me

14. Then back to back the brithers twa
    Gaed in among the throng
    And they laid doon the Hielandmen
    Wi' swords baith sharp & lang

15. The first ae stroke that Forbes struck
    He gart McDonald reel

And the neist ae stroke that Forbes struck
The brave McDonald fell.

16. And siccan a Pitlarichie
I'm sure ye never saw
As was among the Hielandmen
When they saw McDonald fa'.

17. And when they saw that he was dead
They turned and ran awa
And they turned him in Leggat's den
A mile abeen Harlaw.

18. Some rade, some ran and some did gang
They were o' sma record

But Forbes and his merry men
They slew them a' the road.

19. On Mononday at mornin'
The battle it began
On Saturday at gloamin'
Ye'd kentna wha had won.

20. Gin onybody spier at you
For them that cam awa
Ye can tell them plain & plain enough
They're sleepin' at Harlaw.

King Henry Fifth's Conquest of France

CHILD NO. 164

THE musical record for this ballad is fuller than one might have expected, and fairly continuous for the last century and a quarter. The earliest variants are Scottish, of the early nineteenth century; those of the mid-century belong to England; and the latest are from New England.

All these belong to the same family, and are of a fairly common type. All except the American versions have an end refrain of one phrase.

This group of tunes is so steeped in the common stuff of British folk-melody that it is very difficult to follow it back with any assurance. It may have a not too distant relative in the tune of the "Oxfordshire Tragedy," which Chappell found in several ballad operas of around 1730. He was "strongly impressed" that it might be an old minstrel tune, and he prints it among tunes of the Elizabethan era. Cf. Chappell, *Popular Music,* [1855-59], I, pp. 190-91.

TUNES WITH TEXTS

GROUP A

1. "The Battle of Agincourt"

C. K. Sharpe MS. (Macmath transcript, p. 32). Also in Child, 1882-98, V, p. 420; text, III, p. 323, and V, p. 245.

a I

1. As our king lay musing on his bed,
    He bethought himself upon a time
Of a tribute that was due from France,
    Had not been paid for so long a time.
        Fal, lal, etc.

2. He called for his lovely page,
    His lovely page then called he,
Saying, You must go to the king of France
    And bring home the tribute that's due to me.

3. O then went away this lovely page,
    This lovely page then away went he;
And when he came to the king of France,
    Low he fell down on his bended knee.

4. "My master the king salutes thee well,
    Salutes thee well, most graciously;
You must go send him his tribute home,
    Or in French land you soon will him see."

5. "Your master's young and of tender years,
    And darna come to my degree;
Go bid him play with his tenish balls,
    For in French lands he dare no me see."

6. O then returned this lovely page,
    This lovely page then returned he,
And when he came to our gracious king,
    Low he fell down on his bended knee.

7. "What news, what news, my trusty page?
    What is the news you have brought to me?"
"Such tidings from the king of France
    As I'm sure with him you can ner agree.

8. "He says you're young and of tender years,
    Not fit to come into his degree,
He bids you play with these tenish balls,
    That with them you may learn to play."

9. "Recruit me Cheshire and Lancashire,
    And Derby Hills that are so free;
No marryd man nor no widow's son;
    For no widow's curse shall go with me."

10. They recruited Cheshire and Lancashire,
    And Derby Hills that are so free:
No marryd man, nor no widow's son;
    They were a jovial good company.

11. He counted oer his merry men,
    Told them by thirty and by three,
And when the[y] were all numberd oer
    He had thirty thousand brave and three.

12. O then we marchd into the French land,
    With drums and trumpets so merrily;
And then bespoke the king of France,
    "Lo, yonder comes proud King Henry."

13. The first that fird, it was the French,
    Upon our English men so free,
But we made ten thousand of them fall,
    And the rest were forc'd for there [sic] lives to flee.

14. Soon we entered Paris gates,
    With drums and trumpets sounding high.
O then bespoke the king of France,
    "Have mercy on [my] men and me.

15. "Take home your tribute, the king he says,
    And three tons of gold I will give to thee,
And the finest flower that is in all France
    To the Rose of England I will give free."

The text above is conflated from Child's a text (III, p. 323) and the variant readings from C. K. Sharpe's MS. which he lists on V, p. 245.

Sir Andrew Barton

CHILD NO. 167

In accordance with the chances of tradition, which include refashioning into print and out of it again, and willful alteration by individuals as well as unconscious change, the life history of this ballad cannot justly be separated from that of its avatar, "Henry Martin" (No. 250). The present division is made only out of deference to Child's example and for the sake of consistency of method.

Apparently "Sir Andrew Barton" was already a very popular song in the sixteenth century; and this favor it retained, as many broadsides remain to testify, throughout the seventeenth, and well into the eighteenth, century.

The earlier copies are all in tetrameter quatrains or double quatrains. Where a direction for a tune is given, it is always, "Come follow my Love, &c.," which, I believe, can only be the tune of the "Fair Flower of Northumberland" (No. 9), a song that Deloney liked well enough to include in his *Jacke of Newbrie*, c. 1597. The musical tradition for the "Fair Flower," so far as it is now known, is late, and Scottish, but quite consistent and uniform. Its metre is 6/8, and perfectly suited to "Barton." But no copy of the tune as early as the seventeenth century appears to have survived.

Other broadsides of the seventeenth century are extant, directed to be sung to the tune of "Sir Andrew Barton," which would suggest that the present song supplanted the other in familiar use and in turn gave its name to the tune. (Cf., e.g., Roxburghe Collection, I, 44, "A Comparison of the Life of Man"; Huth Collection, Harvard College Library, II, 291, "A Warning for all Lewd Livers," printed W. O. for A. M., sold by J. Deacon.) White-letter copies of "Sir Andrew" carry no indications of a tune.

A number of versions have turned up in recent tradition in this country which seem to preserve more elements of the earlier form of the ballad than of the commoner "Henry Martin" variety; but they are impossible to disentangle—if in fact we ought to try—and will be dealt with more conveniently under the latter head, q.v. (*post*, No. 250).

The tunes here gathered are all from New England, with one exception. The exception was brought to California by a migratory worker from Wisconsin, and may have been carried thither from Maine along the lumberman's trail. All bear pretty clear marks of a single melodic tradition.

TUNES WITH TEXTS

2. "Andrew Bardeen"

Flanders, 1937, p. 8. Sung by Euclid I. Williams, Lower Waterford, Vt., c. 1934. From *Country Songs in Vermont*, collected by Helen Hartness Flanders; copyright 1937 by Helen Hartness Flanders.

p I

1. Three loving brothers in Scotland did dwell
    And loving were the three.
  They each cast lots to see which of the three
    Should go robbing around the salt sea,
  They each cast lots to see which of the three
    Should go robbing around the salt sea.

2. The lot it fell upon Andrew Bardeen,
    The youngest of all the three,
  And for to maintain his two older brothers
    Went robbing around the salt sea.

3. He had not sailed but one summer night,
    When daylight did appear:
  He saw a ship sailing very far off,
    And at last it came sailing quite near.

4. "Who's there, who's there?" cried Andrew Bardeen.
    "Who's there that sails so nigh?"
  "We are the rich merchants from Merrie England
    And no offense. Let us by!"

5. "Oh no! Oh no!" said Andrew Bardeen,
    "Oh no! That never can be.
  Your ship I'll have, and your cargo, too,
    And your bodies I'll sink in the sea."

6. Now when this news reached Merrie England
    (King George he wore the crown)
  That his ship and his cargo were taken away,
    And his brave men they were all drowned,

7. "Go build me a ship," says Captain Charles Stewart,
    "A ship both stout and sure,
  And if I don't fetch this Andrew Bardeen,
    My life shall no longer endure."

8. He had not sailed but one summer's night
    When daylight did appear.
  He saw a ship sailing very far off—
    At last it came sailing quite near.

9. "Who's there? Who's there?" cried Captain Charles
    Stewart,
    "There that sails so nigh?"
  "We are the bold brothers from Merrie Scotland
    And no offense. Let us by."

10. "Oh no! Oh no!" cried Captain Charles Stewart,
    "Oh no! that never can be;

Your ship I'll have and your cargo, too,
  And your bodies I'll carry with me."

11. Then they drew up a full broadside
  And each to the other let pour.
They had not fought but a very short time
  When Captain Charles Stewart gave o'er.

12. "Go home, go home," says Andrew Bardeen,
  "And tell your king for me
That he may reign king of the merrie dry land,
  But that I will be king of the sea."

5b. "Andrew Briton," or "The Three Brothers"

Barry, 1939, p. 64. Sung by Lamont Forbuss, Monson, Me.

a M (inflected VII)

1. There were three brothers in old Scotland,
  Three brothers and only three;
And they did cast lots, and they did cast lots,
  To see who should maintain the whole three.

2. The lot it fell to young Andrew Britón,
  The youngest of the three,
That he should turn robber upon the salt sea,
  To maintain his two brothers and he.

3. They had not been sailing past two in the night,
  Before a loft ship they did spy;
At length she came sailing far off and far on,
  And at length she came sailing close by.

4. "Who's there, who's there?" cries Andrew Britón,
  "Who's there a-sailing so nigh?"
"It's a rich merchant ship from old merry England,
  Will you please, sir, to let us pass by?"

5. "O no, O no," cries Andrew Britón,
  "O no, such a thing ne'er can be;
We'll take your ship, your cargo too,
  And your mariners drown in the sea!"

6. When the news went back to old merry England,
  King George was wearing the crown;
"A rich merchant ship has been taken and robbed,
  And the mariners all of them drowned."

7. "Go build me a ship," cries Captain Charles Stewart,
  "Go build it firm and secure;
And if I don't show you young Andrew Britón,
  My life I'll no longer endure!"

8. He had not been sailing past two in the night,
  Before a loft ship he did spy;
At length she came sailing far off and far on,
  And at length she came sailing close by.

9. "Who's there, who's there?" cries Captain Charles Stewart,
  "Who's there a-sailing so nigh?"
"It's two bold pirates from old Scotland,
  Will you please, sir, to let us pass by?"

10. "O no, O no," cries Captain Charles Stewart,
  "O no, such a thing ne'er can be;
We'll take your ship, your cargo too,
  And your mariners drown in the sea."

11. "Fire on, fire on," says Andrew Britón,
  "I value you not one pin;
If you're good brass on the outside,
  We'll show you bright steel within."

12. They fought, they fought full four hours long
  While cannon like thunder did roar;
They fought, they fought full four hours long,
  When Captain Charles Stewart gave o'er.

13. "Send word right back to old merry England,
  And tell King George for me,
If he reigns king o'er old England,
  Young Andrew reigns king o'er the sea!"

8. "Andrew Batan"

Sung by Warde H. Ford, Central Valley, Calif., Christmas Day, 1938. Learned from his uncle, Charles Walker, of Crandon, Wis., who had it from a Scottish logger in Coeur d'Alene, Idaho, in 1906. LC/AAFS, rec. No. 4194(B1). Also in LC/AAFS, rec. No. L58(A2); and on Folkways rec. No. P4001(B2). Collected by Mrs. Sidney Robertson Cowell.

a M/D

1. There once were three brothers from merry Scotland,
  From merry Scotland were they;
They cast a lot to see which of them
  Would go robbing all o'er the salt sea.

2. The lot it fell to Andrew Batan,
   The youngest one of the three,
   That he should go robbing all o'er the salt sea
   To maintain his three brothers and he.

3. He had not sailed but one summer's eve,
   When a light it did appear;
   It sailed far off and it sailed far on
   And at last it came sailing so near.

4. Who art, who art, cried Andrew Batan,
   Who art that sails so nigh?
   We are the rich merchants from old Eng-a-land
   And I pray you will let us pass by.

5. O no, O no, cried Andrew Batan,
   O no, that never can be;
   Your ships and your cargo I'll take them away
   And your merry men drown in the sea.

6. When the news reached old Eng-a-land
   What Andrew Batan had done,
   Their ships and their cargo he'd taken away
   And all of their merry men drowned.

7. Build me a boat, cried Captain Charles Stuart,
   And build it strong and secure,
   And if I don't capture Andrew Batan
   My life I'll no longer endure.

8. He had not sailed but one summer's eve,
   When a light it did appear;
   It sailed far off and it sailed far on
   And at last it came sailing so near.

9. Who art, who art, cried Captain Charles Stuart,
   Who art that sails so nigh?
   We're the jolly Scots robbers from merry Scotland
   And I pray you will let us pass by.

10. O no, O no, cried Captain Charles Stuart,
    O no, that never can be.
    Your ship and your cargo I'll take it away,
    And your merry men drown in the sea.

11. What ho, what ho, cried Andrew Batan,
    I value you not one pin,
    For while you show me fine brass without
    I'll show you good steel within.

12. Then broadside to broadside these ships they stood
    And like thunder their cannon did roar;
    They had not fought but two hours or so,
    Till Captain Charles Stuart gave o'er.

13. Go home, go home, cried Andrew Batan,
    And tell your king for me,
    While he remains king upon the dry land,
    I'll remain king of the sea.

Johnie Armstrong

CHILD NO. 169

WHETHER or no "Ihonne Ermistrangis dance," mentioned in *The Complaynt of Scotland*, 1549, had anything to do with the extant tune, no musical record has survived with this ballad which is not probably related to a single tune-family. The first record of a tune, called "Good night and God be with you," appears in the Skene MS., No. 109, transcribed in Dauney, *Ancient Scotish Melodies*, 1838, No. 16, p. 222. All our melodic records with clear textual connections are early nineteenth-century Scottish ones. The tune exists under a variety of later names. Cf. Stenhouse, *The Scots Musical Museum*, 1853, IV, No. 356, p. 335. Stenhouse observes that the tune is in Oswald's *Caledonian Pocket Companion* (Bk. IX, p. 13, according to Glen), and "would appear to be the progenitor of that class of airs so frequently noticed under the name of *Todlen Hame—*

Lament for the Chief—Robidh donna gorradh, and several others." Miss Gilchrist refers to *The Scots Musical Museum*, No. 275, for "Todlen Hame," and notes that the air is now familiar as "My Ain Fireside," and in Ireland as "The Old Head of Denis" (*JEFDSS*, III, No. 3 [1938], p. 191).

The tune indications in the early broadsides are not very serviceable: "To a pretty northern tune called, Fare you well, guilt Knock-hall," "To a pretty new northern tune," "To a Northern Tune." Douce Ballads, II, fol. 151ᵛ, Bodleian Library, Oxford ("The married wives Complaint of her unkind husband &c.") has "jonny armstrong" for its tune—along with "True love rewarded with loyalty," and "a very pleasant new tune." The metre is consistently that of LM quatrains.

TUNES WITH TEXTS

GROUP A

3. "Johnie Armstrang"

Scott, 1833-34, I, opp. p. 416; text, p. 407. Words from Allan Ramsay, *The Ever Green*, 1724 (Child's C); Ramsay learned them from "a gentleman called Armstrong."

m I

1. Sum speikis of lords, sum speikis of lairds,
    And sick lyke men of hie degrie;
    Of a gentleman I sing a sang,
    Sum tyme called Laird of Gilnockie.

2. The King he wrytes a luving letter,
    With his ain hand sae tenderly,
    And he hath sent it to Johnie Armstrang,
    To cum and speik with him speedily.

3. The Eliots and Armstrangs did convene;
    They were a gallant cumpanie—
    "We'll ride and meit our lawful King,
    And bring him safe to Gilnockie.

4. "Make kinnen and capon ready, then,
    And venison in great plentie;
    We'll wellcum here our royal King;
    I hope he'll dine at Gilnockie!"—

5. They ran their horse on the Langholme howm,
    And brak their spears wi' mickle main;
    The ladies lukit frae their loft windows—
    "God bring our men weel hame agen!"

6. When Johnie cam before the King,
    Wi' a' his men sae brave to see,
    The King he movit his bonnet to him;
    He ween'd he was a King as weel as he.

7. "May I find grace, my sovereign liege,
    Grace for my loyal men and me?
    For my name it is Johnie Armstrang,
    And a subject of yours, my liege," said he.

8. "Away, away, thou traitor strang!
    Out o' my sight soon mayst thou be!
    I grantit never a traitor's life,
    And now I'll not begin wi' thee."—

9. "Grant me my life, my liege, my King!
    And a bonny gift I'll gie to thee—
    Full four-and-twenty milk-white steids,
    Were a' foal'd in ae yeir to me.

10. "I'll gie thee a' these milk-white steids,
    That prance and nicker at a speir;
And as mickle gude Inglish gilt,
    As four o' their braid backs dow bear."—

11. "Away, away, thou traitor strang!
    Out o' my sight soon mayst thou be!
I grantit never a traitor's life,
    And now I'll not begin wi' thee!"—

12. "Grant me my life, my liege, my King!
    And a bonny gift I'll gie to thee—
Gude four-and-twenty ganging mills,
    That gang thro' a' the yeir to me.

13. "These four-and-twenty mills complete
    Sall gang for thee thro' a' the yeir;
And as mickle of gude reid wheit,
    As a' thair happers dow to bear."—

14. "Away, away, thou traitor strang!
    Out o' my sight soon mayst thou be!
I grantit never a traitor's life,
    And now I'll not begin wi' thee."—

15. "Grant me my life, my liege, my King!
    And a great great gift I'll gie to thee—
Bauld four-and-twenty sisters' sons,
    Sall for thee fecht, tho' a' should flee!"—

16. "Away, away, thou traitor strang!
    Out o' my sight soon mayst thou be!
I grantit never a traitor's life,
    And now I'll not begin wi' thee."—

17. "Grant me my life, my liege, my King!
    And a brave gift I'll gie to thee—
All between heir and Newcastle town
    Sall pay their yeirly rent to thee."—

18. "Away, away, thou traitor strang!
    Out o' my sight soon mayst thou be!
I grantit never a traitor's life,
    And now I'll not begin wi' thee."—

19. "Ye lied, ye lied, now, King," he says,
    "Altho' a King and Prince ye be!
For I've luved naething in my life,
    I weel dare say it, but honesty—

20. "Save a fat horse, and a fair woman,
    Twa bonny dogs to kill a deir;
But England suld have found me meal and mault,
    Gif I had lived this hundred yeir!

21. "She suld have found me meal and mault,
    And beef and mutton in a' plentie;
But never a Scots wyfe could have said,
    That e'er I skaith'd her a puir flee.

22. "To seik het water beneith cauld ice,
    Surely it is a greit folie—
I have asked grace at a graceless face,
    But there is nane for my men and me!

23. "But had I kenn'd ere I cam frae hame,
    How thou unkind wadst been to me!
I wad have keepit the Border side,
    In spite of all thy force and thee.

24. "Wist England's King that I was ta'en,
    O gin a blythe man he wad be!
For anes I slew his sister's son,
    And on his breist bane brak a trie."—

25. John wore a girdle about his middle,
    Imbroider'd ower wi' burning gold,
Bespangled wi' the same metal,
    Maist beautiful was to behold.

26. There hang nine targats at Johnie's hat.
    And ilk ane worth three hundred pound—
"What wants that knave that a King suld have,
    But the sword of honour and the crown?

27. "O where got thou these targats, Johnie,
    That blink sae brawly abune thy brie?"—
"I gat them in the field fechting,
    Where, cruel King, thou durst not be.

28. "Had I my horse, and harness gude,
    And riding as I wont to be,
It suld have been tauld this hundred yeir,
    The meeting of my King and me!

29. "God be with thee, Kirsty, my brother,
    Lang live thou Laird of Mangertoun!
Lang mayst thou live on the Border syde,
    Ere thou see thy brother ride up and down!

30. "And God be with thee, Kirsty, my son,
    Where thou sits on thy nurse's knee!
But an thou live this hundred yeir,
    Thy father's better thou'lt never be.

31. "Farewell! my bonny Gilnock hall,
    Where on Esk side thou standest stout!
Gif I had lived but seven yeirs mair,
    I wad hae gilt thee round about."

32. John murder'd was at Carlinrigg,
    And all his gallant companie;
But Scotland's heart was ne'er sae wae,
    To see sae mony brave men die—

33. Because they saved their country deir
    Frae Englishmen! Nane were sa bauld,
Whyle Johnie lived on the Border syde,
    Nane of them durst cum neir his hauld.

7. "Johnnie Armstrong"

Harris MS., No. 19. Also in Child, 1882-98, V, p. 420. From Mrs. Amelia Harris; learned from an old nurse during childhood in Perthshire, late eighteenth century. Noted by her daughter.

169. JOHNIE ARMSTRONG

a I/Ly, ending on the octave

There liv'd a man in the northwest land,
 His name was Johnnie Armstrong,
He had neither lands nor rents,
 But he keepit eight score o' gallant men.

The Death of Queen Jane

CHILD NO. 170

ALL the tunes of this ballad are comparatively recent—so, indeed, are the texts as well—and all are closely related. Nearly all are in genuinely triple rhythm. The earliest record, full of accidentals, is that of Kinloch, 1827. Gilchrist has recovered one that goes back to c. 1845; and R. W. Gordon has recorded a version that can be traced to Ireland, c. 1880. The rest are later, and come from Devon, Somerset, and Dorset; and from Kentucky and Virginia. It should be observed that three of the Appalachian variants are in common time; but this would appear to be a local idiosyncrasy, stretching the basic triple time in the drawling mountain fashion.

One may suspect that nursery influence has been at work here upon a carol tune (perhaps "When Joseph and Mary").

The melodic tradition, in any case, relates to that of Child No. 54.

In an appendix (1882-98, V, p. 293), Child has printed a version of "The Duke of Bedford," certain stanzas of which, depicting the funeral ceremonies, he declares to be a plagiarism from the present ballad. The same song, under various titles, has been picked up on both shores of the Atlantic: cf., e.g., Sharp, *One Hundred English Folksongs*, 1916, pp. 50-51, and the references he gives on pp. xxvi-xxvii of the same work. A Vermont copy may be added: Flanders and Brown, *Vermont Folk-Songs and Ballads*, 1931, p. 219 ("Two Dukes"). The tunes of these are rhythmically like the ballad on Queen Jane and may perhaps be related.

TUNES WITH TEXTS

GROUP A

3. "Queen Jane"

Sharp MSS., 959/1001. Also in Sharp, *JFSS*, V, No. 20 (1916), p. 257; Sharp, 1916, p. 68; and Sharp, Selected Ed. [1920], II, p. 30. Sung by Mrs. Sweet (61), Somerton, Somerset, August 2, 1906.

a I

1. Queen Jane was in labour
   For six days or more
   Till the women got tired
   And wished it all o'er.

2. Good women, good women
   Good women if you be
   Will you send for King Henry
   King Henry I must see.

3. King Henry was a sent for,
   King Henry did come home
   For to meet with Queen Jane my love[1]
   Your eyes look so dim.

4. King Henry King Henry
   King Henry if you be
   Will you have my right side cut open[2]
   You will find my dear baby.

5. Queen Jane my love, Queen Jane my love
   Such things were never known
   If you open your right side
   You will lose your dear baby.

6. King Henry, King Henry
   King Henry if you be
   Will you build your love a castle
   And lie down so deep
   For to bury my body
   And to christen my dear baby.

7. King Henry went mourning
   And so did his men
   And so did his dear baby
   For Queen Jane did die in.[3]

8. And how deep was the mourning
   How wide was the bands
   How yellow was the flower my boys
   She carried in her hands.

9. How she hold[4] it, how she rumpled it,
   How she hold it in her hand
   Saying the flower of old England
   Shall never detain[5] me long.

10. There was fiddling there was dancing
    The day the babe was born
    To see that Queen Jane my love
    Lying so cold as a stone.

[1] *JFSS*: beloved
[2] *JFSS*: opened
[3] *JFSS*: die-en
[4] *JFSS*: rolled
[5] *JFSS*: retain

5. "Queen Jane"

Sharp MSS., 4152/2994. Also in Sharp and Karpeles, 1932, I, p. 231(B). Sung by Mrs. Margaret Dunagan, St. Helen's, Lee County, Ky., October 12, 1917.

170. THE DEATH OF QUEEN JANE

m M (−VI; inflected VII)

1. King Henry was sent for
   All in the time of her need;
   King Henry he came
   In the time of her need.

2. King Henry he stooped
   And kissed her on the lips.
   What's the matter with my flower,
   Makes her eyes look so red.

3. King Henry, King Henry,
   Will you take me to be,
   To pierce my side open
   And save my baby.

4. O no, Queen Jane,
   Such thing never shall be;
   To lose my sweet flower
   For to save my baby.

5. Queen Jane she turned over
   And fell in a swound;
   Her side were pierced
   And her baby was found.

6. How bright was the mourning,
   How yellow were the bed,
   How costly was the shroud
   Queen Jane were wrapped in.

7. There's six followed after
   And six carried her along;
   King Henry he followed
   With his black mourning on.

8. King Henry he wept
   And wrung his hands till they're sore.
   The flower of England
   Shall never be no more.

Mary Hamilton

CHILD NO. 173

THIS poignant ballad, whenever it arose, has been greatly favored in the last century and a half, particularly, of course, among the Scots and singers with Scottish connections.

There are about a dozen and a half apparently independent records of a tune, of which perhaps half form a single close group (D), late in the records, the others appearing to be distinct and usually separate. It is a little odd that whereas all the verbal texts are in CM, three of the oldest musical records are in LM. Two of these unfortunately lack words; but the third shows that the second and fourth lines were lengthened by the simple addition of "O" at the end of the line. Probably the same means was employed in the other two copies also. All the other tunes are CM four-phrase tunes. The homogeneous group is confined to the Major galaxy. A triple rhythm is the rule, usually in a 6/8 form, slowed sometimes to 3/4 in singing.

There is very considerable divergence among the texts, and this variety is matched by the outlying tunes:—a fact which has been noted earlier as characteristic of another ballad that may have arisen late, "Sir Patrick Spens" (No. 58). It is more usual for a ballad with firm roots in tradition to present a homogeneity in the musical records. Whether the present variation makes for the theory of a late origin, one cannot confidently say. I incline to that belief, but would not lean on it very heavily. Professor Davis joins A. H. Tolman in believing in a sixteenth-century origin. Cf. his recent discussion in *More Traditional Ballads of Virginia*, 1960, pp. 247-249.

Child has noted echoes of six other ballads in this one; to which I believe is certainly to be added "Geordie" (No. 209), reinforced by a tune-relation; and possibly "The Cruel Mother" (No. 20), to which Sharpe's tune of the present ballad also points. Such abundant indebtedness once again suggests a late but popular birth.

To attack the well-known essay of Andrew Lang, which reconverted Child (who wanted only to be persuaded) to the older date for the ballad, and which has held the field undisputed since 1895, would be presumptuous unless it were done exhaustively, or with the citation of new and positive evidence. Here it is improper to attempt the former, and it remains impossible to do the latter. It may be allowable, however, to remark that the weight of his argument rests on two piers, neither of which is entitled to the confidence he gives it. One is that ballads were no longer being composed in the old manner in eighteenth-century Scotland, and that that style was "utterly obsolete and unimitated," "entirely superseded by new kinds of popular poetry" (*Blackwood's Magazine*, CLVII [1895], pp. 388, 385). To this it can be replied that the line between crea-

tion and re-creation in this area is not easily to be drawn, and that nothing is more abundantly supported by evidence of the last two centuries, in the volumes of Child, Greig, and others, than the following: the style of the old balladry was so far from being obsolete in Scotland that it is mainly eighteenth-century Scottish forms of the ballads which give us English-speaking folk our clearest sense of ballad-style. Moreover, when he talks about "new" styles, he is simply comparing the work of the professional ballad-monger, or broadside poetaster, or sophisticated or semi-sophisticated versifier, with a sort of poetry the difference of which from the other no one knew better than himself—a difference which is, of course, undisputed. But if it is easy to show that the mass of poets which produced the broadsides was turning such things out by the score as early as the sixteenth century, it is equally easy to prove that the Mrs. Browns of eighteenth-century Scotland did not merely repeat what they had memorized from other singers, but actually re-created the song in other words (and musical notes) drawn from a reservoir of conventional language, theme, and phrase to which the community had equal rights—just as the community at large had rights of pasturage and cultivation in the eighteenth century to the Common Land of the district. Lang forgets that on one side of his opposition he has nothing to pose, only because the evidence was inevitably unwritten at the time: there was no *corpus delicti* to produce. One side of the evidence was written, the other was oral, until such time as the romantic revival instigated a *recording* of the other side as well.

The other main support to his argument is the great variety in the recorded texts. "We have," he says, "been invited to suppose that, about 1719, a Scot wrote a ballad . . . ; that his poem underwent, in seventy years, even more vicissitudes than most other ballads encounter in three or perhaps even five centuries" (p. 389). To this it is fair to reply that the demonstration by numbers in the field of popular poetry *proves* nothing, and serves at best as a straw in the wind. That, moreover, the rate of variational activity may depend on the vitality of the tradition; and, granted the vitality which can be demonstrated in eighteenth-century Scotland, more evidence of textual variation might easily be produced of a living ballad in seventy years than could be shown in a moribund or dead ballad, by written record, in three or five hundred years.

It will probably continue to be impossible to prove conclusively either an early or a late date for the present ballad. The object of the foregoing remarks is simply to suggest that nothing yet has been said on either side which need commit us to a decision.

TUNES WITH TEXTS

GROUP A

3. "Mary Hamilton"

Lady John Scott's Sharpe MS., NL Scotland MS. 843, fol. 13.

p I

1. There lived a knight into the North,
    And he had daughters three, O;
  The ane o' them was a barber's wife,
    The other a gay ladie, O.

2. The youngest o' them to Scotland is gane
    The Queen's Mary to be, O;
  And for a' that they could say or do
    Forbidden she wouldna be, O.

.   .   .   .

3. "Busk ye, busk ye, Mary Hamilton,
    O busk ye to be a bride, O;
  For I am gaen to Edinbro' town
    Your gay wedding to bide, O.

4. "You must not put on your robes of black
    Nor yet your robes of brown, O;
  But you must put on your yellow gold stuffs,
    To shine thro' Edinbro' town, O."

5. "I will not put on my robes of black,
    Nor yet my robes of brown; O, [*sic*]
  But I will put on my yellow gold stuffs,
    To shine thro' Edinbro' town, O.["]

6. As she went up the Parliament Close,
    A riding on her horse, O;
  There she saw many a Burgess' lady
    Sit greeting at the cross, O.

7. "O what means a' this greeting here?
    I'm sure its nae for me, O;
  For I'm come this day to Edinbro' town
    Weel wedded for to be, O."

8. When she gaed up the Parliament stair,
    She gied loud lauchters three, O;
  But ere that she had come down again,
    She was condemn'd to die[, O].

9. "O little did my mother think,
    That day she cradled me, O;
  That I wad gae sae far frae hame
    A shamefu' death to dee, O.

10. "O little did my mother think
    The day she prinn'd my gown, O;
  That I was to come sae far frae home
    To be hang'd in Edinbro' town, O.

.   .   .   .

11. "Yestreen the Queen had four Maries,
    This night she'll hae but three, O;
  There was Mary Beaton, and Mary Seaton,
    And Mary Carmichael, and me, O."

This looks like a bowdlerized version of Child's D (from Motherwell's MS. not then printed).

GROUP C

5. "Marie Hamilton"

Harris MS., No. 9; text, fol. 10 b. Also in Child, 1882-98, V, p. 421; text, III, p. 394(J). From Mrs. Amelia Harris; learned from an old nurse during childhood in Perthshire, late eighteenth century. Noted by her daughter.

m D/Æ

1. My mother was a proud, proud woman,
    A proud, proud woman and a bold;
  She sent me to Queen Marie's bour,
    When scarcely eleven years old.

2. Queen Marie's bread it was sae sweet,
    An her wine it was sae fine,
  That I hae lien in a young man's arms,
    An I rued it aye synsyne.

3. Queen Marie she cam doon the stair,
    Wi the goud kamis in her hair:
  "Oh whare, oh whare is the wee wee babe
    I heard greetin sae sair?"

4. "It's no a babe, a babie fair,
    Nor ever intends to be;
  But I mysel, wi a sair colic,
    Was seek an like to dee."

5. They socht the bed baith up an doon,
    Frae the pillow to the straw,
  An there they got the wee wee babe,
    But its life was far awa.

6. "Come doon, come doon, Marie Hamilton,
    Come doon an speak to me;

.   .   .   .
.   .   .   .

7. "You'll no put on your dowie black,
    Nor yet your dowie broun;
  But you'll put on your ried, ried silk,
    To shine through Edinborough toun."

.   .   .   .

8. "Yestreen the queen had four Maries,
    The nicht she'll hae but three;
  There was Marie Bethune, an Marie Seaton,
    An Marie Carmichael, an me.

9. "Ah, little did my mother ken,
    The day she cradled me,
  The lands that I sud travel in,
    An the death that I suld dee."

10. Yestreen the queen had four Maries,
    The nicht she has but three;
    For the bonniest Marie amang them a'
    Was hanged upon a tree.

The text here printed is from Child. In the MS., the first stanza reads:

My mother was a proud woman;
A proud woman and a bold.
She sent me to Queen Marie's bour,
When scarce eleven years old.

GROUP D

6. [Mary Mild]

Greig and Keith, 1925, p. 109(2); text, (B). Also, from different singers, in Vaughan Williams MSS., III, p. 357; Davis, 1929, p. 590; text, p. 422(B); and on Caedmon rec. No. TC 1146(A7). From Mrs. Walker, Rayne; learned in the Huntly district.

a I

The variants appear in the copy in Colin Brown, *The Thistle*, 1884, according to Miss Gilchrist (*JEFDSS*, III, No. 1 [1936], p. 60). She quotes Brown, whom I have not seen, as saying that this tune had "always" been associated with the ballad in the highlands of Perthshire. There seems to be no earlier record of the tune.

1. Last nicht there were four Maries,
    The nicht they'll be but three;
    There was Mary Seaton, an' Mary Beaton,
    An' Mary Carmichael, an' me.

2. O little did my mother think,
    When first she cradled me,

That I wad be sae far fae hame
An' hang on a gallows tree.

3. They tied a napkin roon my e'en,
    To nae lat me see to dee;
    They neither tell't my father or mother
    That I was awa ower the sea.

4. But I mysel am Mary Mill [*sic*],
    The flower o a' the three;
    But I hae kill't my bonnie wee son,
    An' weel deserved to dee.

5. But ye'll bury me in the aul kirkyard
    Beneath the aul yew tree,
    Where we pull'd the gowans an' ringed the rowans,
    My sisters an' brother an' me.

6. O what care I for a nameless grave
    If I've hope for eternity?
    For it was for the blood of the dyin lamb,
    That's granted through grace unto me.

GROUP E

11.1. "The Four Maries"

Duncan MSS., "Airs," p. 522. Sung by Miss Susan Strachan; from her mother. Noted November 24, 1916.

m I/M

Yestreen there were four Maries,
The nicht there'll be but three;
There was Mary Seaton, and Mary Beaton,
And Mary Carmichael and me.

Captain Car, or, Edom o Gordon

CHILD NO. 178

OF THIS fine ballad, three tunes, all of the second half of the last century, have been recorded from tradition. There is, however, an older claimant for the place of honor: the Elizabethan tune supposed to be referred to in *Much Ado* as the "sick tune" (III. iv. 42). A ballad called "Sick, sick, &c." was licensed to be printed on March 24, 1578; another ballad on an incident of 1578, to the tune of "Sicke and sicke," is, as Chappell notes (*Popular Music* [1855-59], I, p. 226), in the *Harleian Miscellany*, X, p. 272. The latter is in eight-line CM stanzas rhyming alternately, with a four-line burden in the same metre as that of the A-text of "Captain Car." The present ballad is itself in CM quatrains followed in each case by the burden; but if the burden is to be sung to the same notes as the stanza, four lines will suit the tune as well as eight or twelve. The tune in question Chappell has found in Anthony Holborne's *Cittharn Schoole*, 1597, and in one of the Cambridge University lute MSS. (Dd. iv. 23). He prints a transcript, without saying which copy he follows (*loc.cit.*). The result is unsatisfactory in any case; and not much more can be said for other versions.*

It is possible, if unlikely, that a ballad on a local incident in Scotland could be carried into England, and be Anglicized, and gain such currency that seven years after the actual event its burden would have become the accepted name of its tune. Since, however, burdens of this detachable kind are very rare in English balladry; since this one is not found in any other copy; and since, finally, it is not in the least appropriate to the ballad, which concerns matters very different from illness: it is easier to suppose that the burden got attached to this copy of the ballad when someone decided to sing the ballad to the tune of a pre-existent song with this burden—a song which itself has not survived, perhaps a song of the plague, something earlier and less artistic than Thomas Nashe's "Adieu, farewell earth's bliss," which yet has a very similar refrain. It is interesting that in the same work in which Nashe published his beautiful poem, he inserted a parody of the burden in question. (Cf. the extract published in Chappell, *loc.cit.*)

I take it, therefore, that the association of this tune and burden with our ballad is likely fortuitous and transient. The nineteenth-century tunes, on the contrary, though interestingly variant, are clearly related. They are forms of a tune in common use, however: the "Boyne Water" family. The earliest to be printed for this ballad is that in the second (1869) edition of Ritson's *Scotish Songs*. Its immediate provenience is not stated. Close variants are found with "Sir James the Rose" (Child No. 213). Greig and Keith, *Last Leaves*, give five examples; and it occurs with "Hardyknute," "Gil Morice" (Child No. 83), "Macdonald of the Isles" (No. 228), and no doubt elsewhere. The next copy to appear was Christie's, from an old Banff-shire woman, who died in 1866 at the age of eighty and whose memory might therefore carry the tradition back to the beginning of the century and probably beyond. Christie has as usual given the tune a second strain: if there was one in the singer's version, it is yet unlikely that the whole tune had a compass of an octave and a sixth.

* See further, Claude M. Simpson, *The British Broadside Ballad and Its Music*, New Brunswick, 1966, pp. 660-61.

TUNES WITH TEXTS

4. "Edom o' Gordon"

Christie, I, 1876, p. 56. From an old woman in Buckie, Banffshire (d. 1866, aged 80).

m π³

It fell about the Martinmas,
  When winds blew shrill and cauld,
Said Edom o' Gordon to his men,
  "We maun draw to a hauld.
And whatna hauld sha!l we draw to,
  My merrie men and me?
We will gae to the house o' Rodes,
  To see that fair ladye."

[*Etc.*]

Christie "epitomizes" his text from Percy's *Reliques* (cf. Wheatley ed., 1910, I, p. 143) and Ritson's *Scotish Songs* (cf. ed. of 1869. II, p. 362).

5. "Edom o' Gordon"

Greig MSS., IV, p. 6; text, Bk. 753, XLIII, p. 21a. Also in Greig-Duncan MS. 785 (Walker transcript), p. 89; and Greig and Keith, 1925, p. 113. From Mrs. Coutts, Ellon.

p π¹

178. CAPTAIN CAR, OR, EDOM O GORDON

1. It fell aboot a Martmas time,
    When the win' blew shrill & caul',
Says Edom o' Gordon to his men,
    We maun draw to some ha'.

2. What ha', what ha', my merry men,
    What ha', what ha' quoth he;
I think we'll gang to Towie's Hoose,
    And see the fair ladie.

3. She thocht it was her ain dear lord
    That she saw ridin' hame,
But 'twas that traitor Edom o' Gordon
    That recked nae sin or shame.

4. Gie o'er your hoose, Lady Campbell, he cries,
    Gie o'er your hoose to me;
Or I will burn you this nicht,
    And a' your bairnies three.

5. I winna gie o'er my hoose, she says,
    To laird nor yet to loon,
Nor yet to ony rank robber
    That comes fae Auchindoun.

6. The lady fae the battlements
    She leet twa bullets flee,
But it missed its mark wi' Gordon,
    For it only grazed his knee.

7. . . . .
    To bring the faggots near.

8. Haud yer (your) tongue—
    I've paid ye lang yer fee;

And canna ye sit here the nicht,
    And bear the reek wi' me.

9. Haud (your) yer tongue—
    I've paid ye lang yer hire;
And canna ye sit here the nicht,
    And bear wi' me the fire?

10. Up & spak' her young son there,
    Sat on the nurse's knee,—
Open the door & lat me oot,
    For the reek it's chokin' me.

11. I would gie a' my gowd, my child,
    My silver & my fee,
For ae blast o' the western wind
    To blaw the reek fae me (thee).

12. Then up it spak' her daughter dear,
    . . . .
To row her in a pair o' sheets
    And throw her o'er the wa.

13. They rowed her in a pair o' sheets,
    And threw her o'er the wa',
But on the point o' Gordon's sword,
    She got a deadly fa'.

14. Then Gordon turned her o'er & o'er again,
    And oh, her face was white,—
I micht hae spared that bonnie face
    To been some man's delight.

15. He turned her o'er & o'er again
    And oh, her face was wan,
    . . . .

16. And syne he turned till his men,
    . . . .
For Towie's Hoose is in a flame,
    Nae langer need we stay.

Because of the placement of ellipses, the division between the last stanzas is confusing in the MS. The arrangement here follows that in Greig and Keith, 1925, p. 111.

The Bonny Earl of Murray

CHILD NO. 181

It is odd that Child did not note that this ballad appeared in the second edition of Thomson's *Orpheus Caledonius*, 1733, II, p. 8, an earlier date by seventeen years than that of the text he prints. It is the same text, except for variant spellings, and the readings *ha'e* for *have* in lines 2 and 3, and *ye* for *you* in line 2. Since Child says the song was not in the ninth edition of Ramsay's *Tea-Table Miscellany*, 1733, it would appear that Thomson is to be credited with its first printing, both text and tune. He was followed, according to Glen (*Early Scottish Melodies*, 1900, p. 119), by Barsanti, *A Collection of Old Scots Tunes*, 1742. The tune is also said to be in Oswald's *Caledonian Pocket Companion*, V [c. 1753], p. 14.* It was reprinted also in Neil Stewart's *Collection of Scots Songs* (1772, according to Glen); in Johnson's *Museum*; Ritson's *Scotish Songs*; R. A. Smith's *Scotish Minstrel*; Rimbault's *Musical Illustrations*; and Eyre-Todd's *Ancient Scots Ballads*. A late copy, collected from tradition in the 1920's in North Carolina, shows a curious,

if distant, kinship, with this earliest of the ballad's musical records.

Christie gives a fresh tune which he traces back to his great-grandmother, c. 1760, in Buchan. Christie says his paternal grandmother sang this tune to "Young Grigor's Ghost" (Buchan, *Gleanings*, 1825, p. 26); and notes that it appears with "Frennet Hall" ("Fire of Frendraught," Child No. 196) in Johnson's *Museum*, III [1790], p. 286.

Two versions of another tune have appeared in our own century, one from tradition in Rye, New York, but going back to Scotland (variant 4); the other from a source unknown in Diack's *New Scottish Orpheus*, 1923-24 (variant 5). This has a mournful beauty, but seems not very folklike, or at any rate balladlike. Among the revivalists, however, it is the tune most likely to be known.

* Date according to J. C. Dick, ed., *The Songs of Robert Burns*, 1903, p. xli.

TUNES WITH TEXTS

GROUP A

1. "The Bonny Earl of Murray"

Thomson, 1733, II, p. 8. Also in Johnson, II [1788], No. 177, p. 185 (repr. 1853); Ritson, 1794, II, p. 29; Smith [1820-24], IV, p. 101; Rimbault, 1850, p. 68; and Eyre-Todd [1894], p. 128.

m M (–IV)

1. Ye *Highlands* and ye *Lawlands*,
   Oh! where ha'e ye been:
   They ha'e slain the Earl of *Murray*,
   And they laid him on the Green.

2. Now wae be to thee *Huntly*,
   And wherefore did ye sae;
   I bad you bring him wi' you,
   But forbad you him to slae.

3. He was a braw Gallant,
   And he rid at the Ring;
   And the bonny Earl of *Murray*,
   Oh! he might have been a King.

4. He was a braw Gallant,
   And he play'd at the Ba',
   And the bonny Earl of *Murray*,
   Was the Flower amang them a'.

5. He was a braw Gallant,
   And he play'd at the Glove,
   And the bonny Earl of *Murray*,
   Oh! he was the Queen's Love.

6. Oh! lang will his Lady,
   Look o'er the Castle-*Down*,
   E'er she see the Earl of *Murray*,
   Come sounding through the Town.

GROUP B

3. "The Bonny Earl of Murray"

Christie, I, 1876, p. 202. Passed down in the family from Christie's maternal great-grandmother, of Buchan, and dated back to 1760.

a M/D

Ye Highlands, and ye Lawlands,
O where have you been?
They have slain the Earl of Murray,
And they laid him on the green.
"Now wae be to thee, Huntly!
And wherefore did you sae?
I bade you bring him wi' you,
But forbade you him to slay."
[Etc.]

Christie's text is from *The Tea-Table Miscellany* (cf. ed. 1871, II, p. 158).

GROUP C

4. "Highlands and Lowlands"

Parsons and Roberts, *JAF*, XLIV (1931), p. 297. Sung by Mrs. May F. Hoisington of Rye, N.Y. Learned in 1906 from a Scot who had heard it from a kinsman of the Murray family.

p I/Ly

Ye highlands and ye lowlands,
Oh where ha' ye been?
They have slain the earl of Moray
And have laid him on the green.
He was a bra' gallant
And he playèd at the glove
And the bonny Earl of Moray
He was the queeny's love.

Ye highlands and ye lowlands,
Oh where ha' ye been?
They have slain the Earl of Moray
And have laid him on the green.
He was a bra' gallant
And he playèd at the ring
And the bonny Earl of Moray
He might ha' been the king.

Oh wae's me for ye, Huntley,
And wherefore did ye sae?
I bade ye him to capture
And forbade ye him to slay.

He was a bra' gallant
And he playèd at the ring
And the bonny Earl of Moray
He might ha' been the king.

Oh lang may his lady
Look fra' the castle doon
Ere the bonny Earl of Moray
Comes sounding through the toon.

5. "The bonnie Earl o' Murray"

Diack, II, 1923-24, p. 28. Also in Goss, 1937, p. 80(B).

p I/Ly

Copyright 1924 by Paterson's Publications Ltd. Copyright renewed. Reprinted by permission of the publishers and their American agents, Carl Fischer, Inc., New York.

Ye Hielands and ye Lowlands,
O where ha'e ye been?
They hae slain the Earl o' Murray,
And laid him on the green;
He was a braw gallant,
And he rade at the ring;
And the bonnie Earl o' Murray,
He micht ha'e been a king!
O lang will his leddy
Look owre frae castle Doune,
Ere she see the Earl o' Murray
Come soundin' thro' the toon!

Noo wae be to thee, Huntly,
And wherefore did ye sae?
I bade ye bring him wi' ye,
But forbade ye him to slay:
He was a braw gallant,
And he play'd at the ba';
And the bonnie Earl o' Murray
Was the flow'r amang them a'.
O lang will his leddy
Look owre frae castle Doune,
Ere she see the Earl o' Murray
Come soundin' thro' the toon!

The Laird o Logie

CHILD NO. 182

THE three tunes on record that I have seen for this ballad appear to have no kinship, nor can one do much for them in the way of illustration. They are of approximately the same era. Two are in duple rhythm, the other in triple. Mrs. Harris's is a four-phrase, Motherwell's a six-phrase, and Christie's, as usual in his handling, an eight-phrase, or two-strain, tune. All three are hexatonic, but of different modes.

Mrs. Harris's tune is transparently a variant of the "Hind Horn" family. But it is odd in its revelation of kinship to the old "Duke of Norfolk" tune (cf. Playford, *The English Dancing Master*, 1651 and subsequently). Now, since Scott had a version of the present ballad which was sung to "Logan Water," the weight of tradition is thrown to Mrs. Harris for the tune.

For "Logan Water" is the "Hind Horn" tune. Under the first name, it was well known in the seventeenth and eighteenth centuries. The tune appears in Ramsay's *Musick*, c. 1726, as noted by J. C. Dick, ed., *Songs of Robert Burns*, 1903, p. 458, q.v. also for a number of other references. Cf. also Glen, *Early Scottish Melodies*, 1900, pp. 49-50.

Christie had so liberal an idea of the legitimate powers of an editor that it is puzzling to know what ought to be done in the way of reconstruction. The second strain is pretty certainly due to him; but the final itself, in both strains, seems so much less in keeping than E for this tune that one doubts whether E be not the true tonic. If so, the tune would be brought into the D/Æ field.

TUNES WITH TEXTS

GROUP A

1. "Young Logie"

Harris MS., No. 17; text, fol. 16. Also in Child, 1882-98, V, p. 421; text, III, p. 455(D). From Mrs. Amelia Harris; learned from an old nurse during childhood in Perthshire, late eighteenth century. Noted by her daughter.

p D/Æ

1. Pretty is the story I hae to tell,
    Pretty is the praisin o itsel,
  An pretty is the prisner oor king's tane,
    The rantin young laird o Logie.

2. Has he brunt? or has he slain?
    Or has he done any injurie?
  Oh, no, no, he's done nothing at all,
    But stown a kiss frae the queen's marie.

3. Ladie Margaret cam doon the stair,
    Wringin her hands an tearin her hair;
  Cryin, Oh, that ever I to Scotland cam,
    Aye to see Young Logie dee!

4. "Had your tongue noo, Lady Margaret,
    An a' your weepin lat a bee!
  For I'll gae to the king my sell,
    An plead for life to Young Logie."

5. "First whan I to Scotland cam,
    You promised to gie me askens three;

  The first then o these askens is
    Life for the young laird o Logie."

6. "If you had asked house or lands,
    They suld hae been at your command;
  But the morn, ere I taste meat or drink,
    High hanged sall Young Logie be."

7. Lady Margaret cam doon the stair,
    Wringin her hands an tearin her hair;
  Cryin, Oh, that ever I to Scotland cam,
    A' to see Young Logie dee!

8. "Haud your tongue noo, Lady Margaret,
    An a' your weepin lat a bee!
  For I'll counterfiet the king's hand-write,
    An steal frae him his richt hand gloe,
  An send them to Pitcairn's wa's,
    A' to lat Young Logie free."

9. She counterfieted the king's hand-write,
    An stole frae him his richt hand gloe,
  An sent them to Pitcairn's wa's,
    A' to let Young Logie free.

10. The king luikit owre his castle-wa,
    Was luikin to see what he cald see:
  "My life to wad an my land to pawn,
    Yonder comes the young laird o Logie!"

11. "Pardon, oh pardon! my lord the king,
    Aye I pray you pardon me;
  For I counterfieted your hand-write,
    An stole frae you your richt hand gloe,
  An sent them to Pitcairn's wa's,
    A' to set Young Logie free."

12. "If this had been done by laird or lord,
    Or by baron of high degree,
    I'se mak it sure, upon my word,
    His life suld hae gane for Young Logie.

13. "But since it is my gracious queen,
    A hearty pardon we will gie,
    An for her sake we'll free the loon,
    The rantin young laird o Logie."

The text here given is from Child. In the MS. the first stanza reads:

Prettie is the storie I hae to tell,
    An prettie is the praisin o' itsel;
Prettie is the prisoner oo'r King's ta'en,
    The rantin' young Laird o' Logie.

GROUP B

2. "May Margaret"

Motherwell, 1827, App'x., No. 25; text, App'x., p. xxii. Tune from Andrew Blaikie, Paisley.

a M/D (or if A, p D/Æ; if C tonic, a I/Ly; if G tonic, p I/M)

The last two lines of each quatrain must have been repeated to the tune.

Lament, lament na, May Margaret,
    And of your weeping let me be,

For ye maun to the king himsell
    To seek the life o' young Logie.

GROUP C

3. "The Laird of Ochiltrie"

Christie, II, 1881, p. 170. Tune from Jenny Meesic, c. 1850.

a I/M

O listen gude people to my tale,
    Listen to what I tell to thee,
The king has taken a poor prisoner,
    The wanton laird of Ochiltrie.
When news came to our guidly queen,
    She sicht and said richt mournfullie,—
"O what will come of lady Margaret,
    Wha bears sic love to Ochiltrie?"
                              [Etc.]

Christie's text follows that in David Herd, *Ancient and Modern Scottish Songs*, 1776, I, p. 21.

Dick o the Cow

CHILD NO. 185

As CHILD notes, Ritson called attention to an allusion in Nashe's *Have with you to Saffren Walden*, 1596, which would indicate that this ballad, or something like it, was known at that date: "Dick of the Cow, that mad demi-lance northren borderer, who plaied his prizes with the lord Jockey so bravely." A reference in 1613 and another in 1688 make up the sum of surviving seventeenth-century allusion to Dick. No other occurs till the copy of the ballad sent to Percy in 1775, from which Child prints his copy a. A second copy, Child's b, was printed by Caw in *The Poetical Museum*, 1784, the first ever to be published. Scott followed this in his *Minstrelsy*, 1802, and in the 1833 edition conflated it with a third, which had been taken down from singing in 1816 and printed, with its proper tune, in *Albyn's Anthology*, II [1818], p. 31. The tune, slightly modified, also appeared in the revised *Minstrelsy*. There is a very imperfect copy of the same tune in Lady John Scott's MS., NL Scotland

MS. 840, with fifty-two stanzas of text. So far as I have discovered, no other tune has been sung or printed. The copy of 1818 is here given as the most painstaking and accurate. The others have no difference worthy of record. It ought perhaps to be noted that the refrain varies somewhat in the three basic texts; but as printed in a, it may probably only be intended as a short indication of kind and position—this would accord with the accurate transcript of c. The refrain in Caw's version is entirely omitted by Scott; but if it is accurately reported, as coming after the first and fourth line in an identical form, another tune would seem to be implied—or at least a considerable variation of the one we have: to be more specific, such a tune as that of "Jock o the Side" (No. 187), in Campbell's version, which came from the same family as his "Dick o the Cow" (the Shortreeds, father and son[s]).

TUNE WITH TEXT

"Dick o' the Cow"

Campbell, II [1818], p. 30. Also in Lady John Scott's MS., NL Scotland MS. 840; and Scott, 1833-34, II, opp. p. 62. Sung by Robert Shortreed, Liddesdale, 1816.

m I

The variant is as in the *Minstrelsy*, cited above.

1. Now Liddesdale has layen lang in,
    Lal de ral, lal de ral, lal de ral, la lal de:
   There is nae riding there at a';
    Lal de ral, lal de ral, lal de ral, la dal de:

   The horses are grown sae lither fat,
    They downa stur out o' the sta'.
    Lal lal de ridle la di, fal lal de ridle la di,
    Fal lal di lal la, fal lal di ridle la.

2. Fair Johnie Armstrang to Willie did say—
    "Billie, a-riding we will gae;
   England and us have been lang at feid,
    Ablins we'll light on some bootie."—

3. Then they are come on to Hutton Ha';
    They rade that proper place about;
   But the Laird he was the wiser man,
    For he had left nae gear without.

4. For he had left nae gear to steal,
    Except sax sheep upon a lee:
   Quo' Johnie—"I'd rather in England die,
    Ere thir sax sheep gae to Liddesdale wi' me."—

5. —"But how ca' they the man we last met,
    Billie, as we cam' o'er the know?"—
   "That same he is an innocent fule,
    And men they call him Dick o' the Cow."—

6. "That fule has three as gude ky of his ain,
    As there are in a' Cumberland, billie," quo' he:—
   "Betide me life, betide me death,
    These ky shall go to Liddesdale wi' me."—

7. Then they have come on to the poor fule's house,
    And they hae broken his wa's sae wide;
   They have loosed out Dick o' the Cow's three ky,
    And ta'en three co'erlets frae his wife's bed.

8. Then on the morn when the day was light,
    The shouts and cries rase loud and hie;
   —"O had thy tongue, my wife," he says,
    "And o' thy crying let me be!

[329]

9. "O had thy tongue, my wife," he says,
    "And o' thy crying let me be;
   And aye where thou hast lost ae cow,
    In gude suith I shall bring thee three."

10. Now Dickie's gane to the gude Lord Scroop,
     And I wat a dreirie fule was he;
    —"Now had thy tongue, my fule," he says,
     "For I may not stand to jest wi' thee."—

11. "Shame fa' your jesting, my Lord!" quo' Dickie,
     "For nae sic jesting grees wi' me;
    Liddesdale's been in my house last night
     And they hae awa my three ky frae me.

12. "But I may nae langer in Cumberland dwell,
     To be your puir fule and your leal,
    Unless you gi' me leave, my Lord,
     To gae to Liddesdale and steal."—

13. "I gi'e thee leave! my fule," he says—
     "Thou speakest against my honour and me;
    Unless thou gi' me thy trowth and thy hand,
     Thou'lt steal frae nane but whae sta' frae thee."—

14. —"There is my trowth and my right hand,
     My head shall hang on Hairibee;
    I'll ne'er cross Carlisle sands again,
     If I steal frae a man but whae sta' frae me."—

15. Dickie's ta'en leave o' lord and master,
     I wat a merry fule was he!
    He's bought a bridle and a pair of new spurs,
     And pack'd them up in his breek thie.

16. Then Dickie's come on to Pudding-burn house,
     E'en as fast as he might drie;
    Then Dickie's come on to Pudding-burn,
     Where there were thirty Armstrangs and three.

[*2 stanzas here in Scott*]

17. "I'm come to plain o' your man, fair Johnie Armstrang,
     And syne o' his billie Willie," quo' he;
    "How they've been in my house last night,
     And they hae ta'en my three ky frae me."—

18. —"Ha!" quo fair Johnie Armstrang, "we will him hang."—
     —"Na," quo' Willie, "we'll him slae."—
    Than up and spak another young Armstrang,
     "We'll gie him his batts and let him gae."—

19. But up and spak the gude Laird's Jock,
     The best falla in a' the cumpanie;
    —"Sit down thy ways a little while, Dickie,
     And a piece o' thy ain cow's hough I'll gie ye."—

20. But Dickie's heart it grew sae grit,
     That the ne'er a bit o't he dought to eat—
    Then was he aware of an auld peat house,
     Where a' the night he thought for to sleep.

21. Then Dickie was ware of an auld peat house,
     Where a' the night he thought for to lye—
    And a' the prayers the pure fule prayed
     Were, "I wish I had amends for my gude three ky!"—

[*1 stanza here in Scott*]

22. The lads that hungry and weary were,
     Abune the door-head they threw the key;
    Dickie he took good notice o' that,
     Says—"There will be a bootie for me."—

23. Then Dickie has into the stable gane,
     Where there stood thirty horses and three;
    He has tied them a' wi' St. Mary's knot,
     A' these horses but barely three.

24. He has tied them a' wi' St Mary's knot,
     A' these horses but barely three;
    He's loupen on ane, ta'en another in hand,
     And away as fast as he can hie.

25. But on the morn, when the day grew light,
     The shouts and cries raise loud and hie—
    —"Ah! whae has done this?" quo' the gude Laird's Jock,
     "Tell me the truth and the verity."—

26. "Whae has done this deed?" quo' the gude Laird's Jock;
     —"See that to me ye dinna lie!"
    —"Dickie has been in the stable last night,
     And has ta'en my brother's horse and mine frae me."—

27. —"Ye wad ne'er be tald," quo' the gude Laird's Jock;
     "Have ye not found my tales fu' leil?
    Ye ne'er wad out o' England bide,
     Till crooked, and blind, and a' would steal."—

28. —"But lend me thy bay," Fair Johnie can say,
     "There's nae horse loose in the stable save he;
    And I'll either fetch Dick o' the Cow again,
     Or the day is come that he shall die."—

[*1 stanza here in Scott*]

29. He has ta'en the Laird's jack on his back,
     A twa-handed sword to hang by his thie;
    He has ta'en a steil-cap on his head,
     And galloped on to follow Dickie.

30. Dickie was na a mile frae aff the town,
     I wat a mile but barely three,
    When he was o'erta'en by Fair Johnie Armstrang,
     Hand for hand on Cannobie lee.

[*4 stanzas here in Scott*]

31. Then Johnie let a speir fu' laigh by his thie,
     Thought weil to hae slain the innocent, I trow;
    But the powers above were mair than he,
     For he ran but the puir fule's jerkin through.

32. Together they ran, or ever they blan;
     This was Dickie the fule and he—
    Dickie could na win at him wi' the blade o' the sword,
     But feld him wi' the plummet under the e'e.

33. Thus Dickie has feld Fair Johnie Armstrang,
     The prettiest man in the south country—
    —"Gramercy!" then can Dickie say,
     "I had but twa horse, thou hast made me thrie!"—

34. He's ta'en the steil-jack aff Johnie's back,
     The twa-handed sword that hang low by his thie;
    He's ta'en the steil-cap aff his head—
     —"Johnie, I'll tell my master I met wi' thee."—

35. When Johnie wakened out o' his dream,
        I wat a dreirie man was he:
    —"And is thou gane? Now, Dickie, than
        The shame and dule is left wi' me.

36. "And is thou gane? Now, Dickie, than
        The deil gae in thy cumpanie!
    For if I should live these hundred years,
        I ne'er shall fight wi' a fule after thee."—

37. Then Dickie's come hame to the good Lord Scroop,
        E'en as fast as he might hie—
    —"Now, Dickie, I'll neither eat nor drink,
        Till hie hanged thou shalt be."—

38. —"The shame speed the liars, my Lord!" quo' Dickie;
        "This was na the promise ye made to me!
    For I'd ne'er gane to Liddesdale to steal,
        Had I not got my leave frae thee."—

39. —"But what garr'd thee steal the Laird's Jock's horse?
        And, limmer, what garr'd ye steal him?" quo' he;
    "For lang thou mightst in Cumberland dwelt,
        Ere the Laird's Jock had stown frae thee."—

40. —"Indeed I wat ye lied, my Lord!
        And e'en sae loud as I hear ye lie!
    I wan the horse frae Fair Johnie Armstrang,
        Hand to hand on Cannobie Lee."

41. "There is the jack was on his back,
        This twa-handed sword hang laigh by his thie,
    And there's the steil-cap was on his head;
        I brought a' these tokens to let thee see."—

42. —"If that be true thou to me tells,
        (And I think thou dares na tell a lie,)
    I'll gie thee fifteen punds for the horse,
        Well tald on thy cloak-lap shall be."

       [2 stanzas here in Scott]

43. He's gien him twenty punds for the gude horse,
        A' in goud and gude monie;
    He's gien him ane o' his best milk ky,
        To maintain his wife and children thrie.

44. Then Dickie's come down thro' Carlisle toun,
        E'en as fast as he could drie;
    The first o' men that he met wi'
        Was my Lord's brother, Bailiff Glozenburrie.

45. —"Well be ye met, my gude Ralph Scroop!"—
        "Welcome, my brother's fule!" quo' he;
    "Where didst thou get Fair Johnie Armstrang's horse?"
        —"Where did I get him? but steal him," quo' he.—

       [3 stanzas here in Scott]

46. He's gi'en him twenty punds for the gude horse,
        Baith in goud and gude monie;
    He's gi'en him ane o' his best milk ky,
        To maintain his wife and children thrie.

47. Then Dickie lap a loup fu' hie,
        And I wat a loud laugh laughed he—
    —"I wish the neck o' the third horse were broken,
        If ony of the twa were better than he."

48. Then Dickie's come hame to his wife again,
        Judge ye how the poor fule had sped:
    He has gi'en her twa score English pund,
        For the thrie auld coverlets taen aff her bed.

49. —"And tak thee these twa as gude ky,
        I trow as a' thy thrie might be;
    And yet here is a white-footed nagie,
        I trow he'll carry baith thee and me.

50. "But I may nae langer in Cumberland bide,
        The Armstrangs they would hang me hie."—
    So Dickie's ta'en leave at lord and master,
        And at Burgh under Stanmuir there dwells he.

"This celebrated Border (or rather Liddesdale) Ballad, is here given, as taken down by the present Editor, from the singing and recitation of a Liddesdale-man, namely, Robert Shortreed, Esq. Sheriff-substitute of Roxburghshire, in the autumn of 1816. In consequence of which the public are now in full possession of what partly appeared in the *Hawick Museum* 1784 [i.e., Caw's *Poetical Museum*], and afterwards a more perfect edition in the Minstrelsy of the Scottish Border, 1802. This popular Ballad is thus completed, by its melody being united to it; which seems to the present Editor to have a strong English *gout*, rather than a true Scottish flavour; but in this point he may be wrong; however it is certainly a spirited air, and highly worthy of musical record." [*Campbell's note.*]

Jock o the Side

CHILD NO. 187

THAT there was a song on this subject known familiarly before the end of the sixteenth century is proved, as has been noted by Hyder Rollins, by a ballad in Bodleian Rawlinson MS. Poet. 185, fols. 9-10, the date of which is not later than 1592. It is to be sung to the tune of "Hobbinole and Iohn A Side." For the sake of the stanzaic pattern, the first stanza is here given. Cf., for the rest, Rollins, *Old English Ballads*, 1920, pp. 325ff.

Assist me now, you dolefull dames,
sing hevely now my ioyes do weare,
Sound forth your rewfull morning plantes,
lament my sorofull, wayling cheare;
Lament with me, for I am he
Who lives (alas!) and faine would die,
Oh paine, sorofull paine, paine that nipes me sore.

The ballad "Iohn a Side" may probably have been that which has survived in the Percy Folio (Child's A), where it appears, as usual for that MS., without any refrain. Nothing is clearer than the fact that whoever compiled the Percy Folio had no interest in *singing* his songs.

The next text, and the earliest extant in print, is that in Caw's *Poetical Museum*, 1784, which is said to be given "from an old manuscript copy." It is four stanzas shorter than the decapitated Folio copy, and differs considerably in names, narrative, and language, and has a fifth-line refrain (Child Ba). Nine years earlier (1775), Percy had received a very defective copy (C) taken down as imperfectly remembered by an "old person." Most of the stanzas are badly disordered, but the first one shows the same pattern as the Caw copy, and almost the identical refrain. It is, in fact, clearly to be made out that Ba and C were derived from copies differing in no essential respect. There is enough difference in phraseology, however, to show that this form had a certain currency, about the mid-eighteenth century.

The copy in Campbell's *Albyn's Anthology* was, as we are explicitly told, transcribed, both "the melody and particularly the words . . . from the singing and recitation of Mr. Thomas Shortreed, who learnt it from his father." Child has little hesitation in declaring it to have been derived from Caw, in spite of numerous verbal differences. I take it that both could equally well derive from a common original at one or two removes, as is probably the case with C, though the C copy is too mutilated for certainty. But Campbell's copy differs in the refrain pattern, introducing a refrain-line after the first, as well as after the fourth, regular line of the stanza. This alteration, of course, markedly affects the tune. I believe that Campbell himself may have been responsible for the change: his words seem to me to imply that he was conscious of having taken more liberties with the melody than with the words, as they were sung. But not, we are to understand, such liberties as to destroy the basic authenticity of the record.

Campbell's tune is of that very rare kind, of which we have other examples in Nos. 110 and 144, where an interpolated phrase after the first throws the balance off, so that the main cadence, the "turn" of the tune, comes on an odd phrase. The phenomenon is so unusual that the examples of it in Anglo-American folksong can probably be counted on one hand. The outstanding example of it is the "Arthur a Bland" tune (cf. No.

126), where, however, the tune is of only five phrases. The present tune belies the look of its text, and has really eight phrases, because the refrain-lines divide each into two full-length musical phrases. The shape of the tune fails to correspond with the stanzaic pattern, inasmuch as the latter breaks at the end of the fourth musical phrase ("Staid at hame"), whilst the tune has its natural emphases at the ends of the third and the fifth phrases.

At first glance, it might be guessed that the pattern of the sixteenth-century "Iohn a Side" (as exemplified by the stanza quoted above) conformed to such a tune, the refrain after line one, and the long final refrain-line which doubtless occupied two full musical phrases, seeming to lend itself to the present scheme. But it can hardly have been so: there appears to be one line too many in the second half of the stanza, and the first refrain-line would need to be extended by partial verbal repetition. I have not found the tune of "Hobbinole" (for Hobby Noble?); but it must have agreed with the scheme of "Greensleeves," to which "Assist me now, you doleful dames" could easily be sung.

Scott appears to have got his text of the present ballad from Campbell and to have published it sixteen years earlier than did Campbell, at the same time inserting three stanzas from Caw which had been omitted by Shortreed. (Cf. Child, 1882-98, III, p. 475.) But it is noteworthy that Scott, no singer, quite discards all trace of refrain from his copy. This is, in fact, his regular habit—another illustration of how undependable are printed texts without their tunes.

In 1882, Bruce and Stokoe took strong exception to Campbell's tune—"which, in our opinion, was written for any purpose except that of having these ballads sung to it" (*Northumbrian Minstrelsy*, p. 41). *These* refers to "Dick o the Cow" (No. 185), "Hobbie Noble" (189), and the present ballad, all of which the editors mistakenly accuse Scott of assigning to this single tune. Bruce and Stokoe themselves print a tune (from Telfer's MS. of the mid-nineteenth century) which has very little about it to suggest the earlier tune, yet which may have some distant relation. The supposition would appear the more likely in that their tune is pretty distinctly related to one collected by Kidson, which in its turn ends with a phrase very close to the Shortreed tune. Both the Northumbrian and Kidson tunes are lacking the "fal lal diddle" etc. refrains of the earlier copies, and make their refrain by repeating the last line to a new musical phrase. One suspects that a chief reason why the Northumbrian editors took such violent exception to the earlier tune was the lack of dignity they felt in "fa ding diddle" syllabifying. Association is much in these matters; and if the song were sung at a moderate pace, with a refrain like that of "The Three Ravens" substituted—"with a down, down derry; heigh down down derry"—repugnance might be abated. For, in its way, Shortreed's is a capital tune, even in Campbell's handling. Given towardly circumstances—a long evening in a bothy, an excellent memory, a flexible voice, plenty of support in the choral refrains—the song would go far to make one forget cold, damp, and aching bones. To be sure, so performed it would be interminable. But who would not regard that as a great merit?

GROUP A

1. "Jock o' the Side"

Campbell, II [1818], p. 28. Also, inaccurately, in Lady John Scott's MS., NL Scotland MS. 840. From the singing and recitation of Thomas Shortreed, Liddesdale; learned from his father.

m D

1. Now Liddesdale has ridden a raid,
       Wi' my fa ding diddle, lal low dow diddle:
   But I wat they had better hae staid at hame;
   For Michael o' Winfield he is dead,
       And JOCK O' THE SIDE is prisoner ta'en.
       Wi' my fa ding diddle, lal low dow diddle.

2. For Mangerton house Lady Downie has gane,
       Her coats she has kilted up to her knee;
   And down the water wi' speed she rins,
       While tears in spaits fa' fast frae her e'e.

3. Then up and spoke our gude auld Lord—
       —"What news? what news, sister Downie, to me?"
   —"Bad news, bad news, my Lord Mangerton;
       Michael is killed, and they hae ta'en my son Johnie."

4. "Ne'er fear, sister Downie," quo' Mangerton;
       —"I have yokes of ousen, eighty and three;
   My barns, my byres, and my faulds a' weil fill'd,
       And I'll part wi' them a' ere Johnie shall die.

5. "Three men I'll send to set him free,
       A' harneist wi' the best o' steil;
   The English louns may hear, and drie
       The weight o' their braid swords to feel."

6. Lord Mangerton then orders gave,
       —"Your horses the wrang maun be shod;
   Like gentlemen ye mauna seim,
       But look like corn caugers ga'en the road.

7. "Your armour gude you mauna shaw,
       Nor yet appear like men o'weir;
   As country lads be a' array'd,
       Wi' branks and brecham on each mare."—

8. Sae now their horses are the wrang way shod,
       And Hobbie has mounted his grey sae fine;

Jock's on his lively bay, Wat's on his white horse, behind,
       And on they rode for the water of Tyne.

9. At the Cholerford they all light down,
       And there, wi' the help of the light o' the moon,
   A tree they cut, wi' fifteen nogs on each side,
       To climb up the wa' of Newcastle toun.

10. But when they cam to Newcastle toun,
       And were alighted at the wa',
    They fand their tree three ells ower laigh,
       They fand their stick baith short and sma'.

11. Then up and spak the Laird's ain Jock,
       —"There's naithing for't; the gates we maun force."—
    But when they cam the gate untill,
       A proud porter withstood baith men and horse.

12. His neck in twa the Armstrangs wrang,
       Wi' fute or hand he ne'er play'd pa!
    His life and his keys at anes they hae ta'en,
       And cast the body ahind the wa'.

13. Now sune they reach Newcastle jail,
       And to the prisoner thus they call—
    —"Sleeps thou, wakes thou, Jock o' the Side,
       Or art thou weary of thy thrall?"—

14. Jock answers thus, wi' dulefu' tone,
       —"Aft, aft, I wake—I seldom sleep;
    But whae's this kens my name sae weil,
       And thus to mese my waes does seik?"—

15. Then out and spak the gude Laird's Jock,
       —"Now fear ye na, my billie," quo' he;
    "For here are the Laird's Jock, the Laird's Wat,
       And Hobbie Noble, come to set thee free."—

16. —"Now haud thy tongue, my gude Laird's Jock,
       For ever, alas! this canna be;
    For if a' Liddesdale was here the night,
       The morn's the day that I maun die.

17. "Full fifteen stane o' Spanish iron,
       They hae laid a' right sair on me;
    Wi' locks and keys I am fast bound
       Into this dungeon dark and dreirie."—

18. —"Fear ye na' that," quo' the Laird's Jock;
       "A faint heart ne'er wan a fair ladie;
    Work thou within, we'll work without,
       And I'll be sworn we'll set thee free."—

19. The first strong door that they cam at,
       They loosed it without a key;
    The next chain'd door that they cam at,
       They garr'd it a' to flinders flee.

20. The prisoner now upon his back,
       The Laird's Jock has gotten up fu' hie;
    And down the stair, him, irons and a',
       Wi' nae sma' speid and joy, brings he.

21. Sae out at the gates they a' are gane,
The prisoner's set on horseback hie;
And now wi' speid they've ta'en the gate,
While ilk ane jokes fu' wantonlie:

22. —"O Jock! sae winsomely's ye ride,
Wi' baith your feet upon ae side;
Sae well ye're harniest, and sae trigg,
In troth ye sit like ony bride!"—

23. The night, tho' wat, they did na mind,
But hied them on fu' merrilie,
Until they cam to Cholerford brae,
Where the water ran like mountains hie.

24. But when they cam to Cholerford,
There they met with an auld man;
Says—"Honest man, will the water ride?
Tell us in haste, if that ye can."—

25. —"I wat weel no," quo' the gude auld man;
"I hae lived here threty years and thrie,
And I ne'er yet saw the Tyne sae big,
Nor running anes sae like a sea."—

26. Then out and spak the Laird's saft Wat,
The greatest coward in the cumpanie—
"Now halt, now halt, we needna try't;
The day is come we a' maun die!"—

27. "Puir faint-hearted thief!" cried the Laird's ain Jock,
"There'll nae man die but him that's fie;
I'll guide thee a' right safely thro';
Lift ye the pris'ner on ahint me."—

28. Wi' that the water they hae ta'en,
By ane's and twa's they a' swam thro';
—"Here are we a' safe," quo' the Laird's Jock,
"And puir faint Wat, what think ye now?"—

29. They scarce the other brae had won,
When twenty men they saw pursue;
Frae Newcastle toun they had been sent,
A' English lads baith stout and true.

30. But when the Land-serjeant the water saw,
—"It winna ride, my lads," says he;
Then cried aloud—"The prisoner take,
But leave the fetters, I pray, to me."—

31. —"I wat weil no," quo' the Laird's Jock;
"I'll keep them a'; shoon to my mare they'll be:
My gude bay mare—for I am sure
She has bought them a' right dear frae thee."—

32. Sae now they are on to Liddesdale,
E'en as fast as they could them hie;
The prisoner is brought to's ain fire-side,
And there o's airns they mak him free.

33. —"Now Jock, my billie," quo' a' the three,
"The day is com'd thou was to die;
But thou's as weil at thy ain ingle side
Now sitting, I think, 'twixt thee and me!"

GROUP B

3. "Jock o' the Syde"

Telfer MS., No. 41, p. 20. Also in Bruce and Stokoe, 1882, p. 37.

p D/Æ

In Bruce and Stokoe, the cadence-note of phrase 3 is C instead of B.

The text is taken from Caw's *Poetical Museum*, 1784, of which the only material differences from that in *Albyn's Anthology* (variant 1 above) are the two stanzas that follow Campbell's fifth, as follows:

"The Laird's Jock ane, the Laird's Wat twa;
O! Hobbie Noble, thou ane maun be!
Thy coat is blue, thou hast been true
Since England banish'd thee to me."

Now, Hobbie was an English man,
In Bewcastle-dale was bred and born;
But his misdeeds they were sae great
They banish'd him ne'er to return.

a stanza following Campbell's 20, thus:

"Now, Jock, my man," quo' Hobbie Noble,
"Some o' his weight ye may lay on me";
"I wat weel no," quo' the Laird's ain Jock,
"I count him lighter than a flee."

and the final stanza, as follows:

They hae garred fill up ae punch bowl,
And after it they maun hae anither;
And thus the night they a' hae spent,
Just as they'd been brither and brither.

Archie o Cawfield

CHILD NO. 188

THE first tune to be published for this ballad, which is perhaps a *rifacimento*, or secondary form, of "Jock o the Side," is Christie's, which he got from his grandfather. It has resemblances to other Scottish songs, most notably, perhaps, to "The Beggar Laddie" (Child 280). Cf., e.g., Greig and Keith, *Last Leaves*, 1925, pp. 228-29, especially 1f and 2; Christie, I, 1876, p. 100.

The Maine editors, in a very interesting note, show that the ballad must have been brought over to this country as early as the beginning of the eighteenth century, and that it was re-modelled to suit the affair of John Webster, who appears to have been rescued from jail in a fashion sufficiently similar to suggest the adaptation. Cf. Barry, Eckstorm, and Smyth, *British Ballads from Maine*, 1929, p. 395. Bryant discovered a Pitts broadside of the early nineteenth century, called "The Bold Prisoner," which gives the older ballad in greatly weakened and abbreviated form (Bryant, *History of English Balladry*, 1919, pp. 436-37; Barry, Eckstorm, and Smyth, 1929, p. 399). Greig recovered one version, of the Peter Buchan variety (Child C), from his redoubtable Bell Robertson, which is at least better

than the Pitts broadside. It is interesting that no fewer than eight more or less fragmentary versions of the ballad and its cognates have been collected in this country in the present century, one as far West as Michigan, the rest in New England.

This ballad, speaking now more particularly of the words, is a good instance of a kind of variation of which more account will have to be taken. It is not gradual nor unconscious, but a deliberate making over to suit the changing times. The adaptation, if successful, goes on its own traditional way, and may be again remade at a later date. These are the sharp corners in oral tradition. It is probable that many of our most esteemed ballads have once, and more than once, been subjected to such treatment; and, no doubt, "in the fatness of these pursy times," the process will recur with increasing frequency, if anything at all is left of recognizable tradition. Though it be a kind of vandalism, leading to what in more recent decades has proved disintegrative in effect, there is little question that formerly it has given a new lease of life to many a song which would otherwise have perished.

TUNES WITH TEXTS

GROUP A

1. "The Three Brothers"

Christie, I, 1876, p. 98. Tune sung by Christie's maternal grandfather and arranged by his father.

m M

As I walked on a pleasant green,
    'Twas on the first morning of May,
I heard twa brothers make their mane,
    And hearken'd well what they did say.
The first he gave a grievous sigh,
    And said, "Alas! and wae's me!
We ha'e a brother condemned to death,
    And the very morn must hangèd be."
                                        [*Etc.*]

Christie's text is abridged from Buchan, 1828, I, p. 111.

GROUP B

3. "Bold Archer"

Collinson and Dillon, I, 1946, p. 20.

a I

1. It was all in the month of June,
       Just as the flowers were in full bloom,
   A castle was built upon Kensal Green,
       All for to put bold Archer in.

2. O, now our brother in prison do lay,
       Condemned to die is he
   If I had eleven such brothers as he,
       It's soon the poor prisoner I'd set free.

3. Eleven, says Richard, is little enough,
       Full forty there must be,
   The chain and the bars will have to be broke,
       Before bold Archer you can set free.

4. Now ten for to stand by our horses' reins,
   And ten for to guard us round about,
   And ten for to stand by the castle door,
   And ten for to bring bold Archer out.

5. Now Dickie broke locks and Dickie broke bars,
   Dickie broke everything he could see,
   He took bold Archer under his arm,
   And carried him off most manfully.

6. They mounted their horses, away they did ride,
   Archer, he mounted his horse likewise.
   They rode till they came to their family,
   And there they dismounted bold and free.

7. And there they ordered the music to play,
   It played so sweet and joyfully,
   And the very first dancer among them all
   Was bold Archer, whom they set free.

Stanzas 2 and 3 are sung with the slight differences noted in the melodic variants above.

GROUP C

7. "Billy and Johnny"

Barry, Eckstorm, and Smyth, 1929, p. 393. From Mrs. Fred P. Barker, Brewer, Me. Tune noted by Mrs. C. Carter.

p I (–VI)

There was eighty weight of good Spanish iron,
Between his neck-bone and his knee.
But Billy took Johnny up under his arm,
And carried him away, most manfully

Billy broke locks and Billy broke bars,
And Billy broke all that he came nigh,
And Billy took Johnny up under his arm,
And carried him away most manfully.

Hughie Grame

CHILD NO. 191

CHILD says this ballad "is not so old as the middle of the sixteenth century" (1882-98, IV, p. 9). The earliest broadsides, which are the first surviving records of it, belong to the last quarter of the seventeenth century, and are English, though with one or two traces of Scots about them (Child A, 9[4]: thou'st ner gang doun). Some of them are directed to go "to a pleasant new northern tune." In 1720, D'Urfey published the broadside copy (*Pills*, 1719-20, VI, p. 289), directing it to be sung to "Chevy Chase," but without giving the tune. The Chevy Chase tunes of his day, however, are CM, not LM tunes, and one assumes that the indication is mistaken.

Burns sent a traditional copy to Johnson for the fourth volume of the *Scots Musical Museum* (No. 303); but without the tune, which he said he had forgotten. Johnson printed this text with presumably an arbitrary tune which he seems to have taken from Oswald's *Caledonian Pocket Companion*, there called "Drimon Duff" (VIII, [c. 1756],* p. 12, according to J. C. Dick, ed., *The Songs of Robert Burns*, 1903, p. 362). This tune has been repeated in several nineteenth-century collections; but, as Alexander Keith has noted, the evidence is lacking that it was ever mated in tradition with "Hughie Grame." None the less, its roots are in the folk, and evidence may yet be found for the present connection.

Thus far, we have nothing properly avouched as a traditional tune for this ballad. In the Blaikie MS., however, is a tune called "Good Lord Scroope alias Hughie Graham." There are no words, and the tune has an end-refrain of two phrases. Among Child's texts, only D, a late Roxburghe copy (second half of the eighteenth century), and I, from early nineteenth century, have any refrain. There it is also an end-refrain, but in D, of one line, "He derry derry down." It is possible that this is only an indication of the kind of syllabication employed, not an accurate rendering. The I version has a two-line end-refrain, "Fall all the day, fall all the dandy,/ Fall all the day, fall the

dandy O." Fifty years later, Christie gives a tune from Banffshire tradition which appears to me distinctly related to the Blaikie tune. The thrice-repeated first phrase is a noticeable feature of both. As usual, Christie has filled up a second strain of four phrases, accommodating a second quatrain instead of a refrain. But he has not followed his usual practice of returning in the last two phrases to the phrases of the first strain. Instead, the pattern of the second strain here is two phrases repeating in alternation. These phrases are made out of the last phrase of the first strain, and I believe were (before Christie extended them) two phrases of probably syllabifying refrain. Confirming this surmise we have Greig's tune, an obvious relative from the same region, and with a two-phrase syllabified end-refrain of similar character. Here, then, is the central melodic tradition of this ballad.

We have still to take account of a tune from Liddesdale, of the middle or second half of the nineteenth century. This tune, given by Bruce and Stokoe, 1882, doubtless from James Telfer's MS., is farther from the center. It is in 3/4 instead of duple time, and it has no refrain. It is plagal; the rest are authentic (though Christie's is mixed). But it, too, leans to π^3 skeletally, and its plagalism is pretty well forgotten after the first bar or two. If we push the rhythm into a duple one by making quarter-notes of the first two eighths in each bar, the tune looks more like the others; and there would be no incongruity in adding the refrain-phrases of either Blaikie's or Greig's. The tune, we conclude, may well be a cousin of those. But it is also a variant of the one in C. K. Sharpe's MS. to "Otterburn" (No. 161) printed in Child, 1882-98, V, p. 419. It has lately been sung and recorded with the present ballad by Ewan MacColl.

It should also be mentioned that the Christie tune suggests "The Keeper" (e.g., Sharp's *One Hundred English Folksongs*, 1916, p. 178), and the Greig tune, Mrs. Harris's "Sir Colin" (*ante*, No. 61, variant 1).

TUNES WITH TEXTS

GROUP A

1. "Hughie Graham"

Johnson, IV, [1792], No. 303, p. 312 (repr. 1853). Also in Smith [1820-24], IV, p. 22; Chambers, 1844, p. 24; Maver, 1866, No. 360, p. 180; and Eyre-Todd [1894], p. 208. From James Oswald, *The Caledonian Pocket Companion*, VIII, [c. 1756], p. 12.

m D/Æ

1. Our lords are to the mountains gane,
   A hunting o' the fallow deer,
   And they hae gripet Hughie Graham
   For stealing o' the Bishop's mare.

2. And they hae tied him hand and foot,
   And led him up thro' Stirling town;
   The lads and lasses met him there,
   Cried, Hughie Graham thou art a loun.

3. O lowse my right hand free, he says,
   And put my braid sword in the same;
   He's no in Stirling town this day,
   Daur tell the tale to Hughie Graham.

4. Up then bespake the brave Whitefoord,
   As he sat by the bishop's knee,
   Five hundred white stots I'll gie you,
   If ye'll let Hughie Graham gae free.

5. O haud your tongue, the bishop says,
   And wi' your pleading let me be;
   For tho' ten Grahams were in his coat,
   Hughie Graham this day shall die.

6. Up then bespake the fair Whitefoord,
   As she sat by the bishop's knee;
   Five hundred white pence I'll gee you,
   If ye'll gie Hughie Graham to me.

7. O haud your tongue now lady fair,
   And wi' your pleading let it be,
   Altho' ten Grahams were in his coat,
   Its for my honor he maun die.

8. They've taen him to the gallows knowe,
   He looked to the gallows tree,
   Yet never colour left his cheek,
   Nor ever did he blin' his e'e.

9. At length he looked round about,
   To see whatever he could spy;
   And there he saw his auld father,
   And he was weeping bitterly.

10. O haud your tongue, my father dear,
    And wi' your weeping let it be;
    Thy weeping's sairer on my heart,
    Than a' that they can do to me.

11. And ye may gie my brother John,
    My sword that's bent in the middle clear,
    And let him come at twelve o'clock,
    And see me pay the bishop's mare.

12. And ye may gie my brother James
    My sword that's bent in the middle brown
    And bid him come at four o'clock,
    And see his brother Hugh cut down.

13. Remember me to Maggy my wife,
    The niest time ye gang o'er the moor,
    Tell her, she staw the bishop's mare,
    Tell her, she was the bishop's whore.

14. And ye may tell my kith and kin,
    I never did disgrace their blood;
    And when they meet the bishop's cloak,
    To mak it shorter by the hood.

This text = Child's B.

2. "Good Lord Scroope alias Hughie Graham"

Blaikie MS., NL Scotland MS. 1578, No. 102, p. 32.

a Anomalous (–III; inflected VI)

3. "Hughie Graham"

Christie, II, 1881, p. 82. From Banffshire tradition.

m I

Our lords are to the mountains gane,
    A-hunting o' the fallow deer,
And they ha'e grippit Hughie Graham
    For stealing o' the bishop's mare.
And they ha'e tied him hand and foot,
    And led him up through Stirling town;
The lads and lasses met him there,
    Cried, "Hughie Graham thou art a loun."

[*Etc.*]

Christie follows the text in Johnson's *Museum*, IV, [1792], No. 303, p. 312 (cf. variant 1 above).

4. "Hughie Grame"

Greig and Keith, 1925, p. 118; from Duncan MS., No. 446. From Mrs. Lyall, Skene, as learned from a schoolgirl, c. 1870.

a M/D

He lookèd east, he lookèd west,
     He lookèd far across the sea;
And there he spied his agèd father,
     Standing weeping bitterly.
Tey ammarey, O Londonderry,
Tey ammarey, O London dee.

GROUP B d

5. "Oh! the Grahams and hey! the Grahams"

Telfer MS., No. 6, p. 3. Also in Bruce and Stokoe, 1882,
p. 34; and Stokoe and Reay, n.d. [1893?], p. 98. From
Liddesdale tradition.

m D

Gude Lord Scroope's to the hunting gane,
     He has ridden o'er moss and muir,
And he has grippit Hughie the Græme,
     For stealing o' the Bishop's mear.

[*Etc.*]

The text is Child's C, from Scott's *Minstrelsy*, 1803, III, p. 85. For
Scott's traditional versions, see Child's C, H, and I in his fourth volume,
pp. 518-20.

The Lochmaben Harper

CHILD NO. 192

THIS ballad, except for gradual dilapidation as the nineteenth century wore on, shows a marked degree of consistency, both text and music. The extant tradition extends from the end of the eighteenth to the end of the nineteenth century, but we lack a late tune because of the fact that Bell Robertson, though she learned her vast store of ballads from singers, could not or would not "unlock her silent throat" in song even when death approached.

Child notes that the Stationers' Register for 1564-65-66 has entries of ballads about a blind harper or harpers. Whether these had anything to do with ours is not known. But as possible evidence that the present ballad has travelled some way from its source, we might note the neglect of the harper's blindness as a factor in the story. Beyond calling him blind, only one version, I believe (Child B), even mentions the possibility of a blind man's having difficulty in identifying one horse from another in a strange stable, let alone knowing whether every man of his audience had his eyes closed in slumber. We may suppose that originally more was done with this element of the story than has come down to us.

TUNES WITH TEXTS

1. "The Blind Harper of Lochmaben"

Glenriddell MSS., 1791, XI, p. 45, HCL transcript, 25241.49, p. 66.

a D/Æ, ending on the octave

The MS. gives 12/8 as the time-signature.

Heard ye e'er of the silly Blind Harper
That long lived in Lochmaben Town
How he wad gang to fair England
To steal King Henry's wanton Brown?
Sing faden dilly and faden dilly
Sing faden dilly and deedle Dan.

2. "Oh heard ye e'er of a silly blind Harper"

Johnson, VI [1803], No. 579, p. 598 (repr. 1853). Contributed by Robert Burns.

a D/Æ, ending on the octave

1. O heard ye of a silly Harper,
   Liv'd long in Lochmaben town,
   How he did gang to fair England,
   To steal King Henry's wanton brown?
   How he did gang to fair England
   To steal King Henry's wanton brown.

2. But first he gaed to his gude wife
   Wi' a' the speed that he cou'd thole:
   This wark, quo' he, will never work,
   Without a mare that has a foal.
       This wark, &c.

3. Quo' she, thou has a gude grey mare,
   That'll rin o'er hills baith low & hie;
   Gae tak' the grey mare in thy hand,
   And leave the foal at hame wi' me.
       Gae tak', &c.

4. And tak' a halter in thy hose,
   And o' thy purpose dinna fail;
   But wap it o'er the wanton's nose;
   And tie her to the grey mare's tail:
       But wap, &c.

5. Syne ca' her out at yon back yeate,
   O'er moss and muir and ilka dale,
   For she'll ne'er let the wanton bite,
   Till she come hame to her ain foal.
       For she'll, &c.

6. So he is up to England gane,
   Even as fast as he can hie,
   Till he came to King Henry's yeate;
   And wha' was there but King Henry?
       Till he, &c.

7. Come in, quo' he, thou silly blind Harper;
   And of thy harping let me hear.
   O! by my sooth, quo' the silly blind Harper,
   I'd rather hae stabling for my mare.
       O! by my, &c.

8. The King looks o'er his left shoulder,
   And says unto his stable groom,

Gae tak the silly poor Harper's mare,
And tie her 'side my wanton brown.
    Gae tak, &c.

9. And ay he harped, and ay he carpit,
Till a' the Lords gaed through the floor,
They thought the music was sae sweet,
That they forgat the stable door.
    They thought, &c.

10. And ay he harpit, and ay he carpit,
Till a' the nobles were sound asleep,
Than quietly he took aff his shoon,
And saftly down the stair did creep.
    Than quietly, &c.

11. Syne to the stable door he hies,
Wi' tread as light as light cou'd be,
And whan he open'd and gaed in,
There he fand thirty good steeds & three.
    And whan, &c.

12. He took the halter frae his hose,
And of his purpose did na' fail;
He slipt it o'er the Wanton's nose,
And tied it to his grey mare's tail.
    He slipt, &c.

13. He ca'd her out at yon back yeate,
O'er moss and muir & ilka dale,
And she loot ne'er the wanton bite,
But held her still gaun at her tail.
    And she, &c.

14. The grey mare was right swift o' fit,
And did na fail to find the way,
For she was at Lochmaben yeate,
Fu' lang three hours ere it was day.
    For she, &c.

15. When she came to the Harper's door,
There she gae mony a nicher and snear,

Rise, quo' the wife, thou lazy lass,
Let in thy master and his mare.
    Rise, quo', &c.

16. Then up she raise, pat on her claes,
And lookit out through the lock-hole,
O! by my sooth then quoth the lass,
Our mare has gotten a braw big foal.
    O! by my, &c.

17. Come haud thy peace, then foolish lass,
The moon's but glancing in thy ee,
I'll wad my haill fee 'gainst a groat,
It's bigger than e'er our foal will be.
    I'll wad, &c.

18. The neighbours too that heard the noise,
Cried to the wife to put her in,
By my sooth, then quoth the wife,
She's better than ever he rade on.
    By my, &c.

19. But on the morn at fair day light,
When they had ended a' their chear,
King Henry's wanton brown was stawn,
And eke the poor old Harper's mare.
    King Henry's, &c.

20. Alace! alace! says the silly blind Harper,
Alace! alace! that I came here,
In Scotland I've tint a braw cowte foal,
In England they've stawn my guid grey mare.
    In Scotland, &c.

21. Come had thy tongue, thou silly blind harper
And of thy alacing let me be,
For thou shall get a better mare,
And weel paid shall thy cowte foal be.
For thou shall get a better mare,
And weel paid shall thy cowte foal be.

The Death of Parcy Reed

CHILD NO. 193

JAMES Telfer sent Sir Walter Scott a copy of this ballad "exactly as it is sung by an old woman of the name of Cathrine Hall, living at Fairloans, in the remotest corner of Oxnam parish": this was said in 1824. Telfer further remarked that the ballad had its own tune, "a very mournful air" (Child, 1882-98, IV, pp. 520-21), but obviously did not enclose it with the text, or there would have been no need to describe it. Kitty Hall's text was nowhere printed at the time, and when in 1844 a text was published by Richardson at Newcastle, as a twelve-page pamphlet, with an introduction by Robert White, although the title page read "an old ballad taken down by James Telfer from recitation," the text was actually remade and nearly doubled in length. This "improved" text of Telfer's was reprinted in 1846 in Richardson's *Borderer's Table Book*, and again by J. H. Dixon in the same year. The editors of *Northumbrian Minstrelsy* reprinted it with a tune in 1882; and in 1890 Child reprinted it once again as his B text (IV, pp. 26-28). By 1892 Child had recovered Kitty Hall's untouched version in the Abbotsford correspondence, and now for the first time printed it in the Additions and Corrections of Vol. IV, pp. 520-21. No other copy, I believe, has been recovered except Child's A, which Robert White, who wrote the notes for the 1846 copy, himself collected (but did not publish) from a different source in 1829. In view of these facts, the procedure of the 1882 editors of *Northumbrian Minstrelsy* is a little blameworthy. As the only custodians of a tune for the ballad, they say nothing about its source. If they had recovered the tune from tradition, they would probably have had a different text from any yet printed. But in the Child MSS. at Harvard (XXVII, No. 2032) is a newspaper article contributed by John Stokoe to the *Newcastle Courant* in 1880, and containing the information that the tune is called "Lord Trowend" in old MSS. The tune appears in the article as it later was printed in *Northumbrian Minstrelsy* (1882, p. 42). One wishes for more light on these old MSS., on their nature, age, number, authority, and whereabouts. But in a separate MS. of tunes, 'Mr. Telfer's Tunes,' now in the library of the Society of Antiquaries, Newcastle-upon-Tyne, is one called "Hey sae green as the rashes grow," which proves to be the tune in question. A title, "Lord Trowend," has been faintly pencilled above. Presumably, Stokoe took his copy from this MS., which differs only in one note.

It may be observed that the tune belongs to the family of which "Loch Lomond" is a member. Cf. *post*, No. 199 ("Bonnie House o' Airlie").

TUNE WITH TEXT

"Hey sae green as the rashes grow" ["Lord Trowend"]

Telfer MS., No. 5, p. 3; text, Child, 1882-98, IV, p. 520. Also in Bruce and Stokoe, 1882, p. 42. Tune taken down by James Telfer, perhaps from the singing of Kitty Hall (originally from Northumberland), Fairloans, Roxburghshire, from whom he obtained the text.

m I/M

1. O Parcy Reed has Crozer taen,
     And has deliverd him to the law;
   But Crozer says he'll do warse than that,
     For he'll gar the tower of the Troughend fa.

2. And Crozer says he will do warse,
     He will do warse, if warse can be;
   For he'll make the bairns a' fatherless,
     And then the land it may lie lea.

3. O Parcy Reed has ridden a raid,
     But he had better have staid at hame;
   For the three fause Ha's of Girsenfield
     Alang with him he has them taen.

4. He's hunted up, and he's hunted down,
     He's hunted a' the water of Reed,
   Till wearydness has on him taen,
     I the Baitinghope he's faen asleep.

5. .   .   .   .   .   .
     .   .   .   .   .   .
   And the fause, fause Ha's o Girsenfield,
     They'll never be trowed nor trusted again.

6. They've taen frae him his powther-bag,
     And they've put water i his lang gun;
   They've put the sword into the sheathe
     That out again it'll never come.

7. 'Awaken ye, awaken ye, Parcy Reed,
     For I do fear ye've slept owre lang;
   For yonder are the five Crozers,
     A coming owre by the hinging-stane.'

8. 'If they be five and we be four,
     If that ye will stand true to me,
   If every man ye will take one,
     Ye surely will leave two to me.

[342]

9. 'O turn, O turn, O Johny Ha,
      O turn now, man, and fight wi me;
   If ever ye come to Troughend again,
      A good black nag I will gie to thee;
   He cost me twenty pounds o gowd
      Atween my brother John and me.'

10. 'I winna turn, I canna turn;
       I darena turn and fight wi thee;
    For they will find out Parcy Reed,
       And then they'll kill baith thee and me.'

11. 'O turn, O turn now, Willie Ha,
       O turn, O man, and fight wi me,
    And if ever ye come to the Troughend again
       A yoke of owsen I will gie thee.'

12. 'I winna turn, I canna turn;
       I darena turn and fight wi thee;
    For they will find out Parcy Reed,
       And they will kill baith thee and me.'

13. 'O turn, O turn, O Thommy Ha,
       O turn now, man, and fight wi me;
    If ever ye come to the Troughend again,
       My daughter Jean I'll gie to thee.'

14. 'I winna turn, I darena turn;
       I winna turn and fight with thee;
    For they will find out Parcy Reed,
       And then they'll kill baith thee and me.'

15. 'O woe be to ye, traitors a'!
       I wish England ye may never win;
    Ye've left me in the field to stand,
       And in my hand an uncharged gun.

16. 'Ye've taen frae me my powther-bag,
       And ye've put water i my lang gun;
    Ye've put the sword into the sheath
       That out again it'll never come.

17. 'O far ye weel, my married wife!
       And fare ye weel, my brother John!
    That sits into the Troughend ha
       With heart as black as any stone.

18. 'O fare ye weel, my married wife!
       And fare ye weel now, my sons five!
    For had ye been wi me this day
       I surely had been man alive.

19. 'O fare ye weel, my married wife!
       And fare ye weel now, my sons five!
    And fare ye weel, my daughter Jean!
       I loved ye best ye were born alive.

20. 'O some do ca me Parcy Reed,
       And some do ca me Laird Troughend,
    But it's nae matter what they ca me,
       My faes have made me ill to ken.

21. 'The laird o Clennel wears my bow,
       The laird o Brandon wears my brand;
    Whae ever rides i the Border side
       Will mind the laird o the Troughend.'

The Fire of Frendraught

CHILD NO. 196

THE incident which gave rise to this ballad occurred in 1630. In the Skene MS., which has been dated in the preceding decade, there is a tune called "Ladie Rothemayis Lilt." Dauney supposes that this was the tune to which the ballad would have been sung, on the principle that tunes already associated with a family would be used by minstrels when celebrating that family's history. Such a rule would be hard to prove, but nothing forbids its happening now and again. In the present case, one may admit that it would be easy to fit two quatrains (CM) to the tune. More telling would be a relation between this and later versions found in tradition. But the melodic material found here and in the nineteenth century tunes of this ballad is too common to support any confident assertions. The second strain of the Skene tune appears to be allied with the familiar "Boyne Water" family, and so does the late Greig tune from Mrs. Coutts, which, as Keith rightly observes, has further con-

nections with "Sir James the Rose" (No. 213), "Sweet William and Fair Annie" (73-74), and, we may add, the same singer's "Edom o' Gordon" (178). The Greig tune and Christie's are also more distantly related. But, indeed, affiliations are far too frequent in this tribe to serve for evidence. The Skene tune is very much the sort of thing we find in Playford's *English Dancing Master* (cf., e.g., "All in a Garden Green," Margaret Dean-Smith edition, 1957, p. 60).

Christie gives a tune from Banffshire tradition. Its second strain we may safely disregard as very much his own. This tune is a π^3 plagal, and should be closely compared with Greig's tune, which is a π^4 plagal and bears a different time-signature. Christie's predilection for a 3/4 signature is a noteworthy feature of his volumes. If we reduce both tunes to the same time, it is not difficult to see that Greig's tune is a dominant counterpart of Christie's.

TUNES WITH TEXTS

1. "The Fire of Frendraught"

Christie, I, 1876, p. 58. From Banffshire tradition.

p π^3

The eighteenth of October,
    A dismal tale to hear,
How good Lord John and Rothiemay
    Were both burnt in the fire.

When steeds were saddled and well bridled,
    And ready for to ride,
Then out came she and fause Frendraught,
    Inviting them to bide.
                                        [*Etc.*]

Christie says his text is "epitomized" and refers the reader to Motherwell's *Minstrelsy*, 1827, p. 161, and Chambers' *Scottish Ballads*, 1829, p. 85.

2. [Frendraught]

Greig MSS., IV, p. 6; text, Bk. 753, XLIII, p. 25. Also in Greig and Keith, 1925, p. 122. From Mrs. Coutts of Ellon.

p π^4

1. On the twenty-third October,
    A dismal tale to hear,
How good Lord John & Rothiemay
    Were burned in the fire.
        (doon by)

2. Lady Frendrat she sent messengers
    To call the Gordons a',
That the ancient feud might be forgot,
    And in peace they'd reap & saw.

3. The horses were from the stable brocht,
    And a' were bound to ride,
When out came Lady Frendrat gay,
    Cries, Abide, Lord John, abide.

4. Ye'll stay & sup wi' us to-night,
    And tomorrow we shall dine;
'Twill be a token o' richt goodwill,
    Atween your hoose & mine.

5. The horses were ta'en to the stable again,
    Which made them for to stay;
The horses were to the stable sent,
    And got both corn & hay.

6. When bells were rung & mass was sung,
    And a' man bound to bed,
Good Lord John & Rothiemay
    In a high chamber were laid.

7. They hidna been lang to their beds,
 And scarcely fa'en asleep,
When smoke & flames aboot them came,
 Which made them for to weep.

8. . . . .
 . . . . . .
The door is lockit & the window barred,
 And together we baith maun dee.

9. . . . .
And there they saw false Lady Frendrat
 A-walkin' on the green.
. . . . . .
 And unconcerned was she.

10. (Lord John cried) open the door Lady F.—
 And let us oot, cried he;
For the door is lockit & the window barred,
 And dead men soon we'll be.

11. . . . .
For the keys wis doon in the deep draw-wall,
 And widna be found till day.

12. Johnnie Chalmers was a bonnie boy,
 Jist new come fae the King,
And on the first alarm o' fire
(And when he saw the fire begun)
 He lightly leapt the wa'.

13. Come doon, come doon, my master dear,
 Come o'er the wa' to me;
And I'll kep you in my airms twa,
 One fit I winna flee.
. . . . . .

14. He drew the ring fae his finger,
 Which wis baith lang & sma',
And give it to my lady gay,
 But let not my mother ken.

15. And tell her now to mak' her bed
 Aye langer to the breid;
For the day will never dawn again
 That I'll lie by her side.

16. And bid her train her young son up,
 That when a man he'd be,
Upon this hoose for this cruel deed
 Avenged he will be.
. . . .

17. As for you, my good Lord John,
 My heart is very sore
But as for you, Rothiemay,
 I wish 'twere ten times more.

18. Woe be to you, false Lady F.—
 A murderess are ye;
For ye brought us

19. Woe be to you, false Lady F.—
 And ill death may ye dee;
For ye . . . . . .
. . . . . .

20. And when that ye for pardon seek,
. . . . . .

21. Oh, gin I were a little bird,
 Wi' feathered wings & gray,
I'd fly aboot Lady F's gates,
 Crying vengeance till I die.

APPENDIX

3. "Ladie Rothemayis Lilt"

Skene MS., NL Scotland Adv. MS. 5.2.15; transcribed in Dauney, 1838, No. 4, p. 218.

a I/Ly, ending on III

The Bonnie House o Airlie

CHILD NO. 199

A TUNE for this ballad appeared in print almost as early as printed records of the text. The differences between later copies, whether printed or traditional, and this earliest recorded version are so slight as to indicate that oral tradition has never escaped control by one or other publication. The mode is I/M and authentic, usually with a plagal initial upbeat on the lower fifth. In two copies, the seventh slips in unobtrusively, and Christie has varied his second strain with a flattened seventh—editorially, we may assume.

Latterly, however, the earlier form has tended to be supplanted by a plagal tune, melodically akin, and universally familiar today with the more modern text of "The bonny banks of Loch Lomond." This is sung in Major, π^1, and I/M variants.

Eyre-Todd (variant 13) has substituted, without vouching authority, the tune belonging especially to "The Gypsy Laddie" (No. 200), q.v.

Kinloch (variant 12), in 1827, mated this ballad with the "Cowdenknowes" tune (No. 218). If there was traditional authority, no other evidence of it has appeared.

TUNES WITH TEXTS

GROUP A

1. "The Bonny House o' Airlie"

Smith [1820-24], II, p. 2. Also in G. Thomson [1822-23], I, p. 34; Graham, 1848-49, II, p. 130; and Maver, 1866, No. 102, p. 51.

p I/M

1. It fell on a day, a bonny simmer day,
    When the leaves were green and yellow,
  That there fell out a great dispute
    Between Argyle and Airlie,
  That there fell out a great dispute
    Between Argyle and Airlie.

2. Argyle he has taen a hundred o' his men,
    A hundred men and fifty,
  And he's awa, on yon green shaw,
    To plunder the bonny house o' Airlie.

3. The lady looked owre the hie castle wa';
    And oh! but she sighed sairly,
  When she saw Argyle and a' his men,
    Come to plunder the bonny house o' Airlie.

4. "Come down to me," said proud Argyle;
    "Come down to me lady Airlie,
  Or I swear by the sword I haud in my hand,
    I winna leave a stanin stane in Airlie."

5. 'I'll no come down, ye proud Argyle,
    Until that ye speak mair fairly,
  Tho' ye swear by the sword that ye haud in your hand,
    That ye winna leave a stanin stane in Airlie.

6. 'Had my ain lord been at his hame,
    But he's awa wi' Charlie,
  There's no a Campbell in a' Argyle,
    Dare hae trod on the bonny green o' Airlie.

7. 'But since we can haud out nae mair,
    My hand I offer fairly;
  Oh! lead me down to yonder glen,
    That I may nae see the burnin o' Airlie.'

8. He's taen her by the trembling hand,
    But he's no taen her fairly,
  For he led her up to a hie hill tap,
    Where she saw the burnin o' Airlie.

9. Clouds o' smoke, and flames sae hie,
    Soon left the wa's but barely;
  And she laid her down on that hill to die,
    Whan she saw the burnin o' Airlie.

GROUP B

11. "The Bonnie House o' Earlie"

Barry, Eckstorm, and Smyth, 1929, p. 266. From Mrs. James McGill of Chamcook, New Brunswick, November 1927.

m I/M

1. It fell on a day, a bonnie simmer's day,
    When the corn grew ripe an' yellow,
  There fell oot a great dispute
    Between Argyll an' Earlie.

2. The Duke o' Montrose he's written tae Argyll
   Tae com' in the mornin' early
An' lead in his men by the back o' Dunkeld
   Tae plunder the bonnie hoose o' Earlie.

3. The Ladye looked ower her winda sae high
   An' O but she looked weary,
For there she espied the great Argyll
   Com' tae plunder the bonnie hoose o' Earlie.

4. "Com' doon, com' doon, Lady Margaret," he says,
   "Com' doon an' kiss me fairly,
For afore the morn is clear daylicht
   Ah'll no leave a stanin' stane in Earlie."

5. "I wadna kiss thee, great Argyll,
   I wadna kiss thee fairly,
Tho before the morn was clear daylicht
   Gin ye suldna leave a stanin' stane in Earlie."

6. He's taen her by the waist sae sma',
   Sayin' "Ladye, where is your dowie?"
"O, it's up, it's doon the bonnie burn side
   That rins thro the plantin's o' Earlie."

7. They socht it up, and they socht it doon,
   They socht it late an' early,
They foun' it in the bonnie balm tree
   That stan's in the bowlin' green o' Earlie.

8. He's taen her by the left shoulder,
   An' O, but she grat sairly,
An' he's led her doon tae yon green bank
   Till they plundered the bonnie hoose o' Earlie.

9. "O, it's a hae seven braw sons," she said,
   "An' the youngest ne'er saw his daddie,
An' gin I had as mony mair
   I'd gae them a' tae Prince Charlie.

10. "O, gin my lord had bin at hame,
    As this nicht he's wi' Charlie,
There dauna a Campbell in a' the west
    Hae plundered the bonnie hoose o' Earlie."

2. The great Montrose has written to Argyll,
   And that the fields they were fairly,
And no to keep his men at hame,
   But come and plunder bonnie Airly.

3. The lady was looking oure the castle wa',
   She was carrying her courage sae rarely,
And there she spied him, gley'd Argyll,
   Coming for to plunder bonnie Airly.

4. "Wae be to ye, gley'd Argyll,
   And are ye there sae rarely?
Ye micht hae kept your men at hame,
   And no come to plunder bonnie Airly."

5. "And wae be to ye, Lady Ogilvie,
   And are ye there sae rarely?
Gin ye had bow'd whan first I bade,
   I never wad hae plunder'd bonnie Airly."

6. "O gin my gude Lord had been at hame,
   As he is wi' prince Charlie,
There durst na a rebel on a' Scottish grund
   Set a foot on the bonnie green o' Airly."

7. "But ye'll tak me by the milk-white hand,
   And ye'll lift me up sae rarely;
And ye'll throw me out oure my ain castle wa',
   Lat me never see the burning o' Airly."

8. He has tane her by the milk-white hand,
   And he has lifted her up sae rarely,
He has thrown her out oure her ain castle wa',
   And she never saw the plundering o' Airly.

9. Now gley'd Argyll he has gane hame,
   Awa frae the plundering o' Airly,
And there he has met wi' Captain Ogilvie,
   Coming over the mountains sae rarely.

10. "O wae be to ye, gley'd Argyll,
    And are ye there sae rarely,
Ye micht hae kept your men at hame,
    And na gane to plunder bonnie Airly."

11. "O wae be to ye, Captain Ogilvie,
    And are ye there sae rarely?
Gin ye had bow'd whan first I bade,
    I never wad hae plunder'd bonnie Airly."

12. "But gin I had my lady gay,
    Bot and my sister Mary,
Ae fig I wadna gie for ye a',
    Nor yet for the plundering o' Airly."

GROUP C

12. "Bonny House of Airly"

Kinloch, 1827, App'x. to p. 100; text, p. 104.

a I/Ly

1. O gley'd Argyll has written to Montrose,
   To see gin the fields they war fairly;
And to see whether he shou'd stay at hame,
   Or come to plunder bonnie Airly.

GROUP D

13. "The Bonnie House o' Airlie"

Eyre-Todd [1894], p. 198.

a I/M

199. THE BONNIE HOUSE O AIRLIE

It fell on a day, and a bonnie summer day,
    When the corn grew green and yellow,
That there fell out a great dispute
    Between Argyle and Airlie.

The Duke o' Montrose has written to Argyle
    To come in the morning early,
And lead in his men by the back o' Dunkeld,
    To plunder the bonnie house o' Airlie.
                [*Etc.*]

Eyre-Todd took his text from John Finlay's *Scottish Historical and Romantic Ballads*, 1808, II, p. 25 (Child Ab).

The Gypsy Laddie

CHILD NO. 200

THIS great favorite is one of those ballads which, if we had the re-ordering of Child's canon, might well be moved forward into the first hundred. Its connection with history is even more precarious than that of "Sir Patrick Spens" (No. 58), and only less so than that of "King John and the Bishop" (No. 45). For the tradition which associates the ballad with the Earl of Cassilis has, as Child shows, not a shred of historical fact behind it. At any rate, the romantic theme of "All for Love, or the World well lost" is one to the perennial appeal of which, so long as there are social distinctions, human nature will continue to respond.

Well over a hundred musical records of the last three centuries, most of them from tradition in our own, attest this popularity. It is fair to divide these into three main classes. The first class has one of the longest traditional sequences observable in all British balladry. Its earliest appearance is in the Skene MS., *ante* 1630; its latest is current today. The name which it bears in the Skene MS. is "Lady Cassiles Lilt," and Child, as well as later students, failed, I believe, to note the full implications of this fact. Child says that we have no evidence that the ballad was associated in tradition with the Cassilis family until the end of the eighteenth century. But this tune yields such evidence. For it is indisputably the same tune as the one found with our ballad in Johnson's *Museum* and in a number of recent traditional versions. The Skene tune was never translated from tablature until Dauney published it in 1838, and anyhow it is obvious that later variants have developed traditionally, not by derivation from that or any other authoritative record. The most reasonable explanation of such a phenomenon is that the ballad was associated with the family which gave its name to the tune much earlier than explicit statements survive to show, and earlier indeed—supposing the ballad in anything like its later form to have been circulating around 1630—by nearly a hundred years than the first extant record of the text.

The Skene tune is of the highest interest in other ways as well. It is a two-strain tune, and both its strains, but especially the second, have had sufficient vitality to engender independent tunes which are very widespread in tradition. For the second strain is none other than the earliest recorded appearance of that ubiquitous melodic formula—the thrice-repeated sequence (IV) V VI 1 1 VI V (IV)—which we had first occasion to notice in connection with "Lady Isabel and the Elf-Knight" (No. 4), and have seldom since lost sight of. It is today in America one of the two or three most generally employed formulae in folk song. Where this formula is found, another, (IV) V bVII 1 (2) bVII V (IV), which has been called "Boyne Water," is never far away, for the latter is but the dominant counterpart of the former—a continuation (a fifth higher, a fourth lower) of the pentatonic scale. It is therefore not surprising to find another group of the ballad's variants in some form of this latter scheme, which does not arise immediately from the original tune. The combinations and permutations of these two patterns are very suggestive for the student of folk-tune variation. By means of them, the different variants of this whole group oscillate in an arc stretching from π^1 to D/Æ. Scottish, English, and American traditions find these forms congenial.

The second large group belongs again to a familiar type of English folk-tune, of which there are two generally distinguishable branches among our variants. One branch falls into the Ionian-Mixolydian area, the other into the Dorian-Æolian. Most of these open with a familiar descending sequence twice repeated: a formula widely known and met not infrequently with other ballads; for example, in its major style, "The Bailiff's Daughter of Islington" (No. 105), and, in its minor, perhaps actually most familiar in Cecil Sharp's very favorite setting of a Somerset variant of the present ballad.

In the first of these two branches, the tunes are more or less evenly divided between major and Mixolydian varieties, and all are authentic. In the second branch, about a third are plagal Dorian tunes, the rest authentic Æolian. This class as a whole probably has a right to be considered the main line of English tradition for this ballad; but some Scottish, one or two Irish, and a fairly large number of American variants are included in it.

The third class is melodically the least consistent of the three, but it is loosely held together by the opening of the first phrase, rising emphatically on the major triad, by the lively character of the tunes, and by the major or Mixolydian tonality. In this class, also, there is generally an end-refrain, more or less elaborate, with nonsense syllables. Frequently this burden is as long as the stanza itself. There is an almost equal division of variants between authentic and plagal tunes. A few of the latter have fallen closes on the lower dominant. Probably, this whole class has a distant relation to the second class, but the recollection seems very dim, and a new and stronger influence has intervened. All or most of the members of this newer tradition, it should be added, are American.

TUNES WITH TEXTS

GROUP A

2. "Johnny Faa, or the Gypsy Laddie"

Johnson, II [1788], No. 181, p. 189 (repr. 1853). Also in Ritson, 1794, II, p. 176; Smith [1820-24], III, p. 90; Hogg, Second Series, 1821, p. 192 ("Wae's Me for Prince Charlie"); G. Thomson [1822-23], IV, p. 35; Maver, 1866, No. 61, p. 31; and Eyre-Todd [1894], p. 14.

a M

4. "Black Jack Davy"

Sung by Bascom Lamar Lunsford of Turkey Creek, N.C., March 1949, in the Library of Congress, Washington, D.C. LC/AAFS, rec. No. 9474(A1). Also in Lunsford and Stringfield, 1929, p. 4. Learned from Selma Clubb, Buncombe County, c. 1925. Collected by Mrs. Rae Korson and Duncan Emrich.

a π²

1. The gypsies came to our Lord's yett,
   And vow but they sang sweetly;
   They sang sae sweet, and sae compleat,
   That down came the fair lady.
   When she came tripping down the stair,
   And a' her maids before her;
   As soon as they saw her weel fair'd face,
   They coost the glamer o'er her.

2. Gae tak frae me this gay mantile,
   And bring to me a plaidie;
   For if kith and kin and a' had sworn,
   I'll follow the gypsie laddie.
   Yestreen I lay in a weel-made bed,
   And my good lord beside me;
   This night I'll ly in a tenant's barn,
   Whatever shall betide me.

3. Oh! come to your bed says Johny Faa,
   Oh! come to your bed, my deary;
   For I vow and swear by the hilt of my sword,
   That your lord shall nae mair come near ye.
   I'll go to bed to my Johny Faa,
   And I'll go to bed to my deary;
   For I vow and swear by what past yestreen,
   That my lord shall nae mair come near me.

4. I'll make a hap to my Johny Faa,
   And I'll make a hap to my deary;
   And he's get a' the coat gaes round,
   And my lord shall nae mair come near me.
   And when our lord came hame at e'en,
   And speir'd for his fair lady,
   The tane she cry'd, and the other reply'd,
   She's awa wi' the gypsie laddie.

5. Gae saddle to me the black, black steed,
   Gae saddle and mak him ready;
   Before that I either eat or sleep,
   I'll gae seek my fair lady.
   And we were fifteen well made men,
   Altho' we were nae bonny;
   And we are a' put down for ane,
   The earl of Cassilis' lady.

1. Black Jack Davy come a-riding through the woods
   He sang so loud and merrily,
   His voice rang out on the green grass lea
   And he charmed the heart of a lady,
   He charmed the heart of a lady.

2. How old are you, my pretty little Miss,
   How old are you, my honey?
   Well, she smiled so sweet with a te-he-hee,
   I'll be sixteen next Sunday,
   I'll be sixteen next Sunday.

3. O will you come and go with me,
   Come go with me, my honey?
   We'll go away to the deep blue sea,
   You'll never want for money,
   You'll never want for money.

4. As she put on her Sunday shoes
   All made of Spanish leather
   And he put on his old cork boots
   And they both rode off together,
   And they both rode off together.

5. The landlord come a-riding in
   Inquiring for his lady.
   O one of his maids then said to him,
   She is gone with Black Jack Davy,
   She is gone with Black Jack Davy.

6. Then bridle and saddle my old gray mare
   And hand me down my derby
   And I'll ride east and I'll ride west
   And overtake my lady,
   And overtake my lady.

7. Well, he rode east and he rode west
   He rode to the deep blue sea

And there he found with tears in his eyes
   O there he found his lady,
   O there he found his lady.

8. Will you forsake your house and home
   Your husband and your baby?
  Will you forsake all else on earth
   And go with Black Jack Davy,
   And go with Black Jack Davy?

9. Last night I slept on the cold cold ground
   Beside the Black Jack Davy,
  I'll sleep tonight in a warm feather bed
   Between my husband and baby,
   Between my husband and baby.

GROUP Ab

8. "The Davy"

Sung by Mrs. Carrie Grover, Gorham, Me., 1941. LC/
AAFS, rec. No. 4454(B1). Collected by Alan Lomax. Also
in Grover, n.d., p. 116.

a π²

1. The Squire came home late at night
   Inquiring for his lady,
  The servant made him this reply,
   "She's gone with the Gypsy Davy."

Refrain

Too-riddle ink tom toor de lie (?Toor de linktum)
   Too riddle ink tom tido
The servant made him this reply,
   "She's gone with the Gypsy Davy."

2. "Go harness up my milk-white steed,
   The gray is not so speedy.
  I'll ride all night and I'll ride all day,
   Till I overtake my lady."

[*Refrain as before, changing line three*]

3. He rode till he came to the river's side
   It looked so dark and dreary
  There he espied his lady fair
   Along with the Gypsy Davy.

[*Refrain as before, lines three and four changing*]

4. "Would you forsake your house and home
   Would you forsake your baby?

Would you forsake your own wed lord,
   And go 'long with the Gypsy Davy?"

[*Refrain as before*]

5. "Yes, I'd forsake my house and home,
   Yes, I'd forsake my baby,
  Yes, I'd forsake my own wed lord,
   And go 'long with the Gypsy Davy."

[*Refrain as before*]

6. "Last night I lay on a bed of down
   My baby lay beside me
  Tonight I'll lay on the cold cold ground
   Along with Gypsy Davy."
Toor de linktum toor de lie
   Toor de linktum tido
Tonight I'll lay on the cold cold ground,
   Along with the Gypsy Davy.

GROUP AC

21. [The Gypsy Laddie]

Sharp MSS., 3375/2468. Also in Sharp and Karpeles, 1932,
I, p. 234(B). Sung by Mrs. Mary Norton (37), Rocky
Fork, Tenn., September 2, 1916.

a D/M

1. The squire he came home at night
   Enquiring for his lady.
  The answer that came back to him:
   She's gone with the gypsy Davy.
   [She's gone with the gypsy Davy.][1]

2. Go saddle up my milk-white horse,
   And go saddle up my pony,
  And I will ride both night and day
   Till I overtake my lady.

3. How can you leave your house and land
   And how can you leave your baby,
  And how can you leave your kind husband
   To go with the gypsy Davy?

4. It's I can leave my house and land,
   And I can leave my baby,
  And I can leave my kind husband
   To go with the gypsy Davy.

5. Go pull off them high-heeled pumps
   That's made of Spanish leather,
  And give me your lily-white hand,
   We'll bid farewell for ever.

[1] 1932 reading; not in MS.

42. "Gipsies-O"

Collinson, *JEFDSS*, V, No. 1 (1946), p. 14. Also (edited) in Collinson and Dillon, 1952, p. 43. Sung by Harry Cox, Catfield, Norfolk, 1946.

a I

1. Oh seven gipsies all in a gang,
   They were brisk and bonny-o.
   They went till they came to the Earl Castle's hall (*sic*)
   And there they sang so sweetly-o.
   Sweetly-o, sweetly-o;
   They went till they came to the Earl Castle's hall,
   And there they sang so sweetly-o.

2. They sang so sweet and so complete
   Until downstairs came a lady-O,
   And as soon as they saw her pretty, pretty face,
   They cast their gazes over her.
   Over her, over her, etc.

3. She gave to them a bottle of wine.
   She gave to them some money-O.
   She gave to them some far finer things
   'Twas the gold rings on her fingers-O.
   Fingers-O, fingers-O, etc.

4. She pulled off her high-heeled boots,
   Put on her highland plaidie-O.
   "Last night I slept with my own wedded lord,
   And tonight with the gipsies' laddy-O."

5. When her dear lord came home that night
   Inquiring for his lady-O,
   The waiting maid made her reply,
   "She is gone with the black-guarded gipsies-O."

6. "So come saddle me my best black horse,
   Come saddle it quite swiftly-O,
   So I may search for my own wedded wife,
   Who is gone with the black-guarded gipsies-O."

7. He rode high and he rode low,
   He rode brisk and bonny-O,
   He rode till he came to a far water-side
   And there he found his lady-O.

8. "What made you leave your house and land,
   What made you leave your money-O,
   What made you leave your own wedded lord,
   To follow the black-guarded gipsies-O?"

9. "I know I've left my house and land,
   I know I've left my money-O,
   But here I am and here I remain,
   So fare-you-well my honey-O."

10. Seven gipsies all in a gang
    They were brisk and bonny-O.
    To-night they are all condemned to die,
    For stealing Earl Castle's lady-O.

71. [Wraggle Taggle Gipsies]

Sharp MSS., 2308/2103. Sung by Shepherd Haden (83), Bampton in the Bush, August 21, 1909.

m D

1. There was three gipsies came to the door
   And they sang brisk and bonny O
   And they sang high and they sang low
   And downstairs ran the lady O.

2. Then she pulled off her new silk gown
   And round her shoulders a blanket thrown
   And round her shoulders a blanket thrown
   For to toddle with the draggle tail gipsies O.

3. When the old Lord he came home
   Enquiring for his lady O
   The housemaid made him this reply
   She's gone with the draggle tail gipsies O.

4. Bridle me my milk white steed
   And saddle him so bonny O
   That I may ride and seek for my dear
   Who is gone with the draggle tail gipsies O.

5. Then he rode all that night long
   And part of the next morning O
   And there he saw his own true love
   A setting with the draggle tail gipsies O.

6. How could you leave your house & land?
   How could you leave your money O?
   How could you leave your new wedded lord
   To toddle with the draggle tail gipsies O?

7. What care I for house or land?
   What care I for money O
   I don't care a fig for my new wedded lord.
   I'll toddle with the draggle tail gipsies O.

8. Last night I lied on a warm feathered bed
   And my new wedded lord by my side O.
   And to night I'll lie in the cold open field
   Along with the draggle tail gipsies O.

6. What makes you leave your house & land?
   What makes you leave your money too
   What makes you leave your new wedded Lord
   To follow the draggletail gipsies O?

7. What care I for house or land
   What care I for my money O?
   What care I for my new wedded Lord
   I'll follow the draggletail gipsies O.

8. Last night you could lie on a good feather bed
   And into the arms of your Johnny too.
   And now you must ride on the wide open land
   Along with the draggletail gipsies O.

73. "The Draggletail Gipsies"

Sharp MSS., 264/373. Also in Sharp and Marson, 1904, p.
18; Sharp, 1916, p. 13; and Sharp, Selected Ed. [1920], I,
p. 13. Sung by Mrs. Overd, Langport, Somerset, August 4,
1904.

a Æ

1. There was three gipsies a come to my door
   One sung high & the other sung low
   The one sung high & the other sung low
   And the other sung bonny bonny brisky O.

2. This lady come down in a silken gownd
   Put on her spanish livery O
   Says she this night I'll resign
   To follow the draggletail gipsies O.

3. Twas late at night when her Lord came home
   Inquiring for his lady O
   The servants replied on every side
   She's gone with the draggletail gipsies O.

4. Come saddle me my milk white steed,
   Come bridle me my pony too
   That I might ride & seek for my bride.
   She's gone with the draggletail gipsies O.

5. Then he rode high and he rode low
   He rode through woods and copses too
   He rode till he came to the woodside
   And there he found his lady O.

83. "Gypsy Laddie"

Sung by Robert Shiflett, Brown's Cove, Va., July 15, 1961.
LC/AAFS, rec. No. 12,004(A2). Collected by George Foss.

a D/Æ

The F's are frequently uncertain in this singer's intonation.

1. Young Gipsy Davy came merrily by
       Whistling loud and gaily,
   He whistled and sang till the green woods rang,
       Charmed the heart of a lady.

2. Merrily down the castle stair
       Came this fair young lady,
   In her hand so fine was a glass of wine
       To drink a health to Davy.

3. Her own ?grim ["engram"] lord came home that night
       Inquiring for his lady,
   The waiting-maid cried as she replied,
       She's gone with (the) Gipsy Davy.

4. O saddle with speed my milk-white steed,
       Quickly make him ready,
   I will ride this night till broad daylight,
       Till I overtake my lady.

5. He rode that night, he rode next day,
       Till he came to the banks of the river,

On the other side his wife he spied
   Beside her gipsy lover.

6. Turn back, turn back, my own fair one,
   Turn back to your {lord? / home?} and baby,
   How can you roam from your (own) fair home
   To follow a gipsy laddie?

7. I won't turn back, I shan't turn back,
   For neither lord nor baby;
   I would give your home and the rest you own
   For one sweet kiss from Davy.

8. Last night on a bed of down you lay,
   Your baby lay by you.
   Tonight you will lay on the cold cold clay,
   With the gipsy lad beside you.

9. I won't turn back, I shan't turn back,
   For all your words of honey;
   I wouldn't give a kiss from the gipsy's lips
   For all your lands and money.

10. Take off, take off your costly glove
   That's made of Spanish leather,
   Your hand I will grasp in a farewell clasp,
   'Twill be farewell forever.

GROUP C

101. "Black Jack Davy"

Sung by Mrs. T. M. Davis, Fayetteville, Ark., November 15, 1953. LC/AAFS, rec. No. 11,894(B18). Collected by Mary Celestia Parler.

a I/M

1. Black Jack Davy came a-riding o'er the plains
   Singing his song so gaily O.
   He sang so loud he made the echoes ring,
   And charmed the heart of a lady O.

2. He says, little Miss, will you go with me?
   Will you be my baby O?
   I swear by the sword that hangs at my side,
   You never'll want for money O.

3. Will you forsake your house and home?
   Will you forsake your baby O?
   Will you forsake the one that loves you
   To go with Black Jack Davy O?

4. O yes, I'll forsake my house and home,
   Yes, I'll forsake my baby O,
   Yes, I'll forsake the one that loves me
   To go with Black Jack Davy O.

5. Then pull off that little black glove you wear
   Made out of Spanish leather O,
   Place your little white hand in mine,
   And here we'll part forever O.

6. She pulled off that little black glove she wore,
   Made out of Spanish leather O,
   Placed her little white hand in his,
   And there they parted forever O.

7. Well, they rode all night and they rode all day,
   Till the sun set in the evening O,
   There they came to a dark salt lake,
   And looked so dark and dreary O.

8. O once I had a home so fine,
   And jewels very costly O,
   Now I sit me down in rags
   By the side of the gipsy draily O.

9. Last night I slept on a new feather bed,
   By the side of my darling baby O,
   Tonight I sleep on an old straw bed
   With the gipsies piled all around me O.

During her childhood, Mrs. Davis learned two different versions of this ballad: one from her father, which is given above, and another from her mother, which Mrs. Davis in turn taught to her daughter, Mrs. Oleava Houser (see variant No. 102).

120. "Black Jack David"

Brown MSS., 16 a 4 J. Also in Schinhan, *Music, Brown Collection*, IV, 1957, p. 88(E1). Sung by Dr. I. G. Greer. Collected by C. Alphonso Smith and Thomas Smith, n.d. Another copy, unidentified in Brown MSS., 16 a 4 J, nearly identical with this, probably also from Dr. Greer.

p I/M

Four stanzas not preserved with tune. The full text of this singer is given as follows in Belden and Hudson, *Folk Ballads, Brown Collection*, II, 1952, p. 165(E):

1. Black Jack David come ridin' through the woods,
   Singin' so loud and merry
   That the green hills all around him ring,
   And he charmed the heart of a lady,
   And he charmed the heart of a lady.

2. 'How old are you, my pretty little miss,
   How old are you, my lady?'
   She answered him with a 'tee, hee, hee,
   I'll be sixteen next summer.'

3. 'Come, go with me, my pretty little miss,
   Come, go with me, my lady;
   I'll take you across the deep blue sea
   Where you never shall want for money.

4. 'Won't you pull off those high heel shoes
   All made of Spanish leather;
   Won't you put on some low heel shoes?
   And we'll ride off together.'

5. She soon pulled off those high heeled shoes
   All made of Spanish leather;
   She put on those low heeled shoes
   And they rode off together.

6. 'Twas late at night when the land-lord come
   Inquirin' for his lady.
   He was posted by a fair young maid:
   'She's gone with Black Jack David.'

7. 'Go saddle me my noble steed,
   Go bridle me my derby;
   I'll ride to the east, I'll ride to the west,
   Or overtake my lady.'

8. He rode till he came to the deep below;
   The stream was deep and muddy.
   Tears came tricklin' down his cheeks,
   For there he spied his lady.

9. 'How can you leave your house and land,
   How can you leave your baby,
   How can you leave your husband dear
   To go with Black Jack David?'

10. 'Very well can I leave my house and land,
    Very well can I leave my baby,
    Much better can I leave my husband dear
    To go with Black Jack David.

11. 'I won't come back to you, my love,
    Nor I won't come back, my husband;
    I wouldn't give a kiss from David's lips
    For all your land and money.

12. 'Last night I lay on a feather bed
    Beside my husband and baby;
    Tonight I lay on the cold damp ground
    Beside the Black Jack David.'

13. She soon run through her gay clothing,
    Her velvet shoes and stockings;
    Her gold ring off her finger was gone,
    And the gold plate off her bosom.

14. 'Oh, once I had a house and land,
    A feather bed and money,
    But now I've come to an old straw pad,
    With nothing but Black Jack David.'

Bessy Bell and Mary Gray

CHILD NO. 201

THE historico-legendary event that gave rise to this fragmentary song would appear to assign its earliest commencement to the year 1645 or '46. But, as Child failed to observe, or thought not worth noting, there was a song with the title "Bessy Bell" in existence as early as 1629, in which year, on June 22, Martin Parker's "Fourepence halfepenney Farthing," to be sung to that tune, was licensed to Francis Grove (Pepys Ballads, I, f. 274; reprinted Hyder Rollins, *A Pepysian Garland*, 1922, pp. 323ff.). An alternative tune named for Parker's ballad is "A Health to Betty," and it could be surmised that the two names referred to the same song. I believe that they did not: the currency of a new ballad could be increased by naming more than one familiar tune to which it would go. "A Health to Betty" is preserved as a country dance tune in Playford's *English Dancing Master* (1651 and subsequently) and was used over and over again with new sets of words, for more than a century (cf. Chappell, *Popular Music* [1855-59], I, pp. 366-67; D'Urfey, *Pills*, 1719-20, II, p. 110; etc.). It does not resemble the tune of "Bessy Bell," which also recurs throughout the eighteenth century, both with Allan Ramsay's words and, with new ones, in a number of ballad operas (*The Beggar's Opera*, 1728; *The Highland Fair*, 1731; *The Mock Doctor*, 2nd ed., 1732; *An Old Man Taught Wisdom*, 1735; *The Plot*, 1735). Presumptive evidence that the "Bessy Bell" named in 1629 was the same *tune* as that later sung under that title lies in the fact that Parker's words fit the tune so well. His internal rhyme in every other line brings out the rocking motion of the tune, of which the first and third phrases of the first strain fall into echoing halves; and his second and fourth lines have the feminine cadence which is so characteristic a feature of the tune. His stanzas are for a double-strain tune, as the refrain at every stanza's end makes clear, in spite of the print's breaking the third and seventh lines into two short rhyming lines. It should be observed that Parker's ballad goes only with effort to the alternative tune of "A Health to Betty."

The Guthrie version, as transcribed from tablature by Nellie Diem, is a plagal major, while most of the later versions that I have seen, from *Orpheus Caledonius* onward, are Mixolydian variants. (*The Beggar's Opera* copy is an exception.) There is very little difference among these later copies, except in degree of editorial ornamentation, and it would appear that no traditional variants were picked up in the record of the eighteenth or nineteenth century.

The tune which Greig collected at the opening of the present century is by bare possibility an ill-recollected variation of the old tune, but few readers will see any relation. It is a plagal tune, and may have been slightly influenced by "Green grow the rashes O"—which the mention of *rashes* in the text would have encouraged. The singer, Mrs. Gillespie, said that she had heard the song sung also to that tune. Her tune for "Bessy Bell" (variant 5 below) is less attractive by far than the earlier one, but much more characteristically traditional, and has the look of being worn down to a repetitive burden. It may be thought more in keeping with the melancholy text.

In the nineteenth century, if not before, the song came to rest—or the contrary?—in the nursery. Since the story had already disappeared in Ramsay's *rifacimento*, and since there was little chance that his added stanzas would appeal to the folk memory, it was not unnatural that something ludicrous should be tagged to the traditional first stanza by way of conclusion. Child has printed this nursery text from Halliwell (*Nursery Rhymes of England*, 1874, No. 484, p. 246). It seems to have had some circulation in print, both in Britain and in America.

A word of comment may be ventured on the ancient text, in so far as it has survived. Its compressed and condensed state gives it the air—which it may very well have lacked in a fuller form—of a sardonic commentary, like the "Twa Corbies," upon the chances of worldly pride. Walter Scott, however, found it the repository, "to a Scottish ear, of much tenderness and simplicity" (*Poetical Works*, 1833-34, I, p. 45). One may wonder if he was not to some extent reading into the song feelings that were derived from the local tradition which he so tenderly relates. Child's cautious remarks deserve to be pondered before we let our tears flow uncontrolled. The lover, he says, "who ought to have had his place in the song, appears only in [prose] tradition, and his reality [i.e., assuming the ladies to have been historical] may be called in question. It is not rational that the young women should seclude themselves to avoid the pest and then take the risk of the visits of a person from the seat of the infection. To be sure it may be doubted, notwithstanding the tenor of the ballad, whether the retirement of these young ladies was voluntary, or at least whether they had not taken the plague before they removed to their bower. In that case the risk would have been for the lover, and would have been no more than he might naturally assume" (1882-98, IV, p. 76). Child quotes close historical analogies in support of the last, more ingratiating and pathetic, hypothesis; and we may readily grant that it would have improved the narrative element of the ballad. As it is, we may wonder at the incalculable chances of tradition, which have kept such a fragment alive for so long a time. It is another demonstration of the fact that the lifeblood of traditional balladry does not lie in the story alone.

TUNES WITH TEXTS

GROUP A

4. "Bessy Bell"

Thomson, 1733, I, opp. p. 3. Also in Johnson, II [1788],
No. 128, p. 134 (repr. 1853); Smith [1820-24], IV, p. 21;
and Graham, 1848-49, II, p. 96; and Maver, 1866, No. 68,
p. 34.

a M, ending on 3

O Bessy Bell and Mary Gray,
  They are twa bonny Lasses,
They bigg'd a Bower on yon Burn-brae,
  And theek'd it o'er wi' rashes.
[Fair Bessy Bell I loo'd yestreen,
  And thought I ne'er cou'd alter;
But Mary Gray's twa pawky Een,
  They gar my Fancy falter.

Now Bessy's Hair's like a Lint-tap;
  She smiles like a May Morning,
When Phoebus starts frae Thetis' Lap,
  The Hills with Rays adorning:
White is her Neck, saft is her Hand,
  Her waste and Feet's fu' genty;
With ilka Grace she can command;
  Her Lips, O wow! they're dainty.

And Mary's Locks are like the Craw,
  Her Een like Diamonds glances;
She's ay sae clean, redd up and braw,
  She kills whene'er she dances:

Blyth as a Kid, with Wit at will,
  She blooming tight and tall is;
And guides her Airs sae gracefu' still,
  O Jove! she's like thy Pallas.

Dear Bessy Bell and Mary Gray,
  Ye unco sair oppress us;
Our Fancies jee between you twa
  Ye are sic bonny Lasses;
Wae's me! for baith I canna get,
  To ane by Law we're stented;
Then I'll draw Cuts, and take my Fate,
  And be with ane contented.]

[Bracketed text by Allan Ramsay.]

GROUP B a

5. "Bessy Bell and Mary Gray"

Greig and Keith, 1925, p. 130; from Duncan MS., No. 474.
Sung by Mrs. Gillespie.

a π^4, ending on V

Bessie Bell an' Mary Gray
  They were twa bonnie lasses,
They biggit their boo'r on yon burnside,
  An' thickit it owre wi rashes.

The Baron of Brackley

CHILD NO. 203

OF THIS excellent ballad, the records, verbal and musical, are rather scanty. It seems not to have achieved more than a regional currency; but at least we are spared the spectacle of dilapidation that too often discomfits us in these walks.

The tunes which are preserved have little in common, but perhaps enough, in metre and melodic contour, to relate them to a single family. (Miss Gordon's tune surely derives from Christie's.) Christie's tune dates, he says, from about 1816 in Buchan tradition, and was "arranged"—whatever that may mean—by his father. In this case, at least, it is unlikely that the second half of the tune was invented by the editor. It is, properly regarded, not a two-strain tune, but is composed, like other dactylic or anapaestic ballad-tunes, of four long phrases. There may be some distant kinship, most marked in the final cadence, between this and "Hay Tutti Taiti." There would be no doubt that the final is tonic, were it not that the Lady John Scott tune raises a query whether the second which ends the first phrase of Christie's tune might not have been the earlier tonic. Such a decision would throw both tunes into the same modal region, since the other has an Æolian cast. But Lady Scott's can be taken as pure major in its first three phrases: it is only the last phrase that is Æolian. So that, conversely, the π^2 character of Christie's tune as it stands may be thought closer to the modal norm than would be π^4, the other possibility. Lady Scott's tune may remind some readers of Sharp's Somerset tune, "O Sally, my dear" (Cecil J. Sharp and Charles L. Marson, *Folk Songs from Somerset*, 3rd series, 1906; *ante*, No. 44, vt.12). Where she got it has not been ascertained. Comparison may also be made with some of the tunes for "Queen Jane" (No. 170).

TUNES WITH TEXTS

GROUP Aa

1. "The Baron of Brackley"

Christie, I, 1876, p. 20. Obtained by Christie's father, c. 1816, from tradition in Buchan.

a π^2 (or π^4, ending on *VII*)

Down Dee side came Inverey, whistling and playing,
He's lighted at Brackley yates at the day dawing.
Says, "Baron o' Brackley, O are ye within?
There's sharp swords at the yate will gar your blood spin."
[*Etc.*]

Christie "epitomizes" his text from Jamieson's *Popular Ballads*, 1806, I, p. 102.

2.3. "Baron of Brackley"

Archive, School of Scottish Studies, rec. No. 1964/67/A6. Sung by Anne Neilson, Glasgow. Collected by Norman Buchan. Transcribed by Ailie Munro.

a π^2

1. In Deeside cam Inverey, whistlin an playin,
   An he was at Brackley's yetts ere the day was dawning

2. 'Oh, are ye there, Brackley, an are ye within?
   There's sherp swords are at your yett, will gar your
      bluid spin.'

3. 'Then rise up, my baron, an turn back your kye,
   For the lads frae Drumwharran are drivin them by.'

4. 'Oh, how can I rise up, an how can I gyan,
   For whaur I hae ae man, oh I'm sure they hae ten.

5. 'Then rise up, Betsy Gordon, an gie me my gun,
An though I gyan oot, love, sure I'll never come in.

6. 'Come, kiss me, my Betsy, nor think I'm tae blame
But against three-an-thirty, wae is me, what a fame.'

7. When Brackley was mounted, an rade on his horse,
A bonnier baron ne'er rade owre upon.

8. Twa gallanter Gordons did never sword draw,
But against three-an-thirty wisnae evens ava.

9. Wi their dirks an their swords, they did him surroond,
An they've slain bonnie Brackley wi monie's the wound.

10. Frae the heid o the Dee tae banks o the Spey,
The Gordons shall mourn him an ban Inverey.

11. 'Oh, come ye by Brackley's yett, or come ye by here?
Oh, saw ye his lady, a-rivin her hair?'

12. 'Oh, I come by Brackley's yett, an I come by here,
An I saw his fair lady; she was makin guid cheer.

13. 'She was prancin an dancin and singin for joy
An she vowed that that nicht she wad feast Inverey.

14. 'She laughed wi him, drank wi him, welcomed him ben;
She was kind tae the villain had slain her guid man.'

15. Through hedges and ditches ye cannot be sure,
But through the woods o Glentanor you'll skip in an hour.

16. Then up spak the babe on the nanny's knee:
It's afore I'm a man avengèd I'll be.

GROUP Ab

3. "The Baron of Brackley"

Lady John Scott MS., NL Scotland MS. 840.

a Æ

1. Inverey cam down Dee side whistling and playing
He lighted at Brackley yetts, ere the day-dawing
Cries Baron o Brackley are ye within?
There's sharp swords at your yett will gar yer blude spare.

2. His Ladye she rose to the window she went
She heard her Kye lowing over hill and over bent
She cried, rise up then Brackley and turn back yer Kye
For the Lads o' Dumwharran are driving them bye.

3. Theres sheep in the aitneuk [?Etnach] an' goats on the brae
An' a' will be harried by young Inverey
Rise up, Rise up Brackley an' be not afraid
They are but herd-wuddifas [?hir'd widdifus] wi' kilted
plaids.—

4. How can I [?gae out] and turn them again
Where'er I hae ae man I wot they hae ten
Then rise up my maidens tak rokes in your hand
An turn back the kye I hae you at command.

5. Gin' I had ae husband as it seems I hae nane
He wadna bide in the bower an see his kye taen.
Then up raise the Baron and cried for his graith
Saying, Ladye I'll gang tho' to leave thee I'm laith.

6. Oh kiss me my ladye and gie me my spear
I aye was for peace tho I never feared war
Farewell then my ladye, nor think me to blame
I weel may gae out but I'll never come hame.

7. When Brackley was busket & strode thro' the close
A gallanter baron neer sprang on a horse
When Brackley was mounted an rode o'er the green
He was as bauld a baron as ever was seen.

8. Tho' there cam' wi fause Inverey thirty & three
There was nane wi Bonnie Brackley but his Brother & he
Twa gallanter Gordons did never sword draw
But against four & thirty wae's me—what are twa?

9. At the head of the aitneuk [?Etnach] the Battle began
At little Aquhulzie they killed the first man
First they killed ane and syne they killed twa
And they killed Bonnie Brackley the flower o' them a'—

10. Wi swords and wi daggers they did him surround
An' they've pierced Bonnie Brackley wi' mony a wound
Frae the head o' the dee to the banks of the Spey
The Gordons may mourn him and curse Inverey.

11. Oh! cam ye by Brackley yetts were ye in there
Saw ye his ladye dear reiving her hair
Oh I cam by Brackley yetts I was in there
An' I saw his ladie dear making good cheer

12. That ladye she feasted them carried them ben[?]
She laughed wi' the men that her Baron had slain
She kept them till evening she bade them be gane
An' shewed them the road that she [sc. they?] might na be
ta'en

13. Through Birse and Aboyne she says hie ye [?attour]
Over the hills o' Glentanner ye'll ride in an hour
Theres grief in the kitchen theres mirth in the ha'
For the Baron o' Brackley is dead and awa'.

3.1. "Betsy Gordon"

Archive, School of Scottish Studies, rec. No. 1955/63/A7.
Sung by Duncan Burke, Perth. Collected by Hamish Henderson and Peter Kennedy. Transcribed by Ailie Munro.

203. THE BARON OF BRACKLEY

a D/Æ

Did you come by Brackley; did ye come by Dee?
And did you see a lady; she was speiring for me?
She was whistlin' and singin; she was combing her hair.
She was whistlin'; she was singin; she was combing her hair

(spoken) This is called "Betsy Gordon".

For he builded it out, an he builded it in,
And he built a false window to roll himsel in
'Wad ye rise, Betsy Gordon, and gie me my gun!
For it's when I go oot, love, I'll never come in.'

(she says)

'If I had a man, as I hae got nane,
Wad he lie in his bed an see his kye gane?

(he says)

'Wad ye rise, Betsy Gordon, an gie me my gun?
For it's when I go oot, I shall never come in.'

Jamie Douglas

CHILD NO. 204

CHILD has reprinted as an appendix a broadside of late seventeenth- or early eighteenth-century date, called "Arthur's Seat Shall Be My Bed, etc.," or "Love in Despair." This is obviously a piece cobbled for print out of scraps of traditional song and invented stanzas. The first two stanzas are untraditional and serve ill as a prologue. The third has still less to do with the narrative and shifts the rhyme-scheme to couplets. The fourth is the true commencement, and starts with the title line. The fifth departs again from the narrative and drops again into couplets. Its first two lines are favorites in folk-song and are still current (cf. the ubiquitous "Died for Love"). The rest of this stanza and the next belong to some song about a jilted girl (or boy) who is defiant under the blow (cf. "Early, Early" and "Werena my heart licht I wad die"). The seventh stanza is again in couplets; but it and the next are a restatement of matter found in the song now to be mentioned.

Allan Ramsay was the first to publish the beautiful lament of a forsaken girl, "Waly, Waly, Gin Love be Bony" (*Tea-Table Miscellany*, c. 1724). This appears to be genuinely traditional stuff and may very probably antedate the song described above. Its fifth stanza is identical in all important respects with the "Arthur's Seat" stanza of the other, and its sixth and tenth stanzas with the tenth and eleventh of the other. As mentioned above, also, the seventh and eighth stanzas of the other correspond in matter to two stanzas, the seventh and fourth, of "Waly, Waly." It appears indeed quite probable that the broadside, although earlier in point of record, was made out of imperfect recollections of "Waly, Waly." As Child notes, the third stanza of "Waly" closely corresponds with a proverbial stanza in a MS. of about 1620, which appears again in a medley in the 1666 edition of Forbes' *Songs & Fancies*.

When Thomson printed "Waly, Waly" in *Orpheus Caledonius* in 1725, he introduced a stanza about cockle-shells and "siller" bells. This latter reappears in all but one of the fuller texts of our present ballad, "Jamie Douglas." The ballad-texts also usually make use, variously, of seven out of ten of the other stanzas printed by Ramsay as "Waly, Waly." Most texts, however, use no more than one or two of these stanzas.

The earliest text of "Jamie Douglas" to see print was a five-stanza fragment given by David Herd in *Ancient and Modern Scottish Songs*, 1776, I, p. 144, entitled only "Tune, Wally, wally up the bank." Now Herd also gives "Waly, Waly" in Ramsay's text, in the same volume (I, p. 81). It is interesting that there is no connection, other than in the titles, between these two texts of the ballad and the song. Herd includes in the ballad the cockle-shells stanza, but this, it will be recalled, was not in the Ramsay text of "Waly" (nor indeed in the "Arthur's Seat" broadside). What we have here is excellent evidence that "Jamie Douglas," in the second half of the eighteenth century, was sung to the tune of the better known song.

Similar testimony is offered fifty years later than Herd by Motherwell (1827, App'x., p. xvii), who says that the ballad is often so sung, although he himself gives another tune.

Child says that the ballad "must date from the last quarter of the seventeenth century" (1882-98, IV, p. 92, note ‡). He may not have meant that it would have had to be made immediately after the events it purports to celebrate, but that, at least, would be a natural assumption. He points out that stanza eight of "Waly Waly," "When we came in by Glasgow town," hardly suits the song, but is quite fitting in the ballad, and suggests: "it may have been taken up from this ballad . . . or from some other" (*loc.cit.*).

It appears to me an entirely unwarranted inference that the song "Waly Waly," as R. Chambers declared (*Songs of Scotland Prior to Burns*, ed. of 1880, p. 280), and as G. F. Graham agreed (*Songs of Scotland*, 1848-49, I, p. 101), forms, without room for doubt, part of the ballad of "Jamie Douglas." There is, on the contrary, every reason to suppose that the makers of "Jamie Douglas," like the cobbler of "Arthur's Seat," made free use of a popular song to fill out their ballad, and sang the latter to the same tune. As counterweight for the inappropriate —but traditionally conventional—stanza about Glasgow town in the song, we may set the still less appropriate borrowing in most of the ballad-texts of the lament for lost maidenhood, and other touches befitting a deserted damsel, and quite unsuited to the Marchioness' married state. Her eldest son, the Earl of Angus, was in fact a promising lad of ten or more by the date of separation: in this light, her remarks look oddly unmaternal.

> But gin I had wist or I had kist
> That young man's love was sae ill to win,
> I would hae lockt my heart wi a key o gowd,
> And pinnd it wi a sillar pin.
>
> (Child F 3)

There is little doubt, then, as to which way the borrowing went, and we may suppose that the ballad was made with the tune of "Waly Waly" in mind and regularly sung to it. How old the tune may be I have no skill to say; but it was in print so early and so constantly that it has suffered little change from traditional transmission.

There remain to be mentioned two other quite beautiful tunes. One is the M/D setting which Motherwell printed for the ballad "Jamie Douglas" in 1827 (App'x., No. 9). This has no discernible relation with any form of the "Waly Waly" tune. The last is the haunting and lyrically free tune that Sandburg has found in this country, a plagal major set to the two stanzas, "cockle shells" and "love is bonny" (1927, p. 16). This melody appears to be a "sport," with no affiliations in tradition.

GROUP A

1. "Waly, Waly"

Thomson, 1733, I, opp. p. 71; less simply in [1725].

a I (inflected VII)

1. O Waly, Waly, up yon Bank,
    And Waly, Waly, down yon Brea;
   And Waly by yon River's side,
    Where my Love and I was wont to gae.

2. Waly, Waly, gin Love be bonny,
    A little while when it is new;
   But when it's auld, it waxes cauld,
    And wears away, like Morning Dew.

3. I leant my Back unto an Aik,
    I thought it was a trusty Tree;
   But first it bow'd, and sine it brake,
    And sae did my fause Love to me.

4. When Cockle-shells turn siller Bells,
    And Muscles grow on ev'ry Tree;
   When Frost and Snaw shall warm us a',
    Then shall my Love prove true to me.

5. Now *Arthur-Seat* shall be my Bed,
    The Sheets shall ne'er be fyl'd by me;
   Saint *Anton*'s Well shall be my Drink,
    Since my true Love has forsaken me.

6. O *Martinmas* Wind, when wilt thou blaw,
    And shake the green Leaves off the Tree?
   O gentle Death, when wilt thou come?
    And take a Life that wearies me.

7. 'Tis not the Frost that freezes fell,
    Nor blawing Snaw's Inclemency;
   'Tis not sic Cauld that makes me cry,
    But my Love's Heart grown cauld to me.

8. When we came in by *Glasgow* Town,
    We were a comely Sight to see;
   My Love was cled in the black Velvet,
    And I my sell in Cramasie.

9. But had I wist before I kiss'd,
    That Love had been sae ill to win;
   I'd lock'd my Heart in a Case of Gold,
    And pin'd it with a silver Pin.

10. Oh, oh! if my young Babe were born,
    And set upon the Nurse's Knee,
   And I my sell were dead and gane,
    For a Maid again I'll never be.

GROUP B

5. "Jamie Douglas"

Motherwell, 1827, App'x., No. 9; text, App'x., p. xvii. From A. Blaikie, Paisley.

a M/D (or a I/Ly, ending on II)

O come down stairs Jamie Douglas
    O come down stairs and speak to me,
And I'll set thee in a fine chair of gowd
    And I'll kindly daut thee upon my knee.

Bothwell Bridge

CHILD NO. 206

OF THE four tunes extant for this ballad, two are authentic, π^1, and nearly alike. The other two are respectively π^3 and Æolian; but the last gives such slight notice to the sixth as to be virtually D/Æ. The second strain, also, of the Æolian tune looks trumped up and artificial: the simpler π^3 tune looks genuine. This second pair is also closely related.

It is harder to decide whether the two pairs themselves have any kinship. If we reduce them all to the same metre, we are tempted to imagine the plagal form as a counterpart to the other pair. But to suppose such a development is, I believe, to argue a late and sophisticated origin; and it may be that the relation is fanciful and hypnotically induced by rhythmical similarities only. Lacking a more abundant supply of variants, we can reach no security, nor even determine which of the types has the greater weight of tradition behind it. To be sure the Blaikie copy looks rudest and most primitive: I have not discovered whence it came.

This ballad appears not to have been found by Greig, nor is it (as yet) in the archive of the School of Scottish Studies.

TUNES WITH TEXTS

GROUP A

2. "Earlistoun"

Chambers, 1844, p. 26. Tune from John Shortrede of Jedburgh.

a π^1

GROUP B

3. "Bonny Billie"

Blaikie MS., NL Scotland MS. 1578, No. 54, p. 20.

p π^3

4. "The Battle of Bothwell Brigg"

Scott, 1833-34, II, opp. p. [246]; text, p. 237.

m Æ

1. "O, billie, billie, bonny billie,
    Will ye go to the wood wi' me?
  We'll ca' our horse hame masterless,
    An' gar them trow slain men are we."—

2. "O no, O no!" says Earlstoun,
    "For that's the thing that mauna be;
  For I am sworn to Bothwell Hill,
    Where I maun either gae or die."—

3. So Earlstoun rose in the morning,
    An' mounted by the break o' day;
  An' he has joined our Scottish lads,
    As they were marching out the way.

4. "Now, farewell, father, and farewell, mother,
    And fare ye weel, my sisters three;
  An' fare ye weel, my Earlstoun,
    For thee again I'll never see!"—

5. So they're awa' to Bothwell Hill,
     An' waly they rode bonnily!
   When the Duke o' Monmouth saw them comin',
     He went to view their company.

6. "Ye're welcome, lads," the Monmouth said,
     "Ye're welcome, brave Scots lads, to me;
   And sae are you, brave Earlstoun,
     The foremost o' your company!

7. "But yield your weapons ane an a';
     O yield your weapons, lads, to me;
   For gin ye'll yield your weapons up,
     Ye'se a' gae hame to your country."—

8. Out then spak a Lennox lad,
     And waly but he spoke bonnily!
   "I winna yield my weapons up,
     To you nor nae man that I see."—

9. Then he set up the flag o' red.
     A' set about wi' bonny blue;
   "Since ye'll no cease, and be at peace,
     See that ye stand by ither true."—

10. They stell'd their cannons on the height,
      And showr'd their shot down in the howe;
    An' beat our Scots lads even down,
      Thick they lay slain on every knowe.

11. As e'er you saw the rain down fa',
      Or yet the arrow frae the bow,—
    Sae our Scottish lads fell even down,
      An' they lay slain on every knowe.

12. "O hold your hand," then Monmouth cry'd,
      "Gie quarters to yon men for me!"—
    But wicked Claver'se swore an oath,
      His Cornet's death revenged sud be.

13. "O hold your hand," then Monmouth cry'd,
      "If onything you'll do for me;
    Hold up your hand, you cursed Græme,
      Else a rebel to our King ye'll be."—

14. Then wicked Claver'se turn'd about,
      I wot an angry man was he;
    And he has lifted up his hat,
      And cry'd, "God bless his Majesty!"—

15. Than he's awa' to London town,
      Aye e'en as fast as he can dree;
    Fause witnesses he has wi' him ta'en,
      And ta'en Monmouth's head frae his body.

16. Alang the brae, beyond the brig,
      Mony brave man lies cauld and still;
    But lang we'll mind, and sair we'll rue,
      The bloody battle of Bothwell Hill.

Lord Derwentwater

CHILD NO. 208

ONE of the most interesting things about this ballad is its thoroughly popular tone, in view of its late date. It is made, of course, out of the stuff of earlier balladry, produced and recombined in the interests of a new hero, who was beheaded February 24, 1716. Tradition can be traced back to about the middle of the eighteenth century, or a very little earlier. Child's ten variants show that the ballad had a good purchase on life in the first half of the nineteenth century, in Scotland and the north of England. Lately it has been found in Florida.

Motherwell's tune is an excellent example of folk music. Its feeling is major, but it ends on the second, so as to make a graceful return to the beginning. Technically, therefore, it may be classed as Dorian. It has many relatives in tradition, one of the best known, possibly, being Cecil Sharp's "Outlandish Knight" (*One Hundred English Folksongs*, 1916, p. 29), Child No. 4, *ante*, variant 28a.

Vaughan Williams' second tune, from Hampshire (variant 3), is also major in its first three phrases, but it has a dropped close, and might be regarded as Mixolydian. It has to my ear more major feeling than Mixolydian. The tune at any rate is soundly traditional, and is obviously related to Motherwell's.

TUNES WITH TEXTS

GROUP A

1. [Lord Derwentwater]

Motherwell, 1827, App'x., No. 4; text, p. 350. From A. Blaikie, Paisley.

a D

1. Our King has wrote a long letter,
   And sealed it ower with gold;
   He sent it to my lord Dunwaters,
   To read it if he could.

2. He has not sent it with a boy,
   Nor with any Scots lord;
   But he's sent it with the noblest knight,
   E'er Scotland could afford.

3. The very first line that my lord did read,
   He gave a smirkling smile;
   Before he had the half of it read,
   The tears from his eyes did fall.

4. "Come saddle to me my horse," he said,
   "Come saddle to me with speed;
   For I must away to fair London town,
   For to me there was ne'er more need."

5. Out and spoke his lady gay,
   In child bed where she lay;

"I would have you make your will, my lord Dunwaters,
   Before you go away."

6. "I leave to you, my eldest son,
   My houses and my land;
   I leave to you, my youngest son,
   Ten thousand pounds in hand.

7. "I leave to you, my lady gay,
   You are my wedded wife;
   I leave to you, the third of my estate,
   That'll keep you in a lady's life."

8. They had not rode a mile but one,
   Till his horse fell owre a stane;
   "Its a warning good enough," my lord Dunwaters said,
   "Alive I'll ne'er come hame."

9. When they came to fair London town,
   Into the courtier's hall;
   The lords and knights of fair London town,
   Did him a traitor call.

10. "A traitor, a traitor," says my lord,
    "A traitor how can that be?
    An it be nae for the keeping five thousand men,
    To fight for King Jamie.

11. "O all you lords and knights in fair London town,
    Come out and see me die;
    O all you lords and knights in fair London town,
    Be kind to my ladie.

12. "There's fifty pounds in my right pocket,
    Divide it to the poor;
    There's other fifty in my left pocket,
    Divide it from door to door."

3. "Lord Ellenwater"

Gamblin and Vaughan Williams, *JFSS*, III, No. 13 (1909), p. 270. Sung by Mrs. Goodyear (74), Axford, Hampshire, August 1907.

a M (inflected VII)

1. The king he wrote a long letter,
   And sealed it up with gold,
   And sent it unto Lord Ellenwater,
   For to read it if he could.

2. The first three lines Lord Ellenwater read,
   It made his heart to revive;
   And the next three lines Lord Ellenwater read,
   The tears fell from his eyes.

3. He callèd for his stable groom,
   To saddle his milk-white steed,

   That up to London I might go,
   For I am sure there never was more need.

4. He put one foot all in his stirrup,
   Another across his steed,
   Three drops of blood fell from his nose,
   As he mounted his milk-white steed.

5. "That token's enough," Lord Ellenwater said,
   "That I never no more shall return,
   .   .   .   .
   .   .   .   .

6. "Here to you, my gay lady,
   Which is my wedded wife,
   .   .   .   .   an estate
   To maintain you all the days of your life.

7. "Here is fifty thousand pounds in one pocket,
   To be given away to the poor,
   Fifty thousand in the other pocket,
   Shall be strewed from door to door."

8. There stands the old grim man
   With the shining axe all in his hand,
   Saying, "Come, you, along here, Lord Ellenwater,
   For your life is at my command."

9. The people all amazed stood
   And well enough they may
   For he jumped three times upon his legs
   After they had cut off his head.

Geordie

CHILD NO. 209

LIKE the textual tradition, the musical tradition for this ballad is confused and crossed between the Scottish and English forms. If we accept Burns's text (Child A) as approximating the old norm of Scottish tradition, we find that norm accompanied by a series of variant tunes all belonging to a very familiar family best identified as the "Gypsy Laddie" (No. 200). Child's headnote, in fact, makes passing reference to a casual and probably accidental connection between "Geordie" and the Earl of Cassilis, a leading figure in the "Gypsy Laddie" tradition. At any rate, the Scottish tunes seem not to establish any independent tradition for the present ballad. The group under discussion can be read as members of the Dorian-Mixolydian galaxy, all authentic: most of them M/D, that is, lacking the third. Yet it might be argued that they are really I/M tunes, and all plagal, with finals on the lower fifth. Half are in 3/4, half in common time.

The second, and largest, group is English, mainly from the Southwest, but with scattered examples eastward and as far north as Lincolnshire, with two or three from the Appalachians as well. This is definitely the strongest English tradition, and is clearly connected with the later ballad about George of Oxford, which itself goes back to the seventeenth century. None of these preserves the burden of the earliest broadsides. The tune is of a favorite English pattern, found in a great variety of permutations and associations with other song-texts, both religious and secular. "Walsingham" is perhaps the earliest of these ("How should I your true love know"), but Lucy Broadwood and Anne Gilchrist (in *JFSS*, III, p. 191) noted affiliations also with "The man that lives," "The Truth sent from above," "Dorcas," "The Sinner's Dream," "There is a fountain," "The Holy Well," "The Carnal and the Crane" (No. 56), and an old Scottish psalm-tune, "Coleshill." (Cf. *JFSS*, IV, pp. 16, 20.) Others might be added: "Bailiff's Daughter" (No. 105), "Searching for Lambs." All of these are plagal tunes swinging between the Æolian and Dorian modes. There are one or two arguable variants, including a characteristic Scottish one (Greig and Keith's 2) found with many other ballads and not at all typical here.

A third group belongs to the "Boyne Water" family (also frequent with "Barbara Allan," No. 84 [Group D]). Variants are found from Aberdeenshire to the Ozarks, from Yorkshire to North Carolina and Arkansas. The modal center is again Æolian and Dorian, with π^4 and π^3 variants in America. Most are authentic tunes.

A fourth, not very homogeneous, group has, again, relationship with "Barbara Allan" in another tradition. Its spread is from Sussex to North Carolina. It is definitely in the major area (π^1, I/Ly, I/M), and always plagal.

TUNES WITH TEXTS

GROUP A

1. "Geordie"

Johnson, IV [1792], No. 346, p. 356 (repr. 1853). Also in Smith [1820-24], II, p. 68; and Maver, 1866, No. 448, p. 224. From Robert Burns.

a M/D

1. There was a battle in the north,
    And nobles there was many,
    And they hae kill'd Sir Charlie Hay,
    And they laid the wyte on Geordie.

2. O he has written a lang letter,
    He sent it to his lady;
    Ye maun cum up to Enbrugh town
    To see what words o' Geordie.

3. When first she look'd the letter on,
    She was baith red and rosy;
    But she had na read a word but twa,
    Till she wallow't like a lily.

4. Gar get to me my gude grey steed,
    My menzie a' gae wi' me;
    For I shall neither eat nor drink,
    Till Enbrugh town shall see me.

5. And she has mountit her gude grey steed,
    Her menzie a' gaed wi' her;
    And she did neither eat nor drink
    Till Enbrugh town did see her.

6. And first appear'd the fatal block,
    And syne the aix to head him;
    And Geordie cumin down the stair,
    And bands o' airn upon him.

7. But tho' he was chain'd in fetters strang,
    O' airn and steel sae heavy,
    There was na ane in a' the court,
    Sae bra' a man as Geordie.

8. O she's down on her bended knee,
    I wat she's pale and weary,
    O pardon, pardon, noble king,
    And gie me back my Dearie!

9. I hae born seven sons to my Geordie dear,
    The seventh ne'er saw his daddie:
    O pardon, pardon, noble king,
    Pity a waefu' lady!

10. Gar bid the headin-man mak haste!
    Our king reply'd fu' lordly:

O noble king, tak a' that's mine,
　　But gie me back my Geordie.

11. The Gordons cam and the Gordons ran,
　　　And they were stark and steady;
　　And ay the word amang them a'
　　　Was, Gordons keep you ready.

12. An aged lord at the king's right hand
　　　Says noble king, but hear me;
　　Gar her tell down five thousand pound
　　　And gie her back her Dearie.

13. Some gae her marks some gae her crowns,
　　　Some gae her dollars many;
　　And she's tell'd down five thousand pound,
　　　And she's gotten again her Dearie.

14. She blinkit blythe in her Geordie's face,
　　　Says, dear I've bought thee, Geordie.
　　But there sud been bluidy bouks on the green,
　　　Or I had tint my laddie.

15. He claspit her by the middle sma',
　　　And he kist her lips sae rosy:
　　The fairest flower o' woman-kind
　　　Is my sweet, bonie Lady!

4. "Gight's Ladye"

Greig MSS., II, p. 22. Also in Ord, 1930, p. 408. From William Walker, May 3, 1907.

a D

It is odd that the copy in the *Bothy Songs*, though note for note the same, and with the same first stanza, as Greig's copy, is attributed to a different source. On the possibility that the two were alike throughout—for Greig's twenty-three stanzas are missing—the Ord text, with twenty-three stanzas, is given here. The source is said to be James B. Allan, Glasgow.

1. Will ye gang to the Hielands, my bonnie love?
　　Will ye gang to the Hielands, Geordie?
　I'll tak' the high road gin ye tak' the low,
　　And I'll be in the Hielands afore ye.

2. I'd rather for to stay on the bonnie banks o' Spey
　　To see a' the fish boaties rowin',
　Afore that I would gang to your high Hieland hill
　　To hear a' the black kye lowin'.

3. He had not been in the high Hieland hills
　　Months but barely twa, O,
　When he was put in a prison strong
　　For hunting the deer and the roe, O.

4. Where will I get a little wee boy
　　That is both true and steady,
　That will run on to the bonnie Bog o' Gight
　　Wi' a letter to my ladye?

5. Oh, here am I, a bonnie wee boy
　　That is baith true and steady,
　And I'll run on to the bonnie Bog o' Gight
　　Wi' a letter to your ladye.

6. When you come where the grass grows green
　　You'll slacken your shoes and run, O;
　And when you come where the bridge is broke
　　You'll bend your bow an' swim, O.

7. And when you come to the bonnie Bog o' Gight
　　You'll neither shout nor call, O,
　But you'll bend your bow to your left breast
　　Then leap in over the wall, O.

8. When he came where the grass grew green
　　He slackened his shoes and ran, O,
　And when he came where the bridge was broke
　　He bent his bow and swam, O.

9. And when he came to the gates of Gight
　　He did neither shout nor call, O,
　But he bent his bow to his left breast
　　And he leaped in over the wall, O.

10. When that the ladye the letter looked on,
　　I wat little laugh got she, O;
　Afore she had read it half-way down
　　A saut tear blinded her e'e, O.

11. Gae saddle to me the grey horse, she cried,
　　The broon never rode so smartly,
　And I'll awa to Edinburgh town
　　And borrow the life o' my Geordie.

12. When she came to the pier o' Leith
　　The puir folk stood thick and mony.
　She threw the red gowd right them among,
　　Bade them pray for the life o' her Geordie.

13. When that she came to Edinburgh town
　　The nobles there were mony,
　Ilka ane wi' his hat on his head,
　　But hat in hand stood Geordie.

14. O has he killed, or has he robbed,
　　Or has he stolen ony?
　Or what's the ill that my love has done
　　That he's going to be hanged shortly?

15. He has not killed, he has not robbed,
　　He has not stolen ony,
　But he has hunted the King's young deer,
　　So he's going to be hanged shortly.

16. Will the red gowd buy aff my love, she said,
    Will the red gowd buy aff Geordie?
Ten thousand crowns, if ye pay down,
    Ye'll get on your hat on your Geordie.

17. Then out it speaks Lord Montague
    (O woe be to his body),
This day we hanged young Charlie Hay,
    The morn we'll hang your Geordie.

18. She's taen the silk mantle frae her neck,
    And, O, but she spread it bonnie;
Wi' his hat in her hand she has begged all around,
    Till she's begged the life o' her Geordie.

19. Some gave crowns and some gave pounds,
    Some gave dollars mony;
The King himself gave five hundred crowns
    To get on her hat on her Geordie.

20. Then out it speaks Lord Montague
    (O wae be to his body),
I wish that Gight had lost his head,
    I might enjoyed his ladye.

21. But out it speaks the ladye herself,
    Ye need ne'er wish my body;
O ill befa' your wizened snout,
    Would ye compare wi' my Geordie?

22. Now since she's on her high horse set,
    And on behind her Geordie,
There was ne'er a bird so blythe in a bush
    As she was behind her Geordie.

23. First I was lady at bonnie Auchindoun,
    And next I was mistress at Kincraigie,
But now I'm guidwife at the bonnie Bog o' Gight,
    And I've ventured my life for my Geordie.

He has stole six of the ?crowns ?white deer
And has sold [them] ?in Den Caney.

3. Come bridle my milk white steed,
   Come saddle me my pony
That I might ride to the Goodluck bridge [judge?],
   There I'll beg for the life of Georgie.

4. When she arrived at the ?red shire hall,
   Where people there were many,
Down on her bended knees did fall,
   Crying spare me the life of Georgie.

5. The judge looked over his left shoulder,
   ?When [he] saw her grief of ?misery,
He said young woman you are too late,
   For he is condemned already.

6. She turned her heavy eyes around
   And fixed them upon Georgie.
As you are ?confessed and die you must,
   May the Lord have mercy on you.

7. Georgie shall be hung in the chains of gold,
   Such chains as [his?] never be any,
And he is one of the royal blood
   And he courted a royal lady.

8. He shall be buried in a coffin of gold,
   Such coffin as there never was any.
Then on his tombstone it shall be wrote,
   He's ?long ?won the heart of a lady.

9. I wish I were on yonder hill,
   Where oft times I've been many,
With a sword and pistol all by my side,
   There I'd fight for the life of Georgie.

The text given is that which accompanies the tune at I, p. 436 of the MSS., since only one stanza of text is found with the tune at III, p. 394. The latter differs from the first stanza above only in line three, which reads "O there I spied a fair pretty maid."

GROUP B

11. "Georgie"

Vaughan Williams MSS., III, p. 394; also I, p. 436. Also in Sharp MSS., 980/; and Sharp, 1908-12, II, p. 47. From Cambridgeshire, c. 1906.

p D/Æ

1. As I walked over London Bridge
   One midsummer morning early,
   There I spied a pretty fair maid,
   She was ?mounted for her Georgie.

2. Georgie has stole no house nor land [horse nor cow?],
   Nor has he murdered any.

GROUP C

40. "Georgie"

Sung by Mrs. Georgia Dunaway, Fayetteville, Ark., May 10, 1951. LC/AAFS, rec. No. 10,821(A7). Also in Randolph, I, 1946, p. 164(D). Learned from her father, c. 1900. Collected by Mrs. Irene Carlisle.

a π³

1. As I went over London's bridge,
   'Twas early in the morning,
There I spied a pretty fair maid
   Pleading for the life of Georgie.

2. Go saddle up my milkswhite steed,
   And bridle them so gaily,
That I may ride to the King's castle town
   And plead for the life of Georgie.

3. She rode all day and she rode all night
   Till she was weak and weary;
While throwing back her fine yellow hair
   She pleads for the life of Georgie.

4. She took from her pocket a purse of gold,
   Saying here is money a-plenty.
Lawyers, lawyers, fee yourselves,
   And spare me the life of Georgie.

5. George stepped up then unto the lawyer,
   Saying, I have not murdered any,
But I've stole sixteen of the king's white steeds
   And sold 'em in Boheeny.

6. Up stepped the lawyer then to George,
   Saying, George, I'm sorry for you,
For your own confession has condemned you to die,
   May the Lord have mercy upon you.

7. George walking up and down the street
   A-bidding adieu to many,
A-bidding adieu to his own dear girl,
   Which grieved him the most of any.

8. George shall be hung with a golden cord,
   For of such there is not many,
Because he came from a royal race,
   And he courted a handsome lady.

9. I wish I were over on yon hillside
   Where kisses are a-plenty;
With a sword and a pistol by my side
   I would fight for the life of Georgie.

50. [Geordie]

Sharp MSS., 3416/2507. Also in Sharp and Karpeles, 1932,
I, p. 240(A). Sung by William F. Wells, Swannanoah,
N.C., September 9, 1916.

p I, ending on II

1. As I crossed over London's Bridge
   One morning bright and early,
I spied a maid for bide the way
   Lamenting for poor Charlie.

2. Charlie was the son of a poor man
   Who was loved by a fair lady.
It's by his own confession he must die.
   May the Lord have mercy on him.

3. Charlie never murdered any one.
   He stole sixteen of the king's white staff
And sold them in Virginee.

4. The king looked over his right shoulder
   And thus he says to Charlie:
It's by your own confession you must die.
   May the Lord have mercy on you.

5. The king looked over his left shoulder
   And thus he says to Charlie:
It's by your own confession you must die.
   Jinny have mercy on you.

Bonnie James Campbell

CHILD NO. 210

THE tune which has the best claim to traditional association with this poignantly beautiful elegy appeared with it about fifty years after the first extant (fragmentary) text. Where it came from one cannot say, or even whether R. A. Smith arbitrarily set it to the words. It has been reprinted in later collections so often that it is unlikely to be dislodged. The rhythm of the song is so powerful in any case as almost to compel its tunes, despite varying contours, into a mutual resemblance.

The first tune is clearly related to other Scottish melodies, in particular "Todlen hame," which, as Glen has noted, goes under various names: "My ain fireside," "Armstrong's Farewell," "Robie douna gorrach," "Earl Douglas's Lament," "Lude Lament," and so forth. The same stuff went into the making of "Whistle and I'll come to you, my lad." In its earliest form, it appears to be a π^1 plagal tune, ending on the second to avoid the immediate restatement of the tonic at the opening of the next stanza. It seems likely that the final ending was a feminine one, like that of the first phrase:

This ending can be seen in a number of comparable tunes, e.g., "Todlen butt and Todlen ben" in *Orpheus Caledonius*, 1733, II, No. 41.

The melody, like those of other dactylic ballads (e.g., "Queen Jane," Child No. 170), has (four) long phrases, which confirms one's judgment that the words should be printed as long couplets.

TUNES WITH TEXTS

1. "Bonnie George Campbell"

Smith [1820-24], V, p. 50. Also in Maver, 1866, No. 303, p. 152; Moffat, 2nd ed. [1896], p. 68; and Eyre-Todd [1894], p. 20.

p π^1, ending on II

Hie upon Hielands, and laigh upon Tay,
Bonnie George Campbell rode out on a day;
He saddled, he bridled, and gallant rode he,
And hame cam his guid horse, but never cam he.

Out cam his mother dear, greeting fu' sair,
And out cam his bonnie bryde riving her hair,
"My meadow lies green, and my corn is unshorn,
My barn is to build, and my baby's unborn."

In the second edition, Smith changed lines three and four of the second stanza to:

"The meadow lies green, the corn is unshorn,
But bonnie George Campbell will never return!"

and added a third stanza, as follows:

Saddled and bridled and booted rode he,
A plume in his helmet a sword at his knee,

But toom cam his saddle, all bloody to see,
Oh hame cam his guid horse but never cam he.

4. "James Campbell"

Sung by Frank Proffitt, August 1961, at Pinewoods Camp, Plymouth, Mass. Recorded by Evelyn K. Wells. Also (with other variations) on Folk-Legacy rec. No. FSA-1, 1962.

a π^2

Booted and spurred and bridled rode he,
A plume in his saddle and a sword at his knee.
Back come his saddle, all bloody to see,
Back come the steed but never come he.

A-ridin' in the Highlands, steep was the way,
Ridin' in the Lowlands, hard by the Tay.
Out come his mother, with feet all so fair,
Out come his sweetheart, a-reivin' of her hair.

The meadow's all a-fallin' and the sheep is unshorn,
The house is a-leakin' and the baby's unborn,
But bonny James Campbell nowhere could be seen,
For back come the saddle but never come he.

Booted and spurred and bridled rode he,
A plume in his saddle and a sword at his knee.
Home come the saddle all bloody to see,
Home come the steed but never come he.

Bewick and Graham

CHILD NO. 211

THE single tune which has been preserved for this fine ballad comes apparently from Northumbrian tradition, and is printed only in Bruce and Stokoe, without information as to source. It is not among James Telfer's tunes in manuscript. What makes one more confident that it was derived from tradition is the fact that whoever set it down (?Stokoe) had trouble in noting the time of bars two and four. As they are given, they look like an attempt to fit free singing into the strait jacket of regular barring. If these two bars are lengthened to 4/4, we should probably have something closer to what was sung. The same thing may have occurred at the cadence of phrase three, or the singer may not have found a pause necessary.

There are not very many ballad-airs in genuine triple time. This one suggests the "Young Beichan" (Child No. 53) tradition. The final cadence makes it Mixolydian, but up to that point it could as well be major and plagal.

TUNE WITH TEXT

"The Bewick and the Græme"

Bruce and Stokoe, 1882, p. 25.

a M

1. Gude Lord Græme is to Carlisle gane,
   Sir Robert Bewick there met he,
   And arm in arm to the wine they did go,
   And they drank till they were baith merrie.

2. Gude Lord Græme has ta'en up the cup—
   "Sir Robert Bewick and here's to thee!
   And here's to our twa sons at hame!
   For they like us best in our ain countrie."—

3. "O were your son a lad like mine,
   And learn'd some books that he could read,
   They might hae been twa brethren bauld,
   And they might hae bragg'd the Border side.

4. But your son's a lad, and he's but bad,
   And billie to my son he canna be."

   .   .   .   .

5. "Ye sent him to the schools and he wadna learn,
   Ye bought him books and he wadna read."—
   "But my blessing shall he never earn
   Till I see how his arm can defend his head."

6. Gude Lord Græme has a reckoning call'd,
   A reckoning then called he;
   And he paid a crown, and it went roun',
   It was all for the gude wine and free.

7. And he has to the stable gane,
   Where there stude thirty steeds and three,
   He's ta'en his ain horse amang them a',
   And hame he rade sae manfullie.

8. "Welcome, my auld father!" said Christie Græme,
   "But where sae lang frae hame were ye?"—
   "It's I hae been at Carlisle town,
   And a baffled man by thee I be.

9. "I hae been at Carlisle town,
   Where Sir Robert Bewick he met me;
   He says ye're a lad, and ye are but bad,
   And billie to his son ye canna be.

10. "I sent ye to the schools and ye wadna learn,
    I bought ye books and ye wadna read,
    Therefore, my blessing ye shall never earn,
    Till I see with Bewick thou save thy head."

11. "Now God forbid, my auld father,
    That ever sic a thing suld be;
    Billie Bewick was my master and I was his scholar,
    And aye sae weel as he learned me."

12. "O hald thy tongue, thou limmer loon,
    And of thy talking let me be;
    If thou disna end me this quarrel soon
    There is my glove, I'll fight wi' thee."

13. Then Christie Græme he stooped low,
    Unto the ground you shall understand—
    "O father put on your glove again,
    The wind has blown it from your hand."

14. "What's that thou says, thou limmer loon,
    How dares thou stand to speak to me?
    If thou do not end this quarrel soon,
    There's my right hand, thou shalt fight with me."

15. Then Christie Græme's to his chamber gane,
    To consider weel what then should be,
    Whether he should fight with his auld father,
    Or with his billie Bewick, he.

[372]

16. "If I suld kill my billie dear,
    God's blessing I shall never win;
    But if I strike at my auld father,
    I think 'twould be a mortal sin.

17. "But if I kill my billie dear,
    It is God's will, so let it be;
    But I make a vow ere I gang frae hame,
    That I shall be the next man's dee."

18. Then he's put on his back a gude auld jack,
    And on his head a cap of steel,
    And sword and buckler by his side,
    O gin he did not become them weel!

19. We'll leave off talking of Christie Græme,
    And talk of him again belyve,
    And we will talk of bonnie Bewick,
    Where he was teaching his scholars five.

20. When he had taught them well to fence,
    And handle swords without any doubt,
    He took his sword under his arm,
    And he walk'd his father's close about.

21. He looked atween him and the sun,
    And a' to see what there might be,
    Till he spied a man in armour bright,
    Was riding that way most hastilie.

22. "O wha is yon that cam this way,
    Sae hastilie that hither came?
    I think it be my brother dear!
    I think it be young Christie Græme.—

23. "Ye're welcome here, my billie dear,
    And thrice ye're welcome unto me!"
    "But I'm wae to say I've seen the day
    When I am come to fight wi' thee.

24. "My father's gane to Carlisle town
    Wi' your father Bewick there met he:
    He says I'm a lad and I am but bad,
    And a baffled man I trow I be.

25. "He sent me to schools and I wadna learn;
    He gae me books and I wadna read;
    Sae my father's blessing I'll never earn
    Till he see how my arm can guard my head."—

26. "O God forbid, my billie dear,
    That ever such a thing suld be;
    We'll take three men on either side,
    And see if we can our father's agree."

27. "Oh haud thy tongue now, billie Bewick,
    And of thy talking let me be;
    But if thou'rt a man, as I'm sure thou art,
    Come o'er the dyke and fight wi' me."—

28. "But I hae nae harness, billie, on my back,
    As weel I see there is on thine,"—
    "But as little harness as is on thy back,
    As little, billie, shall be on mine."—

29. Then he's thrown off his coat o' mail,
    His cap of steel awa flung he;
    He stuck his spear into the ground,
    And he tied his horse unto a tree.

30. Then Bewick has thrawn aff his cloak,
    And's psalter-book frae's hand flung he;
    He laid his hand upon the dyke,
    And ower he lap most manfullie.

31. O they hae fought for twa lang hours,—
    When twa lang hours were come and gane
    The sweat drapp'd fast frae aff them baith,
    But a drop o' blude could not be seen.

32. Till Græme gae Bewick an akward stroke,
    An akward stroke strucken sickerlie;
    He has hit him under the left breast,
    And dead-wounded to the ground fell he.

33. "Rise up, rise up, now, billie dear!
    Arise and speak three words to me!—
    Whether thou's gotten' thy deadly wound,
    Or if God and good leeching may succour thee?"—

34. "O horse, O horse, now, billie Græme,
    And get thee far from hence with speed,
    And get thee out of this country,
    That none may know who has done the deed."—

35. "O I have slain thee, billie Bewick,
    If this be true thou tellest to me;
    But I made a vow ere I came frae home,
    That aye the next man I wad be."—

36. He has pitched his sword in a moodie hill,
    And he has leap'd twenty lang feet and three,
    And on his ain sword's point he lap,
    And dead upon the ground fell he.

37. Twas then came up Sir Robert Bewick,
    And his brave son alive saw he.
    "Rise up, rise up, my son," he said,
    "For I think ye hae gotten the victorie."—

38. "O haud your tongue, my father dear!
    Of your pridefu' talking let me be!
    Ye might hae drunken your wine in peace,
    And let me and my billie be.

39. "Gae dig a grave baith wide and deep,
    And a grave to haud baith him and me;
    But lay Christie Græme on the sunny side,
    For I'm sure he wan the victorie."

40. "Alack! a wae!" auld Bewick cried,
    "Alack, was I not much to blame?
    I'm sure I've lost the liveliest lad
    That e'er was born unto my name."—

41. "Alack! a wae!" quo gude Lord Græme,
    "I'm sure I hae lost the deeper lack!

I durst hae ridden the Border through,
 Had Christie Græme been at my back.

42. "Had I been led through Liddesdale,
 And thirty horsemen guarding me,
 And Christie Græme been at my back,
  Sae soon as he had set me free!

43. "I've lost my hopes, I've lost my joy,
 I've lost the key but and the lock;
 I durst hae ridden the world around,
  Had Christie Græme been at my back."

Bruce and Stokoe take their text from Scott's *Minstrelsy* (e.g., Scott, *Poetical Works*, 1833-34, III, p. 69).

The Duke of Athole's Nurse

CHILD NO. 212

For all these late romantic Scottish ballads which employ the favorite feminine ending in the second and fourth phrases, we are very likely to find the same two or three tunes being handed about in abundantly variant forms. The commonest, probably, are the "Binorie" type and the "Gypsy Laddie."

The A-group of the present ballad belongs to the first of these, the "Binorie" family. All the tunes properly belong in the Æolian camp; they are plagal, but the lower range reaches sometimes to the octave and sometimes to lower III, and hence

they may alternatively be regarded as authentic tunes ending an octave above.

The second class is represented by only one example, Greig's 2 (variant 9). The second and third phrases of it are closely paralleled in Greig's first "Geordie" (No. 209) tunes, 1a and 1b. Those tunes are M/D and Æolian, the present one clearly Mixolydian. All belong to the "Gypsy Laddie" family, but the present tune is farther than usual from the traditional center.

TUNES WITH TEXTS

GROUP Aa

4. "The Duke of Athole's Nurse"

Greig MSS., IV, p. 129; text, Bk. 717, VII, p. 74. From Alexander Robb; learned from his grandmother, who was born c. 1780 at Mill of Crimond.

p D/Æ

1. As I cam in by the Duke of Atholl's (Athole's) gates
   I heard his yule nurse singin
   And aye as she sang and her bonnie voice rang
   Till hills and dales were ringin

2. Oh, I am the bonnie Duke of Atholl's nurse
   And the post it does well become me
   And I would gie a' my half-year's fee
   For a kiss and a sicht o' my Johnny.

3. He leant him in over his saddle bow
   And he has gien her kisses mony,
   Says, Keep weel, keep weel your half year's fee
   You'll get twa sichts o' your Johnny.

4. But ye have my heart and another has my hand,
   And what can I do wi' ye?
   But gin I hae your heart and another has your hand
   What the better will I be of you?

5. But you'll go doon to yonder ale house
   And drink or the day be a-dawnin'
   And spare nae the beer tho' it be dear
   And the wine keep constantly drawin.
   And gin I be a woman as surely as I am
   I will come and clear ye o' your lawin.

6. Her seven brothers were standin' near by
   And they heard them thus talkin
   And they hae said amon' themselves
   We'll go and clear this lawin.

7. So he went down to yonder ale house
   And drank till the day was a-dawnin'
   And he spared nae the beer although it was dear
   And the wine he kept constantly drawin.

8. But he lookit over the castle wa'
   To see gin the day was a-dawnin
   And there he spied seven well armed men
   They were comin wi' their swords well drawn.

9. O Landlady, O Landlady what shall I do
   For my life it is nae worth a farthin
   For here they come seven well armed men
   I'll be dead or the day be a-dawnin.

10. But she's castin aff her petticoat
    Likewise her goon & her apron
    And she has gien him the mutch frae aff her heid
    And she set the young squire to the bakin.

11. Oh when they came up to the gates
    Sae loudly as they rappit
    Oh when they came up to the door
    Sae loudly as they chappit.

12. Oh cam there a stranger here last night
    To drink or the day was a-dawnin
    Come show us the room that the stranger is in
    For we've come to clear his lawin.

13. Oh there cam a stranger here last night
    But he went ere the day was a-dawnin
    For he bocht but a pint and he paid it ere he went
    So he didna leave ony lawin.

14. But they socht him up & they socht him doon
    And they spared nae the feather beds a-turnin
    And aye as they gaed but and aye as they gaed ben
    They said Bonnie lassie are ye bakin'.

15. They socht him up and they socht him doon
    And spared nae the curtains a-rivin
    And aye as the auld wife gaed but and ben
    She scolded her maid at the bakin'
    And she said I have had mony a maid
    But the marrows o' you I never had bakin'.

16. They socht him up and they socht him doon
    Through kitchie and ha' a-rankin'
    But for a' that they ca'd and a' that they socht
    They left the young squire busy bakin.

GROUP B

9. "The Duke of Athole's Nurse"

Greig and Keith, 1925, p. 136(2); from Duncan MS., No. 11. Sung by Mrs. Gillespie.

a M

1. As he cam in by yon toon en',
   She heard his bridles ringin,
   An' when he cam in by the Castle wa',
   He heard her bonnie voice singin.

2. "O I'm the Duke o' Athole's nurse,
   My post is very weel becomin,
   But I wad gie a' my half year's fee
   For ae sicht o my leman."

3. "Ye say ye're the Duke o Athole's nurse,
   An' your post it is very weel becomin;
   Keep weel, keep weel your half year's fee,
   Ye'll get twa sichts o your leman."

4. He leaned him ower his saddle bow,
   An' cannily kissed his dearie;
   Said, "Ye hae my heart, but another has my han',
   What better can ye be o me?"

5. "Gin I hae your heart, an' another has your han',
   These words hae fairly undone me;
   But let us set a time, an' tryst to meet again,
   Then in good friendship ye'll twine me.

6. "Ye'll do ye doon to yon tavern house,
   An' drink till it be dawin,
   An' as sure as I'm a woman true,
   I'll come an' clear your lawin.

7. "Ye'll spare not the wine, although it be fine,
   Nor any drink though it be rarely;
   But ye'll aye drink to the bonnie lassie's health
   That's to clear your lawin fairly."

8. Then he's done him doon to yon tavern house,
   An' drank till the day was dawin,
   An' ilka gless he drank, he drank the lassie's health,
   That was comin to clear his lawin.

9. "It's a wonder to me," the squire he did say,
   "That my bonnie lassie's sae delayin;
   She promised as sure as she loved me,
   She wad be here by the dawin."

10. He's teen him up to a shott window,
    A little before the dawin,
    An' there he spied her brothers three
    Wi' their swords a' weel drawn.

11. "O where shall I rin, or where shall I gang,
    Or where shall I gang an' hide me?
    She that was to meet me in friendship this day
    Has sent her brothers to slay me."

12. He's gane to the landlady o the house,
    To see gin she could save him.
    She dressed him in her ain clothin,
    An' she set him to the bakin.

13. She gae him a suit o her ain female claes,
    An' set him to the bakin;
    The birds never sang mair sweet on the bush,
    Than the young squire sang at his bakin.

14. As they came in at the ha' door,
    Sae loodly as they rappit,
    An' when they cam upon the floor,
    Sae loodly as they chappit.

15. "O had ye a quarterer here last nicht,
    Who drank till the day was dawin?
    Come show us the room where the quarterer lies in,
    An' we'll shortly clear his lawin."

16. "There was nae quarterer here last nicht
    That drank till the day was dawin.
    He called for a pint, an' he paid it ere he went,
    Ye've got naething to do wi his lawin."

17. One of them bein in a very merry mood,
    To the young squire fell a-talkin;
    The wife took her foot an' she gae him a kick,
    Says, "Haste ye, bonnie Annie, wi your bakin."

18. They socht the house up, an' they socht the house doon,
    An' they spared nae the curtains for the rivin,
    An' ilka ane o them, as they passed by,
    They kissed the bonnie lassie at her bakin.

Sir James the Rose

CHILD NO. 213

OF this rather tasteless ballad, not popular but popularized, and apparently much affected in Scotland, the melodic tradition is fairly consistent and perhaps basically one. With the exception of Christie's first tune (Christie, I, 16), which he claims to be able to trace back traditionally for a century and a quarter, it is obvious that all the tunes were meant for texts that had a masculine rhyme at 2 and 4—that is, for the ballad generally attributed to Michael Bruce.

The main line of the melodic tradition belongs in the D to Æ province, inclining uneasily in a few exceptional cases toward the major. The latter look as though they had forgotten their earlier outlines and their true tonic; and viewing them in isolation, one would hardly relate them to the others.

Perhaps a more general observation is in order at this point. In connection with these abnormal variants, e.g., Greig's Id (vt. 20), it is natural, in the light thrown by the large majority of examples, to conclude that the final here is not the true tonic. The cast of the tune still remains recognizably the same, with the same modal feeling, when we put it into the context to which it belongs. But just here we must be on guard. We ought probably to be cautious in restoring or imposing that earlier tonic-final when the tune has shown a tendency to adopt a different one. For a song is not sung in a context of variants: it is a solitary. When we meet it so, the (new) final may make an entirely satisfactory resting-point for our now ignorant ears, so that we class the tune unquestioningly in the mode of that final. Or we may be in doubt between the final and one or even two or three alternative possibilites, according to whether the emphases and cadences of earlier phrases have made us aware of certain pivotal notes. But doubtless it is in just this way that modal changes often occur. There is a weakening of the tonal center; and from the various possibilities which the phrases of the tune successively offer, sometimes one will be chosen for anchor, sometimes another. But the choice is not unlimited: it will naturally be among the notes important to the tune as it stands—resting places which, when final, generate a mode close at hand, and out of corresponding segments of the same scale, whether pentatonic, hexatonic, or heptatonic.

Thus, for example, in Greig's Id (vt. 20) below, the mass of evidence shows that the tune as here transposed "ought" to end on A. The cadence B-A would have been perfectly natural. But the lower seventh (here G) has been planted at strategic points throughout, and that note's own fourth above and fifth below make melodic pivots which reinforce its importance. By the time we reach the end of the third phrase, the "lower seventh" has thus established itself as a quite satisfactory anchor for the tune, and is so stated in the final cadence. Thus the tune has changed from P/Æ to M/D, both plagal. We should, I believe, be wary of denying this new development because of previous knowledge, and of insisting that the "true" tonic is still A. The temptation, I repeat, is strong to do so—nor have I been able to resist it; but to yield is to make our melodic sensibilities slaves to historical event and accidental knowledge which in the next instance may probably be denied us. Thus all our judgments as to mode become more, instead of less, subjective, in comparison with the solid objectivity of a rule that the final is tonic. I believe, therefore, that we should give up that anchorage only when driven from it by the strongest pressures.

The main tradition here, to revert to our starting-point, is closely tied up with that of "Gil Morrice" (Child No. 83). The tune was used also with "Young Johnstone" (No. 88), "Fause Foodrage" (No. 89), and with the notorious "Hardyknute," to which it is mated in Johnson's *Museum*. It is often π^4, and plagal; not seldom D/Æ, plagal.

TUNES WITH TEXTS

GROUP A

6. "Sir James the Rose"

Christie, I, p. 18. From Aberdeenshire tradition.

m π^4

Of all the Scottish northern chiefs,
　　Of high and warlike name,
The bravest was Sir James the Rose,
　　A knicht of meikle fame.
The chieftain of the brave clan Ross,
　　A firm, undaunted band;
Five hundred warriors drew their sword,
　　Beneath his high command.

　　　　　　　　　　[*Etc.*]

Christie's text is "epitomized" from that of Michael Bruce in Alexander Whitelaw, *The Book of Scottish Ballads*, 1844, p. 41.

18. "Sir James the Rose"

Karpeles MSS., No. 5319; text, p. 4874. Also in Karpeles, *JEFDSS*, III, No. 1 (1936), p. 58(4). Sung by Mrs. James Welsh, Ferryland, Newfoundland, August 1, 1930.

m D

1. Of all the Scottish northern chiefs
   Of high and warlike fame,
   The bravest was Sir James the Ross,
   A knight of mighty fame.

2. The fair Mathilda dear he loved,
   A maid of high renown

   . . . .

   And bid her wed Sir James the Ross.

   . . . .

3. Art thou asleep Mathilda dear?
   Awake, my love, I say,
   A luckless lover on thee calls
   A long farewell to take.

4. For I have slain Sir Donald Graham,
   His blood lies on my sword,
   And far, far distant are my men,
   They can't assist their lord.

5. To Skye I'll now direct my way
   Where my two brothers abide
   And rouse the combat of the . . .
   And combat on my side.

6. O do not go, the maid replied,
   With me till morning stay,
   For dark and distant is the road
   And dangerous is the way.

7. All night I'll watch you in the park,
   My faithful page I'll send
   To run and raise the Ross's clan
   Their master to defend.

8. Swift ran the page o'er hill and dale
   Till in a lonely glen
   He met the fierce Sir John Graham
   With fifth of his men.

9. Where goest thou, little page, he said,
   So late who did thee send.
   I have to raise the Ross's clan
   Their master to defend.

10. For he have slain Sir Donald Graham,
    His blood lies on his sword,
    And far, far distant are his men
    That can't assist their lord.

11. Tell me where is Sir John the Ross,
    I will thee well reward.
    He sleeps within Lord Bohun's park
    Mathilda is his guide.

12. Outside the gate Mathilda stood,
    To her the Graham did say:
    Saw you Sir John the Ross
    Last night did he pass this way?

13. Last day at noon, Mathilda said,
    Sir John the Ross passed by,
    He spurred his steed with furious move,
    'Tis onward fast did hie.

14. By this he's in Edinburgh
    If horse and men holds good.
    'Tis false, said he, your page told me
    He sleeps within your wood.

15. She wrung her hands and tore her hair,
    Brave Ross you are betrayed
    And wounded by those means, she cried,
    Of when I hoped thine aid.

16. By this the gallant knight awoke,
    The virgin's squeaks he heard,
    And up he rose and drew his sword
    As the undaunted band appeared.

17. Last day your sword my brother slew,
    His blood yet dim with shine,
    And e'er the setting of the sun,
    Yours will reek on mine.

18. Your words are great, replied the chief,
    But deeds approve the man,
    Set by your band and hand to hand
    We'll try what valour can.

19. Four of his men, the bravest four,
    Fell down beneath his sword,
    But still he scorned the high revenge
    That sought their hearty lord.

20. Behind him beastly came the Graham
    And pierced him through the side
    And spurting came the purple blood

    . . . .

21. The sad Mathilda saw him fall.
    O spare his life, she cried.
    Lord Bohun's daughter begs his life,
    Let her not be denied.

22. Her loving voice the hero heard,
    And raised his death-closed eyes
    And fixed them on the weeping maid
    And weakly thus replied:

23. In vain Mathilda begs the life
    Of death's arrest denied,
    My race is run, adieu my love,
    And closed his eyes and died.

20. "Sir James the Rose"

Greig MSS., III, p. 63. Also in Greig and Keith, 1925, p. 141(1d). Sung by A. Robb, New Deer, December 1907.

213. SIR JAMES THE ROSE

p P/Æ, ending on *VII*

Of all the Scottish northern chiefs
Of high & mighty name
The bravest was Sir James the Rose,
A knicht o' mickle fame.

The Braes o Yarrow

CHILD NO. 214

ALTHOUGH the textual tradition of this ballad cannot be followed very far into the eighteenth century, it seems clear that a ballad lay behind Hamilton of Bangor's overwrought piece on the subject ("Busk ye, busk ye"); and the ramifications of the tunes which in one way or another are connected with the ballad are ancient and honorable.

It will be well to begin with the steadiest and best established, even if most recent, tradition. This is that of the North-East of Scotland, where Greig and Duncan collected no less than twenty-two examples, of which Keith printed six. The tune is very characteristic and fairly consistent. It is always plagal; almost always D/Æ, but sometimes π^4 or Æ; and all the variants are in triple time. It generally opens with a phrase that divides into two identical, or very similar, descending figures, but sometimes opens with an upward sequence. As Keith has noted, it is found with a number of ballads: "Geordie," "Barbara Allan," "Willie's Drown'd" (all in Christie), Greig's "Tifty's Annie," and others.

The tunes of this group that start with an ascending figure have a discernible allegiance to the simpler forms (many examples of which we have already encountered) of "Boyne Water" in its second strain. Tunes with fuller and more unmistakable affiliation form our second, small group. The traditional connection of this family with the ballad, however, rests on early hearsay and late evidence. Kidson's tune (variant 36), which came from Eskdale tradition, was sung by Mrs. Calvert of Gilnockie, who was the granddaughter of Scott's Tibbie Shiel, from whom she seems to have got it. Perhaps on the strength of Kidson's note (*Traditional Tunes*, 1891, p. 22), J. C. Dick asserts that Tibbie Shiel sang the ballad to this tune (Dick, ed., 1903, p. 379). As Kidson gives it, it is the second

strain of "Boyne Water." But the tune which Dick prints (*op. cit.*, p. 79) is a form of "Boyne Water" with both strains. He gives it as from Oswald's *Caledonian Pocket Companion*, V [c. 1753],* p. 26, where it was called "The Rashes" (variant 34). The "Boyne Water" tune in an older form is printed by Moffat from a MS. of 1730-35 (*Minstrelsy of Ireland* [1897], p. 340, App'x., No. XII).

It remains to say that the "Boyne Water" tradition has also been found in connection with the "Yarrow" ballad in New England. Cf. Barry, Eckstorm, and Smyth, *British Ballads from Maine*, 1929, pp. xxxvi, 195, and 291. But that tradition is associated with such a multitude of ballads in this country that we need not be so impressed with the fact as Barry appears to have been.

The fourth type is found with the words of Hamilton's poem "Busk ye, busk ye" in Thomson, 1733 ("The Braes of Yarrow"); and appears in many other collections with insignificant alterations. Editorial annotation by Lucy Broadwood connects it with Greig's "The Scauldin Wife," "The Back o' Benachie," "The Lion's Den" (cf. *JFSS*, V, No. 19 [1915], p. 114). It should also be compared with the following ballad, No. 215. Recently recovered variants follow the outline of the older "Busk ye" tune. The latter, in turn, is certainly sib to the still older "An thou wert mine ain thing," familiar in its *Beggar's Opera* form ("O what pain it is to part"), and of which an ancestor appeared in Gordon of Straloch's lute MS., c. 1627 (NL Scotland MS., Adv. 5.2.18). An early version of it, transcribed from the Leyden MS. and bearing the name of "The lady's goune," is given by G. F. Graham, *The Songs of Scotland* (variant 41, not reprinted here).

* Dates according to Dick, *op.cit.*, p. xli.

TUNES WITH TEXTS

GROUP A

2. "The Dowie Dens o' Yarrow"

Ord, 1930, p. 426.

p D/Æ

1. There lived a lady in the south,
   You could scarce have found her marrow;
   She was courted by nine gentlemen,
   And the ploughman laddie o' Yarrow.

2. As he came ower yon high, high hill,
   And down yon glen so narrow,

There he spied nine gentlemen
Come to fight with him on Yarrow.

3. If I see all, there's nine to ane,
   And that's an unequal marrow;
   But I will take you three by three,
   And I'll slay you all on Yarrow.

4. Then three he slew, and three withdrew,
   And three lay deadly wounded,
   Till her brother John stepped in behind
   And pierced his body through.

5. Go home, go home, ye false young man,
   And tell your sister sorrow,
   That her true love John lies dead and gone
   In the dowie dens o' Yarrow.

6. As she came ower yon high, high hill,
   And down yon glen so narrow,
   It's there she spied her brother John
   Returning home from Yarrow.

7. O, brother, dear, I've dreamt a dream,
    And I fear it will prove sorrow,
For I dreamt that you were spilling blood
    In the dowie dens o' Yarrow.

8. O, sister, dear, I'll read your dream,
    And I'm sure it will prove sorrow,
Your true love John lies dead and gone,
    A bloody corpse in Yarrow.

9. She wrung her hands and tore her hair
    Wi' muckle grief and sorrow,
For she dearly loved her true love John,
    The ploughman laddie o' Yarrow.

10. This lady's hair being three-quarters long,
    And the colour of it was yellow,
She's tied it round her middle jimp,
    And she carried him home from Yarrow.

11. O, daughter, dear, dry up your tears,
    And dwell no more in sorrow,
And I'll wed you to one of a higher degree
    Than the ploughman laddie o' Yarrow.

12. O, father, ye hae seven sons,
    Ye can wed them a' to-morrow,
But a fairer flower than my true love John
    There never bloomed in Yarrow.

13. Now this lady, she being in distress
    For her love who died on Yarrow,
She flung herself in her father's arms,
    And died through grief and sorrow.

They made up a plot themsells amang
    To fight for her in Yarrow.

3. "Oh bide at hame my true love John
    Oh bide at hame my marrow.
For my cruel brother will thee betray
    In the dowie dens o' Yarrow.["]

4. As he gaed up yon lang lang bog
    He gaed wi dool and sorrow
He spied ten men all watering their steeds
    In the dowie dens o' Yarrow.

5. Oh, are ye come to sell your land
    Come here to beg or borrow
Or are ye come to wield your brand
    In the dowie dens o' Yarrow.

6. I'm neither come to sell my land
    Come here to beg or borrow
But I am come to wield my brand
    In the dowie dens o' Yarrow.

7. Oh three he slew and three he drew
    And three he did lay low
When her brother John came by a bush
    And ran his body thorough.

8. O lady hie thee to yon glen
    Hi thee wi' dool and sorrow
For your true love John lies dead and gone
    In the dowie dens o' Yarrow.

9. Oh sister sister make my bed
    Oh make it long and narrow
For my true love died for me yestreen
    I'll die for him the morrow.

28. "The Dowie Dens o' Yarrow"

Greig MSS., III, p. 34; text, Bk. 721, XI, p. 3. Also in
Greig-Duncan MS. 785 (Walker transcript), p. 112; and
Broadwood, *JFSS*, V, No. 19 (1915), p. 110. Sung by John
Potts, Peebleshire, September 3, 1907; noted by Lucy E.
Broadwood.

p π⁴

GROUP B

34. "The Rashes"

Oswald, V [c. 1753],* p. 26. Also in Dick, ed., 1903, No.
82, p. 79.

m D/Æ, ending on V

1. There lived a lady in the West,
    Some said she had no marrow
She was courted by nine gentlemen
    And a plowman lad in Yarrow.

2. Late at e'en and drinking wine
    As oft they'd done before o

* Date according to Dick, *op.cit.*, p. xli.

36. "The Dowie Dens of Yarrow"

Kidson, 1891, p. 22. Sung by Mrs. Calvert, Gilnockie, Eskdale; learned from her grandmother, Tibbie Shiel.

a D

1. There lived a lady in the west—
   I ne'er could find her marrow;
   She was courted by nine gentlemen,
   And a ploughboy lad in Yarrow.

2. These nine sat drinking at the wine,
   Sat drinking wine in Yarrow;
   They made a vow among themselves,
   To fight for her in Yarrow.

3. She washed his face, she kaimed his hair,
   As oft she'd done before, O!
   She made him like a knight sae bright,
   To fight for her in Yarrow.

4. As he walked up yon high, high hill,
   And down by the holmes of Yarrow;
   There he saw nine armèd men,
   Come to fight with him in Yarrow.

5. "There's nine of you, there's one of me,
   It's an unequal marrow;
   But I'll fight you all one by one,
   On the dowie dens of Yarrow."

6. There he slew, and there they flew,
   And there he wounded sorely;
   Till her brother, John, he came in beyond,
   And pierced his heart most foully.

7. "Go home, go home, thou false young man,
   And tell thy sister, Sarah,
   That her true love, John, lies dead and gone,
   On the dowie dens of Yarrow."

8. "Oh, father, dear, I dreamed a dream,
   I'm afraid it will bring sorrow;
   I dreamed I was pulling the heather bell,
   In the dowie dens of Yarrow."

9. "Oh, daughter, dear, I read your dream,
   I doubt it will prove sorrow;
   For your true love, John, lies dead and gone,
   On the dowie dens of Yarrow."

10. As she walked up yon high, high hill,
    And down by the holmes of Yarrow,
    There she saw her true love, John,
    Lying pale and dead on Yarrow.

11. Her hair it being three quarters long,
    The colour it was yellow;
    She wrapped it round his middle sma',
    And carried him hame to Yarrow.

12. "Oh, father, dear, you've seven sons,
    You may wed them a' to-morrow;
    But a fairer flower I never saw,
    Than the lad I loved in Yarrow."

13. This fair maid being great with child,
    It filled her heart with sorrow;
    She died within her lover's arms,
    Between that day and morrow.

GROUP C

40.1. ["The Dowie Dens of Yarrow"]

Sung by Jock Higgins, Blairgowrie, Perthshire, September 11, 1962. Collected by Ewan MacColl and Peggy Seeger.

p I

1. There was a lady in the North
   Ye'd scarcely find her marrow.
   She was courted by nine gentlemen
   To fight for her on Yarrow.

2. For nine days a' a–drinkin' wine,
   A' drinkin' wine in Yarrow
   They made a vow among themselves
   To fight for her in Yarrow.

3. O she washed his face and she kamed his hair
   O often she's done before O
   To make him like a knight so bright
   To fight for her in Yarrow.

4. For he walked up yon high high hill
   And down in a down of Yarrow
   There he spied nine arrum'd men
   Come to fight with him in Yarrow.

5. For three he slew and three he drew
   And three lay deadly wounded
   When her brother John came in beyond
   And wounded him sae cru'lly.

6. O it's Father dear, I dreamed a dream,
   I hope it does not prove sorrow
   I dream'd my true love lies dead and gone
   In the dowie dens of Yarrow.

7. O daughter dear, I've read your dream
   Your dream it does prove sorrow

For your true love John lies pale and wan
   In the dowie dens of Yarrow.

8. So she walked up yon high high hill
   And down in the dens of Yarrow
   There she saw her true love John
   Lyin pale and wan in Yarrow.

9. Her hair it hung three-quarters long
   And the color of it being yellow
   She tied it roond her middle small
   And carried him home to Yarrow.

10. O Father dear, you have seven bonny sons.
    You could wed them all tomorrow
    But the bonniest flour that ever ye had
    I woo'd with him in Yarrow.

Rare Willie Drowned in Yarrow, or, The Water o Gamrie

CHILD NO. 215

KEITH has pertinently declared that there is no compelling need to identify the song of "Willie drowned in Yarrow" with the ballad of "Willie drowned in Gamrie" (Greig and Keith, *Last Leaves*, 1925, p. 145). But I find myself not disposed to part company with Child on the point. If we add to the fact that there is no water of Gamrie (unless the sea) the further significant, almost total, absence of rhyme in the Gamrie forms of the ballad, we shall conclude, I believe, that Child was not taking a long shot. There is the connection in subject and the sharing of stanzas; and comparing two of the latter, we are likely to infer a substitution of name in the second:

> She sought him east, she sought him west,
>   She sought him brade and narrow;
> Sine, in the clifting of a craig,
>   She found him drowned in Yarrow. (Child 215 A4)

> She sought it up, she sought it down,
>   She sought it braid and narrow;
> An in the deepest pot of Gamerie,
>   There she got sweet Willie. (Child 215 D13)

Cf. also stanzas F9, G8, H15, and Greig's own stanza 14. There is, at any rate, equally no compelling need to separate the two, as Keith does; and we may properly reckon the tunes printed with "Rare Willie" as belonging to the tradition of this ballad.

There is a long continuity in the musical tradition so understood. Our earliest records of the tune go back to the Blaikie MSS. of 1683 and 1692. The line runs through the eighteenth- and nineteenth-century collections with divergences enough to show that tradition has not depended solely on print; and turns up finally in Ohio, in the twentieth century. Nearly everywhere the tune is I/M and plagal.

TUNES WITH TEXTS

GROUP A

1. "Sweet Willy"

Blaikie MS., NL Scotland MS. 1578, No. 1, p. 1.

p I/M

3. "Willie was drowned in Yarrow"

Greig MSS., III, p. 34; text, Bk. 721, XI, p. 6. Also in Greig-Duncan MS. 785 (Walker transcript), p. 121; and Broadwood, *JFSS*, V, No. 19 (1915), p. 115. Contributed by Lucy Broadwood, as sung by John Potts, Whitehope Farm, Innerleithen, Peebleshire, September 3, 1907.

p I/M

The variant reading is given in the *Journal, loc.cit.*, above.

> Her hair it was five quarters long
>   The colour of it was yellow
> She tied it round his middle sae sma'
>   And she dragged him out o' Yarrow.

> Oh mother mother make my bed
>   Oh make it long and narrow
> For never a young man shall lie by my side
>   Since Willie was drowned in Yarrow.

5. "Willy's rare, and Willy's fair"

Thomson, 1733, II, p. 110. Also in Ritson, 1794, I, p. 142; Johnson, VI [1803], No. 525, p. 542 (repr. 1853); Maver, 1866, No. 416, p. 208; Christie, I, 1876, p. 64; and Eyre-Todd [1894], p. 136 (as from *The Caledonian Musical Repository*, 1809).

p I (VII in grace-note)

Willy's rare, and *Willy's* fair,
    And *Willy's* wond'rous bony;
And *Willy* heght to marry me,
    Gin e'er he marry'd ony.

Yestreen I made my Bed fu' brade,
    The Night I'll make it narrow;
For a' the live-long Winter's Night,
    I lie twin'd of my Marrow.

O came you by yon Water-side,
    Pu'd you the Rose or Lilly;
Or came you by yon Meadow green,
    Or saw you my sweet *Willy*?

She sought him East, she sought him West,
    She sought him brade and narrow;
Sine in the clifting of a Craig,
    She found him drown'd in *Yarrow*.

The Mother's Malison, or, Clyde's Water

CHILD NO. 216

ELEMENTS of this ballad are common to certain other ballads earlier in the canon, and have foreign analogues as well. The most prominent is "Annie of Lochryan" (No. 76), with which, however, it would be too fanciful to claim a connection in the melodic tradition.

For the present ballad there is clearly but one melodic family, and no useful purpose is served by subscribing to Keith's four. But the tune-type is, as he says, met in other associations: "The Gardener" (No. 219), "Lang Johnnie More" (251), "Pitcaithly's Wells," "There cam a Laddie frae the North," "The False Lover Won Back" (218) and elsewhere. It should be observed how even here there is an occasional infusion of the "Gypsy Laddie's" second strain ("Lady Cassilis"). Characteristically, the second half of the tune is consistently more stable than the first half, and the last phrase is steadiest of all. It may be relevant that that phrase has much in common with the most characteristic phrase in the well-known "Comin' thro' the Rye." The tune stays safely within the major galaxy, being variously π^1, I, I/M, and M. It is always plagal, or, alternatively, authentic with an ending on the octave.

TUNES WITH TEXTS

GROUP A

2. "Clyde's Water"

Greig MSS., I, p. 76; text, Bk. 711, I, p. 31. Also in Greig and Keith, 1925, p. 149(2a). Sung by Miss N. Watson, Whitehill, New Deer, October 1905.

p π^1

1. Young Willie stands in his stable
   And combing down his steed
   {And looking through his white fingers
   {His nose began to bleed.

   Repeat last two lines

2. Bring corn, corn to my horse
   And meat unto my men
   {For I'm awa to Maggie's bowers
   {I'll win or she lie doon.

   Repeat

3. O stay, O stay this ae nicht Willie
   O stay and dinna gang
   {For there is a noise in Clyde Waters
   {Wid fear a thousand men.

   Repeat

4. It's I've a steed in my stable
   Cost me twice twenty pounds
   {And I'll put trust in his fore legs
   {Tae carry me safe along.

   Repeat

5. As I rode o'er yon high high hill
   And down yon dreary glen
   It's o spare me spare me Clyde waters
   O spare me as I gang
   Make me the wreck as I come back
   But spare me as I gang.

6. As I rode o'er yon high high hill
   And down yon dreary glen
   It's I hae reached at Maggie's window
   Rise up and lat me in
   For my boots are full of Clyde waters
   And I'm frozen tae the chin.

7. It's up arose her mother dear
   A' for tae speak tae him
   It's my stable's full of horse she says
   My barn's full of hay.
   And my bowers are full of gentlemen
   So ye can't get in till day.

8. He turned his horse right round about
   Wi' the saut tear in his e'e
   I never thought tae come here this nicht
   And be denied by thee.

9. As he rode o'er yon high hill
   And down yon dreary glen
   The rush that ran in Clyde waters
   Took Willie's can[e] frae him.   *Rep[eat]*

10. As Willie he sat saddle o'er
    To catch his cane again
    The rush that ran in Clyde waters
    Took Willie's hat frae him.   *Rep[eat]*

11. His brother being on the other side
    Cries Willie will ye droon.
    Oh had ye tae yer high horse heid
    He'll learn ye how to swim.

12. It's up she rose her Maggie dear
    All in a frightful dream
    For she dreamt that Willie was here last nicht
    And she widna lat him in.

13. Go to yer bed my daughter dear
    Lie doon and tak yer rest
    For it's nae the space of half an hour
    Since Willie left yer gate.

14. Then to her chamber she went with speed
And how quickly she put on
Now she is off tae Clyde waters
As fast as she can run.

12.1. "Clyde's Water"

Archive, School of Scottish Studies, rec. No. 1952/28/A6.
Sung by Willie Edward, Craigellachie, Banffshire. Collected by Hamish Henderson. Transcribed by James Porter.

p I/M

1. "So sleep ye, Maggie? Waukin Maggie?
Rise, come let me in,
For my boots are fu o Clyde water,
An I'm soakin tae the skin."

2. "So who is that at my window,
So fain he would be in?"
" 'Tis your true lover Willie dear;
Frae Scotland he has come."

3. "It's I hae nae lover there-oot," she cried;
"I hae nae lover but een.
It's the ae true love that I dae hae,
Was here late yestreen."

4. "So well fair ye well then, false Maggie,
Since better canna be.

Oh, I'll awa the road I cam,
Nae mair come thee to see."

(Lapse of memory)

5. His brother stands upon yonder banks,
Says, "Fie man, will ye droon?
So turn ye roon t'yir high horse heid,
An learn how to swim."

6. "Oh why could I turn to my high horse head,
An learn how to swim?
It's the deepest pot in aa the Clyde,
An here that I maun droon."

7. . . . "Oh mother dear,
Come rede my drowsy dream;
I dreamt sweet Willie was at my gates:
Nae yin wad let him in."

8. "Lie still, lie still, my Maggie dear
Lie still an tak your rest;
Since your true love was at your gates,
'Tis full three quarters past."

9. It's Maggie rose, put on her clothes,
An to the Clyde she went;
The first step noo that she took in,
It took her tae the knee.

10. The next step noo that she took in,
It took her tae the chin;
In the deepest pot in aa the Clyde,
She found her Willie in.

11. "So you have got a cruel mother,
And I have got another,
But here we lie in Clyde water,
Like sister and like brother."

The Broom of Cowdenknows

CHILD NO. 217

WHEN this ballad first began to be recorded, in the second half of the eighteenth century, it had, apparently, no refrain or burden. Had it had the old familiar burden, "O the broom, the bonny bonny broom," etc., it seems probable that the transcribers would have set that down. The first appearance of a refrain in a dependable text is that in Child D, which was taken down by Motherwell from singing. There the refrain is merely a fifth-line repeat with a syllabic bridge: still no burden. The burden first appears with the ballad in Child G (from Scott's *Minstrelsy*), where, however, it is used only as an introductory stanza, not repeated. It is only with Buchan's texts, Child L and M, that the burden makes its conventional appearance, and with a few texts that succeed his in date.

Nevertheless, it is clear that the musical tradition of the ballad is integral with that of the old song-tune which is intimately associated with this burden from its first appearance in the middle of the seventeenth century. The tune is unmistakable, and we have a number of early records of it, some of them unfortunately hard to decipher from the tablature in which they are written. The tune, wherever it clearly appears, ends on the second degree and is major in cast, whether straight Ionian, π^1, I/M, or Mixolydian. It is also authentic.

The tune in its authentic form enters the ballad tradition in the nineteenth century records, and continues into the present century (Group Ab). One of these variants is Christie's, who says he can follow it back for a hundred years in Buchan tradition.

TUNES WITH TEXTS

GROUP Aa

6. "The Broom of Cowdenknows"

Johnson, I [1787], No. 69, p. 70 (repr. 1853). Also in Ritson, 1794, I, p. 118; Smith [1820-24], II, p. 45; Thomson [1822-23], III, p. 32; Graham, 1848-49, I, p. 56; and Eyre-Todd [1894], p. 40.

a I, ending on II

GROUP AC

9. "Ochiltree Walls"

Motherwell, 1827, App'x., No. 10; text, App'x., p. xviii.

a M/D

O May, bonnie May, is to the yowe buchts gane
    For to milk her daddies yowes,
And ay as she sang her voice it rang
    Out ower the tap o' the knowes, knowes, knowes,
    Out ower the tap o' the knowes.

17. "The Ewe-Bughts"

Greig MSS., III, p. 117; text, Bk. 731, XXI, p. 87. Sung by A. Robb, April 1908.

a M/D

1. Bonnie Mary to the ewe-bughts is gane
    To milk her daddy's Ewes,
  And aye as she sang & her sweet voice it rang
    Right over the tops o' the knowes—knowes,
    Right over the tops o' the knowes.

2. There was a troop of gentlemen,
    Cam' merrily riding by
  And ane o' them is to the Ewe-bughts gane
    To see Mary milkin' her kye.

3. "Milk on, milk on, my bonnie bonnie lass,
    Milk on, milk on," said he;
  "Milk on, milk on, my bonnie bonnie lass,
    And ye'll show me oot owre the lea."

4. "Ride on, ride on, stout rider," she said,
    ["]Your steed is baith stoot & strang,
  It's oot o' the Ewe-bughts I winna gang
    For fear ye do me wrang."

5. He has ta'en her by the milkwhite hand,
    And by the grass-green sleeve,
  And laid her doon on the dewy dewy grass
    And never spiered her leave.

6. He's gien her a silver comb,
    To comb doon her yellow hair,
  And he has gien her guineas three,
    For fear she'd never get mair

7. He has mounted his milk-white steed,
    And after the rest o' his men;
  And a' that they did say to him
    Was, "Dear master, you've tarried lang."

8. She has pitten her milk pail on her head,
    And she's gane singin' hame;
  And a' that her father did say unto her,
    Was, "Dear daughter you've tarried lang."

9. "There's been a tod in your bughts, father,
    And the like o' 'im I never saw,
  For afore he had ta'en the boggie that he's ta'en
    I wad raither he had ta'en them a'.

10. "And the nicht it is misty & dark, father,
    Come ye to the door & see,
  And the Ewes gaed skippin' oot owre the knowes
    And they widna bught in for me.

11. "Woe be to your shepherd, father,
    Some ill death may he dee,
  He's bigget the bughts owre far frae the hoose,
    And he's trysted a man to me.

12. "And he was a man & a bonnie man,
    And a bonnie man was he,
  And aye as he spak & he lifted his hat,
    And he had a bonnie blinkin' eé."

13. It fell once upon a day
    She was cain' oot her father's kye,
  And by cam' the same troop o' merry gentlemen,
    And they winket the bonnie lassie by.

14. And one of them did say unto her
    "Oh have ye got a man?"
  So saucily she did reply,
    Says, "Oh I've got one at home."

15. "Ye lee, ye lee, ye weel-faur'd maid,
    Sae lood's I hear ye lee;
  For don't ye mind on the dark & misty nicht
    That I was in the bughts wi' thee?

16. ["]And I gave you a silver comb
    To comb doon your bonnie yellow hair,
  And I did give you guineas three
    For fear ye'd never gotten mair?"

17. He's taen her by the waist sae sma',
    And he's set her on ahin',
  Says, "Your father can ca his kye when he likes,
    But ye'll never ca them again.

18. "I am Laird o' Youghal Tree Wells,
    I have 20 ploughs & 3,
  And I hae gotten the bonniest lass,
    That's in a' the north countrie."

The False Lover Won Back

CHILD NO. 218

GREIG showed that this pretty ballad, as both Child and Keith have called it, had a firm hold in his region, although Child had recovered but two texts. We might say it had 'sprung from the ashes,' to use Child's phrase for "Henry Martin," of the old and too cruel "Child Waters" (No. 63).

The main melodic tradition is perhaps plagal major. Christie's tune, which he derives from a Buchan singer about the opening of the nineteenth century, is a charming pentatonic. Greig's first tune (our variant 2), mixed I/M, is recognizably close, although of course lacking Christie's second strain. In exchange, it has a fifth phrase, with bridge, for refrain.

Greig's Wallace tune (variant 3) is an interesting example of modal variation. Enough of the previous tune is left to establish a clear relationship, but this one ends convincingly on the lower

sixth, and without other evidence would certainly be called Æolian. And so it probably ought to be considered. According to Keith this tune is found with other folk-songs, but I am unable to point to any close variants. Phrases two and four are, however, common formulae.

The remaining tune appears to be independent of the others. It has a close family resemblance to the first part of "I'm a' doun for lack o' Johnnie" (G. F. Graham, *The Songs of Scotland*, 1848-49, II, p. 36), an air made notable by its use in Max Bruch's "Scottish Fantasia." But possible other and older affiliations are with "O an ye were deid, guidman," and "Corn Riggs" (cf., e.g., Alfred Moffat, *The Minstrelsy of Scotland*, 2nd ed. [1896], pp. 100 and 236).

TUNES WITH TEXTS

GROUP A

1. "The Place where my love Johnnie dwells"

Christie, I, 1876, p. 144. From a Buchan singer, c. 1800.

m π^1

1. The sun shines high on yonder hill,
     And low on yonder town;
   In the place where my love Johnny dwells,
     The sun gaes never down.
   "O when will ye be back, bonny lad,
     O when will ye be hame?"
   "When heather hills are nine times brunt,
     And a' grown green again."

2. "O that's ower lang awa', bonny lad,
     O that's ower lang frae hame!
   For I'll be dead and in my grave,
     Ere ye come back again."
   He put his foot into the stirrup,
     And said he maun gae ride;
   But she kilted up her green claithing,
     And said she wou'dna bide.

3. The firsten town that they came to,
     He bought her hose and sheen;
   And bade her rue and return again,
     And gang nae farther wi' him.
   "Ye likena me at a', bonny lad,
     Ye likena me at a'."
   "It's sair for you likes me sae weel,
     And me nae you at a'."

4. The nexten town that they came to,
     He bought her a braw new gown;
   And bade her rue and return again,
     And gang nae farther wi' him.
   The nexten town that they came to,
     He bought her a wedding ring;
   And bade her dry her rosy cheeks,
     And he would tak' her wi' him.

5. "O wae be to your bonny face,
     And your twa blinkin' een!
   And wae be to your rosy cheeks!
     They've stown this heart o' mine.
   There's comfort for the comfortless,
     There's honey for the bee;
   There's comfort for the comfortless,
     There's nane but you for me."

2. "The false lover won back"

Greig MSS., IV, p. 56; text, Bk. 759, XLIX, p. 88. Also in Greig and Keith, 1925, p. 155(1). From Miss Annie Shirer, as learned from the singing of Miss Kate Morrice, a very old woman of Kininmonth.

[390]

m I/M

1. The sun shines high on yonder hill,
   And low in yonder dell;
   The place where me & my love dwells
   The sun goes never doon, bonnie love,
   The sun goes never doon.

2. Go saddle to me the bonnie black steed,
   Or saddle to me the broon,
   That I may ride all around, bonnie love,
   That I may ride all around.

3. It's when will ye be back, bonnie love,
   Or when will ye be hame?
   When the heather hills are nine times brunt,
   And a' growin' green again, bonnie love,
   And a' growin' green again.

4. Oh, that's owre lang to bide awa',
   Oh, that's owre lang frae hame;
   The baby that's nae born yet
   Will be owre lang wintin' its name, bonnie love,
   Owre lang wintin' its name.

5. He turned aboot his high horse' [sic] heid,
   And fast awa' rode he;
   And she kilted up her gay clothing,
   And fast, fast followed she, bonnie love,
   And fast, fast followed she.

6. The first intoon[1] that they cam' till,
   He bocht her hose & sheen;
   And he bade her rue & return noo,
   And nae mair follow him, bonnie love,
   And nae mair follow him.

7. It's love for love that I do want,
   And love for love again;
   It's hard when I like you sae weel,
   And you nae me again, bonnie love,
   And you nae me again.

8. The neist in toon that they cam' till,
   He bocht her a broch & a ring;
   And he bade her rue & return noo,
   And nae mair follow him, bonnie love,
   And nae mair follow him.

9. It's love for love that I do want,
   And love for love again;
   It's hard when I like you sae weel,
   And you nae me again, bonnie love,
   And you nae me again.

10. The neist in[2] toon that they cam' till,
    He bocht her a wedding goon;
    And he bade her dry her rosy cheeks,
    And he would tak' her wi' him, bonnie love,
    And he would tak' her wi' him.

11. It's love for love that I do want,
    An' love for love again;
    And there's nane but you for me, bonnie love,
    And there's nane but you for me.

12. There's comfort for the comfortless,
    And honey for the bee;
    And there's nane for you but me, bonnie love,
    There's nane for you but me.

13. So it's love for love that I hae got
    And love for love again;
    So turn your high horse heid aboot,
    And we will ride for hame, bonnie love,
    And we will ride for hame.

[1] i.e., firsten toon
[2] i.e., niesten

3. [The False Lover won Back]

Greig and Keith, 1925, p. 155(2); from Duncan MS., No. 510. Sung by William Wallace, Leochel-Cushnie.

a Æ

The sun shines high on yonder hill,
   An' low in yonder glen;
   An' in the place where my love dwells
   The sun gangs never doon.

GROUP B

5. [The False Lover won Back]

Greig and Keith, 1925, p. 155(3); from Duncan MS., No. 286. Sung by Mrs. Gillespie.

p I

It's love for love that I wad gie,
   Love I wad tak again;
   It's hard that I like you sae weel,
   An' you nae me again, bonnie love,
   An' you nae me again.

The Gardener

CHILD NO. 219

THIS piece rests uneasily in Child's collection. It is both too little of a ballad, generating virtually no story, and too sophisticated and fanciful in symbolism. It will perhaps do for a folk-song which has been framed as situation. He says, "Be mine, fair maid." She retorts, "Indeed not!" For narrative this is hardly better than the dramatic prologue of which Joseph Addison was said to have been so inordinately fond: "A certain king said to a beggar, 'What hast to eat?' 'Beans,' quoth the beggar. 'Beans?' quoth the king. 'Yea, beans, I say,' and so forthwith we straight begin the play."

The earliest copy of a tune, Kinloch's, from Northern tradition, is the farthest from what appears to be normal. If the final be tonic, the tune is plagal D/Æ; but its feeling is definitely major, and the final is pretty certainly on the sixth. This brings it into closer relation with the other variants, which are all major (π¹, I/M), plagal, and with which it has other traits in common. Note that, without the tune tradition's being modified beyond recognition, these few members nevertheless vary in number of phrases from five to six to eight (ten, counting repetition). Greig's (b) tune will suggest Christie's "The Place where my love Johnny dwells" (*ante*, No. 218); and, generally, the melodic tradition of this and the preceding ballad seem interconnected.

It did not escape Child's notice that the textual tradition of this ballad had got mixed up with Mrs. Habergham's seventeenth century song, "The Seeds of Love," as handed down orally, and with "The Sprig of Thyme" ("Once I had plenty of thyme"): two very popular songs in the west of England and elsewhere. On these complications, see Chappell, *Popular Music* [1855-59], II, pp. 520-23; Baring-Gould and Sheppard, *Songs and Ballads of the West*, 1895, notes on Nos. VII and CVIII, pp. xv, xlii; Baring-Gould, Sheppard, and Bussell, *Songs of the West*, 1905, notes pp. 3-4; Child, 1882-98, V, pp. 258-60; also Sharp's *One Hundred English Folk Songs*, 1916, Nos. 33 and 34, and the notes on p. xxix. There is, however, no discernible connection between the numerous variants of the English song-tunes and those of our present, Scottish, "ballad."

TUNES WITH TEXTS

3. "The Gardener Lad"

Greig MSS., III, p. 57. Also in Greig and Keith, 1925, p. 157(a). Sung by Alexander Robb, New Deer, December 1907.

p I/M

Lady Margret stood in her bow'r door,
As straucht's a willow wand,
An' by there cam the gard'ner lad,
Wi a red rose in his hand;
An' by there cam the gard'ner lad,
Wi a red rose in his hand.

5. "The Gardener"

Kinloch, 1827, App'x. to p. 74; text, p. 74.

p D/Æ; or, if on C, a I/Ly, ending on VI

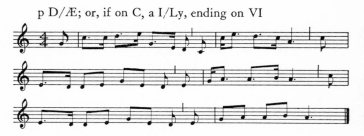

1. The gard'ner stands in his bouer door,
      Wi' a primrose in his hand,
   And bye there cam a leal maiden,
      As jimp as a willow wand;
   And bye there cam a leal maiden,
      As jimp as a willow wand.

2. "O ladie can ye fancy me,
      For to be my bride;
   Ye'se get a' the flowers in my garden,
      To be to you a weed.

3. The lily white sall be your smock,
      It becomes your body best;
   Your head sall be buskt wi' gelly-flower,
      Wi' the primrose in your breist.

4. Your gown sall be the Sweet William;
      Your coat the camovine;
   Your apron o' the sallads neat,
      That taste baith sweet and fine.

5. Your hose sall be the brade kail-blade,
   That is baith brade and lang;
   Narrow, narrow, at the cute,
   And brade, brade at the brawn.

6. Your gloves sall be the marigold,
   All glittering to your hand,
   Weel spread owre wi' the blue blaewort
   That grows amang corn-land."

7. O fare ye weil, young man, she says,
   Fareweil, and I bid adieu;
   Sin ye've provided a weed for me
   Amang the simmer flowers,
   It's I'se provide anither for you,
   Amang the winter-showers:

8. The new fawn snaw to be your smock,
   It becomes your bodie best;
   Your head sall be wrapt wi' the eastern wind,
   And the cauld rain on your breist.

Katharine Jaffray

CHILD NO. 221

THIS ballad, in late reshaping, whether Scots or Irish or English, has enjoyed a widespread popularity, for reasons not hard to guess. It has been found in our century in Aberdeen, Somerset (or Devon), County Connaught, Massachusetts (from County Tyrone), Vermont (from County Cork), New Brunswick, and Nova Scotia.

Phillips Barry has a valuable note on this ballad in connection with Irish tradition (Flanders, *et al.*, *The New Green Mountain Songster*, 1939, pp. 143-44). In it he calls attention to a tune in Petrie, *The Complete Collection of Irish Music*, 1902-05, No. 544, "The fairy troop." This is probably the first record of the tune that is still current with our ballad today. The title is explained by a phrase in a version that Child quotes in part in his headnote (1882-98, IV, p. 218):

> He smiled and this did say,
> 'They might have been some fairy troops,
> That rode along this way.'

One could easily be persuaded that all variants belong to the same tribe. All (save that from Vermont) are authentic, all except two are in the major domain, whether I/Ly, I/M, I, or M. All are long-phrase tunes, properly taking two lines of quatrain text before making a real cadence. All have a strongly marked rhythm, and more than half of them agree in a conspicuous mid-cadence on the major third.

The Greig tune and a recent one from Leitrim (variants 10 and 11) are alike in a mode different from all the rest, and the third phrase of one is like the first of the other. It is possible that they split off from the main family, but they have been assimilated to other patterns, and may stand as independent D/Æ authentic tunes.

TUNES WITH TEXTS

GROUP A

1. "Katherine Janfarie"

Christie, II, 1881, p. 16. From Buchan tradition.

m I

a I

> There was a may, and a weel far'd may,
>   Liv'd high up in yon glen;
> Her name was Katherine Janfarie,
>   She was courted by mony men.
> Up then came lord Lauderdale,
>   Up frae the Lowland border;
> And he has come to court this may,
>   A' mounted in good order.

> *[Etc.]*

Christie takes his text from Scott's *Minstrelsy*, 1833, III, p. 122.

5. "The Squire of Edinboro' town"

Fox, *JIFSS*, I (1904), p. 45. Sung by Ann Carter, Belfast, 1904, who learned it in childhood from her grandmother in County Galway. Tune recorded by Mrs. Fox, text by Mrs. Elizabeth Wheeler.

1. There was a Squire of Edinboro' Town,
     A Squire of high degree;
   He fell in love with a country girl,
     And a comely girl was she.

2. There was a farmer in the East
     That had an only son;
   He fell in love with this comely girl,
     Till he thought he had her won.

3. He got consent from father and mother,
     From old and young likewise;
   And still she cried, "I am undone,"
     And the tears fell from her eyes.

4. She wrote her love a letter,
     And sealed it with a ring,
   That she was to be married,
     And to a farmer's son.

5. He wrote her back an answer,
     To be sure to dress in green;
   A suit of the same he would put on,
     Her wedding for to see.

6. He lookèd East and he lookèd West,
     And looked all round his land;
   And mounted four-and twenty men,
     All of the Scottish clan.

7. He rode East and he rode West,
    He rode all round his lands,
Until he rode to the wedding-house door;
    Of the company he asked no leave,

8. Saying, "Happy is the man they call the groom,
    And he who enjoys the bride;
But another young man may love her as well,
    And take her from his side."

9. Then out spake the angry groom,
    And an angry man was he:
"If 'tis for fight that you come here,
    I am the man for thee!"

10. "It's not for fight that I come here,
    But friendship for to show.
Give me one kiss from your bonny bride's lips,
    And away from you I'll go."

11. He took her by the waist so small,
    And by the grass-green sleeves,
And led her outside of the wedding-house door,
    Of the company he asked no leave.

12. The drums did beat, the fifes did play—
    So glorious to be seen—
And he brought her away to Edinboro' Town,
    With the company dressed in green.

6. [Green Wedding]

Sharp MSS., 1119/1113. Sung by Robert Parish (84), Exford, September 5, 1906.

a I

1. There was a squire lived in the East
    A squire of high degree
Came courting of a country girl
    A comely girl was she
Until her father he heard of it
    And an angry man was he
He requested of his daughter dear
    To shun his company.

2. There was a farmer lived close by
    Who had an only son
Came courting of this country girl
    Until he thought he had her won
He gained consent from her father & mother
    The old & young likewise
Until at last she cried I am undone
    And the tears fell from her eyes.

3. She wrote the squire a letter
    And sealed it with her hand
Saying this very day I am to wed
    Unto another young man
The first few lines that he looked on
    He smiled & thus did say
O I may deprive him of his bride
    All on his wedding day.

4. He wrote her back another
    To be sure to be dressed in green
A suit of the same I will put on
    At yr wedding I'll be seen
A suit of the same I will put on
    To yr wedding I'll prepare
Saying my dearest dear I'll have you yet
    In spite of all that's there.

5. He looked the East he looked the West
    He looked all over his land,
He mounted them all eight score men
    All of a Scottish band
He mounted them on milk white steed
    And a single man rode he
Then all the way to the wedding hall went
    The company dressed in green.

6. When he got to the wedding hall
    They unto him did say
You are welcome Sir, you are welcome Sir
    Where have you spent the day?
He laughed at them he scorned at them
    He unto them did say
O you might have seen my tars of troop [sic]
    Come riding by this way.

7. The Squire he took a glass of wine
    And filled it to the brim.
Here is health unto the man, said he
    The man they call the groom.
Here's health unto the man said he
    The man who may enjoy his bride
For another might love her just as well
    And take her from [sic] his Bride.

8. Then up spoke he the intended one
    And an angry man was he
If it's to fight that you come here
    Why it's I'm the man for thee
No it's not to fight that I come here
    But merely friendship for to show
So give me a kiss from your bonny young Bride
    And away from thee I'll go.

9. He took her by the waist so small
   And by the grass green sleeve
   He led her from the wedding hall
   To the company asked not leave.
   The band did play and the bugles did sound
   Oh, most glorious to be seen.
   Then all the way to Headingbourn Town
   Went the company dressed in green.

"The words I copied from an M.S. copy which Parish lent me."
[*Sharp's MS. note.*]

GROUP B

10. "Katharine Jaffray"

Greig and Keith, 1925, p. 161; from Duncan MS., No. 225.
Sung by Robert Alexander, Udny.

a D/Æ

With this tune, cf. those of "The Duke of Gordon's Daughters"
(No. 237).

1. Lochnagar cam fae the West
   Into the low countrie,
   An' he had coorted Katharine Jaffray,
   An' stole her heart away.

2. Hame he cam, ane Amosdale,
   Cam fae the north countrie,
   An' he has gained her father's heart,
   But an' her mother's tee.

3. A bridal day it then was set,
   An' the bridal day cam on,
   An' who appeared among the guests
   But Lochnagar himsel?

4. A glass was filled o good red wine,
   Weel drunk between them twa:
   Said he, I'll drink wi you, bridegroom,
   An' syne boun me awa.

5. "A few words wi your bridesmaiden
   I hope you'll grant me then:
   I'm sure before her wedding day
   I would have gotten ten."

6. Out spoke then the first groomsman,
   An' an angry man was he,
   Says, "I will keep my bonnie bride
   Until the sun gae tee;

7. "Until the sun gae tee," he said,
   "Until the sun gae tee,
   An' deliver her ower to her bridegroom,
   Which is my duty to dee."

8. But he's taen her by the middle jimp,
   An' never stoppit to ca',
   He's taen her by the milk-white han'
   An' led her through the ha'.

9. He leaned him ower his saiddle-bow,
   An' kissed her cheek an' chin,
   An' then he wissed them a' good nicht,
   An' hoised her on ahin.

10. He drew a trumpet fae his breist,
    An' blew baith lood an' shrill;
    A hunner o well-airmed men
    Cam Lochnagar until.

11. A hunner o weel-airmed men,
    Wi milk-white steeds an' grey,
    A hunner o weel-airmed men
    Upon his wedding day.

12. Horsemen rode, an' bridesmen ran,
    An' ladies in full speed,
    But you wadna hae seen his yellow locks
    For the dust o his horse' [*sic*] feet.

13. She turned in the saiddle-bow,
    Addressed her late bridegroom,
    Says, "The compliments I got fae you,
    I'll return them back again."

14. So Katharine Jaffray was mairriet at morn,
    An' she was mairriet at noon;
    She was twice mairriet in ae day,
    Ere she keest aff her goon.

11. "The Green Wedding"

BBC Sound Archives, rec. Nos. 22016 and 18759. Sung by
Thomas Moran, Mohill, County Leitrim, December 1954.
Collected by Seamus Ennis.

a D/Æ

1. There was a Squire in Edinburgh town
   And a wealthy Squire was he
   And he hadn courted a country girl
   And a comely lass was she.

2. He got consent from father and mother
   From old and young likewise
   But still she cried I am undone
   While the tears roll from my [*sic*] eyes.

3. She wrote her love a letter and
   She sealed it with her hand
   That she was going to be wed
   Unto another man.

4. The very first line that he looked over
   He smiled and this did say:
   Well, I might deprive him of his bride
   All on his wedding day.

5. He wrote her back a letter to
   Be sure and dress in green
   And a suit of the same I will put on
   For your wedding I'll prepare.

6. He looked East and he looked West
   He looked all over his land
   And he had a-mounted eight score men
   All of ?his Scottish land.

7. He mounted two on every steed
   And a single man rode he
   So now they are gone to Edinburgh town
   With the company dressed in green.

8. You're welcome, you are welcome, Lord,
   Where have you been all day,
   Or did you see those fairy troops
   That rode along this way?

9. They filled him a glass of the new port wine
   He drank to the company round.

O happy is the man, he says,
   The man they call the groom.

10. Happier is the man, he said,
    That will enjoy the bride,
    For another might like her as well as him
    And take her from his side.

11. Oh and out he spoke the young bridegroom,
    And an angry man was he.
    If it was to fight that you come here,
    I am a man for thee.

12. It was not to fight that I come here,
    For friendship I mean to show.
    Give me one kiss from your bonny bonny bride,
    And away from you I'll go.

13. He took her by the middle so small
    And by the green grass sleeve
    And he marched her out of the wedding-house-door
    Of the company he asked no leave.

14. They laughed at him, they scoffed at him,
    They smiled and this did say,
    Well it must have been some fairy troop
    That stole your bride [spoken] away.

Bonny Baby Livingston

CHILD NO. 222

CHILD's A-text of this ballad is from Mrs. Brown, and she gave it in two variant forms. It is another example of the re-creative practice of a singer immersed in oral tradition. (Cf. "Mrs. Brown and the Ballad," *California Folklore Quarterly*, IV [1945], p. 129.) Child remarks: ". . . the fact seems to be that, at the time when she recited to Jamieson [i.e., her version 222 Ab, printed in Jamieson, *Popular Ballads and Songs*, 1806, II, p. 135], she was not in good condition to remember accurately" (1882-98, IV, p. 231). But it is not a matter of accurate memory when there is no ultimate text to which to be faithful.

It is a noteworthy fact that all Child's other texts (B-E and the unnumbered text of C. K. Sharpe in App'x., V, p. 261) contain something like the following stanzas from Buchan's MS. (Child B 13, 14):

> 'O day, dear sir! O day, dear sir!
>   O dear! if it were day,
> And me upon my father's steed,
>   I soon shoud ride away.'

> 'Your father's steed is in my stable,
>   Eating good corn and hay,
> And ye are in my arms twa;
>   What needs you lang for day?'

So also does Greig's text (Greig MSS., Bk. 762, LII, p. 89; *Last Leaves of Traditional Ballads and Ballad Airs*, 1925, p. 162). Now, it has not been remarked that Mrs. Brown's unique text of "The Bonny Birdy" (Child No. 82) contains the equivalent of these stanzas, where in part they are used as a burden. "The Bonny Birdy" is a sort of moralized and refined "Little Musgrave" (No. 81), for which we lack any corroborative tradition. Since Mrs. Brown's version of No. 222 departs from otherwise universal traditional testimony on the point just quoted, we may presume that what she added to No. 82 she subtracted from No. 222. Her copy of the latter also departs from all other copies in its happy, romantic conclusion, which we may tentatively credit to the singer's temperamental bias.

The only tune which undoubtedly belongs to this ballad appears to be that preserved by C. K. Sharpe. It is sufficiently characteristic. If the final be read as tonic, we should consider it π^3 authentic. But without supporting analogues, we may suppose the tune to end on the second, in which case it will pass for an authentic π^1 with equal satisfaction.

There may be other tunes for this ballad not yet located: one is said to be in the elusive Bunyan MS. It is curious that in Motherwell's note book at Harvard, in a list of tunes to be got, the name occurs of "Barbra Livingston," with a cross before it, perhaps indicating "mission accomplished." But Motherwell's tune has vanished.

Another tune has been, perhaps rashly, attributed to this ballad, under the title, "There cam' a Laddie frae the North." The text of the ballad so named corresponds ill with Child's No. 222. In it, there is no abduction. On the contrary, the Hieland laddie deserts the lass from Dundee, leaving her to bear her shame at home as she may. After reaching the highlands, he begins to think long, and, encouraged by his mother, returns to Dundee to marry the lass and fetch her home to Strathspey. A version of this may be seen in John Orr's *Bothy Songs and Ballads*, 1930, p. 103, but without a tune. A traditional tune, with a very fragmentary text, has been recovered lately in the North, and will be found in the *Addenda*, p. 502, of the present work, Vol. IV of the full edition. But it has as much resemblance to "Comin' thro' the Rye" as it does to Sharpe's tune here printed.

TUNE WITH TEXT

[Bonny Baby Livingston]

Child, 1882-98, V, p. 421; text, p. 261. From C. K. Sharpe's "first MS. collection, p. 24" (=William Macmath transcript, p. 32, Harvard College Library).

a π^3

1. Bonny Anny Livieston
        Went out to see the play,
    By came the laird of Glenlion,
        And [he's] taen hir quite away.

2. He set hir on a milk-white steed,
        Himself upon a gray,
    He's teen hir oer the Highland hills,
        And taen hir quite away.

3. When they came to Glenlion's gate,
        The[y] lighted on the green;
    There was mony a bonny lad and lass
        To wolcome the lady hame.

4. They led hir through high towers and bowers,
        And through the buling-green,
    And ay when they spake Erse to hir
        The tears blinded hir een.

5. Says, The Highlands is no for me, kind sir,
        The Highlands is no for me;
    If that ye would my favour win,
        Take me unto Dundee.

6. "Dundee!" he says, "Dundee, lady!
        Dundee you shall never see;
    Upon the laird of Glenlion
        Soon wadded shall ye be."

7. When bells were rung, and mas was sung,
        And all were bound for bed,
    And bonny Annie Livieston
        By hir bridegroom was laid.

8. "It's O gin it were day!" she says,
    "It's O gin it were day!
    O if that it were day," she says,
    "Nae langer wad I stay."

9. "Your horse stands in a good stable,
    Eating both corn and hay,
    And you are in Glenlion's arms,
    Why should ye weary for day?"

10. "Glenlion's arms are good enough,
    But alais! the'r no for me;
    If that you would my fevour win,
    Taike me unto Dundee.

11. "Bat fetch me paper, pen and ink,
    And candle that I may see,
    And I'll go write a long letter
    To Geordie in Dundee.

12. "Where will I get a bonny boy,
    That will win hose and shoon,
    That will gang to my ain true-luve,
    And tell him what is done?"

13. Then up then spake a bonny boy,
    Near to Glenlion's kin,
    Says, Many time I hae gane his erand,
    But the lady's I will rin.

14. O when he came to broken brigs
    He bent his bow and swame,
    And when he came to grass growing
    Set down his feet and ran.

15. And when he came to Dundee gate
    Lap clean outoer the wa;
    Before the porter was thereat,
    The boy was in the haa.

16. "What news? what news, bonny boy?
    What news hes thou to me?"
    "No news, no news," said bonny boy,
    "But a letter unto thee."

17. The first three lines he looked on,
    A loud laughter gied he,
    But or he wan to the hinder en
    The tears blinded his eie.

18. "Gae saddle to me the black," he says,
    "Gae saddle to me the broun,
    Gae saddle to me the swiftest steed
    That eer took man to towen."

19. He burst the black unto the slack,
    The browen unto the brae,
    But fair fa on the siller-gray
    That carried him ay away!

20. When he came to Glenlion's yett,
    He tirled at the pin,
    But before that he wan up the stair
    The lady she was gone.

21. "O I can kiss thy cheeks, Annie,
    O I can kiss thy chin,
    O I can kiss thy clay-cold lips,
    Though there be no breath within.

22. "Deal large at my love's buriell
    The short bread and the wine,
    And gin the morn at ten o clock
    Ye may deal as mukle at mine."

23. The taen was biried in Mary's kirk,
    The tither in St. Mary's quire,
    And out of the taen there grew a birk,
    And the ither a bonny brier.

24. And ay they grew, and ay they threw,
    Till they did meet aboon,
    And a' that ere the same did see
    Knew they had true lovers been.

Eppie Morrie

CHILD NO. 223

EWAN MACCOLL alone has recorded a tune for this very spirited, if brutal, ballad of bride-stealing. He learned his tune from his father; the text has come mainly from Maidment by way of Child, with some help from Samuel Wylie of Falkirk. The tune is certainly embedded in the folk idiom, as witness the triadic alternation of the first two phrases between tonic minor and subtonic major. Compare the first strain of "The Piper of Dundee." Partial analogues are not uncommon: compare again the Macmath version of "Trooper and Maid" (Child No. 299). In MacColl's vigorous rendition, the melody does splendid service here.

TUNE WITH TEXT

"Eppie Morrie"

Sung by Ewan MacColl, Riverside rec. No. RLP 12-621(A1), ed. K. S. Goldstein. Tune learned from his father; text conflated.

p D/Æ

1. Four and twenty hielan' men
   Cam' frae the Carron side,
   To steal awa' Eppie Morrie,
   For she wadna' be a bride, a bride,
   She wadna' be a bride.

   [Repeat last line throughout.]

2. Then oot it's came her mither, then,
   It was a moonlicht nicht;
   She couldna see her dochter
   For the waters shone sae bricht, sae bricht.

3. "Haud awa' frae me, mither,
   Haud awa' frae me!
   There's no' a man in a' Strathdon
   Shall wedded be wi' me, wi' me."

4. They've taken Eppie Morrie, then,
   And a horse they've bound her on;
   And they ha' rid to the minister's hoose
   As fast as horse could gang, could gang.

5. Then Willie's ta'en his pistol out
   And set it to the minister's breist;
   "O, marry me, marry me, minister,
   Or else I'll be your preist, your preist."

6. "Haud awa' frae me, Willie!
   Haud awa' frae me!
   I daurna avow to marry you,
   Except she's willing as thee, as thee."

7. "Haud awa' frae me, good sir,
   Haud awa' frae me!
   There's no' a man in a' Strathdon
   Shall married be by me, by me."

8. They've taken Eppie Morrie, then,
   Sin better couldna be,
   And they hae rid ower Carron side
   As fast as horse could flee, could flee.

9. Then mass was sung and bells were rung
   And they're awa' to bed,
   And Willie and Eppie Morrie
   In ane bed they were laid.

10. He's ta'en the sark frae off his back
    And kicked awa' his shoon,
    And thrawn awa' the chaumer key,
    And naked he lay doon, lay doon.

11. "Haud awa' frae me, Willie,
    Haud awa' frae me!
    Before I lose my maidenhead
    I'll try my strength with thee, with thee."

12. He's kissed her on the lilly breist
    And held her shouthers twa,
    And aye she grat and aye she spat
    And turned to the wa', the wa'.

13. "Haud awa' frae me, Willy,
    Haud awa' frae me!
    There's no' a man in a' Strathdon
    Shall married be wi' me, wi' me."

14. A' through the nicht they warssled there
    Until the licht o' day,
    And Willie grat and Willie swat
    But he couldna streitch her spey, her spey.

15. Then early in the morning
    Before the licht o' day,
    In came the maid o' Scallater,
    Wi' a gown and shirt alane, alane.

16. "Get up, get up, young woman!
   And drink the wine wi' me."
   "You micht hae ca'd me maiden
   For I'm sure as hale as thee, as thee."

17. "Weary fa' you, Willie, then,
   That ye couldna prove a man;
   You micht hae ta'en her maidenhead,
   She would hae hired your hand, your hand."

18. "Haud awa' frae me, lady,
   Haud awa' frae me!
   There's no a man in a' Strathdon
   Shall wedded be wi' me."

19. Then in there came young Breadalbane
   With a pistol on each side.
   "O, come awa', Eppie Morrie
   And I'll mak' you my bride, my bride."

20. "Go, get to me a horse, Willie,
   Get it like a man,
   And send me back to my mither
   A maiden as I cam', I cam'."

21. The sun shines o'er the westlin hills
   By the lamplicht o' the moon;
   "O, saddle your horse, young John Forsythe
   And whistle and I'll come soon, come soon."

Lizie Lindsay

CHILD NO. 226

THE most characteristic and familiar setting of this still favorite song is the one contributed by Robert Burns to the *Scots Musical Museum* (variant 1). It is a major tune in triple time, the second phrase of which—elsewhere the first also—takes off on a plagal up-beat. There is something of "Ewe-Buchts, Marion" in this tune: that is, it has well-established traditional connections. Some copies lack the fourth, some the fourth and seventh, but the variations are not wide.

In the other branch of the melodic tradition for this song, represented by Christie and Greig, the mode is D/Æ and Æolian. Greig's tune is closer to the major tradition, but neither his nor Christie's is a mere transposition into the relative minor. Here, too, the presumable laws of traditional modal change have operated, though we lack evidence of intermediary stages.

TUNES WITH TEXTS

GROUP Aa

1. "Leezie Lindsay"

Johnson, V [1796], No. 434, p. 446 (repr. 1853). Also in Smith [1820-24], II, p. 100; and Eyre-Todd [1894], p. 148. From Robert Burns.

m I

The variant readings a and b are from R. A. Smith's copy.

Will ye go to the Highlands Leezie Lindsay,
  Will ye go to the Highlands wi' me
Will ye go to the Highlands Leezie Lindsay
  My pride and my darling to be.

3. "Lizzie Lindsay"

Child, 1882-98, V, p. 421; text, IV, p. 524. Sent by W. Walker; from the singing of George Nutchell (*sic*), Edzell Castle, Forfarshire, October 5, 1891. He learned it 58 years before from his step-grandmother, who was then 80.

m I/Ly

1. "Will ye gang to the Highlands, Lizzie Lindsay?
     Will ye gang to the Highlands wi me?
   Will ye gang to the Highlands, Lizzie Lindsay,
     My bride an my darling to be?"

2. She turned her round on her heel,
     And a very loud laugh gaed she:
   "I'd like to ken whaur I'm ganging,
     An wha I am gaun to gang wi."

3. "My name is Donald Macdonald,
     I'll never think shame nor deny;
   My father he is an old shepherd,
     My mither she is an old dey.

4. "Will ye gang to the Highlands, bonnie Lizzie?
     Will ye gang to the Highlands wi me?
   For ye shall get a bed o green rashes,
     A pillow an a covering o grey."

5. Upraise then the bonny young lady,
     An drew till her stockings an sheen,
   An packd up her claise in fine bundles,
     An away wi young Donald she's gaen.

6. When they cam near the end o their journey,
     To the house o his father's milk-dey,
   He said, Stay still there, Lizzie Lindsay,
     Till I tell my mither o thee.

7. "Now mak us a supper, dear mither,
     The best o yer curds an green whey,
   An mak up a bed o green rashes,
     A pillow an covering o grey.

8. "Rise up, rise up, Lizzie Lindsay,
     Ye have lain oer lang i the day;
   Ye should hae been helping my mither
     To milk her ewes an her kye."

9. Out then spak the bonnie young lady,
     As the saut tears drapt frae her ee,
   "I wish I had bidden at hame;
     I can neither milk ewes or kye."

10. "Rise up, rise up, Lizzie Lindsay,
　　There is mair ferlies to spy;
　For yonder's the castle o Kingussie,
　　An it stands high an dry."

11. "Ye are welcome here, Lizzie Lindsay,
　　The flower o all your kin,
　For ye shall be lady o Kingussie,
　　An ye shall get Donald my son."

a D/Æ

Up spoke Lady Dysie's old mother,
　　An' a rude spoken woman was she:
"I would like to know where she is gaun,
　　Or wha she is gaun to gang wi."

"My father he's laird o Kinkussie,
　　My mother she's lady the same,
My name it is Donald Macdonald,
　　To tell it I never think shame."

Then oot spak young Lady Dysie,
　　An' a weel spoken lady was she:
"Ye'll pack my clothes in small bundles,
　　An' awa wi young Donald I'll gae."

GROUP Ab

7. "Donald Macdonald"

Greig and Keith, 1925, p. 164; from Duncan MS., No. 258.
Sung by George Innes, Portnockie; learned in Banffshire,
mid-nineteenth century.

Bonny Lizie Baillie

CHILD NO. 227

THIS ballad appears not to have held its ground so well in tradition as others intrinsically no better. So far as I know, no new copies have appeared since Buchan's day, and Christie did not include it in his collection.

For our copy of an air, we are indebted to Burns and the *Museum* (No. 456). But according to Glen, *Early Scottish Melodies*, 1900, p. 201, the tune and six stanzas had earlier appeared in William Napier's *Selection of Scots Songs*, 1792, Vol. II. Technically, if the final be tonic, the mode is Dorian; but the tune has more Æolian feeling, and a more comfortable tonic would be the fourth below the final. R. A. Smith (IV, p. 90) gives the same tune, with a slight change in timing at the mid-cadence.

TUNE WITH TEXT

"Lizae Baillie"

Johnson, V [1792], No. 456, p. 469 (repr. 1853). Also in Smith [1820-24], IV, p. 90. From Robert Burns.

p D; or, if tonic D, a Æ

1. [Lizae Baillie's to Gartartan gane,
   To see her sister Jean;
   And there she's met wi' Duncan Graeme,
   And he's convoy'd her hame.]

2. My bonny Lizae Baillie,
   I'll row ye in my plaidie
   And ye maun gang alang wi' me
   And be a Highland Lady.

3. "I am sure they wad nae ca' me wise,
   Gin I wad gang wi' you, Sir;
   For I can neither card nor spin,
   Nor yet milk ewe or cow, Sir."

4. "My bonny Lizae Baillie,
   Let nane o' these things daunt ye.
   Ye'll hae nae need to card or spin,
   Your mither weel can want ye."

5. Now she's cast aff her bonny shoen,
   Made o' the gilded leather,
   And she's put on her highland brogues,
   To skip amang the heather:

6. And she's cast aff her bonny gown,
   Made o' the silk and sattin,
   And she's put on a tartan plaid,
   To row amang the braken:

7. She wad nae hae a Lawland laird,
   Nor be an English lady;
   But she wad gang wi' Duncan Graeme
   And row her in his plaidie.

8. She was nae ten miles frae the town,
   When she began to weary;
   She aften looked back, and said,
   "Farewell to Castlecarry.

9. "The first place I saw my Duncan Graeme
   Was near yon holland bush.
   My father took frae me my rings,
   My rings but and my purse.

10. "But I wad nae gie my Duncan Graeme
    For a' my father's land,
    Though it were ten times ten times mair
    And a' at my command."

11. Now wae be to you, logger-heads,
    That dwell near Castlecarry,
    To let awa sic a bonny lass,
    A Highlandman to marry.

The *Museum* text is that of Herd, *Ancient and Modern Scottish Songs*, 1776, II, p. 3, except for lacking the first stanza, which is here supplied therefrom.

Glasgow Peggie

CHILD NO. 228

THE center of the melodic tradition for this ballad appears to be an authentic Dorian tune. Christie establishes this tradition with his tune from Banffshire. In succeeding examples collected by Greig there is a slighter emphasis on III and VI, and III is entirely absent from several copies. Greig's Crighton (c) tune (variant 12), although technically M/D, has much more of a major feeling. It has extended its range another degree upward, and its strong emphasis on a major triad anchored on the fourth degree would cause it to be classified as an I/M plagal tune, if there were no other variants by which to test it. Miss Macmath's tune (variant 13) has quite succumbed to the major, keeping the added degree upward, and anchoring on the degree just below the old tonic, so as to be authentic I/M.

TUNES WITH TEXTS

GROUP Aa

3. "The Highland Lads"

Greig MSS., I, p. 33; text, Bk. 726, XVI, p. 26. Sung by J. W. Spence, Rosecroft, Fyvie, July 1905.

a M/D

1. Highland lads are brisk and braw
     Highland lads are young and airy
   But I'll awa to Glesga toon
     And steal awa yon bonnie lassie.

2. When her father got word o' this
     Oh but he was wondrous angry
   Says "Ye may steal awa my ousen & my kye
     But ye winna steal awa my lovely Peggy."

3. Keep weel aul' man your ousen & your kye
     For I've got cows and ewes already
   I winna steal awa your ousen & your kye
     But I'll steal awa your lovely Peggy.

4. He's mounted her on his milk-white steed
     Jumped up himself on his little gray nagie
   And they rode thirty miles afore it was lang
     So he's ta'en awa his lovely Peggy.

5. They rode o'er hills & they rode o'er dales
     They rode through moors & mosses many
   Until that they met the Earl o' Argyle
     He was ridin' oot wi' his young son bonnie.

6. It's oot & spak the Earl o' Argyle
     And oh but he was wondrous angry
   To see the bonniest lass in a' the countryside
     Gaun ridin awa wi' a Hielan laddie.

7. They rode o'er hills, they rode through dales
     They rode through moors & mosses money
   Until that they came to yon low glen
     There he's lighted down wi' his lovely Peggy.

8. Their bed was o' the good green grass
     Their blankets & sheets o' the ferns bonnie
   He's rolled up his plaid, laid it below her head
     And she's lain her doon wi' her Hielan' laddie.

9. There is blankets & sheets in my father's hoose
     And they're a' washed & dried already
   And oh, wadna he right angry be at me
     For lyin' doon wi' a Hielan' laddie.

10. There is 500 acres of good land
      And it's a' ploughed & sown already
    And oh wadna he richt angry be at me
      For lyin' doon wi' a Hielan' laddie.

11. He's ta'en her up to yon high hill
      When that the sun was yet shining clearly
    Says "A' that is yours as far as ye can see
      For lyin' doon wi' a Hielan laddie."

12. A' that I promised you at the first
      Was a wee-cot hoose & a little kail yardie
    But noo ye are the lady o' all the Isle of Skye
      For lyin' doon wi' the Hielan laddie.["]

12. "A Highland Laddie"

Greig MSS., III, p. 138. Also in Greig and Keith, 1925, p. 166(c). Sung by Miss Lizzie Crighton, Bonnykelly.

a D/M; or, if on G, p I/M

As the troops gied up thro' Glasgow toon,
The Highland clan they were a' lively,
The bonniest lass that e'er I saw
Was a Glasgow girl & her name was Peggy.

GROUP Ab

13. "Glasgow Peggy"

Macmath MS., p. 115; text, p. 93. Also in Child, 1882-98,
V, p. 422; text, p. 266(G). Sung by Miss Jane Webster,
Kirkcudbrightshire, 1892; learned more than 50 years
before.

a I/M

1. It was on a day, and a fine summer's day,
    When the Lowlands they were making ready,
   There I espied a weelfar'd lass,
    She was gaun to Glasgow, and they ca' her Peggy.

2. It's up then spak a silly auld man,
    And O but he spak wondrous poorly!
   Sayin, Ye may steal awa my cows and my ewes,
    But ye'll never steal awa my bonny Peggy.

3. "O haud yer tongue, ye silly auld man,
    For ye hae said eneugh already,
   For I'll never steal awa yer cows and yer ewes,
    But I'll steal awa yer bonny Peggy."

4. So he mounted her on a milk-white steed,
    Himsel upon a wee grey naigie,
   And they hae ridden ower hill and dale,
    And over moors and mosses many.

5. They rade till they cam to the head o yon glen,
    It might hae frightened anybody;
   He said, Whether will ye go alongst with me,
    Or will ye return back again to your mammie?

. . . .

6. Their bed was o the green, green grass,
    And their blankets o the bracken sae bonnie,
   And he's laid his trews beneath their head,
    And Peggy's laid doun wi her Heilan laddie.

7. They lay till it cam to the break o day,
    Then up they rose and made them ready;
   He said, Whether will ye go alongst with me,
    Or will ye return back again to your mammie?

8. "I'll follow you through frost and snow,
    I'll follow you through dangers many,
   And wherever ye go I will go alongst with you,
    For I'll never return back again to my mammie."

9. "I hae four-and-twenty gude milk-kye,
    They're a' bun in yon byre sae bonny,
   And I am the earl o the Isle o Skye,
    And why should not Peggy be called a lady?

10. "I hae fifty acres o gude land,
    A' ploughed ower and sawn sae bonny,
   And I am young Donald o the Isle o Skye,
    And wherever I'm laird I'll make ye lady."

Stanzas 2 through 10 are from Child.

Earl Crawford

CHILD NO. 229

GREIG did not find this ballad, and it has left but a meager record. To the unique tune preserved by Christie, one may be added from the Blaikie MS., of unknown provenience. These are certainly related, though not very obviously. The Blaikie tune, although it lacks its fourth, is distinctly Mixolydian; the other lacks the Mixolydian note and is I/M. Blaikie's tune lacks the repetition of the second half which appears to be indicated in Buchan's text, as also in Christie's.

Christie's note on this ballad contains an interesting generalization, which will go far to justify his editorial practice. He says he "has known instances where one person, who had the Air from another, sung it in a different and more melodious style from having a finer musical taste. It is, therefore, almost impossible to find out the true set of any traditional air, unless the set can be traced genuinely to its composer" (*Traditional Ballad Airs*, I, p. 68). And if it can be so traced, how traditional is it?

TUNES WITH TEXTS

1. "Earl of Crawford"

Blaikie MS., NL Scotland MS. 1578, No. 126, p. 39.

a M (–IV)

2. "Earl Crawford"

Christie, I, 1876, p. 68; text, Child, 1882-98, IV, pp. 277 (Aa), 280(Ab). From Mrs. Mary Thomson, the nurse of Christie's children, 1867; learned from her mother.

a I/M

1. O we were sisters, sisters seven,
    We were a comely crew to see,
 And some got lairds, and some got lords,
    And some got knichts o hie degree;
 And I mysel got the Earl o Crawford,
    And wasna that a great match for me!

2. It was at fifteen that I was married,
    And at sixteen I had a son;
 And wasna that an age ower tender
    For a lady to hae her first-born!
 And wasna, etc.

3. But it fell ance upon a day
    I gaed into the garden green,
 And naebody was therein walking
    But Earl Crawford and his young son.

4. 'I wonder at you, ye Earl Crawford,
    I wonder at you wi your young son;
 Ye daut your young son mair than your Lillie;
    [I'm sure you got na him your lane.']

5. [He turned about upon his heel,
    I wite an angry man was he;
 Says, If I got nae my young son my lane,
    Bring me here the one that helpet me.]

6. ['O hold your tongue, my Earl Crawford,
    And a' my folly lat it be;
 There was nane at the gettin o oor son,
    Nae body only but you and me.']

7. He set her on a milk-white steed,
    Her little young son her before;
 Says, Ye maun gae to bonny Stobha,
    For ye will enter my yates no more.

8. When she cam to her father's bowers,
    She lichtit low down on the stane,
 And wha sae ready as her auld father
    To welcome Lady Lillie in?

9. 'O how's a' wi you, my daughter Lillie,
    That ye come here sae hastilie?
 And how's a' wi' the Earl o Crawford,
    That he didna send a boy wi thee?'

10. 'O haud your tongue now, my old father,
    And ye'll lat a' your folly be;
 For ae word that my merry mou spak
    Has parted my good lord and me.'

11. 'O haud your tongue, my daughter Lillie,
    And a' your follies lat them be;
 I'll double your portion ten times ower,
    And a better match I'll get for thee.'

12. 'O haud your tongue now, my old father,
     And a' your folly lat it be;
    I wouldna gie ae kiss o Crawford
     For a' the goud that ye can gie.

13. 'Whare will I get a bonny boy,
     That's willin to win meat and fee,
    What will gae on to Earl Crawford
     And see an 's heart be fawn to me?'

14. 'O here am I, a bonny boy,
     That's willin to win meat and fee,
    That will go on to Earl Crawford's,
     And see an 's hairt be faen to thee.'

15. When he cam to the yates o Crawford,
     They were a' sitting down to dine:
    'How comes it now, ye Earl Crawford,
     Ye arena takin Lady Lillie hame?'

16. 'Ye may gae tell her Lady Lillie,
     And ye maun neither lee nor len,
    She may stay in her father's bowers,
     For she'll not enter my yates again.'

17. When he cam back to her father's yates,
     He lichtit low down on his knee:
    'What news, what news, my bonny boy?
     What news, what news hae ye to me?'

18. 'I'm bidden tell you, Lady Lillie—
     I'm bidden neither to lee nor len—
    She may stay in her father's bowers,
     For she'll not enter my yates again.'

19. She stretched out her lily hand,
     Says, 'Adieu, adieu to ane and a!
    Adieu, adieu to Earl Crawford!'
     Wi that her sair heart brak in twa.

20. Then dowie, dowie her father raise up,
     And dowie, dowie the black put on,
    And dowie, dowie he mounted the brown,
     And dowie, dowie sat thereon.

21. And dowie rade to the yates o Crawford,
     And when to Crawford's yates he came,
    They were a' dressd in the robes o scarlet,
     Just gaun to tak Lady Lillie hame.

22. 'Ye may cast aff your robes o scarlet—
     I wyte they set you wondrous weel—
    And now put on the black sae dowie,
     And come and bury your Lady Lill.'

23. He took his hat into his hand,
     And laid it low down by his knee:
    'An it be true that Lillie's dead,
     The sun shall nae mair shine on me.'

Child's Aa text consists of the text printed by Christie (I, p. 290) from the recitation c. 1867 of Mrs. Mary Robertson, mother of Mrs. Thomson, with bracketed additions (st. 4⁴, 5, 6) from a version contributed by Mrs. Thomson in 1890 (Ab). (The text possessed by Christie apparently also included these lines, but he did not print them.) Stanza 14, interpolated here from a note in Child (IV, p. 280), is likewise from Ab.

The Earl of Errol

CHILD NO. 231

THE melodic tradition for this ballad falls easily into three groups—if we admit the Blaikie tunes to the canon on the strength of the title "Kate Carnagie." The first group has the strongest claim to be considered the proper tune, although it is found elsewhere as well, as Keith has noted ("Laird o' Drum," No. 236; "Lang Johnnie More," No. 251; and "Maybe I'll be married yet"). Here there is always a second strain or burden. Both Christie's tunes are intrinsically (*bar* editing) π^1 plagal.

The Blaikie tunes are very much alike. Here there is question of the true tonic. To me, the feeling is major, with no inclination toward the Mixolydian; and I suppose the tonic to be properly a fifth below the final, therefore authentic and I/Ly. There is no burden or second strain.

It is regrettable that there is no good text mated to a tune for this ballad. See the versions in Child.

TUNES WITH TEXTS

GROUP A

1. "What needs I my apron wash?" or "The Countess of Errol"

Christie, I, 1876, p. 206.

p π^1

Christie took the tune from his father's *Collection of Strathspeys*, c. 1820, there given as "The Countess of Errol." Since the words of this ballad were deemed "unsuited" to his own work, Christie substituted a sentimental text for the true words.

a I/M

Errol it's a bonnie place,
　It stands upon a green, O;
The roses they grow red an' white,
　An' the apples red an' green, O.

Errol O, Errol O,
Errol o the green,
The lady's lost the richts o it,
An' noo she lies her leen, O.

GROUP C

6. "Kate Carnagie"

Blaikie MS., NL Scotland MS. 1578, No. 48, p. 17.

a I/Ly, ending on V

GROUP B

4. "The Earl of Errol"

Greig and Keith, 1925, p. 170(1); from Duncan MS., No. 3. Sung by Mrs. Gillespie, 1905; from 50 years' recollection.

Richie Story

CHILD NO. 232

ALL the tunes recorded for this ballad are related. They are mainly authentic major, but may lack either the seventh or the fourth, and may extend their range downward to the plagal limit. To the same family belongs "Galla Water" (*Scots Musical Museum*, No. 125), for which we should expect earlier records, there being apparently none prior to that in Oswald's *Caledonian Pocket Companion*, VIII [1756],* p. 28, according to Glen, *Early Scottish Melodies*, 1900, p. 102. To the same melodic tradition seem likewise to belong "Ay wakin O" (cf. Johnson's *Museum*, Nos. 382, 213, etc.) and a tune, undeniably close to ours, in D'Urfey, *Pills*, 1719-20, V, p. 42, to which J. Muir Wood

called attention (see Child, 1882-98, IV, p. 299). The latter therefore would be the tribal progenitor. Keith has observed an Irish relative in Joyce, *Ancient Irish Music*, 1873, No. 11, p. 12 (repr. 1912).

Dick's references for "Galla Water" are given in *The Songs of Robert Burns*, 1903, pp. 397-98. He remarks: "In many modern copies it is corrupted by closing on the key-note, with the introduction of the leading note." If these are the signs of corruption, most copies of the *ballad*-tune display them.

* Date according to Dick, ed., *The Songs of Robert Burns*, 1903, p. xli.

TUNES WITH TEXTS

3. "Richie's Lady"

Christie, I, 1876, p. 72. In Buchan tradition "from time immemorial."

a I

1. There were ladies in yon ha',
   Seven ladies in Cumbernaudie;
   The youngest and fairest o' them a'
   Has faun in love wi' her footman laddie.
   He gaed down the garden green,
   In amang the birks sae bonnie;
   And there he saw his lady gay,
   Wi' ribbons on her shoulders mony.

2. "Here's a letter to thee, Madam;
   Here's a letter to thee, Lady;
   With Earl Hume's humble desire,
   Your servant for to be, Lady."
   "I'll ha'e nane o' his letters, Richie;
   Nane from Earl Hume, Richie;
   But I'll ha'e him that I like best,
   And I'll ha'e nane but you, Richie."

3. "Say na' that to me, Lady,
   Say na' that to me, Lady;
   For I ha'e neither lands nor rents,
   For to maintain you wi', Lady."

"Say na' that again, Richie,
   Say na' that again, Richie;
The House o' Athole it is mine,
   Taranadie shall be thine, Richie."

4. He gaed from the garden green,
   Thinking he would shun his lady;
But quickly she follow'd after him,—
   Says, "Ye maun leave your comrades, Richie.
To the Borders we maun gae,
   I'll gae to them wi' thee, Richie;
For gin my father hear o' our love,
   High hangèd ye will be, Richie."

5. "To the Borders we will gae,
   We will to them gang, Lady;
But tho' your father hear o' our love,
   It's me he daurna' hang, Lady."
As they rode by her sister's bowers,
   Her sisters they were wondrous sorry;
They bade her cast off her robes o' silk,
   And gang and beg wi' her Richard Storie.

6. As they rode thro' yon burrow town,
   Her gold watch, it shone sae bonny,
And mony a ane saluted her;
   But nane thought that she was to be his Lady.
As they were riding up yon high hill,
   The Lady, she grew wondrous weary;
She lookèd over her left shoulder,
   Says, "I wish I were at the Cumbernaudie!"

7. "Oh, are ye not sorry, Lady?
   Oh, are ye not sorry, Lady?
To leave your home and kindred dear,
   And follow Richard Storie, Lady!"
"What needs I be sorry, Richie?
   What needs I be sorry, Richie?
When I get him that I like best,
   And what is laid before me, Richie."

8. As they rode by yon bonny House,
   They heard music sounding bonny;

[410]

And four-and-twenty gallant knichts,
  Came out to welcome Richie's Lady.
A coach and four was soon prepar'd,
  A coach and four was soon made ready;
And now she rides in her coach and four,
  And blesses the day that made her his Lady.

APPENDIX

7. "The Scotch Wedding"

D'Urfey, 1719-20, V, p. 42.

a I

Andrew Lammie

CHILD NO. 233

ACCORDING to Jamieson, *Popular Ballads and Songs*, 1806, I, p. 128, the music to which this ballad usually went "is of that class which, in Teviotdale, they term a *Northern Drawl*; and a Perthshire *set* of it, but two notes lower than is commonly sung, is to be found in Johnson's *Scots Musical Museum* [i.e., No. 175], to the song 'How lang and drearie is the night, &c.'"

If Jamieson is correct, the recent tradition, which, thanks to Greig, is fairly full for this ballad, is not of great age. The tune to which he refers does conform to the rhythmical scheme of traditional variants, and agrees (necessarily, of course, because of the verbal pattern) in the feminine cadence at 2 and 4. But, melodically, it is too far removed from the rest to trace a connection. Presumably, he did not mean pitch by "two notes lower," for folk-singing has little to do with pitch. He could hardly have meant that there was a Teviotdale tune in the same key literally two degrees higher; but he may have meant that such a tune would approximate what he had in mind. If he meant to imply a shift from major to minor, the tune would be impossible to reconstruct with any assurance.

The tradition as it has been recovered is sufficiently consistent, but diverse in its over-all unity, so that it makes a fine study in variation, ranging all the way from π^4 to π^1 in modal change, and keeping rhythmically steady.

The variants fall without too much forcing into three groups, of which the middle one is perhaps most characteristic. The first is typically D/Æ, plagal, with mid-cadence moving up from minor III to IV, and feminine; first-phrase cadence on the lower flat seventh. The second group swings from Dorian to π^2, plagal. Both Motherwell's and Christie's variants are M/D, and agree so closely that one wonders if Christie (or his father, who published it earlier) did not follow Motherwell, only adding a Dorian third in his second strain. The third group is major and π^1, again plagal. Perhaps the most typical medial and final cadence throughout is that of a fall from a fourth above; but some copies rise one degree, instead. The opening phrases are quite unstable.

As Keith has pointed out, the tune family occurs elsewhere: with "Barbara Allan" (No. 84) and, especially, with "Yarrow" (cf. No. 214).

TUNES WITH TEXTS

GROUP Aa

7. "Tifty's Annie"

Andersson, *Budkavlen*, XXXIII (1954), p. 42. Sung by Mrs. Ethel Findlater, Dounby, Orkney, in the summer of 1938.

p D/Æ

At mill o Tifties lived a man
   In the neighbourhood of Fyvie.
He had a lovely daughter fair
   Who was called Bonnie Annie.

Her bloom was like the springing flower
   That salutes the rosy morning,
With innocence and graceful smile
   Her beauteous form adorning.

GROUP Ab

10. "Mill o' Tiftie's Annie"

Motherwell, 1827, App'x., No. 28; text, App'x., p. xxii. Also in Maver, 1866, No. 398, p. 199; and Christie, I, 1876, p. 48. Tune from A. Blaikie, Paisley.

p D/M

Variant a is the only significant difference between Christie's tune and Motherwell's. In this phrase Christie concurs with Maver.

At Mill o' Tiftie liv'd a man,
   In the neighbourhood o' Fyvie;
He had a lovely daughter fair,
   Was called bonnie Annie.
Her bloom was like the springing flower,
   That salutes the rosy morning,
With innocence and graceful mein [*sic*]
   Her beauteous form adorning.

11. "Tifty's Annie"

Greig and Keith, 1925, p. 178(1b); text, p. 175. From Duncan MS., No. 351. Tune from George F. Duncan, from a MS. of his parents, c. 1886; text from his sister, Mrs. Gillespie, Glasgow, as learned in Buchan in the 1850's.

p M

1. At Mill o Tifty there lived a man
      In the neighbourhood o Fyvie;
   He had a lovely daughter fair,
      Was callèd bonnie Annie.

2. Her bloom was like the springing flower
      That hails the rosy morning,
   With innocence and graceful mien
      Her beauteous face adorning.

3. Lord Fyvie had a trumpeter
      Whose name was Andrew Lammie;
   He had the airt to gain the heart
      O' Mill o Tifty's Annie.

4. Proper he was, baith young an' gay,
      His like was not in Fyvie,
   Nor was there one that could compare
      Wi this same Andrew Lammie.

5. Lord Fyvie he rode by the door
      Where livèd Tifty's Annie;
   His trumpeter rode him before,
      Even this same Andrew Lammie.

6. Her mother called her to the door,
      Said, "Come here to me, Annie;
   Did ye ever see a prettier man
      Than the trumpeter o Fyvie?"

7. Naething she said, but sighed fu' sore,
      Alas for bonnie Annie!
   She durst not own her heart was won
      By the trumpeter o Fyvie.

8. At nicht when a' gaes to their bed,
      A' sleeps fu' soun but Annie;
   Love so oppressed her tender breast,
      Thinking on Andrew Lammie.

9. "Love comes in at my bedside,
      An' love lies doon beyond me,
   Love so oppressed my tender breast,
      An' love will waste my body.

10. "The first time me an' my love met
      Was in the woods o Fyvie;
   His lovely form an' gracefu mien
      Soon gained the heart o Annie.

11. "He called me mistress; I said No,
      I'm Mill o Tifty's Annie;
   Wi apples sweet he did me treat,
      An' kisses soft an' many.

12. "It's up an' doon in Tifty's den,
      Where the burn rins clear an' bonnie,

I've often gane to meet my love,
      My bonnie Andrew Lammie."

13. But alas! her father came to know
      That the trumpeter o Fyvie
   Had had the airt to gain the heart
      O' his daughter bonnie Annie.

14. Her father soon a letter wrote,
      An' sent it to Lord Fyvie,
   To say his daughter was bewitched
      By his servant Andrew Lammie.

15. Then up the stair his trumpeter
      He called him soon an' shortly:
   "Pray tell to me what's this you've done
      To Tifty's bonnie Annie?"

16. "Woe be to Mill o Tifty's pride,
      For it has ruined many;
   He'll not have it said that she should wed
      The trumpeter o Fyvie.

17. "In wicked airt I had nae pairt,
      Nor therein was I canny;
   True love alone the heart has won
      O' Tifty's bonnie Annie.

18. "Where will I get a boy so kind
      That'll carry a letter canny
   An' will rin on to Tifty's toon,
      Gie it to bonnie Annie?

19. "Tifty he has daughters three,
      An' they're a' wondrous bonnie,
   But ye'll ken her amo' them a',
      Gie it to bonnie Annie.

20. "It's up an' doon in Tifty's den
      Where the burn rins clear an' bonnie,
   There will ye gang, an' I'll attend;
      My love, I long to see ye.

21. "Thou must gang to the brig o Sleuch,
      An' there I'll gang an' meet ye,
   An' there we will renew our love,
      Before I gang an' leave ye."

22. "My love, I go to Edinburgh toon,
      An' for a while maun leave ye":
   She sighed fu' sair, an' said nae mair
      But "I wish that I were wi ye."

23. "I'll buy to you a bridal goon,
      My love, I'll buy it bonnie;
   I will thee wed when I come back
      To see my bonnie Annie.

24. "If ye'll be true an' constant too,
      As I am Andrew Lammie,
   I will thee wed when I come back
      To view the lands o Fyvie."

25. "I'll be true an' constant too
      To thee, my Andrew Lammie;
   But my bridal bed it will be made
      In the green churchyard o Fyvie."

26. "The time is gone, an' now comes on,
      My dear, that I must leave ye;

If longer here I should appear,
　　Mill o Tifty he wad see me."

27. "I now for ever bid adieu
　　　To thee, my Andrew Lammie;
　　Ere ye come back, I will be laid
　　　In the green churchyard o Fyvie."

28. He hied him to the head o the house
　　　To the high house-top o Fyvie;
　　He blew his trumpet loud an' shrill,
　　　Twas heard at Mill o Tifty.

29. Her father locked the door at nicht,
　　　Laid up the keys fu canny;
　　An' when he heard the trumpet sound,
　　　Said, "Your coo is lowing, Annie."

30. "My father dear, I pray forbear,
　　　Reproach nae mair your Annie,
　　For I wadna gie that ae coo's low
　　　For a' the kye in Fyvie.

31. "I wadna for my braw new goon,
　　　Nor a' your gifts sae many,
　　That it were known in Fyvie's lands
　　　Sae cruel ye are to Annie.

32. "But if ye strike me, I'll cry out,
　　　An' gentlemen will hear me;
　　Lord Fyvie he'll be riding by,
　　　An' he'll come in an' see me."

33. At that same time the Lord came in,
　　　Said, "What ails thee, my Annie?"—
　　"It's a' for love that I maun dee,
　　　For bonnie Andrew Lammie."

34. "Pray, Mill o Tifty, gie consent,
　　　An' let your daughter marry."—
　　"It will be wi some higher match
　　　Than the trumpeter o Fyvie."

35. "If she'd been come o as high kin
　　　As she's adorned wi beauty,
　　I wad hae teen her to mysel,
　　　An' made her my ain lady."

36. "Fyvie's lands are far an' wide,
　　　An' they're a' wondrous bonnie,
　　But I wadna gie my ain true love
　　　For a' the lands o Fyvie."

37. Her father struck her wondrous sore,
　　　As also did her mother,
　　Her sisters also did her scorn,
　　　But woe be to her brother!

38. Her brother struck her wondrous sore
　　　Wi cruel strokes an' many;
　　He broke her back at the ha' door
　　　For liking Andrew Lammie.

39. "Alas, my father an' mother dear,
　　　Why so cruel to your Annie?

My heart was broken first by love,
　　My brother broke my body.

40. "Ye neighbours hear, baith far an' near,
　　　An' pity Tifty's Annie,
　　Who dies for loving one poor lad,
　　　My bonnie Andrew Lammie.

41. "No kind o vice e'er stained my life,
　　　Nor hurt my virgin honour;
　　My youthfu heart was won by love,
　　　But death will me exoner.

42. "O mother dear, now make my bed,
　　　An' lay my face to Fyvie;
　　Thus will I lie, an' thus will die
　　　For my dear Andrew Lammie."

43. Her mother then she made her bed,
　　　An' laid her face to Fyvie;
　　Her tender heart it soon did break,
　　　An' she never saw Andrew Lammie.

44. Lord Fyvie he did wring his hands,
　　　Said, "Alas for bonnie Annie!
　　The fairest flower cut down by love
　　　That ever sprang in Fyvie.

45. "Woe be to Mill o Tifty's pride,
　　　He micht have let them marry;
　　I wad hae gien them baith to live
　　　Within the lands o Fyvie."

46. Her father sair now laments
　　　The loss o his dear Annie,
　　An' wishes he had gien consent
　　　To wed wi Andrew Lammie.

47. When Andrew hame from Edinburgh came
　　　Wi muckle grief an' sorrow,
　　Said, "My love has died for me to-day,
　　　I'll die for her to-morrow.

48. "Now I will rin to Tifty's den
　　　Where the burn rins clear an' bonnie;
　　Wi tears I'll view the brig o Sleuch,
　　　Where I parted wi my Annie.

49. "Then I will rin to the green churchyard,
　　　To the green churchyard o Fyvie;
　　Wi tears I'll water my love's grave
　　　Till I follow Tifty's Annie."

50. Ye parents who dear children have,
　　　In crossing them be canny;
　　Or when too late ye may repent,
　　　Remember Tifty's Annie.

Mr. Duncan's text, written from his mother's singing in Buchan, 1885,
is inaccessible. According to Keith (*Last Leaves*, p. 272), it has these
differences from Mrs. Gillespie's: omitted sts. 49-50; gave sts. 23-26 in
the order 25, 26, 23, 24; put st. 42 between 39 and 40. "Otherwise the
differences are verbal and slight at that." (Cf. note, *ante*, p. xii, on the
Duncan MSS.)

The Earl of Aboyne

CHILD NO. 235

THREE types of melody appear to have been used for this ballad. The best established is our A group, found in the Blaikie and Harris MSS. of the early nineteenth century, and recorded by Christie in the form used by his maternal grandmother. The tune is major in tonality, of duple rhythm, and usually has a full authentic octave plus the plagal range. We may sub-divide the copies into three classes, of I/Ly, Major, and I/M, the last being plagal and of more recent vintage. As Keith points out, the type is affiliated with "The Mill, Mill O," printed many times in the eighteenth century and later, and used in various ballad-operas and by Burns ("When wild war's deadly blast").

The second type is represented by Mrs. Gillespie's copy, and she sang also another tune to the same ballad-text. As Keith notes, the present is the tune of the popular "Bonnie Lass of Fyvie"; it has easy connections with "Binorie" (Child No. 10), which was Mrs. Gillespie's other tune for "Aboyne." In its present form it is a plagal major.

TUNES WITH TEXTS

GROUP Aa

2. "The Earl of Aboyne"

Christie, I, 1876, p. 22. From his maternal grandmother.

m I/Ly

> The Earl o' Aboyne to Lunnon's gane,
>   And a' his nobles wi' him;
> Sair was the heart his fair lady had,
>   Because she didna win wi' him.
> As she was walking in her garden green,
>   Amang her gentlewomen,
> Sad was the letter that came to her,—
>   That her lord was wed in Lunnon.
>   [*Etc.*]

Christie's text is a collation, based on the way he heard the ballad sung and on the version in Buchan's *Gleanings*, 1825, p. 71.

GROUP B

7. "The Earl o' Aboyne"

Greig and Keith, 1925, p. 182(3); text, p. 180. From Duncan MS., No. 16. Sung by Mrs. Gillespie.

pI

1. The Earl o Aboyne to London's gane,
       An' a' his nobles wi him [O],
   An' sair was the heart that his fair lady got
       Because she couldna win wi him [O].

2. As she was walkin on the green,
       Among her gentle women,
   Sad was the letter that this fair lady got,
       That her lord was wed in London.

3. "O is it true, my Jean," she said,
       "O Jean my gentlewoman?
   O is it true, my Jean," she said,
       "That my lord is wed in London?"

4. When she lookt ower her castle wa,
       She saw twa boys rinnin:
   "What news, what news, my bonnie little boys,
       What news hae ye fae London?"

5. "Good news, good news, my lady fair,
       For the lord o Aboyne he is comin;
   Ere he won within twa miles o the place,
       Ye'll hear his bridles ringin."

6. "O my grooms all, be well in call,
       An' hae your stable shinin;
   Wi corn an' hay spare none this day,
       For the lord o Aboyne he's comin.

7. "O my minstrels all, be well in call,
      An' hae your harps a-tunin;
   Wi the finest o springs spare not the strings,
      Sin the lord o Aboyne he's comin.

8. "My cooks all, be well in call,
      An' hae your spits a-rinnin;
   Wi the best o roast ye'll spare nae cost,
      For the lord o Aboyne he's comin.

9. "My housemaids all, be well in call,
      An' hae your floors a-shinin;
   Ye'll cover the stair wi the herbs sweet an' fair,
      An' the floors wi the finest o linen.

10. "An' dress my body in the finest array,
       My hood o the finest linen,
    My apron shall be o the good silk gauze,
       Sin the lord o Aboyne he's comin."

11. Sae stately's she stept down the stair,
       To see gin he was comin;
    Her gown was o the good green silk,
       Fasten't wi the red silk trimmin.

12. She called on Kate her waitin-maid,
       On Jean her gentlewoman:
    "Gae bring me a glass o the very best wine
       To drink his health that's comin."

13. She's gane out to the close, taen him fae his horse,
       Said, "Ye're welcome for your comin";
    She's gane to the close, taen him fae his horse,
       Says, "Ye're thrice welcome fae London."

14. "If I be half as welcome as ye say,
       Come kiss me for my comin,

For to-morrow should hae been my weddin day
   Gin I'd stayed ony langer in London."

15. She turned about wi a disdainful look
       To Jean her gentlewoman:
    "If to-morrow should hae been your weddin day,
       Go kiss your miss in London."

16. "O my nobles all, now turn your steeds,
       I'm sorry for my comin;
    Tonight we'll alight at the bonnie Bog o Gight,
       An' to-morrow take horses for London."

17. "O Thomas, my man, rin after him,
       An' see gin I'll win wi him."—
    "O I hae been pleadin sair for you,
       But a mile an' ye'll no win wi him."

18. A year an' mair she lived in care,
       An' doctors wi her dealin,
    But in a crack her bonnie heart did brak,
       An' letters gaed to London.

19. When he saw the letters sealed in black,
       He fell in grievous weepin:
    "If she be deid whom I loe best,
       If I'd but her heart a-keepin."

20. Fifteen o the noblest lords
       That London could afford him,
    From their hose to their hat let them be in black,
       To mourn for my bonnie Peggy Irvine.

21. The further he went the sairer he wept,
       "If I'd but her heart a-keepin [O],
    For I'd rather hae lost all the lands o Aboyne
       Than lost my bonnie Peggy Irvine [O]."

The Laird o Drum

CHILD NO. 236

THE main melodic tradition of this favorite ballad-version of King Cophetua is a lively tune in duple time, authentic, and basically π^1 even where the gaps are supplied either as Ionian or as Mixolydian. Of this type Greig collected a dozen examples, and these are given added weight by Christie's fancy copy.

Another half-dozen tunes are impossible to group, and have been ordered on the hypothesis that they would have conformed to the type except for deflecting influences from other tunes. D departs from the strong duple rhythm, and is a plagal Mixolydian variant of the tune which the same singer had already sung as π^1 to "Tifty's Annie" (No. 233).

The musical record, it might be observed, lends no corroboration to the assumption that the secondary forms of the ballad have grown traditionally from the earlier.

TUNES WITH TEXTS

GROUP A

5. "Laird o' Drum"

Greig-Duncan MS. 785 (Walker transcript), p. 160; from Duncan MS., No. 3. Also in Greig MSS., II, p. 6; and Greig and Keith, 1925, p. 185(1b); text, p. 183. Sung in 1905 by Mrs. Gillespie, who learned it from Betty Milne, Fyvie, c. 1862.

a π^1

1. The laird o Drum's a-huntin gane
   All in a mornin early,
   An' there he spied a weel-faur'd maid
   A-shearin her father's barley.

2. "O will ye fancy me, fair maid,
   Or will ye marry me, O,
   An' gang an' be the leddy o Drum
   An' lat your shearin be, O?"

3. "O I maunna fancy you, kind sir,
   Nor lat my shearin be, O,
   For I'm ower low to be leddy o Drum,
   An' your miss I would scorn to be, O.

4. "My father he's an auld shepherd man,
   Keeps hoggs on yonder hill, O,
   An' ilka thing he bids me do,
   I'm always at his will, O."

5. "But ye'll pit aff the gowns o grey,
   Pit on the silk an' scarlet,
   An' come an' be the leddy o Drum,
   An' ye'll neither be miss nor harlot."

6. "I canna wear your gowns o silk,
   They wid harrel at my heel, O,
   But weel can I wear the colour o the ewe,
   It becomes my body weel O."

7. Now he has to her father gane
   Keepin hoggs on yonder hill, O:
   "I'm come to marry your ae dachter,
   If ye'll gie your good will, O."

8. "My dachter can neither read nor write,
   She was never taught at school, O,
   But weel can she milk baith cows an' ewes,
   For I learned the lassie mysel, O.

9. "She'll work in your barn, she'll winnie your corn,
   She'll gang to mill or kill, O;
   In time o need she'll saddle your steed,
   An' draw your boots hersel, O."

10. "I'll learn the lassie to read an' write,
    I'll pit her to the school, O,
    An' she'll never need to saddle my steed,
    Nor draw my boots hersel, O.

11. "But fa will bake my bridal breid,
    Or fa will brew my ale, O,
    An' fa will welcome the leddy o Drum,
    Is mair than I can tell, O."

12. There was four an' twenty gentlemen
    Stood at the gates o Drum, O,
    But neer a een pit his han' till his hat
    When the leddy o Drum cam in, O.

13. But he has taen her by the han',
    An' led her but an' ben, O,
    Says, "Ye're welcome hame, my Leddy Drum,
    For this is a' your ain, O."

14. An' he has taen her by the han'
    An' led her through the ha', O,
    Says, "Ye're welcome hame, my Leddy Drum,
    To your bowers een an' a', O."

15. Then up an' spak his ae brither,
    "Ye've deen us muckle wrang, O;
    Ye've marriet a wife neath your degree,
    A disgrace to a' oor kin, O.

16. "It's Peggy Coutts is a bonnie bride,
       An' Drum is big an' gaucey,
   But he micht hae chosen a higher match
       Than just a shepherd's lassie."

17. Out then spak the laird o Drum,
       Says, "I've done ye nae wrang, O,
   For I've marriet a wife to work an' win,
       An' ye've marriet een to spen', O.

18. "The firstan wife that I did wed,
       She was far abune my degree, O,
   I durstna gang in the room she was in
       But my hat low by my knee, O.

19. "For the first wife that I did wed,
       She lookit doon on me, O;
   She widna walk to the gates o Drum,
       But the pearlins abune her bree O.

20. "An' she was adored but for her gold,
       An' Peggy for her beauty, O,
   An' she micht walk to the gates o Drum
       In as good company, O."

21. Yet four an' twenty gentle knights
       Stood at the gates o Drum, O,
   An' there wasna een amang them a'
       Wid welcome Peggy in, O.

22. But he has taen her by the han',
       An' led her in himsel, O,
   An' pit the keys into her lap,
       An' styled her Leddy Drum, O.

23. An' twice he kissed her cherry cheek,
       An' thrice her cherry chin, O,
   An' twenty times her comely mou,
       Said, "Ye're welcome, Leddy Drum, O."

24. When they had eaten an' drunken weel,
       An' a' were bound for bed, O,
   The laird o Drum an' the shepherd's dachter
       In ae bed they were laid, O.

25. "Gin ye had been o as high kin
       As ye're o low degree, O,
   We might hae baith gane doon the street
       Mang the best o company, O.

26. "An' o a' yon four an' twenty knights
       That gaed in at the yett o Drum, O,
   There neer was een but wid lifted his hat
       When the leddy o Drum cam in, O."

27. "I tell't ye weel ere we were wed,
       Ye was far abune my degree, O,
   But noo I'm wed an' in your bed laid,
       I'd scorn to carry your keys, O.

28. "I tell't ye weel ere we were wed,
       Ye was far too high for me, O,
   But noo I'm wed an' in your bed laid,
       An' I'm just as good as ye, O.

29. "When I am deid an' you are deid,
       An' baith in ae grave laid, O,
   They wid need to look wi very clear een
       To ken your mould by mine, O."

GROUP D

23. "The Laird o Drum"

Greig MSS., I, p. 150; text, Bk. 716, VI, p. 1. Also in Greig and Keith, 1925, p. 186(3). Sung by Miss Annie Ritchie, Whitehill, March 1906.

p M

1. The Laird o' Drum is a huntin' gone
   A' in a mornin' early
   There he spied a weel faured maid
   She was shearin' her father's barley.

2. Will ye gang wi' me he said
   And let your sheerin' be o'
   Or will ye gang and be Lady o' Drum
   Or will ye fancy one o'.

3. I canna gang wi' you she said
   Nor lat my shearin' be o'
   For I'm owre low to be Lady o' Drum
   And you'r miss I'd scorn to be o'

4. I canna wash your cheena cups
   Nor mak a cup o' tea o'
   But weel can I milk oor ewe
   Wi' the cogie on my knee o'

5. I'll shak your barn, I'll winnow your corn
   I'll gang to mull or kiln o'
   In the oor o' need, I'll paddle your steed
   And I'll dry your boots mysel o'.

6. I canna wear your silken dress
   It scarce come to my knee o'
   But weel can I the colour o' the ewe
   For It sets my body weel o'.

7. But fa will bake my bridal bread
   And brew my bridal ale o'
   Fa'll welcome my bonnie bridie hame
   It's mair nor I can tell o'.

8. O I can bake your bridal bread
   And brew your bridal ale o'
   And fa' can welcome your bonnie bridie hame
   I think ye're fittest yoursel' o'.

9. There were four & twenty lairds & lords
   Stood at the gates o' Drum o'
   And in the ha' amo' them a'
   He styled her the Lady o' Drum o'.

10. When a' had eaten and a' had drunk
    And all were bound for bed o'
    The Laird o' Drum and the shepherd's daughter
    Both in one bed were laid o'.

11. And ye had been as guid as me
As guid as me said he o'
We might have been in the high parlour
Among good company o'.

12. I told you long ere you wedded me
I was far below your degree o'
But now since we're in one beddie laid
Ye'll be forced to be daen wi' me o'.

13. Wasn't Adam & Eve, our first parents
When they eat the forbidden tree o'
Waur was a' oor gentry then
Am not I as good as they

14. Gin you & I were seven years deid
And both dug up again o'.
I think they wid see wi' a very clear e'e
That wid ken your mould by mine o'.

The Duke of Gordon's Daughter

CHILD NO. 237

FORMALLY, this ballad is somewhat anomalous, possibly unique. Other ballads which have a feminine ending on lines one and three are clearly dactylic or anapaestic, and generally (I believe) go to triple-time tunes of twelve bars instead of the usual sixteen. The evidence of the variants seems to prove that basically the present ballad is metrically of the same kind, and should be read as six-stress couplets (or three-stress quatrains). But the melodic tradition is clearly one, and none of the variants is in triple time: all are duple, either 2/4 or 4/4. The verbal rhythm is thus treated as containing a good many consecutive unstressed syllables, as may be seen if some of the lines are read with only three stresses:

> Till Lady Jéan fell in lóve with Captain Ógilvie,
> And awáy with hím she would gáe.

In one variant in 2/4 (Greig's 1d; variant 6 below), the singer evidently found it necessary to insert an extra bar in the third phrase in order to accommodate so long a line. The result was a tune of thirteen bars instead of the regular twelve. Of the variants in common time, three are eight-bar tunes, a half-bar being added to each phrase-ending. The secondary accents are thus brought into prominence, and the usual CM or ballad-metre is the result. But in a fourth case (variant 9), there are but seven bars. This situation appears to have arisen from the singer's having swung uncertainly between two possibilities, the first-phrase cadence being held for the extra half-bar, the second and third not.

All the tunes collected belong to the same family, but may be sub-divided into three groups for present purposes. The first is plagal, the second authentic by means of lessening the characteristic octave plunge of the earlier forms. These variants all properly belong to the D/Æ or Æolian field, but the oldest copies are given the leading-note instead of a flattened seventh. Greig's hypermetrical copy, 1d, is also singular in deserting the usual pattern for its mid-cadence and final cadence; and one is tempted to see it as an authentic Dorian (really M/D) variant ending on the fifth.

TUNES WITH TEXTS

GROUP Aa

4. "The Duke of Gordon's Daughters"

Greig MSS., II, p. 9; text, Bk. 715, V, p. 62. Also in Greig and Keith, 1925, p. 189(1b). Sung by Mrs. Milne, New Deer, May 1906.

m D/Æ

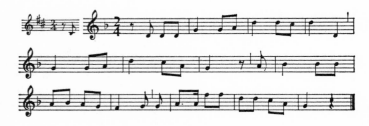

The Duke o' Gordon had three pretty daughters
    Lizbeth, Marget, & Jean,
They wadna stay at Castle Gordon
    They boud be in Bonnie Aiberdeen.

They hadna been in bonnie Aiberdeen
    A Twelvemonth & a day
Till Jeannie Gordon fell in love wi' Captain Noble
    And awa' wi' him she gae.

Oh but I'm weary wanderin',
    Oh but my fortune's been bad
It sets not the Duke o' Gordon's daughter
    To follow a sodger lad.

If I were at the bonnie hills o' Foudlan,
    Where mony merry nichts I have been
I wad get the road tae Castle Gordon
    Without either stockins or sheen.

6. "The Duke of Gordon's Daughters"

Greig and Keith, 1925, p. 189(1d); from Duncan MS., No. 338. Sung by Mrs. Harper, Cluny; learned from her mother.

p D/Æ

GROUP Ab

7. "The Duke of Gordon's Daughters"

Greig and Keith, 1925, p. 189(1a); text, p. 187. From Duncan MS., No. 14. Sung by Mrs. Gillespie and George F. Duncan; learned from their parents, c. 1885.

237. THE DUKE OF GORDON'S DAUGHTER

a D/Æ

1. The Duke o Gordon had three bonnie daughters,
   Eliza, Marget, an' Jean,
   An' they widna stay at Castle Gordon,
   But went to bonnie Aberdeen.

2. They hadna been in bonnie Aberdeen
   A year but an' a day,
   Lady Jean's fa'en in love wi Captain Ogilvie,
   An' from him she winna stay.

3. Word cam to the Duke o Gordon,
   In the chamber where he lay,
   That Lady Jean's fa'en in love wi Captain Ogilvie,
   An' from him she winna stay.

4. "Go saddle to me the black horse,
   Yoursel ride on the grey,
   An' we'll reach bonnie Aberdeen
   By the dawnin o the day."

5. They were not a mile from bonnie Aberdeen,
   A mile but barely three,
   When the Duke met his twa daughters
   To bear him company.

6. "Where is your sister, maidens?"
   He unto them did say;—
   "Lady Jean's fa'en in love wi Captain Ogilvie,
   An' from him she winna stay.

7. "O pardon, O pardon us, father,
   O pardon us," they did say;
   "Lady Jean's fa'en in love wi Captain Ogilvie,
   An' awa wi him she did gae."

8. When he cam to bonnie Aberdeen,
   An' stood upon the green,
   An' there he saw Captain Ogilvie
   A-trainin o his men.

9. "O woe be to you, Captain Ogilvie,
   An ill death may ye dee,
   For takin to you my daughter
   High hangit ye shall be."

10. The Duke he wrote a broad letter,
    An' sent it to the King,
    Said, "Ye'll cause hang Captain Ogilvie
    If ever ye hanged a man."

11. "I will not hang Captain Ogilvie
    For nae lord that I see;
    I'll cause him put off the lace an' scarlet,
    An' put on single livery."

12. Word cam to bonnie Captain Ogilvie
    In his chamber where he lay,
    To put off the lace an' scarlet,
    An' don the single livery.

13. "If this be for bonnie Jeanie Gordon,
    A' this an' mair wid I dree;
    If this be for bonnie Jeanie Gordon,
    It's thrice welcome to me."

14. Lady Jean had not been married
    Years but only three,
    When she had twa babies at her fit
    An' anither on her knee.

15. "O but I'm weary wanderin,
    O but I think lang:
    It ill sets the Duke o Gordon's daughter
    To follow a single man.

16. "Woe to the hills an' the mountains,
    Woe to the frost an' snow,
    My shoes an' stockins are a' torn,
    Nae farther can I go.

17. "But O, gin I were at the bonnie hills o Foudland,
    Faur mony merry days I hae been,
    I wid get the road to Castle Gordon
    Withoot either stockins or sheen."

18. When she cam to bonnie Castle Gordon,
    An' stood upon the green,
    The porter let oot a loud huzza,
    "Here comes our Lady Jean."

19. "O ye're welcome hame, Jeanie Gordon,
    You an' your bairnies three;
    Ye're welcome here, Jeanie Gordon,
    But awa wi your Ogilvie."

20. Now over the seas went the Captain,
    As a soldier under command;
    A message soon followed after
    To come an' heir his brother's land.

21. "Come hame, come hame, Captain Ogilvie,
    An' heir your brother's land,
    Come hame, ye pretty Captain Ogilvie,
    An' be Earl o Northumberland."

22. "O what does this mean, Captain,
    Where are my brother's children three?"—
    "They are a' deid an' buried,
    Northumberland is waitin for thee."

23. "Then hoist up your sails," said the Captain,
    "An' let us be joyful an' free,
    For I'll to Northumberland an' heir my estates,
    An' then my dear Jeanie I will see."

24. When he cam to bonnie Castle Gordon,
    An' stood upon the green,
    He was the prettiest young man
    That ever they had seen.

25. "Ye're welcome here, Captain Ogilvie,
    Ye're thrice welcome to me,
    Ye're welcome here, Captain Ogilvie,
    To your wife an' bairnies three."

26. "The last time I was at your gates
     Ye widna let me in;
   I am come for my wife an' my children,
     Nae ither friendship I claim."

27. "Come in, my pretty Captain Ogilvie,
     Drink the red beer an' the wine,
   An' we'll count ye oot gold an' silver
     Until that the clock strikes nine."

28. "I winna come in," said the Captain,
     "I'll drink neither your red beer nor wine,
   I want neither your gold nor your silver,
     I've enough in Northumberland."

29. Down the stairs cam bonnie Jeanie Gordon,
     The tears were blindin her ee,
   Down cam bonnie Jeanie Gordon
     Wi her bairnies three.

30. "Ye're welcome, my bonnie Jeanie Gordon,
     You an' my young family;
   We'll haste an' go to Northumberland,
     An' a countess ye shall be."

9. "The Duke o' Gordon's Daughter"

Greig MSS., IV, p. 23. Also in Greig and Keith, 1925, p. 189(1c). Sung by John Johnstone, New Deer.

a D

Gin I were at the bonnie hills o' Foudlan'
Where aft times I hae been,
I wad gang to bonnie Castle Gordon,
Tho' I'd neither stockings nor sheen.

Glenlogie, or, Jean o Bethelnie

CHILD NO. 238

THE melodic tradition of this ballad is remarkably consistent. All the variants are of one tribe, all are in triple time, most are π^1, or all but pentatonic. The first accent is always the tonic; the first cadence-point (really the middle of the tune) almost always on the second; the second half, or long phrase, invariably swings down from the tonic to the lower octave and back, like a hammock. It is something of an offense to the music to cut its phrases in two in order to make arbitrary quatrain stanzas. Long rhymed couplets (the second line sometimes repeated) are more natural counterparts of the tune.

TUNES WITH TEXTS

GROUP A

10. "Glenlogie"

Archive, School of Scottish Studies. Sung by John Adams. Collected by Hamish Henderson for the School of Scottish Studies; transcribed by Francis M. Collinson.

a I, ending on the octave

1. There was nine and nine horsemen
      Rode through Banchory Fair,
   An' bonnie Glenlogie
      Was the floo'er o' a' there
   An' bonnie Glenlogie
      Was the floo'er o' a' there.

2. There was nine and nine ladies
      Sat in the Queen's dine,
   An' bonnie Jeannie o' Bethelnie
      Was the floo'er o' twice nine
   An' bonnie Jeannie o' Bethelnie
      Was the floo'er o' twice nine.

3. She has callèd his footboy
      That walked by his side,
   Saying, Who is your master
      And where does he bide?
   Saying, Who is your master
      And where does he bide?

4. He is stylèd Glenlogie
      When he is at home,
   But he's of the noble Gordons
      And his name is Lord John.

5. Glenlogie, Glenlogie,
      If ye will prove kind,
   A maiden's love laid on you,
      Must she die in her prime
   A maiden's love laid on you,
      Must she die in her prime.

6. He's turned aboot lichtly,
      As Gordons dee a',
   My thanks, Lady Jean,
      My love's promised awa'.
   My thanks, Lady Jean,
      My love's promised awa'.

7. She has called her father's chaplain,
      A man of great skill,
   And he has wrote a letter
      And indited it well
   And he has wrote a letter
      And indited it well.

8. When Glenlogie got the letter
      A licht lauch gied he;
   But ere he read it over
      A tear dimmed his e'e.
   But ere he read it over
      A tear dimmed his e'e.

9. Go saddle my black horse,
      And bring it to the green;
   But ere they had it ready
      He was twa mile him leen*
   But ere they had it ready
      He was twa mile him leen.

10. Pale and wan was she
       When Glenlogie gaed in,
    But red and rosy grew she
       When she kent it was him,
    But red and rosy grew she
       When she kent it was him.

* him leen = alone

[423]

The Rantin Laddie

CHILD NO. 240

So FAR as a musical tradition exists for this ballad, it belongs to the familiar "Binorie" type. Copies are preserved in two favorite patterns, both known in other connections. One was sent by Burns to the *Scots Musical Museum*, and later repeated in R. A. Smith. The other was collected by Greig at the beginning of our own century. All are D/Æ plagal, and in common time. Keith cites also *Museum*, No. 320 ("The Cruel Mother") as a relative.

Very lately, Ewan MacColl has given us a fine Mixolydian tune, distinct from all others, as from his own family tradition.

TUNES WITH TEXTS

GROUP A a

1. "The Rantin Laddie"

Johnson, V [1796], No. 462, p. 474 (repr. 1853). Also in Smith [1820-24], IV, p. 6 (with a parallel text). From Robert Burns.

p D/Æ

Aften hae I play'd at the cards and the dice,
    For the love of a bonie rantin laddie;
But now I maun sit in my fathers kitchen neuk
    And Be-low a bastard babie.
For my father he will not me own,
    And my mother she neglects me,
And a' my friends hae lightlyed me,
    And their servants they do slight me.
But had I a servant at my command,
    As aft times I've had many,
That wad rin wi' a letter to bonie Glenswood,
    Wi' a letter to my rantin laddie.
Oh, is he either a laird, or a lord,
    Or is he but a cadie,
That ye do him ca' sae aften by name,
    Your bonie, bonie rantin laddie.
Indeed he is baith a laird and a lord,
    And he never was a cadie;
But he is the Earl o' bonie Aboyne,
    And he is my rantin laddie.
O ye'se get a servant at your command,
    As aft times ye've had many,
That sall rin wi' a letter to bonie Glenswood,
    A letter to your rantin laddie.
When lord Aboyne did the letter get,
    O but he blinket bonie;
But or he had read three lines of it,
    I think his heart was sorry.
O wha is daur be sae bauld,
    Sae cruelly to use my lassie?

For her father he will not her know,
    And her mother she does slight her;
And a' her friends hae lightlied her,
    And their servants they neglect her.
Go raise to me my five hundred men,
    Make haste and make them ready;
With a milkwhite steed under every ane,
    For to bring hame my lady.
As they cam in thro' Buchan-shire,
    They were a company bonie,
With a gude claymor in every hand,
    And O, but they shin'd bonie.

GROUP A b

3. "The Rantin Laddie"

Greig MSS., II, p. 5; text, Bk. 717, VII, p. 99. Also in Greig and Keith, 1925, p. 194(b). Tune from Andrew Findlay, New Deer, June 1906; text from Rev. J. C[alder].

p D/Æ

The Reverend J. Calder's text is referred to Findlay's tune in the MS.

1. My father feed me far far awa
   I was far awa as Kircaldy
   He's feed me hame to an auld widow wife
   And wi' her lives a bonnie rantin' laddie.

2. On this side the burn & on yon side the burn
   And it's oh but the burn rins bonnie
   And yon man promised to marry me
   If ever he married any.

[424]

3. If I had been wise I'd taen my love's advice
I'd da'en as my bonnie love bade me
I micht have been married at Martinmas
And awa wi' the bonnie rantin laddie.

4. But I wasna wise nor yet took advice
Nor did as my bonnie lovie bade me
So I now maun sit in my father's kitchie nook
Singin' ba to my bonnie bastard bairnie

5. My father has come trippin' doon the stair
Wi' shy shy looks and angry
Says Is't to a laird or is't to a lord
Or is it to a caddie.

6. My father is a very proud man
My mother she's gone & left me
My friens & relations they a' do me forget
And my father's servant men they hate me.

7. It's nae to a laird nor yet to a lord
Nor is it to a caddie
But it is to the young Earl of Aboyne
Tho' they ca' him the bonnie rantin' laddie.

8. And where will I get a bonnie wee boy
That will carry a letter cannie
That will run on to the Castle o' Aboyne
Wi' a letter to the bonnie rantin' laddie.

9. As ye gang up by bonnie Deeside
The banks they are a' bloomin' bonnie
Oh then ye will spy the castle o' Aboyne
Doon among the bushes sae bonnie.

10. As he gaed up by bonnie Deeside
The banks they were bloomin' bonnie
And there he spied the Earl o' Aboyne
Doon among the bushes sae bonnie

11. Oh where are you going my bonnie wee boy
Where are ye going my caddie
I'm gaen on to the Castle o' Aboyne
Wi' a letter to the bonnie rantin' laddie.

12. Ye needna gang farther my bonnie wee boy
Ye needna gang farther my caddie
For I am the Earl o' Aboyne
Tho they ca' me the bonnie rantin' laddie.

13. He took the letter & he read the letter
And oh but it was bonnie
But lang ere he had the letter far read
The tears fell thick and many

14. Oh where will I get twenty-four gentlemen
And as many of young ladies
That will mount on milk-white steeds
To welcome home my Peggy.

15. Oh here I'll get twenty four young gentlemen
And as mony ladies
That will mount on to milk-white steeds
And welcome home your Peggy.

16. As we cam' thro' by bonnie Aiberdeen
The folks they were a' makin' ready
But said I to them ye needna buckle braw
To welcome home my Peggy.

17. I shall na bide lang at Aiberdeen,
Nor yet into this low country
But I shall run into the Castle o' Aboyne
To be Aboyne's young lady.

GROUP C

5. "The Rantin Laddie"

Sung by Ewan MacColl, Riverside rec. No. RLP 12-622
(B4), ed. K. S. Goldstein. Learned from his father.

a M

1. "Oft hae I played at the cards and dice
Wi' my ain dear rantin laddie,
But noo I maun sit in my faither's ha'
And sing ba to my bastard baby.

2. "If I'd been wise as I've been nice,
And done what my bonnie lad tauld me,
I'd ha' been married a year or mair,
And been wi' my rantin laddie.

3. "My faither dear he knows me not,
An' my mither she ignores me,
My friends and relations a' slight me,
And the servants they quite hate me.

4. "Gin I had ane horse at my command,
As oft times I've had mony,
I would ride it on to the gates o' Aboyne
Wi' a letter to my rantin laddie."

5. "Is your love a laird or is he a lord,
Or is he but a caddie,
That ye sae aft ca' on his name,
Your ain dear rantin laddie?"

6. Then oot and spak' a kitchie boy,
Says "Though I'm but a caddie,
It's I will run to the gates o' Aboyne,
Wi' a letter for your rantin laddie."

7. When he was near tae the banks o' Dee,
The birds they sang sae bonny,
And there he spied the Earl o' Aboyne,
That they ca' the rantin laddie.

8. And when he looked the letter on,
But O, and he was sorry,
"They've been cruel and fell unkind,
Tae my ain dear rantin lassie."

9. "My faither dear, he knows me not,
My mither she ignores me,
My frien's and relations a' slight me,
And the servants they quite hate me."

10. "Gae get to me five hundred men,
And they'll ride oot sae bonnie,
And we'll bring the bonnie lassie back to Aboyne,
My ain dear rantin lassie."

11. When she was up ahint his back,
Wrapped in a hielan' plaidie,
The birds in the trees sang not sae sweet,
As the bonnie, bonnie rantin lassie.

12. And they rode on through Buchanshire,
And Buchan it shone bonnie,
"Rejoice, rejoice, ye bonnie mays
And see that ye be na' sorry."

13. Gin ye lay your love on a lowland lad,
Be sure that he'll betray ye,
But lay your love on a hielan' lad,
He'll do a' he can to raise ye.

The Baron o Leys

CHILD NO. 241

PERHAPS the most striking feature in this surprisingly light-hearted song of plenary indulgence is the instant forgiveness by the Lady of Leys for her husband's escapade. All Child's copies except Kinloch's (B) display this tolerance; a fact which prompts the suggestion that Kinloch's punctuation at the crucial point mistakes the intention of the ballad. Instead of:

> But word's gane down to the Lady o' Leys
> That the Baron had got a babie:
> 'The waurst o news!' my lady she said,
> 'I wish I had hame my laddie,'
> (B,8)

we should read:

> The waurst o news my lady she said,
> 'I wish I had hame my laddie,' &c.—

meaning the lady did not scold. Compare the Skene copy (Child's A):

> The warst word she said to that was,
> 'I wish I had it in my arms';

the Buchan (Child C):

> She clapped her hands, and this did say,
> 'I wish he were in my arms';

the Greig copy:

> The very first word that the lady she spoke,
> Was, 'I wish I had hame my laddie.'

This ballad, incidentally, better deserves the title of "The Rantin Laddie" than does its predecessor. Adding to the obvious parallels of Child Nos. 110 and 217, mention may be made of Baring-Gould's "The Witty Shepherd." Cf. Baring-Gould and Sheppard, *A Garland of Country Song*, 1895, p. 65.

In the general spate of pathetic melodies of the "Binorie" type which accompany these ballads with feminine endings on lines two and four, it is an agreeable relief to find one of which the tradition is clearly a merry one, in keeping with the mood of the text. It seems clear that although the tunes recorded or mentioned for this ballad have few close resemblances, all the singers had in mind a brisk 6/8 measure with a characteristic cadence of an octave drop. The tune Burns sent to the *Scots Musical Museum* (No. 237) has in its first strain, as Stenhouse rightly notes, much of "Jenny come down to Jock" (for which cf., e.g., Ritson, *Scotish Songs*, ed. of 1869, I, p. 264; R. Chambers, *The Songs of Scotland Prior to Burns*, 1880, pp. 109ff.). Nor is it difficult to see resemblances in the second strain, as he also points out, to "Saw ye Johnny comin'" (cf. *Museum*, No. 9). The latter suggestion is not incompatible with Glen's counter-suggestion that Sheridan's "Here's to the maiden of bashful fifteen" is the related tune (*Early Scottish Melodies*, 1900, p. 139). The second strain of Sheridan's tune has, indeed, a good deal of the folk idiom. For earlier parallels, cf. "Jamaica" in Playford, *English Dancing Master*, 4th ed., whence also "The Jolly Trades-Men" in D'Urfey's *Pills*, 1719-20, VI, p. 91, and doubtless "Country Gardens."

The tune, as Burns gave it, is apparently a D/Æ one, the first strain being a true pentatonic of the fourth class (– II, VI). To me it appears that Greig's tune is probably a worn-down variant of this or a similar tune. We have seen more than once already a tendency in tradition to shorten the range of old airs with a wide gamut; and the drop here of a fifth on the cadence seems a palpable substitute for the earlier octave drop. Likewise the tune's upper reach is shortened by one degree. From another singer, Greig collected this ballad to the tune of "Wha'll be King but Charlie," which has the same characteristic octave drop, the same rhythm of 6/8 and is also Æolian. (Cf. Graham, *The Songs of Scotland*, 1848-49, I, p. 138.)

TUNES WITH TEXTS

1. "The Linkin Laddie"

Johnson, III [1790], No. 237, p. 246 (repr. 1853). Also in Herd MSS., I, p. 233. From Robert Burns.

a D/Æ (π^4 in the first strain); or possibly a I/Ly, ending on *VI*

Waes me that e'er I made your bed,
Waes me that e'er I saw ye,
For now I've lost my maiden head,
And I ken na how they ca' ye!

My name's weel kend in my ain countrie,
They ca' me the linkin laddie:
An ye had na been as willing as I,
Shame fa' them wad e'er hae bade ye.

2. "The Baron o' Leys"

Greig and Keith, 1925, p. 195; from Duncan MS., No. 204. Sung by Mrs. Petrie, Alford.

241. THE BARON O LEYS

a M/D

The Baron o Leys has to London gane,
An' shown his folly fairly,
He shod his horse wi siller sheen,
An' turned a rantin laddie.

The Dæmon Lover (The House Carpenter)

CHILD NO. 243

THE earliest copies of this ballad are English broadsides of the Restoration period. They are directed to be sung to three alternative tunes, of which the first was probably that most closely associated with the ballad—though not originally, since the wife in question here was from Plymouth, not Bristol. The Pepys broadside, IV, f. 101, given as Child's A (another is Pepys, I, f. 502), is "To a West-country tune called 'The Fair Maid of Bristol,' 'Bateman,' or 'John True.'" Copies in Brit. Mus. c.22 f.6, fol.24, and Bodleian Douce Ballads, II, fol.249ᵛ, omit "Bateman." Child cites others, which do not, I believe, add information on tunes. I have not discovered any of the three tunes mentioned and have no confidence that any of them was that printed in Chappell, *Popular Music* [1855-59], I, p. 198, as "Peascod Time." The tune should at any rate have been a CM tune, unlike that for Child's text B (mid-eighteenth century), which is LM. (Keith cites an earlier edition of B from a collection of 1737. Cf. Greig and Keith, *Last Leaves*, 1925, p. 196.) The outlines of B, but not the metre, are closest to the text which has been most popular in recent tradition in this country. But the very beautiful variant collected by Hammond, from Dorset, and later set by Vaughan Williams, is a perhaps solitary offspring of the LM variety (variant 82).

To judge by the few airs, either Scots or English, which have been recovered in Britain (Ireland yielding none to my inquiries), the ballad was sung there to tunes mainly in a major tonality. The Dorset variant (Group Ab) mentioned above is Dorian. On the other hand, Laidlaw wrote Scott that the tune he had heard was "very solemn and melancholy" (Jan. 3, 1803; quoted Child, 1882-98, IV, p. 369). There is a fair number of other, American, variants in a major tonality; but I believe they derive from the typically D/M pattern which comprises the central tradition for this ballad in this country. Of it a very large number of examples have been recorded, for this is still one of the best loved of the Child ballads, whatever its original credentials. The tune-variants are nearly always attractive, often remarkably so; indeed, probably none of the ballads, unless we except No. 79, gives a richer impression of the American melodic tradition.

The majority of these tunes are of extended range (plagal plus authentic), and conform with surprising consistency to a contour of which the mid-cadence is ♭VII-V, the first phrase ends on I, and the two first accents are on V and ♭VII. When the pattern becomes heptatonic, the result is generally Dorian. Variants also occur on either side of this norm: D/Æ, π⁴, Æ; and M and I/M—even to I/Ly. But the farther from the norm, the more the tune inclines to lose its characteristic outlines, to forget its tonic and end on another final (V, V, or II), to pick up accidentals, and to become aware of other tunes from which it may borrow hints. These cases, which show the tradition deteriorating, are difficult to analyze and classify, and frequently unsatisfying musically. But they are valuable for study, as showing how tunes become loosened from their moorings. The tune may vary the cadence-point of its first phrase from I to II, or IV to V, without losing its identity so long as it keeps a mid-cadence on V. But with the loss of that anchorage, the outlines begin to grow unrecognizable; and it may be that another reader would prefer to dissociate the sub-groups after Ab, or Ac, to Ah from the family of Aa altogether. I have not done so, out of a feeling that they still dimly aim at approximating a common archetypal musical image. But one of the melancholy possibilities of a study like the present is that the *idée fixe* may reside nowhere but in the editor's own head.

TUNES WITH TEXTS

GROUP A a

9. [The Daemon Lover]

Sharp MSS., 4594/3213. Also in Sharp and Karpeles, 1932, I, p. 254(M). Sung by Mrs. Virginia Bennett, Burnsville, N.C., September 13, 1918.

m M/D

1. Well met, well met, my own true love,
   Well met, well met, said he.
   I've just returned from the salt, salt sea,
   And it's all for the sake of thee,
   And it's all for the sake of thee.
   I've just returned from the salt, salt sea,
   And it's all for the sake of thee.

2. I could have married a king's daughter fair,
   I'm sure she would have married me,
   But I refused those golden crowns,
   And it's all for the sake of thee.

3. If you could have married a king's daughter fair,
   I'm sure you are to blame,
   For I am married to a house-carpenter,
   And I think he's a nice young man.

4. I pray you leave your house-carpenter
   And go away with me;
   I'll take you down where the grass grows green
   On the banks of the Aloe Dee.

5. Have you anything to support me on
To keep me from slavery?
Have you anything to supply my wants
To keep me from slavery?

6. I have three ships on the ocean wide,
Sailing towards dry land;
Three hundred and sixty sailor men
Shall be at your command.

7. She took her babe up in her arms,
And kisses gave it three,
Saying: Stay at home with your papa dear
And keep him company.

8. She dressed herself in silk so fine,
Most beautiful to behold.
As she marched down by the brine water side,
Bright shined those glittering golds.

9. She had not been on the sea two weeks,
I'm sure it was not three,
Till she lay on deck of her true lover's boat
And wept most bitterly.

10. Are you weeping for your silver and gold,
Or is it for your store,
Or is it for your house-carpenter
You never shall see any more?

11. I'm not weeping for my silver and gold,
Neither for my store;
'Tis all for the love of my darling little babe
I never shall see any more.

12. She had not been on sea but three weeks,
I'm sure it was not four,
Till a leak sprung in her true lover's boat,
And sank it to rise no more.

13. Accursed, accursed be all sea-men,
Accursed for ever more.
They've robbed me of my darling little babe,
I never shall see any more.

"Mrs. Bennett is Sam Bennett's second wife. She is a Kentucky woman raised on Sandy River on the edge of the blue grass country—a very sad-looking dour woman, very unlike the ordinary mountain-type of woman. Nearly all her songs she learned from her mother. She sings very beautifully in a very free way, but has a great dislike to tragedies and 'bluggy' songs, e.g. Young Hunting. For this reason she refused to sing The Cruel Mother which was one of her mother's songs." [*Sharp's MS. note.*]

53. "The House Carpenter"

Barry, Eckstorm, and Smyth, 1929, p. 306(B). Sung by Mrs. Susie Carr Young, Brewer, Me.; traditional in her family. Tune recorded by George Herzog, 1928.

p π⁵; or a π⁴, ending on V

She took her baby [on her knee]
And she gave it kisses three,
Saying, "Stay at home, you sweet pretty babe,
Keep your father company."

They had not been out more than two weeks,
I'm sure it was not three,
Before this lady began to weep,
And she wept most bitterly.

"O, do you weep for the gold that you left,
Or the dangers of the sea?
Or is it for fear of that house-carpenter
That you left when you came with me?"

"I do not weep for the gold that I left,
Or the dangers of the sea;
But it's all for the love of that little baby
That I left when I came with thee."

GROUP A b

75. "If you will leave your house carpenter"

Sung by Mrs. John Williams (née Violet Selena Hankins), Iowa City, Iowa. Learned in 1865-70, in Penn Township, Johnson County, Iowa, probably from Mrs. Tim Tierney. Text noted by her son Charles Williams, September 16, 1921; tune recorded by Mrs. Flora Brennan, February 5, 1922.

a M

"If you will leave your house carpenter
And go away with me,
I'll take you where the sweet winds blow
On the banks of sweet Italy."

This gallant lady had cause for to weep,
And she wept most bitterly
. . . .

"It is not for your gold I weep,
It is not for your store,
But O it is for the darling sweet babe
That I left on yonder shore."

78. "The Ship Carpenter"

Sung by Clay Walters, Salyersville, Ky., 1937. LC/AAFS, rec. No. 1580(A, B1); also LC/AAFS, rec. No. L58(A5). Collected by Alan and Elizabeth Lomax.

a D

Cf. the same singer's other version, *ante*, variant 13.

1. Well met, well met, my own true love
   Long I've been searching for thee
   I've been all across the salt roaring sea
   And it's all for the sake of thee.

2. Oh, I could have married the king's daughter fair
   She all the same would have had me
   But I refused that rich crown of gold
   And it's all for the sake of thee.

3. If you could have married the king's daughter dear
   I'm sure that you are to blame
   For I wouldn't have my husband to hear tell of thee
   For ten thousand pounds of gold.

4. Oh, I am married to a ship carpenter
   And a ship carpenter I obey
   And by him I have a little son
   Or I would go along with thee.

5. What have you to maintain me on?
   Is it houses, land, gold, and fee?
   I've seven loaded ships a-sailing on the sea
   Besides the one that brought me to land.

6. She picked up her baby all in her arms
   And kissed it sweetlie embraced
   And laid it down on a soft bed of down
   And bid it to go to sleep.

7. As they walked down by the seashore
   The water is set running so bold
   The sides was lined with silver so bright
   And the top was the purest of gold.

8. As they sailed all on the sea
   The music did seem so sweet
   She thought of her babe she had left behind
   And set herself down to weep.

9. Are you weeping for my gold, said he?
   Are you weeping for fee?
   Or are you weeping for some other man
   That you love far better than me?

10. I'm not a-weeping for your gold
    Neither am I a-weeping for fee
    But I'm weeping to return to dry land again
    My poor little babe to see.

11. If you had ten thousand pounds of gold
    And would give it all unto me
    You never should return to dry land again
    Your babe you never will see.

12. What hills, what hills, my own true love,
    That look so white like snow?
    It's the hills of Heaven, my own true love
    Where all righteous people go.

13. What hills, what hills, my own true love,
    That look so dark and low?
    It's the hills of Hell, my own true love,
    Where you and I must go.

14. Straight news, straight news to the ship carpenter
    Straight news come back to the land
    The ship that his own dear wife sailed in
    Went sinking to the sand.

15. Sailors may be the worst of men
    That lead poor women astray
    The sailor has ruined the ship carpenter
    By deluding his poor wife away.

82. "Well Met, Well Met, My Own True Love"

Hammond, *JFSS*, III, No. 11 (1907), p. 84. Sung by Mrs. Russell, Upwey, Dorset, January 1907.

a D

This variant was superbly set for mixed voices by Vaughan Williams in 1915.

Well met, well met, my own true love,
Long time have I been absent from thee.
I am lately come from the salt sea,
And 'tis all for the sake, my love, of thee.

I have three ships all on the salt sea,
And (by) one of them has brought me safe to land.
I've four and twenty mariners on board;
You shall have music at your command.

The ship, my love, that you shall sail in,
It shall be of the fine beaten gold.
I've four and twenty mariners on board;
It is a beauty for to behold.

88. "Well Met, Well Met, My Old True Love"

Treat, *JAF*, LII (1939), p. 46. Sung by Mrs. M. G. Jacobs, Bryant, Wisc., September 1933 and September 6, 1938; learned from her mother.

p D

1. "Well met, well met, my old true love.
   Well met, well met," said he.
   "I have just returned from the salt, salt sea;
   And 'twas all for the sake of thee,
   And 'twas all for the sake of thee."

2. "I once could have married a king's daughter fair,
   And she would have married me.
   But I refused that rich crown of gold,
   And it's all for the sake of thee."

3. "If you could have married a king's daughter fair
   I'm sure you're much to blame,
   For I am married to a house carpenter,
   And I think he's a fine young man."

4. "If you'll forsake your house carpenter
   And go along with me,
   I will take you where the grass grows green,
   {On the banks of the Sweet Willee }
   {On the banks of the Sweet Liberty} ,,

5. "If I forsake my house carpenter
   And go along with thee,
   What have you got for my support,
   And to keep me from slavery?"

6. "I have six ships sailing on the sea,
   The seventh one at land,
   And if you'll come and go with me
   They shall be at your command."

7. She took her babe into her arms
   And gave it kisses three,
   Saying, "Stay at home, my pretty little babe
   For to keep your father company."

8. She dressed herself in rich array
   To exceed all others in the town,
   And as she walked the streets around
   She shone like a glittering crown.

9. They had not been on board more than two weeks,
   I'm sure it was not three,
   Until she began to weep
   And she wept most bitterly.

10. "Are you weeping for your houses and your land,
    Or are you weeping for your store,
    Or are you weeping for your house carpenter
    You never shall see any more?"

11. "I'm not weeping for my houses nor my land,
    Nor I'm not weeping for my store,
    But I'm weeping for my pretty little babe
    I never shall see any more."

12. They had not been on board more than three weeks,
    It was not four I'm sure,
    Until at length the ship sprung a leak,
    And she sank to arise no more.

13. "A curse, a curse to all sea men!
    A curse to a sailor's life!
    For they have robbed me of my house carpenter
    And taken away my life."

GROUP AC

98. "The House Carpenter's Wife," or "The Daemon Lover"

Sung by Fred High, High, Ark., March 20, 1951. LC/AAFS, rec. No. 10,818(B10). Collected by Mrs. Irene Carlisle.

p M

1. Well met, well met, my own true love,
   Well met, well met, says he;
   I'm just returning from the salty water sea
   And it's all for the sake of you—
   And it's all for the sake of thee.

2. I once could have married a king's daughter O,
   And she would have married me.
   But I've just received [*for refused?*] the rich crown of gold,
   And it's all for the sake of you—
   And it's all for the sake of thee.

3. Well, if you could have married a king's daughter O,
   I'm sure you are to blame,
   For I have married a house carpenter
   And I think he's a nice young man—
   And I think he's a nice young man.

4. Will you leave your own true love
   And go along with me?
   I'll take you where the grass grows green
   On the banks of sweet Willie—
   On the banks of sweet Willie.

5. What have you got to maintain me on,
   Or keep me from slavery?

6. I have seventeen fine ships on board,
      Seventeen boatsmens or more,
   Seventeen that's a-sailing for sea,
      That shall be at your command—
      That shall be at your command.

7. She called her babe all to her knee,
      And kisses she give him three.
   Says, Stay at home, my sweet little babe,
      Keep your poppy good company—
      Keep your poppy good company.

8. She dressed herself all neat and clean,
      All ?fested o'er with green.
   Every town that she passed through
      They would take her to be some queen—
      They would take her to be some queen.

9. They hadn't been on sea two weeks,
      I'm sure it was not three,
   Till this young lady begin to weep,
      And she wept most bitterly—
      And she wept most bitterly.

10. Are you weeping for silver or for gold,
      [Or] Are you weeping for fear?
   Or are you weeping for the house carpenter
      That you left when you come with me here—
      That you left when you come with me here?

11. I'm am not weeping for silver or for gold,
      Or I am not a-weeping for fear,
   But I am weeping for the sweet little babe
      That I left when I come with you here—
      That I never shall see any more.

12. They hadn't been (gone) on sea three weeks,
      I'm sure it was not four,
   Till this young lady she sprang from the ship,
      And she sank for to rise no more—
      And she sank for to rise no more.

13. A curse, a curse to all sea-men,
      A curse, a curse, cried she.
   You've robbed me of my sweet little babe
      And stolèd my life away—
      And stolèd my life away.

111. "House Carpenter"

Sung by Dan Tate (66), with banjo, Fancy Gap, Va., July 10, 1962. LC/AAFS, rec. No. 12,006(A26). Collected by George Foss.

m M (inflected VII)

Well met, well met, my old true love,
   Well met, well met, said she.
For seven long years I've been sailing on the ocean
   And it's all for the love of thee.

For I could have married a king's daughter dear,
   Being she would have married me.
But I refused her crown of gold,
   It was all for the love of thee.

129. "The Daemon Lover," or "Well Met"

Sung by Mr. Dol Small, Nellysford, Va., September 13, 1950. LC/AAFS, rec. No. 10,004(A2). Collected by Maud Karpeles and Sidney Robertson Cowell.

m I/Ly

1. Well met, well met my old true love,
      Well met, well met says she.
   I'm just returning from the salt salt sea,
      And it's all for the sake of thee.
   I'm just returning from the salt salt sea,
      And it's all for the sake of thee.

2. I could have married a king's daughter,
      And she would have married me.
   But I did slight the crowns of gold
      And it's all for the sake of thee.
   But I did slight the crowns of gold
      And it's all for the sake of thee.

3. If you could have married a king's daughter,
      I'm sure you are to blame,
   For I have married a house carpenter
      And they say he's a nice young man.
   For I have married a house carpenter
      And they say he's a nice young man.

4. Won't you forsake your house carpenter,
      And go along with me?
   I'll take you where the grass grows green,
      On the banks of sweet Willie.
   I'll take you where the grass grows green,
      On the banks of sweet Willie.

5. The ship had not been gone yet quite two weeks,
    I'm sure it was not three,
   Before this lady she began to weep,
    And she wept most bitterly,
   Before this lady she began to weep,
    And she wept most bitterly.

6. Are you weeping for your house carpenter,
    Or are you weeping for your store?
   Or are you weeping for your sweet little babes
    Whose face you'll see no more?
   Or are you weeping for your sweet little babes
    Whose face you'll see no more?

7. I'm not a-weeping for my house carpenter,
    Neither am I weeping for my store.
   But I am a-weeping for my sweet little babes
    Whose face I'll see no more.
   But I am a-weeping for my sweet little babes
    Whose face I'll see no more.

8. Now this is a warning to all young men
    Who try to get themself a wife.
   They'll take you from your house carpenter,
    And they'll cause you to lose your life.
   They'll take you from your house carpenter
    And they'll cause you to lose your life.

Young Allan

CHILD NO. 245

FOR this ballad four fairly distinct tunes, or tune-families, have been recorded. Christie's tune, which he says he can trace back to eighteenth century tradition, is unique, so far as the record goes. The characteristic fourth phrase is found as the opening of other ballads: e.g., cf. Nos. 32 86, 97, 209 (Kinloch).

The second type occurs in a dozen examples collected by Greig and Duncan. The tune is usually π^3, authentic, but occasionally includes also the plagal range.

It may be observed that the ship endowed with human intelligence and purpose, noted by Child as "by far the most in-teresting feature" of the ballad, had all but vanished by the beginning of the present century. Only one of Greig's copies (Bell Robertson's, without a tune) keeps it surely. Another shows a trace, but almost diminished to a metaphor—had we not known of supernaturally responsive boats since Homer (see Child's headnote). Indeed, on a particularly memorable night during the siege of Troy, in Pandarus' house, one of the distinguished company told such a magical tale, while the storm howled outside. (Cf. Chaucer, *Troilus and Criseyde*, Bk. III, line 614.)

TUNES WITH TEXTS

GROUP A

1. "Young Allan"

Christie, I, 1876, p. 252. From the singing of an old woman of Buckie, Banffshire, who died at 80 in 1866; her father was a famous ballad-singer in Buckie in the eighteenth century.

m M

As all the skippers o' Scarboro'
  Sat drinking at the wine;
There fell a-roosing them amang,
  On an unsealy time.
And some there roos'd their hawk, their hawk,
  And some there roos'd their hound;
But young Allan roos'd his comely cog,
  As she stood on dry ground.

[*Etc.*]

Christie's text is "epitomized" from Buchan (*Ancient Ballads and Songs of the North of Scotland*, 1828, II, p. 11), with some alterations from his memory of the sung version.

GROUP B

2. "Young Allan"

Duncan MSS., "Airs," p. 10; "Words," p. 177. From William Duncan, Rothienorman, who learned it from farm servants in boyhood. Words from Mrs. Gillespie. Noted 1905.

a π^3

1. A' the sailors in Merry London
   An they were drinking wine
   They fell a reasoning among themselves
   About some unlucky time.

Chorus:

Young Allan he grat an he wrang his hands
  An kent na well fer to dae
For the wind wis loud an the waves wis proud
  An weel a be lost by sea.

2. Some o thim praised their ladies gay
   An some o thim their wine
   But Young Allan he praised his bonnie new ship
   For she cost him mony a pound.

Chorus.

3. O what will ye wager wi me my boys
    O what will ye wager wi me
  That there's nae a ship in a' the coast
    To morrow will sail wi me.

    Chorus.

4. Except the rose o the heckling game
    An the decks o the dorminee
  An the muckle black snake wi her lee lang end
    I winna count in the three.

    Chorus.

5. Out it spake a little wee boy
    That sat by young Allan's knee
  Said ye lee ye lee young Allan he cried
    Sae loud's I hear you lee.

    Chorus.

6. My father has a bonnie boat
    To morrow will sail wi thee
  An thirty times the lee lang nicht
    She'll turn the wind wi thee.

    Chorus.

6a. There's nane o' them took to their ships
    Till they got mess an' dine,
  An' they took fare weel o' their sweethearts,
    An' took to their ships syne.

    Chorus.

7. They sailed east an they sailed west
    Out our the ragin main
  Till they saw the Rose o the Heckling Game
    Sink down among the fame.

    Chorus.

8. They sailed east an they sailed west
    Out our the ragin main
  Till they saw the deck o the Dorminee
    Wi her top mast rent in twain.

    Chorus.

9. They sailed east an they sailed west
    Out our the ragin main
  Till the muckle Black Snake wi her lee lang end
    Sank never to rise again.

    Chorus.

10. O where will I get a boy sae kind
    That'll tak my helm in hand
  Till I go up to my high top mast
    To look out for some dry land.

    Chorus.

11. Here am I a little wee boy
    That'll tak yere helm in hand
  Till ye gang up to your high top mast
    To look out for some dry land.

    Chorus.

12. Come down come down young Allan he cried
    Ye see not what I see
  For through an through yere bonnie ship's sails
    I see the Greenland (sic) Sea.

    Chorus.

13. O where will I get a clever boy
    That'll tak my ship in hand
  An if he brings me safe on shore
    he'll wed my daughter Ann.

    Chorus.

14. Hell hae the ae half o' my gear
    An the third part o my land
  An if he brings me safe on shore
    Hell wed my daughter Ann.

    Chorus.

15. Here am I a clever wee boy
    That'll tak yere ship in hand
  An gin I bring ye safe on shore
    Ill wed your daughter Ann.

    Chorus.

16. I'll hae the ae half o your gear
    An the third part o your land
  An gin I bring ye safe to shore
    Ill wed your daughter Ann.

    Chorus.

17. Y'ell tak [four an] twenty feather beds
    An busk yere bonnie ship roun
  An as much o the canvas claith
    As gar her gang hale an soun.

    Chorus.

18. An where ye want an iron nail
    Yell ca' a siller pin
  An where ye want an oaken spale
    Yell beat the yellow gold in.

    Chorus.

19. An where he wanted an iron nail
    He caad a siller pin
  An where he wanted an oaken spale
    He beat the yellow gold in.

    Chorus.

20. The firstan shore that they came tull
    It was the shore o ?Lynes
  Wi guns an swords they held them out
    An widna lat them in.

    Chorus.

21. The nextan shore that they came tull
    Wis bonnie Aberdeen

Wi pipes play'n an merry dancin
They welcomed young Allan in.

Chorus.

22.   I'll hae the a half o yere gear
      An the third part o yere land

An since Ive brought ye safe on shore
I'll wed yere daughter Ann.

Chorus.

"There should be another verse, stating that he drowned him, instead of giving him his daughter." [*Duncan's MS. note*].

The Grey Cock, or, Saw You My Father?

CHILD NO. 248

THE text of this ballad is in no very satisfactory state. As it stands in the first printed form, Herd's of 1769, there are but four stanzas (one, four, six, and seven of the text printed by Child) and it can hardly be maintained that the three added in 1776 are a great improvement, or do more than bridge the most palpable gaps in the readiest way. We still do not guess why the lassie asks after her father or mother—unless to throw some one off the track, or to make the conventional *three*, the first two of which are always rejected. But indeed, of whom should she ask such a question at all, since what she would most wish to conceal is that she is waiting to admit her lover. If the answer, and not merely her rationalizing thought, be given in the second stanza, the wonder is increased: some one knows too much and is acting as go-between, or knows not enough and is acting presumptuously. And why should the lassie ask the go-between about her own parents, or how should Johnnie, cooped up as he is, be able to send a messenger? Stanza three is a paltry and unballadlike modern invention.

We may suppose, then, that we have some very unskillful cobbling, more in the manner of the broadside hack than of hugger-mugger tradition. Child is quite right, surely, in hazarding a guess that the opening is indebted to "Sweet William's Ghost" (No. 77), where it makes complete sense. It is a *revenant*, there, who tirls at the pin, and elicits the question:

> Is that my father, or is it my brother,
> Or is it my true-love John?

Or so it might run if we had a closer text for parallel. The pointlessness of the opening in the present context makes it almost certain that something of the other kind lies behind this. One notes besides that the palpably *earthly* character of the returning lover in Herd's third stanza, with John's face reddening angrily while he waits for the family to settle to sleep, is established in the later addition.

If such be the truth, we may infer that this is a humorous or serio-comic *rifacimento* of a tragic ballad. Here, then, we might assume at an earlier stage a serious use of the "bird of dawning" to warn the spirit to take his departure. And in fact that is what happens in "Sweet William's Ghost" (No. 77): "Up and crew the red, red cock, And up and crew the gray"— and the lover vanishes into the grave. Child noted (1882-98, IV, p. 389) that an Irish ballad "descriptive of the visit of a lover's ghost to his betrothed" had been cited (from P. W. Joyce) by A. P. Graves, in *Irish Songs and Ballads*, 1880 (Child's date is 1882), "in which the woman, to protract the interview, says:

> O my pretty cock, O my handsome cock,
> I pray you do not crow before day,
> And your comb shall be made of the very beaten gold,
> And your wings of the silver so gray"—

almost the same words as the lassie utters in the present song. Joyce published the whole song in his *Old Irish Folk Music and Songs*, calling it "The Lover's Ghost" (see variant 12; there are slight verbal differences in the passage quoted). But in this Irish version the situation is reversed, and it is the girl who returns to her living lover.

It is to be noted that Karpeles' Newfoundland texts (variants 3, 4, 5, of which the last is given here) restore the roles of the lovers and are much closer to the pattern of "The Grey Cock" than are the first two stanzas of Joyce. Yet the last stanza of Joyce corresponds to stanzas in the Karpeles versions, and also to both versions from Nova Scotia, where, however, it is again the girl who returns. This element, proper to the *revenant*, is of course lacking in the Scottish ballad. The last stanzas of Karpeles' texts, on the other hand, as well as similar verses in several other versions, seem imported as the familiar commonplace for "never," and not quite at home in this context. Interestingly enough, Sharp's text from North Carolina, sadly corrupted, ends with desertion, which is a natural result when the "never" figure is used of the living rather than the dead. There is surely no necessary reason for believing with the Maine editors that the cock in the song is a supernatural bird. Where in ghost lore is it suggested that it is not an earthly cock which warns spirits of the approach of day—and, for that matter, earthly lovers as well? In the famous lines of Child No. 77 B, so often discussed, it is most definitely with this middle earth that chanticleer has to do: "Cocks are crowing a merry mid-larf."

It is probably idle to speculate on the possibility that Shakespeare had in mind ancestors of these songs when he wrote Ophelia's lines. But the question, "How should I your true love know?" follows naturally enough after the opening enquiry of this ballad in its earlier state; and the answer that the lover is dead would be an appropriate sequence in the narrative, which would proceed with the ghost's return. The "St. Valentine's Day" song, however, seems to belong to the more lighthearted and worldly branch. Its second stanza comes close to versions of "The Grey Cock." There was, of course, a plentiful supply, in Elizabethan England and elsewhere, of songs on the night visit. (Cf. C. R. Baskerville, *PMLA*, XXXVI [1921], pp. 565-614. Neither are Shakespeare's two songs in the same metre; nor is either of them in the metre of "The Grey Cock," although "St. Valentine's Day" is in CM, like "Sweet William's Ghost." By an odd coincidence, one Irish tune on this subject (Petrie, *Complete Collection of Irish Music*, No. 580) with the telltale title "Song of the Ghost," but lacking words, is a suggestively close variant of the older forms of "How should I your true-love know." (Cf. "Walsingham," in Chappell, *Popular Music* [1855-59], I, p. 123.)

In view of all this textual crossing and counter-crossing, it is curious to observe that the extant tunes as well have apparent interconnections. The "Saw you my father?" form of the ballad appeared in English and Scottish record at almost the same moment; and "The Lover's Ghost" may have been circulating in Ireland not long after. The tune of the first was given by Neil Stewart, *A Collection of Scots Songs*, Edinburgh, 1772, according to Glen (*Early Scottish Melodies*, 1900, p. 55) and often thereafter. It is a major, authentic, tune on a familiar pattern which could be either Scots or English, but more probably English. A second subgroup, but related none the less, begins with a Newfoundland tune. The range has been shortened upwards, but falls easily. The tune starts in the major, then develops a strongly Mixolydian feeling, then (in two variants) abandons the earlier tonic and drops a fifth for its final. Technically, then, it is a major. The Irish tunes, and those from Nova Scotia, make a third subgroup inclining to minor modes. Hughes' copy (variant 8) is a mixed M/D. Joyce's (variant 12 below) is an authentic tune with an inflected VI, major in ascending, minor in descending, passages; hence D-Æ impartially. The Irish tunes are unusually beautiful and interesting.

TUNES WITH TEXTS

GROUP A a

1. "O Saw ye my Father?"

Johnson, I [1787], No. 76, p. 77 (repr. 1853). Also in Urbani, II [1794], p. 45; Smith [1820-24], VI, p. 78; Graham [1848-49], I, p. 102; Chappell [1855-59], II, p. 731; and Eyre-Todd [1894], p. 140.

a I

1. O Saw ye my Father, or saw ye my Mother,
   Or saw ye my true love John
 I saw not your Father, I saw not your Mother,
   But I saw your true love John.

2. It's now ten at night, and the stars gi'e nae light,
   And the bells they ring, ding dong;
 He's met wi' some delay, that causeth him to·stay,
   But he will be here ere long.

3. The surly auld carl did naething but snarl,
   And Johny's face it grew red;
 Yet tho' he often sigh'd, he ne'er a word reply'd,
   Till all were asleep in bed.

4. Up Johny rose, and to the door he goes,
   And gently tirled the pin;
 The lassie taking tent, unto the door she went,
   And she open'd, and let him in.

5. And are you come at last, and do I hold ye fast,
   And is my Johny true!
 I have nae time to tell, but sae lang's I like mysell,
   Sae lang shall I love you.

6. Flee up, flee up, my bonny gray cock,
   And craw when it is day;
 Your neck shall be like the bonny beaten gold,
   And your wings of the silver grey.

7. The cock prov'd false, and untrue he was,
   For he crew an hour o'er soon;
 The lassie thought it day, when she sent her love away,
   And it was but a blink of the moon.

GROUP A b

5. "The Lover's Ghost," or "The Little Fishes"

Karpeles MSS., No. 5148; text, p. 4661. Also in Karpeles, 1934, II, p. 108. Sung by Matthew Aylward, Stock Cove, Bonavista Bay, Newfoundland, September 20, 1929.

a I (but M feeling)

1. She said unto her mamma, she said unto her dada:
   There's something the matter with me
 There's something the matter and I don't know what it is
   And I'm weary from lying alone.

2. John he came there at the very hour appointed,
   He tapped at the window so gay.
 This fair maid arose and she hurried on her clothes
   And let her true love John in.

3. She took him by the hand and on the bed she laid him,
   Felt he was colder than clay.
 If I had my wish and my wish it would be so,
   This long night would never be morn.

4. Crow up, crow up, my little bird.
   And don't crow before it is day
 And your cage shall be made of the glittering gold, she says,
   And your doors of the silver so gay.

5. Where is your soft bed of down, my love, she cries,
   And where is your white holland sheet,
 And where is the fair maid that watches on you
   While you are taking your long silent sleep.

6. The sand is my soft bed of down, my love, he cried,
   The sea is my white holland sheet,
 And long hungry worms will feed off of me
   While I'm taking my long silent sleep.

7. O when will I see you, my love, she cries,
   And when will I see you again?
 When the little fishes flies and the seas they do run dry
   And the hard rocks they melt with the sun.

GROUP AC

8. "The light of the moon"

Hughes, II, 1915, p. 64. Learned "from my old nurse, Ellen Boylan," County Derry.

m M/D

It was on a moonlight night when the stars were shining bright,
    A young maid was sighing all alone.
She was sighing for her father, lamenting for her mother,
    Shedding tears for her true lover John.

Young John he's come at last and the doors were bolted fast,
    And slowly he tinkled on the ring.
And up this maid arose and she bundled on her clothes,
    And it's all to let her true lover in.

O ye bird of early dawn, O ye well-feathered bird,
    Do you not crow before it is day,
And I will make your comb of the weather beaten gold
    And your wings of the light silver grey.

Now this bird he crew false, he crew very, very false,
    He crew two long hours before it was day,
And she thought that it was day and she sent her love away
    But it was only the light of the moon.

Reprinted by permission of the publishers, Boosey & Hawkes, Inc.

9. "Fly Up My Cock," or "The Grey Cock" ["Lover's Ghost"]

BBC Sound Archives, rec. No. 24841. Sung by Robert Cinnamond, Ireland, August 1955. Collected by Sean O'Boyle.

a D

I. . . . .   tender
    Where to find him I don't know
    But may kind Providence protect him
    And send me back my Woodley O.
                [Wu(d)lly? = Willie?]

2. As May lay sleepin' her lover came creepin'
    To her bed-chamber door so slow,
    Sayin' Arise up, rise up, O lovely Mary.
    Weep no more for your Woodley O.

3. May arose and put on her clothing,
    Till her bed-chamber door did go,
    And 'twas there she found her true love Woodley
    And his face was as white as snow.

4. Laddy, where are the blushes
    That you had some years ago?
    O Mary dear, it is death has changed them
    For I'm the ghost of your Woodley O.

5. It's seven long years that I have been writing
    To the Bay of Biscay O,
    But cruel death brought me no answer
    From my own true Woodley O.

6. They spent some time in conversation
    Concerning their courtship of years ago,
    And 'twas then they kissed and shook hands and parted
    As the cocks they began to crow.

7. When she saw him disappearing,
    Down her cheeks the tears did flow.
    He says, Mary dear, Sweetheart darling,
    Weep no more for your Woodley O.

12. "The Lover's Ghost"

Joyce, 1909, No. 408, p. 219. Learned by Joyce during his childhood in Glenosheen, County Limerick.

a D—Æ (inflected VI)

"Oh, you're welcome home again," said the young man to his
    love,
  "I am waiting for you many a night and day.
You are tired, you are pale," said this young man to his dear:
  "You shall never again go away."
"I must go away," she said, "when the little cock will crow,
  For here they will not let me stay:
But if I had my wish, Oh, my darling," she said,
  "This night should be never never day."

"Oh my pretty pretty cock, oh, my handsome little cock,
  I pray you will not crow before day;
And your comb shall be made of the very beaten gold,
  And your wings of the silver so grey!"

But oh, this pretty cock, this handsome little cock,
  He crew loud a full hour too soon:
"Oh, my true love," she said, "it is time for me to part,
  It is now the going down of the moon!"

"And where is your bed, my dearest dear?" he said,
  "And where are your white holland sheets?
And where are the maidens, my dearest love," he said,
  "That wait on you while you are asleep?"
"The clay is my bed, my dearest dear," she said,
  "The shroud is my white holland sheet;
The worms and the creeping things are my waiting maids,
  To wait on me whilst I am asleep."

Henry Martyn

CHILD NO. 250

"THE ballad," Child remarks, "must have sprung from the ashes of 'Andrew Barton,' of which name Henry Martyn would be no extraordinary corruption" (1882-98, IV, p. 393). *Must* is more than *may* to so cautious a scholar and the observation would at first glance seem tantamount to saying that No. 250 is a secondary form of No. 167. Nevertheless, it is obvious that he regarded them as distinct ballads, or he would not have given them separate places in the canon.

On what grounds, however, is not at all easy to determine. We should be able to assume that in Child's opinion every ballad in the collection either had a popular origin or is a surrogate for such a ballad, a more authentic form not having survived. Unquestionably, the present ballad is genuinely traditional. Not only is it still very much alive in oral circulation, but we have no hint of illegitimacy in origin, no suggestion by Child of traffic in the black market of the broadside press. What is the meaning of his metaphor, "sprung from the ashes"? In what sense is the new phoenix another, and in what is it the same? The phrase was only too happily chosen: it cannot be reduced to precise statement. It expresses perfectly Child's sense of a vital, spontaneous genesis for the younger ballad. But *ashes* imply, surely—for we must try to compel a statement from the myth—that there was a real cessation: the earlier ballad died. Had there been no actual break in the tradition there could be no justification for separating the two versions by number. Yet in the same sentence, Child suggests that the later name is a "corruption" of the earlier. In balladry, "corruption" is one of the clearest marks of genuine oral transmission. It implies the opposite of deliberate, willful alteration: an unconscious, uncontrolled substitution, produced by mishearing, misunderstanding, or forgetfulness. But such a change cannot occur in connection with beginnings: baptism is a deliberate act. What is implied, then, is continuity in oral tradition; between the last singer to use the name Barton and the first to use Martin there could be no gap either geographical or temporal. In that case, no matter how great the changes which ensue, the ballad is a single entity, and 167 and 250 are the same ballad. To uphold the alternative, of baptism, we should have to meet awkward questions, if we wished to cling to the old orthodoxy. For it would mean, would it not, that someone had possessed himself of a written text of the old ballad of "Andrew Barton"—note that it must have been *written*, because oral transmission has been rendered impossible by death—and deliberately made up a new ballad along similar lines, and called it "Henry Martin." This act of conscious invention would have to have been performed by a single individual some time in the eighteenth century, for the oral tradition of "Henry Martyn" goes back as far as 1800 and the "Barton" tradition is alive into the eighteenth century. But such an origin, and so late, would at once throw "Henry Martyn" out of the traditional canon, in obedience to the teaching of Gummere, who thought he was following Child in declaring that "only a definition by origins really defines" (*The Popular Ballad*, 1907, p. 14). For how could an interloper like this be other than an impostor? Therefore, if "Henry Martyn" be a genuine traditional ballad—and Child accepted it as such—and if it sprang from the ashes of an earlier but extinct authentic traditional ballad—and Child says it "must have" done so—: Child's most devoted disciples are caught on the horns of an interesting dilemma. They must reject their master's decision or give up their basic definition.

The easiest way out of the difficulty would be to regard the two ballads as in reality one, which has survived into the present century in a considerably altered form, like "Lady Isabel" (No. 4) and a good many others. Nor do I see reason, in the light of the dozens of variants which have been collected since Child's death, to deny a closer connection than he suspected.

In particular, the editors of *British Ballads from Maine* set down four heads under which they find a close correspondence between certain American texts and the older ballad. (Cf. *ibid.*, pp. 248-58.) These points are: (1) the name of the hero; (2) the name of the king; (3) the name of the pursuer; (4) the defeat of the pirate. Among these more recent variants, we find the name given as Andrew Bartin (Battan, Batan, Bardan, Bardun, Bardeen, Bardee, Bodee), or Andrew Martine, and Bolender (?Bold Andrew) Martin. The last two obviously exhibit a transitional stage in which the first name preserves the old, the last name the new, form. Bodee, it should be said, appears in Child's D; and the king in his C version is Henrie. In other versions, the king's name is revised to George. None of Child's versions except American E introduces a pursuer; but in this and other copies lately recovered, that character is named Stewart—Captain Charles Stewart, revised, for plausible reasons suggested by the Maine editors, from the Howard of the earlier ballads.

The "Henry Martyn" ballads fall into two classes, those in which the pirate is killed, as in "Sir Andrew Barton," and those in which he is victorious. The majority make the pirate the victor, and it is worthwhile to try to account for this shift. Both classes exist in two forms, a short and a long. In the first there is only one encounter; in the second there are two. Now, the earlier "Barton" ballads take account of two battles, one against a merchant, in which the pirate wins, the other against an avenging naval captain, in which the pirate is worsted. It is the second battle that gets fully described: the first is merely mentioned. It is obvious, in the general diminishment that has overtaken traditional balladry in latter days, that the two sea-fights would come to be described in more and more repetitive terms, so that except for the outcome, the incident would tend to be merely duplicated. With resemblance carried to such a point, the inclination to drop the one or the other encounter would be fairly sure to prove irresistible. Then, according to which fight is omitted, the pirate ends victorious or defeated. If the ballad recounts a fight between the pirate and a merchantman, in which the latter is defeated, there is no difficulty. It is simply a matter of forgetting the old termination and stopping short with the triumph of iniquity. Here, a reversal of fortune in the narrative follows as a matter of course. But where two fights are mentioned and the pirate remains victor, we need further explanation. We find it in a crossing with another pirate ballad, "Captain Ward and the Rainbow" (No. 287). In the "Henry Martyn" texts (and not in the "Barton" texts) there are often two striking features which provide confirmation of this influence. The first is that Martin is made to cry defiance before the battle in terms like the following (from Child E, 1882-98, V, p. 303):

> 'Come on! come on!' says Andrew Bartin,
> 'I value you not one pin:
> And though you are lined with good brass without,
> I'll show you I've fine steel within.'

The second is a final taunt after Bartin (or Martin) has defeated his antagonist:

'Go home! go home!' says Andrew Bartin,
  'And tell your king for me,
That he may reign king of the merry dry land,
  But that I will be king of the sea.'

(*Ibid.*)

Both these features are characteristic of "Captain Ward," and Child himself without hesitation pronounces them importations from that ballad. A good example of the simple mechanism of the iniquitous reversal is to be seen in Maine A (*British Ballads from Maine*, pp. 248-50), where the defeat of the merchantman is conveyed largely by implication and is in turn the provocation of Captain Charles Stewart's expedition. The latter is described in—*mutatis mutandis*—identical terms; an additional stanza recounts the battle with its routing of justice; and Battam's final taunt to the king, as above, ends the ballad.*

Child's A text of "Sir Andrew Barton" is in anapaestic tetrameter quatrains, a metre which perfectly accords with the 6/8 of the tune, "Come follow, my love." The B texts of that ballad are also in tetrameters, basically iambic—a metrical scheme which fits the tune readily enough. All the extant variants of that tune which I have seen are Scottish. It is noticeable that the one Scottish (Scotch-Irish more accurately) copy of

"Henry Martyn" printed by Child is also in LM, again anapaestic. One other northern variant recorded by Kidson compromises by having the metrical scheme 4.4.4.3. The vast majority, however, of the variants collected in the present century—in fact, perhaps all—are in CM anapaestic quatrains, or extensions, by refrain and repetition, to five- or six-line forms with or without a bridge. The musical tradition is strong and relatively homogeneous. Except in the prevailing 6/8 rhythm, I myself find little in the tune-family of "Henry Martyn" to suggest that of "Come follow, my love," with its constant tetrameter phrases. But it is possible that there may once have been a clearer connection. At any rate, the "Henry Martyn" family is one of the most widespread and interesting of all the melodic patterns current in tradition today.

Modally, the tunes run all the way from Ionian to Æolian, in heptatonic and hexatonic forms. Broadly speaking, there are two groups, one authentic, the other plagal. The authentic has the wider modal spread, the plagal confining itself to Ionian, I/M, and Mixolydian. The mid-cadence of the authentic tunes is nearly always on V, the first-phrase cadence on I; of the plagal tunes, the mid-cadence is generally III II, the first-phrase cadence on lower V.

* For a detailed analysis, coming to a conclusion opposite to the above, and distinguishing Nos. 167 and 250 as separate ballads, cf. A. K. Davis, Jr., *More Traditional Ballads of Virginia*, 1960, pp. 290-97.

TUNES WITH TEXTS

GROUP A a

8. "Andy Bardean"

Hubbard and Robertson, *JAF*, LXIV (1951), p. 49. Also in Hubbard, 1961, p. 32. Sung by Milas E. Wakefield, Ogden, Utah, August 12, 1948; learned in 1889 from Arlie Day at a sawmill in Huntington Canyon, Emery County, Utah.

a I

1. Three loving brothers from Old Scotland,
   Three loving brothers were they,
   They all cast lots to see which would go
   A-robbing all on the salt sea.

2. The lot it fell to young Andy Bardean,
   The youngest one of the three,
   To maintain himself and his brothers too
   He went robbing all on the salt sea.

3. He had not sailed scarce three cold winters' nights
   When a ship he did espy,
   Sailing far off, a-sailing far off,
   And at length it came sailing close by.

4. "Who's there, who's there?" cried Andy Bardean;
   "Who's there that sails so nigh?"
   "We're three merchant vessels from old England shore.
   Won't you please to let us pass by?"

5. "Oh no, oh no," said Andy Bardean,
   "Such a thing as that never could be,
   For I'll take your ship and your cargo, boys,
   But your bodies I'll sink in the sea."

6. Then broadside to broadside the two vessels sailed,
   And cannons did loudly roar
   Until Andy Bardean gained the victory,
   And the rich merchant vessel gave o'er.

7. The news soon reached to the ears of the king.
   Young Alfred then wore the crown.
   He said, "Is there anyone here I can find
   That will run young Andy Bardean down?"

8. "Go build me a ship," said Captain Charles Stewart;
   "Go build it strong and sure,
   And if I don't bring in that young Andy Bardean,
   My life I'll no longer endure."

9. The ship it was ricketed and ready for sail
   With guns and men galore,
   And one cold, frosty morning the anchor she weighed
   And sailed from old England shore.

10. They had not sailed scarce three cold winter nights
    When a ship he did espy,
    Sailing far off, sailing far off,
    And at length it came sailing close by.

11. "Who's there, who's there?" cried Captain Charles Stewart,
    "Who's there that sails so nigh?"
    "We're three bold robbers from old Scotland shore:
    Won't you please to let us pass by?"

12. "Oh no, oh no," cried Captain Charles Stewart,
    "Such a thing as that never could be,
    For I'll sink your ship and your cargo, boys,
    But your bodies I'll carry with me."

13. Then broadside to broadside the two vessels sailed,
    And cannons did loudly roar
    Till Captain Charles Stewart was forced to give up,
    And he sailed for Old England shore.

14. "Go back, go back," cried Andy Bardean,
    "And tell your king for me
    That he may reign king over the dry land,
    But I shall reign king on the sea."

12. "Henry Martin"

Vaughan Williams MSS., II, p. 272. Also in Vaughan
Williams, *JFSS*, IV, No. 17 (1913), p. 302. Sung by Mr.
Peter Verrall and his wife, Harriet, Horsham, Sussex, Oc-
tober 8, 1904.

a M

In Scotland, in Scotland, there lived brothers three,
In Scotland there lived brothers three,
And they did cast lots o'er the three, o'er the three, o'er the three,
To know which was to turn robber all on the salt sea, the salt
    sea,
To maintain his two brothers and he.

The lot it fell on Henry Martin,
The youngest of the three,

To go a scotch-robbing all on the salt sea, the salt sea,
To maintain his two brothers and he.

They had not sailed three cold winter's nights . . .

31. "Andrew Marteen"

Flanders and Olney, 1953, p. 73. Sung by Hanford Hayes,
Staceyville, Me., September 22, 1940. From *Ballads Migrant
in New England*, edited by Helen Hartness Flanders and
Marguerite Olney; copyright 1953 by Helen Hartness
Flanders.

p I (but inflected VII)

1. In bon-ey Scotland three brothers did dwell,
   Three brothers did dwell, the three,
   And all did cast lots to see which of them
   Would go robbing down on the salt sea.
   And all did cast lots to see which of them
   Would go robbing down on the salt sea.

2. The lots they fell on Andrew, fourteen,
   The youngest of those brothers three,
   That he should go robbing down on the salt sea
   To maintain his two brothers and he.
   That he should go robbing down on the salt sea
   To maintain his two brothers and he.

3. As he was a-sailing one fine summer's morning
   Just as the day did appear,
   He spied a large vessel a-sailing far off
   And at last she came sailing quite near.

4. "Art thou, art thou?" cried Andrew Marteen,
   "Art thou, a-sailing so high?"
   "A rich merchant-ship from Old England's shores
   And please will you let me pass by?"

5. "O no, O no," cried Andrew Marteen,
   "It's a thing that can't very well be;
   Your ship and your cargo I will take away,
   And your body feed to the salt sea."

6. The news it went back to Old England's shore.
   King Henry he wore the crown.
   His ship and his cargo were all cast away
   And his mariners they were all drowned.

7. "Come build me a boat," cried Captain Charles Stewart,
   "And build it both safe and secure,
   And if I don't bring in that Andrew Marteen,

My life I will never endure.
And if I don't bring in that Andrew Marteen,
My life I will never endure."

8. As he was a-sailing one fine summer's morning,
Just as the day did appear,
He spied a large vessel a-sailing far off,
And at length it came sailing quite near.

9. "Art thou, art thou?" cried Captain Charles Stewart,
"Art thou a-sailing so high?"
"A Scotch bone-y robber from Old Scotland's shore,
And it's please will you let me pass by?"

10. "O no, O no," cried Captain Charles Stewart,
"It's a thing that can't very well be;
Your ship and your cargo I will take away,
And your body feed to the salt sea."

11. "Fire on, fire on!" cried Andrew Marteen,
"Your talk I don't value one pin.
Your brass at your side makes a very fine show
But I'm pure steel within."

12. Broadside to broadside those two came together;
Their cannons like thunder did roar.
When Captain Charles Stewart took Andrew, fourteen,
And they hung him on Old England's shore.

GROUP A b

33. "Henry Martin"

Sung by Philip Tanner, Gower, South Wales. Columbia rec. No. 372-M (CA 16052). Also on Caedmon rec. No. TC 1146(B3).

a D

1. There livèd in Scotland three brothers three,
In Scotland there lived brothers three.
And they did cast lots for to see which of them,
which of them, which of them,
Should go sailing all on the salt sea.

2. The lot it fell out on young Henry Martin
The youngest of these brothers three,
That he should go sailing all on the salt sea,
salt sea, salt sea,
To maintain his two brothers and he.

3. We had not long been sailing on a cold winter's morning,
Three hours before it was day,
Before we espièd a lofty tall ship,
a tall ship, a tall ship,
Coming sailing all on the salt sea.

4. "Hallo, hallo," cried bold Henry Martin,
"How dare you come sailing so nigh?"
"We're a rich merchant ship bound for old England,
old England, England,
Will you please for to let us pass by?"

5. "O no, no, no," cried bold Henry Martin,
"That never, no never can be.
For I am turned pirate to rob the salt sea,
salt sea, salt sea,
To maintain my two brothers and me."

6. "Take down your toproyal, cut away your mainmast,
Come hither in under my lee.
For I will take from you all of your flowing [?glowing] gold,
flowing [?glowing] gold, flowing gold,
And return your fair bodies to the sea."

7. Then broadside and broadside we valiantly fought,
We fought for four hours or more.
Till Henry Martin gave her a dead shot,
a dead shot, a dead shot,
And down to the bottom she goes.

8. Bad news, bad news, you English heroes,
Bad news I have for to tell;
There's one of your rich ships lies sunk off the land,
off the land, off the land,
And all of your merry men drowned.

36. "Henry Martyn"

Sharp MSS., 510/. Also in Sharp and Marson, 2nd series, 1905, p. 6; Baring-Gould and Sharp [1906], No. 10(2), p. 22; and Sharp, 1916, p. 1. Sung by Lucy White, Hambridge, April 19, 1905.

a D

O no no says Henry Martyn
O no that never can be
For I am turned robber all on the salt seas salt seas salt seas
For to maintain my two brothers & me.

Lang Johnny More

CHILD NO. 251

ALL the variants of this simple piece of Scottish pride belong together. Nearly all are plagal π^1, or virtually π^1, tunes in a quick duple rhythm with a refrain. The mid-cadence is usually on V, the first cadence on II. Two subtypes may be distinguished, according as the tune uses the full authentic plus plagal range, or only the plagal.

Child calls attention to the close parallel between this ballad and "Johnie Scot" (No. 99). The present improves upon the other by transferring the physical advantage of the King's champion, a fearsome "Talliant" (Italian), to the hero himself.

The transfer is more in accord with the national reputation; and the ballad, parody or not, has clearly superseded the other in popular esteem in its homeland.

A story was told in the First World War of a company of Cockneys being withdrawn from engagement at the front, to be relieved by Highlanders. As they passed one another, the height of the Highlanders excited some humorous jibes from the English; to which the Scots, looking down good-naturedly, replied, "Ay, and when ye get hame, ye can tell them ye've seen the so'diers."

TUNES WITH TEXTS

GROUP A a

8. "Lang Johnnie More"

Archive, School of Scottish Studies, rec. No. 1952/27/A6. Also on Caedmon, rec. No. TC 1146(B4). Sung by John Strachan, Fyvie, 1952. Collected by Hamish Henderson. Transcribed by Francis M. Collinson.

m π^1

1. There lives a man in Ryvie's land,
   An' anither in Auchindore,
   Bit the bravest among them a'
   Wis Lang Johnnie More.

   Chorus:

   A reedle a, nilden naddie,
   A reedle a, nilden nee.

2. Young Johnnie wis a cliver youth,
   A sturdy, stoot an' strang,
   An' the sword that hung by Johnnie's side
   Was fully sax feet lang.

   Chorus.

3. An' if a' be true that they do say,
   An' if a' be true we hear,
   Young Johnnie's on to fair England,
   The king's standard to bear.

   Chorus.

4. He hidnae been in fair Londin
   A year but barely three,
   The fairest lady in a' Londin
   Fell in love wi young Johnnee.

   Chorus.

5. Word's gane up, and word's gane doon,
   An word's gane to the king,
   That a muckle Scot has fau'n in love
   Wi's daughter, Lady Jean.

   Chorus.

6. 'A' if a' be true that they do say,
   An' that ye tell to me,
   This michty Scot shall strett the rope
   An' hangit he shall be.'

   Chorus.

7. But oot it spake young Johnnie then;
   This word's pronounced he:
   'While I hae strength to wield my blade,
   Ye daurna ha' hung me.'

   Chorus.

8. But the English lads are cunnin' rogues
   An' roon' him they did creep,
   and they gie'd him drams o' lodomy
   Till he fell fast asleep.

   Chorus.

9. When Johnnie wakent frae his sleep,
   A sorry man wis he,
   Wi' his jows an' hands in iron bands
   An' his feet in fetters three.

   Chorus.

10. 'Faur will I get a bonnie boy,
    Will win baith meat an' fee,
    An' will run on til my uncle
    At the fuit o' Benachie?'

    Chorus.

11. 'Oh here am I, a bonnie boy,
    Will win baith meat an' fee,
    An' will rin on tae your uncle
    At the fuit o' Benachie.'

    Chorus.

12. 'Fen ye come on to Benachie,
    Pey it neither chap nor ca',
    Sae weel's ye'll ken aul' Johnnie there,
    Three fit abeen them a'.

    Chorus.

13. 'Ye'll gie to me this braid letter
    Seal'd wi' my faith an' troth,
    An ye'll bid him bring alang wi him
    The body Jock o Noth.'

    Chorus.

14. 'Fat news, fat news, my bonnie boy,
    You never was here afore?'
    'Nae news, nae news, bit a braid letter
    Frae your nephew, Johnnie More.'

    Chorus.

15. Benachie lies very low,
    An the tap o Noth stands high,
    Bit, fir aa the distance that lies atween,
    They heard auld Johnnie cry.

    Chorus.

16. When on the plain the champions met,
    Two grisley ghaists to see,
    There was three feet atween their brous
    An their shouders braid yairds three.

    Chorus.

17. Those men they ran owre hills and dales
    And over mountains high,
    Till they arrived in fair England
    At the dyin o the day.

    Chorus.

18. When they arrived at fair Londin,
    The yetts were lockit in,
    An fo was there but a trumpeter
    Wi' a trumpet in his haun?

    Chorus.

19. 'Fat's the maitter?' old Johnnie says,
    'Oh fat's the maitter wi them,
    That the drums do beat, an' the bells do ring,
    An make sic a dolefu din?'

    Chorus.

20. 'Naething's the maitter,' the keeper said,
    "Naething's the maitter to thee,
    'Bit a wechty Scott to strett the rope,
    An to-morrow he maun dee.'

    Chorus.

21. 'Open the yetts', aul Johnnie said,
    'Open the yetts, I say.'
    The tremmlin keeper smilin said,
    'Bit I haena got the key.'

    Chorus.

22. 'Open the yetts,' said Jock o' Noth,
    'Open them at my call.'
    An wi his fuit he his dung in
    Three yaird-widths o the wall.

    Chorus.

23. Syne they are doun throu fair Londin
    An doun by the toun-haa,
    An there they saw young Johnnie More
    Staund on the English waa.

    Chorus.

24. 'Ye're welcome here, my uncle dear,
    Ye're welcome here to me;
    Ye'll lowse the knot an slack the rope
    An tak me fae the tree.'

    Chorus.

25. 'Oh is't for murder, or for theft,
    Or is't for robberie?
    If it be for onie o these crimes,
    Thir's nae remeid for thee.'

    Chorus.

26. 'It's nae for murder, nor for theft,
    Nor yet for robberie;
    It's aa for loving a fair lady,
    This gyaun tae gar me dee.'

    Chorus.

27. 'Bring back his sword,' said Jock o Noth,
    'An freely to him gie,
    Or I hae sworn a braid Scots oath
    I'd gar five million dee.'

    Chorus.

28. 'Oh faur's the lady?' said Jock o Noth,
    'Sae fair's I would her see.'
    'She's lockt up in her ain chamber,
    The king he keeps the key.'

    Chorus.

29. So they hae gane afore the king,
    Wi courage bauld an free,
    Their armour brisht had sic a licht,
    It almost blinnd his ee.

    Chorus.

30. 'Faur is the lady?' said Jock o Noth
    'Sae fain I would her see,
    For I hae sworn a solemn oath,
    She's gyaun to Benachie.'

    Chorus.

31. 'Oh tak the lady,' the king he says,
    'Ye're welcome to her for me.
    Fir I niver thocht ye hid sic men,
    At the back o Benachie.'

    Chorus.

32. 'If I had kent,' said Jock o Noth,
    'Ye'd winner sae mickle at me,
    I wid a brocht ye bigger men
    Bi sizes three times three.'

    Chorus.

33. 'Bit wae betide that little wee boy,
    That tidings brocht to me:
    Let all England say what they will,
    It's hangit he shall be.'

    Chorus.

34. 'Oh if ye hang that little wee boy
    That's tidings brought to thee,
    He will attend the burial,
    An rewarded he shall be.'

    Chorus.

35. 'Oh tak the lady,' the king he said,
    'Ye're welcome to her for me;
    Oh tak the lady,' the king he said,
    'An the boy he shall go free.'

    Chorus.

36. 'A priest, a priest,' young Johnnie cried,
    'To join my love an me!
    'A clerk, a clerk', the king he cried,
    'To seal her tocher wee.'

    Chorus.

37. But oot it spak auld Johnnie then;
    This word's pronounced he:

'Oh he has lands and rents eneuch,
An' he'll seek nae gowd fae thee.'

Chorus.

38. They've taen the lady by the hand,
    An set her prison free;
    Wi drums beatin an fifes playin,
    They've on to Benachie.

    Chorus.

36. "The Beggar Man"

Archive, School of Scottish Studies, rec. No. 1958/8/A6.
Sung by Annie McDonald. Collected by Hamish Henderson. Transcribed by Alex Sinclair.

a M

A beggar man cam oer the lea
Seekin oot for charitie
. . . .
Would ye ludge a beggar man?
    Larity a tow-row-ray.

The night bein dark an somewhat wet
It's doon by the fireside the auld man sat
Doon . . . .
An aye as he riddled he sang
    Larity a tow-row-ray.

The Kitchie-Boy

CHILD NO. 252

THE Brown copy of this ballad differs from the rest in its metrical scheme, being in tetrameter quatrains (LM) instead of "ballad-metre" (CM). Mrs. Brown's tune has not survived, but presumably it would have been in a different line of tradition from those we have.

Greig's second tune once includes an unaccented Dorian sixth (variant 2). It is also authentic. Mrs. Harris's tune for "Sweet William's Ghost" (No. 77) is a near relation in a different metre.

TUNES WITH TEXTS

GROUP A

2. "The Kitchie-Boy"

Greig MSS., IV, p. 90; text, Bk. 769, LIX, p. 5. Also in Greig and Keith, 1925, p. 207(2); text, p. 206(B). From Annie Robb, Strichen.

a D

1.
    She's fa'en in love wi' her kitchie boy,
      And the greater was her shame.

2. He's gien him a ship, a ship,
    A ship o' muckle fame,
  And he sent him awa' to Flanders,
    And never see land again.

3. The ship being fair, the day being rare
    That that ship took the sea,

    .   .   .   .   .   .

He put a mask upon his face,
  For fear she wad him ken.

4. The lady she stood in her bower[1] door,
    Beheld baith[2] dale and doon,
  And she beheld a bonnie ship
    Cam' sailin' to the toon.

5. Bonnie, bonnie was the ship,
    And bonnier was her men;
  And bonnier was the bonnie skipper
    That was bringin' her thro' the faem.

6. Come up, come up, skipper, she said,
    Come up wi' me and dine;
  I thank you for your offer, lady,
    But I really hinna time.

  .   .   .   .

Oh, got ye't on the sea, sailor,
  Or got ye't on the sand?
Or got ye't at Flanders far
  Upon a droont man's hand?

I got not it on the sea, lady,
  I got not it on the sand;
But I got it at Flanders far
  Upon a droont man's hand.

For sorrow she tore her green mantle,
  For grief she tore her hair,—
Alas, alake, it's my love Willie,
  And I'll never see him mair.

[1] Variant in MS. ha'
[2] Variant in MS. a'

The Heir of Linne

CHILD NO. 267

So FAR as a melodic tradition can be made out for this ballad, it seems to lie adjacent to the "Cowdenknowes" tunes. Christie's tune, which he claims to follow back into the eighteenth century, is another one of those with ambiguous finals. The second half is doubtless Christie's drawing-room variation of the first half. The range is implausible. If the final be tonic, the tune is a plagal π^2; but the final might, if the "Cowdenknowes" pattern were more closely followed, be A: then possibly π^3 authentic. Christie quite properly refers to "O Mary turn awa" (*Scots Musical Museum*, No. 541) as a variant, and the latter tune ends on E. If E be tonic here, the tune becomes π^4, plagal. But also, G is a conceivable tonic: then π^1.

Greig's first tune (variant 3 below) seems of a different rise. It, clearly, is in a major tonality, though it lacks its sixth, by chance, as well as its seventh. But its final is not in doubt, and the tune is definitely I/M, plagal.

TUNES WITH TEXTS

1. "The Laird o' Linne"

Christie, I, 1876, p. 112. From family tradition traceable to mid-eighteenth century, in Buchan.

Disregarding second strain:
If tonic G, a π^1, ending on V, or p π^1, ending on V
If tonic D, p π^2

1. O yonder he stands, and there he gangs,
   The weary heir o' Linne;
   Yonder he stands on the cauld causey,
   And nane bids him come in.
   But it fell ance upon a day,
   The sheets were laid in fauld;
   And poor Willie found he had nae friends,
   And it was wondrous cauld.

2. "Oh, one sheave o' your bread, nourice,
   And one glass o' your wine;
   And I will pay you o'er again,
   When I am Laird o' Linne."
   "Oh, one sheave o' my bread, Willie,
   And one glass o' my wine;
   But the seas will be dry ere ye pay me again,
   For ye'll never be Laird o' Linne."

3. But he mind't him up, and he mind't him down,
   And he mind't him o'er again;
   And he mind't him on a little wee key,
   That his mother ga'e to him.
   He did him to the House o' Linne,
   He sought it up and down,
   And there he found a little wee door,
   And the key gaed slippin' in.

4. And he got gowd, and he got gear,
   He got gowd stor'd within;
   And he got gowd, and he got gear,
   Thrice worth the lands o' Linne.
   He did him to the tavern straight,
   Where nobles were drinking therein;
   The greatest noble among them a'
   Was near to Willie o' kin.

5. And some of them bade him fish to eat,
   And some of them bade him a fin;
   And some of them bade him nothing at a',
   For he'd never be father's son.
   But out it spake an aged knicht,
   And vow but he spake slie,—
   "I'll sell you your father's land back again,
   All for the third pennie."

6. "I take witness upon you here," he says,
   "I take witness upon thee,
   That you will sell me my father's land again,
   All for the third pennie."
   Then he took out a little wee coffer,
   And he set it on his knee;
   And he told the gowd doun on the table roun',
   Says, "Tak' up your third pennie."

7. "Come ben, come ben, my good nourice,
   I'll pay you, when you come ben,
   For the seas are not dry, and I'll pay you back again,
   For I'm again the Laird o' Linne."
   Poor Willie, that night at eight o'clock,
   Had his stockings abeen his sheen;
   But ere the morrow at twelve o'clock,
   He was convoy'd by lords sixteen.

GROUP B

3. "The Heir of Linne"

Greig MSS., IV, p. 20; text, Bk. 765, LV, p. 31. Also in
Greig and Keith, 1925, p. 212(1). From Alexander Robb,
New Deer.

p I/M (–VI)

He min't him up, & he min't him doon,
    And he min't him owre again;
He min't himsel' on a little key
    That his mother gae to him;
She bade him keep it till he should need it
    As sair's ony mither's ae son.

Witness, witness, witness, he said,
    It's witness I take o' thee
That ye'll gie me my father's lands back again,
    And for the third pennie.

Lady Diamond

CHILD NO. 269

THE melodic tradition for this ballad is probably single, though there is considerable variety in the four recorded tunes. It cannot, however, be claimed that there is much individuality in any of them.

Christie's tune is a clear plagal I/M, built in the order of "Gypsy Laddie" (No. 200) in the first strain, and allied in its second strain to the "Valentine's Day" tribe. It is to be compared especially with Greig's second tune (variant 4 below), and with Christie's tune for Child No. 270.

Duncan's tune (1 in Greig and Keith; here variant 3) is a π^1 tune, starting off somewhat like Christie's. Greig's second tune (variant 4 below) at first glance bears quite a different look from the other. It is an I/Ly tune, making use both of

authentic and plagal ranges. But it is noteworthy that its first half is authentic, its second half plagal. Now, on the contrary, Duncan's tune is really plagal in the first three phrases, but in the last phrase with its repetition, authentic, on the lower octave. The result is that, while both tunes are in adjoining modes, Greig's second tune starts as the authentic counterpart of the other's plagal opening. The parallel may be seen perhaps even more clearly if we compare Greig's second tune with Christie's opening phrase. Here is illustrated another way in which melodic variation can take place, even without a change of mode. Incidentally, Greig's second tune is probably badly barred in the last phrase, needing correction from the third cadence onward.

TUNES WITH TEXTS

GROUP Ab

2. "Lady Daisy"

Christie, II, 1881, p. 218 ("The Crusader's Farewell"). From the singing of a native of Banffshire, c. 1850.

p I/M

Christie's text has not been given because he set his tune to other words, feeling that those of "Lady Daisy" were "unsuited" to his work.

GROUP AC

3. "Eliza's Bowers, or Lady Diamond"

Duncan MSS., "Airs," p. 11, and "Words," p. 73. Also in Greig and Keith, 1925, p. 213(1). Sung by Mrs. Gillespie, Glasgow, in 1905; learned from her mother c. 1850.

m π^1

1. There lived a King an' a very great King
   A King o great renown [muckle fame?]
   He had a lovely daughter fair
   And Eliza was her name, name, an Eliza was her name.

2. Word's gaen up an word's gaun down
   An word's gaen to the King
   That Eliza goes right roun' about
   But to whom they dina keen, keen, but to whom they
   dinna keen

3. When bells were rung an mess wis sung
   An a' were bound for bed
   The King came to Eliza's bower
   But he was not a welcome guest, guest, he was not a
   welcome guest

4. . . . .
   . . . .
   Come tell to me Eliza dear
   To whom you go so round, round, to whom you go so
   round

5. Is't till a laird or is't tull a lord
   Or to any Baronee
   Come tell to me Eliza dear
   An I pray ye dinna lee, lee, an I pray ye dinna lee

6. Its nae tull a laird nor yet tull a lord
    Nor yet tull a Baronee,
  But its to Rodger the Kitchen boy
    What occassion hae I to lee, lee, what ocassion hae I
        to lee

7. He's called his merry men a' by one
    By one by two an' by three O
  At last came Rodger the Kitchen boy,
    An he dashed him to a tree, tree, an he dashed him to a
        tree

8. He's te'an out this bonnie boy's heart
    Put it on a plate o gold
  An he's sent it to Eliza's bower
    Because she was so bold, bold, because she was so bold

9. Adieu, adieu, adieu father
    I bid this world adieu
  Since my bonnie love has died for me
    I'll die for him also, so, I'll die for him also.

GROUP Ad

4. "Lady Dysie"

Greig MSS., IV, p. 126; text, Bk. 769, LIX, p. 19. Also in
Greig and Keith, 1925, p. 214(2). Sung by John Johnstone,
New Deer.

m I/Ly

They hae taen the little boy's heart,
    And stuck it on a spear,
And they've carried it to Lady Dyzie's bower,
    For a token that he'd been there.

Farewell father, and farewell mother,
    Farewell brothers three;
Ye thought ye had taken the life o' one,
    But you've taken the lives o' three.

Farewell father, an' farewell mother,
    Farewell pleasure and joy;
He died for me, I'll die for him,
    Tho' he was but a kitchen boy.

The Suffolk Miracle

CHILD NO. 272

ALL the oldest broadsides of this ballad are directed to be sung to the tune of "My Bleeding Heart." I have not identified a copy of this tune. To judge by its use with broadside ballads, it accommodated best the iambic tetrameter quatrain in couplet rhymes, and was most favored in the latter part of the seventeenth century. But it may be Elizabethan, for all that. The name, as noted by Rollins, *Pepys Ballads*, III, 1930, p. 21, comes from the first line of a broadside called, "A Warning to All Lewd Livers. . . . To the tune of *Sir Andrew Barton*" (*Roxburghe Ballads*, Part VII, Vol. III, 1875, ed. W. Chappell, pp. 22-28). But "Sir Andrew Barton" itself, as we have seen, was directed to be sung to "Come follow my love" (cf. No. 167). The latter tune, in extant copies, none so early as the seventeenth century, is properly in 6/8 metre, corresponding to the text, of Elizabethan date, of its own proper ballad. Cf. "The Fair Flower of Northumberland" (No. 9).

The extant tunes for the present ballad, at any rate, all seem to belong to a widespread type, favorite for lugubrious themes such as pathetic deaths, awful portents, and moralizing carols. To it belong "Death and the Lady," "Christmas now is drawing near at hand," "The Iron Peel," "Died for Love," etc. For some of these, cf. *JFSS*, V, No. 18 (1914), pp. 7ff. and the references there given. Also cf. Sharp, *One Hundred English Folksongs*, 1916, No. 22 and the notes. The simpler forms of this tradition conform with a most wooden and tedious regularity to an iambic dimeter rhythm, with every other accent held to the length of an added foot, e.g.,

> A handkerchief ($\smile$/)
> She said she tyed ($\smile$/)
> About his head ($\smile$/)
> And that they tryed ($\smile$/), etc.

Musically, this rhythm is best expressed in 3/2 time. But the variants of this type which have been recovered, both in England and in America, are surprisingly irregular in their timing, as will be evident in even the few examples that follow for the present ballad. The phrases of a tune of this sort will accommodate, without being unduly taxed, a line of six stresses, or of five, or of four; and all these varieties may be illustrated in the texts below. Pentameter couplets are generally found in "Death and the Lady" and the hymns; but the secular pieces appear to favor tetrameters.

So far as I have discovered, "The Suffolk Miracle" is no longer sung in England, and there is no indication that it has ever been current in Scotland—an odd fact, in view of its subject-matter and the very wide geographical spread of its continental analogues. Nor, I believe, has it been recovered in Ireland. The American copies are mostly Mixolydian. Sharp's copy from Small (variant 1 below) is especially close to familiar forms of "Died for Love" ("The Butcher's Boy").

Among the seventeenth-century broadsides, "My bleeding heart" as a tune for a ballad is frequently paired with "In Crete" as alternative or equivalent. The latter title comes from the first line of a ballad formerly well known and referred to by Nashe and Deloney. "My bleeding heart" is the opening of Martin Parker's subsequently popular ballad, earlier cited (*Roxburghe Ballads*, III, p. 23), and although the text therefore cannot be so old, it is barely possible that the tune merely took on another name, to identify it more readily. "In Crete" is given by Claude Simpson from William Ballet's lute-book (Claude M. Simpson, *The British Broadside Ballad and Its Music*, 1966, p. 363) and the tune has survived in more than one copy. As Simpson prints it, the 3/4 metre looks unfriendly to the iambic tetrameter couplets of our ballad-text; but it may as easily be read in 3/2 time, and is perfectly suitable to "The Suffolk Miracle."

TUNES WITH TEXTS

GROUP Aa

1a. "The Suffolk Miracle"

Sharp MSS., 4263/3062. Also in Sharp and Karpeles, 1932, I, p. 264(D). Sung by Adolphus G. Small, Nellysford, Nelson County, Va., May 22, 1918.

a M

1. There was[1] an old and wealthy man,
   He had a daughter great and grand.
   She were neat, handsome and tall,
   She had a handsome face withall.

2. A many a squire came this way,[2]
   This handsome lady for to see;
   But at length there were a widow's son,
   'Twas found he were her chosen one.

3. It's when her[3] old folks came this to know
   They sent him[4] two thousand miles from home,
   Which broke this young man's tender heart
   To think that he and his love must part.

4. It were[5] on a cold and stormy night,
   He started for his heart's delight;
   He rode till he came to the place he knew,
   Says he: My love, I've come for you.

5. It's your father's request, your mother's heed,
   I've come for you all in great speed,
   And in two weeks or a little more,
   I'll set you safe at your father's door.

6. They rode till they came to the old man's gate,
   He did complain his head did ache.
   With a handkerchief that he[6] had out,
   With it she tied[7] his head about.

7. They rode till they came to the old man's stile,
   Says he: My love, let's tarry awhile.
   Alight, alight, alight, says he,[8]
   And I will put your steeds away.

8. She knocked upon her father's door,
   The sight of her love[9] she saw no more.
   It's welcome home, my child, says he.
   What trusty friend hath[10] come with thee?

9. It's the one I love, I love so well,
   I love him better than tongue can tell.
   Which[11] made the hair stand on the old man's head,
   To think that he'd been twelve months dead.

10. Then princes grand and judges too
    Were sent for to witness this great one do (wonder?).[12]
    It's although[13] he had been twelve months dead,
    The[14] handkerchief were around his head.

11. Now this is warning to young and old
    Who love your[15] children better than gold;
    For if you love them give them their way
    For fear that love will lead astray.[16]

The following changes were made in Small's 1950 recording (1b, below):

[1] 1950: were
[2] 1950: There were many a guy there came this way.
[3] 1950: the
[4] 1950: her
[5] 1950: was
[6] 1950: she
[7] 1950: bound
[8] 1950: she
[9] 1950: lover
[10] 1950: friends has
[11] 1950: It
[12] 1950: Summons'd were to witness this grave's undo
[13] 1950: though
[14] 1950: Her
[15] 1950: their
[16] 1950: For fear their love may lead astray

2. "The Suffolk Miracle"

Sharp MSS., 3385/2483. Also in Sharp and Karpeles, 1932, I, p. 262(B). Sung by T. Jeff Stockton, at Hogskin Creek, Flag Pond, Tenn., September 4, 1916.

a M

1. Sing courting, courting, courting, cane,[1]
   But all the courtships was[2] in vain.
   As soon as her parents this came to know,
   They send[3] her three hundred miles or more.

2. It's first they vowed and then they swore
   Back home she should not come no more.
   This young man was taken sad,
   No kind of news could make him glad.
   His day had come, his hour had passed,
   Unto his grave he must go at last.

3. Although he had[4] twelve months been dead,
   He arose and rode this milk white steed.
   Your mother's cloak, your father's steed,
   My love, I've come for you with great speed.

4. They rode more swifter than the wind
   At last, at last, three hours or more,
   At last, at last, three hours or more,
   He sought[5] her at her father's door.

5. Just as they got within the gate,
   He did complain his head did ache.
   She drew her handkerchief from around her neck
   And bound it round her lover's head.

6. She reached around to kiss his lips.
   She says: My love, you're colder than the clay.
   When we get home some fire we'll have,
   But little did she know he'd come from his[6] grave.

7. Go in, go in, my love, go in,
   Till I go put this steed away.
   Her knocking at her father's door,
   The sight of her love she saw no more.

8. This old man arose, come putting on his clothes,
   Saying: You're welcome home, dear child, to me,
   You're welcome home, dear child, to me.
   What trusty friend did come with thee.

9. Did you not send one I did adore,
   I loved so dear, could love no more?
   Him a-knowing he had twelve months been dead,
   It made the hair rise on the old man's head.

10. The very next morning this was to do,
    This young man raise and him to view.
    Although he had twelve months been dead,
    The handkerchief was around his head.

11. Come parents all, both old and young,
    Your children love more precious than gold.
    For in love let them have their way,
    For love brings many to their grave.

¹ 1932: cain (*sic*)
² 1932: were
³ 1932: sent
⁴ 1932: has
⁵ 1932: sot
⁶ 1932: the

6. "The Suffolk Miracle"

Creighton and Senior, 1950, p. 89(B). Sung by William Gilkie, Sambro, N.S.

m D

1. There was a squire lived in this town
   He was well known by the people round,
   He had a daughter of beauty bright
   And she alone was his heart's delight.

2. There was a squire a-courting came
   But none of them could her fancy gain
   Until a lad of low degree
   He fell in her arms and she fancied he.

3. It's when her father he came to hear
   He separated her from her dear,
   Four score miles or better he had her sent
   To her uncle's house and her discontent.

4. This fair one unto her bed of down
   She heard a deep and a deadly sound,
   She heard a deep and a deadly sound
   Saying, "Unloose those bandages that's lightly bound."

5. She looked out of her window clear
   And saw her true love on her father's mare,
   Saying, "Your mother's orders you must obey
   And your father's anger to satisfy."

6. She jumped on to the mare's behind
   And they rode off with contented mind,
   They rode on till this sad mourn he made
   Saying, "My dearest dear how my head do ache."

7. She had a handkerchief of holland clear
   And around her true love's head she bound,
   She kissed his lips and this sad mourn she made
   Saying, "My dearest dear you're as cold as clay."

8. They rode along to her father's cot,
   Loud for her father she thus did call,
   Saying, "Father dear did you send for me?"
   And by such a young man she namèd he.

9. Her father knowing this young man was dead
   Caused every hair to stand on his head,
   He wrung his hands and he wept full sore
   But this young man's darling wept ten times more.

10. She arose, to the churchyard goes,
    She riz the corpse that was lying once dead,
    She riz the corpse that was nine months dead
    With a holland handkerchief tied round his head.

11. So come all young men and maidens,
    It's never be persuaded by your parents dear,
    For when love and virtue it is all gone
    There's no recalling it back again.

King Edward the Fourth
and a Tanner of Tamworth

CHILD NO. 273

THE earliest extant broadsides of this ballad name no tune, but speak of "an excellent new tune"—the usual meaningless formula. That there was a favorite tune associated with the ballad in Elizabeth's day is clear from a passage quoted by Chappell (*Popular Music* [1855-59], II, p. 392) from *Noctes Templariae*, in the Harleian MSS., dated (he says) 1599: "Poet Natazonius saluted him to the tune of *The Tanner and the King*"; but no tune has survived under that name.

It is possibly worth noticing that the early texts show abundant substitution of dactyls for trochees—which could most easily be accommodated by a tune in 6/8 metre, or its equivalent. A number of short second lines appear to contain an extra (fourth) foot; and this would necessitate filling up the mid-cadence.

Of the varieties of the poems given in Child's appendices, the first, "The Kyng and the Barker," in a very rough CM, has no surviving tune. The second, the "delectable Historie," has no named tune, but is in the same metre as the ballad proper, with which it has much in common. The third, "King Henry II and the Miller of Mansfield," is in a quite different metre, clearly dactylic and 3/4; with six-line stanzas, the last two lines of each being written in couplet form, but with internal rhyme that breaks them into shorter, more lyrical, units. Most, if not all, of the copies of this piece direct it to be sung to "The French Levalto" [Lavolta, Lavalto]. A tune of that name rescued by Rimbault from a MS. collection of music for virginals (then belonging to T. Birch, of Repton, Derbyshire) is printed with the text in question, by Chappell, *op.cit.*, I, p. 169, and is a variant, undoubtedly, of the one intended. In his *Illustrations of Percy's Reliques*, 1850, p. 39, Rimbault claimed ownership of the MS. which he might have sold or exchanged by the date of Chappell's publication (c. 1855). It seems to have vanished. No date is given for the MS., but the tune sounds Elizabethan. *The Fitzwilliam Virginal Book* (ed. J. A. Fuller Maitland and W. Barclay Squire, 1899, reprint 1963, Vol. II, CLV, p. 180) contains a setting of the tune for virginals, by William Byrd. Both Chappell and Rimbault took it to be English, and we do not care to deny this. But it is an unnoticed fact that the tune has much in common with the one employed by Gay, in *The Beggar's Opera*, for Polly's song, "The Turtle thus with plaintive crying," and the latter air is called "Le printemps rappelle aux armes." So that there would appear to be French associations of at least a century and a half with this graceful melodic idea. See, too, Simpson, *op.cit.*, pp. 237-38, who cites Dutch and French versions as well as English, but believes that no recorded form of the tune "was set down with the ballad in mind."

If there is little help to be got from the early broadsides, there appears to be a clear melodic line of tradition, howsoever it chances to exist, between the three known records, of dates and places far separated, transmitted from oral sources as the tune of one of the secondary forms of this ballad, "The King and the Tinker." (Cf. Child, V, *loc.cit.*) One was noted in Ireland in the eighteenth century, one in Scotland (apparently) at the beginning of the present century, and one quite recently from Ontario, Canada. Although there is an unmistakable kinship, each has its own individuality, and it is hardly conceivable that the later copies owe anything directly to their printed predecessors. Unfortunately, the textual record is very deficient, and in this case, *faute de mieux*, has been filled with the traditional copy printed in 1846 by J. H. Dixon, later by Robert Bell.

TUNES WITH TEXTS

1. "The King and the Tinker"

Petrie, 1902-05, No. 399. "From O'Neill's Collection, 1787."

a D (inflected VI and VII)

1. And now, to be brief, let's pass over the rest,
   Who seldom or never were given to jest,
   And come to King Jamie, the first of our throne,
   A pleasanter monarch sure never was known.

2. As he was a hunting the swift fallow-deer,
   He dropt all his nobles; and when he got clear,
   In hope of some pastime away he did ride,
   Till he came to an alehouse, hard by a wood-side.

3. And there with a tinkler he happened to meet,
   And him in kind sort he so freely did greet:
   Pray thee, good fellow, what hast in thy jug,
   Which under thy arm thou dost lovingly hug?

4. By the mass! quoth the tinkler, its nappy brown ale,
   And for to drink to thee, friend, I will not fail;
   For altho' thy jacket looks gallant and fine,
   I think that my two-pence as good is as thine.

5. By my soul! honest fellow, the truth thou hast spoke,
   And straight he sat down with the tinkler to joke;
   They drank to the King, and they pledged to each other,
   Who'd seen 'em had thought they were brother and brother.

6. As they were a-drinking the King pleased to say,
   What news, honest fellow? come tell me, I pray?

There's nothing of news, beyond that I hear
The King's on the border a-chasing the deer.

7. And truly I wish I so happy may be
Whilst he is a hunting the King I might see;
For altho' I've travelled the land many ways
I never have yet seen a King in my days.

8. The King, with a hearty brisk laughter, replied,
I tell thee, good fellow, if thou canst but ride,
Thou shalt get up behind me, and I will thee bring
To the presence of Jamie, thy sovereign King.

9. But he'll be surrounded with nobles so gay,
And how shall we tell him from them, sir, I pray?
Thou'lt easily ken him when once thou art there;
The King will be covered, his nobles all bare.

10. He got up behind him and likewise his sack,
His budget of leather, and tools at his back;
They rode till they came to the merry green wood,
His nobles came round him, bareheaded they stood.

11. The tinkler then seeing so many appear,
He slyly did whisper the King in his ear:
Saying, They're all clothed so gloriously gay,
But which amongst them is the King, sir, I pray!

12. The King did with hearty good laughter, reply,
By my soul! my good fellow, it's thou or it's I!
The rest are bareheaded, uncovered all round.—
With his bag and his budget he fell to the ground,

13. Like one that was frightened quite out of his wits,
Then on his knees he instantly gets,
Beseeching for mercy; the King to him said,
Thou art a good fellow, so be not afraid.

14. Come, tell thy name? I am John of the dale,
A mender of kettles, a lover of ale.
Rise up, Sir John, I will honour thee here,—
I make thee a knight of three thousand a year!

15. This was a good thing for the tinkler indeed;
Then unto the court he was sent for with speed,
Where great store of pleasure and pastime was seen,
In the royal presence of King and of Queen.

16. Sir John of the Dale he has land, he has fee,
At the court of the King who so happy as he?
Yet still in his Hall hangs the tinkler's old sack,
And the budget of tools which he bore at his back.

The text is from J. H. Dixon, *Ancient Poems, Ballads, and Songs of the Peasantry of England*, Percy Society Publications, Vol. 17, 1846, pp. 109-112. The tune reprinted by permission of the publishers, J. B. Cramer & Co., Ltd.

Our Goodman

CHILD NO. 274

THE melodic stuff of this ballad is so fluid that it is difficult to handle. It keeps taking the shape of, or borrowing phrases from, other and more familiar tunes, most of them popular, but not ballad, tunes. Especially in the American variants, traces will be noted of "Uncle Ned," "Susanna," "Ain't goin' to rain no more," "Polly-wolly-doodle," "Son of a Gambolier," "Jingle Bells," "The Derby Ram." Yet it hardly seems necessary to separate the variants into different families, or to regard them as belonging to truly unrelated traditions. The Scottish, English, Manx, Irish, and American copies appear to show enough features in common to convince one that all the singers were aiming at a roughly similar melodic ideal, in spite of the great divergences in their realizations of it. The most convenient divisions, therefore, are the objective ones of plagal and authentic, and modal variation between I/Ly and I/M. The tune almost never leaves the major galaxy: only twice in the copies seen.

The earliest version on record, that in *The Scots Musical Museum*, is one of the most elaborate, being swelled out by phrases inserted in recitative; but the tune is entirely present, apart from excrescences, in the first four long phrases. Its second half is twice restated thereafter, so that four stanzas of Herd's text, plus two interpolated short couplets, are required for one full musical statement. Most of the others are far simpler, several of them being worn down to two long phrases. Refrains and repetitions are handled in a number of ways, more quickly observed than described. Clearly the basic stanza is composed of long couplets, not of quatrains; some violence is done to the melodic phrases when they are broken into shorter units.

More variants are found in a full major scale than in other scales; but I/M is a close second. Half as many variants as in major are in π^1, and half as many variants as in π^1 are in I/Ly. About two-thirds of the total are plagal tunes; and all are in some form of duple time: 2/2, 2/4, 4/4, and, rarely, 6/8.

An extended study of this song has been made by Joseph Hickerson, who has gathered a very large number of versions. He will, one may hope, publish in due time.

TUNES WITH TEXTS

GROUP Ab

3. "Our Goodman"

Duncan MSS., "Airs," p. 118; "Words," p. 590. Also in Greig and Keith, 1925, p. 216(1). Sung by Mrs. Gillespie, Glasgow, 1905. From local tradition.

a D/Æ

Duncan names other singers who used the same tune, Mrs. Petrie, Mrs. Kindness. Mrs. Gillespie, he says, also sang to it "Molly Leigh." Duncan MSS., "Airs," p. 115.

1. Hame cam oor goodman, an' hame cam he,
An' he got a horse in a stall where nae horse should be.
"An' how cam this horse here, an' how can it be?
An how cam this horse here withoot the leave o' me?"
    (*Spoken*) "A horse?" quo' she; "Ay, a horse," quo he.
"Ye aul' blin' dottered carle, blinner mat ye be,
It's but a little milk coo my minnie sent to me."
    (*Spoken*) "A milk coo"? quo' he; "Ay, a milk coo," quo' she.
"Far hae I ridden an' muckle hae I seen,
But a saddle on a milk coo saw I never neen."

2. Hame cam oor goodman, an' hame cam he,
An' he got a pair o' boots where nae boots should be.
"How cam this boots here, an how can it be?
An how cam this boots here withoot the leave o' me?"
    (*Spoken*) "Boots"? quo' she, "Ay, boots," quo' he.
"Ye aul' blin' dottered carle, blinner mat ye be,
It's but a pair o' water stoups my minnie sent to me."
    (*Spoken*) "Water stoups"? quo' he; "Ay, water stoups," quo she.
"Far hae I ridden, an' muckle hae I seen,
But laces upon water stoups saw I never neen."

3. Hame cam oor goodman, an' hame cam he,
An' he got a staff in the hoose where nae staff should be.
"How cam this staff here, an' how can it be?
Or how cam this staff here withoot the leave o' me?"
    (*Spoken*) "A staff?" quo' she; "Ay, a staff," quo he.
"Ye aul' blin' dottered carle, blinner mat ye be,
It's but a little pottage stick my minnie sent to me."
    (*Spoken*) "A pottage stick?" quo' he; "Ay, a pottage stick," quo' she.
"Far hae I ridden an' muckle hae I seen,
But siller heids on pottage sticks saw I never neen."

4. Hame cam oor goodman, an' hame cam he,
   An' there he saw a man's hat where nae hat should be.
   "How cam this hat here, or how can it be?
   Or how cam this hat here withoot the leave o' me?"
       (*Spoken*) "A hat?" quo' she; "Ay, a hat," quo' he.
   "Ye aul' blin' dottered carle, blinner mat ye be,
   It's but a hen's nest my minnie sent to me."
       (*Spoken*) "A hen's nest?" quo' he; "Ay, a hen's nest,"
       quo' she
   "Far hae I ridden an' muckle hae I seen,
   But ribbons aboot hen's nests saw I never neen."

5. Hame cam oor goodman, an' hame cam he,
   An' there he saw a muckle coat where nae coat should be.
   "How cam this coat here, an' how can it be?
   Or how cam this coat here withoot the leave o' me?"
       (*Spoken*) "A coat?" quo' she; "Ay, a coat," quo' he.
   "Ye aul' blin' dottered carle, blinner mat ye be,
   It's but a pair o' blankets my minnie sent to me."
       (*Spoken*) "Blankets?" quo' he; "Ay, blankets," quo' she.
   "Far hae I ridden, an' muckle hae I seen,
   But buttons upon blankets saw I never neen."

6. Hame cam oor goodman an' hame cam he,
   An' he got a man i' the bed where nae man should be.
   "O how cam this man here, an' how can it be?
   An' how cam this man here withoot the leave o' me?["]
       (*Spoken*) "A man?" quo' she; "Ay, a man," quo' he.
   "Ye aul' blin' dottered carle, blinner mat ye be,
   It's but a little milkmaid my minnie sent to me."
       (*Spoken*) "A milkmaid?" quo' he; "Ay, a milkmaid,"
       quo' she.
   "Far hae I ridden an' muckle hae I seen
   But lang-bearded milkmaids saw I never neen."

Stanza six above accompanies the tune, where it appears with some variations, as follows:

> He got a man i' the hoose,
> Where nae man should be.
> Hoo cam this man here, an' hoo can it be?
> Or hoo, cam' this man here withoot the leave o' me?

14. "Came Home the Other Night"

Sung by Elizabeth Law, from Jackson County, Ohio, tradition. LC/AAFS, rec. No. 11,454(A6). Recorded by Anne Grimes.

Came home last night as drunk as I could be
I saw another man's horse tied where my horse ought to be.
My kind wife, my loving wife, my dearest wife, I say,
Whose horse is this horse tied where my horse ought to be?
You fool, you blind fool, can't you very well see?
It's a milk-cow that (your?) mama sent to me.
A long ways I've travelled, thousand miles or more,
I never saw a saddle on a milk-cow before.

p I/Ly

20. "Hame Drunk on Sunday"

Greig MSS., III, p. 144. Also in Greig and Keith, 1925, p. 216(2). Sung by William Carle, December 1908.

a I

Cf. "The Hedgehog" (Greig MSS., IV, p. 159; from A. Robb).

> Hame drunk on Sunday nicht,
>   Hame drunk cam' I,
> And there I spied on my wife's bed
>   A man's hat did lie.
>
> What's this, my dear love,
>   What's this I see?
> Oh that is just a c.[hamber] p.[ot]
>   My grannie sent to me.

35. "The Three Nights' Experience, or The Three Good Nights"

Sung by Bascom Lamar Lunsford of South Turkey Creek, N.C., 1949. Learned c. 1925 from Sam Hunnicut, who was brought up in Yancy County, N.C. LC/AAFS, rec. No. 9475(A1).

I came home the third night drunk as I could be,
Saw a head on the pillow where my head ought to be.
"Come here, my little wifie, explain this thing to me.
See a head on the pillow where my head ought to be."
"You old fool, you blind fool, can't you never see?
It's nothing but a cabbage-head my mammy sent to me."
"I've been around the country a thousand miles or more
But a mustache on a cabbage-head I never saw before."

GROUP E

41. "Our Goodman"

Sharp MSS., 4839/. Sung by George Noble (82), Ross Workhouse, September 1, 1921.

a I

My old man went out one day
And at night he came in
What horse in the stable
What horse can that be?

What horse can this be, my love,
What horse can this be?
O don't you know it's a milking cow
My mother sent to me

Its miles that I've travelled
Ten thousand miles or more
But a saddle on a milking cow
I never saw before.

I came home the first night drunk as I could be,
Saw a horse in the stable where my horse ought to be.
"Come here, my little wifie, explain this thing to me.
See a horse in the stable where my horse ought to be."
"You old fool, you blind fool, can't you never see?
Nothing but a milk-cow your mammy gave to me."
"Been around the country a thousand miles or more
But a saddle on a milk-cow's back I never saw before."

I came home the second night drunk as I could be,
Saw a coat a-hanging on the rack where my coat ought to be.
"Come here, my little wifie, explain this thing to me.
See a coat a-hanging on the rack where my coat ought to be."
"You old fool, you blind fool, can't you never see?
Nothing but a bed-quilt your mammy gave to me."
"I've been around the country a thousand miles or more
But a pocket on a bed-quilt I never saw before."

GROUP H

54. "Three Nights of Experience"

Scarborough, 1937, p. 417(B); text, p. 234. Sung by Orville O'Quinn, Council, Buchanan County, Va.

p I/Ly

1. The first night when I came home,
    Just drunk as I could be,
  I saw a horse in the stable
    Where my horse ought to be.

2. Come here, my little wifie,
    Explain this thing to me.
  What's that horse doing in the stable
    Where my horse ought to be?

3. You blind fool, you crazy fool,
    Can't you never see
  Nothing but a milch cow
    Your granny sent to me?

4. I've travelled this wide world over,
    About a thousand miles or more,
  But a saddle on a milch cow's back
    I never did see before.

5. The second night when I came home,
    Just drunk as I could be,

I saw a coat on the rack
  Where my coat ought to be.

6. Come here, my little wifie,
    Explain this thing to me.
  What's that coat doing on the rack
    Where my coat ought to be?

7. You blind fool, you crazy fool,
    Can't you never see
  Nothing but a bed-quilt
    Your granny sent to me?

8. I've travelled this wide world over,
    About a thousand miles or more,
  But a pocket on a bed-quilt
    I never did see before.

9. The third night when I came home
    Just drunk as I could be,
  I saw a head on a pillow
    Where my head ought to be.

10. Come here, my little wifie,
    Explain this thing to me.
  What's that head doing on the pillow
    Where my head ought to be?

11. You blind fool, you crazy fool,
    Can't you never see
  Nothing but a cabbage head
    Your granny sent to me?

12. I've travelled this wide world over
    About a thousand miles or more,
  But a mustache on a cabbage head
    I never did see before.

Get Up and Bar the Door

CHILD NO. 275

It seems very odd that this ballad has acquired no traditional currency in England. It has been popular in Scotland and is known in various forms, *fabliau* or folk-tale, in many parts of Europe and the Near East. From Scotland it has been brought to the United States, probably before the present century. It has been collected north and south in this country, and as far west as the Ozarks and Oklahoma. At any rate, the *Museum* seems to have been the primary agent of dissemination into popular currency.

All the other known copies of a tune are easily recognizable variants of the same melodic idea. All are in the major tonality. The chief variations lie in the refrain: some variants lack it, some have an extra final phrase, some two, and some three. All but one or two copies have the feminine cadence with "O" in the second and fourth phrases.

TUNES WITH TEXTS

GROUP A

1. "Get up and bar the Door"

Johnson, III [1790], No. 300, p. 310 (repr. 1853). Also in Ritson, 1794, I, p. 226; Smith [1820-24], I, p. 29; and Graham, 1848-49, II, p. 62.

m I/Ly

The tune appears, in union with "Does haughty Gaul invasion threat?" in G. Thomson, *A Select Collection of Original Scottish Airs*, 2nd ed. [1804], I, p. 47.

1. It fell about the Martinmass time,
   And a gay time it was then, O
   When our goodwife got puddings to make
   And she's boil'd them in the pan O.

2. The wind sae cauld blew south & north,
   And blew into the floor, O.
   Quoth our goodman, to our goodwife,
   "Gat up and bar the door" O.

3. "My hand is in my hus'if skap,
   Goodman, as ye may see O,
   And it shou'd nae be barr'd this hundred year,
   It's no be barr'd for me O."

4. They made a paction 'tween them twa,
   They made it firm and sure; O
   That the first who should speak the foremost word,
   Shou'd rise and bar the door O.

5. Then by there came two gentlemen,
   At twelve o'clock at night, O
   And they could neither see house nor hall,
   Nor coal nor candle light O.

6. Now, whether is this a rich man's house,
   Or whether is it a poor, O
   But never a word wad ane o' them speak,
   For barring of the door, O.

7. And first they ate the white puddings,
   And then they ate the black O,
   Though muckle thought the goodwife to hersel,
   Yet ne'er a word she spake O.

8. Then said the one unto the other,
   "Here, man, tak ye my knife O
   Do ye tak aff the auld man's beard,
   And I'll kiss the goodwife, O.

9. "But there's nae water in the house,
   And what shall we do than." O
   "What ails ye at the pudding broo,
   That boils into the pan O."

10. O up then started our goodman,
    An angry man was he, O
    "Will ye kiss my wife before my een,
    And scald me wi' pudding bree." O

11. Then up and started our goodwife,
    Gied three skips on the floor, O
    "Goodman, you've spoken the foremost word,
    Get up and bar the door, O."

12. "The Barrin' o' the Door"

Duncan MSS., "Airs," p. 282. Sung by Mrs. Gillespie, March 22, 1907.

p I

It fell aboot a Martinmas time,
An' a gay time it was then, O,
When oor good wife had puddins to mak
An' she boil'd them in the pan, O.
The barrin o' oor door weel, weel, weel,
An the barrin' o' oor door weel.

The Friar in the Well

CHILD NO. 276

THE seventeenth-century broadsides of this ballad designate the melody not by name but descriptively: "To a merry tune." This is reassuring, but not of much help. Better service is rendered by the stanza-pattern and refrain, which are identical with that of "Sir Eglamore," a song already met in connection with "Sir Lionel" (No. 18). The tune of "Sir Eglamore" was very popular in the later seventeenth century, and many texts were set to it. It is usually a plagal major.

In Playford's *Dancing Master*, 1651, and thereafter in successive editions till 1684, according to Chappell, *Popular Music* [1855-59], I, p. 274, is found a tune entitled "The Maid peept out at the window, or the Frier in the well." This tune is certainly a Dorian variant of the "Eglamore" tune, and very flavorsome. But see, for subsequent melodic change, Claude M. Simpson, *The British Broadside Ballad*, 1966, pp. 240-42. No extant copy of our ballad contains the line, "The maid peept out," and if that was the opening, we must presume a considerably altered narrative from the one we have. There was no need for the maid to peep unless she was the aggressor in the adventure. Yet the tune's secondary title, its close relation to the other, with the identity in refrain, seem conclusive. It is a curious fact that two nineteenth-century traditional copies of "Sir Lionel" (No. 18, Child's E) substitute a friar as here in place of the knight—a friar who is a "jovial hunter." Child's conjecture upon the point (1882-98, I, p. 209) is that *friar* is a corruption of "Rylas, or some like name"; but in view of the melodic interchange it is possible that the friar jumped without premeditation out of the well into high romance—"to a merry tune."

There appear to be no Scottish traditional copies of the present ballad more recent than those of Buchan and Kinloch, and the melodic tradition which would have gone with those was unfortunately not recorded. The Scottish refrains imply a quite different tune from the English: a five-phrase tune, or one with an extended fourth phrase.

Child believes the Scottish form of the ballad to be "derived from print" (presumably English?), and cites a passage in Skelton's *Colyn Cloute* as evidence that the English ballad was known in the first quarter of the sixteenth century. We can hardly do so well for the Playford tune; but it may certainly be as old as Elizabeth's day, and the stanza pattern has been noted as early as 1568, in Wager's play, *The longer thou livest, the more fool thou*. (Cf. *California Folklore Quarterly*, III [July 1944], pp. 192ff.)

A solitary version, with a rollicking tune, was found in Dorset by Hammond at the beginning of the present century. It has only very recently been published. Although the text is palpably close to the old broadside, there is no kinship between the old and new tunes.

TUNES WITH TEXTS

GROUP A

1. "The Maid peept out at the window, or the the Frier in the Well"

Playford, 1651, ed. Dean-Smith, 1957, p. 36.

pD

1. As I lay musing all alone,
   fa, la, la, la, la
   A pretty jeast I thought upon;
   fa, la, la, la, la

Then listen a while, and I will you tell
Of a fryer that loved a bonny lass well.
   fa, la, la, la, la
   fa, la, la, lang-tre-down-dilly

2. He came to the maid when she went to bed,
   Desiring to have her maidenhead,
   But she denyëd his desire,
   And told him that she feard hell-fire.

3. "Tush," quoth the fryer, "thou needst not doubt
   If thou wert in hell I could sing thee out:"
   "Then," quoth the maid, "thou shalt have thy request;"
   The fryer was glad as a fox in his nest.

4. "But one thing," quoth she, "I do desire,
   Before you have what you require;
   Before that you shall do the thing,
   An angel of mony thou shalt me bring."

5. "Tush," quoth the fryer, "we shall agree,
   No mony shall part my love and me;
   Before that I will see thee lack,
   I'le pawn the grey gown from my back."

6. The maid bethought her of a wile
   How she the fryer might beguile;
   While he was gone, the truth to tell,
   She hung a cloth before the well.

p I

7. The fryer came, as his covenant was,
With money to his bonny lass;
"Good morrow, fair maid!" "Good morrow!" quoth she.
"Here is the mony I promised thee."

8. She thankt the man, and she took his mony:
"Now let us go to 't," quoth he, "sweet hony:"
"O stay," quoth she, "some respite make,
My father comes, he will me take."

9. "Alas!" quoth the fryer, "where shall I run,
To hide me till that he be gone?"
"Behinde the cloath run thou," quoth she,
"And there my father cannot thee see."

10. Behind the cloath the fryer crept,
And into the well on the sudden he leapt;
"Alas," quoth he, "I am in the well!"
"No matter," quoth she, "if thou wert in hell.

11. "Thou sayst thou couldst sing me out of hell,
Now prithee sing thy self out of the well:"
The fryer sung with a pittiful sound,
Oh help me out, or I shall be dround!

12. "I trow," quoth she, "your courage is coold."
Quoth the fryer, I was never so foold,
I never was servd so before.
"Then take heed," quoth she, "thou comst there no more."

13. Quoth he, For sweet Saint Francis sake
On his disciple some pitty take:
Quoth she, Saint Francis never taught
His scholars to tempt young maids to naught.

14. The fryer did entreat her still
That she should help him out of the well;
She heard him make such pittious moan
She helped him out, and bid him be gone.

15. Quoth he, Shall I have my mony again,
Which thou from me hast beforehand tane?
"Good sir," said she, "there's no such matter;
I'le make you pay for fouling my water."

16. The fryer went all along the street,
Droping wet, like a new-washed sheep;
Both old and young commended the maid
That such a witty prank had plaid.

The text is Child's A, taken from the Rawlinson Ballads, 566, fol. 63, 4°.

GROUP B

2. "The Friar in the Well"

Purslow, 1965, p. 33; from Hammond MSS., Nos. D 629 D 661. Sung by Mr. J. Penny, Poole, Dorset, October 1906; and Mr. F. Stockley, Dorset, November 1906.

1. It's of an old friar as I have been told,
(Fal-the-dal-diddle-i-dee)
He courted a young maid just sixteen years old,
(Fal-the-dal-diddle-i-dee)
He came to the maid as she lay on her bed,
And swore he would have her maidenhead,
To my fero-lero-liddle,
Sing twice to my lanky-down-derry-o!

2. "Oh! no," said the maid, "for you know very well,
If we do such things we should go to Hell".
"No matter, my dear, you need have no doubt,
If you was in Hell I could sing you out".

3. "Oh! then", said the maid, "you shall have this thing,
But you to me ten shillings must bring."
And while he went home the money to fetch,
She thought to herself how the old friar she could catch.

4. Now while he was gone, the truth to tell,
She hung a cloth in front of the well,
He knocked at the door, the maid let him in,
"Oh! now, my dear, Oh! let us begin."

5. Then "Alas!" cried the maid, all crafty and cunning,
"I think I hear my father a-coming",
So behind the cloth the old friar did trip,
And into the well he happened to slip.

6. The friar called out with a pitiful sound,
"Oh! help me out or I shall be drowned",
"You said you could sing my soul out of Hell,
Well, now you can sing yourself out of the well".

7. So she helped him out and bid him be gone,
And the friar he wanted his money again,
"Oh! no", said the maid, "I'll have none of the matter,
For indeed you must pay me for dirtying the water".

8. So out of the house the old friar did creep,
Dripping his arse like a newly-dipped sheep,
And young and old commended the maid,
For the very pretty trick she had played.

The Wife Wrapt in Wether's Skin

CHILD NO. 277

It appears sensible to make several classes among our materials for this still living and lively ballad. The first two are Scots tradition; the last three English (and American). In nearly all cases the verbal refrain has remained steady enough to locate it in one or another melodic tradition—a laudable if uncommon virtue in refrains.

Class A corresponds with Child's A and B texts and appears to have died out, giving way in Scotland to the "Cooper of Fife" form with its highly characteristic refrain. It may be observed in passing that Child's Ab (from Miss Agnes Macmath) belongs, by its refrain, to this later class, although going back two generations from 1893. C. K. Sharpe is the sole preserver of his beautiful but melancholy tune for the older tradition (variant 1). It is interesting that it was transmitted by Walter Scott, although he lacked musical knowledge to write notes himself. Also to be mentioned is the fact that Child B, the Harris copy, is said in the Harris MS. to go to the tune of "My Jo Janet," although sharing the "Hollin green hollin" refrain. Sharpe's tune is a minor one (π^3, authentic plus a plagal opening).

Class B, still Scottish, though found also in America, is a lively 6/8 tune, with a tonality that swings from Ionian to D/Æ, with examples in π^1, I/M, and D on the way. It is likely to become still better known, for it has been taken up and performed on stage, radio, and phonograph records. It is usually found in the major scales, and is almost always plagal or mixed. The two minor variants (15 and 16), very fine in themselves, may have tangled with the tune of "Muirland Willie," which is as old as Allan Ramsay's day. That tune appears in the *Orpheus Caledonius* (1733, I, opp. p. 56) and many later collections.

Class C is found only in the U. S., and appears at its most characteristic in the Appalachian region, where it inclines toward the Dorian; it is usually in 6/8. Variants have occurred in Maine, Vermont, Missouri, and California (from Wisconsin). There is always, for refrain, some form of "Jennifer, gentle, and Rosemary," on the second phrase, and on the fourth, "As the dew flies over the green valley." We have met this refrain elsewhere (*ante*, p. 000, vt. 4). It seems likely that the tune may be Scots. Cf., e.g., in Greig's collection, the tunes for Child Nos. 41 and 63. It resembles still more closely a Northumbrian variant of Child 2 (i.e., "Whittingham Fair," Bruce and Stokoe, *Northumbrian Minstrelsy*, 1882, p. 79); and perhaps its nearest affiliations lie with the latter ballad.

Class E, "Dandoo," is again found only in the U. S.: Virginia, Kentucky, Mississippi, and Missouri. All the variants are in the major tonality, and all plagal. Three are I/M, two π^1, and one Ionian. Half are in common time, half in 6/8; most are eight-phrase tunes, with refrain on phrases two, four, seven, and eight.

TUNES WITH TEXTS

GROUP A

1. "Hollin green Hollin"

Lady John Scott's Sharpe MSS., NL Scotland MS. 843, fol. 7. From Sir Walter Scott, May 1825.

m π^3

1. She wadna bake, an' she wadna brew;
   (Hollin, green hollin;)
   For the spoiling o' her comely hue;
   (Bend your bow, Robin.)

2. She wadna wash, she wadna [w]ring.
   Hollin, green hollin;
   For spoiling o' her gay goud ring,
   Bend your bow, Robin.

3. Robin he's gane to the fauld,
   Hollin, green hollin;
   And catch'd a weather by the spauld,
   Bend your bow, Robin.

4. And he has killed his weather black,
   Hollin, green hollin;
   And laid the skin upon her back,
   Bend your bow, Robin.

5. "I daurna pay you for your kin,
   Hollin, green hollin;
   But I can pay my weather's skin,
   Bend your bow, Robin.

6. "I daurna pay my lady's back,
   Hollin, green hollin;
   But I can pay my weather black,
   Bend your bow, Robin."——

7. ——"O, Robin, Robin, lat me be!
   Hollin, green hollin;
   And I'll a good wife be to thee,
   Bend your bow, Robin.

8. "Its I will wash, and I will wring,
      Hollin, green hollin;
   And never mind my gay goud ring,
      Bend your bow, Robin.

9. "Its I will bake, and I will brew,
      Hollin, green hollin;
   And never mind my comely hue,
      Bend your bow, Robin."——

10. ——"O, blessings on your bonny mow',
      Hollin, green hollin;
    It never smack'd sae sweet as now;
      Bend your bow, Robin!"——

The text is from Jamieson, *Popular Ballads and Songs*, 1806, I, p. 321 ("Sweet Robin").

2. "Hollin Green Hollin"

Campbell, II [1818], p. 5. Also in Maver, 1866, No. 324, p. 162 ("Border Melody"). Sung by Mr. Lee, Jedburgh, from local tradition.

a minor

GROUP B

5. "The Wee Cooper o' Fife"

Duncan MSS., "Airs," p. 271; "Words," p. 509. Also in Greig and Keith, 1925, p. 219(1a); and Ford, ed. of 1904, p. 192. Sung by Mrs. Gillespie, 1905. Learned from her father.

p I

"From Mrs. Gillespie, the Rev. J. B. Duncan got another version, which is almost precisely the form given by Whitelaw, *Book of Scottish Song* (p. 333)." [*Greig and Keith's note.*]

1. There wis a wee cooper wha lived in Fife
   Nickity nackity noo' noo' noo'
   An he has gotten a gentle wife
   Hey Wullie Wallacky how John Dougall
   A lane quo Rushety roue' roue' roue'

2. She widna bake she widna brew
   Nickity nackity noo' noo' noo'
   For the spoilin o her comely hue
   Hey Wullie Wallacky how John Dougall
   A lane quo rushety roue' roue' roue'

3. She widna card nor she widna spin
   Nickity nackity noo' noo' noo'
   For the shamin o her gentle kin
   Hey Wullie Wallacky how John Dougall
   Alane quo rushety roue' roue' roue'

4. She widna wash an she widna wring
   Nickity nackity noo' noo' noo'
   For the spoilin o her gouden ring
   Hey Wullie Wallacky how John Dougall
   Alane quo rushety roue' roue' roue'

5. The cooper's awa to his woo pack
   Nickity nackity noo' noo' noo'
   He's laid a sheep's skin on his wife's back
   Hey Wullie Wallacky how John Dougall
   Alane quo rushety roue' roue' roue'

6. I'll no thrash you for your proud kin
   Nickity nackity noo' noo' noo'
   But I will thrash my ain sheep's skin
   Hey Wullie Wallacky how John Dougall
   Alane quo rushety roue' roue' roue'

7. O I will bake an I will brew
   Nickity nackity noo' noo' noo'
   I'll never mair think on my comely hue
   Hey Wullie Wallacky how John Dougall
   Alane quo rushety roue' roue' roue'

8. I will card an I will spin
   Nickity nackity noo' noo' noo'
   An never mair think o my gentle kin
   Hey Wullie Wallacky how John Dougall
   Alane quo rushety roue' roue' roue'

9. O I will wash an I will wring
   Nickity nackity noo' noo' noo'
   An never mair think on my gouden ring
   Hey Wullie Wallacky how John Dougall
   Alane quo rushety roue' roue' roue'

10. A ye wha hae gotten a gentle wife
    Nickity nackity woo' woo' woo'
    Send ye for the cooper o Fife
    Hey Wullie Wallacky how John Dougall
    Alane quo rushety roue' roue' roue'

15. "The Wee Cooper o' Fife"

Gilchrist, *JFSS*, II, No. 9 (1906), p. 223. Sung by William Wells, Sunderland Point, July 1906; learned from his father.

m D (inflected IV)

There was a wee cooper wha lived in Fife,
Nickety, nackety, noo, noo, noo,
He took himself a gentle wife,
Hey, Willie Wallacky, How, John Dougal,
Alinkarashity, rue, rue, rue!

29. "Old Wetherskin"

Sung by Mrs. Lena Bourne Fish, East Jaffrey, N.H., 1941. LC/AAFS, rec. No. 12,056(A10). Recorded by Anne and Frank Warner.

a D

1. I married a wife in the month of June,
   Gentle fair Jenny, Rosa, Marie
   I think I married a little too soon
   As the dew flies over the mulberry tree,
   I think I married a little too soon
   As the dew flies over the green valléy.

2. She would not card and she would not spin,
   Gentle fair Jenny, Rosa, Marie
   She was 'fraid of soiling her lily-white skin
   As the dew flies over the mulberry tree,
   She was 'fraid of soiling her lily-white skin
   As the dew flies over the mulberry tree.

3. So while I was tilling my meadow and land,
   Gentle fair Jenny, Rosa, Marie
   She sat in the parlor with folded hands
   As the dew flies over the mulberry tree,
   She sat in the parlor with folded hands
   As the dew flies over the mulberry tree.

4. One day I came in from jogging the plow,
   Gentle fair Jenny, Rosa, Marie
   Saying, Good Wife, is my dinner done now?
   As the dew flies over the mulberry tree,
   Saying, Kind Wife, is my dinner done now?
   As the dew flies over the mulberry tree.

5. There's bread and there's cheese upon the shelf,
   Gentle fair Jenny, Rosa, Marie
   'f you want any dinner, go get it yourself
   As the dew flies over the mulberry tree,
   If you want any dinner, go get it yourself
   As the dew flies over the mulberry tree.

6. Down to the sheep-pen I went with haste,
   Gentle fair Jenny, Rosa, Marie
   And I killed the bell wether without any waste
   As the dew flies over the mulberry tree,
   And I killed the bell wether without any waste
   As the dew flies over the mulberry tree.

7. Then I took up my knife and went whip whip whip,
   Gentle fair Jenny, Rosa, Marie
   And off went the wether's ?pelt strip strip strip
   As the dew flies over the mulberry tree,
   And off went the wether's pelt strip strip strip
   As the dew flies over the mulberry tree.

8. I then threw the hide upon my wife's back,
   Gentle fair Jenny, Rosa, Marie
   And with two sticks I went whickety-whack
   As the dew flies over the mulberry tree,
   And with two sticks I went whickety-whack
   As the dew flies over the mulberry tree.

9. I'll tell my brothers and all of my kin,
   Gentle fair Jenny, Rosa, Marie
   For to wallop your wife is surely a sin
   As the dew flies over the mulberry tree
   For to wallop your wife is surely a sin
   As the dew flies over the mulberry tree.

10. You may tell your brothers and all of your kin
    Gentle fair Jenny, Rosa, Marie
    That I'm bound to tan my old wether's skin
    As the dew flies over the mulberry tree
    I'm bound to tan my old wether's skin
    As the dew flies over the mulberry tree.

11. She then cooked my dinner and set up the bed.
    Gentle fair Jenny, Rosa, Marie
    It's Yes, Sir and No, Sir at every word
    As the dew flies over the mulberry tree
    It's Yes, Sir and No, Sir at every word
    As the dew flies over the mulberry tree.

12. She cooked my food well, she did card and spin,
    Gentle fair Jenny, Rosa, Marie
Since the day that I tanned my old wether's skin
    As the dew flies over the mulberry tree
Since the day (that) I tanned my old wether's skin
    As the dew flies over the green valléy.

GROUP E

37. "The Old Man Who Lived in the West"

Hudson and Herzog, 1937, No. 12. Sung by Mrs. Theodosia Bonnett Long, Saltillo, Lee County, Miss., between
1923 and 1930. Noted by Miss Mary Ila Long.

p I

1. There was an old man who lived in the West,
   Dandoo, dandoo,
   There was an old man who lived in the West,
   Clim a clation, cling-go
   There was an old man who lived in the West,
   He had a wife that was none of the best,
   Lick the ladle, eelie badum,
   Mealy and the cling-go.

2. And this old man came in from plow,
   Dandoo, dandoo,
   And this old man came in from plow,
   Clim a clation, cling-go
   And this old man came in from plow,
   And asked his wife for his breakfast now,
   Lick the ladle, eelie badum,
   Mealy and the cling-go.

3. "There's a crust of bread lies on the shelf,
   Dandoo, dandoo,
   There's a crust of bread lies on the shelf,
   Clim a clation, cling-go
   There's a crust of bread lies on the shelf,
   If you want any more you'll get it yourself,"
   Lick the ladle, eelie badum,
   Mealy and the cling-go.

4. Oh, this old man walked to his sheep-pen
   Dandoo, dandoo,
   Oh this old man walked to his sheep-pen,
   Clim a clation, cling-go
   Oh this old man walked to his sheep-pen,
   And off he jerked a wether's skin,
   Lick the ladle, eelie badum,
   Mealy and the cling-go.

5. He wrapped it all round his wife's own back,
   Dandoo, dandoo,
   He wrapped it all round his wife's own back,
   Clim a clation, cling-go
   He wrapped it all round his wife's own back,
   And with a switch he made it crack,
   Lick the ladle, eelie badum,
   Mealy and the cling-go.

6. "I'll tell my father and all my kin,
   Dandoo, dandoo,
   I'll tell my father and all my kin,
   Clim a clation, cling-go
   I'll tell my father and all my kin,
   That you wipped me in a wether's skin,"
   Lick the ladle, eelie badum,
   Mealy and the cling-go.

7. "You may tell your father and all your kin,
   Dandoo, dandoo,
   You may tell your father and all your kin,
   Clim a clation, cling-go
   You may tell your father and all your kin,
   I'll do what I please with my own wether's skin,"
   Lick the ladle, eelie badum,
   Mealy and the cling-go.

49. "The Wife Wrapt in Wether's Skin"

Wilkinson MSS., 1935-36, p. 96. Sung by Z. B. Lam, Stand-
ardsville, Va., November 9, 1935.

p π¹

1. Little old man lived in the West, Dandoo!
   Little old man lived in the West,
   Tu ma clish tu ma clash tu ma cling-o.
   Little old man lived in the West,
   And he had a wife, she was none of the best.
   Tu ma ling ling liddy may liddy may go,
   Tu ma clish tu ma clash tu ma cling-o.

2. Little old man come in from his plough,
   Says: Ain't you got breakfast ready now?

3. A little piece of bread and meat laying on the shelf,
   And if you want anymore you can get it yourself.

4. Little old man went out to the sheep pen,
   And out he drawed the old wether by the shin.

5. Hung the old wether up by the shin,
   And off he drawed his old wooly skin.

6. Throwed the old wether skin cross his wife's back,
   And two little sticks went whickity-whack,

7. I'll go home and tell my father and mother, and all my kin,
   How you tanned the old wether skin.

The Farmer's Curst Wife

CHILD NO. 278

OF THE various styles of verbal refrain exhibited in the copies of this still favorite ballad, it does not appear that any demarcate a strong and separate musical tradition. The majority of variants are four-phrase tunes, with the second and fourth phrases carrying nonsense syllables. About a third of the total are five-phrase tunes, with refrains of the same style, extended to a fifth line. About one-seventh elaborate into six-phrase tunes, of which a majority have refrains on the second, fifth, and sixth phrases, and fewer on the third and sixth. About a quarter of the total, also, give over the second phrase to whistling; but of these variants some are four-phrase tunes, some five-phrase; most are American, the rest English and Irish. The Scots eschew the whistle. Burns's refrain (variant 42)—(2) "Hey and the rue grows bonnie wi thyme," and (4) "And the thyme it is wither'd and rue is in prime"—is unique for this ballad. But a Michigan copy (variant 27) also has a flower refrain, corrupted: (2) "Jack a fie gent to rosim Marie," and (4) "As the dew flies over the green vallee." There would seem to be some sort of connection between the verbal tradition of a Virginia copy (Davis's I) with (2) "Old Marindy, Marowly," (4) "With his left leg, right leg, over leg, under leg," (5) "Old Marindy, Marowly," and that of a Michigan copy, with (2) "Brave old Anthony Marala," (4) "By the right leg, left leg, upper leg, under leg," (5) "Brave old Anthony Marala." For the rest, there promises no ready advantage from sorting out the varieties of fol-lols, dols, and diddles, since they do not appear to signalize distinct species of tune.

The underlying idea of a melodic scheme, in spite of great superficial variation, appears to be three successive descending phrases, each commencing on the octave above the tonic, the first and third following the major triad and cadencing on the tonic, the second with cadence on the dominant, the fourth opening near the subdominant and also descending. The overall pattern is thus roughly as follows:

But this pattern is always departed from in one way or another, according to varying melodic or harmonic impulses. It should be noted that something on these lines is rooted in the British folk tradition. Analogous tunes are the Elizabethan "Carman's Whistle," "My father was born before me," and Sheridan's "Here's to the maiden" (e.g., Chappell, *Popular Music* [1855-59], I, pp. 137ff., and II, pp. 446, 744). Moreover, Dixon informs us that his Sussex copy, Child's A, with a whistling chorus, was sung and whistled to the tune of "Lilli burlero," the soloist repeating the stanza for the second strain, and the chorus whistling all the refrain lines. That tune, even if Purcell had a finger in it, is out of the common well, though not so close to our pattern here.

The modal range of the variants is small, from I/Ly to Mixolydian and very often hexatonic. There are some eight anomalies, debatable, or not ending on the tonic, or bi-modal. The melodic range is often more than an octave, plagal plus authentic. All variants are in some form of duple rhythm, most frequently 6/8.

TUNES WITH TEXTS

GROUP A a

2. "The Devil and the Farmer"

Hammond, *JFSS*, III, No. 11 (1907), p. 131. From an unnamed singer at Beaminster, Dorset, June 1906.

a I, ending on the octave

1. There was an old farmer in Yorkshire did dwell.
   [*Whistle*]
   He had an old wife and he wished her in Hell.
   Sing fa la la la, fa la la la,
   Sing fa la la liddle la day.

2. Oh! the Devil came in when he was at plough,
   [*Whistle*]
   Saying, "One of your family I will have now."
   Sing Fal la la la, fal la la la, sing fal la la liddle la day.

3. "Now Oh! Mr. Devil, and which do you crave?"
   [*Whistle*]
   "Your ugly old wife, and she I will have."
   Sing Fal la la la, etc.

4. So they bundled the old woman into a sack.
   [*Whistle*]
   The Devil he lugged her away on his back.
   Sing Fal la la la, etc.

5. So when Mr. Devil he came up to his door:
   [*Whistle*]
   "In there you must go [for to bide evermore]."
   Sing Fal la la la, etc.

6. There she spied three young devils a-hanging in chains.
   [*Whistle*]
   She took off her pattens, got smashing their brains.
   Sing Fal la la la, etc.

7. So they to the Devil for mercy did call:
   [*Whistle*]
   "This ugly old woman she will kill us all."
   Sing Fal la la la, etc.

8. So they bundled the old woman out over the wall.
   [*Whistle*]
   She came down [on the earth a most terrible fall].
   Sing Fal la la la, etc.

9. So the women are ten times worse than the men,
   [*Whistle*]
   Since they've been into Hell and got kicked out again.
   Sing Fal la la la, etc.

6. There were two little divils a playing with chains,
   She upp'd with her stick, and knocked out their brains.

7. There were two other divils looked over the wall
   They said, "Take her away or she'll murder us all."

8. So the divil he hoisted her up on his back,
   And back to the old man hurried the pack.

9. They were seven years going and nine coming back,
   Yet she asked for the scrapings she left in the pot.

10. Said he, "My good man, here's your wife back again.
    For she wouldn't be kept, not even in Hell!

11. Now, I've been a divil the most of my life,
    But I ne'er was in Hell till I met with your wife."

12. So it's true that the women are worse than the men,
    For they went down to Hell and were threw out again.

7. "The Women are Worse than the Men"

O'Lochlainn, 1939, p. 108. Learned from D. Maguire, Belfast, 1912. Also, titled "Killyburn Braes," in O'Sullivan, *JIFSS*, XVIII (1921), p. 28, as sung by a sailor in Ardglass, County Down, c. 1915.

a I, ending on the octave

1. Is it true that the women are worse than the men
   Right fol right fol tiddy fol lay
   Is it true that the women are worse than the men,
   That they went down to hell and were thrown out again,
   With your right fol-lol tiddy fol lol
   Fol-the-dol-lol-the-dol, lol-the-dol-lay.

2. Now there was an old man lived at Kellyburn braes
   And he had a wife was the plague of his days.

3. The divil he came to the man at the plough,
   Saying, "One of your family I must take now."

4. Said he, "My good man, I've come for your wife,
   For I hear she's the plague and torment of your life."

5. So the divil he hoisted her up on his back,
   And landed at Hell's hall-door with a crack.

18. "The Farmer's Curst Wife"

Sharp MSS., 4876/3346. Sung by Thomas Taylor, Ross Workhouse, September 10, 1921.

p I

1. It was of a farmer in Cheshire did dwell
   Sing fal the lal laddy I day.
   And by the old devil was known very well.
   Sing fal the lal laddy I day.

2. The devil came to him one day to his plough
   Saying: One of your family I must have now.

3. I don't want thee nor thy son Jack,
   But it's thy old bitch of a wife I'll have.

4. The old devil he tumbled her into his sack
   Just like an old pedlar a-carrying his pack.

5. He took her and threw her down at hell's door,
   And bade her stay there not to rise any more.

6. Up come the young devils all fettered in chains,
   She up with her patterns and beat out their brains.

7. So you see now the women they're worse than the men,
   If you send them to heaven they get sent back again.

GROUP A d

26. "The Devil and the Farmer's Wife"

Sung by Ezra Barhight, March 11, 1956. Recorded by Ellen Stekert; sent by her to the Editor.

p I

1. There was a man when he was first born,
    (Poor) Old Anthony Rōwley
   There was a man when he was first born,
   He had no horse to plow his corn,
       With his right leg, left leg, upper leg, under leg,
   Poor Old Anthony Rōwley

2. So he hitched the pigs with his old sow,
    (Poor) Old Anthony Rōwley
   He hitched the pigs with his old sow
   And plowed up the corn the devil knows how
       With his right leg, left leg, upper leg, under leg,
   Poor old Anthony Rowley.

3. Well the devil he came to the old man's plow,
    Poor old Anthony Rowley
   The devil he came to the old man's plow,
   "It's your oldest son that I'm after now."
       With his right leg, left leg, upper leg, under leg,
   Poor old Anthony Rowley.

4. "You cannot have my oldest son,
    Poor old Anthony Rowley
   You cannot have my oldest son,
   You'll have to take the old woman or none."
       With (his) right leg, left leg, upper leg, under leg,
   Poor old Anthony Rowley.

5. So the devil he took her all onto his back,
    Poor old Anthony Rowley
   The devil he took her all onto his back
   And like an old fool he went carrying his pack
       With his right leg, left leg, upper leg, under leg,
   Poor old Anthony Rowley.

6. Well he carried her over three fields more,
    Poor old Anthony Rowley
   (Well) he carried her over three fields more,
   At length he came to his old trap door
       With his right leg, left leg, upper leg, under leg,
   Poor old Anthony Rowley.

7. There sat little devils all bound in chains,
    Poor old Anthony Rowley
   There sat little devils all bound in chains,
   She up with a shovel, knocked out their brains,
       With their(?) right leg, left leg, upper leg, under leg,
   Poor old Anthony Rowley.

8. Then one little devil all with a red cap,
    Poor old Anthony Rowley
   (Poor) One little devil all with a red cap
   (She) up with her shovel, gave him a slap
       With his right leg, left leg, upper leg, under leg,
   Poor old Anthony Rowley.

9. Then three little devils peeped over the wall,
    Poor old Anthony Rowley
   Then three little devils peeped over the wall,
   Crying, "Carry her back, she'll brain us all
       With her right leg, left leg, upper leg, under leg."
   Poor old Anthony Rowley.

10. So the devil he took her all onto his back,
    Poor old Anthony Rowley
    The devil he took her all onto his back
    And like an old fool he went carrying her back
        With his right leg, left leg, upper leg, under leg,
    Poor old Anthony Rowley.

11. Well he carried her over three fields more,
    Poor old Anthony Rowley
    Well, he carried her over three fields more,
    At length he came to the old man's door,
        With his right leg, left leg, upper leg, under leg,
    Poor old Anthony Rowley.

12. (Well), that shows the women are worse than the men,
    Poor old Anthony Rowley
    That shows the women are worse than the men,
    They'll go to hell and come back again
        With their right leg, left leg, upper leg, under leg,
    Poor old Anthony Rowley.

GROUP A e

33. "The Farmer's Curst Wife"

Sung by Horton Barker, near Chilhowie, Va., 1939. LC/AAFS, rec. No. 2837(B1). Also in LC/AAFS, Album 1, rec. No. 1(B); and on LC/AAFS, rec. No. L1(A2). Collected by Herbert Halpert. Other records of this song as Barker sang it are preserved in Davis, 1960, p. 321(BB); Schinhan, *Music, Brown Collection*, IV, 1957, p. 116; and in Folkways LP rec. No. FA 2362, Side 2, Band 5.

a π[1]

14. There's one advantage women have over men:
They can go to Hell and come back again.
Sing heigh, etc.

The texts given by Davis and Schinhan differ in particulars from the text printed above. Barker felt no literal obligation to a fixed reading.

GROUP Ag

42. "Kellyburnbraes"

Johnson, IV [1792], No. 379, p. 392 (repr. 1853). Also in Thomson, IV, 1805, p. 182; Maver, 1866, No. 222, p. 111; and Goss, 1937, p. 126(B). From Robert Burns, with words written for the *Museum* by him.

a I

1. There was an old man at the foot of the hill,
If he ain't moved away he's livin' there still.
Sing heigh! diddle-eye, diddle-eye, fie!
Diddle-eye, diddle-eye, day!

2. He hitched up his horse and he went out to plow,
But how to get around he didn't know how.
Sing heigh, etc.

3. The Devil came to his house one day,
Says, "One of your family I'm a-gonna take away."
Sing heigh, etc.

4. "Take her on, take her on, with the joy of my heart;
I hope by gollies you'll never part!"
Sing heigh, etc.

5. The Devil put her in a sack,
And the old man says, "Don't you bring her back."
Sing heigh, etc.

6. When the Devil got her to the forks of the road,
He says, "Old lady, you're a terrible load."
Sing heigh, etc.

7. When the Devil got her to the gates of Hell,
He says, "Punch up the fire, we want to scorch her well."
Sing heigh, etc.

8. In come a little devil a-draggin' a chain;
She upped with the hatchet, and split out his brains.
Sing heigh, etc.

9. Another little devil went climbin' the wall,
An' says, "Take her back, Daddy, she's a-murderin' us all."
Sing heigh, etc.

10. The old man was a-peepin' out of the crack,
And saw the old Devil come a-waggin' her back.
Sing heigh, etc.

11. She found the old man sick in the bed,
And upped with the butterstick and paddled his head.
Sing heigh, etc.

12. The old woman went whistlin' over the hill.
"The Devil wouldn't have me, so I wonder who will?"
Sing heigh, etc.

13. This is what a woman can do:
She can outdo the Devil and her old man, too.
Sing heigh, etc.

1. There lived a carl in Kellyburnbraes,
Hey, & the rue grows bonie wi' thyme,
And he had a wife was the plague of his days
And the thyme it is wither'd and rue is in prime.

2. Ae day as the carl gaed up the lang-glen,
Hey and the rue grows bonie wi' thyme;
He met wi' the d-v-l, says, how do ye fen?
And the thyme it is wither'd and rue is in prime.

3. I've got a bad wife, Sir, that's a' my complaint,
Hey, &c.
For, saving your presence, to her ye're a saint,
And, &c.

4. It's neither your stot nor your staig I shall crave,
Hey, &c.
But gie me your wife, man, for her I must have,
And, &c.

5. O, welcome most kindly! the blythe carl said;
Hey, &c.
But if ye can match her ye're waur than ye're ca'd,
And, &c.

6. The d-v-l has got the auld wife on his back,
Hey, &c.
And like a poor pedlar he's carried his pack,
And, &c.

7. He's carried her hame to his ain hallan door,
Hey, &c.
Syne bade her gae in for a b— and a w—
And, &c.

8. Then straight he makes fifty, the pick o' his band,
   Hey, &c.
   Turn out on her guard in the clap of a hand,
   And, &c.

9. The carlin gaed thro' them like ony wud bear,
   Hey, &c.
   Whae'er she gat hands on, cam near her nae mair,
   And, &c.

10. A reekit, wee deevil looks over the wa',
    Hey, &c.
    O help, Master, help! or she'll ruin us a',
    And, &c.

11. The d-v-l he swore by the edge o' his knife,
    Hey, &c.
    He pitied the man that was ty'd to a wife,
    And, &c.

12. The d-v-l he swore by the kirk and the bell,
    Hey, &c.
    He was not in wedlock, thank Heaven, but in h—,
    And, &c.

13. Then Satan has travell'd again wi' his pack,
    Hey, &c.
    And to her auld husband he's carried her back,
    And, &c.

14. I hae been a d-v-l the feck o' my life,
    Hey and the rue grows bonie wi' thyme;
    But ne'er was in h—ll till I met wi' a wife,
    An' the thyme it is wither'd, and rue is in prime.

3. O, it's neither your son nor your daughter I crave,
   It's your old scolding wife and it's her I must have.

4. So he hobst her up all on his back,
   And like a bold peddlar went a-packing his pack.

5. As they drew near the high gates of Hell,
   Sing, rake back the coals, boys, and we'll roast her well.

6. O, two little devils come a-rattling their chains,
   She hauled back her cudgel and knocked out their brains.

7. Two more little devils peeped over the door,
   She hauled back her cudgel, killed ninety-nine more.

8. Two more little devils peeped over the wall,
   Says, Take her back Daddy, or she'll kill us all.

9. So he hobst her up all on his back,
   And like a bold peddlar went a-packing her back.

10. Here's your old scolding wife and it's her I won't have,
    She ain't fit for Heaven, she shant stay in Hell.

11. O it's seven year going and seven coming back,
    She called for the 'baccer she left in the crack.

12. O the women they are so much better than men,
    When they go to Hell they get sent back again!

GROUP B

67. "The Devil and the Farmer's Wife"

Sung by Mrs. Carrie Grover, Gorham, Me., 1941. LC/AAFS, rec. No. 4454(B2). Also on LC/AAFS, rec. No. L58(B2). Recorded by Alan Lomax.

p Æ

1. Oh, the Devil he came to the farmer one day
   (Whistle)
   Saying you owe me a debt and I will 'a my pay,
   To my right fol-lol-fol-laddi-i-day.

2. It is not your children or you that I crave
   (Whistle)
   But your old scolding wife and it's her I must have
   To my right fol-lol-fol-laddi-i-day.

3. Oh, take her, oh take her, with all my heart
   (Whistle)
   And I hope you and she will never part,
   To my right fol-lol-fol-laddi-i-day.

GROUP Ah

52. "Little Devils"

Ritchie, 1955, p. 144. Also in Ritchie, 1953, p. 23, and on Folkways LP rec. No. FA 2302(A2), ed. K. S. Goldstein. Sung by the Ritchie family, Viper, Ky. Learned from an uncle, Jason Ritchie, Ball Mountain, Ky.

a I/M, ending on VI

1. There was an old man and he lived near Hell,
   (Whistle)
   He had a little farm and upon it did dwell,
   Sing heigh O rattle ding day.

2. O the devil came to him one day at his plow,
   (Whistle)
   There's one in your family I have to have now,
   Sing heigh O rattle ding day.

4. So the Devil he mounted her onto his back
   (Whistle)

   And like a bold pedlar went carrying his pack,
   To my right fol-lol-fol-laddi-i-day.

5. Nine little devils were hanging in chains
   (Whistle)

   She up with a poker and knocked out their brains,
   To my right fol-lol-fol-laddi-i-day.

6. She climbed on a stool for to make herself higher
   (Whistle)

   She threw round her left leg and knocked nine in the fire,
   To my right fol-lol-fol-laddi-i-day.

7. Nine little blue devils peeped over the wall
   (Whistle)

   Oh, take her back, Dad, or she'll kill us all,
   To my right fol-lol-fol-laddi-i-day.

8. So the Devil he mounted her onto his back
   (Whistle)

   And like a bold pedlar went carrying her back.
   To my right fol-lol-fol-laddi-i-day.

GROUP C

68. "The Farmer's Curst Wife"

Archive, School of Scottish Studies, rec. No. 1953/237/B14.
Sung by Willie McPhee, Blairgowrie, Perthshire (born in
Helensburgh, Dunbartonshire). Collected by Hamish Hen-
derson. Transcribed by Francis M. Collinson.

m D

1. Oh the Devil, he cam tae the man at the plew,
   Right fa lah right fal de larriddle,
   Sayin', "Here I come for your auld wife noo."
   Right fal deedle ah riddle ay.

2. "Oh, tak her awa wi aa my hairt,"
   So he humped her away like a pedlar's pack.

3. Oh, when he cam to the gates o Hell,
   He flung her doon: "Get in there, auld Nell."

4. For there were six devils chained up wi a chain,
   For she lifted her crutch an she lashed oot their brains.

5. For there six more lookit over a wall,
   Sayin, "Take her away, or she will kill us all."

6. An he humped her again like a pedlar's pack,
   For she taen seven year comin an seven gaun back.

7. Oh, when he cam back tae the man at the plew,
   Sayin, "Here I'm back wi your auld wife noo."

8. For she's too bad for Heaven; they won't have her in Hell,
   So here she's back; ye can try her yersel."

GROUP D

69. "The Devil and the Farmer's Wife"

Recorded by Peter Shepheard from Seamus Ennis of
Dublin, 1963; probably collected in Ireland. Sent to the
Editor by Peter Shepheard.

a D

1. There was an old couple that lived on a hill
   (whistled phrase)
   If they're not gone away then they're living there still
   With me wig fo(l) lay folligity fol di do(l) lay

2. Well the Devil he came to the man at the plough
   (whistled phrase)
   Saying one of your family I'll take away now
   With me wig fo(l) lay folligity fol di do(l) lay

3. Now which of me family do you like best
   (whistled phrase)
   It's your old scolding wife it's her I like best
   With me wig fo(l) lay folligity fol di do(l) lay

4. Take her off take her off with the joy of me heart
   (whistled phrase)
   And I hope to the Lord that thee never may part
   With me wig fo(l) lay folligity fol di do(l) lay

5. Well the Devil he bundled her into the sack
      (whistled phrase)
   To the Devil said don't you bring her back
   With me wig fo(l) lay folligity fol di do(l) lay

6. The Devil he hoisted her up on his back
      (whistled phrase)
   And it's hotfoot for Hell with her then he did pack
   With me wig fo(l) lay folligity fol di do(l) lay

7. He carried her on to a heap of stones
      (whistled phrase)
   He left her down there and he jumped on her bones
   With me wig fo(l) lay folligity fol di do(l) lay

8. Then he carried her on till he came to Coult hill(?)
      (whistled phrase)
   And she wept as much there as would turn a mill
   With me wig fo(l) lay folligity fol di do(l) lay

9. And he carried her on till he came to Hell's wall
      (whistled phrase)
   And she skated pissed and she scorned at them all
   With me wig fo(l) lay folligity fol di do(l) lay

10. And then all the Devils ran up in the wall
      (whistled phrase)
   Saying take her home daddy she'll murder us all
   With me wig fo(l) lay folligity fol di do(l) lay

11. So handled(?) he hoisted her up on his back
      (whistled phrase)
   They were nine days going and one coming back
   With me wig fo(l) lay folligity fol di do(l) lay

12. The old man was peeping into the crack
      (whistled phrase)
   He saw the old Devil come winding back
   With me wig fo(l) lay folligity fol di do(l) lay

13. They were nine days going and one coming back
      (whistled phrase)
   She's gone with the scraper she left in her pot
   With me wig fo(l) lay folligity fol di do(l) lay

14. They went into the room the old man was in bed
      (whistled phrase)
   She lifted the butter stick and patted his head
   With me wig fo(l) lay folligity fol di do(l) lay

15. Now the old woman ran away over the hill
      (whistled phrase)
   The Devil won't have her I wonder who will
   With me wig fo(l) lay folligity fol di do(l) lay

16. There's one thing that women have got over men
      (whistled phrase)
   They can go down to Hell and come back again
   With me wig fo(l) lay folligity fol di do(l) lay

The Jolly Beggar

CHILD NO. 279

CHILD, curtly dismissing the attribution of this piece to James V of Scotland, refuses to decide whether its antecedents belong more properly to Scotland or to England. He notes the existence of a seventeenth-century English broadside, but remarks that the Scottish form, although it makes its first appearance a century later, is "far superior." At any rate, clearly, the ballad, in one form or another, has been current for at least three hundred years, and has been well liked in England, Scotland, Ireland, and latterly in this country. The oral and printed traditions are impossible to disentangle, and especially in England, *rifacimenti* of the broadside press have had widespread oral currency.

The ballad has circulated with various styles of refrain: a line after each long couplet, a refrain as the second and fourth line of a quatrain, a burden as second strain. The last style is that with the longest musical tradition of record, and has here been given first place, although one must regard it, on account of its burden-text, as borrowed from yet another piece. The burden text appears first in Herd's MSS., I, No. 5 (Brit. Mus. Add MS. 22311), is printed in his revised collection of 1776, and appears soon after in *The Scots Musical Museum*, No. 266, with the tune, copied thence into a good many other collections. It is major, authentic, and sometimes abbreviated. Something like the tune of the "Derby Ram" has been attracted to it in versions found as far apart as Aberdeenshire and Missouri.

What we have placed in the second class may be especially Irish, though there are several Scottish variants. The refrain pattern is on phrases two and four. The tonality is sometimes debatable, and appears to stretch from major to Æolian; but more than one copy fails to establish its final as tonic. One Irish variant is bi-modal, the first two phrases being really a plagal major, the last two authentic Mixolydian (variant 13).

A quite different style of tune is found with the more genuinely secondary forms of this ballad lately current, as in several variants called "The Tinker," "The Ragged (Dirty) Beggarman," collected in the West of England by Baring-Gould and Cecil Sharp, and in counties farther east and north. Of these, the "plot" is still closer to the old "Jolly Beggar" than is the ballad which follows, i.e., "The Gaberlunyie-Man" (No. 279, Appx.).

TUNES WITH TEXTS

GROUP A

1. "The Jolly Beggar"

Johnson, III [1790], No. 266, p. 274 (repr. 1853). Also in Ritson, ed. of 1869, I, p. 245; Maver, 1866, No. 484, p. 242; and Ford, ed. of 1904, p. 9.

a I

1. There was a Jolly beggar, and a begging he was bound,
   And he took up his quarters into a land'art town,
     And we'll gang nae mair a roving
     Sae late into the night,
     And we'll gang nae mair a roving,
     Let the moon shine ne'er sae bright,
     And we'll gang nae mair a roving.

2. He wad neither ly in barn, nor yet wad he in byre,
   But in ahint the ha' door, or else afore the fire.
     And we'll gang nae mair, &c.

3. The beggar's bed was made at e'en wi' good clean straw and hay,
   And in ahint the ha' door, and there the beggar lay.
     And we'll gang nae mair, &c.

4. Up raise the goodman's dochter, and for to bar the door,
   And there she saw the beggar standin i' the floor.
     And we'll gang nae mair, &c.

5. He took the lassie in his arms, and to the bed he ran,
   O hooly, hooly wi' me, Sir, ye'll waken our goodman.
     And we'll gang nae mair, &c.

6. The beggar was a cunnin' loon, and ne'er a word he spake,
   Until he got his turn done, syne he began to crack.
     And we'll gang nae mair, &c.

7. Is there ony dogs into this town, Maiden, tell me true;
   And what wad ye do wi' them, my hinny and my dow.
     And we'll gang nae mair, &c.

8. They'll rive a' my mealpocks, and do me meikle wrang.
   O dool for the doing o't, are ye the poor man.
     And we'll gang nae mair, &c.

9. Then she took up the mealpocks and flang them o'er the wa',
   The d—l gae wi' the mealpocks, my maidenhead and a'.
     And we'll gang nae mair, &c.

10. I took ye for some gentleman, at least the Laird of Brodie;
    O dool for the doing o't! are ye the poor bodie.
      And we'll gang nae mair, &c.

11. He took the lassie in his arms, and gae her kisses three,
And four-and-twenty hunder mark to pay the nurice fee.
    And we'll gang nae mair, &c.

12. He took a horn frae his side, and blew baith loud and shrill.
And four-and-twenty belted knights came skipping o'er the hill.
    And we'll gang nae mair, &c.

13. And he took out his little knife, loot a' his duddies fa'.
And he was the brawest gentleman that was amang them a'.
    And we'll gang nae mair, &c.

14. The beggar was a cliver loon, and he lap shoulder height,
O ay for sicken quarters as I gat yesternight.
    And we'll gang nae mair, &c.

6. "The Jolly Beggar"

Archive, School of Scottish Studies, rec. No. 1952/33/A17.
Sung by Jeannie Robertson, Aberdeen. Collected by Hamish Henderson. Also on Caedmon rec. No. TC 1146(B8),
recorded by Peter Kennedy; collected by Peter Kennedy and
Alan Lomax. Transcribed by Gillian Johnstone.

a π¹, ending on III

1. There wis a auld beggar man
An' he was dressed in green
An' he was askin' lodgin's
At the place near Aberdeen.

Chorus:

Na mair I'll gang a-rovin a-rovin in the nicht,
Nae mair I'll gang a-rovin till the meen shines
                    [ne'er sae bricht.]

2. He wadna lie in the barn,
Nor yet intae the byre,
He wadna lie in nae ither place
But at the kitchen fire.

3. "For if ye had been a decent lass,
As I took you to be,
I wad 's made you the queen
O' a' the counteree."

4. He put his hand intae his pooch,
He gied her guineas three.

"O tak you this, ma bonnie lass,
For to pay the nurse's fee."

5. He took a horn frae his side,
He blew it loud and shrill,
And four and twenty noblemen
Come trippin' ower the hill.

6. He took a penknife frae his pooch,
He let a' his duddies fall,
And he was the brawest gentleman
That stood amangst them all.

GROUP BA

13. "There Was a Bold Beggarman"

Joyce, 1873, No. 44, p. 45 (repr. 1912). Also in Goss, 1937,
p. 129(D). Learned by Joyce in his childhood.

I—M: first half p I, second half a M

There was a bold beggarman as ever you did see,
    With a hi, with a ho fol-de dan-dy-o;
He asked for a lodging near the house of Tandragee,
    With his toorn-oorn-oorn-oorn-andy-o!

GROUP Bb

15. "Jolly Beggar"

Telfer MS., No. 48, p. 23. Tune noted by William Oliver
of Langraw, 1855.

a Æ

17. "The Jolly Beggar"

Archive, School of Scottish Studies, rec. No. 1952/55/2.
Sung by Norman McCaig, Edinburgh, 1952. Collected by
Hamish Henderson.

aD

1. There was a jolly beggar and a-beggin' he was boun'
   With his fal and his dal and his dandy-o
   And he has taen up his quarters intae some landward toon
   With his teerin owrin' teerin owrin' andy-o

Interlinear refrain throughout

2. He wouldna lie in barn nor yet would he in byre
   But in a-hint the ha' door or else afore the fire

3. The beggar's bed was weel made wi' lynen sheets and hay
   And in a-hint the ha' door the jolly beggar lay.

4. Up raise the gude man's dochter for to bar the door
   When there she saw the jolly beggar standin' on the floor

5. He's taen her in his airms an' till his bed he ran
   "Be canny wi' me noo", she says, "you'll waken oor pair man".

6. The beggar being a cunnin' loon the ne'er a word he spake
   Until he got his jobby deen an' he began to crack

7. Hae ye cats or dogs aboot the place oh lassie tell me true.
   Oh what would ye dae wi' them my hinny and my doo?

8. They would rive a' my mealpocks and gar me curse an' ban.
   Oh the deil gae wi' your mealpocks are ye the beggar-man?

9. She's taen up his mealpocks and thrown them owre the wa'
   The deil gae wi' your mealpocks my maiden-heid's awa

10. He's taen a horn fae his side and blawn it loud and shill
    And four and twenty belted knights came tripperin's owre the hill

11. He's taen oot his little knife let a' his duddies fa'
    And he was the bravest gentleman there was among them a'

GROUP D

36. "Farmer and Tinker"

Sharp MSS., 2365/2138. Sung by Shepherd Hayden (83), Bampton, September 6, 1909.

a M (inflected VII)

Its of an old farmer lived in the West Countree
And he had as fine a daughter that ever my eyes did see
Most night and day as I've heard say that girl was in his eyes
And he never would rest contented until he had gained her joy

Then he dressed himself up in a tinker's suit of clothes
With the breeches hanging round him to the farmer's house he goes
Saying have you any frying pans or candle sticks to mend
Or have you any lodging for I am a single man

Then this young man being so cunning he run & bar the door
He laid this pretty fair maid down flat upon the floor
He laid this pretty fair maid among the proud straw
Until he had gained her maidenhead he never w^d let her go

So now you've had your will of me & brought me here to shame
I'll hope you'll be so cruel as tell to me your name
When I am in my own countree they called me David Four
What pretty pastime we did have in the barn upon the floor.

The Gaberlunyie-Man

CHILD NO. 279, APPENDIX

CHILD has relegated this favorite song to an appendix of "The Jolly Beggar." It is difficult to guess why. The melodic tradition of the two, at any rate, lends no support to this determination, and on grounds of metrical and stanzaic pattern, as well as of plot, there would seem to be better justification for making the present ballad No. 280, and reducing Child's 280 to a later redaction of "Gaberlunyie-Man." Indeed, Child himself calls his 280 "a sort of 'Gaberlunyie-Man' with a romantic conclusion."

The present ballad has had a long life, both textual and melodic. The earlier melodic tradition first appears in Thomson's *Orpheus Caledonius*, 1725, and can be followed to the present century. The later tradition cannot be traced before the last century: in fact, Greig's examples are the earliest discovered. But there may be some distant relation between the two groups.

The first group is mainly inclined to the D/Æ mode, in plagal range.

Greig's and a generous reinforcement of recent copies collected for the School of Scottish Studies are the mainstay of the second class, which contains variants in Mixolydian, M/D, and π^3, all authentic unless they are better considered major or I/M with fallen closes. The tradition is so consistent that it seems safer to accept the final as tonic. All except one are in duple time.

TUNES WITH TEXTS

GROUP A

1. "The Gaberlunzie-Man"

Thomson [1725], fol. 43; and 1733, I, opp. p. 95.

m Æ—D (inflected VI)

1. The pawky auld Carle came o'er the Lee,
   Wi' many good E'ens and Days to me,
   Saying, Good-wife, for your Courtisie,
      Will ye lodge a silly poor Man?
   The Night was cauld, the Carle was wat,
   And down ayont the Ingle he sat;
   My Daughter's Shoulders he 'gan to clap,
      And cadgily ranted and sang.

2. O wow! quo' he, were I as free,
   As first when I saw this Country,
   How blyth and merry wad I be!
      And I wad never think lang.

He grew canty, and she grew fain;
But little did her auld Minny ken
What thir slee twa togither were say'n,
   When wooing they were sae thrang.

3. And O! quo' he, ann ye were as black,
   As e'er the Crown of my Dady's Hat,
   'Tis I wad lay thee by my Back,
      And awa' wi' me thou shou'd gang.
   And O! quo' she, ann I were as white,
   As e'er the Snaw lay on the Dike,
   I'd clead me braw, and lady-like,
      And awa' with thee I'd gang.

4. Between the twa was made a Plot;
   They raise a wee before the Cock,
   And wylily they shot the Lock,
      And fast to the Bent are they gane.
   Up in the Morn the auld Wife raise,
   And at her Leisure pat on her Claise;
   Syne to the Servant's Bed she gaes,
      To speer for the silly poor Man.

5. She gaed to the Bed where the Beggar lay,
   The Strae was cauld, he was away,
   She clapt her hands, cry'd, Walady,
      For some of our Gear will be gane.
   Some ran to Coffers, and some to Kists,
   But nought was stown that cou'd be mist,
   She danc'd her lane, cry'd, Praise be blest,
      I have lodg'd a leal poor Man.

6. Since nathing's awa', as we can learn,
   The Kirns to Kirn, and Milk to Earn,
   Gae butt the House, Lass, and waken my Bairn,
      And bid her come quickly ben.
   The Servant gade where the Daughter lay,
   The Sheets was cauld, she was away,
   And fast to her good Wife can say,
      She's aff with the Gaberlunzie-Man.

7. O fy gar ride, and fy gar rin,
   And haste ye find these Traitors again;
   For she's be burnt, and he's be slain,
      The wearifu' Gaberlunzie-Man.

[481]

Some rade upo' Horse, some ran a fit,
The Wife was wood, and out o' her Wit:
She cou'd na' gang, nor yet cou'd she sit,
     But ay she curs'd and she ban'd.

8. Mean time far hind out o'er the Lee,
Fu' snug in a Glen, where nane cou'd see,
The twa, with kindly Sport and Glee,
     Cut frae a new Cheese a whang:
The Priving was good, it pleas'd them baith,
To lo'e her for ay, he ga'e her his aith;
Quo' she, to leave thee I will be laith,
     My winsome Gaberlunzie-Man.

9. O ken'd my Minny I were wi' you,
Ill fardly wad she crook her mou,
Sic a poor Man she'd never trow,
     After the Gaberlunzie-Man.
My Dear, quo' he, ye're yet o'er young,
And ha' na' learn'd the Beggars Tongue,
To follow me frae Town to Town,
     And carry the Gaberlunzie on.

10. Wi' cauk and keel I'll win your Bread,
And Spindles and Whorles for them wha' need,
Whilk is a gentle Trade indeed,
     To carry the Gaberlunzie-O.
I'll bow my Leg, and crook my Knee,
And draw a black Clout o'er my Eye,
A Cripple or Blind they will ca' me,
     While we shall be merry, and sing.

GROUP B

13. "The Beggar Man"

Greig MSS., I, p. 34. Also in Greig-Duncan MS. 785 (Walker transcript). Sung by J. Greig, New Deer, 1904, as sung by Hugh Begg's grandfather.

a M/D

There was an auld carle cam' owre yon lea
Wi' mony a story telling unto me;
He was lookin' oot for charity,
Will ye lodge a beggar man?
Laddie to my tow-row-ree.

15. "The Beggar Man"

Greig MSS., IV, p. 174. Sung by J. Angus.

a M/D

The MS. gives only the refrain-line:

     Ladle tee a tow row ree.

36. "The Beggar Man"

Archive, School of Scottish Studies, rec. No. 1958/8/A6. Sung by Annie McDonald. Collected by Hamish Henderson. Transcribed by Alex Sinclair.

a M

A beggar man cam oer the lea
Seekin oot for charitie
. . . .
Would ye ludge a beggar man?
     Larity a tow-row-ray.

The night bein dark an somewhat wet
It's doon by the fireside the auld man sat
Doon . . . .
An aye as he riddled he sang
     Larity a tow-row-ray.

24. "The Gaberlunzie Man"

Duncan MSS., "Airs," p. 18; "Words," p. 217. Text also in Greig and Keith, 1925, p. 224. From Mrs. Gillespie, 1905, as sung by Mary Gallen, 40 years earlier. Also from the MS. of G. F. Duncan (1885), who had it from several sources (chiefly his mother).

a M/D

1. There wis an auld carle cam our the lea
   An mony's the fine tale he tell unto me
      Asking meal for charity
   Will ye lodge a leal pu'r man; Laddle lilt te tow, row, ree.

2. The nicht wis caul an the carle wis wat
   An down by the fireside the auld beggar sat
   The dochter he began to clap
   An aye as he rantit an sang; Laddle lilt-te tow, row, row.

3. O wow quoth he if I were as free
   As first when I came to this countrie
   O blyth an merry wid I be,
   An' I wid never think lang. Laddle lilt-te-tow row, row.

4. He wis canty an she wis fain
   But little did her auld mither ken
   What the twa together wer sayin
   When they were sae thrang. Laddle lilt-te-tow, row, row.

5. O says he gin ye were as black
   As the croun o my daddies hat
   'Tis I wid lay thee at my back
   An awa on me ye wid gang. Laddle lilt-te tow, row, row.

6. O said she if I were as white
   As e'er the snaw lay on the dyke
   I'd cleed me braw an leddy like
   An awa wi thee I'd gang. Laddle lilt te-tow, row, row.

7. Gin my mammy kent I were wi you
   Ill faurd'ly wid she crook her moo
   Anather pu'r man she ne'er wid trew
   After the Gaberlunzie man. Laddle lilt-te-tow row, row.

8. O said the beggar ye're yet our young
   Ye hina the clink o the beggin tongue
   Ye hina the clink o the beggin tongue
   An wi me ye canna gang. Laddle lilt te tow row row.

9. I'll ben' my back I'll bue my knee
   I'll tie a black patch on my e'e
   An for a beggar they'll tak me
   An awa wi you I'll gang. Laddle lilt-te-tow row row.

10. Between the twa they made a plot
    To rise a wee before the cock
    An wili-ly they shot the lock
    An fast tae the bents they ran. Laddle lilt-te-tow row, row.

11. She's bent her back she's bou'd her knee
    She's tied a black patch on her e'e

An for a beggar they've ta'en she
An awa wi him she's gane. Laddle lilt te tow row row.

12. Up in the mornin the auld wife raise,
    An at her leisure pat on her claise
    Sine to the servant's bed she gae's
    To spier for the silly pe'er man. Laddle lilt-te-tow, row row.

13. She gid tae the bed whare the beggar lay
    The stray wis caul an he wis away
    She clapped her hands cried wal-la-day
    For some o our gear'ill be gaen. Laddle lilt-te-tow row, row.

14. Some ran to coffer an some ran tae kist
    But nought wis stoun that could be missed
    She danced her lean crying praised be bless't
    I've lodged a leal pu'r man. Laddle lilt-te-tow, row, row.

15. Since naething's awa as we can learn
    The kirn is tae kirn and the milk tae yern
    Gie but the hoose an wauken the bairn
    An bid her come quickly ben. Laddle lilt-te-tow, row, row.

16. The servant gid where the dochter lay
    The sheets wis caul an she wis away
    An fast tae the auld wife she did gae
    Say'n she's awa wi the beggar man. Laddle liltte-tow, row, row.

17. Some rode on horseback some ran on fit
    A' bit the auld wife and she wisna fit
    Aye she rockit fae hip tae hip
    An aye she cursed an bann'd. Laddle lilt-te-tow, row, row.

18. When five long years wis come and gaen
    The auld beggar carl came back again
    He's seekin after charity
    Could ye lodge a leal pu'r man. Laddle lilt te tow row, row.

19. I never lodged a beggar bit ane
    I never had a dochter bit ane
    An awa wi the beggar she his gane
    An I canna tell where nor when. Laddle lilt-te-tow row row.

20. O auld wife auld wife what wad ye gie
    For a sight o ye're dochter Jean to see
    Wi a baby at her fit an anether on her knee
    An ane o the road coming hame? Laddle lilt te tow row row.

The Beggar-Laddie

CHILD NO. 280

THIS ballad, so far as the record shows, seems to have had a very limited circulation, almost entirely confined to the north-east of Scotland. Neither can its tradition be followed back beyond the nineteenth century, though Christie says the air has been a great favorite, sung from "time immemorial." In connection with the preceding ballad, it was suggested that the present one, a "romantic" "Gaberlunyie-Man," from which one of its stanzas "is taken almost bodily," as Child remarks (1882-98, V, p. 116), might better be considered a derivative or secondary form of the "Gaberlunyie-Man" than an independent piece.

Nevertheless, the melodic tradition is perfectly distinct and unusually stable. The commonest variety is a strongly Mixolydian tune, beginning and ending at the octave, and descending to the tonic in the third, or beginning of the fourth, phrase. All the copies are in 3/4 time.

TUNES WITH TEXTS

GROUP Aa

7. "The Beggar Laddie"

Duncan MSS., "Airs," p. 2; "Words," p. 36. Also in Greig and Keith, 1925, p. 229(1d); text, p. 227. Tune as sung by Mrs. Gillespie, Glasgow, 1905; text as remembered by her and her brother, George F. Duncan. Learned from their mother over 50 years before. Tune noted by George F. Duncan.

a M, ending on the octave

1. 'Twas in the pleasant month o' June,
   When woods an' valleys a' grow green,
   An' gentle ladies walk aleen,
       An' Phoebe shines sae clearly.

2. Doon in yon grove I spied a swain,
   A shepherd's sheep club in his hand,
   He was drivin's yowes ootower the knowes,
       A bonnie weel-faur'd laddie.

3. "Come, tell to me what is your trade,
   Or by what airt ye win your bread,
   Or by what airt ye win your bread,
       When herdin' ye gie over.["]¹

4. "Makin' spin'les is my trade
   An' fitin sticks in time o' need,
   But I am a beggar to my trade,
       Noo, lassie, could ye love me?"

5. "I could love you as many fold
   As Jacob loved Rachél of old,
   As Jesse loved his cups of gold,
       My laddie, if you'll believe me" [laddie dear]

6. "Then ye'll tak aff yer robes o' reed,
   An' ye'll pit on the beggin weed,
   An' ye'll follow me hard at the back,
       An' ye'll be the beggar's dawtie."

7. Then she keest aff her robes o' reed,
   And she put on the beggin' weed,
   And she followed him hard at the back,
       And she was the beggar's dawtie.

8. But when they cam to yonder toon,
   They bocht a loaf and they baith sat doon,
   They bocht a loaf and they baith sat doon,
       And the lassie ate wi' her laddie.

9. But the lassie's courage began to fail,
   And her rosy cheeks grew wan and pale,
   And the tears cam trinklin' doon like hail,
       Or a heavy shower in summer.

10. "O, gin I were at yon high hill,
    Where my father's flocks do feed their fill,
    I would sit me doon and greet² a while,
        For the followin' o' my laddie["]

11. "Then ye'll tak aff that beggin' weed,
    An ye'll put on your robes o' reed,
    An ye'll turn ye back the way ye cam
        For I canna bide yer greetin'."

12. "It's betide me weel, or betide me woe,
    It's wi' my beggar I will go,
    And I'll follow him through frost and snow,
        And be the beggar's dawtie."

13. When they cam to yon marble gate,
    Sae boldly as he knocked thereat,
    He rappit lood an' he rappit late,
        An' he rappit there sae rudely.

14. Oot spak the lassie at his back,
    "Oh dear, but ye'll be found in faut,
    Oh dear, but ye'll be found in faut,
      For rappin' there sae boldly."

15. But four an' twenty gentlemen
    Cam oot to welcome the beggar hame,
    And jist as many ladies gay,
      To welcome the young knicht's lady.

16. His brother John stood next the wa',
    He laughed till he was like to fa',

"O brother, I wish we had beggit a'
  For sic a bonnie lassie."

17. "Yestreen I was the beggar's bride,
    This nicht I'll lie doon by his side,
    I've come to gweed by my misguide,
      For I'm noo the young knicht's lady."

Duncan gives the following variants as from his brother, G. F. Duncan:
[1] "When club and you give over."
[2] "weep"

The Keach in the Creel

CHILD NO. 281

This ballad has lived mainly in Scotland, but has been found also in Northumbria, Ireland, and in the northeast of the U. S. and Canada. Considering its subject matter, and the early analogues in *fabliaux* pointed out by Child's infallible finger, it is rather odd that we have no fuller traditional record.

The melodic tradition appears to be at least double, and exceptional variants in Scotland, Northumbria, and Ireland make one wonder about other branches. One type is comparatively steady, I/Ly or major, with a range confined within the octave from lower to upper mediant. The time is 2/4, and there is always a two-phrase end-refrain. This type is our B. It enjoys a vigorous life today, continuous or perhaps resuscitated.

The earlier type is much less steady. Its modal character is so various that it is difficult to guess the true center of the tradition. The variants have here been placed in nearly chronological order, and run from Æ/D through D/M, I—M to I/Ly. These are also all in a duple metre, properly 2/4, and there may probably be a relation between the two classes, type B breaking off from A and crystallizing. But the A type varies in number of phrases: five, six, seven, eight. The three variants with eight phrases simply repeat the tune for a burden.

Our C group stands apart. It consists of a Mixolydian and a major version, closely allied. It is authentic, in 6/8 metre, with an end-refrain of one phrase. Telfer's tune, of the mid-nineteenth century, without words, classed as D, appears to be solitary. In his headnote to this ballad (V, 121), Child adds a first stanza, from a letter of May 12, 1824, written by Telfer to Sir Walter Scott, which presumably belongs to the tune given here (variant 35):

> A bonny may went up the street
>   Some white [f]ish for to buy,
> And a bonny clerk's faen in love with her,
>   And he's followed her by and by, by,
>   And he's followed her by and by.

TUNES WITH TEXTS

GROUP A

1. "Ricadoo," or "The Auld Wyfe and the Peet Creel"

Motherwell, 1827, App'x., No. 29; text, Andrew Crawford MS., Paisley Central Library, PC 1453, pp. 174-77. From the singing of Mrs. Storie of Lochwinnoch, December 12, 1826; learned from her brother, Tam.

p D/Æ; or if tonic B♭, p I/Ly

The tune and the stanza below, contributed by Andrew Blaikie to Motherwell's collection, were apparently also recorded from Mrs. Storie, probably on a different occasion. The fresh text that follows is included here by the kindness of Dr. Emily Lyle, Edinburgh.

> The farmer's daughter gade to the market,
>   Some white fish for to buy,
> The young squire followed after her
>   As fast as he could hie, Ricadoo,
>   Tunaway ricadoo [tunaway ricadoo] a doo a day,
>   Raddle ricadoo,
>   Tunaway.

1. The farmer's daughter gade to the market
     Some white fish for to buy
   The young squire followed after her
     As hard as he could hie, ricadoo
       tun-un-nay, ricadoo,
       tun-un-nay, ricadoo.
       a dee a day, raddle, ricadoo
       tun-un-nay.

2. A gude mornin to you sweetheart she said
     For to see you I am richt glad
   But my faither he locks the door every nicht
     Puts the key below his head, ricadoo, &c

3. But ye maun get a lang ladder
     That's thirty feet and three
   And ye maun gang to the chimney top
     And your brither will let you to me, &c.

4. He has got a lang ladder
     That is thirty feet and three
   He has gane to the chimney top
     And his brither lute him in the creel, ricadoo

5. But the auld wyfe she could nae rest
     For thoughts ran in her head
   I'll lay my life quo the silly auld wyfe
     There a man in our dochter's bed, ricadoo, &c.

6. The auld man he rose up himsel
     To see if it was true
   But she tuke the young squire in her arms
     An the curtains around him drew, ricadoo, &c.

7. Gude morrow to you auld faither she said
   Whar are ye gaun sae soon
   Ye disturbit me of my prayer
   And so did ye last noon, ricadoo &c.

8. O woe to you he said,
   And an ill death may you die
   It was the braid book she had in her arms
   She was prayand for you and me, ricadoo, &c.

9. But the auld wyfe she could nae rest
   Till she got up hersel
   But sumthing or anither tuke the auld wyfe's fit,
   Into the creel she fell, ricadoo.

10. The man upon the chimney top
    He gade the creel a pou
    I'll lay my lyfe quo the auld wyfe
    The deil will hae us aw just now, ricadoo, &c.

11. The man upon the chimney top
    He lute the creel down fa
    He brak three of the auld wyfe's ribs
    Knock't her agane the wa, ricadoo, &c.

12. O the brume and the bonnie bonnie broom
    And the broom that I like weel
    An every auld wyfe that's jealous o her daughter
    May be dangled in the same peet creel, &c.

4. "The Keach i' the Creel"

Bruce and Stokoe, 1882, p. 82. Also in Telfer MS., No. 2,
p. 1. From a Northumbrian private printing of c. 1845.
(Substantially Child's A copy.)

a I/Ly

1. A fair young May went up the street,
   Some white fish for to buy,
   And a bonny clerk's fa'n in luve wi' her,
   An' he's followed her by and by, by;
   He's followed her by and by.

2. "O! where live ye, my bonny lass,
   I pray thee tell to me,
   For gin the night were ever sae mirk,
   I wad come and visit thee."

3. "O! my faither he aye locks the door,
   My mither keeps the key,
   And gin ye were ever sic a wily wicht,
   Ye canna win in to me."

4. But the clerk he had ae true brother,
   And a wily wicht was he,
   And he has made a lang ladder,
   Was thirty steps and three.

5. He has made a cleek but and a creel—
   A creel but and a pin;
   And he's away to the chimley-top,
   And he's letten the bonny clerk in.

6. The auld wife being not asleep,
   Tho' late, late was the hour—
   "I'll lay my life," quo' the silly auld wife,
   "There's a man in our dochter's bower."

7. The auld man he gat owre the bed,
   To see if the thing was true,
   But she's ta'en the bonny clerk in her arms,
   And covered him owre wi' blue.

8. "O! where are ye gaun now, father?" she says,
   "And where are ye gaun sae late?
   Ye've disturbed me at my evening prayers,
   And, O, but they were sweit."

9. "O! ill betide ye, silly auld wife,
   And an ill deeth may ye dee;
   She has the muckle buik in her airms
   And she's prayin' for you and me."

10. The auld wife still lay wide awake,
    Then something mair was said,
    "I'll lay my life," quo' the silly auld wife,
    "There's a man by our dochter's bed."

11. The auld wife now gat owre the bed,
    To see if the thing was true,
    But what the wrack took the auld wife's fit!
    For into the creel she flew.

12. The man that was at the chimley-top,
    Finding the creel was fu',
    He wrappit the rape round his left shouther,
    And fast to him he drew.

13. "O help! O help! O hinny now, help!
    O help! O hinny, do!
    For *him* that ye aye wished me at,
    He's carryin' me off just noo'."

14. "O! if the foul thief's gotten' ye,
    I wish he may keep his haud;
    For a' the lee lang winter nicht
    Ye'll never lie in your bed."

15. He's towed her up, he's towed her down,
    He's gien her a richt down fa',
    Till every rib o' the auld wife's side,
    Played nick nack on the wa'.

16. O! the blue, the bonny, bonny blue,
    And I wish the blue may do weel;
    And every auld wife that's sae jealous o' her dochter
    May she get a good keach i' the creel.

The first stanza is given as it is printed beneath the notes of the tune
and not as it appears with the full text.

GROUP B

14. "The Wee Town Clerk"

Archive, School of Scottish Studies, rec. No. 1952/28/B25.
Sung by Jimmie MacBeath, Portsoy, Banffshire. Collected
by Hamish Henderson. Transcribed by James Porter.

p I, on mediant octave

1. Mysie, she went up the street,
Some fresh fish for to buy,
An the wee toon clerk, he heard her feet
An he followed her on the sly.

Chorus:

Ricky doo dum day, doo dum day,
Ricky dicky doo dum day.

2. "Whit wey will I get to your bed, my love?
Whit wey will I get to your bed?"
"My mither, she locks the door at nicht,
An the key lies under her head."

Chorus.

3. "If ye get a ladder along,
Some sixty steps an three,
An wi a lang rope tae the chimney-top,
And ye'll come in a creel to me."—

Chorus.

4. "It's noo he's got a ladder along,
Some sixty steps an three,
An wi a lang rope to the chimney-top,
An he's come in a creel to me."

Chorus.

5. Nae peace nor rest could the aul wife get;
Strange things cam in her heid;
"I'll wager my life," says the silly aul wife,
"There's a man in my dochter's bower."

Chorus.

6. The aul man rose, pit on his clothes
To see if this was true,
But she caught the Bible in her hand,
An in the curtains drew

Chorus.

7. "Oh, father dear, whit wey ye'r up so late,
When my mither, she ?rocks/locks to the bed at nicht
An the key lies under her head?"

Chorus.

8. "Ye silly aul wife, ye lyin aul wife,
An an ill daith may ye dee!
When your dochter's lyin in her bed,
An she's prayin for you an me."

Chorus.

9. The aul wife she rose an put on her clothes
To see if this was true,
But she caught her fuit in the tummlin-block,
An into the creel she flew

Chorus.

10. Them 'at was at the chimney-top,
They thocht it was naethin new,
But they thocht it was the wee toon clerk,
So up the creel they drew.

Chorus.

11. But when they saw it was the aul wife,
They let the creel doon faa,
An every rib o the aul wife's back
Played nick-nack on the waa

Chorus.

12. It's oh! the blue, the bonnie, bonnie blue,
The blue that I lo'e weel;
Let ilka aul wife be jealous o her dochter
Be rockit in the same aul creel.

Chorus:

Ricky doo dum day, doo dum day,
Aw ricky doo dum day.*

* The chorus as given at the end sometimes replaces the version given
after the first verse.

GROUP C

33. "The Keach in the Creel"

Greig MSS., I, p. 36; text, Bk. 764, LIV, p. 103. Also in
Greig and Keith, 1925, p. 233(3). Sung by J. W. Spence,
1905.

a M

1. A fair maid doon thro' Collieston cam',
   Some fresh fish for to buy—buy;
   The little toon clerk he followed her,
   And he followed her speedily.

2. My father locks his doors at night,
   And carries the keys him wi'—wi',
   An ye canna come to my bedside,
   And neither can I to thee.

3. The clerk he had a little wee boy,
   And a cunning wee boy was he—he;
   And he has made a lang lang ladder,
   Wi' thirty steps & three.

4. He has made a lang lang ladder,
   And pitten't oot owre the lum—lum;
   And he's pitten his maister intil a creel,
   And he's latten him doon the lum.

5. The auld guidman & the auld guidwife
   Gaed to their beds to sleep—sleep;
   But weary fa' the auld carlin',
   For e'en she's wakent yet.

6. The auld guidwife she dreamed a dream,
   I hinna wull that it be true—true,
   A rotten crap oot o' a hole in the wa',
   And cuttit the coverin' blue.

7. The auld guidman he rose himsel',
   To see gin it was true—true;
   She's pitten him in atween her and the wa',
   And happit him owre wi' the blue.

8. Fat are ye daein', my ae dochter,
   And fat are ye daein' my doo—doo?
   I'm prayin' on a prayer-book
   For my aul' mither and you.

9. Pray on, pray on, my ae dochter,
   Be sure you do it right—right;
   For gin ever a woman gaed oot o' her wit,
   And your mither she'll gang this night.

10. The auld guidman & the auld guidwife
    Gaed to their beds to sleep—sleep;
    But weary fa' the auld carlin,
    For e'en she's waken't yet.

11. The auld guidwife she dreamed a dream
    I hinna will that it be true—true,—

The cunning clerk & her ae dochter
Are aneath the coverin' blue.

12. Rise up, rise up, ye aul' carlin',
    The deil to raise you wi'—wi';
    For atween ye & your ae dochter
    I hinna ance winkit an ée.

13. The aul' guidwife she rose hersel',
    To see gin it was true—true;
    She slippit her fit & into the creel,
    And up the tow they drew.

14. They showdit her, they towdit her,
    Frae back to side o' the wa'—wa',
    Till twa or three o' the aul' wife's ribs
    Gaed knick-knack owre in twa.

15. Come help me noo, my aul' guidman,
    Come help me noo, my doo—doo;
    For the man that ye boded me on last nicht,
    And I'm sure he has me noo.

16. Oh gin he hae ye I wish he may haud ye,
    I wish he may grip ye fast—fast;
    For atween ye & your ae dochter
    I hinna got kindly rest.

17. The aul' guidwife she fell oot o' the creel,
    The clerk he jumped into—to;
    And little wee Jack upon the lum
    And up the tow he drew.

18. Sing hey the blue, & sing how the blue,
    And I wish the blue may dae weel—weel;
    And a' the auld wives that wakes at e'en,
    I wish they may rock in the creel, creel, creel,
    And I wish they may rock in the creel.

GROUP D

35. "The Keatch i' the creel"

Telfer MS., No. 3, p. 2. Tune noted by William Oliver of Langraw, 1855.

m I

Jock the Leg and the Merry Merchant

CHILD NO. 282

To BORROW Child's expression, used of "Henry Martin" (No. 250), this ballad "must have sprung from the ashes" of the Robin Hood cycle. It is at any rate a late northern avatar of a greener original, somewhat soiled by a touch of industrialism. Child dates it from the last half of the eighteenth century, and consigns it to the pack of Autolycus.

With the exception of Christie's somewhat fancy copy, Greig's, Duncan's, and Ewan MacColl's from Galloway are the only known examples of the melodic tradition. They fall into two fairly distinct groups, neither of which has much in common with Christie's tune.

The first type is basically D/Æ, if we may trust the final as tonic, and is of that style of melody wherein the first three phrases make much the same beginning on a descending figure.

The second type is similar in starting the first three phrases in the same way. The tune is four-phrased. It is hard to be sure of the tonic. One of the two variants may be a π^1 plagal tune, ending on the lower dominant. The other, which is in large part very close, departs at the mid-cadence and radically in the fourth phrase, and may be I/M, ending on the upper dominant. If the finals be regarded as tonic (a doubtful decision), the first is π^2, authentic, and the second M/D, plagal. This type is also found, as Keith observes, with "The Laird o' Drum."

TUNES WITH TEXTS

GROUP A

2. "Jock the Leg"

Greig MSS., I, p. 134; text, Bk. 715, V, p. 67. Also in Greig and Keith, 1925, p. 235(1b). Sung by Mrs. Mary Milne, New Deer, March 1906.

a D/Æ

1. Jock the Leg and the merry merchant
   Went up to London town, O,
   They had twa packs upon their twa backs
   And I wyte they were weel tied on, O.

   [*Repeat the last two lines of each stanza.*]

2. They traivellèd up & they traivelled doon,
   Till they came to London Inn, O,
   Says Jock the Leg to the merry merchant
   Nae farther will we gang, O.

3. When mass was sung & bells was rung,
   And a' wis bound for bed, O,
   Jock the Leg and the merry merchant
   Were both in one bed laid, O.

4. They hadna been an hour in bed,
   An hour but barely one, O,
   Says Jock the Leg to the merry merchant
   We'll rise & gang again, O.

5. Never a fit says the merry merchant,
   Till daylight I do see, O,
   There's one, they call him Jock the Leg,
   He vows he will rob me, O.

6. Ye'll gang in by Netherdale,
   And in by Coventry, O,
   And I will warrant Jock the Leg
   That he winna trouble thee, O.

7. He gaed in by Netherdale,
   And in by the Coventry, O,
   And woe be to him, Jock the Leg,
   For fast fast followed he, O.

8. Your pack your pack upo' your back,
   Your pack & every pin, O,
   There's nae a neuk in a' your pack
   But my hand shall be in, O.

9. Never a fit, says the merry merchant,
   Will I lowse my pack to thee, O,
   As lang's the sword hings by my side
   I'll fecht until I dee, O.

10. They fought up and they fought down
    Wi' the swords o' the tempered steel, O,
    They fought up and they fought down,
    Till the blood ran owre their heels, O.

11. He's putten his whistle to his mouth
    And he's blown it loud & shrill, O,
    As six o' his well-armèd men
    Came tripping down the hill, O.

12. Ye'll tak' sax o' your bravest men,
    And yersel' the seventh to be, O,
    Gin ye pit me ae fit frae my pack
    Ye'll get it a' for me, O.

13. They fought up and they fought down,
    Till daylight they did see, O,
    Though they should hae fought till that day month
    One fit he wadna jee, O.

14. Ye'll tak' your pack upon your back
    And ye'll traivel by land or sea, O,
    At kirk or market where we meet,
    And ye'll get nae ill frae me, O.

15. I'll tak' my pack upon my back,
    And I'll traivel by land & by sea, O,
    And at kirk or market where we meet,
    I'll *hae* nae ill frae thee, O.

GROUP B

5. "Jock the Leg"

Greig MSS., III, p. 44. Also in Greig and Keith, 1925, p. 236(2a). Sung by Alexander Greig, Oldwhat, New Deer, December 1907.

p π¹, ending on *V*; or a π²

Jock-the-leg & the merry merchant
Went up to London town O,
Wi' their twa packs upon their backs,
And I wyte they were weel tied on, O.

6. "Jock the Leg and the Merry Merchan'"

Duncan MSS., "Airs," p. 442. Also in Greig and Keith, 1925, p. 236(2b). Sung by Mrs. Matheson (60), Torphins Farm, August 24, 1908. Learned in girlhood from John Eggo, Tornaveen district, Kincardine O' Neil parish.

a I/M, ending on *V*; or p M/D

Jock the Leg an' the merry merchan'
Went up throw London toon,
Wi' their twa packs on their twa backs
They were twa pretty men.

The Crafty Farmer

CHILD NO. 283

IN HIS concern with story, Child paid very little attention to metrical considerations; but these may be significant where one is tracing lines of traditional descent. It is of considerable importance to the melodic tradition of the present family of ballads that each of the three types mentioned by Child has a different metre, to which it has pretty faithfully clung.

"The Crafty Farmer," or "Saddle to Rags," is in quatrains of three-stressed lines, basically dactylic or anapaestic, and with or without an end-refrain or burden. The first and third lines do not ordinarily rhyme. "The Farmer's Daughter," or "Maid of Rygate," is in quatrains also, without a refrain, more regularly dactylic or anapaestic, and with a double or feminine rhyme on the first and third lines. There is thus an effect of greater speed, because there is typically no end-pause on lines one and three—and on three the pause is infrequent. "The Yorkshire Bite" is in anapaestic four-stress quatrains, rhyming in couplets, with frequent substitution of iambs for anapaests. There is an end-refrain of one, two, or four phrases, composed of nonsense syllables.

The names given above are not a significant means of distinction, however, and editors tend to use them indiscriminately. The first two kinds have melodic traditions rather similar in effect, but probably distinct. "The Crafty Farmer"—in Devonshire copies called "The Silly Old Man"—is a plagal major tune in 3/8 or 6/8, its mid-cadence coming on the second or fourth degree. Three Scottish variants are, as noted by Keith, common to the song, "Jack Munro." They end not on the tonic, probably, but the sixth, the mid-cadence being on the tonic at the octave, where the tune centers in its earlier phrases. The tune, if read thus, is I/Ly.

The next class, B, has a melodic tradition that appears to stem from "The Rant" ("Give ear to a frolicsome ditty," or "How happy could I be with either"); cf. Chappell, *Popular Music* [1855-59], II, p. 554. This is the tune to which Dixon says that the Northern "Saddle to Rags" is sung (*Ancient Poems, Ballads, and Songs of the Peasantry of England*, 1846, p. 126), although most of the available variants are from Sharp's Somerset collection, and we have no traditional text of "Saddle to Rags" to quite this tune. It is ordinarily major, with mid-cadence on three or five, and sometimes plagal, sometimes authentic.

The third class, frequently called "The Yorkshire Bite," or "Well Sold the Cow," has two melodic subgroups, one major, one minor (our Ca and Cb). Cb has a better defined and more characteristic pattern. Both types are mainly in duple metres, 2/4, 4/4, 2/2, but half a dozen are in 6/8—at least three of them (one from the Orkneys, one English, one found by Sandburg in Chicago) with a "Derry down" refrain (such as that quoted in Logan's *Pedlar's Pack* from a garland of 1782.) The Ca group, major in tonality, is mostly American, but there are Scottish and Irish variants. The Cb group is larger, and contains Dorian, Æolian, and D/Æ tunes mostly. This group is predominantly English, along the East coast from Sussex to Yorkshire (Norfolk examples contributed by Vaughan Williams); with half a dozen Scottish, and three or four from the New England seaboard, traveling westward along the woodsmen's route, from Maine to Wisconsin and beyond. It may be, however, that the whole lot classed as C is linked to the widespread tune-family especially associated with "The King and the Bishop" (Child No. 45).

TUNES WITH TEXTS

GROUP A

1. "The Farmer and the Robber"

Greig MSS., III, p. 175; text, Bk. 753, XLIII, p. 91. Also in Greig and Keith, 1925, p. 237. Sung by J. W. Beattie, New Pitsligo.

a I/Ly, ending on VI

1. I'm gaun to sing a sang,
    And I hope it will gie ye content,
   Aboot an auld fairmer
    Gaun awa' to pay his rent.
   [Sing fal al al al al,
   Sing fal al al al al lee.]

2. As he was riding along,
    Along on the highway,
   A gentleman robber rode up to him,
    And thus to him did say:—

3. How far are ye gaun this way, kind sir?
    Which made the auld man to smile;
   Indeed, quoth the auld man,
    I'm jist gaun six miles.

4. I am an auld fairmer
    Just renting a small piece of ground,
   And the half-yearly rent of it
    Amounts to forty pounds.

5. My landlord he's been absent
   For twelve months or more,
   Which makes the yearly rent of it
   Amount unto fourscore.

6. Ye shouldna hae told me this, kind sir,
   When robbers they're so many,
   And if they meet you on the way
   They'll rob ye o' yer money.

7. The auld man grew crusty,
   Says, I don't care a fig,
   I have it well secured in bags
   Just under the saddle I ride.

8. The robber to the auld man said,
   Deliver up your money,
   Or else your life I'm sure to take,
   For pistols are nae canny.

9. The auld man he grew crusty,
   Says, What's in this world so many;
   Took aff the saddle, threw it over his head,
   Says, Ye fetch it if you should have any.

10. The robber dismounted his horse,
    With courage so stout & bold;
    Away in search of the saddle he ran,
    Gave the auld man his horse to hold.

11. The auld man got foot in the stirrup,
    And then he got on at the stride,
    And syne he set oot at the gallop,
    Ye needna hae bidden him ride.

12. The robber he flew in a passion,
    Because nothing was in the bags,
    He oot with an auld rusty gully
    And he hackit the saddle to rags.

13. As the farmer was riding hame again,
    And riding through yon glen,
    He spied his auld meer Maggie,
    And cries, O Maggie will ye come hame?

14. When he arrived at hame again,
    And told them what he had done,
    The jolly auld wife took aff his saddle,
    And roon the toon she ran.

15. And aye she ran & aye she sang,
    And aye she sang wi' devotion,——
    If ever oor dother happen to be mairriet,
    It will help to enlarge her portion.

16. When they opened the robber's bag,
    'Twas wondrous to behold,
    There were 600 guineas in silver,
    And 600 guineas in gold
    Sing fal al al al lee
    Sing fal al al al al lee.

GROUP B

12. "The Highwayman Outwitted"

Kidson, *JFSS*, I, No. 5 (1904), p. 236. Sung by Mrs. Kate
Thompson, Knaresborough, Yorkshire.

p I

1. It's of a rich farmer in Cheshire,
   To the market his daughter would go,
   Not thinking that any would harm her,
   She'd often been that way before.

2. She was met by a rusty [ruffian] highwayman,
   Who caused the young damsel to stand [stay].
   "Your money and clothes now deliver
   Or else your sweet life is at hand" [you must pay]

3. He stripped this fair damsel stark naked,
   And gave her his bridle to hold,
   And there she stood shivering and shaking,
   Near starved unto death with the cold.

4. She put her left foot in the stirrup,
   And mounted her horse like a man,
   Over hedges and ditches she galloped,
   Crying, "Catch me, bold rogue, if you can.["]

5. The bold rogue he soon followed after,
   Which caused him to puff and to blow.
   Thank God that he never did catch her,
   Till she came to her own father's door.

6. "Oh daughter! dear daughter! what's happened?"
   "Oh father! to you I will tell;
   I was met by a rusty highwayman,
   Thank God! he has done me no harm."

7. "Put the grey mare in the stable,
   And spread the white sheet on the floor."
   She stood there and counted the money,
   She counted five thousand and more.

GROUP Ca

18. "The Oxford Merchant," or
"The Hampshire Bite"

Sung by Warde H. Ford, Central Valley, Calif., 1938. LC/
AAFS, rec. No. 4197(A). Also on LC/AAFS, rec. No.
L58(B3). Collected by Sidney Robertson Cowell.

pI

1. In Oxford there lived a merchant by trade
   He had for his servants a man and a maid,
   A true Hampshire lad he had for his man
   All for to do his business, his name it was John.
      Laddy tell I day, tell I do, laddy laddy tell I day.

2. One morning quite early he called upon John
   And Johnny heard his master and quickly did run.
   "Oh take this cow and drive her to the fair
   For she's in good order and her I can spare."
      Laddy tell I day, tell I do, laddy laddy tell I day.

3. So Johnny took the cow and away he did go,
   He drove her to the fair as far as I do know.
   Before the day was over he sold her to a man
   Who paid him the chink which was six pounds ten.
      Laddy tell I day, tell I do, laddy laddy tell I day.

4. They went to a tavern for to get a drink,
   'Twas there the tradesman laid down the chink.
   Johnny turned to the lady and unto her did say
   "Oh, what shall I do with my money, I pray?"
      Laddy tell I do, tell I day, laddy laddy tell I day.

5. "Sew it up in your coat lining," the lady did say
   "For fear you will be robbed along the highway."
   The highwayman sat behind him a-drinking up his wine
   And said he to himself, "That money's all mine."
      Laddy tell I day, tell I do, laddy laddy tell I day.

6. Then Johnny took his leave and away he did go,
   The highwayman followed after him as far as I do know.
   He overtook the lad upon the highway,
   "You're well overtaken young man," said he.
      Laddy tell I day, tell I do, laddy laddy tell I day.

7. "Oh jump on behind me, oh jump on and ride,
   How far are you going?" Little Johnny replied,
   "About twelve miles, as far as I do know;"

And Johnny jumped a-horseback and away he did go.
   Laddy tell I day, tell I do, laddy laddy tell I day.

8. They rode along together till they came to a dark lane,
   There the highwayman spoke up very plain,
   "Deliver up your money without fear or strife,
   Or in this lonesome valley you'll lose your pleasant life."
      Laddy tell I day, tell I do, laddy laddy tell I day.

9. So Johnny seeing there was no time for dispute
   Came down from the horse without fear or doubt,
   From his coat lining he pulled the money out
   And in the tall grass he strewed it well about.
      Laddy tell I day, tell I do, laddy laddy tell I day.

10. The highwayman suddenly got down, got down from his horse
    And little did he think it was for his loss,
    For while he was picking the money that was thrown
    Little Johnny jumped his horseback and away he did go.
       Laddy tell I day, tell I do, laddy laddy tell I day.

11. The highwayman followed after him and bid him for to stay
    But Johnny never minded him and still rode away
    And home to his master thus he did bring
    Horse, saddle, and bridle and many a fine thing.
       Laddy tell I day, tell I do, laddy laddy tell I day.

12. The servant maid seeing Little Johnny's return
    She went and told his master as near as I can learn.
    The master came out and he looked very cross
    And said, "Have you turned my cow into a hoss?"
       Laddy tell I day, tell I do, laddy laddy tell I day.

13. "Oh no, dearest Master, your cow I have sold,
    But be robbed on the highway by a highwayman bold
    And while he was picking the money in his purse
    All for to make amends I came off with his horse."
       Laddy tell I day, tell I do, laddy laddy tell I day.

14. The saddle bags were opened and there as I've been told
    Ten thousand pounds and (sic) silver and gold
    A brace of loaded pistols. "Oh, Master, I vow,
    I think for a boy I have well sold your cow."
       Laddy tell I day, tell I do, laddy laddy tell I day.

15. "Oh yes, for a boy you have done quite rare;
    Two-thirds of this money you shall have for your share
    And as for the villain with whom you had to fight,
    I think you've played him a true Hampshire bite."
       Laddy tell I day, tell I do, laddy laddy tell I day."

GROUP cb

25. "The Boy and the Cow"

Greig MSS., III, p. 24; text, Bk. 726, XVI, p. 78. Sung by Mr. Spence, Sr., September 1907. Text from his son, Mr. J. W. Spence.

aD

1. There was a rich farmer in Yorkshire did dwell
   For wealth & for riches he many did excel
   And a little Yorkshire boy that he had for his man
   For the doing of his business his name was called John
   With my Fal-al-di-di, raddle-il-de-di.

2. I[t] happened on a day that he called on his man
   The little boy hearing him he instantly ran
   Says tomorrow you must go with my cow to the fair
   For she is in good order & her I can spare

3. The boy went away with the cow in his hand
   At the end of the market there met him three men
   At the end of the market there met him three men
   And he sold her to one of them for six pound ten.

4. The boy went away with the farmers to drink
   And aye now & then they paid him down the clink
   Until to the handmaid the boy this did say
   Oh what shall I do with my money I do pray.

5. "Sew it into your coat lining" said she
   For fear on the highway ye robbed may be
   The highwayman sitting drinking his wine
   Says to himself "All the money it is mine

6. The boy went away to his home for to go
   The highwaym[a]n followed him as I let you know
   The highwaym[a]n followed him & soon did him uptake
   It's well uptaken the boy he did cry.

7. "Come up behind me" the highwayman cried
   "How far have you to go?" the little lad replied
   Two or three miles, for odds that I know
   So the boy jumped on horseback & off they did go.

8. They rode on along till they came to a glen
   Now my dear boy I must tell you very plain
   Deliver your money to me without any strife
   Or else to be sure I must take your sweet life.

9. The boy he had no time to dispute
   Tore his coat money [sic] & the money pulled out
   Tore his coat lining & the money pulled out
   And he showered it among the green grass round about.

10. The highwayman jumped off his horse
    Little did he think that it was to his loss
    He hadn't got the place where the money was unto
    So the boy jumped on horseback & off he did go

11. The highwayman shouted to make him stand
    The boy never minded but rode on alone
    With saddle & bridle & many fine things
    Till he came to the place where his master did dwell

12. He acquainted the handmaid as soon's he came home
    And to acquaint her master she ran to the room

On hearing the news he came out to the close
Crying, "Pocks upon you Jock is my cow turned a horse?"

13. Oh no my dear master I must tell you very plain
    I have been robbed by the highwayman
    And the time he put the money into his purse
    To make you amends I came off with his horse.

14. The bags they were unsighted and told
    Three hundred guineas & more of bright gold
    Besides a pair of pistols loaded near fu'
    The boy cries "Hurrah I hae weel sold your coo.["]

15. The boy for his boldness we'll have to reward
    Three parts of the money was given to his share
    And since that the highwayman lost all his store
    Let him go a robbing till he find more
    With my Fal-al-de-di, raddle il-de-di.

38. "The Lincolnshire Farmer"

Vaughan Williams MSS., III, p. 136. From an unidentified source. Also in Vaughan Williams, *JFSS*, II, No. 8 (1906), p. 174(1). Sung by J. Whitby, Tilney-all-Saints, Norfolk, January 8, 1905.

a Æ

These fragmentary verses, from an unidentified singer, found in Vaughan Williams's MSS., correspond in the main with part of the text printed with the first tune in the *Journal* as above cited.

1. Good people attend and soon you shall hear
   It's of an old farmer lived in Lincolnshire
   A Yorkshire boy he kept for his man,
   For to do his business as you shall understand.

2. Early one morning he called for his man
   For to go to the fair as you shall understand
   Saying boy the cow's in good order and her I can spare,
   Saying boy the old cow you shall take to the fair.

3. Away the boy went with the cow in a band,
   To go to the fair as you shall understand.
   As he was a going he met with three men
   And he sold his old cow for six pound ten.

4. Away they went to the ale house to drink,
   Where the men paid the boy down his chink.
   There sat the old highwayman drinking of wine,
   Said he to myself [sic] all that money is mine.

5. The boy unto the landlady did say,
   What am I to do with my money I pray?
   Sew it up in your coat lining the landlady did say,
   For fear you should be robbed upon the high way.

   . . . .

   Without fear or strife,
   Or this very next minute I'll take away your life.

   . . . .

   Home to his master the boy did run,
   [With] a fine horse and saddle a very fine thing.

   . . . .

   Saying dear master I've well sold your cow.

aM

1. and his name it was John

2. as we understand

4. I'll sew it within your coat lining said she
   For fear on the road you robbèd should be.

6. He quickly alighted without fear or doubt
   He tore his coat lining, the money pulled out,
   Amongst the long grass he strayed it about.

40. "The Yorkshire Bite"

Vaughan Williams MSS., I, p. 114. Sung by Mr. Smith,
?Fowlmere, Cambridgeshire, August ?10, 1907.

John Dory

CHILD NO. 284

THE earliest copy of this ballad, both text and tune, is that in Thomas Ravenscroft's *Deuteromelia*, 1609, sig. B, No. 1. From that copy, apparently, all later versions derive. But Ravenscroft's version was extended into a three-part song, or "Freemans Song of 3 voices"; and it is consequently a question whether the phrases of the tune have not been modified for the purposes of harmonization, quite apart from being dislocated from the stanzaic arrangement.

Ravenscroft's tune, at any rate, appears to be a straightforward major, of a style very popular in Elizabeth's day, however deep in the past its roots may lie. (Child identifies the French king in the ballad as John II, who died in 1364.) The best modern printing of the original is that in Peter Warlock's edition [1928] of the rounds from Ravenscroft's three publications, from which copy it is here given (variant 1b below).

Wooldridge's redaction of Ravenscroft (Chappell, 1893, I, p. 93) is hardly likely to be correct except in its first and last phrases. The major doubt in reading the original as a ballad-tune comes in the third phrase. Since the first voice rests at the beginning of that phrase, we should assume, I take it, that the continuing tune lies in one of the other two voices; and of the two, phrase one is more likely to follow a mid-cadence than phrase two. But the first voice enters again at the end of that phrase (now phrase three), and carries the melodic line up to where it can make a fitting entrance to the fourth phrase. The two melodic half-phrases for the words "holy day" may be amalgamated in three almost equally plausible ways. But it seems likely that the highest line was adopted here for harmonic reasons, and that the natural folk tendency would be to jump to the fourth. Such a solution is actually found in a modern analogue, "A boy he had an augur" (Sandburg, *The American Songbag*, 1927, p. 343), which is probably a burlesque offshoot of another old sea-ballad, "The Golden Vanity" (No. 286).

It seems very probable that the line in Ravenscroft, "John Dory [a] bought him," etc., is on a melodic alternative of the opening phrase, to avoid monotony, and not, as Wooldridge interprets it, on the third phrase of the tune. All this bother, however, can be very happily circumvented by accepting Ravenscroft's part-song as it stands, or, better still, by embracing Vaughan Williams's exhilarating choral setting of it.

"If all the world were paper" (Playford, *The English Dancing Master*, 1651 ed. Dean-Smith, 1957, p. 25) may also be compared with the present tune.

TUNES WITH TEXTS

1a. "As it fell on a holy day"

Ravenscroft, *Deuteromelia*, 1609, No. 1 (AFS facsimile edition, 1961, p. 59). Also in Ritson, 1790, p. 164.

a I

As it fell on a holy day

holy day, and vpon an holy tide a

tide a John Dory bought him an ambling Nag

ambling Nag to Paris for to ride a

And when

1. As it fell on a holy day,
   and vpon an holy tide a,
   Iohn Dory bought him an ambling Nag,
   to *Paris* for to ride a.

2. And when *Iohn Dory* to Paris was come,
   a little before the gate a
   Iohn Dory was fitted, the porter was witted,
   to let him in thereat a:

3. The first man that *Iohn Dory* did meet,
   was good King *Iohn* of France a:
   Iohn Dory could well of his courtesie,
   but fell downe in a trance a.

4. A pardon, a pardon my Liege & my king,
   for my merie men and for me a:
   And all the Churles in merie England,
   Ile bring them all bound to thee a.

5. And *Nicholl* was then a Cornish [man]
   a little beside Bohyde a:
   And he mande forth a good blacke Barke,
   with fiftie good oares on a side a.

6. Run vp my boy vnto the maine top,
   and looke what thou canst spie a:
   Who, ho; who, ho; a goodly ship I do see,
   I trow it be *Iohn Dory*.

7. They hoist their Sailes both top and top,
   the messeine and all was tride a:
   And euery man stood to his lot,
   what euer should betide a:

8. The roring Cannons then were plide,
   and dub a dub went the drumme a:
   The braying Trumpets lowde they cride,
   to courage both all and some a

9. The grapling hooks were brought at length,
   the browne bill and the sword a:
   Iohn Dory at length, for all his strength,
   was clapt fast vnder board a.

1b. "As it fell on a holy day"

Warlock, ed. [1928], p. 27. From Ravenscroft, *Deutero-melia*, 1609, No. 1.

a I

2. "John Dory"

Pleasant Musical Companion, 1686, Bk. II, Pt. II, No. 22. Transcribed by Claude M. Simpson in *The British Broad-side Ballad*, 1966, p. 399.

a I

1e. ["John Dory"]

Reduced by the Editor from Ravenscroft, *Deuteromelia*, 1609, sig. B, No. 1.

a I

The George Aloe and the Sweepstake

CHILD NO. 285

THE early broadsides of this vigorous song are directed to be sung to "The Saylor's Joy." Child (after Ebsworth) notes that a ballad of that name was registered January 14, 1595; but neither ballad nor tune appears to have survived (Child, V, p. 133n).

There is no musical record of our ballad earlier than the present century, wherein it has been collected on both sides of the Atlantic. Its most typical style is a plagal D/Æ tune, in duple time (6/8 or 4/4), with a characteristic refrain rhythmically consistent with the earliest copies, on the second and fourth phrases.

* Agnes D. Cannon, citing G. Malcolm Laws, Jr., *American Balladry from British Broadsides*, 1957, p. 157, attributes the song to Charles Dibdin. Cf. *Western Folklore*, XXIII, January 1964, p. 7n. Laws quotes Frank Shay, presumably out of *American Sea Songs and Chanties* [1948], as his authority; but Laws seems concerned only with the text. Dibdin's song, "Blow high, blow low," in *The Seraglio*, 1776, is an entirely independent and original composition. It is reprinted in Granville Bantock, *One Hundred Songs of England*, Boston, 1914, p. 154.

TUNES WITH TEXTS

GROUP A

6. "High Barbaree"

Whall, 1927, p. 85.

pD/Æ

1. There were two lofty ships from old England came,
Blow high, blow low, and so sailed we:
One was the *Prince of Luther*, and the other *Prince of Wales*,
Cruising down along the coast of the High Barbaree.

2. "Aloft there, aloft!" our jolly boatswain cries,
Blow high, blow low, and so sailed we;
"Look ahead, look astern, look a-weather and a-lee,
Look along down the coast of the High Barbaree."

3. "There's nought upon the stern, there's nought upon the lee,"
Blow high, blow low, and so sailed we;
"But there's a lofty ship to windward, and she's sailing fast and free,
Sailing down along the coast of the High Barbaree."

4. "O hail her! O hail her!" our gallant captain cried,
Blow high, blow low, and so sailed we;
"Are you a man-o'-war or a privateer," said he,
"Cruising down along the coast of the High Barbaree?"

5. "O, I am not a man-o'-war nor privateer," said he,
Blow high, blow low, and so sailed we;

"But I'm a salt-sea pirate a-looking for my fee,
Cruising down along the coast of the High Barbaree."

6. O, 'twas broadside to broadside a long time we lay,
Blow high, blow low, and so sailed we;
Until the *Prince of Luther* shot the pirate's masts away,
Cruising down along the coast of the High Barbaree.

7. "O quarter! O quarter!" those pirates then did cry,
Blow high, blow low, and so sailed we;
But the quarter that we gave them—we sunk them in the sea,
Cruising down along the coast of the High Barbaree.

10. "The Wild Barbaree"

Sung by Mrs. Carrie Grover of Gorham, Me., at Washington, D.C., 1941. LC/AAFS, rec. No. 1485. Also in LC/AAFS, Album 21, rec. No. 103(B1), recorded by Alan Lomax; and in Grover, n.d., p. 133.

pI

1. Two lofty ships of Eng-e-land set sail,
Blow high, blow low, and so sailed we,
And one was Prince of Luther and the other Prince of Wales,
Cruising down round the coast of the wild Barbaree.

2. "Look ahead, look astern, look to wind'ard and to lee,"
Blow high, blow low, and so sailed we,
"There's a lofty ship astern and for us she does make way,"
Cruising down round the coast of the wild Barbaree.

3. "Oh, hail her, oh, hail her," our gallant captain cries,
"Are you a man-o'-war or a privateer?" said he.

4. "I am neither man-o'-war or a privateer," said he,
"But I am a saucy pirate a-seeking for my fee."

5. Then for broadside for broadside these two ships did go,
Till at length the Prince of Luther shot the pirate's mast
away.

6. Then for quarter, for quarter the pirate captain cried,
But the quarter that we gave them was to sink them in the
sea.

7. Oh, we fought them for better than three hours as you see,
But their ship it was their coffin and their grave it was the
sea.

The Sweet Trinity (The Golden Vanity)

CHILD NO. 286

JUDGING by the number of copies secured in this century, the present ballad was never more vigorously alive than now. It appears more than likely that, with the possible exception of a few intrusions of other (usually recognizable) tunes, a single melodic idea governs the whole tradition. To be sure, this assertion is open to challenge; yet perhaps it will seem especially questionable rather to those who have most acquaintance with a song-literature protected from rough handling than to those familiar with such flotsam as the melodic stuff here collected. The rhythmic element is perhaps the most constant part of this congeries: the dipodic nature of it seems unusually pronounced. There is the freest substitution in half-feet, but the recurrence of the heavy stresses is almost inexorably regular; and one feels that the text has always been in especially close touch with its tune.

Child's A text is in a somewhat different stanza-pattern from later copies, and is besides unusually irregular in number of lines to the stanza. In various stanzas, discounting repeated lines, the narrative is carried in two, or in three, or in four lines. It would be normal for the first line to be sung three times, with a refrain-line after the first and second times, and a couplet rhyming line to follow, with either another line rhyming similarly, plus an end-refrain, or a two-line end-refrain. The A text seldom conforms, and it seems to have become separated from its music before it reached print. The tune indicated, "The Sailing of the Low-land," I have not discovered. It may, however, have been the ancestor of the current forms.

These forms are, in the main, major in character, sometimes I/Ly, sometimes π^1, now plagal, now authentic, now mixed. A fairly large sector descends to the lower octave and ends on the upper. There are a few excellent Mixolydian variants, and some M/D and D/Æ and Æ variants about which one is at times in doubt as to the true tonic. They seem to have drifted from the central current in any case. The overwhelmingly favorite degree for a mid-cadence is the lower or upper dominant; for the first phrase, the tonic either above or below, but not infrequently the fifth and sometimes the fourth, second, third, or lower sixth. The number of phrases varies from four to six, with four vastly more favored than other choices.

I can find little justification for local or national subdivisions either on grounds of phrase-number, mode, or melodic line.

TUNES WITH TEXTS

GROUP Aa

2. "The Golden Vanity"

Sharp MSS., 2909/. Sung by William Kingdon (76), Simonsbath, April 27, 1914.

a I, ending on the octave

1. My father had a ship in the North Countree
   It's called by the name of the Golden Vanity
   I'm afraid she will be taken by the Turkish Canoo
   As she sails along the Low lands Low, low low
   As she sails along the Lowlands lowlands low

2. The [first] that spake up was the little cabin boy
   Saying what will you give me if she I will destroy
   O I will give thee gold, and I will give thee store
   And thou shalt have my daughter when I return on shore
   If thou wilt sink her in the Lowlands etc.

3. Then the boy he bent his breast so gallantly he swam
   Some they were at card and others were at dice
   And he let in the water he dazzled all their eyes
   As they sailed along the Lowlands etc[.]

4. Then the boy swam back to the starboard side
   Saying Captain pick me up oh so louderly he cried
   " " " " " or else I shall be drowned
   For I've sunk her in the Lowlands etc.

5. Oh I'll shoot thee I'll stab thee & send 'ee with the tide
   And I'll send their bodies sinking in the Lowlands.

6. And the boy swam round to the near-board side
   Saying Shipmates pick me up or else I shall be drowned.

7. Then his shipmates picked him up }
   And 'twas on the deck he died } bis
   They threw his body overboard
   And sent him in the tide
   And sent his body sinking in the Lowlands

GROUP Ab

27. "The Golden Vanity"

Merrick, JFSS, I, No. 3 (1901), p. 104. Sung by Henry Hills, Shepperton, Sussex, January 1900.

a I

43. "The Golden Vanity"

Sharp MSS., 3763/2783. Also in Sharp and Karpeles, 1932, I, p. 287(E). Sung by Miss N. F. Stoton, Berea, Ky., May 29, 1917.

p π¹

1. It's I have got a ship in the North country,
   She goes by the name of the "Golden Vanity."
   I'm afraid she will be taken by the Spanish galleon,
   As she sails on the Lowlands, Lowlands, low
   As she sails on the Lowlands low.

2. Then up stept a little cabin boy,
   Saying, "Master, what will you give me if I will them
      destroy?"
   "I'll give you gold and silver, and you shall have my
      daughter
   If you'll sink her in the Lowlands low."

3. This boy he undaunted and soon jumpèd in,
   He leant upon his breast and so gallantly did swim;
   He swum till he came to the Spanish galleon,
   As she lies in the Lowlands low.

4. This boy had an auger which bored two holes at once;
   While some was playing cards and the others playing dice;
   He let the water in, and it dazzled in their eyes,
   And he sunk her in the Lowlands low.

5. He leant upon his breast and he swum back again.
   "Oh master, take me up, for I'm sure I shall be slain;
   For I have offended the total of the crew,
   And I've sunk her in the Lowlands low."

6. "I will not take you up," the master he cried,
   "I will not take you up," the captain he replied;
   "I will shoot you, I will kill you, I will send you with
      the tide,
   And I'll sink you in the Lowlands low."

7. He leant upon his breast; and swum round the larboard
      side;
   His strength began to fail him, most bitterly he cried,
   "O messes, take me up, for I'm sure I shall be slain,
   For I've sunk her in the Lowlands low."

8. His messes took him up, and on the deck he died,
   And then they wropped him up in an old cow's hide;
   They threw him over board to go with the wind and tide,
   And they sunk him in the Lowlands low.

1. There was a little ship and she sailed upon the sea
   And she went by the name of the Mary Golden Tree,
   As she sailed upon the lone and the lonesome low,
   As she sailed upon the lonesome sea.

2. There was another ship and she sailed upon the sea
   And she went by the name of the Turkish Roberee,
   As she sailed, etc.

3. Up stepped a little sailor, unto his captain said:
   O captain, O captain, what will you give to me
   If I'll sink them in the lone and the lonesome low,
   If I'll sink them in the lonesome sea?

4. Ten thousand dollars I'll given unto thee,
   And my oldest daughter I'll wedden' unto thee,
   If you'll sink them in the lone, etc.

5. He bowed upon his breast and away swum he,
   Till he came to the ship of the Turkish Roberee,
   As she sailed upon the lone, etc.

6. Then out of his pocket an instrument he drew
   And he bored nine holes for to let the water through
   As they sailed upon the lone, etc.

7. O some had hats and some had caps,
   And they tried for to stop those awful water gaps,
   For they're sinking in the lone, etc.

8. He bowed upon his breast and away swam he
   Till he came to the ship of the Mary Golden Tree
   As she sailed upon the lone, etc.

9. O captain, O captain, won't you take me on board?
   O captain, O captain, be as good as your word,
   For I've sank them in the low, etc.

10. O no, I will neither be as good as my word,
    O no, I will neither take you on board,
    For I'm sailing on the lone, etc.

11. If it wasn't for the love of your daughter and your men
    I would do unto you as I done unto them,
    I would sink you in the lone, etc.

12. He turned on his back and down sank he.
Farewell, farewell to the Mary Golden Tree,
For I'm sinking in the lone, etc.

GROUP Ae

71. "The Golden Willow Tree"

Flanders, 1937, p. 40. Sung by Elmer George, East Calais,
Vt., c. 1934; learned from F. Layton, lumberjack, 40 years
before. From *Country Songs of Vermont*, collected by
Helen Hartness Flanders; copyright 1937 by Helen Hartness Flanders.

a M

1. There was a ship in the south countree,
Saying, oh, the lowlands lie so low;
There was a ship in the south countree,
And it went by the name of the "Golden Willow Tree,"
As she sailed o'er the lowlands, low, down low,
As she sailed o'er the lowlands low.

2. There was another ship in the same countree
Sailing o'er the lowlands lie so low,
There was another ship in the same countree
And it went by the name of the Turkish Shageree,
And she sailed in the lowlands, low, down low,
And she sailed in the lowlands, low.

3. Oh, up speaks one little cabing-boy,
Saying, oh, the lowlands lie so low,
Oh, up speaks one little cabing-boy,
Saying, "What would you give me if the ship I'll destroy
If I'll sink her in the lowlands, low, down low,
If I'll sink her in the lowlands, low."

4. "Oh, I'll give you gold and I'll give you fee,
Saying, oh, the lowlands lie so low,
Oh, I'll give you gold, and I'll give you fee,
And my oldest daughter your wedding-bride shall be,
If you'll sink her in the lowlands, low, down low,
If you'll sink her in the lowlands, low."

5. He bent upon his breast and away swam he,
Saying, oh, the lowlands lie so low,
He bent upon his breast and away swam he,
And he swam till he came to the Turkish Shageree,
As she sailed o'er the lowlands, low, down low,
As she sailed o'er the lowlands, low.

6. He had an instrument was fixed for the use,
Saying, oh, the lowlands lie so low,

He had an instrument was fixed for the use
And he bored nine holes and he bored 'em all to once,
And he sank her in the lowlands, low, down low,
And he sank her in the lowlands, low.

7. Then he bent upon his back and back swam he,
Saying, oh, the lowlands lie so low,
He bent upon his back and back swam he,
And he swam till he came to the "Golden Willow Tree."
As she sailed o'er the lowlands, low, down low,
As she sailed o'er the lowlands, low.

8. O capting, O capting, O take me on board,
Saying, oh, the lowlands lie so low.
O capting, O capting, O take me on board
And be unto me as good as your word,
For I've sunk her in the lowlands, low, down low,
For I've sunk her in the lowlands, low."

9. "Oh no, Oh no, I won't take you on board,
Saying, oh the lowlands lie so low,
Oh no, Oh no, I won't take you on board,
Nor be unto you as good as my word,
If you've sunk her in the lowlands, low, down low,
If you've sunk her in the lowlands, low."

10. "If it wasn't for the love that I have for your men,
Saying, oh, the lowlands lie so low,
If it wasn't for the love that I have for your men,
I would do unto you as I did unto them,
I would sink you in the lowlands, low, down low,
I would sink you in the lowlands, low."

11. He wrote a message and sent it to his friends,
Saying, oh, the lowlands lie so low,
He wrote a message and sent it to his friends,
To let them know of his dreadful end,
And he sank in the lowlands, low, down low,
And he sank in the lowlands, low.

12. He bent upon his head and down swam he,
Saying, oh, the lowlands lie so low,
He bent upon his head and down swam he,
And he swam till he came to the bottom of the sea,
And he lays in the lowlands, low, down low,
And he lays in the lowlands, low.

GROUP Af

74. "The Turkish Rebilee"

Sung by Horton Barker. Folkways LP rec. No. FA 2362
(B2), recorded by Sandy Paton. Learned in boyhood from
Beecher Webster, Nashville, Tenn.

m I/Ly (nearly π1)

1. There was a little ship that sailed on the sea
   And the name of this ship was the Turkish Rebilee;
   She sailed on the lonely, lonesome water,
   She sailed on the lonesome sea.

2. There was another ship that sailed on the sea
   And the name of this ship was the Golden Willow Tree;
   She sailed on the—etc.

3. Up stepped a little sailor, saying what'll you give to me
   If I will [sink] that ship to the bottom of the sea?
   If I'll sink her in—etc.

4. I have a house and I have land
   And I have a daughter that shall be at your command
   If you'll sink her in—etc.

5. He bowed on his breast and away swam he;
   He swam till he came to the Golden Willow Tree;
   He sunk her in—etc.

6. He had a little auger all fit for to bore;
   He bored nine holes in the bottom of the floor.
   He sunk her in the—etc.

7. Some had hats and some had caps
   A-trying to stop the salt water gaps
   As she sunk in—etc.

8. Some were playing cards and some were shooting dice
   While others stood around a-giving good advice
   As she sunk in—etc.

9. He bowed on his breast and away swam he;
   He swam till he came to the Turkish Rebilee.
   "I've sunk her in the—etc."

10. "Now Captain, will you be as good as your word,
    Or either will you take me in on board?
    I've sunk her in the—etc."

11. "No, I won't be as good as my word
    And neither will I take you in on board,
    Though you've sunk her in the—etc."

12. "If it were not for the love I have for your men,
    I'd do unto you as I've done unto them;
    I'd sink you in the—etc."

13. He bowed on his breast and down sunk he,
    A-bidding farewell to the Turkish Rebilee;
    He sunk in the—etc.

aD

3. O captain, O captain, what'll you give to me
   If I'll go and sink the ship of the weeping willow tree,
   As she sailed upon the low de lands deep.

4. I will give to you* gold and I'll give to you a fee,
   Give to you my daughter and married you shall be,
   As we sailed upon the low de lands deep.

5. He bent to his breast and away swum he,
   He swum and he sunk the ship of the weeping willow tree,
   As they sailed upon the low de lands deep.

6. He bent to his breast and back swum he,
   Back to the ship of the golden silveree,
   As they sailed upon the low de lands deep.

7. O captain, O captain, pray take me on my board,
   For I have been just as good as my word,
   I sunk her in the low de lands deep.

8. I know that you've been just as good as your word,
   But never more will I take you on board,
   As we sailed upon the low de lands deep.

9. If it wasn't for the love that I have for your girl,
   I'd do unto you as I did unto them,
   I'd sink you in the low de lands deep.

10. But he turned upon his back and down went he,
    Down, down, down to the bottom of the sea,
    As they sailed upon the low de lands deep.

* 1932: give you.

GROUP Ag

94. "The Golden Vanity"

Sharp MSS., 3420/2510. Also in Sharp and Karpeles, 1932, I, p. 282(A). Sung by Mrs. Jane Gentry, Hot Springs, N.C., September 12, 1916.

1. There was a little ship in the South Amerikee
   That went by the name of the Weeping Willow Tree,
   As she sailed upon the low de lands deep.

2. There was another ship in the North Amerikee,
   She went by the name of the golden silveree,
   As she sailed upon the low de lands deep.

GROUP Ah

102. "The Golden Willow Tree"

Sung by Mrs. Polly Johnson, Wise, Va., 1939. LC/AAFS, rec. Nos. 2758(B) and 2759(A1). Collected by Herbert Halpert.

1. There once was a ship she was a-sailing on the sea
   Crying O the lowlands lonesome low
   There once was a ship she was sailing on the sea
   And she goes by the name of the Golden Willow Tree
   For she's sailing in the lowlands lonesome low
   For she's sailing in the lonesome low.

286. THE SWEET TRINITY (THE GOLDEN VANITY)

a M

2. There was another ship that was sailing on the sea
Crying O the lowlands lonesome low
There was another ship she was sailing on the sea
And she went by the name of the Turkish Ravalie
For she's sailing on the lowlands lonesome low
For she's sailing on the lonesome low

3. There was a young man that was sailing on the sea
Crying O the lowlands lonesome low
There was a young man he was sailing on the sea
. . . .

4. O Captain O Captain O what will you give
Crying O the lowlands lonesome low
O Captain O Captain what will you give
If I'll overtake her and sink her in the low
I will sink her in the lowlands lonesome low
I will sink her in the lowlands low

5. I will give you gold, I will give you fee
Crying O the lowlands lonesome low
I will give you gold, I will give you fee
And my oldest daughter, and (?then) married you shall be
If you'll sink her in the lowlands lonesome low
If you'll sink her in the lowlands low.

6. He turned on his back and away goes he
Crying O the lowlands lonesome low
He turned on his back and away goes he
Till he came along beside of the Golden Willow Tree
[Turkish Reveille]
For she's sailing in the lowlands lonesome low
For she's sailing in the lowlands low.

7. He pulled out his tools all fitten for the use
Crying O the lowlands lonesome low
He pulled out his tools all fitten for the use
And he cut nine gashes a-lettin' in the juice
For she's sailing in the lowlands lonesome low
For he sunk her in the lowlands low.

8. He turned on his back and away goes he
Crying O the lowlands lonesome low
He turned on his back and away goes he
Till he came along beside of the Golden Willow Tree
For she's sailing in the lowlands lonesome low
For she's sailing in the lowlands low

9. O Captain O Captain take me on board
Crying O the lowlands lonesome low
O Captain O Captain take me on board
And be unto me as good as your word
For I've sunk her in the lowlands lonesome low
For I've sunk her in the lowlands low.

Captain Ward and the Rainbow

CHILD NO. 287

This ballad has been a favorite of the broadside press, and the nineteenth-century collectors, Buchan, Kinloch, Baring-Gould, found it in traditional copies. But the melodic tradition is scattered and thin, hardly convincing one that there is any real core. The tunes that have been collected have little in common, and remind one too much of other songs.

The tunes collected by Baring-Gould and Vaughan Williams, in Devon and Norfolk, look, in spite of considerable difference outwardly, as if they had the same basic melodic idea in mind, and perhaps in this B group we come closest to a tradition for our ballad in England.

For Scotland, Greig's two copies, reinforced by Ewan Mac-Coll's of later vintage, are all undoubtedly related, but the tune does duty elsewhere also; for the Child ballads, notably with "Young Allan" (No. 245). Modally, our copies differ from one another.

Phillips Barry's tunes, from New Brunswick and Maine, are both majors, one plagal, the other authentic (variants 9 and 10). They appear to have nothing in common with each other. The Maine copy has echoes of common stuff, e.g., "The Derby Ram."

TUNES WITH TEXTS

3. "Captain Ward"

Vaughan Williams MSS., III, p. 144. Also in Vaughan Williams, *JFSS*, II, No. 8 (1906), p. 163; and in Sharp, 1908-12, II, p. 72. The singer is unidentified in the MSS., but in *JFSS* he is named as Mr. Carter, a fisherman (c. 70), at North End in King's Lynn, Norfolk, January 9, 1905.

a I

1. Come all you gallant seamen bold, all you that "marchy drum" (marched wrong? march along? march to drum?)
   Let's go and look for Captain Ward, for on the sea he roams.
   He is the biggest robber that ever you did hear.
   There's not been such a robber found out [?] for above this hundred year.

2. A ship was sailing from the East and going to the West
   Was loaded with silks and satins and velvets of the best.
   But meeting there with Captain Ward it proved hard to maintain
   He robbèd them of all their wealth and bid them tell their king.

3. O then the King provided a ship of noble fame.
   She's called the Royal Rainbow, perhaps you've heard her name.
   She was well provided for as any ship can be,
   Full thirteen-hundred men on board to bear her company.

4. O then this gallant Rainbow came crossing o'er the main
   Saying, "Yonder lies bold Captain Ward and here we must remain."
   "Go home, go home," says Captain Ward, "and tell your king from me
   If he reigns king on all the land, Ward will reign king on sea."

5. It was eight o'clock in the morning when they began to fight,
   And so they did continue there till nine o'clock at night.
   "Fight on, fight on," says Captain Ward, "this sport well pleases me,
   For if you fight this month and more, your master I will be.

8. "Captain Ward and the Rainbow," or "The Jolly Mariner"

Greig MSS., III, p. 127; text, Bk. 727, XVII, p. 52. Also in Greig and Keith, 1925, p. 240(a). Sung by Miss L. Crighton, Bonnykelly, July 1908.

a M

1. Come all ye jolly mariners
   That love to take a dram
I'll tell ye o' a robber
   That o'er the seas did come.

2. He wrote a letter to his King
   On the eleventh o' July
To see if he wid accept o' him
   For his jovial company.

3. "Oh na, oh na," says the King
   Such things they canna be
They tell me ye are a robber
   A robber on the sea.

4. He has built a bonny ship
   An' sent her to the sea
Wi' fower and twenty mariners
   To guard his bonny ship wi'.

5. They sailed up and they sailed doon
   Sae stately, blythe and free
Till they spied the King's "High Reindeer,"
   Like a leviathan on the sea.

6. "Why lie ye here ye tinker
   Ye silly coordy thief
Why lie ye here ye tinker
   And hold oor King in grief?"

7. They fought from one in the morning
   Till it was six at night
Until the King's "High Reindeer"
   Was forced to take her flight.

8. "Gang hame, gang hame, ye tinkers
   Tell ye yer king frae me
Tho' he reign king upon good dry land
   I will reign king on the sea."

GROUP D

9. "Captain Ward and the *Rainbow*"

Barry, Eckstorm, and Smyth, 1929, p. 348(A). Sung by Edward Holt, St. Andrews, New Brunswick, September 27, 1927. Tune noted by George Herzog, 1928.

a M (but inflected VII)

Cf. Kidson's variant of "The Outlandish Knight" (*ante*, Vol. I, p. 66; Child No. 4, variant 63).

"Go home, go home," cries Captain Ward,
   "And tell your king for me,
If he reigns king on dry land,
   It's I'll reign king on sea."

GROUP D

10. "Captain Ward and the *Rainbow*"

Barry, Eckstorm, and Smyth, 1929, p. 348(B). Tune sent in by Mrs. H. R. Murphy, Rumford, Me., October 1928; text sent in October 1924 by her uncle, Captain L. F. Gott, Bernard, Me.

p I

1. Our King built a ship, 'twas a ship of great fame,
   The *Rainbow* she was called, and the *Rainbow* was her name:
   He rigged her and fitted her and sent her off to sea,
   With five hundred bold mariners to bear her company.

2. She cruised the blue waves over and sailed on many a lee;
   At length a wicked pirate we chanced for to see;
   He bore right down upon her, and hailed in the King's name,
   We knew it was a pirate ship, a pirate of great fame.

3. "We've got you now, you cowardly dog, you ugly, lying thief;
   What makes you rob and plunder, and keep your King in grief?"
   "You lie, you lie," cries Captain Ward, "such things can never be,
   I've never robbed an English ship, an English ship but three."

4. Our guns we trained upon her, as everyone might see;
   "We'll take you back to England, and hanged you shall be,
   Or fill your ship with shot and shell, and sink you in the sea."
   "Fire on! Fire on!" cries Captain Ward, "I value you not a pin,
   If you are brass on the outside, I am good steel within."

5. They fought from six that morning till six o'clock at night,
   And then the gallant *Rainbow* began to take her flight;
   "Go home! Go home!" cries Captain Ward, "and tell your King of me,
   If he reigns king upon the land, I'll reign king on the sea."

The Young Earl of Essex's Victory over the Emperor of Germany

CHILD NO. 288

THE only surviving tunes for this thoroughly English piece are two Scottish variants of the same melodic tribe. The one from the Blaikie MS. has not, I believe, been hitherto printed. It is a plagal Æolian tune, and a very fine one, making provision for an end-refrain of only one line. As it happens, our texts are either for a six-phrase tune or a four-phrase, not one with five phrases. Greig's tune in its stanza-phrases is in duple time (4/4), but in its burden goes to 6/8; if the whole be reduced to 6/8 the resemblance with Blaikie's tune becomes more obvious. Greig's tune is a plagal D/Æ in six phrases: the burden is of the same length as are the broadsides', but different syllables are used. Keith has noted that this tune occurs with other songs, "False Mallie" (Christie, *Traditional Ballad Airs*, I, 1876, p. 232), "I will set my ship in order," "In Strichen you know."

Keith mentions a ballad of 1680-90, to be sung to "Young Essex." No extant copy of the present ballad is of so early a date.

Dr. Johnson, in the Isle of Skye, was reminded of this ballad when his efforts to get exact translations of Gaelic songs were proving fruitless. "They told him," writes Boswell, "the chorus was generally unmeaning. 'I take it, (said he,) Erse songs are like a song which I remember: it was composed in Queen Elizabeth's time, on the Earl of Essex; and the burthen was

"Radaratoo, radarate, radara tadara tandore." ' . . .

When Mr. M'Queen began again to expatiate on the beauty of Ossian's poetry, Dr. Johnson entered into no further controversy, but, with a pleasant smile, only cried, 'Ay, ay: Radaratoo radararate.' " (*Boswell's Life of Johnson, together with Boswell's Journal of a Tour to the Hebrides and Johnson's Diary of a Journey into North Wales*, ed. by George Birkbeck Hill, and rev. by L. F. Powell, Oxford, 1950, Vol. V, p. 201.)

TUNES WITH TEXTS

1. "Young Essex"

Blaikie MS., NL Scotland MS. 1578, No. 60, p. 20.

p Æ

2. "Young Essex"

Greig MSS., II, p. 39. Also in Greig and Keith, 1925, p. 241. Sung by Rev. John Calder, Crimond, July 1908.

p D/Æ

O I winna grant thee thy son back again
Which I this day have taken frae thee,
But he must go on to fair Lunnon Toon,
And appear before the Queen's High Majesty.
Singin' fal the reedle airil al airil al airil
Singin' fal the reedle airil al airil al-ee.

The Mermaid

CHILD NO. 289

The musical tradition of this still favorite ballad has been unusually constant and widespread in one of its two main branches. Sung to varieties of the same tune-type, the piece is known in Scotland, England, and in many parts of America. It is nearly always an authentic major, and the great majority of copies have mid-cadences on V., a first cadence on I. There is difference in the treatment of refrain or burden. A common style has a fifth phrase with the last line repeated, with a bridge leading into the repetition. Some copies then repeat the whole tune, slightly altered, to accommodate a burden. Others repeat the whole tune, but without the fifth phrase in either part. Barry's New Brunswick copy (variant 25 below) is solitary in its three-phrase chorus added to the four-phrase stanza.

The third group, less clearly defined, is a four-phrase tune, with no refrain. Its focus is Æolian but there are slight irregularities, inflected sevenths and in one case a compass of only a fifth. Some of these variants are quite beautiful.

It is to be regretted that Child did not take the occasion of this ballad to divulge some of his mermaid-lore. Perhaps he thought the ballad of too recent origin to deserve exegesis from ancient superstition. But we should like to know more of the comb and glass, whether symbols of self-regard or whether, as some sager say, of plectrum and quince. Child mentions the ill omen of Friday for a sailing-date; and it may be presumed that the ship turned withershins when she sank.

TUNES WITH TEXTS

GROUP A

2. "The Mermaid"

Duncan MSS., "Airs," p. 212. Also in Greig and Keith, 1925, p. 243(c). Sung by Mrs. John Milne, Glasgow, 1905. Learned in girlhood in Portgordon, Banffshire.

a I

25. "Our Gallant Ship"

Barry, Eckstorm, and Smyth, 1929, p. 365. Sent in by Mrs. James McGill, Chamcook, N.B., April 1928; learned in Scotland.

a I

1. On a stormy sea as we set sail,
   Not far, not far from land,

     .   .   .   .

     .   .   .   .

2. Up spoke the Captain of our gallant ship,
     And a fine old man was he,
   "O, I hae a wife in Edinboro toon,
       An this nicht she'll be lookin' for me, for me, for me,
       An this nicht she'll be lookin' for me."
           She may look, she may sigh wi' a watery eye,
             She may look tae the bottom o' the sea, the sea,
             the sea,
             She may look tae the bottom o' the sea.

Three times roun' went our gallant ship,
   And three times roun' went she;
Three times roun' went our gallant ship,
   Till she sank to the bottom o' the sea, the sea, the sea,
   Till she sank to the bottom o' the sea.

   When the stormy seas do roar,
   And the stormy winds do blow,
   And we jolly sailors are toiling up aloft,
   While the landlubbers lie down below, below, below,
   While the landlubbers lie down below.

3. Then up spoke the mate o' our gallant ship,
   An' a brave young man was he,
   "O, I hae a wife in fair Edinboro toon,
   An' this nicht she'll be lookin' for me, etc."

4. Then up spoke the cabin boy on our gallant ship,
   An' a fine wee boy was he,
   "O, I hae a sweetheart in auld Edinboro toon,
   An' this nicht she'll be lookin' for me, etc."

5. Then up spoke the cook on our gallant ship,
   An' a cross old cook was he,
   "O, I hae mair bother wi' ma kettles, pots an' pans,
   Than ye wi' your wives all three, etc."

6. Then three times round went our gallant little ship,
   An' three times round went she,
   An' three times round went the gallant little ship,
   An' she sank to the bottom of the sea.

GROUP B

30. "The Mermaid"

Sung by A. J. Ford, Crandon, Wis., 1937. LC/AAFS, rec.
No. 2236(A1). Collected by Sidney Robertson Cowell.

p I/M

It was Friday morning when we set sail,
   And we were not far from the land,
When the Captain spied a fair mermaid
   With a comb and a glass in her hand.

   O the ocean waves may roll,
      And the stormy winds may blow,
   While we poor sailors go skipping to the tops
      And the landlubbers lie down below.

Well, up spoke the Captain of our gallant ship,
   And a well-spoken man was he,
"I've married a wife in Salem town
   And tonight she a widow will be."

   Chorus.

Then up spoke the Cook of our gallant ship,
   And a red-hot cook was he,
"I care much more for my kettles and my pans
   Than I do for the depths of the sea."

   Chorus.

Then three times round went our gallant ship,
   And three times round went she,
Then three times round went our gallant ship
   And she sank to the depths of the sea.

   Chorus.

GROUP C

35. "The Mermaid"

Telfer MS., No. 13, p. 7. Tune noted by William Oliver of
Langraw, 1855.

a Æ

40. "The Mermaid"

Sung by Mrs. Emma Dusenbury, near Mena, Ark., 1936.
LC/AAFS, rec. No. 3229(A1). Also on LC/AAFS, rec. No.
L58(B6); and in Randolph, I, 1946, p. 203(B). Collected by
Sidney Robertson Cowell and Laurence Powell.

a D/Æ

1. As I sailed out one Friday night
   I was not fur from land,
   When I spied a pretty girl a-combing up her hair
   With a comb and a glass in her hand.

   Chorus:

   And the sea is a-roar, roar, roar,
      And the stormy winds may blow,
   While us poor sailor boys are climbing up the mask,
      And the landlord a-lying down below.

2. Up stepped the captain of our gallant ship,
   A well spoken captain was he,
   Saying we're all lost for the want of a boat,
   And will sink to the bottom of the sea.

   Chorus.

3. Up stepped the mate of our gallant ship,
   A well spoken mate was he,
   Saying we're all lost for the want of a boat,
   And will sink to the bottom of the sea.

   Chorus.

4. I have a wife and children three,
   This night they're looking for me,
   They may look, they may wait till the cold water rise,
   They may look to the bottom of the sea.

   Chorus.

5. I have a mother and sisters three,
   This night they're waiting for me,
   They may look, they may wait till the cold water rise,
   They may look to the bottom of the sea.

   Chorus.

John of Hazelgreen

CHILD NO. 293

The musical tradition—let alone the surprisingly widespread circulation—of this rather too literary piece is somewhat puzzling. There appear to be two distinct lines, and a number of unrelated separate tunes.

The line which seems to have had least to do with print is a simple π^1 plagal four-phrase tune, not very interesting, but perhaps worn down from richer materials analogous to the beautiful "Drowsy Sleeper" tradition (for which cf., e.g., Sharp and Karpeles, 1932, I, pp. 358ff.: "Awake, awake"). Kinloch's (variant 1 below) is the earliest example of this, an I/M tune going to Child B. It is the only example of its type with a mid-cadence on the upper, rather than the lower, dominant; and the other variants are all American. All copies have quite similar melodic contours in the first two phrases.

The other line is historically more interesting, as the tune—but not the ballad-words—can be followed much farther back. With Scott's literary text it first appears as "a border melody" in Campbell's *Albyn's Anthology*. Barry collected it from tradition in New Brunswick. It is still current in Scottish tradition (variant 16). But long before the appearance of "Jock of Hazeldean" or "John of Hazelgreen," this tune was popular, and Glen (*Early Scottish Melodies*, 1900, pp. 39ff.) has pointed out a version of it, "Lashley's March," as early as 1652 in Playford's *New Lessons on the Gittern*. In various forms thereafter, as noted by Glen and by Chappell (*Popular Music* [1855-59], II, pp. 575-76) and confirmed by Day and Murrie (*English Song Books, 1651-1702*, 1940), it reappears in the early songbooks.

TUNES WITH TEXTS

GROUP A

1. "Jock o' Hazelgreen"

Kinloch, 1827, App'x. to p. 206; text, p. 206.

p I/M (–VI)

1. It was on a morning early,
    Afore day licht did appear,
   I heard a pretty damsel
    Making a heavy bier:
   Making a heavy bier,
    I wonder'd what she did mean,
   But ae the tears came rapping down,—
    Crying, "O Jock o' Hazelgreen."

2. "O whare is this Hazelgreen, maid,
    That I may him see."—
   "He is a ticht and proper youth,
    Lives in the south countrie.
   His shoulders broad, his arms long,
    O! he's comely to be seen,"—
   But ae the tears cam rapping doun,
    For Jock o' Hazelgreen.

3. "Will ye gang wi' me, fair maid,
    And I'll marry ye on my son:"—
   "Afore I wad go along wi' you,
    To be married on your son,
   I'd rather choose to bide at hame,
    And die for Hazelgreen!"

4. But he has tane her up behind,
    And spurred on his horse,
   Till ance he cam to Embro' toun,
    And lichted at the corss.
   He coft to her a petticoat,
    Besides a handsome goun;
   He tied a silver belt about her waist,
    Worth thrice three hunder pund.

5. And whan he came to Hazelyetts,
    He lichted doun therein;
   Monie war the brave ladies there,
    Monie ane to be seen;
   Whan she lichted doun amang them a',
    She seem'd to be their queen;—
   But ae the tears cam rapping doun,
    For Jock o' Hazelgreen.

6. Young Hazelgreen took her by the hand,
    And led her out and in:
   Said, "Bonnie lady, for your sake,
    I could be rent and ravin';
   I wad gae a' my lands and rents,
    Though I had kingdoms three,
   If I could hae the great pleasure
    To enjoy thy fair bodie,"

7. "Na mair o' this," his father said,
    "Of your mourning let abee;
   I brought the damsel far frae hame,
    She's thrice as wae for thee:
   The morn is your bridal day,
    The nicht's your bridal e'en,
   And I'll gie ye a' my lands and rents,
    My pleasing son, Hazelgreen."

12. "John of Hazelgreen"

Wilkinson MSS., 1935-36, p. 110(B). Sung by Mr. R. H. Mace, Grottoes, Va., October 30, 1935.

p π¹

m I/M

1. As I were walking down the road,
   Down by the greenwood side,
   I cast my eye on a pretty fair miss;
   And all alone she cried.

2. I drew myself up near to her,
   To listen to what she did say.
   And her only imitation were,
   John over the Hazel Green.

3. His arms were long and his shoulders broad,
   He's the flower of all his kin,
   And his hair hung down like links of gold;
   John over the Hazelgreen.

4. You are welcome home, you are welcome home,
   You are welcome home with me,
   And you may have my only son
   Your husband for to be.

5. Oh I don't want your only son,
   He's neither lord nor king.
   I never expect to be the bride of none,
   But John over Hazelgreen.

6. Forty times he kissed her cheek,
   And forty times her chin.
   And forty times her red ruby lips,
   And led his lady in.

GROUP B

16. "Jock o' Hazeldean"

Archive, School of Scottish Studies, rec. No. 1960/146/B5.
Sung by Mary Robbie, Rathen near Fraserburgh, Aberdeenshire, February 27, 1960. Collected by K. S. Goldstein.

"Why weep ye by the tide, lady
Why weep ye by the tide?
I'll wed ye to my youngest son,
And ye shall be his bride,
And ye shall be his bride, lady,
Sae comely to be seen."
But sye she loot the tear doon fa'
For Jock o' Hazeldean.

"Now let this wilful grief be done,
And dry that cheek so pale;
Young Frank is chief of Errington
And Lord of Langley-dale.
His step is first in peacefu' hall,
His sword in battle keen."
But aye she loot the tear doon fa'
For Jock o' Hazeldean.

The Kirk was deckt at morning-tide,
The tapers glimmered fair;
The priest an' bridegroom wait the bride,
And dame and knight are there.
They sought her baith by bower and ha',
The lady was not seen.
She's owre the Border an' awa'
Wi' Jock o' Hazeldean.

The Brown Girl

CHILD NO. 295

THIS is a very interesting ballad for the student of melodic variation. Reckless though it seem, it hardly belies the homogeneity of musical feeling to set the whole assemblage in one large class; but the differences are none the less striking.

The English and in part the New England tradition rather favors duple time; the Appalachian generally prefers a triple time, and allies the tune with the type associated with "Lord Randall" (No. 12) in this country, and also with "Lamkin" (No. 93). Yet it is impossible to make a significant differentiation on grounds of rhythm, and it has seemed more helpful to give extra importance to differences of range. Further, so few variants are on the minor side of the tonal spectrum, that modal distinctions are less indicative than phrasal pattern. There is a group of squinting tunes, most of which seem to be attempting to es-cape from major to Mixolydian by means of the fallen close on the lower dominant. There are, however, only two or three clearly achieved Mixolydian examples.

One hexatonic variant (variant 41) has clear connections with a common tune of "The Wagoner's Lad" (cf., e.g., Sharp and Karpeles, *Appalachians*, 1932, II, p. 126 [D]). I have admitted Barry's "Fair Sally" from the Whittier Perkins MS. of c. 1790 (variant 26), on grounds of melodic kinship. It is therefore the earliest recorded tune by as much as one hundred years, being almost contemporary with Child's A text—to which, however, it could not possibly be sung. Child has not printed any example of the rhythmic type (anapaestic tetrameter couplets) now almost universally found with this ballad.

TUNES WITH TEXTS

GROUP Aa

1. "Fair Sally"

Barry, Eckstorm, and Smyth, 1929, p. 420(B). Sung by Mrs. Susie Carr Young; learned from her grandmother.

a I/Ly

1. There was a rich lady, from England she came,
Fair Sally she was called and Fair Sally was her name;
Her riches were more than the world e'er possessed,
And her wit and her beauty were more than the rest.

2. There was a rich squire worth ten thousand pounds a year,
And for to court this lady away he did steer,
She being a lady so lofty and so high
That upon this young gentleman she scarce cast her eye.

3. "O Sally, Fair Sally, O, Sally," says he,
"Isn't it a pity you and I can't agree?
For though I do love you, I know you don't me,
Ten thousand times ten thousand my follies I see."

4. When six weeks were over, all over, gone and past,
At length this fair damsel grew lovesick at last;
She being sick and was like for to die,
She sent for this young gentleman whom she did deny.

5. "O Sally, Fair Sally, O Sally," says he,
"O am I a doctor that you sent for me?"
"Yes, you are the one that can kill or can cure,
And without your assistance I am ruined evermore."

6. "O Sally, Fair Sally, O Sally," said he,
"Don't you remember when you slighted me?
'Twas when I did ask you, you answered me with scorn,
And now I'll reward you for what's past and gone."

7. "For what's past and gone, love, forget and forgive,
And grant me a little longer that in this world I may live."
"No, I never will forgive you while during of my breath,
But I'll dance o'er your grave when you're cold in the earth."

8. Then off from her finger (she) pulled diamond rings three,
Saying: "Keep these in remembrance while dancing o'er me;
For I can forgive you, although you won't me,
Ten thousand times ten thousand my follies I see."

9. And now she is dead, as we do suppose,
And left some other lady dressed in her fine clothes.
Come all you pretty fair maids, your sweethearts don't slight,
But be always condescending; so I wish you good night.

20. "Pretty Sally"

Sung by Horton Barker, January 3, 1950. LC/AAFS, rec. No. 10,503(B4). Collected by Sam Eskin.

p I

1. There was a rich lady, from London she came,
   She was called pretty Sally, pretty Sally by name.
   Her wealth it was more than the King he possessed,
   Her beauty was more than her wealth at the best.

2. There was a young doctor was living hard by
   Who on this fair maiden in love cast his eye.
   He courted her nightly a year and a day,
   But still she refused him and ever said nay.

3. O Sally, dear Sally, pretty Sally, says he,
   Can you tell me the reason our love can't agree?
   Your cruel unkindness my ruin will prove
   Unless all your hatred will turn into love.

4. I bear you no hatred nor no other man
   But truly, to marry you I never can.
   Give over your courting, I pray you, be still,
   For you I'll ne'er marry of my own free will.

5. 'Twas soon after this, ere a year had gone by,
   Pretty Sally grew sick and she feared she would die
   So sent for the doctor she once had refused
   She tangled was in love and herself she accused.*

6. O am I the doctor whose skill you would try?
   Or am I the young man you once did deny?
   Yes, you are the doctor can kill or can cure
   Unless you will have me, I'm dying, I'm sure.

7. O Sally, dear Sally, O Sally, says he,
   Don't you remember how you slighted me?
   You treated me coldly, my love you did scorn,
   So now you must suffer for things past and gone.

8. If they are past and gone, dear, forget and forgive,
   And suffer me longer in this world to live.
   I freely forgive you, though me you disdain
   So now I will leave you in sorrow and pain.

9. She took from her fingers the diamond rings three
   Saying, Take these and wear them, and wear them for me.
   I never can forgive you until my dying day,
   But on your grave I'll dance when you're laid in cold clay.

* The singer stumbled momentarily and reversed the third and fourth lines of this stanza.

26. "Fair Sally"

Barry, *JAF*, XXVII (1914), p. 74. From the Whittier Perkins MS., c. 1790.

m I

41. "The Brown Girl"

Sharp MSS., 4599/3217. Also in Sharp and Karpeles, 1932, I, p. 302(I). Sung by Mrs. Virginia Bennett, Burnsville, N.C., September 13, 1918.

a D/M

1. A young Irish lady from London she came,
   A beautiful creature, fair Sally by name.
   Her riches was more than the king did possess,
   Her beauty was more than her wealth at the last.

2. There was a young squire who lived right near,
   A-courting this lady to make her his dear.
   But she was so wealthy, so lofty and high,
   That on this young man she would scarce cast an eye.

3. O Sally, O Sally, O Sally, said he,
   I fear that your beauty my ruin will be,
   Unless that your hatred is turned into love,
   I fear that your beauty my ruin will prove.

4. No hatred for you, sir, nor any other man,
   But to say that I love you is more than I can,
   So quit your intentions and mend your discourse,
   For I never will wed you unless I am forced.

5. He said no more to her, but quickly turned home,
   Saying: You shall be sorry for what you have done.
   For what's past and gone I'll never forgive,
   But when you've been buried I will dance on your grave.

6. Before six weeks had scarce come and passed,
   This beautiful creature lay sick at the last.
   She sent for this young man she once did deny.
   She was pierced to the heart and she knew not for why.

7. He came to her softly, walked to her bedside.
   Have you a pain in your head or a pain in your side.
   O no, sir, dear young man, the rights you've not guessed;
   The pain is a-piercing all in my left breast.

8. O Sally, O Sally, O Sally, said he,
   O don't you remember that you once slighted me?
   I courted for love, you slighted with scorn;
   Now I'll reward you for what you have done.

9. For what's passed and done, sir, I hope you'll forgive,
And grant me some longer in this wide world to live.
That I'll ne'er do, Sally, while I do draw breath,
But I'll dance on your grave when you're laid in the earth.

10. Farewell father and mother, all foes and all friends,
Farewell dear young man, God make you amends.
I'd freely forgive you although you won't me.
Ten thousand times over my folly I see.

GROUP AC

47. "The Brown Girl"

Karpeles MSS., No. 5300; text, p. 4647. Sung by Mr. George Taylor, Grole, Hermitage Bay, Newfoundland, July 23, 1930.

a D

1. A squire from Dover, a squire he came,
He courted pretty Sally, pretty Sally was her name.
She grew so proud and lofty and her portion was so high
And 'twas on a young sailor she scarce winked an eye.

2. O Sally, dear Sally, O Sally dear, said he,
I'm afraid that your false heart and mine won't agree,
And if your hatred don't turn out in love,
I'm afraid that your false heart will ruin reprove.

3. My hatred don't be to you nor to any other man,
For to say that I love you 'tis more than I can.

4. Six long months being over and past,
Sally, pretty Sally grew sick in love at last,
She grew sick in love and she knew not for why,
And she sent for the young man that she had once denied.

5. Saying: Am I the doctor that you do want to see,
Or am I the young man that you have sent for me?
Yes, you are the doctor can kill or can cure,
And the pain that I do feel, my love, is hard to endure.

6. Can't you remember when you slighted me for scorn,
And now I will reward you for what you have done.
For what is gone and past, my love, forget and forgive,
And so spare me a little longer in this world for to live.

7. O yes, I might forget it, love, but never could forgive,
I will dance on your grave my love when you lies underneath.
She took rings from her fingers, 'twas one, two by three
Saying: Take this, lovely Willie, in remembrance of me.

8. In remembrance of me, my love, when I am dead and gone,
And perhaps you might be sorry, love, for what you have done.

Trooper and Maid

CHILD NO. 299

ALL the copies of a tune for this tale of careless love appear to be related. To judge by the extant variants, the center of musical tradition in the U. S. inclines to the Æolian mode, in the authentic range; that of Scots tradition a little earlier is plagal, and closer to the Dorian. But latterly in Scotland a cheerful major form, oftenest hexatonic and authentic, seems to have swept the field.

The good earlier texts probably had a characteristic burden commensurate with the stanza. This has survived in Greig's b, but appears to have tried the patience of many singers and been abridged either to three phrases, or two, or entirely omitted in his other copies. But it appears to have returned in full force in the copies recently collected (Group B).

The mid-cadence favored in America is on V; in Scotland, on II, but latterly V. The first phrase in this country prefers to end on I; in Scotland on lower V, latterly I.

TUNES WITH TEXTS

GROUP Aa

3. "Trooper and Maid"

Child, 1882-98, V, p. 424; text, V, p. 306. From Macmath MS. Sent to Mr. Macmath by his aunt, Jane Webster, Kircudbrightshire, 1895; learned many years before at Airds of Kells from the singing of John Coltart.

p D

1. The trooper lad cam to oor gate,
      And oh! but he was weary,
   He rapped at and chapped at,
      Syne called for his kind deary.

2. The bonnie lass being in the close,
      The moon was shining clearly,—
   "Ye'r welcome here, my trooper lad,
      Ye'r welcome, my kind deary."

3. She's taen his horse by the bridle-reins,
      And led him to the stable,
   She's gien him corn and hay to eat,
      As much as he was able.

4. She's taen the knight by the milk-white hand,
      And led him to her chamber,
   And gied him bread and cheese to eat,
      And wine to drink his pleasure.

5. "Bonnie lassie, I'll lie near ye noo,
      Bonnie lassie, I'll lie near ye,
   An I'll gar a' your ribbons reel
      In the morning or I leave ye."

6. . . . .
   . . . .
   And she put off her wee white smock,
      Crying, "Laddie, are ye ready?"
   * * * * * * * * * * * *

7. The first time that the trumpet played
      Was, Up, up and awa, man!
   The next time that the trumpet played
      Was, The morn's the battle-day, man!

8. "Bonnie lassie, I maun leave ye noo,
      Bonnie lassie, I maun leave ye;
   But, if e'er I come this way again
      I will ca in an see ye."

9. Bread and cheese for gentlemen,
      An corn and hay for horses;
   Pipes and tobacco for auld wives,
      And bonnie lads for lasses.

10. "When will us twa meet again?
      When will we meet and marry?"
   "When cockle-shells turn silver bells,
      Nae langer, love, we'll tarry."

11. So he's taen his auld grey cloak about him noo,
      An he's ower the mountains fairly,
   Crying, "Fare ye weel, my bonnie lass,
      Fareweel, my ain kind deary."

GROUP Ab

12. "Trooper and the Maid"

Sharp MSS., 3393/2491. Also in Sharp and Karpeles, 1932, I, p. 305(B). Sung by T. Jeff Stockton, Hogskin Creek, Flag Pond, Tenn., September 4, 1916.

a Æ/P

a Æ

The printed copy repeats the first two phrases, and gives E instead of D as the third note after the double-bar.

Here's cakes and wines for you, young man,
To eat and drink we're able.
Here's cakes and wines for you, young man,
To eat and drink we're able.
Yes, we're able, we're able,
Here's cakes and wines for you, young man,
To eat and drink we're able.

He pulled off his shoe boot clothes
As he rose from the table,
He pulled off his shoe boot clothes
And into the arms of the lady.
Yes, the lady, the lady,
He pulled off his shoe boot clothes
And into the arms of the lady.

The trumpet now is sounding,
And I must go and leave you.
O soldier, my dear, don't you leave me here,
For if you do I'm ruined for ever.
For ever, for ever,
O soldier my dear, don't you leave me here,
For if you do I'm ruined for ever.

O when will you come back my love,
Or when will we get married.
When conk-shells turn to silver bells,
Then, my love, we'll marry.
Yes, we'll marry, we'll marry,
When conk-shells turn to silver bells,
Then, my love, we'll marry.

1. In the dragoon's ride from out the North
    He came up to a lady,
  And then she knew him by his horse
    And she loved him very dearly
            O dearly, O dearly,

2. She took the horse by the bridal rein,
    To lead him to the stable,
  She said, There's hay & corn for the horse
    So let him eat whilst able,
            O able, O able

3. She said, There's cake & wine for you,
    There's corn & hay for horses.
  There's bread & ale for the King's soldiers,
    Aye, & there's pretty lasses
            O lasses, O lasses!

4. She stepped upstairs, she made the bed,
    She made it plum & easy,
  And into bed she nimbly jumped
    And said, Dragoon, I'm ready.
            O ready! O ready!

5. O he pulled off his armour bright,
    He cast it on the table.
  And into bed he nimbly jumps,
    To kiss whilst he was able,
            O able! O able!

6. They spent the night till break of dawn,
    They saw the light full grieving.
  O hark! I hear the trumpet sound
    Sweet maid! I must be leaving.
            O leaving! O leaving!

7. I would the trumpet ne'er might call,
    O cruel does it grieve me.
  My heart, my very heart will break,
    Because, Dragoon, you leave me.
            O leave me! O leave me!

8. Here's half a crown for Saturday night
    Sheeps'head & lung for Sunday.
  Here's bread & cheese for al[l] the week
    And Devil a bit for Monday.
            O Monday! O Monday!

13. "A Bold Dragoon"

Baring-Gould MSS., LXV(I); text, (A). Also in Baring-Gould, Shepherd, and Bussell, 1905, p. 134. Sung by an old laborer in Dartmoor, 1878. Noted by W. Crossing.

By permission of Mr. G. Hitchcock, on behalf of Baring-Gould Estate.

GROUP B

17. "Trooper and Maid"

Archive, School of Scottish Studies, rec. No. 1954/32/A11.
Sung by Jimmie MacBeath, Portsoy, Banffshire. Also on
Caedmon rec. No. TC 1146(B12). Collected by Hamish
Henderson. Transcribed by James Porter.

a I/Ly

1. A trooper-lad cam here last nicht,
   An oh, but he was weary;
   A trooper-lad cam here last nicht,
   When the moon shone bright an clearly.

Chorus:

Bonnie lassie, I'll lie near ye yet,
Bonnie lassie, I'll lie near ye,
An I'll gar all your ribbons reel
In the mornin or I leave ye.

2. Oh, she took this trooper by the hand;
   Led him til her chamber;
   She's . . . him the bread an wine,
   An the wine it bein like aimber (amber)

   Chorus.

3. For she made this bed baith lang an wide,
   Shaped it like a lady;
   She took her (?) wee coaties owre her heid,
   Said, "Trooper, are you ready?"

   Chorus.

4. "Will ye no come back again?
   Will ye no come back an see me?"
   "When heather growes on yonder k'nowes,
   Bonnie lassie, I'll come an see ye."

   Chorus.

5. She took her wee coatie owre her heid,
   Followed him up to Stirlin;
   She grew so fu' that she cuidna boo,
   An he left her in Dunfermline.

   Chorus.

BIBLIOGRAPHICAL LISTS

Containing the names of editors and titles of works drawn from or referred to in this volume.

PRINTED COLLECTIONS

Albyn's Anthology, see Campbell, Alexander.

Baby's Opera, The. [? London, mid-nineteenth century.]

Bantock, Granville. *One Hundred Songs of England.* Boston, 1914.

Baring-Gould, Sabine, and Cecil J. Sharp. *English Folk-Songs for Schools.* London [1906].

Baring-Gould, Sabine, and H. Fleetwood Sheppard. *A Garland of Country Song.* London, 1895.

————. *Songs and Ballads of the West.* London, 1895.

Baring-Gould, Sabine, H. Fleetwood Sheppard, and F. W. Bussell. *Songs of the West.* London, 1905 (revised by C. J. Sharp).

Barrett, William Alexander. *English Folk-Songs.* London [1891].

Barry, Phillips. *The Maine Woods Songster.* Cambridge, Mass., 1939.

Barry, Phillips, Fannie H. Eckstorm, and Mary W. Smyth. *British Ballads from Maine.* New Haven, 1929.

Barsanti, Francis. *A Collection of Old Scots Tunes.* Edinburgh, 1742.

Beaumont, Francis, and John Fletcher. *The Knight of the Burning Pestle.* London, 1611.

Belden, Henry M. *Ballads and Songs.* Columbia, Mo., 1940.

Belden, Henry M., and Arthur Palmer Hudson, eds. *Folk Ballads from North Carolina (The Frank C. Brown Collection of North Carolina Folklore, II).* Durham, N.C., 1952.

"Blind Harry." *The Actis and Deidis of the illustere and vailzeand Campioun Schir William Wallace, Knicht of Ellerslie, by Henry the Minstrel, commonly known as Blind Harry* [c. 1460], ed. James Moir. Edinburgh and London [1885–1889].

[Boswell, James.] *Boswell's Life of Johnson, together with Boswell's Journal of a Tour to the Hebrides and Johnson's Diary of a Journey into North Wales,* ed. George Birkbeck Hill, rev. L. F. Powell. New York, 1950.

Bremner, Robert. *Thirty Scots Songs.* Edinburgh [? 1749].

————. *A Second Set of Scots Songs.* Edinburgh, 1757.

[Breuer, Hans, ed.] *Die Lieder des Zupfgeigenhansl.* Leipzig, 1912.

The British Orpheus, n.d.

Broadwood, John. *Sussex Songs,* rev. Lucy E. Broadwood. London [1890].

Broadwood, Lucy E. *English Traditional Songs and Carols.* London, 1908.

Broadwood, Lucy E., and J. A. Fuller Maitland. *English County Songs.* London [1893].

Bronson, Bertrand H. *The Ballad as Song.* Berkeley, 1969.

Bruce, John Collingwood, and John Stokoe. *Northumbrian Minstrelsy.* Newcastle-upon-Tyne, 1882.

Bruch, Max. "Fantasie unter freier Benutzung schottischer Volksmelodien," op. 46 ("Scottish Fantasia"). Berlin, 1880.

Bryant, Frank Egbert. *A History of English Balladry.* Boston, 1919.

Buchan, Peter. *Gleanings of Scotch, English, and Irish scarce old Ballads.* Peterhead, 1825.

————. *Ancient Ballads and Songs of the North of Scotland.* 2 vols. Edinburgh, 1828.

Burne, Charlotte Sophia. *Shropshire Folk-Lore.* London [1884–1886].

Bystrón, Jan Stanislaw. *Pieśni Ludowe.* Warszawa, 1927.

Caledonian Musical Repository, The. Edinburgh, 1809.

Campbell, Alexander. *Albyn's Anthology.* 2 vols. Edinburgh, 1816–1818.

Campbell, Olive Dame, and Cecil J. Sharp. *English Folk Songs from the Southern Appalachians.* 1st ed. London and New York, 1917.

Caw, George. *The Poetical Museum.* Hawick, 1784.

Chambers, Robert. *Twelve Romantic Scottish Ballads.* Edinburgh, 1844.

————. *The Songs of Scotland Prior to Burns.* Edinburgh, 1880.

Chappell, Louis W. *Folk-Songs of Roanoke and the Albemarle.* Morgantown, W.Va., 1939.

Chappell, William. *Popular Music of the Olden Time.* 2 vols. London [1855–1859].

————. *Old English Popular Music,* ed. H. E. Wooldridge. London, 1893.

Chappell, William, and Joseph W. Ebsworth, eds. *The Roxburghe Ballads.* 9 vols. London, 1869–1899.

Child, Francis J. *The English and Scottish Popular Ballads.* 5 vols. Cambridge, Mass., 1882–1898.

Christie, W[illiam]. *Traditional Ballad Airs.* 2 vols. Edinburgh, 1876–1881.

Coffin, Tristram P. *The British Traditional Ballad In North America.* Philadelphia, 1950.

Collection of Old Ballads. A., 1723 [Ambrose Phillips?]

Collinson, Francis, arr. "The Prickety Bush," W. Paxton & Co., #80327. London, n.d.

Collinson, Francis M., and Francis Dillon. *Songs from the Countryside.* London, 1946.

————. *Folk Songs from "Country Magazine."* London, 1952.

Combs, Josiah H. *Folk-Songs du Midi des Etats-Unis.* Paris, 1926.

Complaynt of Scotland, The. [? Robert Wedderburn], 1548. Ed. John Leyden, Edinburgh, 1801.

Cox, John Harrington. *Folk-Songs of the South.* Cambridge, Mass., 1925.

————. *Folk-Songs Mainly from West Virginia.* New York, 1939.

————. *Traditional Ballads Mainly from West Virginia.* New York, 1939. Re-ed. George W. Boswell [Philadelphia], 1964.

Creighton, Helen. *Songs and Ballads from Nova Scotia.* Toronto, 1932 [1933].

Creighton, Helen, and Doreen H. Senior. *Traditional Songs from Nova Scotia.* Toronto, 1950.

Cruikshank, George. *The Loving Ballad of Lord Bateman.* London, 1839.

Dale's Collection of Sixty Favourite Scotch Songs. London [1794].

Dauney, William. *Ancient Scotish Melodies.* Edinburgh, 1838.

Davis, Jr., Arthur Kyle. *Traditional Ballads of Virginia.* Cambridge, Mass., 1929.

———. *More Traditional Ballads of Virginia.* Chapel Hill, N.C., 1960.

Day, Cyrus L., and Eleanore B. Murrie. *English Song-Books 1651–1702.* London, 1940 (for 1937).

Dean-Smith, Margaret. *A Guide to English Folk Song Collections.* London, 1954.

Deloney, Thomas. *Jack of Newbrie. London* [c. 1597].

———. *Iacke of Newberie.* 10th ed., London, 1626. In Deloney's *Works*, ed. F. O. Mann. Oxford, 1912.

Diack, J. Michael. *The New Scottish Orpheus.* 2 vols. Glasgow, 1923–1924.

Dibdin, Charles. *The Seraglio.* London, 1776.

Dick, James C. *The Songs of Robert Burns.* London, 1903.

Diem, Nellie. *Beitrage zur Geschichte der Schottischen Musik in XVII Jahrhundert.* Zurich and Leipzig, 1919.

Dixon, James Henry. *Ancient Poems, Ballads, and Songs of the Peasantry of England.* London, 1846.

Douce Ballads, I and II. Bodleian Library, Oxford. After 1660.

[Drummond, William, of Hawthornden]. *Polemo-Medinia inter Vitarvam et Nebernam.* Edinburgh, 1684.

D'Urfey, Thomas. *Wit and Mirth: or Pills to Purge Melancholy.* 6 vols. London, 1719–1720.

Eddy, Mary O. *Ballads and Songs from Ohio.* New York, 1939.

Eyre-Todd, George. *Ancient Scots Ballads. London* [1894].

Fabian, R. *Trick for Trick.* London, 1735.

Fitzwilliam Virginal Book, The, ed. J. A. Fuller Maitland and W. Barclay Squire. London, 1899.

Flanders, Helen Hartness, ed. *A Garland of Green Mountain Song.* Boston, 1934.

Flanders, Helen Hartness. *Country Songs of Vermont.* New York, 1937.

———. *Ancient Ballads Traditionally Sung in New England.* 4 vols. Philadelphia, 1960–1965.

Flanders, Helen Hartness, Elizabeth F. Ballard, George Brown, and Phillips Barry. *The New Green Mountain Songster.* New Haven, 1939.

Flanders, Helen Hartness, and George Brown. *Vermont Folk Songs and Ballads.* Brattleboro, Vt., 1931.

Flanders, Helen Hartness, and Marguerite Olney. *Ballads Migrant in New England.* New York, 1953.

Forbes, John. *Cantus, Songs & Fancies.* Aberdeen, 1666. 3rd ed., Aberdeen, 1682.

Ford, Robert. *Vagabond Songs and Ballads of Scotland.* 2 vols. Paisley, Scotland, 1899–1901. 2nd ed., one vol. Paisley, 1904.

Gardner, Emelyn E., and Geraldine J. Chickering. *Ballads and Songs of Southern Michigan.* Ann Arbor, 1939.

Gay, John. *The Beggar's Opera.* London, 1728.

Gilbert, Davies. *Some Ancient Christmas Carols.* London, 1823.

Glen, John. *Early Scottish Melodies.* Edinburgh, 1900.

Goss, John. *Ballads of Britain.* London, 1937.

Gow, Na[thaniel]. *Vocal Melodies of Scotland.* Edinburgh, n.d.

Graham, George Farquhar. *The Songs of Scotland.* 3 vols. in one. Edinburgh, 1848–1849. 4th ed., 3 vols., Edinburgh, 1854–1856.

Graves, A. P. *Irish Songs and Ballads.* London, 1880.

Greene, Richard Leighton. *Early English Carols.* Oxford, 1935.

Greenleaf, Elisabeth B., and Grace Y. Mansfield, *Ballads and Sea Songs of Newfoundland.* Cambridge, Mass., 1933.

Greig, Gavin, and Alexander Keith. *Last Leaves of Traditional Ballads and Ballad Airs.* Aberdeen, 1925.

Grover, Carrie B. *A Heritage of Songs*, ed. Ann L. Griggs. Bethel, Me., n.d.

Gummere, Francis B. *The Popular Ballad.* Cambridge, Mass., 1907.

Gutch, John Mathew, and Edward F. Rimbault. *A Lytell Geste of Robin Hode.* 2 vols. London, 1847.

Halliwell, J. O. *The Nursery Rhymes of England.* London, 1842.

Harleian Miscellany. X, p. 272. British Museum, *temp. Eliz.*

Hawkins, Sir John. *A General History of the Science and Practice of Music.* London, 1776.

Hecht, H. *Songs from David Herd's Manuscripts.* London, 1904.

Herd, David. *Ancient and Modern Scottish Songs.* 2 vols. Edinburgh, 1776.

Highland Fair, The. London, 1731. (By Joseph Mitchell)

Hogg, James. *The Jacobite Relics of Scotland.* First series, Edinburgh, 1819. Second series, Edinburgh, 1821.

Holborne, Anthony. *The Cittharn Schoole.* London, 1597.

Home, John. *Douglas: a tragedy.* Belfast, 1757.

Hubbard, Lester A. *Ballads and Songs from Utah.* Salt Lake City, 1961.

Hudson, Arthur P., and George Herzog. *Folk Tunes from Mississippi.* New York, 1937.

Hughes, Herbert. *Irish Country Songs.* 2 vols. New York, 1915.

Husk, William H. *Songs of the Nativity.* London [1868].

Huth Collection, HCL II 291. Harvard College Library, late seventeenth century.

Jackson, George Pullen. *Spiritual Folk-Songs of Early America.* New York, 1937.

———. *Down-East Spirituals and Others.* New York [1943].

Jamieson, Robert. *Popular Ballads and Songs.* 2 vols. Edinburgh, 1806.

Johnson, James. *The Scots Musical Museum.* 6 vols. [1787–1803]. Reprinted in 4 vols. with notes and illustrations by William Stenhouse (1839), and by the editor, David Laing. Edinburgh, 1853.

Jovial Crew, The, A ballad opera. [London], 1731. (Anon. [? Roone, Concanan, Yonge]).

Joyce, Patrick Weston. *Ancient Irish Music.* First printed Dublin, 1873. Reissued Dublin, 1905 and 1912.

———. *Old Irish Folk Music and Songs.* Dublin, 1909.

Karpeles, Maud. *Folk Songs from Newfoundland.* London, 1934.

Kidson, Frank. *Traditional Tunes.* Oxford, 1891.

Kidson, Frank, and Alfred Moffat. *A Garland of English Folk-Songs.* London, 1926.

Kinloch, George R. *Ancient Scottish Ballads.* London, 1827.

Kolinski, M. *Ethnomusicology*, vols. XII–XIII, 1968–1969.

Korson, George. *Pennsylvania Songs and Legends.* Philadelphia, 1949.

Langhorne, John. *Owen of Carron: a poem.* London, 1778.

Laws, George M. *American Balladry from British Broadsides.* Philadelphia, 1957.

Leather, Ella Mary. *The Folk-lore of Herefordshire.* Hereford, 1912.

Logan, W. H. *A Pedlar's Pack of Ballads and Songs.* Edinburgh, 1869.

Lomax, John A., and Alan Lomax. *Folk-Song: U.S.A.* New York, 1948.

Long, Eleanor K. *"The Maid" and "The Hangman."* Berkeley, 1962.

Lunsford, Bascom Lamar, and Lamar Stringfield. *Thirty and One Folk Songs from the Southern Mountains.* New York, 1929.

Mackenzie, W. Roy. *Ballads and Sea Songs from Nova Scotia.* Cambridge, Mass., 1928.

Mason, M. H. *Nursery Rhymes and Country Songs.* London [1878] (reprinted 1908).

Maver, Robert. *Genuine Scottish Melodies.* Glasgow [1866].

McGibbon, William. *A Select Collection of Scots Tunes.* London, n.d. [*c.* 1742–1745].

————. *Second Collection of Scots Tunes.* Edinburgh, 1746.

McGill, Josephine. *Folk-Songs of the Kentucky Mountains.* New York, 1917.

Mock Doctor, The. 2nd ed., London, 1732. (By Henry Fielding)

Moffat, Alfred. *Minstrelsy of the Scottish Highlands.* London, n.d.

————. *The Minstrelsy of Scotland.* 2nd ed., London [1896].

————. *The Minstrelsy of Ireland.* London [1897].

————. *Fifty Traditional Scottish Nursery Rhymes.* London [1933].

Moffat, Alfred, and Frank Kidson. *Children's Songs of Long Ago.* London, n.d.

————. *The Minstrelsy of England.* London, 1901.

Morris, Alton C. *Folksongs of Florida.* Gainesville, Fla., 1950.

Motherwell, William. *Minstrelsy: Ancient and Modern.* Glasgow, 1827.

Napier, William. *A Selection of the most Favourite Scots Songs chiefly Pastoral.* 3 vols. London [1792].

Nashe, Thomas. *Have with you to Saffron Walden.* London, 1596.

————. "Adieu, farewell earth's bliss," in *The Complete Works of T. Nashe,* ed. A. B. Grosart. 6 vols. London, 1883–1885.

Newell, William Wells. *Games and Songs of American Children.* New York, 1883.

Novello's School Songs, Set II, IX.

————. *School Songs,* Bk. 245.

Nygard, H. O. *The Ballad of Heer Halewijn.* Helsinki, 1958.

Old Man Taught Wisdom, An. London, 1735. (By Henry Fielding)

O Lochlainn, Colm. *Irish Street Ballads.* Dublin, 1939.

Opie, I. and P. *The Oxford Dictionary of Nursery Rhymes.* London, 1951.

Ord, John. *The Bothy Songs and Ballads.* Paisley, Scotland, 1930.

Orpheus Caledonius, see Thomson, George.

Oswald, James. *A Collection of Curious Scots Tunes.* London, 1742.

————. *The Caledonian Pocket Companion.* 12 vols. London [*c.* 1743–*c.* 1759].

————. *A Collection of Scottish Airs.* London [*c.* 1760].

Peacock, Francis. *Fifty Favorite Scotch Airs.* Aberdeen, 1762.

Penelope; or, *The Fair Disconsolate.* London, 1728. (By John Motley.)

Pepys broadsides. Magdalen College Library, Oxford. After 1650.

Percy, Thomas. *The Percy Letters,* ed. David Nichol Smith and Cleanth Brooks. Baton Rouge, 1944–1957. Vol. IV, *The Correspondence of Thomas Percy and David Dalrymple, Lord Hailes,* ed. A. F. Falconer. Baton Rouge, 1954.

————. *Reliques of Ancient English Poetry.* 3 vols. London, 1765. Later eds. 1767, 1775, 1794.

Petrie, George. *Ancient Music of Ireland from the Petrie Collection.* Dublin, 1877.

————. *The Complete Petrie Collection of Irish Music,* ed. Charles Villiers Stanford. New York, 1902–1905.

Playford, Henry. *Collection of Original Scotch-Tunes.* London, 1700.

Playford, John. *The English Dancing Master.* London, 1650–1651. Reprinted 1933, re-ed. Margaret Dean-Smith, 1957. Other source eds. are 1653, 1665, and 1716.

————. *New Lessons on the Gittern.* London, 1652, 1656.

Pleasant Musical Companion, second book. [London], 1686.

Plot, The. London, 1735. (By John Kelly)

Purslow, Frank. *Marrow Bones: English Folk Songs from the Hammond and Gardiner Mss.* London, 1965.

Raine, James W. *The Land of Saddle-bags.* New York, 1924.

Ramsay, Allan. *The Tea-Table Miscellany.* 1st ed., 4 vols. Edinburgh, 1724–1737.

————. *The Ever Green.* 2 vols. Edinburgh, 1724.

————. *Musick for Allan Ramsay's Collection of Scots Songs.* Edinburgh [*c.* 1726].

————. *The Tea-Table Miscellany.* 2 vols. Glasgow, ed. of 1871.

Randolph, Vance. *The Ozarks.* New York, 1931.

————. *Ozark Mountain Folks.* New York, 1932.

————. *Ozark Folksongs.* Vol. I, Columbia, Mo., 1946.

Ravenscroft, Thomas. *Deuteromelia.* London, 1609. American Folklore Society facsimile, ed. MacEdward Leach. Philadelphia, 1961.

————. *Pammelia.* London, 1609. American Folklore Society facsimile, ed. MacEdward Leach. Philadelphia, 1961.

————. *Melismata.* London, 1611. American Folklore Society facsimile, ed. MacEdward Leach. Philadelphia, 1961.

Rawlinson Ballads, Bodleian Library, 4to Rawlinson 566, fol. 63. After 1660.

Reid Tait, E. S., ed. *The Shetland Folk Book,* II. 1947–1951.

Richardson, M. A. *The Borderer's Table Book.* 8 vols. Newcastle-upon-Tyne and London, 1846.

Rimbault, Edward F. *Nursery Rhymes.* London, n.d.

————. *Musical Illustrations of Bishop Percy's Reliques.* London, 1850.

Ritchie, Jean. *A Garland of Mountain Song.* 1953.

————. *Singing Family of the Cumberlands.* New York, 1955.

Ritson, Joseph. *A Select Collection of English Songs.* 3 vols. London, 1783.

————. *Ancient Songs.* London, 1790.

————. *Scotish Songs.* 2 vols. London, 1794.

————. *Scotish Songs.* Revised ed., 2 vols. Glasgow, 1869.

————. *Robin Hood.* 2 vols. London, 1795.

Rollins, Hyder, ed. *Old English Ballads.* Cambridge, 1920.

————. *A Pepysian Garland.* Cambridge, 1922.

————. *The Pack of Autolycus.* Cambridge, Mass., 1927.

————. *The Pepys Ballads.* 8 vols. Cambridge, Mass., 1929–1932.

Sandburg, Carl. *The American Songbag.* New York, 1927.

Sandys, William. *Christmas Carols; Ancient and Modern.* London, 1833.

Scarborough, Dorothy. *A Song Catcher in Southern Mountains.* New York, 1937.

Schinhan, Jan P., ed. *The Music of the Ballads (The Frank C. Brown Collection of North Carolina Folklore,* IV). Durham, N.C., 1957.

Scots Musical Museum, The, see Johnson, James.

Scott, Sir Walter. *Minstrelsy of the Scottish Border.* 3 vols. Vols. I and II, Kelso, 1802; vol. III, Edinburgh, 1803.

———. *Minstrelsy of the Scottish Border,* ed. J. G. Lockhart. Vols. I-IV of the 12 vol. collection *The Poetical Works of Sir Walter Scott.* Edinburgh, 1833–1834.

Seeger, Charles. "Versions and Variants of the Tune of 'Barbara Allen.'" Publication of the Institute of Ethnomusicology of UCLA. 1966.

Sharp, Cecil J. *English Folk-Song: Some Conclusions.* London, 1907.

———. ed. *Folk Songs of England.* 5 vols. London, 1908–1912. Vol. III, *Folk Songs from Hampshire,* ed. Gustav von Holst, 1909. Vol. IV, *Folk Songs from Various Counties,* ed. Cecil J. Sharp [*c.* 1911].

———. *English Folk-Carols.* London, 1911.

———. *Folk-Song Carols.* London, 1913.

———. *One Hundred English Folksongs.* Boston, 1916.

———. *American-English Folk-Ballads.* New York, 1918.

———. *English Folksongs, Selected Edition.* 2 vols. London [1920].

Sharp, Cecil J., and Maud Karpeles. *English Folk Songs from the Southern Appalachians.* 2 vols., 2nd ed., London, 1932.

Sharp, Cecil J., and Charles L. Marson. *Folk Songs from Somerset.* First series, London, 1904.

Sharpe, Charles Kirkpatrick. *A Ballad Book.* [Edinburgh, 1823]. Reprinted Edinburgh, 1891.

Shay, Frank. *American Sea Songs and Chanties.* New York [1948].

Simpson, Claude M. *The British Broadside Ballad and Its Music.* New Brunswick, N.J., 1966.

Skelton, John. "Colin Cloute," in *The Poetical Works of John Skelton,* ed. A. Dyce. 2 vols. London, 1843.

Smith, Reed. *South Carolina Ballads.* Cambridge, Mass., 1928.

Smith, Reed, and H. Rufty. *American Anthology of Old-World Ballads.* New York, 1937.

Smith, Robert Archibald. *The Scotish Minstrel.* 6 vols. Edinburgh [1820–1824].

———. *The Scotish Minstrel.* 6 vols., 2nd ed., Edinburgh [1825].

Stenhouse, William. *Illustrations of the Lyric Poetry and Music of Scotland* (1839). Vol. IV of James Johnson, *The Scots Musical Museum,* ed. and add. notes by David Laing. Edinburgh, 1853.

Stewart, Neil. *A Collection of Scots Songs.* Edinburgh, 1772.

Stokoe, John, and Reay, Samuel. *Songs of Northern England* [1892].

Taylor, Archer. *"Edward"* and *"Sven i Rosengård."* Chicago, 1931.

Terry, Richard Runciman. *The Shanty Book.* 2 parts. London, 1921–1926.

Terry, Sir Richard R. *Gilbert and Sandys' Christmas Carols.* London [1931].

Thomson, George. *A Select Collection of Original Scottish Airs.* Edinburgh, Vols. I-II, 1793–1799; Vol. III [1802]. 2nd ed., 1804.

———. *A Select Collection of Original Scottish Airs.* Edinburgh, Vol. IV, 1805; Vol. V [1818–1826]; Vol. VI [1841].

———. *The Select Melodies of Scotland* [1822–1823].

Thomson, W. *Orpheus Caledonius.* [London, 1725].

———. *Orpheus Caledonius.* 2 vols., 2nd ed., London, 1733.

Urbani, Peter. *A Selection of Scots Songs.* 4 vols. Edinburgh [1793]–1799.

Valerius, A. *Nederlandtsche Gedenck-Clanck.* Haerlem, 1626. Re-ed. P. J. Meertens, N. B. Tenhaeff, and A. Komter-Kuipers. Amsterdam and Antwerp, 1947.

Vaughan Williams, Ralph. *Folk-Songs for Schools.* London, 1912.

Village Opera, The. London, 1729. (By Charles Johnson)

Wager, William. *The longer thou livest the more fool thou art.* London [*c.* 1568].

Warlock, Peter, ed. *Pammelia and other Rounds and Catches by Thomas Ravenscroft.* London [1928].

Watts, John. *The Musical Miscellany.* 6 vols. London, 1729–1731.

Wells, Evelyn K. *The Ballad Tree.* London, 1950.

Whall, W. B. *Sea Songs and Shanties.* Glasgow, 1927.

Whittaker, W. G. *Collected Essays.* London, 1940.

Williams, Alfred. *Folk Songs of the Upper Thames.* London, 1923.

Wimberley, Lowry C. *Folklore in the English and Scottish Ballads.* Chicago, 1928.

PERIODICALS

Blackwood's Magazine.
    (*Blackwood's Edinburgh Magazine*). Edinburgh, vol. 1 (April 1817)—

Budkavlen.
    Vasa, vol. 1 (1922)—

Bulletin of the Folk-Song Society of the North-East (BFSSNE).
    Cambridge, Mass., vols. 1–12 (1930–1937).

Bulletin of the Tennessee Folklore Society (BTFLS), see Tennessee Folklore Society Bulletin.

California Folklore Quarterly (CFQ).
    Berkeley and Los Angeles, vols. I–V (1942–1946). (Later called *Western Folklore.*)

Colorado Folksong Bulletin (CFB).
    Boulder, Colorado, vols. 1–3 (1962–1964).

Contemporary Review, The.
    London, 1 (January 1866)—

Ethnomusicology, I (1900).

Folklore Fellows Communications.
    Helsinki, I (1910)—

Folk Music Journal (FMJ).
    London, vol. I (1965)—

Journal of American Folklore (JAF).
    Philadelphia, vol. I (April 1888)—

Journal of the American Musicological Society.
    Boston, vol. I (1948)—

Journal of the English Folk-Dance and Song Society (JEFDSS).
    London, vols. I–IX (1932–1963). (Succeeded by *Folk Music Journal*).

Journal of the Folk-Song Society (JFSS).
    London, vols. I–VIII (1899–1931). (Succeeded by *Journal of English Folk-Dance and Song Society*).

Journal of the Irish Folk-Song Society (JIFSS).
Dublin, vols. I–VIII (1904–1910).

Kentucky Folklore Record (KFR).
Bowling Green, Ky., vol. I (1955)—

Memoirs of the American Folk-Lore Society (MAFS).
New York, I (1894)—
Midwest Folklore.
Bloomington, Indiana, vols. I–XIII (April 1951–Winter 1963/
1964).
Musical Quarterly (MQ).
New York, I (January 1915)—

Newcastle Courant.
Articles by John Stokoe printed 1878–1881.
New York Folklore Quarterly (NYFQ).
Ithaca, N.Y., I (February 1945)—
New York Tribune.
August 17, 1902.
North Carolina Folklore (NCF).
Chapel Hill, N.C., vols. I–VI (1948–1958).
Notes and Queries, vols. I– (1850–1855).
Notes from the Pine Mountain Settlement School (NPMSS).
Pine Mountain, Ky., vols. I–? (1919–1949).

Publications of the Modern Language Association (PMLA).
Baltimore, vol. I (1884/1885)—
Publications of the Texas Folk-Lore Society (PTFLS).
Austin, vol. I (1916)—

Rymour Club Miscellanea.
Edinburgh, vol. I (1910)—?

Scottish Studies.
Edinburgh, I (1957)—
Southern Folklore Quarterly (SFQ).
Jacksonville, Fla., I (March 1937)—

Tennessee Folklore Society Bulletin (TFSB).
Murfreesboro, Tennessee, vol. I (1935)—

Vocal Magazine, The.
Edinburgh, I–III (1797–1799). "New series" (publ. James
Sibbald), Edinburgh, 1803—?

Western Folklore (WF).
Berkeley and Los Angeles, vol. VI (1947)—. (Vols. I–V, *see
California Folklore Quarterly.*)

MANUSCRIPTS

Ballet, William, lute-book, *c.* 1599. Trinity College Library, Dublin.
Baring-Gould, Sabine, MSS., 1880–1890. Plymouth Public Library.
Blaikie MS., *c.* 1820. National Library of Scotland, Edinburgh.
Blaikie Lyra-viol MS., 1692. Present location unknown.
Brown, Frank C., MSS., 1912–1943. Library of Congress, photostat.

Cambridge University Lute MSS., *temp. Eliz.* Cambridge University Library.
Child MSS., 1880–1896. Harvard College Library.
Crawfurd, Andrew, MS., ?1826. Paisley Central Library PC1453, Scotland.

Duncan, J. B., MSS., "Folk-Song Airs of the North East," and "Folk-Song Words belonging to the North East, and received from Mrs Gillespie," *c.* 1900–1917. Cecil Sharp House, London.

Edinburgh University Library MS. Dc. 1. 69, *c.* 1650.

Gamble, John, MS. (Drexel MS 4257), *c* 1659. New York Public Library.
Gardiner, George, MSS., 1905–1909. Cecil Sharp House, London.
Garrison, Theodore. "Forty-five Folk Songs Collected from Searcy County, Arkansas." M.A. thesis, University of Arkansas, 1944.
Gilbert, Davies, Carol MS., 1767–1768. Harvard College Library.
Gordon, Robert, of Straloch, lute MS., *see* Straloch MS.
Grainger, Percy, MS., 1905–1906, hectograph copy. New York Public Library.
Greig MSS., *c.* 1885–*c.* 1914. King's College Library, Aberdeen.
Greig-Duncan MS (transcription of W. Walker), 1919. King's College Library, Aberdeen.

Guthrie MS., 1675–1680. Edinburgh University Library.

Harris MS. Before 1880. Harvard College Library.
Hudson MS., "Collection of Folk Songs of the Irish Peasantry," *c.* 1840. Boston Public Library.

Karpeles, Maud, MSS., 1929–1930. Private collection.
Kidson, Frank, collection. "Edinburgh MS.," sent to Kidson from Edinburgh, December 1903, by an unknown correspondent.

Leyden MS., *c.* 1692. University Library, Newcastle.

Macmath MS., *c.* 1880-*c.* 1885. Harvard College Library.
Munnally, Tom. Private collection.

Panmure MS., early seventeenth century. National Library of Scotland, Edinburgh.

Ritson-Tytler-Brown MS., *c.* 1792–1794. Harvard College Library.
Roxburghe Collection. British Museum.

Scott, Lady John MS., *c.* 1830. National Library of Scotland, Edinburgh.
Scott, Lady John, Sharpe MS., *c.* 1820. National Library of Scotland, Edinburgh.
Scott, Sir Walter. Abbotsford MSS. collection, 1783–1830.
———. "Scottish Songs," 1795. Abbotsford MSS., N3.
Sharp, Cecil J., MSS., 1903–1918. Clare College Library, Cambridge, England.
Sharpe, Charles Kirkpatrick, MSS., *c.* 1820. William Macmath transcript, 1893. Harvard College Library.
Shepheard, Peter. Private collection.
Skene MS., *c.* 1620. National Library of Scotland, Edinburgh.
Stekert, Ellen. Private collection.
Straloch lute MS., 1627–1629. National Library of Scotland, Edinburgh.

Telfer, James, MS., 1855. Society of Antiquaries Library, Newcastle-upon-Tyne.

Tytler-Brown MS., *c.* 1800. Aldourie Castle, Inverness-shire. Photostatic copy in National Library of Scotland.

Vaughan Williams, Ralph, MSS., 1903–1913. Cecil Sharp House, London.

Wells, Evelyn K. Private collection.

Wilkinson, Winston, MSS., 1935–1936, 1936–1937. University of Virginia.

Williams, Mrs. John (*née* Violet Selena Hawkins). "Tunes of Old Ballads and Folksongs." Unpublished collection from her singing, ed. Charles A. Williams and Mabel Williams Kemmerer, 1963.

SOUND

Barry, Phillips, Dictaphone Cylinders.
  Harvard College Library.

British Broadcasting Company Sound Archives.
  London.

Brunswick record company.
  Record Nos. 117, 212, 213 (069)

Caedmon record company.
  Record No. TC 1146

Columbia record company.
  Albums M372 and M408; LP record Nos. SL–206, 14489–D, 15336–D, 15654—D, 15763–D (151002), and 37756 (17478 and 17508)

INDEX OF TUNES AND BALLADS QUOTED

Listing variant titles as they appear in this volume. Child numbers are in boldface and variant numbers in Arabic type. The titles in capitals and small capitals are Child's ballad-family titles, infrequently altered by the editor to the form most often traditionally used.

LIBRARY OF CONGRESS CATALOGING IN PUBLICATION DATA

Bronson, Bertrand Harris, 1902-   ed.
  The singing tradition of Child's popular ballads.

  An abridgement of the editor's The traditional tunes
of the Child ballads, 1959-72.
  1. Ballads, English—History and criticism.
  2. Ballads, Scottish—History and criticism.
  3. Ballads, English.   4. Ballads, Scottish.
  I. Child, Francis James, 1825-1896, ed. English and
Scottish popular ballads.   II. Title.
  ML3650.B82 1976   784'.3   75-2980
  ISBN 0-691-09119-6
  ISBN 0-691-02704-8 pbk.